MAGILL'S
LITERARY ANNUAL
1998

MAGILL'S
LITERARY ANNUAL
1998

Essay-Reviews of 200 Outstanding Books
Published in the United States during 1997

With an Annotated Categories List

Volume Two
L-Z

Edited by
JOHN D. WILSON

SALEM PRESS
Pasadena, California   Englewood Cliffs, New Jersey

∞ The paper used in these volumes conforms to the American National Standard for Permanence of Paper for Printed Library Materials, Z39.48-1992.

LIBRARY OF CONGRESS CATALOG CARD NO. 77-99209
ISBN 0-89356-298-X

FIRST PRINTING

PRINTED IN THE UNITED STATES OF AMERICA

MAGILL'S
LITERARY ANNUAL
1998

LOGICAL DILEMMAS
The Life and Work of Kurt Gödel

Author: John W. Dawson, Jr. (1944-   )
Publisher: A. K. Peters (Wellesley, Massachusetts). 361 pp. $49.95
Type of work: Biography
Time: 1906-1978
Locale: Austria and the United States

An integrated study of the intellectual achievement and psychological disorder of the most important logic researcher of the twentieth century

Principal personages:
KURT GÖDEL, a naturalized American logician born to ethnic German
    parents in Brno, Czechoslovakia (then part of Austria-Hungary)
ADELE PORKERT, his wife
ALBERT EINSTEIN, his friend and colleague at the Institute for Advanced
    Studies (IAS) in Princeton, New Jersey
OSKAR MORGENSTERN, a noted economist, and Gödel's friend and IAS
    colleague
JOHN VON NEUMANN, a prominent mathematician, and Gödel's friend
    and IAS colleague

In 1930, shortly after receiving his Ph.D. from the University of Vienna, logician Kurt Gödel announced to friends the discovery of a formally undecidable proposition. He proved that there is a statement in the language of elementary number theory which is true but which can neither be proved true nor false. Thus, he concluded, any formal mathematical system strong enough to include elementary number theory cannot prove its own consistency.

These unexpected results, known as Gödel's incompleteness theorems, not only ran counter to most scientists' implicit assumptions about the ultimate decidability of truth but also seemed to challenge the widespread view that all problems may be solved through scientific inquiry. Paradoxically, Gödel retained that view for the rest of his life and championed scientific inquiry as the best tool for potentially solving any problem. Rather than having discovered limitations on the scope of intelligence in problem solving as Alan Turing, the artificial intelligence pioneer, famously interpreted Gödel's incompleteness theorems, Gödel thought his incompleteness discovery actually affirmed the unique role of the human mind and its dynamism in problem solving. If there were inherent limitations in every fixed logical scheme, he reasoned, then the evolution of intelligence as embodied by computers and machines could never completely surpass the human mind and its capacity to change schemes. Trying to reconcile the contradictions posed by his own epochal discoveries and seemingly anachronistic philosophy, Gödel suffered sporadically from paranoia and eventually, overcome by a fear of being poisoned, died of starvation.

Gödel's biographer, John Dawson, Jr., set himself a formidable task in weaving his subject's intricate ideas in mathematics and logic together with details of his life. As a partial indication of the difficulty of Gödel's work, Dawson reports that there are still many professional mathematicians who have little awareness or understanding of what Gödel accomplished—this, in spite of Gödel's greater posthumous visibility afforded by his prominent appearance in Douglas Hofstadter's best-seller *Gödel, Escher, Bach* (1979). Even stating correctly the essence of a Gödel theorem is a delicate matter requiring some advanced terminology and knowledge of logic or set theory. Dawson presupposes such knowledge in his brief descriptions of Gödel's mathematical ideas and novel methods of proof. Yet Gödel's personal story, with its cast of important supporting characters such as Albert Einstein, likely will compel even a reader with little mathematical background to eagerly continue turning the pages of Dawson's important chronicle.

After establishing himself internationally among mathematicians and logicians with the incompleteness theorems and some groundbreaking work in set theory, Gödel emigrated to the United States in 1940 where his research turned toward philosophy. By presenting Gödel as one who did not believe in chance events, one of Dawson's main themes concerns Gödel's search for hidden causes for all things. Instead of the dour "nothing but the facts" empiricist one might initially expect Gödel to be, this logician's interest in supernatural phenomena (including extrasensory perception, or ESP), his published work asserting that Einstein's field equations imply the possibility of time travel into the past, and his proof of the existence of God reveal a more reflective character. As opposed to maintaining a state of alertness so as to observe the world with maximum accuracy, Gödel suggested that introspection was the right road to true knowledge of concepts and ideas whose existence, he claimed, was every bit as real as the material realm.

Dawson contextualizes the later half of Gödel's research career, with its frequent changes of direction, by relating these shifts in focus to specific distractions in the logician's personal life. Although Dawson's claims in this area are as cautious as those pronounced by his subject (whose desire to avoid confrontation was manifested as his legendary reclusiveness and hesitancy to publicly announce research results), one wonders if Dawson, too, is excessive in singling out hidden causes to flatteringly account for Gödel's seemingly erratic research activity after emigrating to the United States. As evidence to the contrary, Dawson cites the continuing admiration for Gödel by esteemed friends such as Einstein, mathematician John von Neumann, and economist Oskar Morgenstern, as recorded in their personal letters and diaries, which attest to Gödel's continuing brilliance throughout this period. Dawson also compares Gödel's post-emigration research, whose reception was less than warm at its time of publication, with more recent physical and philosophical research which supports many of Gödel's later views.

Dawson's depiction of German-speaking university life in Europe as the backdrop to Gödel's prewar professional years is one of the most historically useful sections in the book. Gödel attended the University of Vienna in 1924 as a student and stayed on as a teacher through 1940, two years after Austria had been taken over by Hitler's political surrogates. Although Gödel remained astonishingly apolitical through World

War II, the letters of Gödel's European colleagues during that period offer grave and conflicting reactions to the events in Europe after the Nazi Party came to power. Some, such as Gödel's thesis adviser Hans Hahn, were murdered in the midst of a chaotic mix of ideologically motivated violence and wanton thuggery. Some, like Gödel in 1940, emigrated to the United States. Others felt compelled against their wishes, but as a professional necessity, to join the fascist Austrian "Fatherland Front" party. Still other university officials zealously joined that party and gladly complied with the German Civil Service order to purge non-Aryans. The picture that emerges from Dawson's excerpts of correspondence among European academics working amidst or having escaped from Nazism is that of a time of tumultuous upheaval. Dawson deftly orchestrates the self-depiction of a few of the Western world's preeminent scientists. Experiencing painful personal traumas as many others did on the one hand, yet charging forth toward exciting intellectual and professional success at the dawn of the atomic and computer age on the other, these accounts provide a brief historical presentation whose complex flavor is deeply memorable.

As Europe was on the brink of war, and despite his family's strong disapproval, Gödel married an Austrian night-club dancer, Adele Porkert, in 1938. Dawson's portrayal of Porkert and her life-long marriage to Gödel, her list of "faults" (such as having a port wine stain on her face), and her inability to mix smoothly with other faculty families at Princeton unfortunately misses an opportunity to shed critical historical light on the prosaic but nevertheless relevant aspects of the personal lives of Gödel and his esteemed friends. Dawson's Gödel is framed nearly always as either a genius on high or a genius run amok; readers miss seeing his more usual aspects—namely, that of a spouse trying to keep his marriage, career, and mental health on track in the face of tensions arising from issues such as cultural difference and personal finance. In spite of indicating more than once how essential Porkert was to Gödel's stability, Dawson does not clarify her special contribution and instead naturalizes Porkert's auxiliary role as that of Gödel's nurturing, if occasionally bothersome, protector, his clumsy yet affectionate sometime mother and sometime lover. Consider that, from before the time of their marriage, Gödel had Porkert pre-taste food for him; that Gödel's friend, Morgenstern, complained of Porkert's coarse manners and strong will, likening her to a washerwoman; and that Gödel's family objected to their son's marriage to Porkert in part because of the aforementioned birth mark. How those for whom logical consistency and general problem solving was utmost could reconcile or ignore their own bourgeois customs and contradictory attitudes is a key, if unnoticed, dilemma not elaborated on by Dawson. One wonders why, at an institution such as Princeton comprised of those among the world's most logically accomplished men, this intellectually elite group did little, if anything, to distinguish itself from other communities in dealing with immediate, everyday problems such as class division and petty personality disputes. That these intellectual supermen had so many normal problems for which their erudite artillery was no match seems astounding.

Dawson carefully tells Gödel's story, using the letters and diaries of colleagues, friends, and family, as well as later interview material and various public records. A patient investigator whose attention to detail goes so far as to describe the breeds of dogs Gödel owned and their role in the Gödel household, Dawson fills in the portrait with helpful commentary and reasonable speculation into his subject's motives and the causes for his idiosyncrasies. Without turning away from Gödel's afflicted inner life, Dawson expresses his admiration for Gödel by including as many perspectives as possible. The biographer's recounting of many unflattering episodes of psychological illness only adds interest to Gödel's work.

Dawson, a professor of mathematics at Pennsylvania State University at York who was selected to catalog Gödel's papers at Princeton's Institute for Advanced Studies (IAS), and who is co-editing an ongoing series of Gödel's *Collected Works* (1986-), evidently had a surfeit of primary data. This data ranged from highly revealing sketches of proofs in rough drafts of letters to colleagues such as von Neumann, and library slips indicating which books Gödel borrowed at which times, to reams of financial statements and letters to his mother and brother from which Dawson attempts to extract more personal information about Gödel. The diaries of Morgenstern and logician Hao Wang also figure prominently in Dawson's portrayal of Gödel's final years. Thus, the biography that emerges is ultimately a personal story in which readers learn about a great intellect's imperfect inner life in fine detail. In what will likely prove to be the definitive Gödel biography for those interested in the logician's life, Dawson's work, with admirable restraint, gives readers nearly every tantalizing detail that the factual record has to offer. It is a classic tale of genius gone mad. *Logical Dilemmas: The Life and Work of Kurt Gödel* is replete with anecdotes such as the following: Shortly after arriving at Princeton, Gödel complained to IAS colleagues about poison gasses coming out of his refrigerator; still at Princeton, he had the screens on his windows removed because he believed they interfered with his breathing; and apparently unaware of potential trouble, he told the Immigration and Naturalization Service official presiding over his test for American citizenship that there were logical contradictions in the American Constitution which could lead to the rise of a communist dictatorship in Washington without breaking any laws.

In the end, however, readers learn much more about Gödel's personal life than they do about his intellectual endeavors, the achievements for which he was eventually awarded the National Medal of Science in 1975. For a thorough account and critical discussion of Gödel's scholarly output, one must look elsewhere. As an introduction to Gödel's role in twentieth century mathematics and logic, or as an in-depth personal profile for those who already know and appreciate Gödel's intellectual contributions, Dawson presents an engaging, penetrating, and significant analysis.

Nathan Berg

Sources for Further Study

Choice. XXXV, September, 1997, p. 151.
Commentary. CIV, September, 1997, p. 48.

Mathematics Magazine. LXX, April, 1997, p. 151.
Nature. CCCLXXXVII, May 22, 1997, p. 362.
New Scientist. CLIV, April 26, 1997, p. 45.
Publishers Weekly. CCXLIII, October 28, 1996, p. 70.

LOITERING WITH INTENT
The Apprentice

Author: Peter O'Toole (1932-   )
First published: 1996, in Great Britain
Publisher: Hyperion (New York). Illustrated. 406 pp. $24.95
Type of work: Autobiography
Time: 1953
Locale: England and Ireland

The Irish stage and screen actor's reminiscences about his schooling in London's "Old Vic" Theater Academy in 1953

> *Principal personages:*
> PETER O'TOOLE, the Irish-born stage and screen actor
> JOHN GABRIEL,
> ROBERT ATKINS, and
> ERNEST MILTON, his teachers

While far from being a dry historical document, Peter O'Toole's second volume of memoirs, offering vivid accounts of his early education in the legendary "Old Vic" Royal Academy of Dramatic Arts, will primarily interest readers who share his craft, those interested in classical dramatic training, and particularly those wanting an insider's peek into London's "Old Vic" in the 1950's. Other readers will likely be less satisfied with O'Toole's extremely stylized, extravagant narrative, which tries hard to be more than Polaroid snapshots of bygone years. Unfortunately, O'Toole simply does not quite meet the high mark he sets for himself.

Ironically, O'Toole's surprising difficulty in reaching a wider audience has less to do with his well-established and acknowledged storytelling abilities than with the stories that he has to tell from this brief period of his life. Autobiographies are, almost by definition, more substance than style. Best-selling, tell-all Hollywood accounts of scandals, romances, and facile opinions concerning people and film projects are notorious for being framed in self-justification and self-aggrandizement. Such formulas are what O'Toole deliberately sets out to reverse, turning most well-trodden expectations about actors' memoirs on their heads. Instead, the actor takes an original road with an elegant, if overdone, descriptive panorama of anecdotes, incidents, accidents, and asides told with a dry, rambling wit that promises more than it delivers.

For example, in one characteristic and offbeat passage, O'Toole recounts one incident in which he admits difficulty explaining his subject, so he instead tries to capture a moment of street-corner hawking in cryptic colors typical of his impressionistic style:

> "The Royal Academy of Dramatic Art. You know, my associates Justice Wrottesley, Bob the Liar and the Flea were only the other day asking me what exactly it was that you studied there and by Jesus would you believe I scarce had the ghost of a notion what to tell them? These are Royal Academy balloons, are they? And the Dramatic Art lies in the selling of the little hoors, does it?"
> "Pop. I'm skint. And I'm only trying to knock out a few shillings."

"I'm fair flush, son."

"Thanks, Daddy, but I don't want to be always cadging."

"No, you wouldn't, Peter, you wouldn't. Give us a kiss. Now. Shove over. Mark them up to a dollar the eight. Your last chance, ladies and gentlemen, to buy these red white blue and yellow Royal Academy balloons! We're practically giving away these dramatic Royal Academy balloons at a mere dollar for eight. Don't miss your Royal Academy balloons!"

"Royal Academy balloons!"

"Two for a florin or a dollar will give you eight. Dramatic balloons!"

"Academic balloons!"

"Artistic balloons!"

"Royal balloons!"

This scene captures the essence of O'Toole's use of language, flavorful and likely true to his memory, but his sketchiness obscures his subject matter. O'Toole's wordplay forces readers—if they are so inclined—either to reread lengthy passages or to take each paragraph slowly, connecting the dots for themselves. Like the first volume in O'Toole's series of memoirs, *Loitering with Intent: The Child* (1992), the emphasis on clever, imaginative style is clearly by design, stretching out material most writers would ordinarily confine to chapters rather than full-length books.

In this second volume, covering only the first year at the "Old Vic" academy, O'Toole does succeed in capturing the flavor of his times, writing with an urbane and literate voice. In this period of his life, he seemingly wants to distance himself from his back-street, impoverished background in the industrial town of Leeds, where he was an altar boy, an athlete, a carouser, and ultimately a member of the Royal Navy.

In his memoirs published to date, O'Toole verbosely shows off how far he has come since his early interest in a career in journalism. Here, his tone is lighthearted, impressionistic, and knowledgeable, as he describes a colorful canvas of classrooms for fencing, stage technique, voice projection, and bone-crushing ballet lessons that helped shape his professional career. Also revealing are his personal, internal responses to his eccentric teachers (notably John Gabriel, Robert Atkins, and Ernest Milton). Colleagues and cronies in their collective life behind the curtains are also drawn in incomplete portraits. Throughout this memoir, no figures are ever developed into fully fleshed-out characters other than the narrator himself, a casualty to be expected in ego-driven romances of one's past. Some individuals, such as the Americans "The Cisco Kid" and "Pocahontas," are anonymous figures for whom O'Toole clearly feels affection, but it is never clear why he holds them in such regard.

Theater devotees will likely find interesting perspectives in O'Toole's insights and analysis of plays being rehearsed at the academy, especially Sir Arthur Pinero's *Trelawny of the Wells* (1898), William Shakespeare's *As You Like It* (1599/1600) and *King John* (1596/1597), and George Bernard Shaw's *You Never Can Tell* (1898). (In the case of the latter play, O'Toole delightfully captures one pivotal moment when his skillful teacher puts a yellow rose in his hand to prevent him from making unconscious arm movements). Were there more of such material in *The Apprentice*, this volume's significance might rise to the lofty goals O'Toole set for it, as it is clear that his eye for stagecraft is one of his strongest suits. When he is focused on the stage itself, he is illuminating, perceptive, and particularly qualified to share his specialist's knowledge of the world he knows best.

In these sections, style and substance appropriately merge, providing vitality and spirit to what might be only dry criticism in another writer's hands. Clearly influenced by the stylistic panache of his oft-praised literary mentor, Shaw, O'Toole jumps from tense to tense and from real-life to on-stage lines. In these passages, O'Toole successfully shows how actors must blur the distinctions between off- and on-stage roles. In these passages, perhaps, readers learn the most about the personality of the writer as he demonstrates, in perfectly overdrawn style and substance, his penchant for dramatic romanticism and his distaste for low-key realism.

Admittedly, O'Toole skillfully captures the spirit of excitement and wonder in a young actor's mind, particularly one accepted into a privileged, elite academy. He evokes the passion and energy of an apprentice's awe, bewilderment, and curiosity about his eccentric surroundings as well as his feelings about joining a long historical train of thespians. He makes the latter point often by repeatedly comparing himself with the nineteenth century Shakespearean tragedian Edmund Kean and by including long lists of actors and plays seemingly unrelated to the point he is trying to make in a particular passage—unless, of course, the point is simple showboating. After all, showboating is the point and theme of this entire volume, and readers should expect theatricality on every level on every page of the second volume of *Loitering with Intent*.

Still, readers expecting the humorous anecdotes that O'Toole and fellow Irish actor-storyteller Richard Harris have made their stock in trade on late-night television talk shows will find few memorable punch lines. Readers seeking reasons for the lengthy descriptions of boardinghouse pranks, parties, and street-corner ogling will also find few moments to remember. Instead, O'Toole begins with images of backstage furnishings and creates a backdrop of Irish and English theater history flavored with impersonal asides regarding the joys of sex and drinking. Then, after this intriguing and promising introduction, O'Toole's biography is told indirectly, through allusions to his roles from Lawrence of Arabia to Pizza Hut commercials, from green novice to learned survivor. Breezy anecdotes of his early education reveal his adoration for actors Richard Burton and Claire Bloom and his early friendship with fellow film-star-in-waiting Albert Finney. O'Toole also includes a puzzling recap of World War II. Only those who have read his first volume will understand that this reflects his obsession with Adolf Hitler. In the interim, glimpses are given into other important influences on his career, such as details about how dramatic English poetry, particularly that of Shakespeare and Dylan Thomas, helped shape O'Toole's artistic taste and sensibilities. Undeniably, there are interesting revelations in this book, but there are perhaps too many home movies, told painstakingly frame by frame, to sustain reader interest in every facet of the life of Peter O'Toole.

These vivid if disconnected descriptions may best be read as they were likely written—in short, open-ended intervals when the reader, like the author, is in the mood to loiter. *Loitering with Intent: The Apprentice* is ultimately a slow-paced read with few page-turners. Many readers will enjoy the colorful atmosphere and creative wordcraft, but this actor's most engaging literary work is likely to come when he covers the film roles that make his career worth reading about in the first place.

Wesley Britton

Sources for Further Study

Booklist. XCIII, December 1, 1996, p. 619.
Boston Globe. February 7, 1997, p. D12.
Chicago Tribune. February 16, 1997, XIV, p. 8.
Los Angeles Times Book Review. February 16, 1997, p. 14.
The New York Times Book Review. CII, February 23, 1997, p. 26.
People. XLVII, February 24, 1997, p. 31.
Publishers Weekly. CCXLIII, December 9, 1996, p. 53.
Sight and Sound. VI, November, 1996, p. 35.
The Spectator. CCLXXVII, July 6, 1996, p. 37.
The Times Literary Supplement. July 12, 1996, p. 13.
Vanity Fair. February, 1997, p. 80.
The Washington Post Book World. XXVII, February 2, 1997, p. 3.

LOOK, LISTEN, READ

Author: Claude Lévi-Strauss (1908-   )
First published: Regarder, Écouter, Lire, 1993, in France
Translated from French by Brian C. D. Singer
Publisher: HarperCollins (New York). Illustrated. 202 pp. $24.00
Type of work: Essays

This collection of essays discusses the nature of the aesthetic experience and the structures which underlie painting, music, and literature

Claude Lévi-Strauss is primarily known as an anthropologist, one of the most influential figures in that field. He is closely associated with the structuralist school of literary theory. Structuralism, as Lévi-Strauss defines it here, is not limited to one discipline but is suited to any subject. In structuralism, the details of specific cases are simplified to reveal a scientific inner structure, such as the grammar which underlies the infinite expressions of language. Lévi-Strauss claims as a structuralist the French composer Jean-Philippe Rameau because he developed a theory of musical chords that greatly reduced the complexity of earlier systems.

The essays in *Look, Listen, Read* are concerned with facets of aesthetic experience. Lévi-Strauss divides the text into six categories, within which he clusters related essays. The essays are not divided into single academic units. They interpenetrate one another by multiple references to the same great figures of (mainly) French art, music, and literature. They are bound by Lévi-Strauss's contemplation of the structures which underlie art, music, and literature as sources of pleasure and as products of human skill.

Lévi-Strauss organizes these six chapters in the following order: "Looking at Poussin," "Listening to Rameau," "Reading Diderot," "Speech and Music," "Sounds and Colors," and "Regarding Objects." The essays deal with a wide range of historical periods and present a bewildering array of authors, artists, and classic and contemporary criticism. Beneath this surface, rich in detail and citation, however, lies a common structure. These collected thoughts, which stem from different places and times, work together to produce a nested argument where each fragment is self-contained yet an integral part of the whole.

Several explicit models for this view of intellectual activity are presented. A striking example is the opening essay in "Looking at Poussin," where Lévi-Strauss discusses the writing technique of Marcel Proust. Another is essay 13, within "Reading Diderot." Here Lévi-Strauss deals with the definition of fractals, patterns which are repeated throughout a structure at all of its scales of size. This concept, drawn from mathematics, is commonly illustrated by the branching of twigs in a tree, a pattern repeated in the larger boughs and in the shape of the whole tree. The image of fractals underlies the structure of *Look, Listen, Read.*

A grounding in art, music, and literary history is essential to understanding these essays (Lévi-Strauss assumes his reader to be familiar with the major artists under

discussion and cites minor painters, musicians, writers, and critics with equal enthusiasm and detail) and to readily change context of reference to the opinions or
characteristic techniques of other artists from other schools and periods. For example,
it seems odd to find that the opening pages of "Looking at Poussin" concern Proust
and the temporal nature of his multivolume novel, *À la recherche du temps perdu*
(1913-1926; *Remembrance of Things Past*, 1922-1932). Proust, after all, is a novelist
of the early twentieth century, while painter Nicolas Poussin lived from 1594 to 1665.
The juxtaposition of genres and eras, however, characterizes this collection. This essay
serves as a veiled statement of purpose for the book. Proust did not write his
monumental novel in chronological order but rather wrote and rewrote, using bits of
text from different times, each to be integrated within a greater structure.

Generally, the other essays in "Looking at Poussin" concern aspects of Poussin's
painting techniques. In the second essay, Lévi-Strauss reflects on the fact that Poussin
preceded his paint compositions with compositions of small statues draped in costume
and placed in different positions to represent the figures which would appear on
canvas. Thus each picture by Poussin the painter is prefigured by several works by
Poussin the sculptor. This characteristic of Poussin echoes Proust's sculpting a literary
whole from temporally distinct fragments.

Look, Listen, Read is accompanied by four color plates, three of which illustrate the
third essay in "Looking at Poussin." Here Lévi-Strauss considers an article by his
contemporary, Erwin Panofsky, about a group of paintings under the same title, *Et in
Arcadia Ego*, and the translations of that title into English and onto canvas. The first
painting is by an Italian painter, Guercino (1591-1666), the other two by Poussin; all
depict groups of shepherds beside a tomb in a pastoral landscape. Lévi-Strauss
analyzes the change in concept and composition of these canvases, particulary the
assimilation and transformation of Death from a large skull in the first painting to
a female divinity in the third. He differs with Panofsky's conclusion that the third
painting reflects a change in concept, a mistranslation of the Latin title (from *I, too, am
in Arcadia* to *I, too, have lived in Arcadia*). The essay posits an essential relationship
between the meaning of the canvas, the technique which forms the personages of the
paintings and the ideas they carry, and the dynamic of the groupings in which these
figures appear.

The fourth essay pursues an analysis of Poussin's painting *Eliezer and Rebecca*
based on its biblical source, color qualities, and the positions of the figures within it.
Lévi-Strauss emphasizes the sculptural quality of Poussin's paintings and reactions to
Poussin's color qualities and compositions from critics of the seventeenth, eighteenth,
and nineteenth centuries.

In the Bible story, Abraham has been led by God to a new homeland, yet when it
comes time for his son to marry he sends a servant, Eliezer, back to his original
homeland and the people of his own blood to seek a bride, Rebecca. Eliezer meets
Rebecca at the well, where she draws water for his camels. Poussin paints the moment
when the title couple stands in the center of a group of women drawing water from
the well. For Poussin's contemporary critics, the lack of camels damaged the painting.

For Lévi-Strauss, this canvas is a fully realized and logical unit. Each figure is modeled to stand alone, yet within the small groups and within the composition as a whole, each figure contributes to a total meaning, a structural conflict between homeland and blood relationships, the kernel of meaning within Abraham's story. Camels, although picturesque, would add nothing to this thoughtful canvas.

Lévi-Strauss offers six essays in the Poussin section, three in the Rameau section, four in "Reading Diderot," five in "Speech and Music," three in "Sounds and Colors," and three in "Regarding Objects." Most are highly idiosyncratic texts which cannot be represented by any sort of group analysis. Moreover, although one section may bear the name of one figure in its title, the essays deal with other figures. In "Reading Diderot," Jean-Jacques Rousseau and Poussin figure heavily, and Lévi-Strauss writes at length about the Abbé Charles Batteux, Denis Diderot's contemporary literary theorist. The common question of these different essays, whether painting should preserve a temporal unity, presenting only the image of one moment, is one posed by Diderot but also considered by Rousseau and Batteux. Poussin's painting of another Bible story, the manna given to the Israelites in the desert, is evoked to counter the position urged by Diderot. Poussin presents several "moments" in his canvases, several points of thought which enable him to tell a whole story in what appears on the surface to be one moment in time.

The title *Look, Listen, Read* alerts the reader to another dynamic besides Lévi-Strauss's interest in the articulation of works to form other works. These essays are concerned with the senses, with the eyes and ears, and with their skilled employment: the reading of art, music, literature. The intersection of the sense with its art or science follows a model familiar to readers of Lévi-Strauss, the diagram where the diachronic and the synchronic meet, the horizontal line intersected by the vertical. One "looks" at Poussin and apprehends the colors and forms of the figures which make up his compositions, his sculptural individuals and three-dimensional groups within a two-dimensional context. Yet the viewer also is a reader who follows the story of Eliezer and Rebecca. Operagoers hear the chord progressions of Rameau as his chorus passes from one key to another. Do they feel the thrill of sorrow felt by eighteenth century listeners, or are they bored? The analysis devoted to Arthur Rimbaud's sonnet "Voyelles" ("Vowels"), one of French literature's most famous precisely because it posits a synesthetic intersection between the worlds of sound, color, and meaning, is as typical of this structure in Lévi-Strauss's collection as the first essay, devoted to Proust, is of the fractal model.

While lamenting that the audience of the twentieth century is deficient in the technical knowledge of musical theory familiar to eighteenth century listeners, Lévi-Strauss presents technical citations from Rameau's contemporaries and two pages of an operatic score as illustration. His analysis of crucial measures from *Castor et Pollux* (1737) illuminates a transition in key which was an innovation in its day, eliciting a dramatic reaction from its audience. Rameau no longer thrills the public. Why is the same operatic score "boring" in the twentieth century? Does the change in reception of Rameau's work reflect a less sophisticated audience? Can music be calculated to convey emotion through melody and harmony? Does technical manipulation produce predictable emotions?

The section "Speech and Music" raises similar questions in different form. Lévi-Strauss juxtaposes prominent twentieth century linguists Roman Jakobson and Ferdinand de Saussure with Jean-Jacques Rousseau and Richard Wagner to explore whether music can convey ideas and emotions, whether it can be understood as a language with a grammar which may be manipulated. Can an operagoer appreciate the meaning of a given work without knowing the language in which it is sung? Lévi-Strauss can.

Lévi-Strauss chooses his contemporary, the late Michel Leiris, as his antagonist over the language of opera. He argues other aesthetic points with other great figures now dead, with Rousseau and Diderot, but also with friends from his own past. One essay in "Sounds and Colors" details an exchange of notes with André Breton which led to Breton's declaration of the principles of surrealism. Lévi-Strauss even probes his own misuse of "abrogation" in an earlier work, a lingering memory of reading other authors, mingled with a rearrangement of letters, changing "orb" to "bro" and finally, by intellectually subterranean paths, placing it in an inappropriate context. This eccentric note follows the personal, but abstract, exchange with Breton.

Who is the reader for this collection of essays? There are few who can match the erudition of the author or his interests. The reader with a good acquaintance with the poet Rimbaud will relish Lévi-Strauss's essay on "Voyelles." If the same reader is also familiar with Breton and his interest in the Symbolist poets, the juxtaposition of the two pieces is a happy one. That same reader would be unlikely to be equally versed in eighteenth century opera and painting or Diderot and the other philosopher scholars of the *Encyclopédie* (1751-1772; *Encyclopedia*, 1965). Certainly, students of art and music will find this book fruitful material for reflection, but they must also be familiar with literature, for Lévi-Strauss does not confine his citations of Rimbaud or Proust to essays directly addressing literary questions. The final section of *Look, Listen, Read* devotes several essays to traditional tales of the Pacific Northwest about artists and the objects they make. These essays unite the themes of aesthetic endeavor and Lévi-Strauss's own work as an ethnographer. They are, perhaps, the most accessible pieces in this remarkable collection, a fractal reflection of the life work of an exceptional scholar.

Anne W. Sienkewicz

Sources for Further Study

Booklist. XCIII, May 1, 1997, p. 1473.
Choice. XXXV, September, 1997, p. 112.
Journal of Anthropological Research. LIII, Winter, 1997, p. 514.
Kirkus Reviews. LXV, April 1, 1997, p. 528.
The New York Times Book Review. CII, June 22, 1997, p. 21.
Publishers Weekly. CCXLIV, April 14, 1997, p. 66.

LOST MAN'S RIVER

Author: Peter Matthiessen (1927-   )
Publisher: Random House (New York). 537 pp. $26.95
Type of work: Novel
Time: The 1950's
Locale: The Florida Everglades

A Florida man returns to his remote hometown, obsessed with finding out the truth about his father's mysterious death in 1910

Principal characters:
> LUCIUS WATSON, the son of E. J. Watson, a prominent pioneer and
> entrepreneur who was shot to death
> SPECK DANIELS, an Everglades poacher, gunrunner, and moonshiner
> HENRY SHORT, a local black man who was a participant, though a
> reluctant one, in the elder Watson's death
> WATSON DYER, a Miami real estate lawyer and the secret namesake of E.
> J. Watson, whose agenda centers on the family's wilderness homestead
> SALLY BROWN, a local resident who struggles to escape the stigma of
> her family's racism and who aids Lucius with his research
> R. B. ("CHICKEN") COLLINS, an elderly and embittered alcoholic who
> seems to be the main custodian of the Watson family secrets

Lost Man's River carries forward the intricately woven family saga, set in the Florida Everglades, that Peter Matthiessen began with his 1990 novel *Killing Mister Watson*. He envisions the series as a trilogy but has said in interviews that "It's all one book. It's just that I chopped the first third away and gave it to Random House. Eventually, I would like to see the whole thing under one cover." The concluding volume is set for publication in late 1998. As reviewer Janet Burroway wrote in *The New York Times*, the project is one of "enormous ambition, laying out the interconnected lives of at least two dozen families whose fortunes and misfortunes betoken the history of the entire state, especially as those lives impinge on that of the pioneer entrepreneur, probable murderer—and certainly murdered—Edgar J. Watson."

The seed for the project was planted when Matthiessen, at the age of seventeen, was on a boat trip through the Everglades with his father and began hearing tales of a notorious killing "that the community was still arguing about," the author recalls. "That's what drew me to it. You could see this myth being shaped, but there were very few hard facts to go by."

Although the people and the landscape in the two books are much the same, *Lost Man's River* and *Killing Mister Watson* differ substantially as fiction, both in writing style and narrative approach. Matthiessen's story is based, however loosely, on an actual historic event, which, apparently, was as puzzling and contradictory to the people of that day as it is in the author's retelling of it. *Killing Mister Watson* was largely written as a fictional form of reportage, investigating the death of E. J. Watson through the viewpoints of early Florida settlers whose ethnic and socioeconomic variety sometimes made the phrase "melting pot" seem almost an understatement but who, nonetheless, were saddled with, as the book's liner notes put it, "the racism that infects the heart of New World history."

The facts of both books' central incident, Watson's killing, are anything but ambiguous. County records show that on October 24, 1910, Watson was confronted by more than twenty armed men on a beach in front of a Chokoloskee Island general store. A medical examiner removed thirty-three pieces of lead from Watson's corpse, but nobody was ever brought to trial for the murder. The reluctance of villagers to "come clean" about the incident, even all these years later, is apparently rooted in an almost unimaginably dense web of blood kinship (both "legitimate" and not), loyalties, and grudges—which, at one point, is described in the book as "people who are all related to each other, back door, front door, and every which way."

Significantly, the book opens with a copy of the Watson family tree. This is not for decoration nor effect. Even the most intrepid of Matthiessen's readers will find themselves referring back to it at some point, trying to clear up confusion over some character's remarks about kinship. Even then, the linkages sometimes remain ambiguous.

The sixty-year-old Lucius who arrives in his old community is a knot of contradictions himself: loner, drifter, college graduate (history), commercial fisherman, hunting guide, outdoorsman with a weakness for alcohol, and melancholic bachelor who has always wanted children. The purpose of his homecoming is not as avocation but as quest—with all of that word's connotations of obsession and excess. Under a pseudonym, he places classified ads in Florida newspapers asking for family stories and reminiscences of the early days in the Everglades on the off chance that one of them might provide some thread he can trace back to his father. However, he gets far more than he bargained for: He receives in the mail—anonymously—a copy of an old deposition filed in a Fort Myers, Florida, courthouse shortly after his father's death. Furthermore, very early in the book, Lucius gets a surprise nighttime visit from a Mikasuki Indian named Billie Jimmie, who says he has been hired to deliver a burial urn of ashes ("Stroke of midnight," says Billie, "them were his very words") and invite Lucius to meet with their mysterious sender at a local bar called Gator Hook.

The odd and seemingly unrelated confluences begin to mount, as do Lucius's questions, problems, and fears. Along the way, readers get a fascinating tour of the region's colorful, awe-inspiring, and often otherworldly landscape, which reviewer Terry Catchpole, writing in *Entertainment Weekly*, calls "a brute beauty." In addition to his novel-writing credentials—*Lost Man's River* is his eighth work of fiction, and he is the only American writer to be nominated for the National Book Award in both the fiction and nonfiction categories—Matthiessen is a naturalist, environmentalist, explorer, and poet, roles that often mesh to brilliant effect in such passages as this one:

> They spent that evening at a motel camp on the Withlacoochee River. While the old man slept off a long day, Lucius drank his whiskey in the shadow of the porch, in the reflections of the giant cypress in the moon mirror of the swamp, deep in forest silence. The gallinule's eerie whistling, the ancient hootings of barred owls in duet, the horn notes of limpkins and far sandhill cranes from beyond the moss-draped walls, were primordial rumorings as exquisitely in place as the shelf fungi on the hoary bark of the great trees.

And he considered how the Watson children, especially the sons, had been bent by the great weight
of the dead father, as pale saplings straining for the light twist up and around the fallen tree, drawing
the last minerals from the punky wood before the great log crumbled into a feast for beetles.

Matthiessen not only has the eye of a born writer but the ear as well. His rendering
of the countless subtleties of his characters' dialects is a marvel in itself, with virtually
every voice seeming just right, regardless of the speaker's age, station, or ethnic
background. For example, one of the people Lucius interviews, an elderly blind man
named Whidden Harden, tells him about

a day in '26, when we was livin on the Watson place, a hurricane day when there was twenty-five
men from Pavilion Key come up the river to find shelter. They had to stand up in the boat, they was
that crowded. That clam skiff was sunk right to the gunwales, and the river lappin in, we couldn't
hardly see no boat at all. Coming up around the bend, them men looked like they was walkin on the
water.

By then, the clams was pretty well thinned out, and in the Depression, the cannery jobs at Caxambas
and Marco was real scarce. The white fellers claimed that the nigra hands had undercut their pay,
so they lynched a black feller at Marco to teach the rest a lesson. Only thing that poor nigra done
wrong was try to make a livin. Them white boys had no education, no ambition, just wanted to feel
they was better than somebody else. Cowards, you know, always in a gang. They was feelin
frustrated, was all it was.

The subject of racism is a constant theme in *Lost Man's River*, as is the destruction
that progress is continuing to wreak on the environment. It is only in the latter case
that the author's own views occasionally intrude on the authenticity of the story, with
characters voicing opinions and assessments that may strike readers as disturbingly
anachronistic, particularly for the 1950's, when the average person was not aware of
the negative impact of technological progress on the environment. Perhaps the chief
environmental bogeyman in the novel comes in the person of Watson Dyer, a slick
Miami attorney with shady motivations. Dyer comes to Lucius asking help to preserve
the family homestead, which he says the National Park Service is preparing to bulldoze
in order to return the wilderness to its natural state. To avoid that outcome, Lucius
agrees to circulate a petition among his relatives in order to pursue an old claim to the
land.

Along the way, he finds that most of the actual participants in the shooting are dead,
the few remaining are very old, and none of their stories fully agree. Some of the people
claim that E. J. Watson used his power and influence to terrorize the community,
spontaneously killing people who got on his bad side, including a worker who once
criticized his wife's cooking. Others describe him in glowing terms: warm, generous,
larger than life, a man with a special fondness for spending time with his babies, which
was not typical of males in that day. For example, Henry Short, in a long deathbed
confession to Lucius, says, "Mist' Lucius, your daddy always *seen* me . . . Seen I was
a *somebody*—some kind of a man, with my own look to me and my own way of workin.
Seen I counted. Seen I weren't just nothin-but-a-nigger. By *seein* me, he give me some
respect, and I was grateful, all them years I knew him." At one point on his trek, Lucius

muses about the contradictions: "He looked like God and he looked like Satan and he looked like Uncle Sam, all three at once." These kinds of paradoxes run deep in human history and myth, from the tale about the blind men all describing different versions of an elephant to Japanese director Akira Kurosawa's classic 1950 film *Rashomon*, in which various observers give radically different accounts of the same event, all of them "true."

Matthiessen did painstaking research into the area's history, one factor that contributed to the project occupying nearly twenty years of his life in between more lucrative nonfiction assignments. In an author's note, however, Matthiessen cautions that *Killing Mister Watson* and *Lost Man's River* "are in no way historical . . . since almost nothing here is history. On the other hand, there is nothing here that could *not* have happened."

Near the end of the book, an acquaintance asks Lucius "Did you get the truth?" Lucius nods and the acquaintance asks, "Well? Feel any better?" Lucius does not answer, but he has established himself as someone who "could never find a truth that satisfied him. That's why he could never let go" of his father's death. Though the ending of *Lost Man's River* is not altogether unresolved, it will still be intriguing to see, in the concluding volume, what use Lucius makes of his newfound "truth."

Carroll Dale Short

Sources for Further Study

Booklist. XCIV, September 15, 1997, p. 180.
Boston Globe. December 14, 1997, p. H1.
Library Journal. CXXII, October 15, 1997, p. 93.
Los Angeles Times. December 8, 1997, p. E4.
Lost Man's River: An Everglades Documentary. 1990, distributed by Mystic Fire (video documentary).
The New York Times Book Review. CII, November 23, 1997, p. 7.
The New Yorker. LXXIII, December 22, 1997, p. 136.
Publishers Weekly. CCXLIV, October 13, 1997, p. 56.
San Francisco Chronicle. November 22, 1997, p. D1.
Time. CL, November 24, 1997, p. 106.

THE MAN MADE OF WORDS
Essays, Stories, Passages

Author: N. Scott Momaday (1934-   )
Publisher: St. Martin's Press (New York). 211 pp. $22.95
Type of work: Essays and miscellaneous prose

This collection of essays, travel accounts, anecdotes, and observations written over Moma-day's career consistently pursues a Native American perspective on language, places, and the spiritual

N. Scott Momaday, author of the Pulitzer Prize-winning novel *House Made of Dawn* (1968) and other works reflecting his Native American background, indicates in a preface to *The Man Made of Words* that "the essays, stories, and passages in this volume . . . were written over a considerable span of time, something over thirty years" and "by different writers" (himself at different stages). Readers may consider the book a collection of "random" prose pieces, but Momaday himself sees a "unified design" in the collection, as well as "something of growth and maturation."

Part 1, "The Man Made of Words," is the longest and most interesting section. Here are gathered the longer essays, key pronouncements by Momaday on such topics as language, the oral tradition, the land, and worldviews. This section shows its seams in the changing terminology—"Indian," "American Indian," "Native American" (and the Canadian version, "First American"). Less noticeable seams appear in subtle changes of attitude (for example, switching to the term "we Americans"). One essay, "The Morality of Indian Hating," written in the militant early 1960's when Momaday was a graduate student at Stanford University, is given an afterword in which he notes its "political" nature and calls it "a kind of anachronism" (but he sticks by his convictions expressed there).

Part 2, "Essays in Place," consists of travel accounts: Visits to religious sites in Russia, Bavaria, and Spain are wedged between visits to Native American sacred places. This sandwich effect emphasizes the continuity in Momaday's quest for the sacred, which he considers another endangered species. Part 3, "The Storyteller and His Art," includes brief essays on people in the arts whom Momaday admires: Native American actor Jay Silverheels, Danish author Isak Dinesen, and American painter Georgia O'Keeffe (American poet John Neihardt and Argentine author Jorge Luis Borges are featured earlier, in part 1). The rest of part 3 consists mostly of anec-dotes—brief encounters making a point—in which Momaday demonstrates the Native American storytelling aesthetic described in his preface.

Overall, *The Man Made of Words* suggests a broad movement in Momaday's career from 1960's-style militancy to 1990's-style mellowing out. Yet literary biographers seeking to use the collection (along with his 1976 work, *The Names: A Memoir*) to piece together Momaday's life and development as a writer will be somewhat frus-trated. Except for "The Morality of Indian Hating," no dates of composition or publication are given, and within the essays Momaday often uses indefinite dates like "twenty years ago" and "one day last summer." Nor is there any indication of how much revision went into the collection.

Still, *The Man Made of Words* affords numerous autobiographical glimpses of Momaday. He was born in 1934 on a homestead near Rainy Mountain Creek in Oklahoma, a part of the southern plains once ruled by his Kiowa ancestors at the height of their culture (see also the introduction to his 1969 work, *The Way to Rainy Mountain*). His mother spoke only English, the language used in the immediate family, but his father's first language was Kiowa, the language used by other relatives on the homestead. When Momaday was still a child, the family moved to the Navajo reservation in New Mexico, where he heard Navajo spoken. This early exposure to several languages likely influenced Momaday's confessed fascination with language, even though he also confesses "real possession" only of English.

One expects a writer to be fascinated with language—a fact at which Momaday's title seems to lightly glance—but for Momaday the explanation is both more complex and crucial. The title *The Man Made of Words* comes from the collection's first essay, "The Arrowmaker," which recounts a Kiowa legend and Momaday's interpretation of it. In the legend, a Kiowa man is making arrows at night when he detects someone watching him through a hole in the tepee. He goes on talking to his wife as if nothing is wrong but tells the presence outside to identify himself by name as a Kiowa. When there is no response, he lets fly an arrow and kills his lurking enemy. The legend offers much food for thought, such as the charming assumption that enemies speak another language. But Momaday interprets the legend as an allegory of existence: Survival depends on one's sense of identity and use of language. The arrowmaker is "the man made of words"—and so is Momaday, who takes the arrowmaker as his prototype and inspiration.

How this allegory applies to Momaday is suggested by other autobiographical glimpses in *The Man Made of Words*. The child from Rainy Mountain Creek has become a cultured man who travels the world, has numerous friends in artistic and intellectual circles, enjoys fine food and wine, has daughters and a dog, and has learned to fly. Left unsaid is that Momaday has spent most of his adult life in universities, first as a student at the University of New Mexico and Stanford University (Ph.D., 1963) and then as an English teacher at the University of California, Berkeley, at Stanford, and at the University of Arizona. How has he remained true to that child from Rainy Mountain Creek, to his Kiowa heritage?

Bridging cultures can be dangerous business, almost a no-win situation involving one's language, identity, values, and ways of thinking. Momaday notes the problems of Native Americans moving from the reservation to the city: "None but an Indian knows so well what it is like to have incomplete existence in two worlds and security in neither." For intellectuals, the cultural gap that must be bridged is even greater. Momaday seems to have achieved some equilibrium by living in academia but identifying with his native culture and writing about it. He is "the man made of words" who has written himself into existence, who has defined his sense of identity through his writing.

In characterizing writing as an existential act, Momaday considers himself lucky to be able to draw on the oral tradition of his Kiowa ancestors. He feels that print culture has debased words by diluting them and making it easy to take them for granted. In the oral tradition, which is always one generation from extinction, words are given their true value, which partakes of the sacred: "Every word spoken, every word heard, is the utterance of prayer." In "On Indian-White Relations: A Point of View" and "The American West and the Burden of Belief," Momaday sees the oral tradition and the print culture as underlying the main difference in worldviews of Native Americans and European immigrants. The print culture of the Europeans led them to "take liberties with words" and led to their "loss of a crucial connection with the real."

As these linkages imply, for Momaday, the "real" always involves the sacred. It is therefore not surprising that his recurrent concern is the decline and loss of the sacred in the modern world. Nor is it surprising that, as he travels the world, he goes in search of remnants of the sacred, which he finds in prehistoric cave art, medieval cathedrals, and the hearts of the Russian people even under communism. Finally, it is not surprising that he describes "the theft of the sacred" from Native Americans as "a subtle holocaust."

For Native Americans, the sacred is disappearing because it often resides in the natural world or particular places, such as Devil's Tower, Canyon de Chelly, Monument Valley, or Wounded Knee. These places have been made sacred by "sacrifice"; to pollute or despoil them is "sacrilege." Yet encroachment upon them is inexorable:

> The sacred places of North America are threatened, even as the sacred earth is threatened. In my generation we have taken steps—small, tentative steps—to preserve forests and rivers and animals. We must also, and above all, take steps to preserve the spiritual centers of our earth, those places that are invested with the dreams of our ancestors and the well-being of our children.

As Momaday's language suggests, there are parallels between the contemporary ecological movement and Native American thinking, particularly in the desire to preserve species and the balance of nature. Yet the ecological movement seems to derive predominantly from Darwinian, scientific-based thinking, as though humans are now in a position to mastermind evolution, for better or worse. With Momaday, the emphasis remains on the "spiritual": The natural world primarily nourishes the soul, and the soul relates to the natural world through feelings, ritual, and tradition.

For Momaday, sacred ground includes the migration route of his Kiowa ancestors, the homestead on Rainy Mountain Creek where he was born, and the New Mexico canyon country where he grew up. He has twice retraced the route of his Kiowa ancestors, who about three hundred years ago migrated from the Montana Rockies to the southern Great Plains. He has also apparently made regular pilgrimages to the Rainy Mountain Creek homestead and to New Mexico. As he says, "There is great good in returning to a landscape that has had extraordinary meaning in one's life. . . . They [such landscapes] become indispensable to our well-being." In his case, the returns to these landscapes seem to have nourished both his identity as a person and his inspiration as a writer.

Harold Branam

Sources for Further Study

Atlanta Journal Constitution. June 29, 1997, p. L9.
Booklist. XCIII, April 15, 1997, p. 1376.
Kirkus Reviews. LXV, March 1, 1997, p. 360.
Library Journal. CXXII, May 1, 1997, p. 104.
The Nation. CCLXIV, June 30, 1997, p. 31.
The New York Times Book Review. CII, June 15, 1997, p. 22.
Publishers Weekly. CCXLIV, March 24, 1997, p. 67.

MAN OF THE CENTURY
The Life and Times of Pope John Paul II

Author: Jonathan Kwitny (1941-   )
Publisher: Henry Holt and Company (New York). Illustrated. 754 pp. $30.00
Type of work: Biography
Time: About 1900 to 1996
Locale: Poland, Vatican City, Rome, and other parts of Italy

This tenth full biography of Pope John Paul II since 1990 is comprehensive and gives special attention to the pope's role in ending the Cold War that existed between the United States and Russia following World War II

> *Principal personages:*
> KAROL "LOLEK" WOJTYLA, a Polish priest who became Pope John Paul II in 1978
> POPE JOHN PAUL I, John Paul II's immediate predecessor
> RONALD REAGAN, fortieth president of the United States
> MIKHAIL GORBACHEV, political leader of the Soviet Union
> MEHMET ALI AGCA, Pope John Paul II's would-be assassin
> LECH WALESA, Polish labor leader, later president of Poland
> GENERAL WOJCIECH JARUZELSKI, Poland's last Communist leader
> POPE PAUL VI, Karol Wojtyla's mentor before Wojtyla became pope

At 754 pages, *Man of the Century: The Life and Times of Pope John Paul II* qualifies as one of the weightiest biographies of the long-serving prelate who, as a Polish national, broke the long-standing tradition, in place for the preceding 455 years, of appointing Italians to the papacy. This comprehensive biography, written by Jonathan Kwitny—formerly a front page feature writer for the *Wall Street Journal* and whose series on the Public Broadcasting System (PBS), *The Kwitny Report*, won the George Polk Award for the best investigative reporting on television—distinguishes itself from the nine other books written about Pope John Paul II since 1990 by honing in on the pope's role in ending the Cold War that had divided the East and West since World War II ended in 1945.

This book, Kwitny's eighth, is essentially an exhaustive example of investigative reporting, comparable in many ways to his earlier, highly successful journalistic efforts such as *Acceptable Risks* (1992), *The Crimes of Patriots: A True Tale of Dope, Dirty Money, and the CIA* (1988), and *Vicious Circles: The Mafia in the Marketplace* (1979). The journalistic approach of *Man of the Century* is evident in its title: As the millennium approaches, it is inevitable that people-of-the-century and people-of-the-millennium books and articles will crowd the shelves of bookstores and the pages of magazines and journals.

The election of Karol Wojtyla, archbishop of Krakow, to pope took the world by surprise. Pope John Paul I, the new pope's immediate predecessor, held office for only thirty-three days before his unexpected death early in October, 1978. When the College of Cardinals was reconvened to select John Paul I's successor, most people foresaw that an Italian would be chosen to assume the role of pope. A few, sensing that the

Roman Catholic church was due for some sort of drastic change, had gone so far as to predict that a non-Italian would be selected, possibly a black cardinal from one of the newly established African nations; these prognosticators, however, were a distinct minority.

As the cardinals met to choose the new pope, the Curia had prepared for distribution to reporters a press release with biographical sketches of sixteen likely candidates. Karol Wojtyla's name was not included on that list, from which most journalists were convinced the new pope would be selected. When the newly elected pope's name was finally made public, the universal response was "Who?" At that point, Wojtyla was little known outside his native Poland. One American, on hearing his name announced, presumed that an Asian had been named pope.

The Polish reaction to Wojtyla's election generally was one of astonishment tempered by considerable hope, although the political leaders in the communist regime that then controlled Poland were deeply troubled by the choice. Many dissident Poles interpreted the appointment as a sure sign that Communism was about to collapse, an interpretation that, in the long term, has proved to be on the mark.

Throughout his life until his election to the papacy, Wojtyla was an outspoken defender of the poor and a strenuous foe of political oppression. He rose to a position of power in the Polish church when he was appointed archbishop of Krakow in 1964. The Polish United Workers' Party, the official, communist-leaning party in power at the time, was unwilling to accede to the church's preferences in selecting an archbishop for this major city. The head of the Polish church in this now classless society was Cardinal Stefan Wyszynski, who was descended from noble stock. The controlling political party did not want a churchman with such high visibility as the archbishop of Krakow to be of noble birth.

Wojtyla came from a relatively poor worker's family. Philosophically, he was the polar opposite of Wyszynski. Zenon Kliszko, Polish minister of religious affairs at the time, selected Wojtyla from among the candidates for the archbishopric because he knew Wojtyla was an independent thinker who would, in a position of power, break from Wyszynski, thereby playing into the Party's hands by embarrassing the church. Kliszko considered Wojtyla the best candidate for the reigning party, not because Wojtyla had communist leanings—he clearly did not—but because he was likely to challenge his ecclesiastical superiors.

A decade later, Pope John Paul II, as the new leader of the Roman Catholic church, embarked on a program that emphasized pacifism, a respect for and acceptance of other religions, and, perhaps most important of all, a willingness to admit error, something unheard of in the papacy as held by formal, authoritarian, and aloof Italian popes for nearly half a millennium. A chink in the Vatican's ecclesiastical armor had begun to appear with the election of Pope John XXIII, who was the most human and approachable of the Italian popes and whose relaxation of certain protocols in many ways paved the way for Pope John Paul II's less formal approach.

The papacy has always, of necessity, been concerned with politics. The church is a unique entity that maintains its own sovereign state, Vatican City, but must also coexist worldwide within other sovereign states, many of which do not support or uphold its most zealously upheld doctrines. Certainly the Communist bloc countries, with their official antireligious doctrines, had a most uncomfortable and uneasy relationship with the church, which many eastern Europeans still supported either overtly or covertly. For this reason, the election of a Polish pope created a substantial political stir throughout Eastern Europe.

A chance remark made by Pope John Paul II during his first week in office, and reported out of context, had broad political implications and caused some political fallout. Addressing a group of reporters in his first days as pope, John Paul II was asked by a reporter whether he planned to return for a visit to his native Poland. The pope's advisers, including the very controlling master of ceremonies and papal adviser Monsignor Virgilio Noe, were off camera when the question was posed. The pope gestured to the advisers and said such a trip necessarily would depend on whether they would let him make it. The Polish government presumed that the pope's widely reported remark referred to its leaders and took umbrage at it, thinking that John Paul II was trying to back them into a political corner, which he indeed was not.

The pope's advisers did their best to keep John Paul II's remarks as noncontroversial as possible, but the pope had a mind of his own. Determined to bring as much warmth and informality as he could to his office, he soon did away with many of the established protocols, substituting "I" and "my" in speeches where previously the royal "we" or "our" would have been used.

In the United States, the Ronald Reagan administration had difficulties with the Roman Catholic church. Reagan was bent on accelerating the nuclear arms race at a time when the Vatican called for a ban on nuclear weapons. Roman Catholic priests called for such a ban from their pulpits across the United States, delivering frequent homilies on the subject.

In California, Bishop Roger Mahoney declared publicly that no Catholic could justify supporting the use of nuclear weapons even for defense. The Vatican gave him a vote of confidence by naming him cardinal of Los Angeles. Elsewhere in California, a referendum to freeze the production of nuclear weapons was supported publicly by Archbishop John Quinn and other prominent churchmen. As far away as New Zealand, a Roman Catholic cardinal was instrumental in preventing the docking of a French ship thought to be carrying nuclear materials.

Kwitny's depiction of Reagan's interaction with Leonid Brezhnev, which resulted in a standoff regarding the production of nuclear weapons and a thaw in the Cold War, is detailed and informative, as is his material on the rise and effectiveness of Mikhail Gorbachev in diplomatic circles. Kwitny presents the two American leaders who were presumably working toward world peace, Reagan and George Bush, as men living in the past, whereas Gorbachev clearly was moving meteorically toward the future. The pope, according to Kwitny, worked quietly behind the scenes to help bring about the détente that the politicians involved apparently could not reach independently.

Kwitny also provides important information on labor's uprisings against Wojciech Jaruzelski's communist regime in Poland and Lech Walesa's rise to political power.

During the period of Poland's greatest political upheavals, Pope John Paul II, who often visited Poland, kept his finger firmly on the pulse of his native land and worked successfully for the institution of free elections there.

When this aim finally came to fruition on June 4, 1989, in what were the first free, multiparty elections in any Eastern European Bloc nation, the Solidarity Party won all 162 of the seats it was permitted to run for in the lower house and 99 of the 100 seats available in the upper house. It is estimated that an astounding 80 percent of the Communist Party members in Poland crossed party lines and voted for Solidarity.

Mehmet Ali Agca, a twenty-one-year-old Turkish fanatic who belonged to a fascist group labeled the Gray Wolves and was reminiscent of an American "skinhead," announced as early as November, 1979, his intention to kill the pope. John Paul II visited Turkey at about that time to seek an accord between the Orthodox church and the Roman Catholic church, from which it had broken off more than nine hundred years earlier. It took Agca a year and a half to carry out his threat. This Islamic militant went to Rome shortly before his planned attack, and on May 13, 1981, was in the Vatican courtyard when John Paul gave his weekly general audience.

Following this audience, as was his custom, the pope made a circuit around the perimeter of the open courtyard in the "popemobile." A shot rang out, and the pope crumpled. His assailant was quickly and easily subdued by some nearby nuns, and the pope was rushed to the hospital, where his life-threatening injuries were attended to.

This close brush with death left the pope weakened for some months, but always forgiving of his would-be assassin, with whom he has since met several times. It took four hours of surgery to repair five serious wounds to the pope's large intestine. One bullet missed a major artery by one-tenth of an inch.

A second assassination attempt was made on Pope John Paul II on May 13, 1982, the first anniversary of Agca's assault on His Holiness. This attempt was made in Fatima by a disgruntled priest who objected to Vatican II. The assailant was subdued, and the pope was not injured. Such attempts, however, limited the pope's mobility and have reduced the extent to which he can mingle with crowds, as he always wished to do.

R. Baird Shuman

Sources for Further Study

America. CLXXVII, November 22, 1997, p. 24.
Booklist. XCIII, August, 1997, p. 1844.
Boston Globe. November 16, 1997, p. L3.
Chicago Tribune. October 31, 1997, II, p. 10.
Library Journal. CXXII, September 15, 1997, p. 79.
National Catholic Reporter. XXXIII, September 26, 1997, p. 12.
The New York Times Book Review. CII, October 19, 1997, p. 11.
Publishers Weekly. CCXLIV, September 15, 1997, p. 70.

MARSHALL McLUHAN
Escape into Understanding

Author: W. Terrence Gordon (1942-   )
Publisher: Basic Books (New York). Illustrated. 465 pp. $35.00
Type of work: Biography
Time: 1911-1979

The authorized biography of the classically trained academician who, as innovative media analyst, transformed and illuminated the way we live in "the global village"

> *Principal personages:*
> HERBERT MARSHALL McLUHAN, Canadian-born academic and media analyst
> CORINNE LEWIS McLUHAN, his wife
> ERIC McLUHAN, his son
> EDMUND CARPENTER, artist, designer, and collaborator with McLuhan
> QUENTIN FIORE, designer and collaborator with McLuhan

For a time, it seemed as if Marshall McLuhan had experienced the inevitable trajectory of modern fame: early years of academic preparation and semi-obscurity, followed by a sudden rise and brief prominence, and then a fall into oblivion with no influence left on those to come. The comet had flashed, the world had wondered, and then it was over.

McLuhan's major publications, with their revealing subtitles and their dates, seem to confirm the story. His first work, *The Mechanical Bride: Folklore of Industrial Man* (1951), was published in 1951 and not followed until 1962 by *The Gutenberg Galaxy: The Making of Typographic Man*. The trilogy (so it seems in retrospect) was completed in 1964 with *Understanding Media: The Extensions of Man*. Following those three seminal volumes came some secondary but still important works, most notably the visually and intellectually stimulating *The Medium Is the Message: An Inventory of Effects* (1967), undertaken in collaboration with Quentin Fiore; *Counterblast*, the journal produced with the noted designer Edmund Carpenter; and a compendium of views edited by Gerald Stearn titled *McLuhan, Hot and Cool: A Primer for the Understanding of and a Critical Symposium with a Rebuttal by McLuhan* (1967). From then until McLuhan's death on New Year's Eve in 1979, there was a series of works that to the casual reader might seem marginal, even derivative, including a compilation of his literary criticism.

Before ten years had passed after his death, the interest in McLuhan's ideas, which had never died (neither the interest nor the ideas) began to re-emerge with publication of the *Letters of Marshall McLuhan* (1988); *Laws of Media* (1989), written in conjunction with and finished by his son, Eric McLuhan; *Essential McLuhan* (1995); and a host of book-length and shorter studies, including recognition by the growing Internet community of McLuhan as its "patron saint." The question Tom Wolfe perceptively had posed back in the 1960's finally was answered: "What if he is right?" Wolfe had asked the question in a major essay about McLuhan—if this Canadian professor was correct in his outlandish theories, what difference would that make?

Now the world knew: McLuhan had been right about many things, and his being right about so many things had made a very big difference. Terrence Gordon's authorized biography helps readers understand what McLuhan was right about and something about how he came to his startling but seemingly inescapable conclusions. This is among the best and rarest of biographies, one that links the history and life of an individual with the growth and development of his ideas.

McLuhan, born in 1911 in Edmonton, Alberta, moved with seeming ease and ability into the academic life. After receiving his undergraduate degree in English literature from the University of Manitoba, where he had enrolled with the intention of becoming an engineer, McLuhan won a coveted scholarship to Cambridge University, where he came under the profound and lasting influence of the great English critic I. A. Richards. It was Richards, through works such as *Practical Criticism* (1929), who suggested to McLuhan that the way to approach a work of art—or, later, any medium of communication between human beings, including most famously the electric light bulb, which McLuhan defined as "pure information"—was to focus on its effect and form, rather than its intent and content. The thought that "The medium is the message" had been seeded; it awaited only its quickening and then delivery to a first indifferent, then astounded, world.

An essential impetus to the development of McLuhan's thoughts on media and their effects was his choice of the English writer Thomas Nashe for his dissertation subject. McLuhan's study of Nashe and Nashe's prose style brought a galaxy of wildly disparate topics into focus to make startlingly yet irrevocable sense. Nashe, a contemporary of William Shakespeare, was a bravura performer in the exuberantly rhetorical prose of his period, yet his works were so seemingly muddled and confused that traditional literary critics had been baffled by him. McLuhan, intuitively at first and later with increasing understanding, supplied the key: Nashe was a transitional figure, an artist at the nexus between the oral age of the Middle Ages (when "reading was necessarily reading aloud" as McLuhan glossed in *The Gutenberg Galaxy*) and the print age of the Renaissance (the transition of "the auditory into visual terms"). It was not Nashe's subject matter (his content) but his technique (his medium) that made the difference. It was a difference, McLuhan claimed, that altered not only the readers' reception of the work but also their very perception of the world around them.

As McLuhan explained in *Understanding Media*, the media are "the extensions of man," taking innate senses and expanding and enlarging them, making people capable of seeing, hearing, and (one hopes) understanding more through and with the media than unaided. The media have a profound and lasting impact on people, and McLuhan rightly understood media in the widest and most inclusive fashion. Thus, the wheel is an extension of the foot; the book, an extension of the eye; and electric circuitry, from radio to TV to computers, an extension of the central nervous system. These media, by altering the environment, change the ratio of senses: the oral/aural world of the Middle Ages favored the sense of hearing, and the visual/print world of the Renaissance favored the sense of sight. Nashe recorded the change from one medium to another and from one perception of the world to another. What McLuhan perceived and announced was that when media change, people change. He also noted that, in the 1950's and 1960's, people were changing again, because the formerly dominant print culture was giving way to the new electronic media. The change in media was giving the world "an ear for an eye," in McLuhan's typically punning way of phrasing a valuable insight. He meant (among other things) that as media changed, so changed the human beings who used them.

Nor was this all, for McLuhan had concluded that media came in two forms, hot and cool, depending on how much information they provided the recipient and how much the individual had to supply for him- or herself. As he explained it in *Understanding Media*:

> A cool medium, whether the spoken word or the manuscript or TV, leaves much more for the listener or user to do than a hot medium. If the medium is of high definition, participation is low. If the medium is of low intensity, the participation is high. Perhaps this is why lovers mumble so.

In other words, television and cartoons are "cool" because their gaps leave so much for the viewer to fill in, while radio and film are "hot" because they give the participant almost all the information needed for the message to be received and absorbed. With this distinction between hot and cool media, and the realization that the electronic revolution had come close to creating the "global village," McLuhan had put into place most of his groundbreaking work. Much of this insight had been heard, and some even acted on by artists and the communications industry, yet precious little had been understood. Years after the fact, we are returning to understand just how, and why, in Tom Wolfe's words, "he was right."

Gordon's biography does an outstanding job in following McLuhan's personal and intellectual development during the years these groundbreaking theories were conceived, developed, and presented. On the personal side, Gordon is completely satisfactory. His sketches of McLuhan's family, in particular of his likable but perhaps lightweight father and his theatrical mother (she was an accomplished performer on the lecture circuit throughout much of her life), shed invaluable light on his intellectual development. Gordon's handling of McLuhan's conversion to Roman Catholicism, which was certainly the keystone and confluence of his personal, spiritual, and intellectual lives, is handled with elegance and understanding. It was perhaps inevitable that a philosopher of the media would be drawn to a church that focused its own attention so closely and intensively on the Word.

Gordon is also exemplary in following McLuhan's personal history. Most academics live lives that may be intellectually fulfilling but that are notably short in personal melodrama. This does not mean that their lives are without interest, even passion. McLuhan's impulsive courtship of his beautiful Texas-born wife, Corinne, and their loving relationship over decades of marriage is a passionate story, and Gordon's telling of it rounds out McLuhan as a very human individual.

The major interest in McLuhan is on his thought, for that is what has made such a difference. When it comes to McLuhan's theories on media, Gordon presents them clearly, outlines them cogently, and remarks perceptively on the reception they received from fellow academics, journalists, and the general public. At the height of his fame during the late 1960's, McLuhan was so well known, if little understood, that *Rowan and Martin's Laugh-In*, a popular television comedy show, could raise a laugh by having a character plaintively implore, "Marshall McLuhan, whatcha doin'?"

What McLuhan was doing was explaining how the media we create in turn re-create us. Hot media, such as radio, fill the recipient with information; there is little for the listener to do *except* listen and be transported on the oral/aural wave. The extreme and the outrageous flourish on radio; thus, both Adolf Hitler's ranting rise to dictatorship and Orson Welles's infamous *The War of the Worlds* broadcast found radio to be the perfect medium. By contrast, television is perhaps the coolest of media, providing the audience with only disjointed fragments of information on its dancing cathode ray tube and forcing the viewer to participate (largely unknowingly, McLuhan perceptively notes) in making sense of its flickering shadows. "Hot" media demand passive audiences; "cool" media, active ones. The change from a dominant "hot" medium (print) to a "cool" one (electronics in general, television in particular) would mean wrenching changes in society. Just as Nashe and the Elizabethan writers had helped usher out as the oral world gave way to the visual, so Jack Parr and his televised cohorts reintroduced the oral culture that has caused the global village to become a reality.

McLuhan did not pretend to fully explain this global village. He realistically described much of his work as "intellectual probes," and he never gathered these probes together in a comprehensive, coherent fashion. Perhaps he never could, given the ever shifting focus of his studies. Even *The Laws of Media*, a reasonably "definitive" work that McLuhan produced with his son, Eric, retains his hallmark questioning, speculative approach. As McLuhan himself once noted, in a world where all is in flux, a fixed point of view can be a dangerous luxury.

Such a point of view, however, is not a luxury but a necessity for a biographer, and Gordon has provided an outstanding point of view of McLuhan and his compelling insights. Even McLuhan himself admitted that his probes were sometimes murky and often infuriating—in fact, he sometimes liked that. As the originator of the probes, he could revel in the responses they provoked. Gordon has clarified and illuminated them, and in doing so he has linked them into a more coherent system that not only explains what McLuhan was saying but also helps us understand why, as Tom Wolfe long ago suspected, it still and so importantly matters that "he is right."

Michael Witkoski

Sources for Further Study

Booklist. XCIV, September 15, 1997, p. 183.
Boston Globe. October 22, 1997, p. D3.
Library Journal. CXXII, October, 1997, p. 92.
Maclean's. CX, October 6, 1997, p. 73.
The New York Times Book Review. CII, November 2, 1997, p. 38.
Publishers Weekly. CCXLIV, August 18, 1997, p. 76.

MASON AND DIXON

Author: Thomas Pynchon (1937-   )
Publisher: Henry Holt (New York). 773 pp. $27.50
Type of work: Novel
Time: The mid- to late eighteenth century
Locale: England, South Africa, South Atlantic, the American colonies, and Scotland

Pynchon uses the establishment of the Mason-Dixon line, eventually dividing slave states from free states, to dramatize some of America's deepest tensions and contradictions

Principal characters:
CHARLES MASON, an English astronomer
REBEKAH MASON, his dead wife, to whose memory he remains devoted
THE REVEREND WICKS CHERRYCOKE, a minister who narrates Mason
    and Dixon's travels to his relatives
JEREMIAH DIXON, an English surveyor
NEVIL MASKELYNE, a royal astronomer who is brother-in-law of the
    famous Clive of India
ARMAND ALLÈGRE, France's greatest chef, who is loved by a mechanical
    duck
ZEPHO BECK, a man who metamorphoses at night into a gigantic beaver
CAPTAIN ZHANG, a *fêng shui* master
BENJAMIN FRANKLIN, an American who chases young women and
    dispenses trite advice
GEORGE WASHINGTON, an American who speaks Yiddish and smokes
    hemp with Mason and Dixon

Next to J. D. Salinger, Thomas Pynchon is the most famous recluse among important twentieth century American authors, having craftily covered his tracks for some thirty-five years as of the publication of *Mason and Dixon.* He majored in engineering physics at Cornell University before switching to English, worked as a technical writer for Boeing from 1960 to 1962, then went underground, surfacing only occasionally with novels that are as idiosyncratic and convoluted as they are brilliant. Few readers will disagree that he can write like the proverbial bat out of—no known address.

The publication of *V.* in 1963 introduced Pynchon's public to an immense, intricate, often savagely humorous vision of a century gone haywire, propelled by chaos and governed by fruitless worldwide quests related in densely symbolic language. *The Crying of Lot 49* (1966) also takes the form of a search, with a protagonist named Oedipa Maas uncovering an international postal conspiracy. The governing theme of this and Pynchon's subsequent novel, *Gravity's Rainbow* (1973), is entropy, a concept borrowed from thermodynamics, which refers to the tendency of all systems, even the universe itself, to run down and move toward disorder through an irretrievable loss of available energy. *Gravity's Rainbow*, which won a National Book Award, has earned a fervent cult following among readers. It features Tyrone Slothrop, an American soldier in London during World War II, who can predict imminent German bombing trajectories and whose fragmentary consciousness roams around the world as Pynchon floods the book with arcane information about physics, statistics, sociology, history, and much more. *Vineland* (1990) is a dark fairy tale about the United States under what Pynchon considers an evil spell: sinister Federal Bureau of Investigation (FBI) plots, the death of 1960's idealism, and the pitiless, reactionary politics of the Nixon and Reagan eras.

Mason and Dixon is a monster of a novel, often an allegorical picaresque, sprawling over three continents and half a century. Its central narrative is factual, featuring two Englishmen, the astronomer Charles Mason (1728-1786) and the surveyor Jeremiah Dixon (1733-1779). From 1763 to 1767, they were engaged by the Royal Society to settle an eighty-year-old dispute by mapping the borders between the proprietorships of Pennsylvania and Maryland. Ten years before the American Revolution, Mason and Dixon divided much of America in two, their line formalizing what was to become a war-causing separation between slave and free states, a mark where some of America's deepest characteristics and contradictions were to focus. The book is Pynchon's reimagining not only of Mason's and Dixon's lives but also of the tensions between science's orderly processes and rationalism and nature's wildness, marvels, and frequent violence.

Compared with the enigmatic complexities of Pynchon's earlier work, this novel is refreshingly linear, with the protagonists fully and concretely drawn. Mason and Dixon are a great buddy duo, acting as halves to each other. Mason is a mopey deist obsessed with the ghost of his beloved dead wife and stewing over his professional disappointments; he is essentially cautious and prudent in temperament. Dixon is a cheerful Quaker, an instinctive radical and populist, an erotic adventurer and genial drinker who finds himself appalled by the cruel slaughter of American Indians and enslavement of Africans. He is a humane bumpkin to Mason's melancholy sophisticate. As an astronomer, Mason looks up; as a surveyor, Dixon looks down; most of their reality is complementary.

The travels and travails of Mason and Dixon are told by the slightly sententious Reverend Wicks Cherrycoke as after-dinner stories to entertain his family. He claims to have been a member of two of Mason and Dixon's expeditions yet recounts many events at which he could not have been present, perhaps relating to the psychic Ronald Cherrycoke in *Gravity's Rainbow*. "What we were doing out in that country," he tells his nephews and nieces, "was brave, scientifick beyond my understanding, and ultimately meaningless, . . . eight years later to be nullified by the War for Independence."

The work's style is a playful pastiche of eighteenth century prose studded with archaic diction and capitalizations, metaphorical, bumptiously Fieldingesque but also slyly Shandyan, occasionally laced with late twentieth century idioms that mix the verifiable with the invented. Pynchon's broad wink at history is affectionate and playful; the paranoid tone of his previous works is here absent, replaced by fantastic comedy as he mixes eighteenth century form with a twentieth century tone.

The novel opens with Mason and Dixon meeting in 1760 to embark on a journey, commissioned by the British Royal Society, to observe the transit of Venus (its passage across the sun) in Cape Town, South Africa. At the Cape they encounter a Dutch-controlled slave culture and are lodged with the libidinous Vroom family, whose nymphomaniac women conduct transits of Venus on land, causing Mason no end of embarrassed arousals. A luscious slave girl visits his bed on orders from her white mistress, who wants him to impregnate her for economic purposes: "The baby, being fairer than its mother, will fetch more upon the Market,—there it begins, there it ends." The Cape of Good Hope proves to be a parable about slavery and free will.

After the pair has returned to England, Mason participates in calendar reform, which will eliminate eleven days from the old calendar and, many fear, from their lives. Then the pair journeys to the wind-blown island of St. Helena, where they encounter the half-crazed, historic astronomer Nevil Maskelyne (1732-1811), whose appointment as astronomer-royal in 1765 was likely at Mason's expense.

Not until page 257 do Mason and Dixon journey to America, where, accompanied by ax men and various motley characters, they establish an eight-yard-wide swath, called "Visto," through 244 miles of wilderness on a straight latitudinal path from Chesapeake Bay over the Alleghenies to the Ohio River. They are shocked by the subjection of American Indians as well as by slavery, reminding them of their South African and St. Helena experiences. At Lancaster, they hear, Indian children and old people had been massacred by local Irregulars, while a regiment of Highlanders refused to help them. Cherrycoke comments that whites in both Cape Town and America "are become the very Savages of their own worst Dreams, far out of Measure to any Provocation."

Toward the book's end, a slave market is graphically described, with twenty African men and women auctioned off. "Not in the Market," puns Dixon to the shilling auctioneer, who begins to whip the slaves after Dixon has successfully appealed to spectators not to buy them. Dixon then seizes the whip, unchains the slaves, and drives away their "owner." He will place the whip, as an "Instrument of Shame," in a Quaker meeting-house. "Where does it end?" Dixon rhetorically asks Mason. ". . . Shall we find all the World Tyrants and Slaves? America was the one place we should *not* have found them."

Before returning to England, Mason and Dixon ruminate remorsefully about the meaning of their labors. Is their line "a conduit for Evil"? Did it denude and degrade a wilderness that should not have been so violated? Was their boundary so many dragon's teeth across the pristine land's free flesh? Their diagnosis is more dystopian than utopian, articulating the novel's tragic heart.

Yet Pynchon's novel also has delights and wonders, presenting many zany and surreal situations. Some provide grand entertainment; others are only silly and sophomoric. Consider the cameos introducing George Washington and Ben Franklin. The not-yet-father of his not-yet-country is a hemp-smoking, folksy, back-slapping real estate hustler. He has an African servant-jester, Gershom, who has converted to Judaism yet regales the company with "Slave-and-Master Joaks." The scene ends with Gershom singing the Hebrew folk song "Havah Nagilah" while "clicking together a pair of Spoons in Syncopation." Franklin sells sunglasses, plays glass instruments, touts his sovereign remedy, Ben's Universal Balm, and performs in a pub as "that Euclid of the Electrick, Philadelphia's own *Poor Richard*." All this is perhaps impossible to sort out intellectually as acceptable scenes in a serious novel, but it may amuse readers as absurdist assaults on revered American icons. The provenance is vaudeville.

Pynchon loves to fill his rambling text with fantastically discursive anecdotes and wholly incredible episodes. Readers meet fanatical Jesuits who plot to construct a secret global communications network using gigantic balloons as satellites; then there are fanatical anti-Jesuits, principally a former Chinese convert named Captain Zhang, who has become a master of *fêng shui;* Popeye, who makes an appearance to offer Mason a helpful gloss on a Hebrew passage, "I am that which I am"; mounds made by natives, or possibly extraterrestrial visitors, shown to possess strangely magnetic powers. Perhaps most memorable are the accounts by France's greatest chef, Armand Allègre, of his persecution by an amorously smitten invisible mechanical duck that pursues him to the New Land and ruins his social life. One must also include Zepho Beck, who is afflicted with "Kastoranthropy," turning into a beaver on nights of a full moon; once an eclipse rehumanizes him before he has felled his usual quota of trees. Then there are a Golem, a talking "Learnèd Dog," an evil electric eel, speaking clocks, a watch that runs on perpetual motion, and a popular Gothic romance, one of whose chapters joins the main plot.

What is Pynchon about in his book? His bizarre curios and marvels are tests of Mason and Dixon's faith in rationalism as well as emblems of America's magnetic appeal to fugitives, dreamers, and eccentrics, to the lost and the disfranchised. Yet on the most significant level, this novel is a relentless and often painful unmasking of the great moral and political diseases that taint the nation to this day: the destruction of forests and pollution of the land, the persecution of the weak and the different, the incessant violence, the ruthless financial speculations, the unscrupulous exploitation of religious needs by self-righteous preachers. The novel describes Mason and Dixon as contributing through their work to the standardization and universalization of time and space, to the elimination of variety and uncertainty. Pynchon also uses the bizarre and fantastic to resist modernization and rationalization, to subvert what are commonly accepted as the laws of nature, to oppose the world's disenchantment. He is a wonderfully gifted writer. Whether *Mason and Dixon* is a masterpiece is too early to tell.

Gerhard Brand

Sources for Further Study

Chicago Tribune. May 11, 1997, XIV, p. 1.
Commonweal. CXXIV, August 15, 1997, p. 20.
The Nation. CCLXIV, May 12, 1997, p. 65.
The New York Review of Books. XLIV, June 12, 1997, p. 22.

The New York Times Book Review. CII, May 18, 1997, p. 9.
Newsweek. CXXIX, April 28, 1997, p. 77.
Publishers Weekly. CCXLIV, April 14, 1997, p. 56.
Time. CXLIX, May 5, 1997, p. 98.
The Times Literary Supplement. June 6, 1997, p. 25.
The Wall Street Journal. May 2, 1997, p. A12.

MAY SARTON
A Biography

Author: Margot Peters (1933-   )
Publisher: Alfred A. Knopf (New York). Illustrated. 474 pp. $30.00
Type of work: Literary biography
Time: May 3, 1912-July 16, 1995
Locale: The United States and Western Europe

This well-researched biography portrays the life and many loves of May Sarton, a prolific lesbian writer who gained her widest audience with the journals and memoirs of her later years

> Principal personages:
> MAY SARTON, an American poet, novelist, and essayist
> GEORGE SARTON, her father, a Belgian-born scientist
> MABEL SARTON, her mother, a British-born artist
> JUDITH MATLOCK, her long-suffering companion of many years

Margot Peters has created a detailed portrait of writer May Sarton, which illuminates the differences between Sarton's life and the image Sarton created for her audience.

Sarton was born in Belgium in 1911, the only child of George Sarton, a withdrawn Belgian scientist, and Mabel Elwes Sarton, an English artist. Even as a toddler, Sarton was willful and bad-tempered; her parents alternated between coddling her and leaving her in the care of others. When staying with others, Sarton exhibited a sad need to adopt them as her family; she craved the family life that was absent in her own home and liked it even more if the family was wealthy. Sarton was always attracted to the affluence that her parents no longer had. She displayed a constant and intense need for attention—from family, friends, and, eventually, audiences. After the start of World War I, the family moved to England, later settling permanently in the United States. Sarton maintained European friendships and kept emotional ties to Europe, however, and visited there often throughout her life.

Sarton was a striking and fashionable woman with a commanding presence. Both women and men were attracted to her, and although she had crushes on men and a few heterosexual affairs, her primary attraction was always to women. Still, she struggled to clarify her sexual identity and did not consider herself to be a lesbian for many years.

Sarton expected to make a career in the theater and worked as an actress and the director of a theater company. During this time a few of her poems were published, but she did not consider writing to be her life's work. In fact, when her father expressed his opinion that the theater was a waste of time that could better be spent advancing a literary career, she replied, "I don't think if I felt my profession was writing I could write a line. . . . It would be madness to give [the stage] up now. . . . It's the only thing I have which doesn't change—poetry is so much a thing of mood." This was reflected throughout her life; she could only produce poetry when she had a muse, that is, when she was in love with a woman—whether the muse returned her love or not.

Sarton's first book of poetry, *Encounter in April*, was published in 1937, followed in 1938 by her first novel, *The Single Hound*. The novel was highly autobiographical, despite her casting the protagonist, based on herself, as a young man.

In 1940, living in the United States with her parents, Sarton was unable to travel to Europe because of the war. In an effort to keep busy, as well as to supplement the money she received from her father, Sarton wrote to a number of small colleges offering to be a guest lecturer on poetry. After receiving fifteen acceptances, she set off on the first of the many lecture tours that became a staple of her working life. Although many of the students she encountered were disinterested in listening to the little-known poet, she built on her experience as an actress and found that she was a talented public speaker and an expressive reader of poetry.

While her writing and lecturing began to provide a foundation for her literary life, her emotional life continued to be chaotic. "So far I have always done what I felt and then found reasons afterward. Usually it wasn't hard," Sarton wrote to a friend at the age of nineteen. This was the creed by which she lived her life. She fell quickly in and out of love with a succession of older, glamorous, well-to-do women, many of whom were unwilling or unable to return her passion. Sarton often focused her passion on married women, once writing to a psychiatrist that she was never attracted to "the typical lesbian." While Sarton seemed compelled to seduce and conquer, and often lost interest once a woman became smitten with her, she generally tried to remain friends with her conquests after her passion wore off. Still, in 1944, when she had a number of female lovers, she wrote to a friend, "I wish that I could marry now. It is time and for the first time in my life I think I am ready *inside*."

Perhaps the need for the solid base that marriage might offer was what drew her to the one stable companion in her life: Judith Matlock. Unlike the other women Sarton pursued, Matlock was neither wealthy, beautiful, brilliant, nor given to the excesses that marked Sarton's emotional, personal, and financial life. Rather than a muse, Matlock was a safe harbor from which Sarton continued to venture on speaking engagements, on trips to Europe, and to other women's beds. Matlock, a Quaker, had little interest in sex, a fact that Sarton used to justify her continuing conquests of other women. Matlock suffered silently, steadfastly maintaining their home in Cambridge, Massachusetts, despite Sarton's often flagrant affairs.

In 1955, Sarton saw the first of several psychiatrists, trying to deal with what Peters refers to as the "frightening schism in her nature"—the chasm between the strong, wise, radiant woman and the insecure, destructive, chaotic child. Sarton preferred conquests to being loved herself, because her inability to be faithful left her feeling guilty. Peters argues that Sarton's writing was necessary for her to maintain her sanity in the face of the guilt she felt, not for loving women, but because she knew her promiscuous behavior hurt both Matlock and many of her conquests.

Alcohol further complicated Sarton's life. Although Peters never labels Sarton as an alcoholic, one could draw that conclusion from the numerous accounts of Sarton's heavy drinking and the rages that came in the wake of these episodes, with Sarton excoriating dear friends and causing embarrassing scenes in public. Peters concludes that Sarton made no effort to moderate her drinking, not only because it enabled her to avoid responsibility for her behavior, but also because she enjoyed the emotional scenes of recrimination and forgiveness that these episodes generated. Eventually, however, Sarton lost many friends as a result of her alcohol-fueled furies.

In 1958, Sarton made a purchase that started a new chapter in her life and led to a wider audience for her writing: With money from her parents' estate, she purchased a farmhouse in Nelson, New Hampshire, leaving the home she had shared with Matlock in Cambridge. In the next ten years, three books that Sarton published both widened her audience and began the self-mythologizing that Peters chronicles. *I Knew a Phoenix* (1959), a collection of revised essays first published in *The New Yorker*, was, according to Peters, "the beginning of the myth May Sarton was starting to create of her life." In these essays, Sarton painted a picture of herself having been nurtured by such extraordinary people that she was destined to be extraordinary herself. *Mrs. Stevens Hears the Mermaids Singing* (1965) was Sarton's first novel in which the protagonist was a homosexual, an aging lesbian who strives for recognition as an artist and a person. It was poorly reviewed and sold few copies at the time but brought Sarton recognition later, in the wake of the feminist and gay rights movements and the proliferation of women's studies departments across the United States. *Plant Dreaming Deep* (1968), which celebrated her home and life in Nelson, brought her adulation from vast numbers of women, and some men, who admired and identified with her creation of a life as a "solitary." In truth, however, Sarton was more dependent on the company of others than one might surmise from *Plant Dreaming Deep*: Old friends, including Matlock, and new admirers visited regularly, and Sarton continued with speaking engagements and travel. *Plant Dreaming Deep* also glossed over many of her problems with her neighbors in Nelson and, as had *I Knew a Phoenix*, pictured her life as more peaceful than it truly was. *Mrs. Stevens Hears the Mermaids Singing* is far more revealing of Sarton's life than the memoir *Plant Dreaming Deep*, Peters argues. The latter book is "imaginative, not factual truth—May's life as she idealized it." Yet it gained for Sarton not only the smattering of critical acclaim and handful of intellectual readers that her novels and poetry had earned her but also a cadre of devoted fans. Gifts and visitors arrived constantly, and many of Sarton's fans fell in love with her, turning her into their muse.

Despite her homosexuality, Sarton did not identify herself as a lesbian writer and did not think most lesbian literature was very good. She considered herself to be a bridge between the homosexual and heterosexual worlds, but as Peters quotes from a reviewer in the *Los Angeles Times Book Review*, a bridge belongs nowhere.

It is interesting to note, as Peters points out, that Sarton injected no sex and very little sensuality into her novels. "Her characters are intensely oral: they smoke, drink, eat, and talk—like Sarton herself." Sarton was a promiscuous seducer but, Peters concludes, used sex as a means of possessing another rather than a route to sensual pleasure.

The success and acclaim Sarton received from *Plant Dreaming Deep* led to more journals and memoirs and to a decrease in her focus on novels and poetry, although Sarton thought journals were a low form of literature. The journals were easy to write, however, and found a ready audience, no matter what type of reviews they received, and she was in demand for speaking engagements throughout the country. This was partly because of the devotion of her new fans, but also because the woman's movement celebrated diaries and journals as a feminist literary genre that reflected women's interior lives.

Despite advancing age and declining health, Sarton continued to write. Her nineteenth and last novel, *The Education of Harriet Hatfield*, was published when she was seventy-seven. Even a stroke did not end her writing: *After the Stroke: A Journal* was published in 1988. Her last journal, *At Eighty-Two*, was published in 1995, the year she died.

Peters's book is exhaustively researched and annotated in detail. It includes more than fifty pages of notes, a sixteen-page index, and a bibliography encompassing Sarton's works, works about her, and related works on literature and several of Sarton's friends and lovers.

Margot Peters's earlier works examined the lives of Charlotte Brontë, George Bernard Shaw, Mrs. Patrick Campbell, and the Barrymore family. Sarton, however, was alive when Peters began this book, and Peters spoke with her frequently in the last five years of her life. Sarton was a voluminous letter-writer, and apparently neither she nor many of those to whom she wrote disposed of their correspondence. She also made copies of letters to others in her diary, at least for a time. When Susan Sherman, Sarton's devoted fan and companion in her last years, was allowed to edit Sarton's letters for publication, the stack of letters to her parents was more than a foot high. Personal interviews and an exhaustive collection of the written word, however, does not guarantee that objective truth or consensus can be reached. In many cases, Sarton's version of an event differs from letter to letter, clashes with the perceptions of others regarding the same event, and then had a rather different interpretation when Sarton's biographer discussed it with her in the last few years of her life.

Although it is impossible to fully pin down the truth of another's life, *May Sarton: A Biography* is a richly detailed and fascinating portrait of a complex and adventurous woman.

Irene Struthers

Sources for Further Study

Atlanta Journal Constitution. April 6, 1997, p. L12.
Booklist. XCIII, March, 1997, p. 1105.
Boston Globe. April 13, 1997, p. N16.
Kirkus Reviews. LXV, January 1, 1997, p. 46.
Library Journal. CXXII, February 15, 1997, p. 136.
The Nation. CCLXIV, June 30, 1997, p. 29.
The New York Times Book Review. CII, April 6, 1997, p. 9.
Publishers Weekly. CCXLIV, January 13, 1997, p. 59.
The Washington Post Book World. XXVII, February 23, 1997, p. 4.

THE MEASURE OF REALITY
Quantification and Western Society, 1250-1600

Author: Alfred W. Crosby
Publisher: Cambridge University Press (New York). 245 pp. $24.95
Type of work: History of science
Time: 1250-1600
Locale: Western Europe

A wide-ranging account of the rise of quantitative thinking in Western Europe in the late Middle Ages and the Renaissance

Alfred Crosby is professor of American studies, history, and geography at the University of Texas, Austin. As that interdisciplinary appointment may suggest, Crosby is an adventurous scholar who ignores conventional academic boundaries. He is also a breezy, entertaining writer. Among his previous books is *Ecological Imperialism: The Biological Expansion of Europe, 900-1900* (1986).

In the preface to *The Measure of Reality: Quantification and Western Society, 1250-1600*, Crosby recounts the genesis of this new book in intriguing terms. He describes *The Measure of Reality* as "the third book I have written in my lifelong search for explanations for the amazing success of European imperialism." In *Ecological Imperialism* and *Germs, Seeds, and Animals: Studies in Ecological History* (1994), Crosby focused on the "biological advantages" the Europeans enjoyed, a theme also taken up by Jared Diamond in *Guns, Germs, and Steel: The Fates of Human Societies* (reviewed in this volume). However, that line of explanation, Crosby writes, seemed insufficient to account for the scale of European dominance. The "textbook answer"— superior European science and technology—failed to satisfy because it merely reframed the question. The answer, he came to believe,

> lay at first not in [Europeans'] science and technology but in their utilization of habits of thought that would *in time* enable them to advance swiftly in science and technology and, in the meantime, gave them decisively important administrative, commercial, navigational, industrial, and military skills. The initial European advantage lay in what French historians have called *mentalité*.

Why, then, were European imperialists "unique in the degree of their success"? It is because they were, according to Crosby, "thinking of reality in quantitative terms with greater consistency than other members of their species."

Strangely, having stated his thesis so straightforwardly, Crosby never attempts to argue it in any systematic way. He characterizes, at some length, what he calls "the Venerable Model"—the old *mentalité*—that the new quantitative model replaced. He considers some of the conditions, such as "the rise of commerce and the state" and "the revival of learning," that nurtured the shift to "quantificational perception" but were not the direct agents of change. Then he offers such evidences of change as the development of clocks and the increasing sophistication of marine charts and astronomical observations. Finally, in a sequence of chapters ("Music," "Painting," and "Bookkeeping,") Crosby discerns a common pattern in seemingly disconnected enterprises: "visualization," the "striking of the match" in the revolutionary process he has proposed to survey. The "habit of visualization," which is second nature to us today, was then a novelty, "a new way not so much of thinking about the infinite and ineffable as seeing and manipulating matters of finite and daily actuality."

Visualization, then, in the special sense intended by Crosby, is a powerful tool of abstraction:

> Record events in chronological order on parchment or paper and you have a time machine. You can step back and observe beginnings and endings simultaneously. You can alter time's direction, and you can halt time so as to imagine individual events. If you are an accountant, you can proceed backward to find a mistake; you can construct a balance sheet like a still photograph of the whirling storm of transactions.

Indeed, visualization is as important as quantification in the changes he describes. Here his analysis overlaps considerably with the work of Walter Ong (see *Magill's Literary Annual*, 1983, for a review of Ong's *Orality and Literacy*), who has explored the transition from a primarily oral culture, where sound is extremely important, to a primarily literate culture, where print and vision play a dominant role, and finally to the electronic culture of the late twentieth century. Print enormously amplifies the distinctive qualities of writing. It permits the recording and dissemination of knowledge on a scale previously unknown, it encourages standardization and particularization, and, in radical contrast to speech, it creates a distance between the transmitter of knowledge and those who receive it.

It is notoriously unfair for reviewers to fault authors for failing to write books they never set out to write, but it is not at all unfair to wonder why an author fails to follow through on his own premise. Except for glancing comments now and then, Crosby does not even begin to show how the putative new European *mentalité* differed from the prevailing *mentalités* in other cultures, nor does he show how this difference was translated into imperialistic triumphs. What Crosby does do, with considerable flair, is bombard the reader with examples of "quantitative thinking." The reach of his net is impressive, and many readers will finish this book without having paused to follow several of Crosby's leads into this or that fascinating subject (for example, his account of the origins of the Julian calendar and the change to the Gregorian calendar).

Even as the reader is jotting down another irresistible source from a Crosby footnote, however, a certain unease may be setting in. Precisely because *The Measure of Reality* covers such an immense sweep of intellectual territory, precious few readers will be equipped to challenge many of the fine points of Crosby's exposition. Still, readers may occasionally stumble on a subject they know well and find Crosby's treatment of it to be far from adequate. In his chapter on music, for example, Crosby begins one section with a characteristically broad and bold statement: "Generally speaking, nothing is more diagnostic of a society's reading of reality than its perception of time." This provocative observation is not really developed, however; rather, in lieu of argument, Crosby, citing music theorist Victor Zuckerandl, writes that "for most peoples and most eras musical time 'is of the nature of poetic rhythm: free rhythm, in the sense that it is not constrained to keep time.'" A page or so later, speaking of fourteenth century French composer Guillaume de Machaut, Crosby declares that Machaut's mastery of complex rhythms was "possible only because a clock was ticking in the composer's mind, the same clock that was ticking in the performers' and listeners' minds." However, the rhythms of some West African music, which required no notation and which was performed in societies without clocks, were extraordinarily complex, so it is simply not true that rhythmic complexity depends on the quantification and the particular time sense that developed in Western Europe during this period.

This may seem like a nit-picking complaint. Consider, though, that the contrast proposed by Crosby is his "evidence" for a very large claim. If the details are frequently wrong, does the thesis still stand? A comparable case is Marshall McLuhan's famous book, *Understanding Media* (1964). McLuhan got many of the details wrong in that book, as he did elsewhere. While he enjoyed a spectacular run as a media guru, specialists fumed and sputtered. Eventually, the McLuhan boom faded, and the specialists made sure that no one on their turf would take McLuhan seriously or even read his books. However, twenty-five years later, with the digital revolution in full bloom, McLuhan returned in triumph as the patron saint of *Wired* magazine and one of the most prophetic thinkers of his time.

Crosby is no McLuhan, but one may ask if *The Measure of Reality*, despite local glitches, will turn out to be correct when all the evidence is in. It is too soon to tell, but Crosby's failure to support his own thesis suggests that if the case can be made persuasively, someone else will have to make it. Nevertheless, he has written an enjoyable and highly stimulating book full of curious lore that encourages readers to look more closely at the habits of thought on which their way of life is built.

John Wilson

Sources for Further Study

Booklist. XCIII, January, 1997, p. 811.
Business Week. April 28, 1997, p. 12E6.
Choice. XXXIV, May, 1997, p. 1556.
Civilization. IV, February, 1997, p. 82.
Journal of Interdisciplinary History. XXVIII, Autumn, 1997, p. 261.
Library Journal. CXXII, January, 1997, p. 118.
Los Angeles Times Book Review. January 26, 1997, p. 4.
The New York Times Book Review. CII, January 26, 1997, p. 24.
Publishers Weekly. CCXLIII, November 25, 1996, p. 62.
The Times Literary Supplement. November 7, 1997, p. 23.

MEMOIRS OF A GEISHA

Author: Arthur Golden (1957-   )
Publisher: Alfred A. Knopf (New York). 434 pp. $25.00
Type of work: Novel
Time: 1929-1985
Locale: Yoriodo and Kyoto, Japan; and New York City

In this gender-switching historical romance, Arthur Golden attempts to look behind the geisha mask

> *Principal characters:*
> NITTA SAYURI, first-person narrator and premier geisha
> SATSU, Sayuri's older sister
> PUMPKIN, a fellow geisha who apprentices with Sayuri
> MAMEHA, a renowned geisha who sponsors Sayuri
> HATSUMOMO, a villainous geisha
> THE CHAIRMAN, Sayuri's benefactor and eventual lover
> NOBU, a war-scarred executive

In his literary debut, Arthur Golden parlays his academic training in Japanese history and culture into a Dickensian first-person narrative of a geisha girl's rise to prominence in pre-World War II Japan. As a product of meticulous research, *Memoirs of a Geisha* provides a detailed portrait of a little-known but much mythologized profession. In other respects, the novel has its weaknesses: The characterizations are often two-dimensional and thin (as was true for Charles Dickens's work at times), set scenes can take on a touristy aesthetic (Sayuri never forgets she is speaking to an American audience), and the style suffers from a forced metaphorical lyricism. Golden knows how to maintain dramatic tension during the narrator's struggle to free herself from slavery and attain geisha status, but her role as a passive observer of Japanese culture flattens the novel once she grows up.

In spite of these lapses, the novel shows Golden's grasp of the 1930's Japanese milieu, which helps the reader immerse him- or herself in a landscape interestingly apposite to the familiar American culture, a secretive world where geishas are obliged to keep quiet about what they learn from powerful men. Practitioners of a profession that has no real equivalent in America, geishas resemble cultured call girls who train for years in the fine arts of dance, music, makeup, fashion, and socializing. Compared to other Japanese women, geishas are exotic cultural creations. Their kimonos, the colorfully decorated robes, are often worth as much as a fine art object. Their white makeup accentuates their skin so as to make their necks and other exposed areas more erotic. Their hairdos are elaborate enough to require geishas to use little wooden cradles for their necks when they sleep, so that these coiffures are not disturbed. In many respects, geishas are the fantastical creations of male desire, and there is an odd dissonance between their artistic ability and their more debased utilitarian function as hostesses and flirts. Ever the master at maintaining appearances, the geisha knows how to act, disguise her true emotions, and use her social wiles to further herself. The geisha possesses the writer's ability to play a role in much the same way that a man may inhabit a female persona in drag, which perfectly suits Golden's technique. On the job, geishas mostly attend teahouse parties, serve sake (Japanese wine), play drinking games, and entertain boorish businessmen with self-conscious glimpses of their wrists or a lewd joke. Compared to the many apprentice years of learning dance and singing, their actual work can resemble drunken fraternity parties.

Nitta Sayuri begins her story as Chiyo, a peasant girl in the small fishing village of Yoriodo. A local fish merchant sells her and her sister into slavery in Kyoto. While her uglier sister is forced into prostitution, Chiyo is suddenly orphaned out to an okiya, or geisha house, where she must work to pay off the price of her purchase and any other expenses she incurs in her apprenticeship toward becoming a geisha. If she fails, she will work in drudgery as a maid for life. The premier geisha of the okiya is Hatsumomo, a beautiful but viciously competitive woman who supports everyone else in the household by attending teahouse parties into the night. Hatsumomo has limitations as a character, as nothing is shown of her but her wicked side, but her instinctual loathing for Chiyo's threatening young beauty enlivens the novel. Hatsumomo entices Chiyo into trying to escape the okiya. Not knowing the consequences of her actions (she is only twelve years old), Chiyo tries to escape and join her sister by climbing over the rooftops of the adjoining okiyas, but she ends up trapped and further in debt than ever. In despair of ever breaking free from her bound servitude, she runs into the chairman of an electrical appliance company, and his unexpected act of kindness persuades her to seek her freedom through becoming a geisha instead of by escaping.

Chiyo decides to rough it out and, with the help of another, nicer "older sister" geisha named Mameha, starts to succeed as an apprentice. Hatsumomo does everything she can to stop her. For example, Hatsumomo follows the newly named Sayuri around Gion, spreading lies about her whenever she can. When it comes time for Sayuri to put her virginity on the auction block, so to speak, and sell her *mizuage* to the highest bidder, Hatsumomo tells prospective older suitors that Sayuri already lost her virginity with a young boyfriend. Sayuri and Mameha must wait until Hatsumomo's treachery turns on her to finally prevail.

In the meantime, readers learn much of the Japanese culture of the 1930's era. Golden includes one set piece of a sumo wrestling scene in which the reader can find correspondences between Hatsumomo's and Sayuri's rivalry and different wrestling techniques. Readers also learn of the concept of a *danna*, a man who pays extravagantly for a geisha's closer attention (the closest geishas ever come to marriage). The geishas are deeply superstitious, relying on their astrological charts to make decisions and having their servants spark flames off a piece of flint on their backs before undertaking a journey. Everyone walks on tatami mats and sleeps on futons.

When Dr. Crab buys Sayuri's virginity, he claims a sample of her hymen blood and places it in a kind of trophy case of vials labeled with the names of his different *mizuages*. After that bizarre fetishistic episode, the high price that Sayuri obtained enhances her social value.

Repeatedly, Golden showcases the extreme sexism of the culture. For all her arts,

Sayuri and her geisha mentors are at the mercy of men's favor. Because the men do not share their serious concerns with them, the geisha do not have much opportunity to grow intellectually. As a result, Sayuri as a character seems peculiarly stunted. Her perspective does not change significantly as she moves through adolescence to adulthood. Sayuri does encounter an artist, Uchida Kosuburo, who carries on like Jackson Pollack in a sloppy atelier, but she remains merely a muse to him, a subject for his next line of paintings. By the last third of the novel, the narrow role of the geisha limits the possibilities of Golden's narrative.

In a profession in which sex appeal is all important, the geishas show a touching simplistic awareness of the topic of sex. Mameha instructs Sayuri in the facts of life, using the metaphor of a male "homeless eel" that looks for a woman's "cave." The possibility of a woman enjoying sex rarely comes up. Sayuri does admit to having one affair with a younger man, just as Hatsumomo does earlier (a practice much frowned upon because it fails to bring in money), but generally their profession encourages a kind of chaste ritualized flirtation. The geishas are too involved in their roles as performers to get much pleasure out of it. Besides, economic necessity often obliges them to cater to distasteful older men. Sayuri's love for the much older Chairman remains idealized and abstract, like a schoolgirl's crush, well into her adult years.

Most problematic of all are Sayuri's metaphors. From the very beginning, she describes her home as drunk, and tipping at the edge of the sea. When she is tired after a journey, she feels "as sore as a rock must feel when a waterfall has pounded on it all day long." These metaphors seem cute at first, a childish affectation, but they never let up. Sayuri characterizes Hatsumomo as a spider, a cat, and finally as a wounded tiger. Such forced poetry becomes contrived and increasingly cloying as the novel progresses. For example, when she finds herself obliged to talk to Nobu when the Chairman is in the room, she says "I turned away from the Chairman with as much difficulty as a hungry child turns away from a plate of food." The metaphor adds little to an understanding of her situation. Later, disappointed in her love, Sayuri finds herself "wading through an ocean of sorrow." In times of great emotion, the metaphors clog the page, sometimes obscuring the subject under discussion. Because Golden can know only so much about what a young Japanese woman of the 1930's might be thinking, Sayuri's associations are often quite banal. As Sayuri gets older, Golden appears reluctant to sacrifice the reader's identification with her youthful self for a more complex adult persona. She remains a pseudo-lyrical conduit for observation long after one would expect her to take a more active role.

By the time Sayuri finds some standing and stability as a geisha, World War II stops her career as everyone struggles to survive amid economic hardships and American bombings. Nobu finds shelter for her at a kimono-making factory in a rural area away from Kyoto. Deprived of much dramatic interest except for Sayuri's waiting for the end of the war, later scenes lack the specificity of detail of the youthful passages. Golden accelerates the sense of time passing and compresses most of Sayuri's later years into a final romance with the Chairman and her exile in America.

Curiously, Sayuri gains the Chairman's love because she fails in her stratagem of getting caught by Nobu in flagrante delicto with the Minister. She tries to guarantee that Nobu will never become her *danna*, but another geisha arranges for the Chairman to see her compromised, and instead of becoming outraged, he professes his long-standing love to her. Curiously, her failure as an actress leads to her success, because the Chairman notes that he could see the desperation behind her heavily made up face. Sayuri's novel-length dreams come true in a *deus ex machina* plot shift.

By the end of the novel, Golden's melodramatic story structure overwhelms the carefully researched historical detail. Readers used to romance clichés will enjoy the latter third of the novel, but the more literary-minded may wonder what happened to all the evocative descriptions. Sayuri's endgame move to the United States collapses her foreign perspective into the familiar just as the novel finds a haven in romantic conventions. She makes one jab at judging her profession by noting how many American wives are just as much kept by men as she is, but she also seems to enjoy her newfound lifestyle in America. Geishas are now an endangered species in Japan, probably because of gains in Japanese women's rights and the gradual usurpation of more Western methods for amusement such as television and movies. Golden conjures up a world in the process of disappearing until all that remains are the works of art themselves—the kimonos as paintings in dress, the traditions in dance and music, the exotic landscape that enriches Sayuri's memoirs.

Roy C. Flannagan

Sources for Further Study

Booklist. XCIV, September 1, 1997, p. 7.
Chicago Tribune. October 19, 1997, XIV, p. 5.
Entertainment Weekly. October 24, 1997, p. 61
Library Journal. CXXII, August, 1997, p. 128.
Los Angeles Times Book Review. November 30, 1997, p. 8.
The New Leader. LXXX, November 3, 1997, p. 18.
The New York Times Book Review. CII, October 5, 1997, p. 16.
The New Yorker. LXXIII, September 29, 1997, p. 82.
Newsweek. CXXX, October 13, 1997, p. 76.
Publishers Weekly. CCXLIV, July 28, 1997, p. 49.
The Times Literary Supplement. December 12, 1997, p. 21.

MONEY
Who Has How Much and Why

Author: Andrew Hacker (1929-   )
Publisher: Scribner (New York). 288 pp. $25.00
Type of work: History, current affairs, and economics
Time: 1950-1997
Locale: The United States

Concerned about the growing gulf between the best-off and the rest of the American people, Hacker analyzes reliable economic data and shows why 80 percent of the American population had a smaller share of the nation's income in the late 1990's than it did twenty years earlier

As 1998 began, Jack Nicholson starred in a popular movie called *As Good as It Gets*. From some perspectives, that phrase might have described the American economy at the same time. Unemployment, inflation, and mortgage rates were low. Despite jitters at the end of 1997, that year brought banner prosperity to most stock market portfolios. There were even projections from Washington to indicate that a flush economy would bring the annual federal budget into the black for the first time in thirty years and as much as three years ahead of the 2002 deadline negotiated between the White House and Congress.

Political scientist Andrew Hacker, however, does not share the view that everything is as rosy as this bright macroeconomic picture might suggest. He worries about the distribution of wealth in the United States. Specifically, he fears what will happen if the growing gap between the best-off Americans and the rest of the nation keeps growing, which Hacker believes is the most likely scenario in the foreseeable future.

Best known for *Two Nations: Black and White, Separate, Hostile, Unequal*, his 1992 study of race relations in late twentieth century America, Hacker follows up with a clear and penetrating exploration of a subject as fascinating as it is controversial: money, who has it, how much, and why. Noting that Americans are both intensely private and immensely curious about personal money matters, Hacker sets himself two tasks.

First, *Money* presents information to answer basic questions about American incomes. Those questions include: How much money do Americans make? What are their sources of income? How do individuals and groups compare with one another financially? How are Americans getting along in the economic world they inhabit? The United States, Hacker observes, is a world leader when it comes to gathering data on earnings. Thus, answers to many of his guiding questions are in the public domain, but Hacker focuses them succinctly by skillfully drawing on government reports from the U.S. Bureau of the Census, the Internal Revenue Service, the Social Security Administration, the Securities and Exchange Commission, and the Department of Labor. Publications from the private sector—*Forbes* and *Financial World*, to mention only two—also provide key material for Hacker's analysis, which uses figures through the year 1995.

Second, Hacker probes deeper by asking why American money gets apportioned as it does. Answers to that question are not so easily obtained, for they involve interpretation that goes beyond the numbers and percentages found in government records or financial reports from the private sector. To respond to issues about why wealth is distributed as it is in the United States, Hacker has to explore American history, reflect on fundamental economic philosophy, and weigh choices that reflect and influence ethical values, public policies, and business practices. In addition, these lines of thought unavoidably lead Hacker to ask whether the nation's allocation of wealth makes good sense. Hacker, at times explicitly but more often by implication, questions that it does. *Money* is so full of facts and figures that no synopsis can report them all, but here are a few examples that are vital for the analysis that separates Hacker's book from run-of-the-mill accounts of the state of American wealth. With the figures adjusted to 1995 values, the amount of money held in American households rose from $2.7 trillion in 1975 to $4.5 trillion twenty years later. In constant dollars, average household income during that same period jumped from $37,365 to $44,938, a gain of 20.3 percent. This rising tide lifted all boats, but far from equally. Not only did the top fifth of the population do twenty-four times better than the bottom fifth, but also, in terms of the amount of the nation's aggregate wealth that was theirs, 80 percent of the American population lost ground—the drop was from 56.7 percent to 51.3 percent.

Looking at the gains made between 1975 and 1995, Hacker emphasizes that far more households had two or more incomes in 1995 than they did two decades earlier. The dual earnings, however, helped the upper quintile much more than the fourth quintile, for example, where average household income grew only $862 between 1975 and 1995. Affecting that disparity was the fact that the number of high incomes rose at the top end of the scale, as did the number of low incomes in the bottom tiers. Meanwhile, although Americans reputedly enjoy a high-wage economy, the median 1995 wages and salaries for full-time workers in forty-two typical occupations charted by Hacker—they include pharmacists, engineers, computer analysts, and college faculty at the high end and hairdressers, waiters, and laundry workers at the low end—amounted to a hardly lavish $24,908. Within this occupation group, the midpoint pay for men and women was $27,976 and $21,112, respectively. Also central to Hacker's concerns about American economic life, large numbers of the nation's children—one out of five—are growing up in homes with incomes of less than $15,000. Since opportunity and money have much to do with one another, Hacker rightly worries that the nation's distribution of wealth means that millions of children, and black children disproportionately, "are deprived of a chance to develop whatever promise they have."

These facts and figures do not appear in a vacuum. Hacker's chief interest is to understand how they came to be what they are and then to assess how desirable the outcomes have been and whether those results might be improved. History, institutions, values—all of those elements play key roles in "America's way with money," a phrase Hacker uses as the title for an insightful chapter in which he argues that "our present distribution is the realized vision of the nation's founders."

In this historical context, Hacker concentrates on James Madison and Alexander Hamilton. Madison's enormous influence on the development of the U.S. Constitution reflected, Hacker believes, that founder's fundamental conviction that disparities in human talent will naturally yield what Madison called an "unequal distribution of property." Hacker does not share Madison's assumption that human nature is inherently disposed in that direction and, thus, that such outcomes are inevitable, but he does think that Americans tend to assume Madison's outlook.

With the help of Adam Smith, the eighteenth century philosopher who promoted free market economics, Alexander Hamilton, the nation's first secretary of the treasury, urged Americans to think that a vigorous industrial economy—especially one in which people entered the market to sell skills and services competitively—was a key to success, happiness, and greatness for the nation and for individual citizen alike. Americans have bought the Hamiltonian vision as well.

According to Hacker, the consequences of accepting these principles from the philosophies of Madison and Hamilton were more problematic than promised. Specifically, the acceptance of Madison's judgments about unequal property distribution created an American predisposition to be too accepting of an economic system that distributes wealth in ways that may become so detrimental that it undermines the very democracy on which the health of the nation depends. Furthermore, the acceptance of Hamilton's judgments about the desirability of ongoing competition in a supposedly free market economy often leaves Americans trapped, probably increasingly so as economic life becomes global, in a system that cares relatively little about basic human needs as it constantly seeks to increase wealth that, in turn, gets distributed unequally.

Running through Hacker's *Money* is a critique of the American variant of capitalism. The nub of his critique is that our economic system is more interested in wealth than in people. Hacker's conviction on that point rests largely on one of his book's recurrent themes: "Our kind of economic system," he writes, "has never made the creation of jobs its first priority. Jobs come into being as and when enterprises need them and disappear when tasks no longer need to be done." Not inevitably but practically, Hacker understands, our economic rationality works that way. Nevertheless, Hacker is not convinced that this rationality serves us nearly as well as we are accustomed to think.

For one thing, ongoing competition in the marketplace is not nearly as open and frequent as the principles of Adam Smith and Alexander Hamilton led people to believe. For example, in his chapter "Hail to the Chief!," a study of the role of the chief executive officer (CEO) in American corporations and organizations, Hacker shows that the very high salaries and perks of these chosen few have more to do with company image than with competition for scarce talent that can individually determine success. At the same time, a mystique exists that somehow this leadership is worth what is spent on it. Indeed, the argument goes, such people would not perform well unless they had such huge incentives to do so. Here, Hacker has his doubts as well. Rare are the CEOs who do their jobs only for the money involved. Using college and university presidents as one example, Hacker points out that most of these executives were initially faculty members who scarcely entered the field of education for the money it paid. Unless these men and women have abandoned their original ideals and commitments, Hacker wonders why their pay should soar, as it often does once they secure a presidential appointment. The conventional argument that grand compensation is necessary to ensure top executive performance is not one that Hacker finds as credible as it sounds.

Meanwhile, most Americans live from paycheck to paycheck, but Hacker finds that they have relatively little resentment toward those who are best-off in the United States, not least because they, too, aspire to that status. Further vindicating his judgment that Americans basically agree with Madison's judgment about unequal distribution of property, Hacker notes not only that the United States has the most glaring income gaps among the world's modernized countries but also that Americans typically hold the belief that "we are entitled to accept with a clear conscience whatever someone else freely offers us." Thus, lotteries and their eager players abound. Pay for professional athletes makes many of them super-rich. In fact, Hacker reports, poor families on welfare are more likely recipients of American resentment than the very wealthy.

Hacker's analysis goes on to report other dimensions of the income disparities that occupy so much of his attention. The median income for black families, for example, rose from $23,806 in 1975 to $25,970 in 1995, but the median amount that black families made in comparison to white families was lower in 1995 than it was twenty years earlier. The most common work for recent immigrants involves jobs that native-born Americans are unwilling to do. The immigrants are paid accordingly. In 1995, American women got $538 for every $1,000 that went to men. Obviously, complex reasons and multiple forces account for these situations, but Hacker is no economic determinist. He believes that human choices—individual and collective— create our socioeconomic world, and, thus, he believes that change is possible. Those affirmations lead him to ask: When it comes to money, what world do we want?

Hacker wants Americans to face that issue openly and honestly. *Money* assists that effort by an analysis that Hacker sums up as follows: "It is one thing for the rich to get richer when everyone is sharing in overall economic growth, and it is quite another for the better off to prosper while others are losing ground or standing still. But this is what has been happening."

Claiming that a reproachful tone will do little good, Hacker says, unconvincingly, that *Money* "should not be read as a plea for income redistribution." Yet, his book, at least implicitly, is just that. If Americans do not make their patterns of income distribution more equal, the nation will pay a rising price for persisting poverty, and most young Americans will not live as well as their parents. "Severe disparities" that produce "excess alongside deprivation," Hacker judges correctly, will "sunder the society and subvert common aims."

John K. Roth

Sources for Further Study

Business Week. July 28, 1997, p. 16.
Choice. XXXV, November, 1997, p. 534.
Commentary. CV, January, 1998, p. 60.
Commonweal. CXXIV, August 15, 1997, p. 28.
Forbes. CLX, September 22, 1997, p. 280.
Library Journal. CXXII, July, 1997, p. 98.
The New York Review of Books. XLIV, August 14, 1997, p. 40.
The New York Times Book Review. CII, July 6, 1997, p. 11.
Publishers Weekly. CCXLIV, May 12, 1997, p. 69.
Washington Monthly. XXIX, September, 1997, p. 52.

MOTHER TONGUE
An American Life in Italy

Author: Wallis Wilde-Menozzi
Publisher: North Point Press/Farrar Straus and Giroux (New York). Illustrated. 373 pp. $25.00
Type of work: Memoir
Time: 1981-1995, with flashbacks
Locale: Northern Italy

A personal account of how the author adjusted to being transplanted from Palo Alto, California, to Parma, Italy, when she moved there in 1981 with her Italian husband

> *Principal personages:*
> WALLIS WILDE-MENOZZI, a writer and wife of Paolo Menozzi
> PAOLO MENOZZI, professor of population biology at the University of Parma
> LIBERO MENOZZI, Paolo's father, a physician who died in Paolo's first year
> ALBA MENOZZI, Paolo's mother
> ROSALIA, Alba's mother
> PIETRO MENOZZI, Paolo's brother, Alba's son, a physician
> ANGELA MENOZZI, Paolo's sister, Alba's daughter
> CLARE, Wallis Wilde-Menozzi's daughter, Paolo's adopted daughter

Mother Tongue is a warm and wonderful book. Its twenty-nine chapters, any of which can be read independently but the sum of which constitute a coherent commentary on the expatriate experience, bristle with fresh ideas and sharp insights. The author's powers of observation are extraordinary, as can be seen, for example, in her description of Signora Biocchi, a nosy neighbor in Parma, who is described as "leaning over her balcony taking her first reconnaissance smoke of the day."

The book is filled with insights that in very few words capture precisely a mood, a reaction, or an immutable truth. In writing about professional translators, Wilde-Menozzi calls them at their best "egoless invisibilities." It is the accuracy and appropriateness of such observations that make *Mother Tongue* a delight to read.

Besides offering insights into Italian life as sensitively and flawlessly as the author has, this book comments cogently on many important facets of life, most of them presented more sharply and strikingly from an expatriate point of view than they could be by an insider in the society being written about. Wilde-Menozzi lives in an identity limbo, delicately poised between two worlds, one she has left in the United States and one into which she has been thrust in northern Italy, where she is relatively happy and well adjusted but where she will never experience the acceptance and feeling of belonging known by those native to the area.

Mother Tongue poses many questions that will interest readers who have followed the feminist movement in recent years. At Stanford University, the author, a single mother with one child, Clare, meets Paolo Menozzi, who has lived most of his life in the ancient Italian city of Parma. Ten months after she and Paolo marry, Paolo is offered a coveted chair at the University of Parma, a position too tempting for him to reject.

As often happens in such cases, the wife and adopted daughter—Wallis and six-year-old Clare—put their lives on hold to follow the career-advancing father, Paolo. This means not only that Wallis must give up her professional affiliation but also that she and her daughter must move into a culture wholly different from the one they know best. Although there is a sense of high adventure in making such drastic leaps in life, the accompanying uncertainty of such wrenching change often is difficult to deal with, as is suggested in the author's recounting of troubled dreams, many of them reported in detail, that all three members of the family have after their relocation.

Wilde-Menozzi has a deep appreciation of Italy's past and of the history of Parma and its environs. She adapts reasonably well to her new life, although to do so, she must create her own goals and practice a level of self-discipline that demands enormous personal commitment. Besides being caught up in an Italian bureaucracy that, throughout its history (which the author recounts with considerable understanding and accuracy), has bewildered both Italians and visitors to their country, Wilde-Menozzi has to cope with the details of running a household in circumstances that sometimes prove daunting. Because Parma has a damp climate, the bed linens and mattresses need frequent airing, which involves removing them from the beds and hanging them out the windows on sunny days so that they can dry out and lose the musty smell that the continual dampness causes. One day when Wilde-Menozzi is performing this ritual, she discovers that a scorpion the size of a child's hand has been lurking in the bed she and Paolo share. She is terrified both by the scorpion and by the thought that it had been in her bed for some length of time. She sucks the offending insect into the vacuum cleaner, then, with great subtlety, employs it symbolically. Immediately after telling about it, she writes of her mother-in-law's surgery that reveals cancer of the stomach, lymph nodes, and liver, a cancer that has lurked undetected in Alba's body just as the potentially dangerous scorpion has lurked undetected in the matrimonial bed.

The author then, with consummate skill, uses her recounting of the initial stages of Alba's terminal illness to reveal other aspects of Italian life. In this society, one does not reveal to someone who is seriously ill that his or her illness is terminal. Alba's doctor, Pietro, also is her son. He tells his mother as she is emerging from the anesthetic that she had gallstones and that they have been removed successfully. This sort of deception continues until Alba's death, although the old woman, reading people's facial expressions and reactions, discovers the truth on her own. Custom prevents her, however, from revealing to her family that she knows her life is nearing its end.

Similarly, friends and neighbors refuse to acknowledge that Alba is terminally ill, nor does anyone in the family suggest such a thing. When asked about his mother, Pietro replies that she is doing well, that she has rallied. When Wallis tells her lawyer neighbor that Alba is losing ground, the neighbor refuses to accept her statement, contradicting it by repeating something that Pietro had told him about his mother's improved condition.

The portions of the book that deal with Alba are consistently touching and revealing. Alba, whose physician husband died when she was thirty years old, leaving her with three children ranging in age from one to five years, has had a remarkably difficult life. She is the illegitimate child of Rosalia, who became pregnant with her at an early age as the result of a dalliance with the master of the household in which she worked as a domestic. She and Alba continue to live in a hovel on the father's estate.

Rosalia often treats Alba badly, in some irrational way blaming her for the shame that her illegitimate birth visited upon the mother. Rosalia often sent Alba, as a small child, to the manor house to beg her father for money, which he grudgingly bestowed. Rosalia, always one step from utter destitution, remained a hopeless spendthrift. On one occasion, when the father gave Rosalia five thousand lire—at that time equivalent to a year's wages for the average working man—Rosalia bought expensive luggage, had new clothes tailored for her and Alba, and went off with her daughter for a month to an expensive resort hotel in the mountains. When her funds were exhausted, she sent Alba to beg her exasperated father for more money.

Wallis gets along well with her mother-in-law, whom she respects and truly loves. At one point, she asks the dying Alba, who as an impoverished widow supported her children by teaching elementary school, whether she has any positive memories of her mother, Rosalia, who not only refused to attend her wedding but also beat her when she returned home after her marriage. Alba, while cataloging many of Rosalia's shortcomings in the account she gives Wallis, portrays her mother as an immature woman with a good heart and a generous nature. Wallis's sensitivity in getting Alba to view her mother positively as her own life ebbs reveals much about Wallis as well as about Alba and Rosalia. Late in the book, Wallis presents another view of Rosalia. Alba's son Pietro was Rosalia's favorite grandchild. He tells about his grandmother and about how she lived, counterbalancing but not contradicting what Alba has revealed about her mother.

The personal vignettes in this book are well drawn. The chapter on Clare deals with the empty nest syndrome, something less common in Italy, where university students usually live at home and stay there until they marry, than in the United States. Clare, in American fashion, leaves the family to live in Bologna, an hour away from Parma, and Wallis presents a sensitive account of what she feels as a result of her daughter being home only on weekends. She also discusses with great sensitivity the biological bond that exists between a mother and a daughter.

Equally well presented is the chapter titled "James," in which Wallis tells about her association with James Gill, a Russian living in Italy, where he is editor of a small literary magazine. As this chapter opens, James is hopelessly ill, contemplating suicide as his condition worsens. He finally dies, and Wallis attends the funeral with Clare. Her understanding of people's reactions to death is shown well in what she says about two of James's friends who attended the funeral: "A husband and wife, inseparable friends of James's, bickered over the directions to a hotel they knew two hours before. Their sharp, nervous comments were shorthand for how his going had set things flying loose in them."

Of considerable interest are the details about Italian education that Wilde-Menozzi reveals. At the secondary level, children are expected to memorize and to obey. They do not deal with current affairs but delve into the distant past in most of their classes. Without asking why, they learn dead languages and ancient history. Wilde-Menozzi reveals that when her daughter was in the second year of secondary school, her teacher called to complain that Clare had "gone outside the theme by expressing a personal view." When Wilde-Menozzi suggested that a fifteen-year-old might have some good ideas and know when to express them, the teacher protested, "No . . . three years from now she will know enough to do so." Wilde-Menozzi concludes that a "student in Italy learns to bow to authority and to understand education as sacrifice. One learns to endure the feeling of no choice."

Clare's intention of entering the university was scuttled when, despite her excellent secondary school record, she failed to pass the entrance examinations. Her mother did not realize that for her daughter to pass, she and Paolo would have to use their influence and demand special consideration because, in a system that is inherently corrupt, that is how admission to the university is gained. The very idea of intervening in this way repelled the author.

Wilde-Menozzi's comments on higher education are cogent. She describes a chaotic system in which there are insufficient classrooms, no laboratory work, no individual classwork, and few libraries. Professors are accountable only to themselves, and classes are so large that no written work is assigned because it cannot possibly be graded. In some instances, the demand for spaces is so pressing that students are divided into two or three groups, each of which is permitted to attend the university for four months every year. Higher education in Italy is virtually free for everyone who attends its universities, but its quality is such that only those students most capable of self-direction emerge as well-educated people.

Mother Tongue is more than just another recounting of an American living abroad. It is a delicate presentation of the dramatic tensions and of the sharpened insights that any multicultural situation necessarily involves. Wilde-Menozzi is to be commended both for her profound understanding of these tensions and for her exceptional, Virginia Woolf-like subtlety in presenting them.

R. Baird Shuman

Sources for Further Study

Booklist. XCIII, June, 1997, p. 1653.
The New York Times Book Review. CII, November 30, 1997, p. 21.
The New Yorker. LXXIII, July 21, 1997, p. 77.
Publishers Weekly. CCXLIV, April 21, 1997, p. 51.

MY LIFE, STARRING DARA FALCON

Author: Ann Beattie (1947-   )
Publisher: Alfred A. Knopf (New York). 307 pp. $24.00
Type of work: Novel
Time: The 1970's to the early 1990's
Locale: Primarily Dell, New Hampshire

In this novel about an odd friendship, Ann Beattie shows how the narrator, Jean Warner, develops her personality because of and in spite of the influence of her friend Dara Falcon

> *Principal characters:*
> JEAN WARNER, a small-town wife
> DARA FALCON, an actress, wandering waif, and catalyst for change
> BOB WARNER, Jean's boring first husband
> TOM VAN SANT, the owner of a nursery, Dara Falcon's onetime fiancé
> FRANK WARNER, Bob's brother, one of Dara's conquests

Unlike much of Ann Beattie's fiction, *My Life, Starring Dara Falcon* does not have at its center a male-female relationship that disintegrates or develops. Rather, Beattie turns her camera-eye vision on a peculiar friendship between the narrator, Jean Warner, and the elusive but charismatic Dara Falcon. The title of the novel suggests the dual role these characters occupy in the narrative. While the plot ostensibly chronicles Jean's attempts to develop her personality amid her husband's smothering extended family, in many ways the novel has less to do with Jean and more to do with the starring role Dara plays in that development. Though mildly flawed by the blandness of the narrator, the novel rises above this problem by Beattie's creation of Dara Falcon. Dara serves as a solid center to this novel, which challenges one's notions about the value and dangers of friendship.

The novel opens in the early 1990's with Jean lounging at a resort with her second husband. She casually picks up *The New York Times* and reads Dara Falcon's obituary. After her initial shock at learning of Dara's death, Jean takes the reader back in time to the early 1970's, when she first met Dara, and then recounts the woman's impact on her life.

As Jean begins the flashback, she is newly wed and living in Dell, New Hampshire, with her husband Bob, a no-nonsense part owner of his family's nursery business. Because he stays all week in Boston with his grandmother and brother while he works on his C.P.A. degree, Jean rarely sees him and instead becomes dependent on Warner extended-family members who still live in Dell—Barbara, her mother-in-law, and Frank and Janey, her brother and sister-in-law, and their brood of children. Because Jean has no family of her own, she feels a desire to be liked by all the Warners and finds herself becoming the family errand girl.

Though Beattie tries to inject some humor into these early descriptions of the family by making them seem quirky—Bob gets Buddy Holly-like glasses, Bob's niece reads aloud in a booming voice for no good reason—these details distract more than they illuminate. One wonders why one needs to know so much about such an obviously boring family. Jean seems to fit into this family's blandness; she is perfectly happy doing very little. She has an occasional weekend meal with her husband or types a local woman's autobiography. Jean does not feel troubled or interested in doing or being anything other than a dutiful family woman until she meets Dara Falcon.

When Dara enters the novel, everything about it changes—the pacing, the descriptions, the amount of reflection. Yet like the first-person narrator, Nick, in F. Scott Fitzgerald's *The Great Gatsby* (1925), who must gather information about Jay Gatsby, Jean learns about Dara gradually—some impressions of her at a birthday party, some from rumors, some from what other people say. Like Gatsby, Dara embellishes her life, so the reader, like Jean, must piece together the elements that seem likely. Also like Gatsby, Dara rises above the rumors and projections to be someone important by the sheer force of her desire to do so.

Dara's life revolves around drama, and when drama does not naturally occur, she creates it. It is not surprising that she is an actress by trade, though she can never support herself very long in this profession. Rather, Dara travels around the country—she has just arrived in New Hampshire from Los Angeles when she first meets Jean—finding ramshackle apartments where she fixes up only one room—her private realm—and leaves the rest to look like a two-bit motel. She takes up with Tom Van Sant, the owner/operator of the rival nursery in town, and uses Jean as their go-between, a role Jean rises to despite her initial misgivings.

These meetings with Tom and Dara serve as the first real excitement Jean has known. No longer does she find herself on the periphery of things; she finally starts doing things for her own pleasure. In fact, the one time she does not go to a family function but instead has drinks with Dara and Tom, she precipitates one of the first rifts in her marriage to the boring and mostly absent Bob.

The intrigues in Dara's life keep Jean's life on edge as well. In an otherwise unpromising day, Dara calls and asks her to bring some rum in a hip flask to a local coffeehouse because she is upset. At another point, desperate for transportation, she coerces Jean into selling her a car for a dollar. When Dara and Tom break up, Dara convinces Jean to be the caretaker for the expensive, gaudy ring Tom had given her on their engagement. By the time Jean accepts this responsibility, Dara has ensnared Jean into believing anything and everything she tells her. Though Jean finds it impossible not to like Dara, much of this friendship seems to be based on her awe of Dara, not on Dara's ability to reciprocate any affection or mutual sacrifice. Ironically, Jean continues to play a passive role even as she begins to develop an appreciation for taking action.

Dara manipulates Jean and others so well because she plays on their need to figure her out. In fact, most of her success as a character comes from the reader's not knowing what to believe. She leads Jean to believe that she is strong and self-reliant, though Jean learns later that she frequently borrowed money and lived primarily from the largesse of others, usually men. She tells Jean how her early life was marked by tragedy—an early pregnancy, family disgrace, hospitalization—yet Jean never gets confirmation for any of these early stories. After Jean learns that Dara embellishes the truth, she sets out to uncover various inconsistencies in her many stories. While Dara tells Jean that Frank, Jean's brother-in-law, pursued her, Frank tells Jean that Dara was mad about him and even wanted him to be part of a suicide pact with her. Dara is consistent only in her inconsistency.

Certainly she likes to do things with gusto—eating, lovemaking, acting—but she also creates unnecessary scenes that disrupt the lives of others. When she begins to date Tom Van Sant, she first must woo him away from his pregnant girlfriend, who eventually has his child out of wedlock. Despite Tom's desire to leave Dara and be with his girlfriend and child during this time, Dara emotionally blackmails him into staying with her. In another, rather unrelated move, Dara also seduces Jean's brother-in-law into an affair.

Probably Dara does the most damage when she begins to intrude actively on Jean's relationships with men. After Jean leaves Bob and begins college, she patterns her life on Dara's example, even creating her own version of Dara's one-room living space. Though Jean's moves toward independence signify a positive turn toward activism, she continues to rely on Dara's acceptance in order to feel secure in her new life. She grows frantic when she does not hear from Dara; she worries when Dara sends her cryptic quotations from Anton Chekhov which she passes off as her own. When Jean takes her first serious lover after her divorce, she insists that he meet and approve of her rash friend. Only when Dara attempts to seduce this lover does Jean realize the wicked side of Dara's personality.

Dara's interest in Jean's men seems to be a ploy to keep Jean from ever really feeling successful. Dara spends the entire novel pushing Jean into a larger arena, showing her by example the benefits of a more open life, but then, in effect, shows her the dangers inherent in risking oneself in a relationship with a man, or with a friend.

The novel has the feel of a memoir in which Jean grows under Dara's mostly perverse tutelage. Her voice provides complete recitations of her moments with Dara, followed by her philosophic musings and commentaries. Because Jean retells incidents from her past, these occurrences seem strangely distant from her, as if she is recounting things that happened to someone else; she seems emotionally numb. Using a pseudo-objective first-person voice works well for the purposes of the novel; readers get to view Dara through the clearer lens that time and distancing allow. Yet this distancing also presents a stumbling block to the reader's attempts to get to know the narrator. She is so coolly objective that one often forgets that she is supposed to be a part of the drama, let alone the main character of the novel. Since Jean changes the most during the course of the novel, the reader expects more detail about her, and, by extension, a greater sense of her personality through her voice. Readers know that Jean is important, but eventually Dara takes over the narrator's voice and then the novel. Beattie perhaps accidentally undermines Jean's change by making Dara such a vivacious person. Dara does share the novel with the narrator, and the novel becomes, in essence, dually focused on what will become of Jean and what will become of Dara.

Certainly Beattie needs the two characters to play off each other, if for no other reason than to point out the huge differences between them. Like Fitzgerald's Gatsby,

Dara partially takes center stage because of the projections of the narrator. Jean's story, however, is not confined to a small period of time. She must relay both her relationship with Dara and her relationships with her family. Unlike much of Nick's tale in *The Great Gatsby*, Jean must also be able to sustain readers' interest in many relationships and situations that do not involve Dara. Unfortunately, Dara is so wonderfully complex that she makes every other character seem dull and lifeless by comparison, particularly the narrator. Thus, when Jean is not speaking of Dara or relaying some aspect of Dara's life and influence, one does not particularly care. Beattie leaves a great deal of the novel for Jean to carry, particularly at the end, and these dull aspects of Jean's life only deflect the reader's interest. The reader wants the novel to be more about Dara and less about Jean, but the fact that Jean is the first-person narrator forces her to be the main focus.

Despite these point-of-view problems, however, *My Life, Starring Dara Falcon* works well on many levels, particularly in the strength of Beattie's characterization and plotting. Beattie consistently points out the positive aspects of Dara and Jean's friendship, as well as the dangers inherent in believing in someone else too strongly. Jean learns about herself during the course of this novel, but only after she learns how to live without Dara Falcon in her life.

Rebecca Hendrick Flannagan

Sources for Further Study

Atlanta Journal Constitution. July 6, 1997, p. L9.
Booklist. XCIII, March, 1997, p. 1203.
Chicago Tribune. May 25, 1997, XIV, p. 7.
The Christian Science Monitor. June 9, 1997, p. 12.
Library Journal. CXXII, May 15, 1997, p. 98
National Review. XLIX, July 14, 1997, p. 54.
The New York Times Book Review. CII, May 11, 1997, p. 10.
Publishers Weekly. CCXLIV, April 7, 1997, p. 71.
The Review of Contemporary Fiction. XVII, Summer, 1997, p. 267.
The Washington Post Book World. XXVII, June 22, 1997, p. 11.
The Yale Review. LXXXV, October, 1997, p. 156.

NEARER, MY GOD
An Autobiography of Faith

Author: William F. Buckley, Jr. (1925-   )
Publisher: Doubleday (New York). 300 pp. $34.95
Type of work: Autobiography and essays

> *An amiably rambling series of personal and intellectual musings on the Christian religion by one of America's most prominent conservative authors*

No less than a novel, an autobiography is a work of art or, at least, of craft. The two forms are opposite sides of the same literary coin: Fiction is a kind of autobiography and vice versa. "An autobiography can distort; facts can be realigned," novelist and journalist V. S. Naipaul has written, "but fiction never lies: it reveals the writer totally." Some autobiographies, especially those of writers, have achieved great literary merit by virtue of their very evasiveness and stylization: Graham Greene's *A Sort of Life* (1971) and Naipaul's own *The Enigma of Arrival* (1987) come to mind. "When you are excited about something is when the first draft is done," admonished Ernest Hemingway, whose standards were as severe as Naipaul's or Greene's, "but no one can see it until you have gone over it again and again until you have communicated the emotion, the sights and the sounds to the reader, and by the time you have completed this the words, sometimes, will not make sense to you as you read them, so many times have you re-read them."

What William F. Buckley, Jr., and/or his publisher have chosen to bill as "an autobiography of faith" is, in Hemingway's terms, a first draft. Less famous writers tend to be edited more stringently. It is necessary to say this, and its truth is self-evident in this book's languid and excessively parenthetical, not to say lazy, discursive, and rambling, style. It is not necessarily a harsh criticism, though, if we call Buckley not a writer in a high-minded literary sense but what he is: a public political figure whose stock in trade is argumentation expressed in spoken and written English. Those who object to Christianity or to Buckley's well-known right wing political views or distinctive and sometimes puzzling persona will find sufficient reason, in their own clusters of prejudices, not to like or, more probably, not to buy and read *Nearer, My God*. More open-minded people will find much of value in this thoughtful and interesting book.

Every writer confronts what Greene shrewdly called "the personally impossible," the necessary evasion of which constitutes the writer's art. Buckley comes up against it rather early in this ostensible attempt at artful self-revelation. His honest and disarming tactic is to shrug amiably and observe that he is better at some kinds of writing than at others. "My mode tends to be argumentative," he explains. "For this I have to offer as an excuse only that when I entered the public arena, everybody (it seemed) was on the other side, and for that reason my polemical inclinations have always been reactive." Buckley seems a rather private man, evidently ill at ease with the prospect of self-revelation, which is fair enough. On the other hand, effusive and

misleading jacket blurbs, such as those perfunctorily given here by Buckley's ideological allies and personal friends William Bennett and Charles Colson, should be
banned; Colson, for example, is deceptively wrong to describe the book as "at times
deeply personal." At most, it is, at times, somewhat personal. Only in its evasiveness
and in a few stilted, yet enjoyable, passages of personal narrative can it be called an
autobiography.

Nearer, My God is a grab-bag assortment of chapters on religious topics on which
its author felt inclined to comment, with only a faintly discernible narrative thread, if
that, connecting the whole—a deficiency of which he is well aware. In the introduction, he relates how the project began "over ten years ago" when someone asked him
to write a book titled *Why I Am Still a Catholic*. "I demurred, using as an excuse that
I had books charted for two book-writing seasons ahead," he writes. "But after a month
or so, I thought to accept the commission, provided I could put off work on the book
until 1992. When I sat down in Switzerland (which is where I write my books) to begin
the project, one thing occurred to me quickly, something else later." The casually
explanatory and workmanlike tone alerts the reader not to expect anything too deeply
personal. He elaborates at some length:

> I didn't want to call this book Why I Am a Catholic for reasons already given. As I put it to bed I
> realize, also, that its tone is not what I'd have hoped for. There is the temperamental problem: I am
> not trained in the devotional mode, nor disposed to it. Moreover, this book is without the gratifying
> narrative one finds in many others, a narrative that generates excitement in the reader who believes
> in the faith . . . and even for the nonbeliever. . . . I was baptized a Catholic and reared as one by
> devoted parents whose emotional and intellectual energies never cloyed. My faith has not wavered,
> though I permit myself to wonder whether, if it had, I'd advertise it: Would I encourage my dinner
> companions to know that I was blind in my left eye? I wish I could here give to my readers a sense
> of my own personal struggle, but there is no sufficient story there to tell.

Two chapters of childhood reminiscences segue awkwardly into one titled "Where
Does One Learn About the Christian God?", which is Buckley's version of the
tiresomely familiar complaint that American schools (private schools, in the case of
Buckley's social circle) no longer feature much reference to religion, Christianity in
particular. Buckley's account of his discovery that the times had changed at his
secondary alma mater provides a good sample of the tone of his concerns as well as
of his writing style:

> The occasion was the fiftieth anniversary of the graduation of my class at Millbrook. We were thirteen
> in the class of 1943, and nine, in 1993, now forgathered. The young headmaster is an enthusiast for
> his mission as educator of young people and as headmaster of a distinguished school. A few weeks
> after we met, he came with his wife to dinner at our house in Stamford and, sharing an evening with
> Millbrook graduate Schuyler Chapin, sometime dean of the School of Arts at Columbia University,
> the subject of religion came up. I asked what were the regularly scheduled religious services
> nowadays at Millbrook. He replied that there weren't any, but that the students were "encouraged"
> to engage in spiritual activities according to their own lights. That rather caught my breath.

He goes on to reproduce the program of the school's cloyingly hyperecumenical
service held in December and an extract from a letter that the school's "master in

charge of spiritual life" sent in reply to his inquiry. He then muses: "How to comment? Yes, the performance, being eclectic, looks eclectic; no surprise. . . . The salient meaning of the Candlelight Service is: *Let Us Not Celebrate Christmas.*" This stuff is ideological softball, unworthy of a batter of Buckley's ability. He is behind the times here—both in the sense in which he prefers to be behind the times and in another sense. He is objecting, rather late, to tendencies which, whether welcome or pernicious, had, by 1997, been *faits accomplis* for a couple of decades. His ingenuous question—"How to comment?"—is telling. Is "to comment" always necessary? Apparently it is, if, by trade, one is a commentator. Almost every effort he makes to write narrative in this book quickly collapses into argument. "The time had come," he writes, concluding the chapter with one such effort, "to explore further some of the profundities, and mysteries, of my religion. Time to make an additional effort to understand my faith, and seek out the means to pass along whatever it is that sustains me to those, if any, who can be helped by my exertions." (The book concludes with two appendices: "Further Commentary on the Millbrook Christmas Celebration" and "A Listing of Religious Activities at Various [private] Schools.")

Miscellaneous topical chapters duly ensue: "On the Evolution of Christian Doctrine"; "Concerning Women as Priests, Divorce, Birth Control, Remarriage"; "On Knowing Malcolm Muggeridge"; "On the Uniqueness of Christ." Almost every chapter is lively and interesting, the notably ill-judged exception being chapter 8, "The Crucifixion Examined, and Imagined." Any young and hungry writers worth their salt learn quickly not to quote excessively from other writers. Why, then, is a writer less young and (one assumes) rather less hungry allowed to take seventeen out of three hundred pages (more than 5 percent of his text), in what is understood to be an autobiography, to quote, in full, someone else's fictionalization of the Crucifixion of Jesus? The book from which Buckley quotes at such length is the English translation of *Il poema dell'Uomo-Dio* (1961-1967; *The Poem of the Man-God*, 1986-1990) by Maria Valtorta; he might, instead, simply have directed the reader to the publisher's North American distributor, as he does, in fact, do in a footnote. Human nature being what it is, however, even wrong decisions can be justified: "My decision, then," writes Buckley, "is that in the only book on the faith I will ever put together I don't want to deprive the reader of what I view, notwithstanding its crudity—perhaps because of it?—as an artful portrayal of the great historical event that preceded, and led to, the Resurrection, a depiction if not inspired by God, inspiring nonetheless."

Yet, even the startling clumsiness or laziness of chapter 8 illuminates one of Buckley's and the book's characteristic virtues, a charming and likeable humanity and generosity of spirit. He casually mentions many famous people with whom he is personal friends, but he himself is at least as famous and accomplished as any of them; so what, in another writer, would be name-dropping is, in Buckley, genuine graciousness and an attractively self-confident urge to speak well of others. The nicest and most memorable sections of *Nearer, My God* are those in which he writes with sincere and uncomplicated emotional warmth of special friends and relatives: his mother; his "contiguous sister," Patricia Bozell; and his collaborator Brent Bozell who, as Buckley notes, died in May, 1997, after many years of painful and trying illness. "I first met Brent at Yale," he writes. "We were drawn together politically by our adamant commitment to the anti-Communist cause. And he became my closest friend."

Ethan Casey

Sources for Further Study

Booklist. XCIV, September 1, 1997, p. 4.
The Christian Century. November 19, 1997, p. 1091.
Christianity Today. XLI, November 17, 1997, p. 59.
Library Journal. CXXII, September 15, 1997, p. 79.
National Catholic Reporter. XXXIV, November 7, 1997, p. 27.
National Review. XLIX, September 29, 1997, p. 54.
The New York Times Book Review. CII, September 28, 1997, p. 16.
Publishers Weekly. CCXLIV, September 29, 1997, p. 84.
Time. CL, November 10, 1997, p. 111.

A NEW BIRTH OF FREEDOM
Human Rights, Named and Unnamed

Author: Charles L. Black, Jr. (1915-   )
Publisher: Grosset/Putnam (New York). 175 pp. $22.95
Type of work: Current affairs and law
Locale: The United States

A veteran legal scholar argues eloquently for a return to judicial activism in the quest for inalienable rights promised in the Declaration of Independence and Abraham Lincoln's Gettysburg address

In *A New Birth of Freedom*, Charles L. Black, Jr., attempts to stem the tide of judicial conservatism that has dominated American constitutional law in the 1980's and 1990's. Black's credentials are most impressive. A professor emeritus at Yale Law School and part-time instructor at Columbia Law School, he was part of the team of attorneys that successfully overcame legally mandated school segregation in the case of *Brown v. Board of Education* (1954), which remains a groundbreaking example of judicial activism, an approach to constitutional law that encourages sweeping judicial initiatives consistent with the text of the Constitution. Black has also been well-published in the fields of constitutional law and civil liberties, previously authoring books such as *Structure and Relationship in Constitutional Law* (1969), *Capital Punishment: The Inevitability of Caprice and Mistake* (1980), and *Decision According to Law* (1981). He has published numerous scholarly articles and spoken publicly to a variety of audiences on these and related topics.

The title of Black's book comes from the Gettysburg address by Abraham Lincoln, to whom the book is dedicated. According to Black, Lincoln's promise of "a new birth of freedom" was meant to be taken seriously and was not just a rhetorical convenience of the moment. Lincoln's promise, however, has not been fully realized because of the failure of Americans to understand the true expanse of rights offered by the U.S. Constitution. This, in turn, is linked to three mistakes of constitutional interpretation: failure to realize the quasi-legal status of rights outlined in the Declaration of Independence, failure to utilize the Ninth Amendment to the Constitution (which strongly suggests the existence of rights not enumerated in the Constitution), and failure to properly implement the "citizenship" and "privileges and immunities" clauses of section 1 of the Fourteenth Amendment. In concert, these mistakes have led to an overall approach to civil liberties and civil rights that systematically deprives Americans of freedoms they should and could be enjoying under the protection of constitutional law.

All three of these alleged mistakes of interpretation are controversial and, therefore, need explanation, which Black supplies in enough detail to make his arguments compelling but not so much as to make his book esoteric or conspicuously academic.

With regard to the Declaration of Independence, Black argues that the nation's founders had the "inalienable rights" mentioned in that document's second paragraph well in mind when they authored the Constitution and, even more particularly, when they added and ratified the Bill of Rights (the first ten amendments to the Constitution). Black reminds readers of the close proximity in time between the Declaration of Independence and the Constitution, which are separated by only about a dozen years, and asserts that the Declaration of Independence had, at the very least, quasi-legal status for the nation's founders. He also suggests that the founders understood the rights to "life, liberty, and the pursuit of happiness" in broad, rather than narrow, terms. Judicial interpretation of the Constitution, however, has been thoroughly dominated by the point of view that the Declaration of Independence has no legal standing whatsoever and that it cannot even be seen as a helpful indicator of what the founders had in mind when they ratified the Bill of Rights. As a result, constitutional interpretation has been denied the richly idealistic legacy that the Declaration of Independence should have provided.

Black further supports his argument for the founders' broad notion of inalienable rights by citing the Ninth Amendment to the Constitution (part of the Bill of Rights), which states that "The enumeration in the Constitution, of certain rights, shall not be construed to deny or disparage others retained by the people." According to Black, this language clearly legitimizes a broad (and flexible) interpretation of constitutionally protected rights and liberties. Jurists, however, have been extremely hesitant to accord the Ninth Amendment any meaningful role in constitutional interpretation, thus artificially narrowing the range of rights and liberties enjoyed by Americans.

Black finally buttresses his argument for a broad interpretation of constitutional liberties by citing the "citizenship" and "privileges and immunities" clauses of section 1 of the Fourteenth Amendment, which, he believes, also indicate the existence of unnamed, but nevertheless inviolable, rights fundamental to genuine civil liberty. Crucial to this section is Black's interpretation of the terms "privileges" and "immunities." For Black, the terms connote an all-inclusive, but as yet indeterminate, range of protections against the intrusiveness of government. In addition, the Fourteenth Amendment, in Black's view, unambiguously extends full protection of individual liberties against incursions by the states as well as the Federal government. Previously, jurists had held (with more certainty than warranted, in Black's view) that the First Amendment protection of free speech, free press, and freedom of religion, for example, applied only to the national government since it (the amendment) specifically prohibits Congress from making laws contravening these rights. Section 1 of the Fourteenth Amendment specifically prohibits the states from violating the "privileges and immunities" of U.S. citizens. Nevertheless, orthodox constitutional interpretation has misfired on both of these issues, according to Black. The Bill of Rights was applied only begrudgingly to the states until well into the twentieth century. Ultimately, this hesitancy to use the Fourteenth Amendment as a means of nationalizing the Bill of Rights abated, but mainstream jurists, for the most part, still have refused to interpret the Fourteenth Amendment as indicative of a broad battery of, as yet, unnamed rights.

In Black's opinion, these mistakes of constitutional interpretation have led to a judicial approach to civil liberties and civil rights that, at best, might accurately be called timid. At worst, it might be seen as one that has served the interests of those with power at the expense of our society's underdogs: racial minorities, the poor, and people with unpopular lifestyles or ideas.

That Black's alternative approach is anything but timid, and that it eschews the protection of privilege, is indicated by his inclusion, among the rights we have failed to recognize, of a substantive freedom from poverty, or what he calls "justice of livelihood." In the realm of American political and legal thought, such a position puts Black outside the mainstream, to say the least. Yet, Black pursues the point with unabashed enthusiasm, arguing that among our inalienable rights are not only those of a negative nature—that is, areas where government must not intrude on individual liberty—but also the positive right to gainful work and, accordingly, sustenance adequate to ensure freedom from want.

This is an extremely important point to make, for it reiterates the belief a majority of Americans held for a brief historical moment during the 1960's. This belief holds that the problems of poverty and homelessness in the United States are not merely economic in nature but also morally problematic, since they represent a major shortfall in civil liberties. In the pantheon of political ideals, economic justice and equality have traditionally come in a distant second to liberty, or freedom, for most Americans. More particularly, civil liberties have always been very important, at least theoretically, to most Americans. Indeed, Americans have taken great pride in their nation's great achievements in the area of civil liberties. On this issue, we have seen ourselves as a beacon for other nations and peoples. Accepting Black's definition of poverty and homelessness as civil liberties issues therefore has the potential of increasing the nation's commitment to meaningful economic equality. In the context of the 1990's, this would be a major turnabout in American public opinion.

While Black does not explicitly tackle other controversial public policy issues in his book, his theory is implicitly applicable, in equally radical or unconventional ways, to such issues as the legalization of marijuana, gay rights, the right to die, and any number of similar areas where government fosters what some observers see as onerous limits on individual freedom. Thus, it would be entirely appropriate to say that Black's ideas are far-reaching and potentially explosive.

Are they right? Given the time period of this book's publication, its ideas would seem to represent a relatively quiet minority within the legal establishment. Champions of judicial conservatism (or judicial restraint) such as Associate Supreme Court Justice Antonin Scalia would appear to have won the day, nor are they shy about publicly proclaiming the superiority of their arguments. Contrary to Black, such figures argue that there is no convincing textual or historical evidence that the Declaration of Independence has legal standing or that it informed the founders' notion of constitutional rights. They argue that the Ninth Amendment merely opens the way for adding new rights and liberties to the Constitution via the amendment process rather than implying that the Constitution is full of numerous, unnamed rights. Applying the standard of "original intent," they find that the Fourteenth Amendment offers essentially limited, rather than expansive, protection against government power.

On a broader philosophical basis, proponents of judicial conservatism argue that judicial activism such as that advocated by Black weakens the authority of law by making the Constitution seem capricious. After all, who is to say what the unnamed rights of the Constitution are? Is there a right to smoke cigarettes in the workplace? Is there a right to tell raucous jokes at a funeral or to pursue sexual relations with consenting children? Most people would say no to these questions. However, the Constitution, Black's opponents argue, is supposed to impose the rule of law, not predilections based on the latest public opinion poll.

Such arguments point out the limits of Black's approach, but they do not completely refute it. It is true that Black cannot prove his case in the same conclusive way that a mathematician or empirical scientist can, but neither can his opponents prove their case conclusively. What Black does achieve is to point out that the arguments for judicial activism and an expansive approach to civil liberties are, at the very least, on a roughly equal footing with those for judicial conservatism. In addition, he is able to neutralize the argument about capriciousness by pointing out that the law also risks the loss of its authority (or legitimacy) when it responds sluggishly or not at all to majority tyranny and other established forms of injustice. The purpose of law, Black reminds us, is not only to provide order but also to approximate justice. Failure to do so puts constitutional law on an ever more slippery foundation.

Black does not belabor this or any other point in his book. Indeed, his presentation throughout is bold and forthright rather than dry and technical. Black's emotional attachment to Lincoln is especially touching. In opposing the great promise of a "new birth of freedom" in Lincoln's Gettysburg address to the "states' rights" advocacy of pre-Civil War southern Senator John C. Calhoun, Black manages to convey an abiding concern for individuals of every stripe as opposed to governments, which, no matter what the level—national, state, or local—are capable of great harm to individuals and decidedly incapable of enjoying the fruits of individual liberty.

This is not to say that Black's modus operandi is to argue entirely from the hip. He offers crisp, sensible reasoning as a basis for all of his conclusions, complementing his heartfelt commitment to a broad conception of constitutional rights with admirable analytic clarity. The result is a charmingly eccentric, highly readable book by a battle-scarred, unapologetic crusader for rights. Furthermore, while one may argue with this book's legal reasoning, there is no question at all about the sincerity of the convictions held by its author.

Ira Smolensky

Sources for Further Study

American Bar Association Journal. Spring, 1997, p. 92.
The New York Times Book Review. September 28, 1997, p. 17.
Publishers Weekly. May 12, 1997, p. 66.

THE NEW LIFE

Author: Orhan Pamuk (1952-   )
First published: Yeni Hayat, 1994, in Turkey
Translated from the Turkish by Güneli Gün
Publisher: Farrar Straus Giroux (New York). 296 pp. $24.00
Type of work: Novel
Time: The 1990's
Locale: Turkey

In Turkish writer Orhan Pamuk's deceptively simple fifth novel, a young man reads a book that changes his life

Principal characters:
OSMAN, the narrator, a student
JANAN, a student with whom he falls in love
MEHMET, a student with whom Janan has fallen in love
DR. FINE, a lawyer turned storekeeper who founds The Great
    Counterconspiracy, a nationalist movement
UNCLE RIFKI, the author of articles on the Turkish railway, of stories for
    children, and of *The New Life,* a novel for adults

Over the course of a dozen years, Turkish writer Orhan Pamuk has accomplished a rather formidable feat, publishing five novels that manage to deal with Turkish subjects while together recapitulating the full range of twentieth century Western literary history. Pamuk's first novel, *Cevdet Bey ve ogullari* (1982; Cevdet Bey and sons), is a work of literary realism. *Sessiz ev* (1983; the silent house) and *Beyaz Kale* (1985; *The White Castle,* 1991) are, as their Kafkaesque titles suggest, more modernist, and *Kara Kitap* (1990; *The Black Book,* 1995) and now *The New Life* are decidedly postmodern works, at once narratively playful and politically engaged. Western reviewers compared the author of *The Black Book,* in which a young lawyer searches throughout Istanbul for his elusive wife, Rueya (dream), eventually taking on the identity of her halfbrother, a journalist who has disappeared, to Don DeLillo and Salman Rushdie, two masters of the kind of postmodern novel Linda Hutcheon calls "historiographic metafiction." The quest structure and assumption of new identities figure even more prominently in *The New Life,* in which Pamuk broadens the playing field and has his characters take up and discard identities with bewildering yet strangely liberating abandon. Yet after the success of *The Black Book, The New Life* seems a bit disappointing, strangely slow despite all of its motion as well as its getting off to a good, indeed brilliantly Borgesian, start.

"I read a book one day and my whole life was changed." Readers of the world, beware: What this opening gambit in Pamuk's narrative chess game implies is about as far removed from the cheerful sentiment expressed in Emily Dickinson's little ditty "There is no Frigate like a Book/ To take us Lands away" as one can go and still be dealing with the same basic trope. Dickinson's poem effaces the colonialist premise upon which her metaphor rides to exotic lands. Pamuk's novel, on the other hand, foregrounds the new colonialism of the global economy and new world order and its consequences for Turkey, where East and West meet, along with old and new. Osman, although not identified by name until quite late in the novel, is another point of intersection, both reader of *The New Life* and narrator of the novel of the same name by an author whose own praenomen suggests that Osman serves, in some oddly angled way, not only as reader's surrogate but also as author Orhan Pamuk's double.

Like Roman Saul on the road to becoming Christian Paul, Osman at his desk is struck by the intensity of the book's light. Metaphorically blinded, he nevertheless believes that it can guide him "through a strange and savage land" and enable him to recast himself, to "find the new life, safe and unscathed by any mishap."

Pamuk's novel is filled with mishaps of one kind or another, from the many, often fatal bus collisions to the more or less fortunate fall Osman recounts at the beginning of chapter 2 with all the directness and simplicity of a folktale for children: "The next day I fell in love." The student of engineering falls for the student of architecture, Janan (soul mate), whom Osman sees carrying the same book (the very same, it turns out) and whom he confuses with a character in the book, the Angel. Yet these meetings of boy and girl, boy and book, are not accidental. They are parts of Janan's plan to restore her boyfriend Mehmet's faith in the book on which Osman has just placed his hopes of a new life (as Janan had earlier). Mehmet is shot, then disappears with Janan in uncertain pursuit. With Osman's life now doubly "off track" following Janan's disappearance as well as the death of his father, a railway worker, the year before, Osman also departs, "searching for something to lighten [his] burden" and hoping that his and Janan's paths—their bus routes—will eventually cross. They do, at the scene of one bus accident, before, at the scene of another, Osman and Janan assume the identities of a young couple less fortunate than they (though like them, also readers of *The New Life*). Thus Osman becomes Ali Kara, like Mehmet a disillusioned reader, and Janan becomes his faithful wife, the book's still faithful reader, Efsun.

As Ali and Efsun, Osman and Janan meet Dr. Fine, who, given the novel's *Alice in Wonderland*-like logic, is not a doctor. Rather, he is a man whose father forced him to abandon his dream of a medical career and become a lawyer. Upon his father's death, Dr. Fine began a new life as a storekeeper, but the great pleasure he derived from this simple pursuit, satisfying his customers' equally simple desires with locally produced goods, ended when his son Nahit read a book that changed his life. Since Nahit's reading led him to renounce his family about the same time that Western goods began driving out Turkish ones, the distraught Dr. Fine turns paranoid, assuming the existence of a great conspiracy. Having lost both his son and his peace of mind, he founds a clandestine, narrowly nationalistic movement, The Great Counterconspiracy, whose activities include assassinating the author of *The New Life* and attempts on the lives of some of its readers. That the shooting of Mehmet is part of the plan is one of the novel's, or life's, little ironies, for Mehmet is actually Nahit, liberated from his earlier life by yet another bus accident. As conspiracies and contingencies proliferate and collide with Pynchonesque abandon, the plot of Pamuk's novel thickens—into (im)pure artifice.

In their own ways, Nahit, Janan, and Osman on the one hand and Dr. Fine and his fellow Counterconspirators on the other find too much, which is to say too little, in this "New Life." For the former, the book offers the answer to the mystery of life, while for the latter it is the cause of all the nation's problems. When Osman finally does locate the rival who is also his double, he finds a Mehmet who has undergone yet another change of name and identity as well as heart. Mehmet is now "Osman," but an Osman who has found the contentment that continues to elude the novel's restless narrator. This Osman neither believes in *The New Life* as Nahit did nor, like Mehmet, rails against it. Instead, he copies it for others. This copying, which constitutes his sole activity but not his sole happiness, is a strange, even paradoxical act, but then so is a "good book" as the former Mehmet now defines it: one that "reminds us of the whole world" *and* "implies things that don't exist. . . . It is futile to look outside the book for a realm that is located beyond the words."

At once disillusioned and liberated, Osman becomes first the other Osman's friend, then his murderer. He rejects the selflessness of Uncle Rifki's children's stories in favor of the violent conclusion of the hard-boiled detective story (with a dash of Edgar Allan Poe's "William Wilson" thrown in for good measure).

Fortunately, there is such a thing as poetic justice, at least in literature. Osman returns to Dr. Fine's to discover Janan recovered from her fever but departed, indeed lost forever. As he later learns, she has married a doctor who has also read *The New Life* with passion yet still managed to live his life in peace. Ever "the unfortunate traveller" and "hapless hero," Osman, the rational student of engineering turned detective, then murderer, finally (or possibly penultimately) becomes "a good family man," marrying the daughter of the family he saw moving in on his street in the novel's first chapter.

Unfortunately, not even the happiness he finds as husband and father is sufficient to offset the restless voyager's, or voyeur's, obsession with finding "the Original Cause." Just as Mehmet earlier felt compelled to track down the book's author, Uncle Rifki (only to become furious when Uncle Rifki claimed that his only aim in writing *The New Life* had been to give adults the same pleasure that his other books had given children), Osman tracks down the candy maker whose wrappers had inspired the Angel figure in *The New Life*. Osman's quest ends late and laughably; the candy maker claims to have been inspired by the film *The Blue Angel* (1959), in which a professor is bewitched by a sexually ambiguous cabaret singer played by Marlene Dietrich.

The joys of hybridity and thus of impurity are, as in Rushdie's novels, evident throughout Pamuk's densely yet delightfully intertextual *The New Life*, a literary recycling project in which textual echoes collide even more frequently than buses. Late in the novel, Pamuk foregrounds his intertextual theme when he has Osman read (and quote from) some of the many books that influenced Uncle's Rifki's writing: American comic books at one extreme, Dante Alighieri's *La vita nuova* (c. 1293) at the other (with its author's own lost love, the angelic Beatrice). To find in any one source the interpretive key to Pamuk's slim yet oddly encyclopedic novel is to miss the author's boat, or bus. Vladimir Nabokov's influence is certainly pervasive but hardly dominant. *Lolita* (1955), *Pale Fire* (1962), and *Speak, Memory* (1951) play their undeniable parts, but only alongside Italo Calvino and Lewis Carroll, Franz Kafka and Milan Kundera, Gabriel García Márquez and Jorge Luis Borges ("Pierre Menard, Author of Don Quixote" in particular), Kōbō Abe and Paul Auster, the very different "road" novels of Jack Kerouac and Ben Okri, plus what the Western reader can only imagine must be an equally vast collection of Turkish texts. "Cleverness spoils everything," Osman says at one point, but it does not spoil a novel that claims to eschew Chekhovian pathos (only to wring some from Osman's situation) in favor of telling a cautionary tale about the dangers of all kinds of fundamentalist readings (Islamic fundamentalist included) while incorporating another Islamic tradition, that of endless interpretation and commentary.

One can well understand why *The New Life* became a best-seller in Turkey. Pamuk's comic novel resonates not only intertextually but also politically and culturally with the clash, or crash, of East and West and the hope of a tolerant but recognizably Turkish secular state versus the rise of Islamic fundamentalism. Above all, *The New Life* deals with simple pleasures rather than all-embracing ideas, the intricacy of accidentally interconnected lives rather than narrowly defined distinctions and boundaries—and of course it deals with survival.

Yet for all of its intelligence and inventiveness, Pamuk's novel will be, for the majority of Western readers, far more interesting, indeed exciting, to think, talk, and write about than to read. Granted, it is by design that its characters are lifeless and abstract, its plot slow and repetitious, but the design nevertheless undermines the novel's considerable charms. One of these charms is the way Pamuk breathes new life into now familiar postmodern self-consciousness and self-reflexivity, as in Osman's trying to "figure out how to inhabit this foreign toy," "this newfangled plaything called the novel," which he calls "the greatest invention of Western culture" even if (sounding here like Dr. Fine) it is "none of our culture's business." Another charm is the way *The New Life* does for its reader what reading a number of books in rapid succession does for Osman, setting up "some sort of murmur among themselves, transforming my head into an orchestra pit where different musical instruments sounded out, and I would realize that I could endure this life because of these musicales going on in my head." In its own intermittently beguiling way, *The New Life* makes the reader believe this, and more besides, playing its witty but at times sad variations on themes supplied by Oscar Wilde ("life follows art") and W. H. Auden ("poetry makes nothing happen").

Robert A. Morace

Sources for Further Study

The Atlantic. CCLXXX, July, 1997, p. 114.
Booklist. XCIII, March 1, 1997, p. 1112.
Chicago Tribune. April 13, 1997, XIV, p. 4.

Library Journal. CXXII, February, 1997, p. 107.
Los Angeles Times Book Review. June 8, 1997, p. 11.
The Nation. CCLXIV, April 7, 1997, p. 38.
The New York Times Book Review. CII, April 6, 1997, p. 8.
Publishers Weekly. CCXLIV, February 3, 1997, p. 93.
The Times Literary Supplement. October 10, 1997, p. 23.
The Wall Street Journal. April 4, 1997, p. A7.
The Washington Post Book World. XXVII, July 13, 1997, p. 11.

NEWS OF A KIDNAPPING

Author: Gabriel García Márquez (1928-   )
First published: Noticia de un secuestro, 1996, in Colombia
Translated from the Spanish by Edith Grossman
Publisher: Alfred A. Knopf (New York). 291 pp. $25.00
Type of work: Political history
Time: 1990
Locale: Colombia

Nobel laureate Gabriel García Márquez recounts a kidnapping campaign that gripped Colombia in the early 1990's

Principal personages:
MARUJA PACHÓN DE VILLAMIZAR, abductee and government
    administrator
BEATRIZ VILLAMIZAR DE GUERRERO, abductee and colleague of Maruja
ALBERTO VILLAMIZAR, politician, husband of Maruja, and brother of
    Beatriz
MARINA MONTOYA, abductee and sister of ambassador Germán Montoya
DIANA TURBAY, abductee and media personality
NYDIA QUINTERO DE BALCÁZAR, mother of Diana
JULIO CÉSAR TURBAY, former president, Liberal Party leader, and father
    of Diana
AZUCENA LIÉVANO, abductee and editor
JUAN VITTA, abductee and writer
RICHARD BECERRA, abductee and cameraman
ORLANDO ACEVEDO, abductee and cameraman
HERO BUSS, abductee and journalist
FRANCISCO "PACHO" SANTOS, abductee and editor-in-chief of *El Tiempo*
HERNANDO SANTOS CASTILLO, publisher of *El Tiempo* and Pacho's father
RAFAEL GARCÍA HERREROS, television priest
CÉSAR GAVIRIA, president of Colombia
PABLO ESCOBAR GAVIRIA, drug trafficker

In September, 1990, publisher Hernando Santos Castillo received word that his son Francisco had been abducted. His first reaction was to say "Thank God." In many parts of the world, such a response might have been unthinkable, yet in the Colombia of Gabriel García Márquez's *News of a Kidnapping* it was understandable. Abductions had become epidemic—but so had killings. As the author notes, "News of a kidnapping, no matter how painful, is not as irremediable as news of a murder."

In *News of a Kidnapping* (originally published in 1996 as *Noticia de un secuestro*), García Márquez takes on the task—he calls it "the saddest and most difficult of my life"—of detailing the Santos abduction and nine others perpetrated in Colombia beginning in August, 1990. He describes this collective kidnapping as a "gruesome drama" that is only one component of a vast "biblical holocaust that has been consuming Colombia for more than twenty years."

García Márquez offers a disturbing glimpse of that national calamity, focusing on the abductions while surveying the circumstances that enabled Colombian militants and drug traffickers like Pablo Escobar Gaviria to attain warlord and even folk hero status, amassing fortunes and entering mainstream politics while masterminding assassinations and kidnappings. According to García Márquez, their ascendance sent a clear message to the public: "The law is the greatest obstacle to happiness; it is a waste of time learning to read and write; you can live a better, more secure life as a criminal than as a law-abiding citizen—in short, this was the social breakdown typical of all undeclared wars."

One of the most problematic outgrowths of this breakdown was the extradition policy that allowed Colombians to be taken from their homeland and tried in the United States. Extradition had resulted in the removal and imprisonment of drug kingpins as powerful as Carlos Lehder Rivas, but it also had raised the stakes of Colombian discord. Using the slogan, "We prefer a grave in Colombia to a cell in the United States," the traffickers, who became known as the Extraditables, seemed willing to deploy all the means at their disposal—kidnapping included—to strengthen their influence and stay out of the reach of the U.S. judicial system.

Such was the backdrop of the abductions documented in *News of a Kidnapping*, which began just after the inauguration of President César Gaviria and just before the convening of a Constituent Assembly intended to bring about the first major Colombian reforms in decades. As their primary victim, the Extraditables targeted an individual closely associated with Colombia's government and mass media—Diana Turbay, director of the television news program *Criptón* and daughter of former president Julio César Turbay (who had signed the extradition treaty). They ensnared her under the pretext that she was being escorted to an interview with the leader of the Army of National Liberation guerrilla movement. Also taken were five of her colleagues: editor Azucena Liévano, writer Juan Vitta, German journalist Hero Buss, and cameramen Richard Becerra and Orlando Acevedo.

At the end of September, two more people—Marina Montoya and Francisco Santos—fell into the hands of the Extraditables; like the other abductees, they were linked by family, friends, and occupation to leading politicians and the mass media. Marina, the sister of Colombian ambassador Germán Montoya, was abducted by three armed men. Francisco was the editor-in-chief of his father's newspaper, *El Tiempo*; his abduction cost the life of driver Oromansio Ibáñez. In November, a group of armed men abducted Maruja Pachón de Villamizar and her colleague and sister-in-law Beatriz Villamizar de Guerrero on their way home from work at Colombia's agency for film promotion. Their driver, Angel María Roa, was killed in the process.

Torn from their daily routines, estranged from their loved ones, and held captive by masked criminals, the abductees underwent profound psychological and physical duress. García Márquez conveys a sense of their displacement by integrating extensive journalistic reporting with "literary" devices—tinkering with chronology, withholding important details, and even introducing "red herrings." Ultimately, his narrative illustrates how the lives of all the involved parties changed in the wake of the kidnappings, which resulted in Marina's and Diana's deaths before the release of the last two hostages, Maruja and Francisco, in May of 1991.

News of a Kidnapping is not the kind of tale most commonly associated with García Márquez, who is best known for the "Magical Realism" of his novels and short stories. Along with the aforementioned narrative devices, however, this nonfiction work includes characters, themes, and events that recall the author's fictional writings. Perhaps most characteristic is the episode in which Diana's mother, Nydia Quintero de Balcázar, correctly senses that her daughter has been killed and confronts Gaviria, blaming the death on him. After the president assures her that she must be mistaken, she tells him she knows Diana has died "Because I'm her mother and my heart tells me so," and ultimately declares her daughter's fate "the story of a death foretold"— recalling García Márquez's 1981 novella *Crónica de una muerte anunciada* (*Chronicle of a Death Foretold*, 1983).

Nydia is but one of the many real-life figures the author portrays with the kind of powerful, near-mythic personality traits found in his fictional characters. Many of the men in the book, for example, seem to personify manifestations of machismo in extremis—such as the glacial stoicism of President Gaviria (Nydia accuses him of having a "soul of stone"), the hearty fellowship of Francisco Santos (which he maintains even with his guards), and the unwavering resolve of Alberto Villamizar (who single-mindedly devotes himself to rescuing his wife).

The power of family units is another García Márquez motif well represented in *News of a Kidnapping*. The affinities he delineates between crime families and the families of key hostages suggest that Colombia, despite its democratic aspirations, remains a nation where family units compete and overlap with gangs, guerrilla groups, and the government as centers of power. With communications between the Extraditables and the government consisting mostly of policy statements and violence, interfamilial contacts established areas of relative accord where progress could be made.

Although some of these contacts occurred in face-to-face meetings, other crucial exchanges took place through electronic and print media. Indeed, *News of a Kidnapping* is as much about news and communications as it is about kidnapping. García Márquez offers many instances of how, with the hostages isolated and the Extraditables on the run, media offered channels where fruitful communication could take place. On more than one occasion, for example, Nydia and other relatives of the hostages staged broadcast events that used secret codes and outright pleas to influence negotiations and boost the morale of the abductees—who, despite their deprivations, were often afforded access to television, radio, and newspapers.

That Colombians as a whole share a desire to transcend their painful predicament by building a sense of community comes across through numerous anecdotes that document what seems to be an almost absurd national desire to celebrate—not only on triumphant occasions like the release of a hostage but also under extremely dire circumstances. Describing the festive atmosphere in the Villamizar home on the night after Maruja and Beatriz's abduction, García Márquez characteristically shrugs, "It can't be helped: In Colombia, any gathering of more than six people, regardless of class or the hour, is doomed to turn into a dance."

Religion, or faith, constitutes another avenue of hope for García Márquez's Colombians. Drug kingpins, hostages, guards, and legislators all profess some form of religious (usually Catholic) belief. Prayers, religious medals, and holy water are used on numerous occasions. Mystical faith even plays a role in the life of Maruja, who rattles her guards by professing atheism but views one of her dreams as a religious omen. In passages redolent with "Magical Realism," Maruja and her husband communicate through supernatural means: García Márquez writes that Alberto would "spend hours staring in the direction where he supposed Maruja was, sending her mental messages until he was overcome by exhaustion" and that Maruja "had responded with all her heart: 'Get me out of here, I don't know who I am anymore after so many months of not seeing myself in a mirror.'"

According to García Márquez, it was ultimately a mystic—the television priest Rafael García Herreros—who emerged after months of abductions, death threats, and desperate communications as the key to the release of the hostages and the subsequent surrender of Escobar, leader of the Extraditables. The breakthrough occurred when the elderly and eccentric clergyman—considered a saint by some and a lunatic by others—made the following declaration on the April 18 broadcast of his long-running series of *God's Minute* television sermons:

> They have told me you want to surrender. They have told me you would like to talk to me. Oh sea! Oh sea of Coveñas at five in the evening when the sun is setting! What should I do? They tell me he is weary of his life and its turmoil, and I can tell no one my secret. But it suffocates me internally. Tell me, oh sea: Can I do it? Should I do it? You who know the history of Colombia, you who saw the Indians worshipping on this shore, you who heard the sound of history: Should I do it? Will I be rejected if I do it? Will I be rejected in Colombia? If I do it: Will there be shooting when I go with them? Will I fall with them in this adventure?

How did the cryptic comments of García Herreros, who died in 1992, trigger the machinations that ended the hostage crisis? The narrative strongly suggests that the answer may lie in García Herreros' appeal as a media personality, one who shunned the greed, violence, and clannishness plaguing Colombia while appealing to its citizens' desire for community, understanding, and peace.

García Márquez, himself a national icon, may have thought of himself as a possible successor to García Herreros when he dedicated *News of a Kidnapping* "To all the protagonists and all my collaborators" as well as "all Colombians—innocent and guilty—with the hope that the story it tells will never befall us again." Throughout 1997, however, reports from Colombia showed the nation to be, in the words of *The New York Times* correspondent Diana Jean Schemo, "in its worst shape in decades, demoralized, angry and broke," and site of approximately 70 percent of the world's kidnappings. National reconciliation still seemed the province of dreamers in a country mired in a leadership crisis and controlled largely by rival militant groups.

David Marc Fischer

Sources for Further Study

Commonweal. CXXIV, September 26, 1997, p. 20.
Los Angeles Times Book Review. June 1, 1997, p. 10.
The Nation. CCLXIV, June 16, 1997, p. 23.
The New York Review of Books. XLIV, October 9, 1997, p. 19.
The New York Times Book Review. CII, June 15, 1997, p. 16.
Publishers Weekly. CCXLIV, April 28, 1997, p. 58.
Time. CXLIX, June 2, 1997, p. 77.
The Times Literary Supplement. July 11, 1997, p. 21.
The Wall Street Journal. June 3, 1997, p. A20.
The Washington Post Book World. XXVII, June 29, 1997, p. 5.

NIGHTMARE ON MAIN STREET
Angels, Sadomasochism, and the Culture of Gothic

Author: Mark Edmundson (1949-   )
Publisher: Harvard University Press (Cambridge, Massachusetts). 224 pp. $22.95
Type of work: Literary criticism
Locale: The United States

Nightmare on Main Street *explores the rise of the gothic sensibility in modern American culture and the inadequate popular cultural responses to its pervasive and negative vision*

Principal personages:
WES CRAVEN, the director of the film *A Nightmare on Elm Street*
TONY KUSHNER, a playwright, author of *Angels in America: A Gay Fantasia on National Themes*
TONI MORRISON, the author of the novel *Beloved*
SIGMUND FREUD, the father of psychoanalysis
PERCY BYSSHE SHELLY, the nineteenth century visionary poet
ANN RADCLIFFE, the eighteenth century gothic novelist

Mark Edmundson's *Nightmare on Main Street* is divided into three disparate, but connected, chapters. In the first chapter, "American Gothic," Edmundson outlines the rise of the gothic sensibility in his own psyche and in popular American culture. In the second chapter, "The World According to Forrest Gump," he examines some cultural themes that constitute a weak and somewhat pathetic response to the premillennial gothic mode. In the third chapter, "S & M culture," he searches for signs of a visionary force that might provide a counterpoint to the negative impact of the gothic impulse on American cultural reality.

Edmundson begins with a premise that hardly needs arguing: Terror and fear are increasingly becoming fundamental features of the American psyche. The American conviction that lust, perversion, and crime are the three pillars of public life, the national obsession with horror and degradation in entertainment, from motion pictures such as *The Texas Chainsaw Massacre* (1974) to the Oprah Winfrey show, and the insatiable desire for real-life gothic, epitomized by the trial of O. J. Simpson, all point to a major shift in the American sensibility from can-do, Emersonian self-reliance to a pervasive sense of danger, dread, and impotence in public and private life.

Edmundson finds that there are three main strains of gothic sensibility in contemporary American life. The first he calls "terror" gothic. Terror gothic has a long and somewhat prestigious history. One can trace its stirrings to the French writer Marquis de Sade and the real-life terrors of the French Revolution. In terror gothic, it is the individual who is menaced, and early literary masters such as Ann Radcliffe and Monk Lewis constructed novels with gothic conventions so compelling that they persist as a model for gothic traumas, both fictional and real, right up to the modern day: a ruthless, dark-browed tyrant, a beautiful and suppliant heroine, a haunted house or landscape, trusty servants, moonlight, eroticism, and knives. These are all ingredients in a formula well known since the middle of the eighteenth century. The question is why do these old gothic trappings reassert themselves so vividly in the 1990's in America. Why, for example, did the murder trial of O. J. Simpson, containing a mystery no less perplexing than the one presented in Ann Radcliffe's novel *The Mysteries of Udolpho* (1794), command center stage and hold the entire nation in thrall? What did the national obsession with Oklahoma City bomber Timothy McVeigh, Michael Jackson, the Menendez brothers, and John Wayne Bobbitt say about the temper of contemporary America? How did these real-life melodramas connect with the fictional terrain of popular motion pictures: *Psycho* (1960), *The Texas Chainsaw Massacre*, and *Silence of the Lambs* (1990)? The gothic mind inevitably sees evil lurking everywhere and sees hypocrisy in all high places. This mind wants slasher films and lurid details. It savors the episode between American ice-skaters Nancy Kerrigan and Tonya Harding as much as the Richard Nixon tapes. It manages, in fact, to take a very few instances of terror and dissembling in public life and distort them into a worldview that fosters unwarranted suspicion and paranoia, if not full-scale *fin de siècle* despair—the ubiquitous "whatever."

Edmundson dubs a second strain of gothic sensibility in American life "apocalyptic." Instead of merely personal menace, the apocalyptic gothic promises to haunt the society at large. Mary Shelley's 1818 novel, *Frankenstein*, is the ur-apocalyptic gothic work. In it, the prototypical mad scientist, in full hubris, tampers with the sacred prerogatives of nature and attempts, through the agency of humankind's puny technology, to usurp the godlike power of creating life. Nothing good can come of it. This basic schema was most successfully exploited in contemporary American film by director Stephen Spielberg in his blockbuster, *Jurassic Park* (1993). In the 1990's, apocalyptic terror was evoked by fear of impending ecological disaster: Global warming, acid rain, and, most especially, acquired immunodeficiency syndrome (AIDS) all entered the national consciousness as righteous revenge for humanity's incessant, egotistical, and immoral tampering with Mother Nature's ways.

Edmundson, who wrote *Towards Reading Freud: Self Creation in Milton, Wordsworth, Emerson and Sigmund Freud* (1990), returns to familiar territory when he describes the third strain of the gothic impulse—"internalized" gothic. It is not enough to be beleaguered from the outside. Since the nineteenth century and the popularization of the ideas of psychoanalytic pioneer Sigmund Freud, it has been well known that the most gripping hauntings, or obsessions, or neuroses, or psychoses, as they are typically referred to today, are generated from within. No outside source can know a person's fears as well as that person knows them. No tortures are so exquisite as the ones that people prepare for themselves. Hence, the spate of popular, contemporary films about characters who are the height of normalcy on the outside but full of demons on the inside. Nothing is as scary as the true self lurking beneath the placid facade. It is no surprise that *A Nightmare on Elm Street*'s Freddy Kruger, the most arresting villain of the 1990's, comes to children in their dreams and mutilates them there, causing them to die in real life. A more powerfully gothic manifestation of Freud's views on the complexity of the dreamlife is hard to imagine.

The danger of the gothic ethos is that it imbues banality with a sense of danger and excitement and that the terrors of America's entertainments are coloring, more and more, the perception of reality so that the inhabitants of America's cosseted suburbs feel ever more at the mercy of satanic cults, bizarre molesters, fratricides, and militiamen despite the relative rarity of these phenomena. The current gothic mode is oddly passive: The average American thinks, primarily, of barricades, not of active vigilantism. Current gothicism is regressive (the 1960's scared the heck out of a lot of people), apocalyptic (the millennium is coming and nothing can be done about that), and reductive (looking for the worst in every situation is a self-fulfilling prophecy). So, what does the current culture do to get itself out of its self-imposed miasma of gothic despair?

Edmundson suggests that it creates a sugary antidote in the form of films such as *Forrest Gump* (1994). In chapter two of *Nightmare on Main Street*, "The World According to Forrest Gump," Edmundson makes the point that the strength of the gothic in the late twentieth century was, at least partly, made possible by the weakness of its cultural adversaries: various forms of easy transcendence and facile promises that gothic terrors can be countered with any number of simple panaceas. *Forrest Gump* was a lightweight and nearly transparent promise that, although one cannot avoid the terrors of life, one can, in fact, ignore them. Another strain of easy transcendence in American life is what Edmundson calls the "Therapeutic Sublime." For men, there is Robert Bly's Iron John men's movement; for women, there is the possibility of running with Clarissa Pinkola Estés's wolves. Everyone, of course, can get in touch with John Bradshaw's adorable inner child. The scary subconscious of Freud, with its battle royal between the ego and the superego, is replaced with a clean, well-lighted place. Human instincts are good; one just needs to follow them more faithfully. If that isn't upbeat enough, there are angels to help. If the gothic is full of unearned traumas, then the world of gauzy Hallmark angels is full of miracles or unearned strokes of good luck. Easy transcendence provides one with a pleasant vacation away from the gothic, but it does not, unfortunately, attack the gothic directly and, consequently, vanquish it. The gothic, confronted with these weak threats to its autonomy, just seems to get stronger. What is needed is a real challenge to its supremacy.

In his third chapter, "S & M Culture," Edmundson tries to envision a future in which the gothic impulse remains unchecked and also attempts to imagine the possibility of a serious and artistic response to the gothic's dominance in American life. Sadomasochism, which is not a historical, erotic fact of life but is, curiously enough, a by-product of civilization, gained currency during the first round of the gothic's hold on Western Culture in the mid-eighteenth century. Furthermore, sadomasochistic culture seems to have been the most likely outcome for the twentieth century's love affair with the gothic. When even *New York* magazine recognized sadomasochism as the sexual mode of the 1990's, could "Main Street" be far behind? In Freudian terms, this all makes sense. The psyche is, after all, the scene of a massive gothic struggle, with the sadistic superego repressing and dominating the helpless ego. That this conflict should take to the streets and bedrooms of America is no more than is to be expected. Is it to be passively endured?

Edmundson reviews the historical record to see how the menace of the gothic in social life has been dealt with before. He finds that both the English visionary poets and the American transcendentalists were able to create viable alternatives to the gothicists' unremitting despair. Nineteenth century English poet Percy Bysshe Shelley countered his wife's *Frankenstein* with the inspiring *Prometheus Unbound* (1820). Prometheus, in a real imaginative leap, refuses to revenge himself on Jupiter and thereby frees himself for an autonomous future unfettered by the ghosts of his past traumas. American poet Ralph Waldo Emerson not only cautions his readers to sever the hold of past hauntings but also warns them of the gothic potential in the things and persons they love most. American poet William Wordsworth, German philosopher Friedrich Nietzsche, and English poet William Blake all battled the gothic head-on; they seemed to recognize that, in Jungian terms, the only way to gain control over the terror of life, the shadow side, was to embrace it.

In Edmundson's view, two modern authors have tried to confront the gothic head-on and have been only moderately successful. American playwright Tony Kushner, in *Angels in America: A Gay Fantasia on National Themes* (1993) created a truly formidable gothic tyrant, Roy Cohn. This powerful New York lawyer is both despicable, as a homosexual homophobe, and mythic, as an uncompromising fighter against fate (which manifests itself in the form of the AIDS virus). Countering Cohn, who is a giant of blind energy, is Belize, a black former drag queen with a gift for goodness. This Kushner play asks a fundamental question: How will the gay community in America keep its humane soul and still appropriate some of Roy Cohn's lust for life, which it needs so badly, in its fight against AIDS? In the end, Kushner's ambitious saga does not satisfactorily answer this question, but Edmundson credits Kushner for asking it in a profoundly serious way. There is no easy transcendence here, only glimpses of the work left to be done. In a similar way, Edmundson sees American writer Toni Morrison, in her novel *Beloved* (1987), as trying to contend with America's biggest gothic demon: racism. In her novel, the burden of guilt for slavery is correctly transferred from blacks to whites, and the sorry weight of past shame is somewhat ameliorated by allowing it to find its true source. This is, Edmundson believes, very good as far as it goes, but it does not give the culture a positive vision of where it might go once racial guilt is successfully assigned.

In looking for an antidote to America's premillennial gothic doldrums, Edmundson disregards religion entirely and, finally, makes a clarion call to artists everywhere to take up the good fight, engage, and use their imaginations in the life-affirming way that is their noble and special gift. What Edmundson eloquently calls for in *Nightmare on Main Street* is a new group of visionary artists to show the way from gothic bleakness to humane renewal, from a grim focus on death to a profound embracing of life in all its manifestations.

Cynthia Lee Katona

Sources for Further Study

Chronicle of Higher Education. XLIV, December 19, 1997, p. A13.
Library Journal. CXXII, October 15, 1997, p. 78.
New York. XXX, October 27, 1997, p. 84.
The New York Times Book Review. CII, October 26, 1997, p. 37.
The Washington Post Book World. XXVII, October 26, 1997, p. 7.

NOAM CHOMSKY
A Life of Dissent

Author: Robert F. Barsky
Publisher: The MIT Press (Cambridge, Massachusetts). Illustrated. 237 pp. $27.50
Type of work: Biography
Time: 1928 to the 1990's
Locale: Philadelphia; Cambridge, Massachusetts; and elsewhere

A biography of the world-renowned linguist, political theorist, and social activist that pays equal attention to Chomsky's contributions to linguistics and his controversial career as an outspoken critic of governmental excesses

Principal personages:
NOAM CHOMSKY, a linguistics professor at the Massachusetts Institute of
Technology (MIT) and an internationally renowned dissident
CAROL CHOMSKY, his wife
WILLIAM (ZEV) CHOMSKY, his father
ELSI CHOMSKY, his mother
ZELLIG SABBETAI HARRIS, a linguistics professor at the University of
Pennsylvania, his mentor
ALAN DERSHOWITZ, a celebrity criminal attorney, his right-wing nemesis
ROBERT FAURISSON, a professor of French literature at Lyon, who has
denied the historical reality of the Holocaust, defended by Chomsky
on free speech grounds

Avram Noam Chomsky is demonstrably the world's most famous and influential intellectual. Author of seventy books and over a thousand articles, Chomsky also happens to be the most cited living person on earth and on the short list of the most cited figures of all time. Possessed of an extremely formidable intellect, a fanatical work ethic, and an equally fanatical devotion to the truth, Chomsky has had an enormous impact on the field of modern linguistics and perhaps an even greater influence on international politics. His many, exhaustively researched, and utterly convincing critiques of the hypocrisy and deception that underlie much of American foreign (and domestic) policy have made Chomsky an internationally renowned spokesman for the libertarian Left while earning him the undying enmity of the American political and media establishment. Too articulate and well versed to be effectively debated by rightist commentators, Chomsky has been systematically denied access to the mainstream media in his own country: a desperate stratagem employed by his enemies that attests Chomsky's power and prestige as a voice of dissent.

While considerable commentary has been produced on Chomsky's linguistic theories and political views, very little has been written about his life and background. There are good reasons for this state of affairs. Apart from his high-profile role as a political activist, Noam Chomsky the man is an intensely private individual who has always sought to keep the focus on the issues he raises, not on himself as a person. Probably some of Chomsky's reticence is a matter of innate temperament, but he also deplores self-aggrandizement and personality cults for personal and political reasons, as ethically unseemly and as symptomatic of the kind of selfish individualism that tends to characterize corporate capitalist culture at its worst. Another factor working against the would-be biographer is that to a great extent Chomsky's intellectual and political work *is* his life—not the kind of thing that makes for scintillating biography.

Robert F. Barsky has understood the special requisites and difficulties posed by his subject and has, accordingly, written a purely intellectual biography. (Readers seeking intimate or merely revealing details about Noam Chomsky's personality, private life, habits, or personal relationships will be sadly disappointed.) Inevitably free of the gossip and more personalized content that typifies conventional biographies, Barsky's narrative is rather dry but not necessarily dull. From an intellectual standpoint, Chomsky's has been a life of enormous risk-taking, adventure, discovery, and controversy. It might even be characterized as heroic.

Chomsky's father, Dr. William (Zev) Chomsky, was a brilliant scholar of Hebrew grammar and a committed exponent of education that fosters independent thinking and social consciousness. His mother, Elsi, was equally gifted in intellect and more politically oriented than her husband. It is abundantly clear, from Barsky's account, that Chomsky inherited his father's interest in linguistics, his mother's leftism, and, collectively, his parents' brains, moral seriousness, and social and political awareness. Another formative influence was, of course, his family's intense involvement in Jewish cultural and political life. Barsky also cites the time and milieu as shaping forces. Growing up Jewish in a predominantly Irish-Catholic and German neighborhood in Philadelphia during the Great Depression, Chomsky had ample opportunity to develop a social conscience.

Chomsky's social conscience manifested itself early. Incredibly, he published his first article—an editorial in his school's newspaper on the fall of Barcelona during the Spanish Civil War—when he was only ten years old. Even at that early age, Chomsky was already fully engaged with current events and quite capable of sophisticated political analysis. Fervently anti-authoritarian, temperamentally predisposed to sympathize with the underdog, he supported the Spanish anarchists in their struggle with Francisco Franco's fascists on the right and Stalin's despotic minions on the left.

In the years immediately following, Chomsky's left-libertarian sympathies were further augmented by life experiences and his reading. Having emerged from the relatively nurturing and sheltered environment of a private country day school, young Chomsky was shocked and dismayed by the conformist rigidity he encountered at Central High School in Philadelphia. He soon regarded high school as a hierarchical institution that promoted competitiveness, jingoistic fervor, and puerile sports fanaticism at the expense of independent, creative thought. At the age of twelve, Chomsky began to venture into New York City, taking the train there from Philadelphia on his own. A frequent destination was the New York office of *Freie Arbeiter Stimme*, an anarchist journal. Now deeply immersed in anarchist social philosophy, Chomsky was an avid reader of such anarchist theorists as Rudolf Rocker, Moishe Shtarkman, and Diego Abad de Santillan. He also read non-Bolshevik Marxists such as Karl

Liebknecht, Rosa Luxemburg, and Karl Korsch. George Orwell's writings, especially his reportage on the Spanish Civil War, were also a major influence, as were the writings of the English philosopher Bertrand Russell.

After graduating from high school in 1945, Chomsky attended the University of Pennsylvania, where he subsequently met Zellig Sabbetai Harris. A brilliant, charismatic, and unconventional linguistics professor who was a pioneer figure in structural linguistics and discourse analysis, Harris had a tremendous impact on Chomsky. Under Harris' tutelage, Chomsky found his intellectual calling in linguistics and produced his undergraduate honor's thesis, "Morphophonemics of Modern Hebrew," in 1949, when he was only twenty years old. A treatise that formed the basis for some of Chomsky's later work, "Morphophonemics" is now considered to be the first example of modern generative grammar.

Harris' politics also had a pronounced effect on Chomsky; he was an influential member of Avukah, a progressive American Zionist organization that fought anti-Semitism and fascism, promoted civil liberties, and advocated a binational (Jewish-Palestinian) state as opposed to the exclusively Jewish state envisioned by the much larger and more conservative B'nai B'rith Hillel Foundation. In light of Chomsky's later run-ins with Zionist hard-liners over Israeli policy toward the Palestinian minority, its Arab neighbors, and American policy toward Israel, Barsky's detailed account of the postwar debate among American Jews over the sociopolitical shape of the Israeli state is particularly fascinating. Barsky does not need to say so, but history has proved Chomsky and Avukah right: Had Israel established itself as a binational state at the outset, it might have been able to avoid much of the mutual hatred and terrible bloodletting that has marked Arab-Jewish relations since 1948.

Through the intervention of friends in academe, Chomsky was appointed to Harvard University's Society of Fellows in 1951, while he was still a graduate student. He found Harvard stuffy and pretentious, but the stipend that came with the fellowship allowed him to devote his time exclusively to writing and research. In 1953, while still at Harvard, Chomsky and his wife, Carol, traveled to Israel to work on a kibbutz. En route to the Middle East by ship, Chomsky had something of an intellectual epiphany about structural linguistics; he decided finally and irrevocably that structuralist theories of language aided and abetted the inherently authoritarian behaviorist concepts of human nature that were just then becoming dominant in Anglo-American intellectual culture. After a stay of six weeks in Israel, the Chomskys returned to the United States, with Noam somewhat disillusioned by the rigid ideological conformity he had observed on the kibbutz. Long-standing plans to immigrate to Israel never materialized.

After receiving his Ph.D. from the University of Pennsylvania in 1955 (on the strength of a single chapter of his dissertation), Chomsky went to the Massachusetts Institute of Technology (MIT) in Cambridge. Within two years he was made an associate professor. Just three years later he was made a full professor—an almost unheard-of occurrence in academe. Five years later, at the age of thirty-seven, he was given an endowed chair. Ten years later, at the still young age of forty-seven, Chomsky was named institute professor, a signal honor usually reserved for the most distinguished of senior faculty near the end of their careers.

Thus assured, early on, of a secure and comfortable university life, Chomsky could have played it safe by quietly going about his research. Instead, true to character, he felt duty-bound to buck the prevailing intellectual vogue by mounting an aggressive attack on the behaviorism of B. F. Skinner in a scathing 1959 review of Skinner's *Verbal Behavior*. Similarly, Chomsky decisively repudiated structural linguistics at high-profile linguistics conferences held in Texas in 1958 and 1959.

Having established himself as a courageous and formidable intellectual maverick in linguistics and philosophy, Chomsky soon broadened his critique of conformity to authoritarianism beyond its academic manifestations in behaviorism and structuralism. Barsky notes that by the early 1960's Chomsky had begun to attack the university as an institution that regularly and cravenly collaborates with state power. In the 1940's, Chomsky had read Dwight Mcdonald in *Politics*, an anarchist journal, and had been impressed with Mcdonald's exhortations to left-libertarian intellectuals on their ethical and political responsibilities, especially in wartime. As America's military involvement in Vietnam escalated and the antiwar movement grew, Chomsky took his own responsibilities as an intellectual with utmost seriousness. He became increasingly active in antiwar circles and found common cause with a wide spectrum of activist groups on the Left that were working in various ways against imperialism, class exploitation, and state-sponsored violence. During this period Chomsky was frequently arrested and jailed and also was placed on Richard Nixon's enemy list. Yet he never wavered in his commitment to truth-telling and social justice.

Still very much an activist in the years since the tumultuous 1960's, Chomsky has continued to publish books and articles on linguistics and political issues at his usual, prodigious rate—even though much of his time is spent keeping up a voluminous correspondence and giving talks all over the world. Since the 1970's Chomsky has also been involved in some rather bitter controversies. Enraged by Chomsky's more moderate Zionism, the bombastic rightist lawyer Alan Dershowitz has vilified him at every opportunity. Chomsky also came under severe media attack for his involvement in the case of Robert Faurisson, a French academic who has written books denying the historical reality of the Holocaust. Though he found Faurrison's views absurd, Chomsky did support Faurisson's free speech rights on libertarian grounds—an elementary but crucial distinction lost on Chomsky's vociferous detractors. More recently, Chomsky has locked horns with proponents of the latest intellectual fashion: French postmodernist theory. Undeceived by the inordinately abstruse verbiage of much postmodernist discourse, Chomsky has denounced its pretensions with refreshing candor.

In the same spirit of directness and clarity, Robert Barsky has written an excellent introduction to Chomsky's life and thought: sympathetic without being fawning, richly informative without being pedantic. Readers will come away from this biography awestruck at Chomsky's almost superhuman intellect, achievements, and moral stature. Still, in the end, Barsky's Noam Chomsky remains an enigmatic figure, impossibly brilliant and accomplished, but somehow too bland and reasonable a person to have engaged in all the fiery battles of his life. There is another story yet to be told.

Robert Niemi

Sources for Further Study

Booklist. XCIII, March, 1997, p. 1211.
Library Journal. CXXII, March 1, 1997, p. 83.
Nature. CCCLXXXVI, April 24, 1997, p. 776.
Publishers Weekly. CCXLIV, February 3, 1997, p. 89.
The Times Literary Supplement. August, 1997, p. 10.
The Washington Post Book World. XXVII, May 25, 1997, p. 4.

THE NUMBER SENSE
How the Mind Creates Mathematics

Author: Stanislas Dehaene
Publisher: Oxford University Press (New York). 274 pp. $25.00
Type of work: Learning theory

In an eminently readable and thoroughly engaging book, Stanislas Dehaene speculates that humans and other mammals are born with an inherent, instinctive knowledge of rudimentary mathematical principles

The burgeoning subject of artificial intelligence, stimulated by humankind's incredible dependence on computers, has drawn people from many disciplines into discourse about the origins of intelligence and learning theory. In 1994, Steven Pinker published *The Language Instinct,* which presents the argument that inherent in humans is a grammatical superstructure that enables people to shape language and to communicate within the language parameters of their societies. Pinker followed this study with *How the Mind Works* (1997), an extended investigation of the origins of human knowledge and intelligence. *The Number Sense,* written by a mathematician turned neuropsychologist, presents for mathematics an argument similar to Pinker's argument that basic grammatical knowledge is inherent and instinctive.

Stanislas Dehaene, citing a considerable body of research, demonstrates not only that humans command a basic understanding of mathematical principles practically from birth but also that some other mammals—notably rats, horses, pigeons, dolphins, and chimpanzees—have similar understandings. Designing research experiments that test an infant's mathematical discernment is challenging. Since 1980, however, a number of such experiments have been designed and orchestrated. American psychologists Rochel Gelman, Elizabeth Spelke, and Prentice Starkey sought to determine whether babies six, seven, and eight months old could make numerical associations between visual and auditory stimuli. For example, someone seeing two flashes of lightning typically expects them to be followed by two claps of thunder. These researchers set out to discover whether infants make the same sorts of associations in this regard as adults. They sought to distinguish between innate behavior and learned behavior. Their experiments involved having infants look at two screens, one with two objects randomly arranged, the other with three objects randomly arranged. The second screen presented a more complex problem than the first; therefore, the infants involved gave it more of their attention initially than they gave the screen with only two objects.

When an auditory element was added, however, by placing a loudspeaker between the screens and having it project drumbeats, the attention of the subjects became related to the sound: If there were two drumbeats, the infants concentrated on the screen with two objects; if there were three, their concentration shifted to the screen with three objects. Such an experiment, of course, is more suggestive than conclusive because infants of six to eight months possess many learned behaviors.

Dehaene outlines Karen Wynn's experiments with infants five months old, in which a Mickey Mouse puppet was placed on one side of a stage within sight of the subjects. A screen then obscured part of the stage and a second puppet was introduced on the other side. In Wynn's experiment, when the screen was raised, sometimes two puppets would appear on the stage, but at other times only one puppet would appear. Wynn videotaped the reactions of the infants in this experiment, equating their surprise reactions to the amount of time they appeared to concentrate in each situation. When the expected two puppets appeared, they concentrated on average one second less than when only one puppet was present. By studying the surprise reaction in these infants, Wynn concluded that, although the infants had never seen both puppets on the stage simultaneously, an expectation had been aroused in them, so that when the screen was finally raised and only one puppet appeared, their expectation was not met.

This experiment, as Dehaene notes, challenges the Piagetian theory that in young children, out of sight means out of mind. Obviously, in this experiment, five-month-old infants expected one plus one to equal two. When it did not, they reacted with a degree of astonishment at not having their expectation met.

Dehaene systematically debunks Jean Piaget's theory that, in newborn children, the mind is a blank slate. He writes, "The child's brain, far from being a sponge, is a structured organ that acquires facts only insofar as they can be integrated into its previous knowledge." Although Piaget's theory often reflects John Locke's notion of the *tabula rasa*, Dehaene points out that John Locke in his *Essay Concerning Human Understanding* (1690) says that many people know that one plus two equals three without knowing any axiom by which this addition can be proved.

Particularly interesting is Dehaene's tracing of how preschool children produce algorithms. He notes that if one asks four-year-olds to add two plus four, such children initially will most likely count "one . . . two" on the fingers of one hand, then "one . . . two . . . three . . . four" on the fingers of their other hand. Then they will count the total. This is a slow, cumbersome procedure. Most children soon realize that they can begin by saying "two," arriving at a correct answer by saying "two, three, four, five, six." Most of them will discover another shortcut, a minimal strategy, as Dehaene calls it, by changing the question from What is two plus four? to What is four plus two?, an operation that requires them to say merely "four, five, six" to answer correctly.

Dehaene compares numerical processing in humans to that of other animals, basing much of what he says on experiments involving rats, horses, dolphins, pigeons, and chimpanzees. He concludes that the human "ability to devise intricate plans for actions, based on both a retrospective memory of past events and a prospective memory of future possibilities, seems to be unique in the animal kingdom."

The thirteen case studies Dehaene presents of people with cerebral lesions and other conditions that affect the brain are especially interesting and cogent. They suggest the specialized functions of various parts of the human brain. In the case of Mr. M., a former architect, a lesion of the inferior parietal cortex left the subject with an ability to do simple addition but robbed him of the ability to subtract or to determine which is the larger of two digits. Although Mr. M. could not tell the author what number falls between one and three, he was quite easily able to tell him what letter falls between A and C.

Clearly, the portion of his brain affected by his lesion caused a selective deficit that, although not totally wiping out his ability to deal with numbers, did severely limit it. This limitation did not affect his ability to deal with language or to deal with numbers in a concrete way. For example, Mr. M. knew that he usually rose at 5 A.M. and worked for two hours before his breakfast at 7 A.M. Even though he was unable to subtract five from seven, he knew how much time elapsed between five and seven o'clock, indicating that he could deal with numbers concretely but not in the abstract. Whereas a problem stated as "7 minus 5" would prove impossible for him to solve, the same problem stated in concrete terms posed no difficulty.

Although examples of mathematical sophistication in Wilhelm von Osten's horse, Hans—whose master spent years schooling it in arithmetic, reading, and music—were subsequently debunked by Oskar Pfungst, experiments with rats conducted in the 1950's and 1960's at Columbia University by Francis Mechner and later validated by John Platt and David Johnson of the University of Iowa were more credible. In these experiments, a hungry rat was placed in a box with two levers. Lever B was connected to a device designed to release food if the lever were pressed. Lever B, however, was impossible to activate unless lever A was first pressed a specific number of times. If the rat pressed lever B prematurely, it not only would receive no food but also would suffer a penalty.

The rats discovered by trial and error that they had to press lever A a specific number of times (stated as n), then press lever B once to receive food. Some of these rats progressed to the point that they knew the number of times they had to press lever A to receive food. Even though that number was changed from an initial four presses to as many as sixteen presses, some rats adapted to these changes and kept track of the numbers of presses they had to make before they pressed lever B.

More startling are some of the experiments Dehaene reports involving Sheba, a trained chimpanzee. Sheba learned to recognize Arabic numbers on cards. The experimenter hid oranges in Sheba's cage, perhaps two under the table and three in a box. When Sheba explored and found all the oranges, she would then be shown cards with numbers on them. She consistently chose the card with the appropriate number. To test further, the researcher placed a card bearing the number 2 somewhere in Sheba's cage and another card bearing the number 3 elsewhere in her cage. When Sheba found the cards and was then shown the range of cards bearing numbers from 1 to 10, she selected the card with the digit 5, clearly suggesting that she was capable of dealing with an abstract mathematical process.

Some of the most interesting material in *The Number Sense* has to do with the origins of numerical systems. Dehaene notes that number systems of base ten and base twenty are grounded in human physical characteristics: Humans have ten fingers and ten toes, all of which are early pressed into use as people learn to count. Among aboriginal people, these means of calculation remain the chief means of counting and of accounting.

It is not uncommon for people at all levels of development to keep track of what they are counting by drawing four vertical strokes crossed by one diagonal stroke to indicate five. It is far easier to visualize numbers if they are recorded in this way. The eye can communicate the number twenty-three to the brain much more readily if it sees ||||| ||||| ||||| ||||| ||| rather than |||||||||||||||||||||||.

Dehaene recalls an episode in the film *Rain Man* (1988), in which Dustin Hoffman plays the role of an autistic man with remarkable mathematical capabilities. He sees a waitress in the restaurant where he is eating drop a box of toothpicks on the floor. He immediately says, "82 . . . 82 . . . 82 . . . that's 246." In other words, he has grouped the number of toothpicks in some manageable way. Dehaene refuses to take this performance at face value but uses it to illustrate one way in which people deal with making approximations, by grouping numbers.

The author tells of the natives of the Torres Straits who "denote numbers by pointing to different parts of their body in a fixed order . . . from the pinkie to the thumb on the right hand (numbers 1 to 5), then up the right arm and down the left arm (6 to 12), through to the fingers of the left hand (13 to 17), the left toes (18 to 22), the left and right legs (23 to 28), and finally the right toes (29 to 33)."

Cultural conventions often determine how various groups of people deal with numbers. Dehaene suggests that speakers of English, when asked to memorize nine random digits and repeat the numbers twenty seconds after their first exposure to them, would fail 50 percent of the time. Speakers of Chinese, however, would have little difficulty reproducing the numbers. This is because the words for Chinese numbers are very brief, causing less memory gap when one tries to memorize a nine-digit list. Memory span in China typically averages nine digits, whereas in English-speaking countries it averages seven.

Much of the information Dehaene presents in *The Number Sense* might revolutionize the way in which elementary and middle school mathematics is taught. This book is profound yet wholly accessible. It is superbly written and persuasively argued.

R. Baird Shuman

Sources for Further Study

Booklist. XCIV, September 15, 1997, p. 188.
Library Journal. CXXII, October 1, 1997, p. 116.
Los Angeles Times Book Review. October 12, 1997, p. 8.
Science News. CLII, November 22, 1997, p. 331.

THE ONE BEST WAY
Frederick Winslow Taylor and the Enigma of Efficiency

Author: Robert Kanigel (1946-   )
Publisher: Viking (New York). Illustrated. 676 pp. $34.95
Type of work: Biography
Time: 1856-1915
Locale: The United States and Europe

Taylor, who enjoyed a conventional upper-class life, developed theories of scientific manage-ment that revolutionized industrial production and helped create the modern obsession with order and efficiency

Shortly before he died in a Philadelphia hospital on March 21, 1915, Frederick Winslow Taylor was heard winding his watch. This final action of the father of scientific management was as appropriate as any last words would have been: The clock was at the center of his struggle to make most of life scientific.

Although one of the goals of Kanigel's account is to resuscitate Taylor's moribund reputation, he is well aware that his subject's overzealous advocacy of efficiency is problematic. In trying to make efficiency an axial value for the world, Taylor alienated numerous workers, for whom he was a soulless slave driver, and even their bosses, who saw him as "an eccentric and a radical" who raised wages while ruling the factory with a stopwatch. To himself, he was a misunderstood crusader who, battling under the banner of science, was bringing peace to the perennial conflict between bosses and laborers. His life, therefore, took place in that "murky territory . . . between the dark country to which [his] critics consign him and the sunny utopia of his own vision."

Frederick Winslow Taylor was born in Germantown, a suburb of Philadelphia, in 1856. The Taylors reared their three children with liberal Quaker values—rationalism, honesty, and tolerance. The private school Taylor attended in Germantown served to reinforce these progressive values. The Taylors' wealth and social position provided Taylor with important opportunities throughout his life: European travel, good school-ing, and easy access to the job market. Despite an undiagnosed astigmatism, he passed Harvard's entrance examination, but he decided on an industrial apprenticeship at the Enterprise Hydraulic Works in Philadelphia.

Taylor was apprenticed as a machinist and became part of a milieu that would possess him for the rest of his life. He became familiar with lathes, drill presses, and milling machines. He found much of this work monotonous and uninteresting, but he believed that doing disagreeable things built character. Nevertheless, like his fellow machinists, he "soldiered," that is, he worked harder when the boss was watching him and slacked off when the boss moved on. To conserve their energy, workmen tried to hide from their bosses what they were actually capable of doing.

At Midvale Steel Company, his next job, Taylor, only twenty-three, was quickly promoted from machinist to machine-shop foreman, overseeing workers who were making the metal tires used on wagon wheels and locomotive wheels. These workers were paid on piece rate; that is, the more wheels they made, the more money they earned, but management could reduce the rate of pay per piece if production increased too much. The workers responded to rate reductions by soldiering, but, as foreman, Taylor was determined to end this practice.

The crux of the matter, as Taylor saw it, was what constituted a day's work. He thought science could provide an answer to this question. He was given permission to conduct metal-cutting experiments to see how fast steel tires could be safely made. He acquired knowledge about how to improve the productivity of the plant's machines and employ less skilled workmen than before. In effect, he was transforming traditional craft knowledge into scientific data, thereby displacing technical expertise from workers to managers.

While conducting these experiments, Taylor managed to obtain a mechanical engineering degree from the Stevens Institute of Technology. During this period, he also won a U.S. Open Tennis Championship with a spoonlike racquet he invented. He participated in theatricals, which he analyzed and tried to reduce to a science. Through them, he formed a close relationship with Louise Marie Spooner, whom he married in 1884. She quickly learned that Taylor was not above applying the techniques of scientific management to the details of their domestic life. She also discovered that his Midvale work took precedence over their marriage.

Taylor was now deeply interested in the time it took for workmen to complete specific tasks. Using a stopwatch to time various jobs, he found that a man could do much more work than previously assumed, but he was unable to obtain a consistent numerical result. He therefore broke operations down into individual movements and established individual times for these. He created detailed instruction cards that explained how tools were to be used, including specific motions and times. He wanted workers to do nothing on their own initiative. To overcome the resistance of his workers to his new system, Taylor paid them handsomely to do the work his way, by his standards, and at the speeds he mandated.

Taylor and his wife lost a large sum of money in the Panic of 1893, and this debacle initiated a period of wanderings for Taylor. He set himself up as a managerial consultant. His base was Germantown, from which he travelled around the country to organize or reform various firms. These experiences convinced him that his talent lay not in making locomotive tires, paper pulp, or ball bearings, but in his methods.

In 1898, a company that would soon be known as Bethlehem Steel hired Taylor to increase its productivity. As in his previous jobs, he instituted new machines and personnel. Although he developed several important innovations, Taylor became most famous at Bethlehem Steel for his study of the loading of pig iron, which focused on a workman named Henry Noll. Taylor had been looking for a strong man of the "mentally sluggish type," and this Dutchman suited his purposes. Using detailed instructions, a stopwatch, and a promised wage hike from $1.15 to $1.70 a day, Taylor trained Noll to carry 92-pound pigs of iron up a ramp onto a freight car over a thousand times a day. His results showed that the total workload could be increased from 13 to 47.5 long tons a day. In sum, Taylor proved that he could more than triple a laborer's output with only a modest pay raise (for the company this meant a labor-cost reduction of more than half). The secret was to keep the workman under load only 43 percent of the day (and entirely free from load the remaining 57 percent).

Despite his successes in increasing Bethlehem Steel's productivity, he was dismissed from the company in May, 1901, ostensibly because of conflicts over his bonus plans and his control of shop management, but also because he treated Bethlehem executives with no more respect than he did Noll. Around the time that Taylor was severing his relationship with Bethlehem Steel, a gruesome murder-suicide in Savannah, Georgia, dramatically changed his life. Four children of the Aiken family were orphaned by the murder of their mother and the suicide of their father. Since the Aikens were related to Taylor's wife, he and Louise decided to adopt them. Thus, at 45, Taylor became a parent. He returned to Germantown, built a new home, and settled into a family life very much like his parents'. Out of this comfortable existence came an influential paper that Taylor delivered at the Saratoga meeting of mechanical engineers in 1903. This talk on shop management, which was published in the *Transactions of the American Society of Mechanical Engineers*, ran to 120 pages. Its theme was that control of work must be taken from the men who did it and placed in the hands of planners. When this new system was put into effect, workers made more money, their company earned higher profits, and consumers paid lower prices. The success of his paper led to an even larger treatise on the art of cutting metals. These two works were translated into several foreign languages, and Taylor's influence spread around the world.

Though these writings made Taylor well-known among engineers, in 1910, an event occurred that made him a celebrity for ordinary Americans. A group of railroad companies petitioned the Interstate Commerce Commission for a rate hike, but Louis Brandeis, the future Supreme Court justice, was sure that the companies did not need the increase, and he created a sensation by asserting that they could save millions of dollars by adopting Taylor's efficiency methods. Almost overnight, Taylor's ideas became the subject of numerous newspaper and magazine articles, and many Americans were converted to Taylor's vision. As a consequence of the publicity, the railroads failed to get their rate increase and Taylor was given the means to spread his ideas to a mass audience, first in a long article for *American Magazine*, and later in a book, *The Principles of Scientific Management* (1911).

The public and Brandeis may have been enamored of Taylor's ideas, but labor leaders continued to criticize them. These criticisms came to a head when workers at the Watertown Arsenal near Boston went out on strike when a boss tried to time a worker. Because of the issues involved, a Special Committee to Investigate the Taylor and Other Systems of Shop Management was formed. Its chairman was William B. Wilson, a former miner, who was sympathetic toward labor, and he accused the scientific managers of de-skilling workers. The stopwatch, which had become a symbol of Taylorism, became the focus of the debate. To managers, it was a tool for enhancing plant efficiency; to workers, it was an attack on their human dignity and an invasion of their privacy. When Taylor testified, he emphasized that his system was a mental revolution, since its locus was in the mental attitudes of workers and managers.

He claimed that his scientific methods helped workers and managers join together to increase production and profits. Wilson responded that the mental attitude of the employer was too arbitrary a foundation upon which to establish the worker's welfare. After the hearings, the committee's report largely backed Taylor's critics, for it stated that a fair day's work could not be determined by a stopwatch, since a workman was not a machine. On the other hand, the committee praised the benefits brought to the workplace by standardization and systematization.

In addition to the attacks on scientific management by labor leaders, Taylor's later life was beset with other difficulties. In 1912, his wife had a nervous breakdown, and, by 1913, Taylor himself was experiencing health problems. He withdrew from the world and found solace amid the relatives and friends who gave him loyalty, respect, and affection. He was increasingly critical of what was happening in the world and to his system. In 1914, when World War I broke out in Europe, he saw the conflict as a colossal stupidity, and, when managers permitted shop committees to help determine piece rates, Taylor insisted, as he always had, that orders should go in only one direction—from the top down. During a trip to Cleveland for a speaking engagement, he caught a cold that turned into bronchitis and then into pneumonia. He entered a city hospital in Philadelphia, where his condition worsened. On the day after his fifty-ninth birthday, watch in hand, he died.

After Taylor's death, his system became almost a religion for some of his followers. They tried to apply the principles of scientific management to farms, cities, businesses of all types, churches, universities, even governments. In 1916, Vladimir Lenin read Taylor in Zurich, and, after the Bolshevik revolution, he saw Taylorism as a way to modernize Russian industry. The Fascists and the Nazis made use of Taylor's ideas, as did the Allies (some historians claim that Taylorism helped the Allies win World War II). Because Taylorism was a philosophy of technology, it is difficult to know how seriously to take all these evaluations. Some of the problem in forming summary judgments about Taylorism can be traced back to the paradoxes of its creator.

Taylor's techniques were not as scientific as he claimed. Indeed, he failed to grasp the true spirit of science, which is the selfless search for the truth about nature. For the genuine scientist, truths about nature can arise from anyone, peasant or prince, but, for Taylor, no truth could ever rise from workers to managers. He was so insistent on worker obedience to his system that it seems doubtful that he was really searching for the truth about human work.

Kanigel's biography of Taylor will be the standard account for years to come, but the reader, after absorbing Taylor's ideas, might well ask: Is this biography the "one best way" to tell his life? If the reader wants a hagiographical account, he can turn to Frank Barkley Copley's two-volume biography published in 1923. If the reader wishes a psychoanalytic study, he can turn to Sudhir Kakar's *Frederick Taylor: A Study in Personality and Innovation*, published in 1970. The strengths of Kanigel's approach are his balanced treatment of Taylor as a man and a visionary, his well-researched and absorbing descriptions of Taylor's technological work, and his probing and insightful analysis of the social, political, and cultural context of Taylor's life and work. On the other hand, one of the weaknesses of Kanigel's treatment is his neglect of intellectual history; for example, he ignores such significant humanist critics of Taylor as Lewis Mumford.

Kanigel shows that he is aware of the trenchant criticisms that have been leveled against Taylor, but his ultimate judgment is that Taylor's legacy has been, on the whole, beneficial. Despite this judgment, the debate about whether Taylor elevated or degraded work continues. Taylor claimed to have quantitative measures for how much he elevated work, but how do you measure the emotional, social, and spiritual costs of degrading work? Kanigel thinks that the central enigma in Taylor is that he failed to grant to his workers the freedom of thought, word, and action he so enjoyed and valued. Ultimately, then, his humanism was shallow. Though one of the first to see human beings as part of technology, he was insensitive to the profound complexity of human motives and values. In his later years, he took up gardening. One wonders: If the rose, rather than the clock, had been the source and symbol of his theories, what kind of system would he have developed?

Robert J. Paradowski

Sources for Further Study

Booklist. XCIII, May 1, 1997, p. 1467.
Business Week. July 7, 1997, p. 21.
Chicago Tribune. May 18, 1997, XIV, p. 1.
Commentary. CIV, November, 1997, p. 62.
Fortune. CXXXVI, July 21, 1997, p. 114.
Kirkus Reviews. LXV, March 1, 1997, p. 355.
Library Journal. CXXII, April 15, 1997, p. 92.
Los Angeles Times Book Review. June 1, 1997, p. 6.
The New Republic. CCXVII, September 1, 1997, p. 25.
The New York Review of Books. XLIV, November 20, 1997, p. 32.
The New York Times Book Review. CII, June 15, 1997, p. 8.
Publishers Weekly. CCXLIV, March 17, 1997, p. 62.
Science. CCLXXVIII, October 24, 1997, p. 594.
Wall Street Journal. IC, June 13, 1997, p. A17.

ONE WORLD, READY OR NOT
The Manic Logic of Global Capitalism

Author: William Greider (1936-   )
Publisher: Simon & Schuster (New York). 528 pp. $27.50
Type of work: Current affairs and economics

William Greider surveys the results of the workings of the capitalist system, offering examples of problems and potential solutions

One World, Ready or Not: The Manic Logic of Global Capitalism explores how the spread of market capitalism is creating a single global marketplace. Diffusion of ideas and introduction of concepts into new places can offer new possibilities, but as William Greider points out, they can also bring problems. He begins with an examination of the worldwide system of production, then shows how it is abetted by finance capital, and finally examines the changes in social reality that result from the spread of capitalism.

Specialists in economic development often argue (though the assertion is contentious) that less developed countries need to enter world markets to boost themselves out of poverty. Modern industry can provide wage-paying jobs and technical training. Employees acquire cash incomes with which to purchase the world's products, and the country as a whole moves along the path toward mechanization and industrialization. The developed countries gain as well, finding low-cost sources of labor and creating new markets by providing cash incomes to employees who will now be both eager and able to buy various manufactured goods.

That is the ideal. Greider offers examples of how it fails to be realized. He reminds readers that the path toward industrialization is not smooth, involving hardships for both the developers and the developing. In a long-run equilibrium, free trade benefits everyone. Greider argues that the long run is never achieved and that the world is in constant disequilibrium, with costs to market participants.

On one end of industrialization are workers. Developing countries compete for jobs primarily through making their labor cheaper. The jobs offered by industrialization therefore tend to improve material standards of living only slightly. In addition to allowing low wages to be paid, a country can make its labor cheaper, in a sense, by allowing various forms of exploitation, including relaxing standards for industrial safety. Greider provides examples of such abuses, including those surrounding a factory fire in Thailand that resulted in the deaths of hundreds of workers. Such a disaster in an industrial country would raise cries of outrage and protest. In this case, the company in question kept similar factories in operation and faced no legal recriminations.

Workers in industrialized countries also suffer from worldwide competition. They find it difficult to demand wage increases, let alone maintain current levels and retain jobs, in the face of low-wage competition. Labor leaders face a paradox inherent in trying to help everyone: To keep wages high, especially in industrial countries, they must restrict competition for jobs, but to help those in poverty they must allow jobs (at low wages) to flow to less developed countries. At best, worldwide competition promotes equalization of wages somewhere in the middle. The true situation, Greider argues, is worse: Competition is pulling everyone down.

The core problem, as Greider sees it, is global overproduction. Factories become bigger to benefit from economies of scale, and production spreads around the world as business tries to diversify across borders, protecting itself from political and economic shocks. Productive capacity thus expands, with each producer assuming that others will fail, making room in the market. On a larger scale, each country tries to run a trade surplus with others, selling products that cannot be sold domestically and refusing to buy the products of others.

In the face of market gluts, producers see their sales and profit margins fall. Rather than cut production, thus idling expensive machinery and factories, they choose to expand even more in an attempt to further exploit economies of scale. They hope to lower costs and prices, thus recapturing market share. On a global scale, this strategy cannot succeed; someone must "lose" and exit the market.

Such losses impose obvious grave economic costs, and such costs prompt action in the political arena. Politicians do not idly sit by while jobs are lost to other countries or as trade deficits accumulate. Governments compete for jobs by offering tax breaks to companies willing to relocate; companies, in turn, juggle their accounting so that profits appear in the least-taxed countries, demonstrating the power of business.

Production and jobs are free to move across borders because finance capital (the money used to finance business construction and expansion) is free to move. Greider sees finance capital as a growing force in the world economy, one that is overwhelming the power of national governments. Capital will always seek the highest rate of return, roaming the world in this search. Rarely does capital concern itself with human rights, worker exploitation, or costs of adjustment; it looks only for profit opportunities. The chase for profits results in tremendous costs as production moves from one location to another: Expensive factories are idled and workers are thrown out of jobs, forced to somehow find something else to do. Economic theory says that in the long run they will adjust and find their most advantageous occupations, but the long run can be a very long time, and even more shocks and dislocations are likely to occur before it is reached.

As a reporter and as editor of *Rolling Stone*, Greider was invited to attend worldwide conferences and tour various countries. His impressions and examples from around the world lend authenticity to his descriptions of worldwide trends, bringing economic concepts from abstraction into reality. Throughout, but especially in describing the plight of workers in developing countries, he writes with a sense of power and drama. He creates what could be impersonal forces, such as finance capital and national governments, as living characters.

Greider admits to a bias toward using American companies as examples and seeing the potential of the United States as a world leader. Greider also sees the United States as an example of problems faced by the industrialized world. Long a source of capital to the world—as well as a major product market, supplier of education, and enforcer of rules of free trade—the United States has become a debtor nation with a large trade deficit. Greider examines the results: American politicians fight to retain jobs, often at the cost of abandoning standards of free trade; they also promote expansion of American companies overseas, seeing that as promoting American business even while it means transferring jobs from domestic factories to ones based in other countries. The profits, it is argued, will flow home, improving America's economic position, but that is little consolation to Americans whose work is now being done in Malaysia or China.

Greider explored how the values of finance capital came to rule American politics in *Secrets of the Temple: How the Federal Reserve Runs the Country* (1987). Here, he provides a few convincing illustrations and generalizations, noting that the force of capital is likely to become larger as the middle class increasingly invests in mutual funds, hoping to benefit from rising financial prices. Greider suggests that current high rates of return reflect not optimism about future earning power but instead a "risk premium" on investments.

Finally, Greider explores the social implications of expanding capitalism. Some countries, such as China, impose political repression as a means of providing a workforce that the world's economy sees as desirable. Under the pressure of global financial forces, the wealthiest countries are being forced to lower standards of living, discard political commitments to social equity, and reduce spending on pensions, health care, and income support. Financial markets, Greider says, err in thinking that saving precedes growth; they demand cuts in deficits (often meaning cuts in social programs) as a means of promoting saving and investment. Greider sees growth as increasing saving, thus making more growth possible.

Greider's proposals for reform link global production, finance, and social standards. He argues that global trade must be controlled so that no country runs persistent and large trade surpluses that damage other countries. This would limit the tendency toward worldwide overproduction and force all countries to face, rather than ignore, the problems of oversupply. Greider argues that the United States, long a champion of free trade, must turn to limited protectionism. Companies that do not defend American jobs, or that transfer them overseas, should not receive government funding or tax breaks. He argues that companies accede to various rules overseas and should do so at home. Furthermore, the finance capital that drives business must be restrained. Greider supports a small tax on capital movements across international borders. Such a tax would both increase stability (because rates of return in different countries could differ by the amount of the tax before a movement of capital became profitable) and provide a source of revenue to pay the social costs of capital movements. In the social arena, international policy should honor labor rights and support higher wages in poor countries. International standards should address such issues as pollution, environmental degradation, and child labor. Greider also advocates worker ownership as a means of moving toward responsible capitalism.

As countries join into one world, it becomes clear that such a world cannot be the one of the industrialized countries; someone is going to have to give up something. Greider notes that the wealthy countries are the obvious choice because poor countries simply cannot afford to make sacrifices. He offers no firm predictions for the future but suggests that people are inventive and will find a new way of thinking about the world that solves the problems he describes. He believes that people will be able to apply knowledge to creating the new technology necessary in this new world, once the market begins to reward such applications. The economic system can correct itself, he argues, but only if prompted in the proper direction.

A. J. Sobczak

Sources for Further Study

Across the Board. I, June, 1997, p. 58.
Business Week. January 20, 1997, p. 14.
Harvard Business Review. LXXV, January, 1997, p. 144.
Los Angeles Times Book Review. January 12, 1997, p. 4.
Multinational Monitor. XVIII, May, 1997, p. 26.
The New York Times Book Review. CII, January 19, 1997, p. 12.
Newsweek. CXXIX, February 10, 1997, p. 67.
Time. CXLIX, March 24, 1997, p. 99.
The Wall Street Journal. January 17, 1997, p. A11.
The Washington Post Book World. XXVII, January 19, 1997, p. 4.

THE ORIGINS OF VIRTUE
Human Instincts and the Evolution of Cooperation

Author: Matt Ridley (1958-   )
Publisher: Viking (New York). 295 pp. $24.95
Type of work: Science

Ridley suggests that the origins of both human behavior and social values can be traced to evolutionary strategies favoring the survival of an individual's genetic code

Matt Ridley's *The Origins of Virtue* covers much the same ground that Robert Wright has already explored in *The Moral Animal* (1994). Both authors summarize the contributions made to the scientific debate about values and their origins by such scholars as Robert Trivers, George Williams, and William Hamilton. Both discuss the relationship between evolutionary strategies and current speculation in the field of game theory. Both interpret a wide range of complex issues so as to make them interesting and understandable to the general reader. The two works are so similar, in fact, that Ridley provides only a slight departure from Wright's argument. Whereas *The Moral Animal* dealt with behaviors having survival value for the individual, family, or tribe, Ridley focuses on much smaller biological units: cells and the genetic code contained in their chromosomes.

Taking Richard Dawkins' concept of "the selfish gene" as its starting point, *The Origins of Virtue* argues that such phenomena as human emotions, altruism, the instinct for reciprocity, and the tendency toward labor specialization are all strategies aimed at passing one's genetic code to a new generation. Even behaviors that may seem counterproductive to the interests of an individual can often be justified as increasing the odds that the genes of one's siblings or other close relatives will somehow be replicated.

To be fair to Ridley, he does expand Wright's thesis in terms of the conclusions he is willing to draw. Whereas Wright limited the prescriptive content of his book to a vague suggestion that nineteenth century utilitarianism accorded best with his own evolutionary model, Ridley explores the origins of a far more complicated ethical system. He uses current theories in the fields of biology and game theory to argue that survival value may be found in such "cooperative virtues" as trusting other people, assisting individuals and societies outside of one's own immediate circle, and reducing the level of international conflict. While none of these suggestions seems revolutionary, Ridley offers an interesting exploration of the possible origins of both productive and counterproductive behaviors by tying their results to the needs for cells to reproduce.

Some readers may find the resulting description of human nature rather cynical. (Ridley, like Wright before him, would argue that he is merely being "realistic.") Nevertheless, the world portrayed in *The Origins of Virtue* is a "nicer" place than that depicted in *The Moral Animal*. Much of this results from the fact that Ridley is less interested than his predecessor in seeing evolution as a way of explaining marital infidelity and humanity's "natural" tendency toward self-interest. In Ridley's kinder, gentler theory of evolution, natural processes underscore the benefits of cooperation. This helps strengthen the connection between values and evolution that is implicit in the work's title. Wright's *The Moral Animal* seemed misnamed because its author spent little time talking about morals. Ridley, on the other hand, takes the biological origins of virtue as his primary topic and interweaves evolution and human behavior throughout the book.

Rather simplistically, *The Origins of Virtue* reduces human behavior to an algorithm for survival. Ridley concludes that the strategy human beings have developed for the propagation of their genetic code might be called "generous reciprocity." According to this theory, cooperation helps one survive, because a group working together is more likely to pass on its genes than are isolated individuals who fall easy prey to hostile forces. Yet individuals who are indiscriminately generous are eliminated as more aggressive individuals supplant them. In a similar way, those who are universally aggressive tend to be isolated as others find little profit in associating with them. This means that the best strategy for survival would be to reciprocate the behavior demonstrated by others—trusting the trustworthy and acting aggressively toward those who are themselves aggressive—while forgiving minor transgressions and thus improving the solidarity of the group. Ridley even believes that human brains developed their capacity to remember, draw inferences, and perform intricate calculations largely as a means of assisting us in reciprocity. The human brain is, in other words, the organ we have developed to keep track of favors owed and debts to be called in.

One of the most persuasive arguments in *The Origins of Virtue* is that the innately human tendency to think reciprocally can explain universal patterns of superstition, religion, and the occult. "We frequently and universally anthropomorphize the natural world as a series of social exchanges. 'The gods are angry because of what we have done' we say to justify a setback in the Trojan war, a plague of locusts in ancient Egypt, a drought in the Namib desert or a piece of bad luck in modern suburbia. I frequently kick or glower at recalcitrant tools or machines, cursing the vindictiveness of inanimate objects, blatant in my anthropomorphism." Reciprocal treatment is such an intuitive part of human behavior that we expect everything around us to act reciprocally. When our favors are not sufficiently rewarded by nature or technology, we lash out in the same way that we would punish an uncooperative member of our own species—and if that does not work, we attempt to increase the size of the bribe.

Ridley's belief that reciprocity is centered in the brain does not mean that he views human behavior as a *rational* series of equations. In fact, Ridley argues that it is through emotions (which he regards as even more uniquely human than reciprocity) that people primarily communicate with one another. By reading the nonverbal cues of others, we attempt to form connections with those who are most likely to be fair in how they treat us (that is, good reciprocators) and to avoid those who are inclined to be selfish. Using once again the approaches of the game theorists, Ridley demonstrates that people can be remarkably perceptive about the signals conveyed in a group. In a game where a person's own score increased through selfish activity while the scores of all players increased through cooperation, players who were not acquainted with one another tended to use trial and error to locate those most likely to be cooperative. Yet when allowed to talk among themselves for as little as half an hour, most individuals knew immediately who was "reliable" and who was going to be motivated merely by selfish gain. The players thus adapted their strategies in such a way as to maximize their return.

The Origins of Virtue explains certain aspects of human behavior by drawing parallels between people and animals. Ridley notes that animals appearing to be "altruistic" usually place the good of their *families* ahead of themselves; they are not merely working for the greater good. Seemingly selfless behavior is thus a strategy developed by a species in order to promote transmission of genetic code at the cost of inconveniencing or even destroying specific individuals. Expanding on this pattern, Ridley explains human altruism as arising, at least in part, from a natural drive to protect kin that has been expanded to the larger kinship of humanity as a whole. "But we are not like animals in every respect," Ridley is quick to point out. "We are unique, we are different, just as every species is unique and different from every other; biology is a science of exceptions, not rules; of diversity, not grand unified theories. That ants are communitarian says nothing about whether man is virtuous. That natural selection is cruel says nothing about whether cruelty is moral." In this way, Ridley's view of humanity differs greatly from that of earlier social Darwinists.

The Origins of Virtue is persuasive when examining social skills that would have benefited the survival of early humans. These skills—which Ridley himself catalogs as "local specialization, cultural conformism, fierce antagonism between groups, cooperative group defence and groupishness"—may explain the origins not merely of social values but of contemporary economic practices as well. For example, local specialization meant that early tribes were able to focus energy on tasks to which they were best suited and for which raw materials were abundant. Since each tribe could then trade its commodities for items produced by neighboring peoples, there was profit in specializing locally even if a variety of raw materials were available: Productivity increased when people were able to concentrate on making a limited number of products; more goods were thus available for trade, and greater material wealth then flowed into the community. As Ridley demonstrates, this same phenomenon helps explain certain aspects of international trade today. Similarly, cultural conformism had survival value for early societies because it meant that individuals did not have to discover everything for themselves but could rely on the collective wisdom of the tribe. An impulse that once protected the individual by accelerating his or her education may now explain seemingly random shifts in fashion and the powerful commercial attraction of a product's "popularity."

Unfortunately, Ridley's book is marred by its ending. After a consistent argument of more than two hundred pages, the author seems to begin a wholly different topic with chapter 11. He suddenly shifts his focus to attack the follies of ecological extremism, "political correctness," and the romanticized case studies of Margaret Mead. Ridley's chapters on these topics, while persuasive by themselves, are only loosely connected to his earlier discussion. The result is that he undermines the effectiveness of the argument he has made patiently throughout the earlier chapters. Many readers will dismiss the book's entire thesis because Ridley proved unable to draw more convincing examples at the end of the work.

Only one of Ridley's final arguments seems at all persuasive. The author uses his discussion of evolution and game theory to suggest that big government is not a natural state of affairs for human beings. "We are not so nasty that we need to be tamed by intrusive government, nor so nice that too much government does not bring out the worst in us, both as its employees and as its clients. . . . The collapse of community spirit in the last few decades, and the erosion of civic virtue, is caused in this analysis not by the spread and encouragement of greed but by the dead hand of government. The state makes no bargain with the citizen to take joint responsibility for civic order, engenders in him no obligation, duty or pride, and imposes obedience instead. Little wonder that, treated like a naughty child, he behaves like one." Human beings, Ridley has demonstrated, tend to protect what is their own and to exploit what is shared by the community as a whole. Though he tries to make this same case in his attacks on ecological extremism, the change of focus seems too abrupt, and he fails as a result.

The Origins of Virtue provides a quick and readable survey of recent thinking about possible connections between evolution and human behavior. General readers will find it informative and thought-provoking, although the book makes no real contribution of its own. In particular, those who have already read Robert Wright's *The Moral Animal* will make few additional discoveries in Ridley's summary of the same material.

Jeffrey L. Buller

Sources for Further Study

Booklist. XCIII, April 15, 1997, p. 1368.
The Economist. CCCXLI, December 7, 1996, p. 5.
Los Angeles Times Book Review. March 30, 1997, p. 3.
National Review. XLIX, June 2, 1997, p. 52.
Nature. CCCLXXXIII, October 31, 1996, p. 785.
New Scientist. CLII, October 19, 1996, p. 49.
The New York Times Book Review. CII, May 11, 1997, p. 13.
Publishers Weekly. CCXLIV, March 10, 1997, p. 60.
The Spectator. CCLXXVIII, January 11, 1997, p. 32.
The Times Literary Supplement. November 29, 1996, p. 3.
The Wall Street Journal. March 26, 1997, p. A17.

OUT TO CANAAN

Author: Jan Karon (1937-   )
Publisher: Viking (New York). 342 pp. $23.95
Type of work: Novel
Time: The 1990's
Locale: Mitford, North Carolina

The fourth installment in Karon's Mitford Series, which includes At Home in Mitford, A Light in the Window, *and* These High, Green Hills

> *Principal characters:*
> TIM KAVANAUGH, an absentminded Episcopal rector
> CYNTHIA COPPERSMITH, his wife, a writer and illustrator of children's books
> DOOLEY BARLOWE, his foster son
> PAULINE BARLOWE, Dooley's biological mother, an impoverished alcoholic
> PERCY and VELMA MOSLEY, the owners of a local diner
> SADIE BAXTER, a wealthy spinster
> LOUELLA, Miss Sadie's companion and best friend
> ESTHER CUNNINGHAM, the mayor of Mitford
> MACK STROUPE, a candidate for mayor
> HAL OWEN, the town veterinarian

Out to Canaan, the fourth book in Jan Karon's series, transpires in Mitford, North Carolina, a town time forgot. In her first book, *At Home in Mitford*, she tells readers that the town's vintage flavor is guarded by citizens who "discourage serious tourism." Mitford's lush private gardens and small-town green set around a war memorial create an ethos that recalls towns from Oxford, Mississippi, to Bath, Maine. *Out to Canaan* continues readers' acquaintance with the soft-spoken and caring rector Tim Kavanaugh, whose marriage to Cynthia Coppersmith, prefigured in the first novel, is now well established. Percy and Velma Mosley, owners of the local grill; eccentric Aunt Rose and Uncle Billy, who view the world from chrome dinette chairs; the young Dooley, taken under Father Tim's wing and brought to town for proper schooling and wider social interaction; and Father Tim's ebullient secretary, Emma—all these reappear and continue their banter and interaction. Even Barnabas, the stray dog that tracks Father Tim down in *At Home in Mitford*, perpetrates his own series of crises. Readers of the series will be happy to continue their acquaintance with this cast of Southern townsfolk, savoring their friendships, difficulties, and epiphanies in Mitford and in the Episcopal congregation at Lord's Chapel. Yet readers picking the book up for the first time will have no trouble understanding the relationships or the narrative continuity because of Karon's skillful weave of memory and event.

Karon's style re-creates life in Southern towns, where highly idiosyncratic personalities live side by side with genteel descendants of families whose aristocratic backgrounds linked them to classical education and the English Romantic poets. Some characters have tasted life in Paris. In one poignant lunchtime conversation, Miss Sadie

Baxter and Father Tim share their reminiscences of Europe.

Miss Sadie personifies the traditional, faded Southern lady. Her failed European romance with a man who became Mitford's most wealthy entrepreneur has left her a frail spinster whom the town reveres for her taste and delicacy. She has a conscience and a sense of the caretaking of old Southern plantation families for their slaves and hired workers. In the contemporary setting of Karon's books, this translates into Miss Sadie's desire to leave her estate, called Fernbank, to the Episcopal Church so the property can be developed as a retirement home for area residents.

Other characters, such as Puny and Emma, have barely enough schooling to get by on but are rich in common sense. They excel in their ability for good hard work. Karon peppers their speech with colloquial aphorisms; in fact, even the highly educated rector has adopted the homey character of Southern sayings. During preparations for company at the rectory, he tells Cynthia that the tablecloth she wants to use is "worn as thin as a moth's wing."

The other ingredient of Southern character that Karon celebrates throughout *Out to Canaan* is the loyalty and compassion that townspeople feel for one another and their town. Leaving nothing to suggestion, Karon makes Mitford's slogan "Mitford Takes Care of Its Own." One of the central plot lines in *Out to Canaan* is the political pretensions of Mack Stroupe and his drive to unseat longtime mayor Esther Cunningham. The speculation about where Stroupe got his money and his fancy new lifestyle is satisfied only near the novel's end, when the high-powered Florida-based Miami Development Company appears in town, positioning itself to buy Fernbank and turn it into a luxury health spa/retreat.

Yet little attention is paid to how town solidarity affects the black population. Only one black character is mentioned: Louella, Miss Sadie's faithful maid, who has returned to help the ailing old lady in her last years in the series opener, *At Home in Mitford*. In *Out to Canaan*, Karon's treatment of Louella reminds readers of phrases heard in the 1960's, as the Civil Rights movement was gathering force. Then Southerners reiterated, "We always took good care of our Negroes; they never complained." Louella's position in Mitford echoes all those sentiments indirectly. She also fills another stereotypical role. The Sunday after Dooley and his mother are united with the youngest missing Barlowe child, Father Tim asks Louella to sing in Lord's Chapel. As she stands to perform, she "raises her hands heavenward" and begins to sing *Amazing Grace* "alone and unaccompanied." Karon cannot resist characterizing her powerful voice as "bronze" as it fills the congregation with the song's moving words. Yet even then, Karon has Father Tim—not Louella—bestow the gift of her song. As he passes his eyes over the congregation, he thinks: "This is for you, Dooley; and for Poo and Jesse, and for you, Pauline, whom the hound of heaven pursued and won. . . . For you, Harley, and you, Lace Turner, and even for you, Cynthia, who was *given to me* so late, yet right on time" (emphasis added).

The openhearted advocacy of the rector in behalf of the small band of stragglers he rescues from poverty, ill health, and isolation is undeniable. Nevertheless, the white man's position and right to arrange the lives of those less privileged than he lives on in these actions. His reference to Cynthia as "given" to him echoes the old idea of wives as property. In fact, their very traditional marriage, with all of its codes and shared moments, recalls many television series of the 1950's, where perfect families resided behind white picket fences in perfectly maintained houses full of happy children and well-adjusted parents. Although the cast at Lord's Chapel Rectory is more polyglot and not technically related, the tone and implication of a happy home as the answer to the world's problems is clear.

Lace and Harley, Jess, Dooley, Pauline, and Poobaw are part of a host of uneducated people whose lives began and were stifled in the ramshackle cabins of the rural poor strung along "the Creek" outside Mitford. Pauline's sad incompetence, poverty, and alcoholism forced her to give her children to various relatives to be raised. In this fourth book, Father Tim's attempt to help Pauline find a job and the last of her scattered children commences after several years of his serving as a surrogate father to her son Dooley. Father Tim drives to Florida with Cynthia and Pauline to retrieve Dooley's younger sister, Jess. When they return, he finds Pauline a job, and she and her children begin a new life together. The Barlowes and Harley and Lace are the only ones of the unfortunate Creek entourage to enter the world of education and middle-class life.

No one can deny that Father Tim is an agent for good and that he tries to maneuver, cajole, and negotiate his flock to wholeness and unselfish interactions with one another. His friends Olivia and Hoppy Harper, as well as veterinarian Hal Owen and his wife, Marge, step in time after time to house those less fortunate than themselves. The town is a model of a community shouldering responsibility for the poor. Yet it is always clear that there are more poor who reside unheeded and unsought along the Creek.

Out to Canaan makes no attempt to break the stereotypical pattern of white Southern largesse lifting African Americans and the underprivileged onto the road toward respectability and success. The rector's dialogues with his secretary radiate class differences. Although Father Tim is clearly in charge of the church office, Emma's bossy, good-natured presence keeps him firmly connected to the real world. She chides him about deadlines, complains about the weather, carries the newest gossip into the office, and generally fusses at him. He dreads her scorn and her barbed remarks about parishioners or his conduct of parish business. Yet theirs is the "affection of unequals." He regards her as his bane but also his responsibility.

Karon's characters, both homespun and educated, seem naively involved in the culture that allowed inequities to pass unnoticed by good Christian folk in the South for decades. Readers are drawn into the circle of interactions and good-humored exchanges that make up the momentum of life in Father Tim's Mitford. Because Karon focuses on the openheartedness of the rector and the honorable solidarity of the town in resisting big money for a Ferndale development deal, readers might not notice that normalcy and decency originate with white residents only. It is easy for middle-class readers to like the main characters and participate in their various adventures without thinking about the imbalance. Readers from the Creek or Louella's community would, no doubt, have another response.

All the Mitford books tell stories of the small-town South with affection and completeness. They do not present the heightened idiosyncrasies of Eudora Welty's Southern folk. There are no shrewd old black women in this novel similar to Welty's Phoenix in "A Worn Path." There is also no eccentric spinster to chill the reader as in William Faulkner's "A Rose for Emily." Nor do Karon's stories reveal the confused torpor of persons caught in a web of failure and delusion that Faulkner presents in *Light in August* (1932). The rough edges of the Mitford rural poor or those with merely standard educations do not grate on readers' sensibilities or create the sometimes surreal effects that Welty and Faulkner achieve, because all burdens and problems are filtered through Father Tim's firm reliance on God's impeccable timing in the affairs of men (and women) and His uncontested goodness. Even Barnabas, the faithful dog, obeys only when people quote Scripture to him.

In *Out to Canaan*, retirement looms before Father Tim and Cynthia as another adventure to be undertaken together. Based on their firm commitment to each other and his long residence in Mitford, they begin to make plans to remodel Cynthia's small yellow house next to the rectory. One can imagine more Mitford books that follow Father Tim into a genial existence in Mitford, where he continues to act as referee, father figure, and friend to townspeople.

Luckily for Mitford and for readers who have a nostalgia for days when faith and family served to take care of most problems, nearly all the crises in this novel are solved. Even Fernbank, which the church withholds from rich Florida outsiders, is purchased by a local antique dealer who has made a stupendous amount of money by selling some of Miss Sadie's antiques. He returns with his new Italian wife and takes up residence. Their appearance signals a contemporary version of the landed gentry and assures Ferndale the kind of care and attention the grand old property deserves.

Perhaps the series' popularity rests on its verisimilitude to what people in the South experienced before Civil Rights advocates began asking the disturbing questions and demanding rights that upset the rationalizations and status quo to which they were accustomed. Or perhaps readers find comfort in reading about situations that can be solved by relying on people's roles in a community where the order of life is relatively stable and people value education, hard work, and honesty. Mitford's security must re-create what many middle-class Americans experienced in the postwar period of the 1950's. Jan Karon's compassionate eye lets them believe that social inequities could have been errors of omission, that most people have good hearts, and that charity played a part in the small-town rural South and small towns elsewhere during the pre-Civil Rights 1960's. Her choice of Canaan as a metaphor for Father Tim's retirement sets Mitford between the promised-land iconography of the Puritans' vision of America and the diversity of contemporary life. It is up to readers to weigh the Southern life that her eye records in the balance with their own visions of contemporary America.

Karen L. Arnold

Sources for Further Study

Booklist. XCIII, April 1, 1997, p. 1268.
Chicago Tribune. June 11, 1997, V, p. 3.
Christianity Today. XLI, September 1, 1997, p. 18.
Denver Post. April 27, 1997, p. G7.
Kirkus Reviews. LXV, March 15, 1997, p. 406.
Library Journal. CXXII, May 1, 1997, p. 140.
Los Angeles Times. July 6, 1997, p. E1.
Publishers Weekly. CCXLIV, May 26, 1997, p. 60.

THE PAPERS OF MARTIN LUTHER KING, JR.
Volume III: Birth of a New Age, December 1955-December 1956

Author: Martin Luther King, Jr. (1929-1968)
Edited by Clayborne Carson (series editor), Stewart Burns, Susan Carson, Peter Holloran, and Dana L. H. Powell
Publisher: University of California Press (Berkeley). Illustrated. 566 pp. $40.00
Type of work: Historical papers
Time: December 2, 1955-December 27, 1956
Locale: Montgomery, Alabama, and other U.S. locations

The third volume in a documentary series on Martin Luther King, Jr.'s life, this collection of primary historical sources portrays the story of the Montgomery bus boycott and the emergence of King as a nationally known civil rights leader

Principal personage:
MARTIN LUTHER KING, JR., pastor and civil rights leader

This collection of historical documents is the third volume in a series being produced by the Martin Luther King, Jr., Papers Project, a documentary history project sponsored by the Martin Luther King, Jr., Center for Nonviolent Social Change in association with Stanford University and Emory University. Together with its predecessors, *Volume I: Called to Serve, January 1929-June 1951*, and *Volume II: Rediscovering Precious Values, July 1951-November 1955*, the volume covers the early career of King and charts the ways in which King's political convictions grew out of his theological training, his skills as a minister, and the social gospel background of his family. *Volume III: Birth of a New Age* specifically focuses on the organization and legal challenges of the Montgomery bus boycott of 1955-1956 and treats this campaign as a pivotal political turning point for King. During the boycott, King and his colleagues honed ideas and practices later utilized in the Civil Rights movement at large. Through the events chronicled in this volume, King himself emerged as a nationally recognized spokesperson of the struggle against segregation.

Correspondence to and from King makes up the bulk of the nearly three hundred documents selected to be printed in the volume. Transcriptions and facsimiles of telegrams or letters are used to illustrate both top-down and bottom-up approaches to understanding the impact of the Montgomery movement. Famous correspondents include President Dwight D. Eisenhower, former First Lady Eleanor Roosevelt, educator Nannie Helen Burroughs, Nobel Prize winner Ralph Bunche, National Association for the Advancement of Colored People (NAACP) executive secretary Roy Wilkins, novelist Lillian Smith, and such luminaries of the emerging Civil Rights movement as Medgar Evers, Septima Clark, and Ella Baker. Printed alongside these missives from or to the well-known are messages exchanged between King and his friends, fellow pastors, and distant supporters who were personally unknown to him. Letters in the latter category—to such people as Lottie Mae Pugh, a student in Suffolk, Virginia, who had written to King for guidance in choosing her own career, or from the impoverished Earline Browning, who had read of the boycott in the *Pittsburgh*

Courier and sent two pairs of her own shoes to be worn by domestic workers walking to work in Montgomery—are representative of the sentiments of common folk across the country who were stirred by reports of King's inspirational oratory and the example of courage and decency he presented in his handling of boycott events. A February 28, 1956, telegram from black and white members of the Longshoremen's and Warehousemen's Union in San Francisco (in which they sent encouragement and expressed their support for the fight for rights in the South) similarly represents the receptiveness of people of different races and regions to the boycott, and the belief held by many that the efforts of the protesters in Montgomery were being made on behalf of an all-encompassing democratic ideal. This correspondence from the great and from people at the grassroots is interspersed with key articles, sermons, and addresses by King—including the one ("The Birth of a New Age," 1956) that gives the volume its title. Minutes or reports of mass meetings are also included, such as the one at which the Montgomery Improvement Association (MIA) was founded in December, 1955. Facsimiles and transcriptions of documents that demonstrate the state's reaction to King's activism include a Federal Bureau of Investigation (FBI) surveillance report on King activities filed with J. Edgar Hoover and the indictment and later testimony and judgment of the court in the state of Alabama's case against King in February and March, 1956.

The majority of documents presented in the book were drawn from the King collections at the King Center in Atlanta and at Boston University, but material also came from some seventy-five other manuscript collections and from private donors who lent their previously unpublished personal papers to the use of the project. The result is an impressive and varied array that tells the story of the boycott from several different angles—legal, political, popular, and official, from court transcript to a leaflet produced on a church mimeograph machine.

The Papers Project's stated goal of presenting a definitive edition of King's papers is a difficult one to achieve, given the copiousness of documentation available. What results from the selection the editors have made is not a definitive history but rather an insider's guide to the major events, feelings, motivations, and personalities that fueled the Montgomery boycott. The editors do an excellent job in presenting that history from multifaceted perspectives and in using documents drawn from different genres, including those in which King speaks in first person and those in which he was a participant with others in a collective endeavor. They also underscore the point that King himself made: that the boycott welled up within the community under the leadership of many, and that circumstance—including the state's legal actions against King—made King, over the course of the months of activism, into the movement's main spokesperson and figurehead.

Despite acknowledgment of the work of a large number of student and postgraduate researchers and interns, evidence of research in this volume, aside from the impressive compilation of documents itself, is quite slim. Headnotes to individual documents offer helpful and enjoyable introductions to major themes and personalities and set the context for the texts that follow. Annotation is sparse and basic. Footnotes offer the reader short general identifications of correspondents and organizations or people mentioned in the text, occasional brief explanations of, or follow-up information on, issues expressed in the text, and identification of source citations or of literary or biblical allusions. The reader is further guided by a detailed chronology in the front of the volume and by a copious calendar of documents at the book's end. The calendar is an especially helpful source for those wishing to pursue further reading and research. It includes the listing of over one thousand King-related items for the period covered by the book (chosen from a project database of some 3,500), including material authored by King and primary and secondary material written to or about him.

The volume begins, appropriately, with a powerful facsimile of a typed leaflet prepared by Jo Ann Robinson and members of Montgomery's Women's Political Council shortly after the arrest of Rosa Parks in the beginning of December, 1955. Parks, a local NAACP leader and graduate of an activist workshop at the famed Highlander Folk School, was arrested on December 1, 1955, after she refused to relinquish her seat to a white passenger and move to the rear of a city bus. Robinson, who worshipped at King's Dexter Avenue Baptist Church, joined other women in calling for a one-day boycott of the bus line in protest over the treatment of Parks and of other individuals who had previously refused to give up their seats on the bus. The subsequent boycott on December 5 was so successful that it led to the formation of the MIA and a long-term, unified spurning of the bus system by Montgomery's black residents. The boycott lasted throughout the year, ending only when the U.S. Supreme Court ruled in *Browder v. Gayle* (1956) that city and state segregation statutes such as those previously in effect in Montgomery public transportation were unconstitutional. The ruling represented a great legal victory for King and the many people who made the boycott work, but it proved to be just the beginning of a much larger struggle for civil rights.

As the selected documents show (and as the editors discuss in their introduction to the volume), the Montgomery boycott proved many things. Among them was the effectiveness of King in articulating the sense of mission that lay behind his own leadership and the dedication of the hundreds of people who participated in the boycott. They showed what an African American community could do operating together under their own leadership. They demonstrated a deep sense of decency and dignity in their actions and experimented with tactics that later would be utilized in the court cases, demonstrations, marches, and sit-ins of the larger Civil Rights movement to follow. When King, Parks, and other boycott leaders were indicted under a 1921 state law regarding conspiracy to interfere with the lawful operation of businesses, the terms for constitutional protest that would be used successfully in the civil rights fights of the future were set: King's position in his trial was that the issue at hand was the legality of Jim Crow laws, not the economic boycott of businesses. He in turn argued that the movement was a case of mass protest, not the action of an elite cadre of individual leaders. His case made headlines in northern newspapers, and King was crowned a national leader, a spokesperson for racial rights and Christian idealism. He used his pulpit and public meetings to articulate the connection between brotherly love, social justice, and spiritual redemption. He used networks of ministers and black fraternities to build a new kind of civil rights base. He strode a fine line between moderation and militancy, and after his home was bombed in January, 1956, he embodied the personal danger involved for those brave enough to openly confront deeply entrenched social and political mores. His leadership linked the Montgomery boycott to ideas embedded in earlier black uplift organizations and benevolent societies. He articulated a larger understanding of civil rights protest in the context of an American tradition in which liberty was defined through processes of rebellion and dissent. Through his embrace of Gandhian principles, he also internationalized those processes, placing the activism in Montgomery in the context of larger anticolonial independence movements, especially the one in India. He began to address issues of social class and the fact that racial discrimination went hand-in-hand with gross economic inequities—themes that later would be more fully played out in the 1960's Poor People's Campaign.

In spite of rifts and disagreements over such things as the involvement of non-southerners in the movement and the extent to which connections to the American Left should be acknowledged, the activists in Montgomery succeeded in acting in unison and winning their immediate goal. That they did all this not just within a firmly Jim-Crowed South but also in an era when the nation's politics were dominated by the Cold War is all the more remarkable. In the events documented by this volume, King grows in stature and positions himself in an independent way relative to older civil rights advocates. In the years to follow the Montgomery boycott, King and his colleagues would expand the scope of civil rights protest beyond transportation issues to include voter registration, residential and school desegregation, access to health care and recreational facilities, and other rights. Montgomery's and King's network of activist ministers and parishioners laid the groundwork for what would become the Southern Christian Leadership Conference, and their protests and arrests provided the foundation for the coming mass movement for civil rights. This volume makes King's private dilemmas and his public actions in this heroic chapter in the early history of the Civil Rights movement both personal and accessible. There is something of inspiration for everyone in its pages.

Barbara Bair

Sources for Further Study

Booklist. XCIII, February 15, 1997, p. 980.
Crisis. CIV, July, 1997, p. 42.
Library Journal. CXXII, March 1, 1997, p. 86.
The Nation. CCLXIV, May 12, 1997, p. 28.

PERSONAL HISTORY

Author: Katharine Graham (1917-   )
Publisher: Alfred A. Knopf (New York). 642 pp. $29.95
Type of work: Memoir
Time: 1875 to the 1990's
Locale: New York City and Washington, D.C.

A candid and probing account of Katharine Graham's family and of her life, with a riveting inside look at the operation and history of her family newspaper, The Washington Post

Principal personages:
KATHARINE MEYER GRAHAM, the influential publisher of *The Washington Post*, 1969-1979
EUGENE MEYER, her father; owner of the newspaper, 1933-1948
AGNES ERNST MEYER, her mother
PHILIP GRAHAM, her husband; publisher of the newspaper, 1946-1963
LESLIE FARBER, Philip Graham's psychiatrist
BEN BRADLEE, the executive editor of the newspaper, 1968-1991
WARREN BUFFETT, a stockholder in the newspaper
BOB WOODWARD, a *Washington Post* reporter
CARL BERNSTEIN, a *Washington Post* reporter
LYNDON B. JOHNSON, the thirty-sixth president of the United States, 1963-1968

Katharine Graham has become such a fixture in Washington, D.C., through her influential *Washington Post* that her rise to power and prestige seems natural and inevitable. How hard could it have been for a woman whose father owned the paper, whose husband edited it for several years, and who then took over after his death? In truth, her dominance took years of struggle. She was beset with self-doubt, with worry that she would lose the paper, and with a set of attitudes about a woman's place in society that seem archaic. She exposes her vulnerability frankly enough to earn her high marks very early in her memoir. What she reveals lays bare the issue of how an executive maintains authority. Over and over again, Graham raises questions about her own competence. That she masters her weaknesses so decisively, however, makes her story not only compelling but far more honest than virtually any book ever written by a corporate leader.

Graham learned a good deal from her shrewd father, a man who came from wealth but who made his fortune on Wall Street using his own hard-earned money. Eugene Meyer resembles his Jewish contemporary Bernard Baruch in many respects. Like Baruch, he believed that he should use his wealth in the public service. When he bought *The Washington Post* in 1933, it was an also-ran among the city's newspapers. Meyer sustained large losses over many years, but he patiently built up the paper's quality and advertising revenues. At the same time, he made the paper a family enterprise. His wife, Agnes, a feisty woman with a taste for the arts and politics, often wrote for the paper and for other periodicals. His children also worked at the paper; Katharine took many different kinds of low-level jobs during summers and periods between school.

Yet even with an ambitious, accomplished mother and a father who did not automatically rule out women in the business world, Katharine Graham did not think of herself as having a career. Certainly she was active in the issues of her time. She was basically a liberal, though she never flirted with communism as did many of her contemporaries at the University of Chicago and elsewhere. She believed in labor unions and progressive policies, but she was never embarrassed about her family's money, and her belief in a capitalist economy never seems to have been shaken by her radical friends.

Perhaps Graham might have considered a career earlier if she had not been romanced by Philip Graham, a brilliant Harvard University law student, a clerk for Supreme Court Justice Felix Frankfurter, and the scion of a family steeped in Florida politics. Philip expected to return home after his education and become a politician, although his father leaned heavily on him to continue the family farming business.

World War II changed everything for Philip and Katharine Graham. Philip served a tour of duty with his usual energy and panache. He was an intense man, prone to drinking too much and to great mood swings. Yet in the early days of his marriage to Katharine, his more erratic qualities rarely surfaced, and she obviously thought of him as a great man who was destined to do great things. Although Philip resisted the idea of joining the *Post*, concerned that Katharine's family money would corrupt him or make it seem as though he had capitalized on her wealth, he could not resist Eugene Meyer's offer to head the paper. Philip was only in his early thirties, and though he had served no apprenticeship in journalism, he had a brilliant mind and Washington contacts that would ensure his getting off to a fast start.

Philip's launch was so meteoric that Katharine Graham became completely swallowed up in his life and career. Even as his manic-depressive personality began to show itself and he began to torture himself with doubts that he could have succeeded without his father-in-law's support, she became even more committed to his quest to dominate the Washington and national media. He acquired several companies— notably *Newsweek*—in his quest to make the Washington Post Company grow and mature.

Philip Graham wielded an influence and became a Washington insider in ways that now might seem close to the unethical. He became so close to Lyndon Johnson and his quest for the presidency that he was virtually Johnson's campaign manager. Katharine Graham repeatedly points out that her husband's actions were not so outrageous at the time, but in the light of later standards that call for a more independent press, his actions seem to cross a dangerous line between reporting the news and making the news.

Unfortunately, Philip Graham's manic-depressive behavior went untreated for several years. Katharine Graham is especially hard on psychiatrist Leslie Farber, who eschewed all use of drugs and tried to treat Graham by having him read existential philosophers. Farber would not even give a name to Graham's condition, believing that labels might make a patient feel that his disorders were incurable or controllable only through medication. Farber was reacting to an era when drugs and electric shock had been administered irresponsibly, but in retrospect, at least, Katharine Graham provides strong proof that Farber erred in the opposite direction. Without any prescriptions, Graham was left to feel guilty over his extreme actions—leaving his wife for a younger woman, impulsively buying properties, and going into profound depressions in which his self-worth plummeted. Graham committed suicide—in part because of his guilt over the pain he had caused his family, in part because his illness seemed untreatable without drugs. At least, this is the impression Katharine Graham conveys (Philip Graham left no suicide note).

A devastated Katharine at first refused to consider replacing her husband at the *Post*. How could she possibly do the job that this titan of journalism had held with such style and verve? The year was 1963—nearly a decade before the start-up of the women's movement. Graham reluctantly took the position as a family responsibility. She deferred to men constantly, however, and they condescended to her. She was often the only woman present at meetings of corporate heads. She never challenged their stupid jokes or speeches that began "Gentlemen and Lady" or "Gentlemen and Mrs. Graham." She felt like a freak, yet she believed that men had a right to dominate business and the marketplace.

Only very gradually did Graham's attitudes change. She admits to having been influenced by Gloria Steinem and women in the *Post* newsroom. One corporate CEO, Warren Buffett, not only thought Graham could make a great publisher but also practically gave her a business-school education to equip her to battle with her male counterparts successfully.

Two events—Watergate and union troubles at the *Post*—seem to have been the making of Katharine Graham. Although the story of Watergate has been told many times, Graham adds one crucial feature: the Nixon administration's effort not merely to intimidate the *Post* but to use Federal Communication Commission (FCC) regulations to economically damage the Washington Post Company. Through political allies in Florida, Nixon associates challenged the FCC license of the Post television station. Ultimately, the *Post* prevailed, but it is still shocking to see how far the Nixon White House was willing to go to destroy its critics.

Graham makes a telling point about herself and the newspaper while recapitulating its role in Watergate. She notes that editor Ben Bradlee and his reporters Bob Woodward and Carl Bernstein were free to report the story without her interference. She did not dictate an editorial line. Yet time and again the Nixon White House treated the *Post* as if every word came directly from Graham. Her point is that a great newspaper is not the voice of one person. A newspaper may have an editorial line, but its reporting of the news cannot be simply a reflection of that line. In subtle ways, however, the editorial and news sides of a paper do influence each other, and Graham is perhaps a little blind to that fact—probably because she is atop the *Post* pyramid of power. Yet her record of conversations with Woodward, for example—conversations he could easily challenge as a formidable figure in his own right—suggest that Graham is on sure ground in rejecting the Nixon line that the *Post* was merely out to get him. Even when she made suggestions about news coverage, she observes, her brilliant but fiercely independent editor, Bradlee, often ignored her.

The most shocking and revealing passages in Graham's book, however, deal with her efforts to settle a pressmen's strike. She believed that for years the *Post* had given in to union demands. It could not afford a strike so long as it had a powerful rival, *The Washington Star*, which would quickly eat up *Post* advertising revenues if it were out of circulation. The *Post* wanted to modernize, eliminate union featherbedding, and revamp its managerial style. It had become all too easy for the union to shut down the presses or delay printing when contracts were being negotiated. With good reason, the union was convinced it could continue to get its way, Graham concedes. When she decided to take a stand, the union simply did not believe her. When she held firm, several pressmen beat a shop manager and destroyed parts of their presses.

The union violence was a turning point for Graham. She continued to negotiate with the union, but she refused to take back workers who had damaged presses. When the union failed to accept her final offer, she hired replacements. Graham still nurses hard feelings about being called a union buster and firmly insists that breaking the union was not her intention. She presents a credible case—even quoting AFL-CIO president George Meany's disapproval of men who destroy their own tools.

Graham's account suggests that in many ways the union destroyed itself. It was all white and arrogant. Graham's replacements included African Americans and women—and some workers who resigned from the union in a state of shock over its uses of violence in the pressroom and threats of violence against those who continued to work at the paper.

Graham's record at the *Post* is one of extraordinary achievement. Yet she never loses sight of the person—the woman—who agonized over business decisions and made many mistakes. Graham admits that she often burst into tears when males criticized her. She had trouble firing incompetent office staff. She did not know how to motivate people, usually dwelling on the paper's mistakes and not acknowledging the many ways in which it had been improved. It took her well over a decade after her husband's death to master her job. Her most impressive trait is that she believes she is still learning. She gives ample credit to the men and women who mentored her during her long road to media ascendancy. Besides being the engrossing story of her own life, her memoir is a moving, informative look at an entire era of newspapering and the role of *The Washington Post* in changing the rules by which newspapers now operate.

Lisa Paddock

Sources for Further Study

America. CLXXVI, March 8, 1997, p. 5.
American Journalism. XIX, April, 1997, p. 53.
Chicago Tribune. March 2, 1997, XIV, p. 1.
The Christian Science Monitor. February, 18, 1997, p. 14.

Forbes. CLIX, April 7, 1997, p. 28.
Harper's Bazaar. February, 1997, p. 108.
Los Angeles Times Book Review. February 16, 1997, p. 3.
The New York Times Book Review. CII, February 9, 1997, p. 13.
The New Yorker. January 20, 1997, p. 60.
Time. CXLIX, February 3, 1997, p. 69.
USA Today. February 21, 1997, p. A15.
Vogue. CLXXXVII, February, 1997, p. 226.
The Washington Post Book World. XXVII, January 26, 1997, p. 1.
Women's Review of Books. XIV, July, 1997, p. 32.

THE PLEASURES OF THE IMAGINATION
English Culture in the Eighteenth Century

Author: John Brewer (1947-   )
Publisher: Farrar Straus and Giroux (New York). Illustrated. 721 pp. $40.00
Type of work: History
Time: 1660-1800
Locale: Britain and the Western European Continent

John Brewer provides a detailed account of the development of the arts during the eighteenth century, a period characterized by significant growth in commercialism associated with the arts and by mass interest in cultural activities

> *Principal personages:*
> SAMUEL JOHNSON, British writer
> DAVID GARRICK, British actor and director
> JOHN MARSH, British musician
> ANNA SEWARD, British writer and critic of Johnson
> THOMAS BEWICK, British illustrator

For many whose views of the history of culture in the West were formed in college survey courses in literature, history, or aesthetics, the conventional view of the eighteenth century is of a period marked by great stability of belief in the fundamentals of great art. Epithets such as "Augustan" or "neoclassic" are used to describe a period in which standards of taste seem to have been firmly established and rules for the production of acceptable art tightly applied. The writings of Joseph Addison and Sir Richard Steele in *The Tatler* and *The Spectator*, and of Samuel Johnson in *The Idler* and *The Rambler*, served as blueprints for shaping character and behavior. Dominating the critical landscape are figures such as Alexander Pope and Samuel Johnson in literature, David Garrick in the theater, and Sir Joshua Reynolds in the visual arts. Received opinion is that restraint and reserve were watchwords for both artistic production and public behavior.

John Brewer, whose credentials certainly rank him among the most knowledgeable and qualified twentieth century scholars of the eighteenth century, presents a decidedly different portrait of that age in *The Pleasures of the Imagination*. Arguing that the zeal for establishing differences between the present age and those that preceded it have caused twentieth century scholars to stress the "order, stability and decorum of eighteenth-century England," Brewer takes a closer look at the various forms of artistic expression that blossomed during the century to show how much controversy actually existed over a number of critical issues that later generations have taken as commonplaces of the age.

Demonstrating an exceptional breadth of knowledge of history, politics, sociology, and the arts, Brewer provides important background to explain why Johnson and Henry Fielding wrote what they did, why and how Sir William Pitt governed, and what excited the many individuals whose private records of the age offer a useful counterbalance to the accepted notions about these turbulent times. Following the advice of

Johnson's philosopher Imlac in *Rasselas*, Brewer chooses not to "number the streaks of the tulip," but rather to exhibit the prominent and striking features of his large subject. When he turns to discussions of individual writers or artists, he does so to "understand a larger historical process" that led to transformations in writing, bookselling, publishing, reading, painting, acting, collecting, and regulating the world of the arts. His aim is to examine and illuminate the emergence of a distinctively British culture that arose during the eighteenth century. This is an important task, Brewer claims, because it was during this time that the notion of what subsequent generations would call high culture (the kind about which Victorian critic Matthew Arnold would write so passionately in the following century) began to be distinguished from folk culture. It was the age in which politeness became the standard of judgment for social behavior, and the period in which the populace at large began to play a role in the creation of, and demand for, the arts.

Written "to build a bridge between the general reader and academic scholarship," *The Pleasures of the Imagination* mixes accounts of the important figures of the age with those of lesser luminaries whose life stories provide insight into daily living in England during the century. Brewer relies less on statistical data and more on biography as his principal means of educating his readers about the cultural developments of this period. Brief sketches of the careers of figures such as novelist Samuel Richardson, actor/director David Garrick, literary lion Samuel Johnson, man-of-letters James Boswell, and others are included principally to show how these figures influenced others in developing the concept of culture. Brewer demonstrates the extent of their influence by reviewing its effect on a number of interesting but now largely forgotten contemporaries. He treats readers to an inside view of cultured life in England revealed in the diaries of Anna Larpent, a woman whose opinions were formed from voracious reading, playgoing, and concert attendance. He shows what life was like for the artist who had to negotiate between the demands of his art and the necessity for making a living by providing an extended sketch of the life of painter Ozias Humphry.

What one learns from studying the careers of these great and small figures in the cultural landscape is that, during the period, the principal forces that influenced culture moved from the court to the marketplace. Extending his examination back into the seventeenth century, Brewer demonstrates how the visual, literary, and performing arts, which were tightly controlled and closely associated with the monarchy during the reigns of Charles I and Charles II (and virtually suppressed during the Puritan interregnum), gradually became the property of the public at large. In the eighteenth century, the marketplace began to dictate what kind of art would be produced, and there emerged a conflict between "art" and "commerce"—a phenomenon that many in the twentieth century believe is unique in their own time. Brewer catalogs ways in which practitioners in a variety of artistic disciplines either refrained from pandering to the public or adapted their work to reach a wide audience.

Unquestionably, the center of culture in Britain during the eighteenth century was the city of London. It is not surprising, then, to find that the bulk of Brewer's study focuses on activities in the capital. Although not all of his contemporaries would have agreed with Samuel Johnson's belief that "when a man is tired of London, he is tired of life," a clear majority of those who sought to make their name and fortune in the arts gravitated to the city. As a consequence, most of the significant changes in both the aesthetic and the commercial dimensions of the arts can be seen in events that took place in London. Brewer traces a number of these developments in separate chapters devoted to writers, readers, publishers, actors, playgoers, musicians, art collectors, antiquarians, and historians.

Some of the vignettes will prove especially interesting to those not familiar with the history of the arts. Among the more intriguing anecdotes is the story of David Garrick's monomaniacal drive to establish William Shakespeare as the predominant English dramatist. Anyone who is the product of a traditional education in the twentieth century is likely to assume that Shakespeare has always been revered among playwrights, and that his prominence as the world's greatest writer has been largely unquestioned since he first began producing plays in the late sixteenth century. Such was certainly not the case, and, as Brewer makes clear, the Bard of Avon owes much to Garrick for his subsequent notoriety. Garrick produced Shakespeare's plays on the eighteenth century stage, organized festivals and events to celebrate his idol, and influenced many who were also instrumental in establishing what has come to be called the Cult of the Bard. Others, too, helped build the legend during this period, among them the publishing house of Tonson, which arranged to have a series of noted literary figures edit Shakespeare's plays at intervals during the century. If, as many scholars assert, Johnson's famous preface to his edition of Shakespeare established once and for all the dramatist's primacy of place in English literature, Brewer's account is a useful reminder of the context in which this essay was written. Johnson writes not merely to proclaim Shakespeare's greatness but also to counter the claims of other critics whose view of the playwright did not match his own; his preface is but one in an ongoing series of polemics that debated the merits of Shakespeare against those of successors whose works were more popular with eighteenth century audiences.

Brewer offers succinct, insightful summaries of a number of other significant developments in the cultural history of Britain: the emergence of the Royal Academy, which influenced the production of painting and sculpture; the growth of the theater, in London and in the provinces; and the influence of booksellers, publishers, and lending libraries on readership and the production of literature (especially novels). Readers are treated to an inside look at the business of the theater through an examination of the production history of one of the century's most popular plays, John Gay's *The Beggar's Opera*. True to his thesis, Brewer focuses not on the aesthetic qualities of the work but on its significance as a cultural phenomenon, influencing dramaturgy and theater business for half a century after its initial appearance early in the century.

Although chiefly concerned with the changes taking place in the cultural landscape of London, Brewer devotes a major section of his study to investigating ways the arts were practiced and promoted in provincial settings: small towns, country houses, regional assemblies, and local theaters. His analysis of these activities, which certainly were prompted by what was occurring in London but which took on their own life and characteristics, is presented through the biographies of three individuals whose contributions to the cultural heritage of Britain were made largely in their hometowns: musician John Marsh, writer Anna Seward, and illustrator Thomas Bewick. Each is chosen by Brewer to illustrate something special about the impact of cultural activities outside the capital. Bewick represents the tradesman-artist who combined his aesthetic talents with his business instincts to advance art in the marketplace, elevating himself socially as he built his fortune through the production of his handiwork. Brewer selects Marsh as his example of the "gentleman amateur" who avoided London in favor of the assemblies that sprang up in small towns, providing venues for talented composers and musicians to demonstrate their artistic prowess. His story provides insight into the influence music had in shaping the lives of the gentry outside England's major city.

The account of Seward's career is of interest for several reasons. A native of Lichfield, the hometown of both Samuel Johnson and David Garrick, Seward was a poet of some talent; she is best remembered, however, as the outspoken critic of Johnson—a role no one in London would have had the courage to take on, and one that few anywhere in Britain would have relished. Seward seemed to be the exception, bravely pointing out Johnson's defects while celebrating sentimental poetry and making the world aware that London had not cornered the market on intelligence or artistic talents.

Brewer's study is accented by more than 240 black-and-white photos and illustrations, and a dozen color plates. These provide visual reinforcement to his argument that the people of the eighteenth century had a vision of themselves quite different from the one formed by their descendants two centuries later. Far from being a time when "cultural hierarchies were respected and the rule of taste prevailed," the age of Pope, Johnson, Reynolds, and Garrick was a time when people saw their society in a state of constant flux. As Brewer demonstrates throughout his perceptive study, it was this "dynamism, variety, and exuberance" that made life exciting. His ability to communicate some of that excitement to his readers is what makes Brewer's *The Pleasures of the Imagination* a truly enlightening work of scholarship.

Laurence W. Mazzeno

Sources for Further Study

Booklist. XCIII, August, 1997, p. 1874.
The Guardian. May 22, 1997, II, p. 12.
Kirkus Reviews. LXV, July 15, 1997, p. 1077.
Library Journal. CXVII, July, 1997, p. 100.
Los Angeles Times Book Review. October 26, 1997, p. 4.
The New Republic. CCXVII, November 24, 1997, p. 42.

The New York Times Book Review. CII, October 26, 1997, p. 22.
Publishers Weekly. CCXLIV, July 14, 1997, p. 74.
The Times Literary Supplement. August, 1997, p. 3.
The Wall Street Journal. October 13, 1997, p. A20.
The Washington Post Book World. XXVII, November 9, 1997, p. 1.

PORTRAITS
A Gallery of Intellectuals

Author: Edward Shils (1911-1995)
Edited, with an introduction, by Joseph Epstein
Publisher: University of Chicago Press (Chicago). 255 pp. $55.00; paperback $17.95
Type of work: Biography
Time: The 1930's to the 1990's
Locale: Chicago, and London and Cambridge, England

A collection of biographical essays about academic figures, mainly humanists and social scientists, introduced by an affectionate memoir about their author

> *Principal personages:*
> NIRAD C. CHAUDHURI, an Indian writer
> SIDNEY HOOK, a socialist political philosopher
> ROBERT MAYNARD HUTCHINS, the president of the University of Chicago
> HAROLD LASKI, an activist professor and founder of the Left Book Club
> ARNALDO DANTE MOMIGLIANO, an historian of the ancient world
> LEO SZILARD, an atomic scientist

The Nobel Prize-winning novelist Saul Bellow once remarked that he knew only three intelligent people in Chicago: the art critic Harold Rosenberg, the classical scholar and translator David Grene, and the sociologist Edward Shils—the editor of *Minerva: A Review of Science, Learning, and Policy* and a member of the Committee on Social Thought at the University of Chicago. *Portraits: A Gallery of Intellectuals* (compiled and introduced by Joseph Epstein, for many years editor of the *American Scholar*) gathers together eleven of Shils's biographical essays, arranged alphabetically from Raymond Aron to Leo Szilard. Some, like those on Sidney Hook, Robert Maynard Hutchins, and Harold Laski, profile widely known figures, while others, like those on Nirad Chaudhuri, Leopold Labedz, and Arnaldo Momigliano, introduce personages barely known to the common reader.

Shils arrived at the University of Chicago as a graduate student in 1932, when Hutchins was already the university's president, expecting to submit himself to dogmatic professors in the German mold who were certain they held all the answers. Instead, he was excited to discover teachers who—acting upon the belief that reality was finite and knowable—were tentative and pluralistic in their approach. In various of the essays collected here, he honors the university as an institution "selflessly and disinterestedly given over to learning without regard for practical ends or profit," passionately committed to the freedom to study important matters "according to one's best lights," and open to the exhilarating conflict and controversy that are necessary to stimulate serious thought. Hinting at a decline in the quality of education since his own student days, Shils abhors the progressive dumbing-down, compromising of standards, and politicization within the academy.

While not focusing specifically upon culture wars and curricular debates, Shils's largely laudatory treatment of Robert Hutchins does bear implicitly on those issues, since he (with strong support from Mortimer Adler of "Great Books" fame) resisted disciplinary specialization and organized the first two years of the undergraduate experience around intensive study of primary texts, intent on stressing the unity, rather than the fragmentation, of all knowledge. Although Hutchins appointed black scholars to his faculty and courageously supported those teachers accused of being fellow travelers, he came to resist departmental autonomy and faculty governance; surprisingly, he also—except for the neo-Aristotelian "Chicago Critics" within English—allowed the humanities to decay. Many of Shils's "portraits" might aptly be called "paradoxes" or "double exposures," exploring as they do such inconsistencies and ambiguities in character.

Shils himself was broadly educated; he particularly admired the writings of Samuel Johnson and Joseph Conrad and calls it "an act of intellectual grace" when one of his professors who is profiled here, the economic historian John Nef, writes T. S. Eliot's name on the blackboard one day, reflecting Shils's own commitment to the popular dispersal of culture and ideas. (The highly cultivated Nef, however, also displayed what amounted to a miniature art museum on his dining room walls.) Epstein, who was Shils's close friend for more than twenty years, claims that Arnaldo Momigliano, an expert in Greco-Roman and Judaic history, was his mentor's only intellectual peer. Shils, however, would probably hesitate to name himself in the same breath as the man he considered perhaps the greatest scholar of any age, rivaling Dutch historian Johan Huizinga and Italian philosopher Benedetto Croce for international renown. Momigliano sought out evidence, was skeptical of theories, and eschewed claims of certainty. His belief that truth about the past is attainable and that, consequently, "reliably true propositions" can be asserted puts him squarely in the midst of crucial debates about the validity of text- or narrative-based history.

Momigliano, like Shils, was Jewish, though he suffered much more for his ethnic heritage. Dismissed from his university position in Turin in the late 1930's, he went to Oxford and then to London before coming to Chicago as a visiting professor after his retirement; eleven members of his family, including his parents, died in the concentration camps. If his uprooting from his homeland proved fortunate intellectually, providing him a scholarly arena he might otherwise have lacked, exile for another of Shils's subjects and another refugee from the Nazi regime, Karl Mannheim, was academically catastrophic, since it left him without close colleagues to sustain him in his work. A number of the men Shils writes about were, in fact, displaced European scholars and researchers forced by reason of birth or political persuasion to exist as outsiders. For example, Leopold Labedz, an insatiable reader who became editor of *Survey: A Journal of East and West Studies*, was born in Poland, where he witnessed anti-Semitic attacks at the university, studied at the Sorbonne, lived in Russia, finally settled in England, and—though a supporter of dissident writers in the Soviet Union—became a Cold War critic of East-West détente. At the opposite end of the spectrum sits the famed physicist and molecular biologist Leo Szilard, author of *The Voice of the Dolphins*. A participant in early experiments on nuclear fission, he later opposed using the bomb and became an activist for civilian control of atomic energy and an advocate of disarmament, which could only be founded upon a comprehensive settlement of the differences between the two superpowers.

As a social philosopher, Shils taught Georg Wilhelm Friedrich Hegel and Thomas Hobbes and Alexis de Toqueville, was a disciple of Max Weber, and an admirer, though not totally uncritical, of John Dewey. In his intellectual minibiography of Sidney Hook—the bookish Jewish boy who grew up to attend City College (the "poor boy's Oxbridge") and become the first American academic to publish scholarly books on Karl Marx, Friedrich Engels, and Vladimir Ilich Lenin—Shils describes Dewey's thought as levelheaded, rational, questioning, nondogmatic, and generous to those who disagree with one's own position, thus open to considering new data and alternative theories in the light of reason. In his consideration of Hook, Shils raises the issue of the participation by teachers and scholars in polemical debate and political affairs outside the academy, finally judging that it was "good" for him to take an active role in American public life.

Raymond Aron, a contemporary of Jean-Paul Sartre and Maurice Merleau-Ponty who criticized the Gaullist position on Israel and French colonial policy in Algeria, was another "publicistic" academic who excelled in occasional journalistic pieces for the intelligent layman and whose influence thus extended well beyond academic sociology and the ivory tower. Since Aron was an early apologist for Max Weber, writing about him allows Shils to delineate the essential nature of Weber's methodology and of his "ethics of responsibility," which demands an "unflinching effort to discover and accept [even] disagreeable truths" as well as a recognition of "the limited range of possibilities of action and the costs as well as benefits of any action," while presupposing the freedom to act.

Although it might seem surprising for Bellow to have singled out as at the very center of Chicago's intelligentsia a man whose name few people outside his academic specialization would recognize, Shils himself is well aware of the vagaries of reputation and renown, as is clear from his well-balanced handling of the career of Harold Laski, another victim of anti-Semitism who denounced the Nazis and became a Zionist during World War II. An anticapitalist and anti-imperialist, and a proponent of collectivist socialism-with-civil liberties, Laski, along with being fully engaged in political activity outside the university, was a longtime professor of political science at the London School of Economics and probably the most prominent Anglo-American academic of his generation; yet today awareness of him has all but disappeared from the intellectual scene—which Shils attributes to a lack of hard thought and a tendency to recycle ideas from earlier books in new forms—though he remained a master teacher.

Given Shils's reputed love for the ethnic mix and variety that, among other things, endeared Chicago to him, what comes as perhaps the greatest surprise in these pages is his apparently sanguine acceptance of the retrograde imperialist sympathies of the Indian author Nirad Chaudhuri, a disaffected academic who published his second volume of autobiographical memoirs at age ninety and who, along with Aron and others, is praised for the courage and indomitability that Shils seems to value above all else. Never himself subject to maltreatment at the hands of the colonizers, Chaudhuri exonerates the British for behaving badly, attributing it to fear and racial prejudice. Because he considered the Indian national character itself as somehow degenerate and thus open to subjugation, and because he believed the appeal of Indian nationalist movements, such as that led by Mohandas Gandhi, to be xenophobic and irrational, Chaudhuri actually favored increased British military might to prevent the calamity he thought inevitable were too much power to be vested in the hands of the people. Not only did he believe that Westernization, while at times vulgar and superficial, was inevitable, but he also thought that Indian society had become so dormant spiritually and creatively that it could only be reanimated by domination and find renewed vitality under Western influence. Political oppression was for him apparently a small sacrifice in order to bring about intellectual and cultural emancipation. For refusing to "run with the mob" and accept the "currently fashionable," Shils somewhat inexplicably judges him as transcending parochialism and rejecting the notion of setting up a "they"—though Chaudhuri's "Other" would appear to be his fellow countrymen who fought for nationalism.

Such occasional myopia notwithstanding, from these reminiscences taken as a whole, Shils emerges as an intellectual of the old school who values the traditions of the past, who is committed to reason, the authority of facts, and the pursuit of truth, but who is fully aware that certainty is hard to come by and that all social and political institutions have their limitations. Because he seeks in his subjects evidence of those things he himself values, there is a certain redundancy in the ideas and a lack of flavor in the writing: The individualizing voice of his subjects is seldom heard, and there are too few telling details—such as Szilard's lunchtime passion for onion rings and heavily sweetened buttermilk consumed at a popular student dive. In that regard, Epstein's lengthy memoir of Shils himself remains the most consistently colorful and affecting, though he does a serious editorial disservice to Shils's readers by not providing the dates or indicating the occasions for which these often fascinating biographical essays were originally composed.

Thomas P. Adler

Sources for Further Study

American Sociologist. XXVII, Winter, 1996, p. 61.
Kirkus Reviews. LXV, April 1, 1997, p. 536.
New Scientist. CLIV, June 14, 1997, p. 43.
The Wall Street Journal. July 21, 1997, p. A20.

PURPLE AMERICA

Author: Rick Moody (1961-)
Publisher: Little, Brown (New York). 298 pp. $23.95
Type of work: Novel
Time: Friday evening through Saturday morning in November, 1992
Locale: Fenwick, Connecticut, and its suburban environs on Long Island Sound

Called to the aid of his terminally ill mother upon her desertion by her second husband, a hapless alcoholic son enters upon a weekend of escalating chaos

Principal characters:
> ALLEN RAITLIFFE, a World War II nuclear scientist turned entrepreneur who dies suddenly in late 1963
> BARBARA "BILLIE" RAITLIFFE, his widow, who has an immobilizing neurological disorder
> DEXTER "HEX" RAITLIFFE, their son, a lonely freelance public relations agent
> LOU SLOANE, Billie's second husband, whose forced early retirement and mental exhaustion after fifteen years of marriage to Billie prompt his abrupt departure
> JANE INGERSOLL, a thirty-eight-year-old single mother and onetime obsession of the teenage Dexter

Purple America marks a new level of accomplishment for Rick Moody, who won the 1992 Pushcart Prize and has been regularly cited as among the most gifted writers of his generation. Moody himself regards *Purple America* as a deliberate corrective to his critical reputation as an essentially cerebral artist. He does not relish having been dubbed the heir apparent to John Updike and John Cheever as the chronicler of what one reviewer calls "the psychedelic twilight of the suburbs." While Moody identifies himself as a "late modern" writer, his literary mannerisms—a baroque rhetorical style, a trenchant eye for the revelatory minutiae of consumer culture, and an acerbic, at times cartoonish, rendering of the physical and psychological indignities of the contemporary human condition—recall the postmodern extravagances of Thomas Pynchon and Don DeLillo. Yet alongside its dazzling linguistic display and comic audacity, *Purple America* evinces a deeply felt compassion for its characters.

The novel unfolds along two narrative tracks, one involving the catastrophic illness of Billie Raitliffe Sloane, the other documenting the escalating breakdowns and resultant spills of an aging nuclear power plant until recently supervised by Billie's second husband, Lou Sloane. Both stories illustrate the desperate, largely futile efforts made by modern society to stave off the ravages of time on humans and machines alike.

Allen Raitliffe, Billie's first husband, had worked on the new weaponry that had ended World War II and initiated the Cold War. Having been present in 1946 at a "minor" laboratory accident that proved fatal to at least one friend, and having witnessed the devastating effects of nuclear testing in the Pacific later that same year, Allen left to invest in the newly prosperous industry of uranium mining. Neither his subsequent infertility nor his sudden death at age thirty-nine is directly tied to those earlier experiences, but there is a gnawing possibility of a cause-and-effect relationship.

Moody tells his tale through a choir of voices, each chapter situated within the perspective of one of the four major characters; a fifth voice is provided to the deceased Allen by the inclusion of several letters written to Billie early in their marriage. All these voices are suspended within the medium of a third-person narrative sensibility that knows more than the characters themselves and regularly drops hints of the consequences attendant upon their choices.

The precipitating event of the narrative is a temporary failure of love: Billie's impersonal abandonment by Lou, who is unable to endure her growing despondency. His desertion stirs Billie to use a despised computer voicing system to summon her only child, thirty-eight-year-old Dexter (Hex), to her eccentrically appointed New England home.

In his own way, Hex is as much a wreck as his mother. A severe alcoholic, he is also emotionally isolated and suffers from a stutter. Once he absorbs the news of Lou's departure, Hex expects to be asked to replace Lou as the mainstay of Billie's care; instead, he learns that she seeks his help not to get on with her life but to end it. The paradox of Billie Raitliffe is that despite the sack of inert bones and spastic muscle in which she lives, she is by far the most acutely sensitive and expressive of Moody's characters, keenly attuned to and appreciative of the pleasures to be had in language, sensation, and human affection. It was exactly that quality that prompted Lou's eagerness to marry her some fifteen years earlier despite her advancing disease.

Glimpses of Lou's earlier tenderness in assuming the most unromantic of tasks (catheterizing and diapering his wife, for example) are matched by equally affecting reminders of the couple's continuing responsiveness to each other long past the point of "normal" sexual engagement. This blending of sexual love and spousal devotion documents the tenacity of human desire.

Another unusual form of sexual love results when Hex takes his mother for a disastrous night out and unexpectedly encounters Jane Ingersoll, a woman with whom he had been infatuated in high school. She has become a single mother of two, outfitted in sufficiently punk fashion to announce her wariness of further attachments. Initially Jane proves as indifferent to Hex as she had been twenty years earlier, for the erstwhile Young Republican misfit of the past is now even less appealing, given his considerable bulk, thick glasses, speech impediment, and general ineptitude. Nevertheless, Jane's compassionate nature increasingly embroils her in Hex's neediness. Their physical relationship becomes even less conventional than that of the Sloanes, for while one of the most delightful sections of the narrative describes the repertoire of kissing techniques the two command, their activity climaxes in Hex's retreat into masturbation as he regards a loosely bound Jane lying on the bottom level of a bunk bed in his childhood bedroom. Yet Jane's empathy deepens into forgiveness, an expression of the grace that undergirds Moody's worldview.

The novel's most lyric evocation of emotional bonds celebrates the love between mother and child. In a work rife with satiric barbs, a heartfelt conversation about motherhood between Billie and Jane is rendered totally without irony. Jane asks, "Do you always think of yourself as a mother now? When do boys begin to resist their mothers for good? Did you ever find that your training as a mom was finally over?"

In a long, whispered monologue, Billie sets forth the contradictory truths that characterize this most intense and irrational of ties:

> You declare them adults . . . whether they want to be or not. . . . The ones that don't get pushed out of the nest . . . love you the most . . . and hurt you worst . . . leave you anyway . . . and you'll get used to the stretches of loneliness . . . and that's when you know you don't want to be merely a mother . . . though a mother is the best thing you have been.

The conversation, occurring halfway through the novel, reframes the provocative opening chapter, comprised mainly of a single four-page sentence describing in biblically inflected prose Hex's act of bathing his helpless mother and coming to know her twisted body more intimately than at any time since his unthinking gestation inside her womb. The comically rendered Freudian overtones of such a moment are inescapable, but Moody also raises the philosophical conundrum such circumstances present:

> Whosoever knows the folds and complexities of his own mother's body, he shall never die . . . whosoever weeps over his mother's condition while bathing her . . . whosoever has formulated a simple gratitude for the fact that *he still has a mother*, but who has nonetheless wondered at the kind of astral justice that has immobilized her thus . . . *he shall never die*.

How, Moody repeatedly asks, do individuals move beyond solipsism and narcissism, beyond their own wounds and appetites and prejudices, to touch the hearts and minds of other individuals, even those for whom they have the deepest feeling? Among its other themes, *Purple America* dramatizes the daunting obstacles that thwart true communication. Billie's powerful sensibility can find an outlet in only the most garbled and incoherent of voices, for her body imprisons her spirit and denies her intimate contact on all levels. Lou's desertion forces her to confront her metaphysical condition. Unable to speak clearly except through a synthesized woman's voice, she falters: "Oh Hex, I am alone."

Similarly, Hex's intrusive stutter turns his every effort to communicate into an alienating ordeal. Unlike his mother, he lacks the rich inner resources that might provide some compensation for his isolation. Throughout the first two-thirds of this day in Connecticut, Hex consumes one drink after another and renders himself steadily less able to manage the escalating challenges he faces: his mother's apparent seizure in the restaurant; his feckless showdown with Lou; his abortive sexual consummation with Jane; his rental car's immolation. If Billie's loss of Lou, the only sure audience for what remained of her voice and her spirit, focuses her death wish, Hex's inability to hear anyone else—even the "adored" mother who has always been the center of his universe—finally unmoors him altogether. Alone with Billie and suffering a severe hangover, he experiences an epiphany:

Hex Raitliffe prays the Great American Prayer . . . the prayer of infants, though to whom he prays
is unclear. . . . G-g-get me out of this, get me out of this one fix, I'll do anything.

Hex's motives are thoroughly ambiguous as he prepares a sleeping-pill cocktail
from the prescriptions Billie has been hoarding. When that measure does not kill her,
he descends into the realm of Grand Guignol and resorts to pillows and plastic bags,
but these also fail to extinguish Billie's vitality. Finally, Hex procures a weapon, only
to be distracted from his mission by the sudden arrival of Lou, Jane, and a police officer
who intends to investigate the matter of the gutted rental car. In the ensuing melee,
"what Dexter Raitliffe has looked for, meanwhile, has come to pass, and he doesn't
know it."

With Billie's death, her consciousness abruptly disappears from the text, as does
Dexter himself, fleeing over a golf course and shedding his clothes even as he sheds
his fantasy of a life with Jane.

The novel does not end on that antic note, however, but with a letter written to Billie
forty-six years earlier by Allen, then observing nuclear weapons testing in the Pacific.
Allen's understated horror at the destructive capabilities of these bombs moves the
text beyond the idiosyncratic stories of Raitliffe mother and son and into the larger
historical canvas against which they have unfolded. In this way, Moody suggests that
a pervasive human death wish operates within the culture both on the societal and the
personal level.

Thus the latest incident at the power plant, although far less dramatically realized
than the family saga, is crucial to Moody's thematic ends. The plant serves as a
reminder of the ominous pact Americans have made with forces that threaten the life
of the planet, and the mask of benign accommodation with the ruptured atom is ripped
away by its failure to protect the populace from its own contamination. Connecticut
Power and Light also demonstrates the true cost of bourgeois prosperity, which relies
on round-the-clock consumption.

The novel's title operates on many levels. In keeping with the operatic passion that
Moody has identified as one of his aesthetic models, the color purple invites associations with royalty, death, and high-flying prose. Purple is the color the vibrant Billie
chose in the 1950's to decorate her new home in the suburbs. It is the color the "purple
bruise of [Hex's] personality," p's posing special difficulty for his stutter. Finally, it is
the startlingly beautiful color of the atomic explosions Allen witnessed in a more
innocent time—one forever lost in the residue of that purple glow.

Barbara Kitt Seidman

Sources for Further Study

Booklist. XCIII, March, 1997, p. 1277.
Chicago Tribune. May 11, 1997, XIV, p. 5.

Elle. April, 1997, p. 122.
Kirkus Reviews. LXV, February 1, 1997.
Library Journal. CXXII, February 15, 1997, p. 163.
Los Angeles Times Book Review. April 20, 1997, p. 12.
The New York Times Book Review. CII, April 27, 1997, p. 7.
Newsweek. CXXIX, April 28, 1997, p. 78.
Publishers Weekly. CCXLIV, March 31, 1997, p. 46.
Time. CXLIX, April 14, 1997, p. 89.
The Washington Post. April 8, 1997, p. B2.

THE PUTTERMESSER PAPERS

Author: Cynthia Ozick (1928-   )
Publisher: Alfred A. Knopf (New York). 236 pp. $23.00
Type of work: Novel
Time: Late twentieth century
Locale: New York City

> *Ruth Puttermesser—a lawyer, a bureaucrat in a city department, and, finally, the mayor of New York—searches for satisfaction in a career and for love and companionship in a relationship reminiscent of George Eliot's, but, as she reaches old age and death, she has found neither*

> *Principal characters:*
> RUTH PUTTERMESSER, a Jewish lawyer living in New York City
> XANTHIPPE, Puttermesser's creation, a golem
> MORRIS RAPPOPORT, Puttermesser's former lover
> RUPERT RABEENO, a painter who specializes in duplicating the works of the masters

Cynthia Ozick—a distinguished novelist, short story writer, playwright, poet, essayist, literary critic, and translator—has collected, in *The Puttermesser Papers*, two short stories and three novellas that have appeared in *The Atlantic Monthly*, *The New Yorker*, and *Salmagundi* over the past fifteen years. The story "Puttermesser: Her Work History, Her Ancestry, Her Afterlife" and the novella "Puttermesser and Xanthippe" have also been published in Ozick's *Levitation: Five Fictions* (1982). All center on Ruth Puttermesser—her name translates as "butterknife"—as she attempts to make sense out of her life.

The first section, "Puttermesser: Her Work History, Her Ancestry, Her Afterlife," relates, in a few pages, those things listed in the title. Puttermesser, in her thirties, realizes that, while others are being promoted in the law firm where she has been employed for a few years, she, a woman and a Jew, will not be promoted; she leaves, taking the position of assistant corporation counsel for the city's Department of Receipts and Disbursements. Again the top positions are denied her, this time because of political patronage. Although her days are spent in the grayness of a bureaucracy, her evenings are enriched by her imagination. She envisions being in paradise, sitting with fudge on one side and a stack of books on the other indulging her desire to study everything from anthropology to chemistry to Roman law. In reality, she studies Hebrew with Uncle Zindel, or so the reader is led to believe until the narrator cries out, "Stop, stop! Puttermesser's biographer, stop! Disengage, please. Though it is true biographies are invented, not recorded, here you invent too much." The truth (or is it?) is that her uncle died long ago; in fact, Puttermesser has never met him. Likewise, her sister is also an invention. Living by herself in the Bronx apartment of her youth, Puttermesser, her parents having retired in Florida, is lonely, and she replaces reality with fantasy. The chapter concludes with the question: "Hey! Puttermesser's biographer! What will you do with her now?"

The answer, elect her mayor of New York City, is found in the next section, "Puttermesser and Xanthippe." However, Puttermesser cannot accomplish this alone.

The chapter opens with the end of her love affair with Morris Rappoport, occasioned because Puttermesser, now forty-six, prefers finishing Plato's *Theaetetus* to making love. This is not her only loss: There is also the loss of bone around her teeth, signaling advanced periodontal disease; her Bronx apartment is destroyed by arson, resulting in the loss of childhood memorabilia; and she will soon lose her position with the Department of Receipts and Disbursements. Thinking herself indispensable because of her vast knowledge of the workings of the department, she is unprepared for her displacement by her boss's college crony. She is demoted, with a corresponding pay cut, to Taxation. She dreams of a city where merit is the basis of appointment and promotion and where employees are educated, prepared, and diligent in their jobs.

Although Puttermesser accepts her unmarried state, she regrets the absence of children, a desire that leads to an extraordinary event: the creation of a golem. As represented in Jewish mythology, golems are voiceless, continually grow, and eventually must be destroyed. Puttermesser, using the dirt from her flower pots and performing ancient rituals, fashions a golem, a creature who, although newly formed, knows all that Puttermesser does and who will do Puttermesser's bidding. Naming herself Xanthippe, the golem protests, in writing, when Puttermesser assigns her domestic chores, arguing that her capabilities are great. The next day, the golem, accompanying Puttermesser to Taxation, follows Puttermesser's injunction to look busy by typing industriously. The pages that she types are later to be revealed as a plan for the "Resuscitation, Reformation, Reinvigoration & Redemption of the City of New York," thoughts formulated by Puttermesser but recorded by Xanthippe. A memo from her former boss arrives requesting information on everything from a list of the city's bank depositories to the procedure for stocking toilet paper in the washrooms, information deemed crucial to the functioning of his department. Puttermesser responds with a memo questioning why she was replaced. The next day, for the first time in ten years, she arrives late and is soon confronted with three additional memos: the first reprimanding her for refusing to provide information, the second for being tardy, and the third firing her.

Puttermesser is out of a job, but not for long. The golem exists for one purpose: "So that my mother should become what she was intended to become," which is mayor of New York City. Puttermesser's vision of "New York washed, reformed, restored," already set forth in the document typed by Xanthippe, can now be realized. With Xanthippe's aid, she is elected, and the period that ensues represents a paradise for New York: The gangs are disbanded, venereal disease disappears, and robberies are nonexistent, all of which is achieved with the guidance of the golem. However, the paradise cannot last. The fall is precipitated when the golem discovers sex, occasioned by a visit from Rappoport. Xanthippe, abandoning her duties as adviser to Puttermesser, searches out lovers in the administration, who, exhausted, soon quit. The city returns to its former squalor and Puttermesser, as the mayor, is ruined. The golem, two years into her existence, is out of control. As a creature of mud, she cannot procreate, but she "yearns hugely after the generative, the fructuous." Reports abound of her attacking and seducing the captain of the Staten Island ferry and of her ravishing the president of the Chase Manhattan Bank.

Realizing she must uncreate the golem, Puttermesser recruits Rappoport, who awakened desire in the golem, as a snare, promising him the head of the department of his choice (her first political appointment, underscoring her decline). When the golem is lured back to her bed, Puttermesser reverses the rituals that bestowed life on her even though Xanthippe pleads in a newly found voice, "O my mother! Do not send me to the elements," echoing her earlier request at her creation, "Do not erase, obliterate, or annihilate me." Afterwards, Puttermesser has the resulting mound of dirt removed from her residence and buried, surrounded by red geraniums, in a city park.

In the third section, "Puttermesser's Paired," Puttermesser, now in her fifties and unemployed, is engrossed in a world of literature, "waiting for life to begin to happen." She longs for a relationship, "a wedding of like souls," of the kind that the Victorian novelist George Eliot experienced with George Lewes. One evening, Puttermesser, in delivering pizza mistakenly brought to her apartment, finds herself at a typical party replete with meaningless conversations. Escaping, she encounters her ideal mate, a young man wearing a cape who belonged in the Victorian era. Ignored, she realizes "youth is for youth." However, on an excursion to the Metropolitan Museum in search of a new reading place, she discovers him making an exact copy of a painting. In the ensuing conversation, he insists, however, that what he does is not a copy but a reenactment.

Thus begins her relationship with Rupert Rabeeno, their time spent reading the fiction of George Eliot to each other. Just as Rabeeno duplicates the art of the great masters, she, although aware that she is twenty years his senior, yearns to duplicate the relationship of Eliot and Lewes. While Puttermesser envisions herself as Eliot and Rabeeno as Lewes, he sees Johnny Cross as his model. Cross, twenty years younger than Eliot, married Eliot eighteen months after Lewes's death. On the day that Puttermesser and Rabeeno marry, he leaves, creating a version of Cross's hurtling himself out of the window on his honeymoon.

The next section, "Puttermesser and the Muscovite Cousin," charts the arrival in New York of Lidia, the granddaughter of Puttermesser's father's sister. Now in her sixties, Puttermesser, remembering her father's grief concerning the family he left in Russia, agrees to help Lidia, who, she believes, is as politically and religiously oppressed as her other Russian relatives had been. To Lidia, however, America is a business opportunity. Eager for dollars, she cleans apartments, cares for children, and peddles Vladimir Lenin medals and other Russian trinkets. After amassing several thousand dollars, she returns to Russia and her boyfriend.

The final section, "Puttermesser in Paradise," mixes the surreal with the realistic. As it happens, Puttermesser, now almost seventy, is thinking of paradise moments before she is brutally murdered by a robber angered over her lack of valuable possessions and, after having died, is then raped. The reader follows her to heaven. Mistaken in her earlier conception of paradise, Puttermesser learns that she will not read and study because, in paradise, all is already known. She discovers that paradise is within herself and is dependent upon her experiences and her imagination. Reliving her past ("Not the record of her life as she had lived it, but as she had failed to live it"), she rewrites the history of her first love. Instead of being intimidated and ultimately ignored by Emil, she marries him and has a child. In paradise, however, "nothing is permanent. Nothing will stay. All is ephemeral." She understands that "a dream that flowers only to be undone will bring more misery than a dream that has never come true at all. . . . The secret meaning of Paradise is that it too is hell." Puttermesser, in life, has found no happiness nor delight in family, friends, mythical creatures, or employment; even literature fails her when she tries to pattern her life after Eliot's. In death, she concludes, "Better never to have loved than loved at all./ Better never to have risen than had a fall."

In *The Puttermesser Papers*, Ozick paints a bleak picture of New York and, perhaps, of all city environments: "the poor lurked and mugged, hid in elevators, shot drugs into their veins, stuck guns into old grandmothers' tremulous and brittle spines, in covert pools of blackness released the springs of their bright-flanked switchblades, in shafts, in alleys, behind walls, in ditches." The city is overrun by vandals, arsonists, and rapists. The inhabitants are self-centered, unsympathetic, and uncaring. Although there is no joy, humor pervades the novel, such as in the portrayal of the inner workings of the city administration (based on the experiences of Ozick's friends) or in the description of the foibles of the deftly drawn characters. For example, Puttermesser's boss at Taxation believes he has been maligned in a novel solely because the protagonist also wears "bow ties and saddle shoes." Her advice sought, Puttermesser encourages his interest in a lawsuit because she "believed in the uses of fancy."

Ozick is often praised for her use of language, and rightly so. In *The Puttermesser Papers*, the reader finds elegant prose with carefully constructed sentences and rich descriptions. She writes as a poet would, understanding the importance of each word. Her fiction is indebted to her Jewish upbringing. Jewish myths, traditions, speech patterns, religious practices and customs, and historical experiences find their place in her fiction. The themes, however, are universal and resonate in all readers.

Barbara Wiedemann

Sources for Further Study

Booklist. XCIII, May 15, 1997, p. 1561.
Chicago Tribune. July 20, 1997, XIV, p. 3.
Library Journal. CXXII, May 15, 1997, p. 104.
Los Angeles Times Book Review. June 15, 1997, p. 2.
National Review. XLIX, September 1, 1997, p. 50.
The New York Times Book Review. CII, June 15, 1997, p. 14.
The New Yorker. LXXIII, December 15, 1997, p. 152.
Publishers Weekly. CCXLIV, April 21, 1997, p. 58.
San Francisco Chronicle. May 25, 1997, p. REV3.
Village Voice. XLII, July 15, 1997, p. 51.
The Wall Street Journal. June 20, 1997, p. A16.

QUESTIONING THE MILLENNIUM
A Rationalist's Guide to a Precisely Arbitrary Countdown

Author: Stephen Jay Gould (1941-   )
Publisher: Harmony Books (New York). 190 pp. $17.95
Type of work: Essays

A scientist reflects on the meaning of a millennium, its end and starting points, and its importance

Stephen Jay Gould is no millenarian. In *Questioning the Millennium*, he neither anticipates nor debunks the advent of a new age of prosperity and peace. Rather, the preeminent Harvard paleontologist and author of *The Panda's Thumb* (1980) and *Full House* (1996) here directs his discriminating mind and great storytelling ability to the historic and scientific significance of units of one thousand years.

Although he writes at the end of the twentieth century and at the end of the second millennium, the scholar Gould offers here no prognostications about life in the twenty-first century and in the third millennium. He is interested in neither scientific prophecy nor science fiction. Nor does he try to explain the psychological forces that often make issues of calendar and millennium matters of religious debate and fanaticism about the end of the world. Tragedies like the Xhosan revolt in South Africa in 1857, the 1890 massacre at Wounded Knee, the rebellion of John Chilembwe in Nyasaland (now Malawi) in 1915, and even the Heaven's Gate mass suicide in 1997 provide a context for Gould to examine the apocalyptic vision in which mass religious hysteria flourishes.

As he suggests in his subtitle, *A Rationalist's Guide to a Precisely Arbitrary Countdown*, Gould approaches the topic of millennia scientifically and focuses on the issues of time organization, astronomy, and history as they pertain to calendars, especially the Christocentric calendar on which millennium countdowns are based. In particular, Gould reflects on three questions that provide an organizational structure for *Questioning the Millennium*. What does the word "millennium" mean? When do millennia start and end? Why do humans consider such temporal transitions so significant?

In the first part of *Questioning the Millennium*, Gould explains how the word "millennium" has evolved from an apocalyptic to a calendric meaning. Starting from its Latin etymological meaning of a unit of one thousand years, the word originally referred to the Second Coming of Christ, which, according to many Christians, would herald a new blessed era of one thousand years followed by the end of the world and the Last Judgment. To reinforce this apocalyptic meaning of "millennium," Gould has incorporated into his book fifteen black-and-white illustrations of hell and judgment, including medieval manuscript illuminations, details from Michelangelo's painting of the Last Judgment in the Sistine chapel in the Vatican, and paintings by El Greco, William Blake, and Pablo Picasso.

Originally, Gould explains, the apocalyptic millennium had no special connection with years divisible by one thousand. Christian Montanists predicted the Second Coming in the second century A.D., the Anabaptist Thomas Müntzer considered the year 1525 fatal, and American preacher William Miller prophesied the end of the world in 1843-1844. Christians have particular reasons for calculating a coming apocalypse in terms of millennia. Working from the biblical tradition that one thousand years is equivalent to one day in the sight of God (Psalm 90:4 and 2 Peter 3:8) and that God created the world in six days (Genesis 1:1-2:1), early Christians concluded that human history would last six thousand years from the moment of creation until the Second Coming. The only question was the starting date, the date of creation. Here Gould cites a variety of Christian authorities who worked on this question in millennial terms. In A.D. 221, the Roman Sextus Julius Africanus calculated fifty-five hundred years to have passed since creation to the birth of Christ and predicted the Second Coming for A.D. 500. Just after A.D. 1000, a Christian monk named Raoul Glaber wrote of the imminent coming of Christ because a one-thousand-year period had passed since the time of Christ. In 1650, Archbishop James Ussher, the Anglican Primate of All Ireland, calculated the year of creation to be 4004 B.C. All these computations have in common the birth of Christ as the principal historical marker for counting back to creation and forward to an apocalyptic millennium. At the same time, Gould suggests, the birth of Christ also has encouraged the semantic transformation of "millennium" from a vision of Armageddon to a significant anniversary date. The apocalyptic millennium thus becomes a calendric commemoration of one-thousand-year intervals of time.

Or does it? In the next part of *Questioning the Millennium*, Gould addresses his second millennial question, namely, when millennia start and end. Here the date of the birth of Christ is, once again, an important focal point for the Christocentric calendar established in the sixth century by a monk named Dionysius Exiguus (Dennis the Short) and still in use today. In typical good humor, Gould notes that Dionysius' calendar placed Jesus' birth four years late; Jesus actually was born in the year 4 B.C., a fact that Ussher's creation date of 4004 B.C. acknowledges. Further, because Europeans lacked the concept of zero in the time of Dionysius, the Christian calendar moved directly from the year 1 B.C. to the year A.D. 1. Not only does this mean that the present calendar is probably five years behind the actual birth date of Jesus, but it also means that centuries and millennia must end with years ending in zero if they are to contain a full hundred or thousand years.

In his discussion of the endpoints of millennia and of the way recent century transitions have been marked, Gould resumes a debate he began in *Dinosaur in a Haystack* (1996). At daybreak on January 1, 1701, Samuel Sewall had four trumpeters herald the start of the eighteenth century on the Boston Common. Although some individuals, including Kaiser Wilhelm II of Germany, advocated welcoming the twentieth century at the beginning of 1900, no major newspapers and magazines of the period marked this occasion until January 1, 1901. Gould uses two journal pages to illustrate this point visually. In one, the British periodical *Nineteenth Century* renames itself *Nineteenth Century and After* with its issue of January, 1901, using a depiction of the two-faced Roman god Janus looking back to the old century as an old man and looking forward to the new century as a youth. In the other, the *Tribune Almanac* issue of January, 1901, proclaims itself the first issue of the twentieth century. Such fin de siècle markings are the legacy of Dionysius' calendar.

In the third part of *Questioning the Millennium*, Gould moves to his final question about the millennium, namely why it is so important for humans to measure time, especially in periods of one thousand years. Time is not easily organized into a calendar, as Gould illustrates by describing the complex rules under which various calendars have operated. Any calendar system, including those of Meso-America, Judaism, Islam, and Christianity, is an imperfect attempt to reconcile several distinct astronomical patterns, including the revolution of the earth on its axis, the phases of the moon, and the revolution of the earth around the sun.

The mathematical fit between day and month, and between month and year, is inexact and leads Gould to a historical discourse on the transition from the old Julian calendar to the present Gregorian one. In the first century B.C., Julius Caesar attempted to adjust the number of days in the yearly calendar to the estimated 365.25 days in the solar year by adding a "leap" day following February 28 in all years divisible by four. As Gould notes, the solar year is actually closer to 365.2422 days, so by the sixteenth century the Julian calendar was ten days fast. Pope Gregory XIII solved this discrepancy by eliminating October 5-14, 1582, and by making two important adjustments to the Julian system of leap years. First, the pope decreed that century years would no longer be leap years; hence, 1700, 1800, and 1900, though divisible by four, were not leap years. Even this fix was not enough. One additional rule was needed to synchronize the calendar with the solar year, namely that century years evenly divisible by four hundred would be leap years. As Gould notes, the year 2000 is distinctive, if not as a century and millennial marker, then as the first leap year evenly divisible by one hundred since A.D. 1600.

Ultimately, the scientist Gould finds the key to millennia in the human fascination with classification, especially in terms of significant numbers. Just as the natural world is organized taxonomically into genus and species, so units of time are defined in terms of seconds, minutes, hours, weeks, days, months, years, centuries, and millennia. The progression of these temporal units can be viewed in the optimistic linear fashion of an evolutionary biologist describing the origin of species as a process of survival of the fittest. Occasionally, however, time also is seen in a more cyclical fashion, in which history repeats itself and all things come around full circle. In articulating this sense of natural and temporal organization and direction, the human mind seeks a model in apparently significant numbers in the natural world, like the unisolar nature of our planetary system; the binary relationship of male and female; the tripling of proton, neutron, and electron; or the decades of human digits. Century and, especially, millennial changes are particularly significant in this regard and show how the concept of millennium reflects both the cyclical and linear views of time.

Gould's inquiry is personal as well as scholarly. *Questioning the Millennium* begins with the author's reactions, at the age of eight, to an article in the January, 1950, issue of *Life* magazine on the twentieth century at midpoint. The retrospectives and projections of this article were a defining experience for Gould and roused in him a lifelong fascination with the millennium. By publishing this article in January, 1950, instead of January, 1951, the editors of *Life* implicitly took a stand on the long-standing controversy of whether centuries start at the beginning or the end of years divisible by one hundred. Despite Dionysius' calendric calculations, which require centuries technically to begin with the year one and to include the years divisible by one hundred to reach arithmetic completion, psychologically, the century seems to turn with the latter rather than the former, that is, with the transition from years ending in 99 rather than 00. Scholarly consensus insisted on celebrating the beginning of the twentieth century in the mathematically correct year 1901, but Gould is convinced that popular consensus will insist on greeting the twenty-first century at the beginning of the year 2000 and will arbitrarily declare the twentieth century to be a century of only ninety-nine years (1901-1999).

Gould concludes *Questioning the Millennium* on a personal note, describing the uncanny ability of his autistic son to identify the day of the week on which any date in history falls. Such calculations are not easy. Because the 365-day year is not simply divisible by the seven-day week or the twelve-month year, a calendar date does not fall on the same day of the week every year; instead, it advances at least one day a year, two in leap years. Gould's son is one of a few mathematical geniuses who have managed ways to make such mental calculations swiftly and accurately. Unfortunately, autism has kept the younger Gould from explaining his method clearly to his scientist father. In the last chapter of *Questioning the Millennium*, Gould takes his readers on a personal quest to crack the code of his son's skill and to suggest ways that such day-date calculations can be accomplished. The need for seemingly complex calculations to determine such a basic aspect of time organization underscores for Gould not only the hidden genius of his autistic son and the arbitrary nature of the traditional calendar but also the inherent beauty of a complex universe that humankind struggles constantly to define and to understand. *Questioning the Millennium* is just one example of that perpetual effort.

Thomas J. Sienkewicz

Sources for Further Study

Boston Globe. November 3, 1997, p. C8.
Library Journal. CXXII, August, 1997, p. 123.
National Business Review. November 28, 1997, p. 48.
National Review. XLIX, September 15, 1997, p. 30.
The New York Times Book Review. CII, November 9, 1997, p. 9.
The New Yorker. LXXIII, October 20, 1997, p. 260.
Publishers Weekly. CCXLIV, July 28, 1997, p. 59.
The Spectator. CCLXXIX, November 15, 1997, p. 44.

RACHEL CARSON
Witness for Nature

Author: Linda Lear (1940-   )
Publisher: Henry Holt and Company (New York). 634 pp. $35.00
Type of work: Biography
Time: May 27, 1907-1960's
Locale: Eastern United States

A well-researched account of Rachel Carson's personal life, writing career, and influence in acquainting Americans with nature, especially the oceans, and the environmental hazards of pesticides

Principal personages:
RACHEL CARSON, American marine biologist and writer
MARIA CARSON, her mother
MARY SCOTT SKINKER, her undergraduate biology professor and mentor
MARIE RODELL, Carson's literary agent and executor
DOROTHY FREEMAN, Carson's closest friend
PAUL BROOKS, Carson's editor, adviser, and friend

Rachel Carson wrote two best-selling books that each were landmarks in science journalism. *The Sea Around Us* (1951) awakened American readers to the vast variety, beauty, and mystery of the oceans. *Silent Spring* (1962) warned that pesticides, if used irresponsibly, would harm wildlife and people. Neither subject was new to the public, but the depth of Carson's treatments and her stylish writing eclipsed books that came before hers, and she became one of America's best-known nonfiction authors.

How did such a triumph come about? What influences shaped her character and developed her writing skill? Carson's biographers, while recognizing her talent and appeal to readers, have been disappointingly vague about these key questions. Carson came to be perceived more as an environmentalist saint than as a person.

That has changed. Linda Lear's biography gives readers a full-fleshed, believable portrait of Carson. Lear creates this by amply supporting a simple thesis: "At the base of it all, there was a ferocious will." Lear interviewed Carson's surviving friends and family, closely examined her publications, and combed through many papers and letters not available to previous biographers. What emerged is not a cheery story. Given Carson's great family responsibilities and precarious finances, it seems that only with fierce willpower could she get any writing done.

Rachel Louise Carson was born on May 27, 1907, in Springdale, Pennsylvania, the youngest of three children. Her father was a rather ineffectual man who struggled to support the family. Her mother was the center of Carson's life. Maria Carson gave up a teaching career to marry and apparently regretted the loss of intellectual stimulus. She focused her considerable intelligence on her youngest child, and her direct influence was profound and lasting. With some gaps, the two lived together until her death in 1958, just six years before Rachel Carson herself died.

The mother instilled in her daughter a deep reverence for nature during frequent walks in the woods and encouraged her talents for drawing and writing. The efforts brought early success. Like other twentieth century literary stars, such as E. B. White, Rachel Carson began publishing stories in *St. Nicholas Magazine*, her first at the age of eleven.

Maria Carson insisted that her daughter attend the Pennsylvania College for Women, although the tuition severely strained family resources. At college, Rachel Carson was regarded as brilliant but standoffish; nevertheless, she made several friendships and attracted two mentors from the faculty. A salient theme of Lear's biography is Carson's need for spiritually close friendships with women as a means of bolstering her confidence and enriching her intellect. One mentor honed her writing. The second, biology professor Mary Scott Skinker, ignited Carson's enthusiasm for the sciences. Accordingly, Carson changed her major from English to biology, a turning point in her life.

Carson continued her studies at Johns Hopkins University, taking a master's degree in zoology in 1932, but the need to earn a living for herself and her family scuttled her bid for a doctorate. In the meantime, however, another turning point occurred. Carson won a fellowship for the summer of 1929 at Woods Hole Biological Laboratory on the Massachusetts coast. The sea had always fascinated her; during that summer, it captivated her. According to Lear, all three of Carson's sea books had their genesis at Woods Hole. It appears that Carson seldom loved things or people, but when she did, the attachment was extraordinarily strong.

Trying to find a college teaching job during the Depression, Carson was guaranteed to fail. Jobs were scarce, and men were preferred. Her fruitless efforts underscore another of Lear's major themes. Carson had to fight widespread biases about women, particularly that they lacked the right sort of intelligence to be scientists—or science writers. Carson tried freelance writing with some success. A third turning point in her life came when the division chief of the Bureau of Fisheries invited her to write public service film scripts and pamphlets. The part-time arrangement led to a full-time job. Carson eventually rose to become principal editor for the U.S. Fish and Wildlife Service before she resigned in 1952. It was a demanding job, but it brought her into contact with leading marine biologists and kept her current on scientific developments.

Carson had to put in a full day of writing at the bureau. When she went home, domestic demands from her mother, sister, and nieces, whom she supported, ate up her time. Still, during late evenings and early mornings, she drove herself to pursue her own writing projects. After a slow start, she placed an article in *Atlantic Monthly* in 1937, wrote on nature themes for newspapers, and published her first book, *Under the Sea-Wind*, in 1941. Critics praised the lyricism of her prose and the deftness with which she explained scientific matters to nonscientist readers while evoking the romance of the sea. Sales were poor, however. The beginning of World War II diverted the public.

Disappointed but not deterred, Carson started her second book, *The Sea Around Us*, with her prose style and exacting research habits fully developed. She worked painstakingly, wrote slowly, and rewrote tirelessly. Lear's discussions of Carson's work habits in writing this book and of her image-laden, sonorous style are astute and lucidly presented, and are among the most engrossing passages of the book. Readers with an interest in literary analysis may wish that Lear had provided even more analysis. Helped by other writers and her agent and friend, Marie Rodell, Carson attracted the attention of William Shawn, editor of *The New Yorker*. He serialized the book in three installments, and it became a sensation among America's intelligentsia. After the book was released, it stayed a best-seller for months and won the National Book Award.

Now a celebrity, Carson felt the confidence to express her philosophy of nature more forcefully. In her acceptance speech for the National Book Award, she criticized the growing elitism among scientists. She insisted that science must not be a specialized, self-contained world unto itself because it can teach people about matters that are a part of the reality of living, and its application in technology was increasingly shaping American life. This theme dominated her later writings, *Silent Spring* especially.

She issued the last of her sea books, *The Edge of the Sea*, in 1955. A sequel to *The Sea Around Us* that dealt with life on the shoreline, it sold well but did not match the pervious book's triumph.

Carson's personal life became more and more difficult through the 1950's. She never married because, according to Lear, her sister's disastrous marriage exposed the precarious nature of marriage and the harm of failed choices. The death of her sister left her responsible for her two nieces, one of whom had an illegitimate son. That niece died, and Carson reared the boy with her mother's help. When her mother died, after a long illness, Carson was worn thin and had difficulty finding time to write. At the same time, she was in great demand as a public speaker and had become prominent in environmental organizations, such as the Audubon Society.

The strain told on her, and she came close to a breakdown, but a new friendship appears to have revived her. The friend was Dorothy Freeman. As Lear movingly describes the developing relation between them, it sounds like Plato's ideal love: emotional openness based on mutual empathy and interests. Together, they concerned themselves with the dangers of technological society to the wilderness and animals. Carson especially perceived a threat to wildlife from commercial fertilizers and pesticides.

With the encouragement of her editor, Paul Brooks, she began research for what developed, after many delays and rewrites, into *Silent Spring*. *The New Yorker* serialized it, and the book became a best-seller, as had happened with *The Sea Around Us*. The response, however, was quite different: Controversy erupted, with scientists and pesticide manufacturers attacking Carson. Her carefully gathered evidence and thorough documentation left her argument impossible to ignore. The book revealed that pesticide manufacturers and users, such as the federal government, applied the poisons with little understanding of, or regard for, their effects on people and wildlife. She confirmed the accusations of environmentalists and alarmed the pesticide industry.

Lear devotes a quarter of the biography to Carson's post-*Silent Spring* life, a turbulent time. Lear's treatment is somewhat disappointing because it lacks balance in characterizing the controversy. Many scientists and pesticide manufacturers denounced Carson, the latter even banding together to hire a public relations agency to ease public fears created by the book. Lear often speaks of these efforts as if they were part of a conspiracy, with an insidious "establishment" arrayed against the lone Carson. Certainly, many of the attacks on her were spiteful and silly. She was dismissed as a mere spinster by the secretary of agriculture and frequently accused of being a Communist. Unfortunately, Lear cites the cranks, those with vested interests who tried to tar her reputation, and overreacting scientists far more often than those readers who raised thoughtful questions about the book. Many scientists joined Carson in her moderate suggestion that insecticides be used with great care, not abandoned, until researchers produced safer methods of pest control. At the same time, she was supported by environmental organizations that wielded considerable political power. Lear does mention such supporters, but she quotes the nincompoops and dwells on the establishment.

On the other hand, Lear shows that Carson attained a measure of heroic tragedy. Even before the book was finished, Carson was ill with breast cancer. In part because of a bungled diagnosis, Lear intimates, Carson had few respites from the pain. She nevertheless maintained a busy schedule of public speaking, including testimony before Congress and a presidential committee. These efforts, coupled with the public alarm created by the book, brought about a sea change in how Americans viewed the environment and the effects of science on their lives. Technological progress, and the economy based on it, she argued, could not be ends in themselves. Although not alone in sounding the theme, she carried the message home. Furthermore, despite the controversy, her illness, and her sad family life, Carson remained calm and dignified.

Carson died at the height of her fame and influence. Her affairs, unfortunately, were left in some confusion. She had not clarified who was to take over rearing her nephew, a task Brooks eventually undertook. Her brother burned some of her papers and quarreled with the literary executor, Rodell. These problems occupy Lear in the biography's closing pages. Readers may well wish to learn, instead, something of Carson's legacy—the effect of her testimony on pending environmental legislation and the long-term influence on American literature and outlook on nature.

Such small disappointments aside, Lear's book portrays Carson as humane, passionate in her ideas, brilliant in forging a prose style to convey the ideas and passion, and admirably resolute; her eloquence was much needed to give the nation perspective on its rapid technological development. More important, Lear helps readers understand how and why a scientist like Carson could become a witness for nature. For this reason, Lear's biography is a valuable contribution to the history of American science.

Roger Smith

Sources for Further Study

Atlanta Journal Constitution. September 28, 1997, p. L10.
Audubon. XCIX, September, 1997, p. 96.
Booklist. XCIII, August, 1997, p. 1862.
Boston Globe. September 21, 1997, p. E1.
Library Journal. CXXII, July, 1997, p. 94.
Los Angeles Times Book Review. September 21, 1997, p. 4.
The New York Times Book Review. CII, October 5, 1997, p. 18.
People Weekly. XLVIII, November 10, 1997, p. 41.
Publishers Weekly. CCXLIV, July 21, 1997, p. 190.
Time. CL, October 6, 1997, p. 97.
The Washington Post Book World. XXVII, September 14, 1997, p. 5.

RADICAL SON
A Generational Odyssey

Author: David Horowitz (1939-   )
Publisher: Free Press (New York). Illustrated. 468 pp. $27.50
Type of work: Autobiography
Time: 1939 to the 1990's

A powerful memoir of David Horowitz's political and spiritual evolution from Left to Right

Principal personages:
DAVID HOROWITZ, an American writer and journalist
BLANCHE HOROWITZ, his mother
PHILIP HOROWITZ, his father
ELISSA HOROWITZ, his wife
PETER COLLIER, his colleague
HUEY NEWTON, the leader of the Black Panther Party

David Horowitz's autobiography, *Radical Son: A Generational Odyssey*, may surprise many readers familiar with his recent work. As a right-wing journalist, Horowitz has maintained and even honed the combative style he learned as an editor of the radically leftist *Ramparts* in the 1960's. His new organ, *Heterodoxy*, offers slashing attacks on the "politically correct" in the intellectual and academic realms.

Yet Horowitz's no-holds-barred approach to journalism is notably absent in his memoir. The tone of *Radical Son* is altogether different from that of *Heterodoxy*, the Horowitz of the book a far cry from his journalistic persona. In part this is the inevitable result of the transition from newsprint to the more rarefied atmosphere of a hardcover book. Much more it is a measure of Horowitz's ambitions. *Radical Son* is meant to be much more than a routine reminiscence.

First and foremost, Horowitz's book is his *apologia pro vita sua*. In it, he attempts to understand and assess a lifelong journey which has seen the shattering of hopes once cherished and compelled him to repudiate ideals that once gave his life meaning. Yet Horowitz the former leftist has not embraced the vacuum of nihilism. A new faith has replaced the old, and he takes this opportunity to elucidate and justify his new convictions. To that extent, like the classical apologias of figures such as Saint Augustine and English theologian John Newman, *Radical Son* proselytizes even as it explains. Like its classical models, it is an effective instrument in advancing its cause.

Adding resonance to Horowitz's apologia is his penetrating account of his relationship with his mother and father. Horowitz's repudiation of the Left inevitably comprehended a break with the radicalism of his parents, both devoted communists. Much of Horowitz's book deals with his long effort to reach an understanding with his father, the poignancy of the gulf between son and father symbolizing in microcosm the distance he has traveled since his youth.

Horowitz is interested in the macrocosm as well. The "generational odyssey" of his title has twin meanings. It refers to his emergence from the world of his parents. It also refers to the larger generation of which Horowitz was a part. He believes that his story sheds light on the vagaries of the young radicals who captured the attention of the nation in the 1960's. Here Horowitz's book shades from memoir into history. With the asperity of a renegade he limns a devastating portrait of a generation blithely uprooting institutions and mores, and blind to its own folly. As Horowitz paints it, the trajectory of his movement from Left to Right is also the arc tracing the flowering and then the failure of 1960's radicalism. Thus *Radical Son* is many things—a personal testament, a family drama, and a generational chronicle. Ultimately, it is most powerful as a record of the salvation of a man and the decline of a movement.

Horowitz was literally born to the Left. His parents were members of the Communist Party, who faithfully adhered to the party line and labored in a variety of party causes. As a "cradle communist," Horowitz attended special party schools and even a summer camp for the children of party activists. At home, he grew up in a heady atmosphere of revolutionary idealism. He learned to mourn convicted communist spies Julius and Ethel Rosenberg as martyrs and to revere figures such as actor Paul Robeson (who was accused of being a communist during the Cold War) as heroes. The McCarthyite mood of the early 1950's touched Horowitz's home when both of his parents lost their jobs as high school teachers because of their Communist Party connections, though their pensions were later reinstated after a court action.

As Horowitz grew older, however, he began to question the simplistic Stalinist verities of his childhood faith. He became acquainted with friends and relatives who had sought alternate paths to the socialist goal. Events such as the Soviet invasion of Hungary and Nikita Khrushchev's 1956 indictment of the crimes of Joseph Stalin undermined Horowitz's once reflexive confidence in communism and the Soviet Union. Even his parents left the party, disillusioned with the bureaucrats who ran it. Yet if communism had lost its romance for Horowitz, socialism had not. He could not bring himself to give up on the dream of remaking humanity and society. As a young man, he cast about for ways to salvage the Left's project while avoiding the mistakes of an earlier generation of revolutionaries. His quest, and the quests of others like him, would result in the New Left movement of the 1960's.

Horowitz slipped almost effortlessly into the vanguard of the new wave of university leftists. He was in the right place at the right time, Berkeley in the early 1960's, doing graduate work in English. Horowitz joined a group of fellow "red diaper babies" who met regularly to discuss socialist ideas. This group put out one of the first radical student journals of the decade. They also organized the first demonstration against American policy in Vietnam and won notoriety for a noisy demonstration at a hearing of the House Committee on Un-American Activities (HUAC). Horowitz wrote a book about the HUAC demonstration which inspired Mario Savio, who later led the Free Speech movement at Berkeley.

Horowitz's growing engagement with political activity led to a disenchantment with his literary studies. He was ambitious to develop a new Marxian analysis of society that would preserve the truth of the Marxist vision while avoiding the authoritarian errors of the old Left. He wanted a humane and liberated Marxism, a Marxism which would be in harmony with the emerging spirit of the age. In 1962, Horowitz left

Berkeley and traveled to Europe with his wife and small child. He devoted himself to writing a series of books criticizing American Cold War policy. These were well received, and some became seminal New Left texts. Horowitz's growing reputation gained for him an entry into several intellectual circles, and in England he became an associate of such luminaries of the Left as Bertrand Russell and Isaac Deutscher.

On the strength of these labors, Horowitz was invited back to the United States in 1968 to help edit *Ramparts*, a fledgling radical journal which was rapidly becoming one of the premier voices of the New Left. Horowitz soon rose to be one of the guiding lights of *Ramparts*. He and his colleagues used the journal to wage what they regarded as a revolutionary struggle against the United States. They even went so far as to publish a story revealing that the National Security Agency had cracked the Soviet intelligence codes.

It was with this spirit of revolutionary enthusiasm that Horowitz became involved with the Black Panthers, and in particular with their leader Huey Newton. Horowitz chose to see the assertive, armed, and self-consciously militant Black Panthers as revolutionaries engaged in a joint struggle with other radicals against the oppressive forces of corporate, capitalistic, white "Amerika." He tried to ignore their violence and the aura of thuggery and criminality that imbued many of their activities. When the Black Panthers needed an accountant to put their party's books in order, Horowitz unhesitatingly recommended Betty Van Patter, a woman he had worked with before. He was horrified when, in 1974, Van Patter disappeared after questioning some suspicious accounts. Despite denials by the Black Panther leadership, Horowitz was convinced that Van Patter had been killed to keep her quiet about party secrets.

For Horowitz, the disappearance of Van Patter crystallized a process of disillusionment with the radical Left which had been building for some time. By the early 1970's, the radical movement was running out of steam. Various splinter groups were veering off in the pursuit of dead ends. Some, such as the Weather Underground, deteriorated into a violent revolutionary nihilism. Horowitz was also deeply uncomfortable with the glorification of the drug culture and sexual liberation that permeated the radical movement. He began to see the whole enterprise that he had been engaged in as a misguided exercise in narcissism, in which the self-regard of the so-called revolutionary was far more important than the consequences of his or her actions for others.

Horowitz then entered a period of transition and turmoil in his life. Letting go of the ideals that had sustained him through his life was not an easy process. Gradually, he found a new direction. A partnership with a fellow refugee from *Ramparts*, Peter Collier, produced a series of best-selling books on prominent American families such as the Rockefellers and Kennedys. Horowitz and Collier also began reevaluating their radical past in a string of publications, burning their bridges with their former associates but gaining a new and appreciative audience as the 1970's gave way to the 1980's. Horowitz voted for Ronald Reagan in 1980 and supported him throughout his presidency because of his staunch anticommunism. The launching of *Heterodoxy* in 1992 completed Horowitz's march to the Right.

Horowitz does not regard himself as an ideologue. He sees his conservatism as the wisdom born of experience. He believes human nature is impervious to ambitious schemes to reshape it. He regards the market as the best means of spurring enterprise and distributing wealth. Where once he had burned to promote equality, he is now more solicitous to preserve freedom. He places his ideas firmly in the tradition of the Founding Fathers, desirous of a government strong enough to protect, but not to oppress, the citizen, anxious for as much liberty for the individual as is consonant with the constraints of human character.

Declaring *Radical Son* a classic would be premature, but Horowitz's memoir is a compelling work. It joins a long line of American autobiographies recounting spiritual journeys. This book, earnest and sober, is a worthy contribution to this tradition.

Daniel P. Murphy

Sources for Further Study

Booklist. XCIII, January 1-January 15, 1997, p. 813.
The Christian Science Monitor. April 7, 1997, p. 13.
Commentary. CIII, June, 1997, p. 64.
Commonweal. CXXIV, May 23, 1997, p. 26.
Human Events. LIII, April 11, 1997, p. 12.
Los Angeles Times Book Review. February 9, 1997, p. 5.
The Nation. CCLXIV, February 17, 1997, p. 30.
The National Review. XLIX, March 24, 1997, p. 50.
The New Leader. LXXIX, December 16, 1996, p. 5.
The New York Times Book Review. CII, February 16, 1997, p. 34.
The Times Literary Supplement. August 1, 1997, p. 11.
The Wall Street Journal. February 3, 1997, p. A12.
The Washington Post Book World. XXVII, February 9, 1997, p. 3.

RAYMOND CHANDLER
A Biography

Author: Tom Hiney (1970-   )
First Published: 1997, in Great Britain
Publisher: Atlantic Monthly Press (New York). Illustrated. 310 pp. $26.00
Type of work: Literary biography
Time: 1859-1959
Locale: Mainly London and Los Angeles

This first new biography of Raymond Chandler in twenty years offers a well-written overview of a troubled life, with new material concerning the famous crime novelist's English public school career and twilight years in London

> *Principal personages:*
> RAYMOND THORNTON CHANDLER, the mystery writer
> CISSY CHANDLER, his adored wife, seventeen years his senior
> A. H. GILKES, the headmaster at Dulwich College
> PHILIP MARLOWE, Chandler's most famous literary creation and alter ego
> "CAP" JOSEPH SHAW, the editor of *Black Mask* magazine
> HAMISH HAMILTON, Chandler's British publisher and long-term
>   correspondent
> BILLY WILDER, the Hollywood director who taught Chandler
>   screenwriting
> HELGA GREENE, Chandler's agent and heir to his estate

Raymond Chandler died in La Jolla, California, in 1959. Tom Hiney, a London journalist, was not born until 1970. His English perspective and his youthful perspective on a much older American writer constitute both the strength and the weakness of his biography. He makes the reader realize how the British feel about Chandler and how the younger generation perceives him. Although Hiney is a competent writer, there is a strong feeling of geographical and chronological distance. Hiney seems most comfortable writing about Chandler's early years in England and his return visits to England before his death. When writing about American pulp magazines or Hollywood, or when trying to summarize Chandler's novels, Hiney sounds like an intelligent foreigner who has read a considerable amount about his subject but remains somewhat confused. When Hiney writes about Chandler's boyhood in Nebraska, for example, he draws on Frank L. Baum's *The Wonderful Wizard of Oz* (1899) for his description of the American Midwest. His only other information about life in that flat, agrarian environment is gleaned from remarks in Chandler's *The Little Sister* (1949) and *The Long Goodbye* (1953).

Hiney's short biography can hardly be called definitive. The reviewer for *The Times Literary Supplement* states correctly that "Frank McShane's excellent 1976 biography remains unrivalled." Hiney's book seems intended to stake a British claim to Raymond Chandler. It will be pleasing to some and exasperating to others that Hiney, representing a new generation of Chandler admirers, believes that "Chandler will outlive most other writers of this century."

Chandler had such a strange transatlantic early life that it is hard to classify him as either American or British. The British, no doubt, would like to claim him because he is extremely important in their country. Chandler was actually born in Chicago in 1888 but moved to England with his mother in 1895, after his father deserted them. He was educated in English schools and acquired English upper-class values.

Hiney devotes considerable space to a description of Dulwich College, where young Chandler studied French, German, and Spanish as preparation for a business career but also immersed himself in the Greek and Roman classics. A major influence in Chandler's early life was A. H. Gilkes, headmaster of Dulwich, who took the place of the young man's absentee father. Hiney thinks that Chandler's character was shaped by this eccentric, bearded giant, who stressed tradition, gentlemanly conduct, education, and morality.

The dynamic interrelationship between Chandler's elitist education and his exposure to the mean streets of America's cities accounts for the piquancy of his style. When Chandler began writing pulp fiction late in life, he needed the money but could not bring himself to write in the lowbrow vernacular characteristic of the pulps. Fortunately, "Cap" Joseph Shaw, editor of the famous *Black Mask* magazine, appreciated the superior literary values Chandler was subtly, somewhat mischievously, inserting into a hackneyed genre. Chandler admired Dashiell Hammett but could see what was lacking in Hammett's fiction—and even more conspicuously lacking in the works of the penny-a-word hacks. Hammett seemed to write in black and white, while Chandler wrote in color.

After being fired from the oil company where he had been an executive with a very comfortable income, Chandler was never free from financial worries until he began writing for the movies. His apprenticeship as cowriter with Billy Wilder on the adaptation of James M. Cain's *Double Indemnity* (1944) is well known. Chandler had mixed feelings about Hollywood. Essentially, he respected the film medium but not many of its practitioners. He wrote:

> An art which is capable of making all but the very best plays look trivial and contrived, all but the very best novels verbose and imitative, should not so quickly become wearisome to those who attempt to practice it with something else in mind than the cash drawer.

Like the reporter in Orson Welles's *Citizen Kane* (1941), Hiney, a professional journalist, goes over the well-worn trail of his subject's life but fails to identify what might be called the "Rosebud," the key that cracks the code. Like the viewer of *Citizen Kane*, however, the reader of *Raymond Chandler: A Biography* may see what the young reporter missed. What was it that drove Chandler to drink, and why did a mere crime writer become, as novelist Evelyn Waugh described him, "the greatest living American novelist"? What keeps Chandler's reputation alive while many other writers—including Sinclair Lewis, Upton Sinclair, John O'Hara, Thomas Wolfe, W. Somerset Maugham, George Bernard Shaw, and Aldous Huxley, to name only a few—are becoming names to which the younger generation reacts with almost no comprehension?

Chandler was a lonely man, a product of a dysfunctional family, a chronic malcontent who threw away a lucrative career in the oil business. He just happened to land in Los Angeles at a time when that city was on its way to becoming the capital of the world. He had the genius to see there a microcosm of what the world was becoming—a world of lonely strangers living on welfare, social security, shoestring entrepreneurship, alcohol, drugs, and dreams. When writers such as Charles Dickens and Jane Austen wrote about their worlds, they wrote about people who knew one another, who interacted, who needed one another; when Chandler wrote about Southern California, he had to write about a world in which people were isolated, lonely, alienated, a world where everybody was from somewhere else. Now that the rest of the world is catching up in terms of alienation and anomie, readers everywhere identify with Chandler's lonely hero Philip Marlowe, who has nothing but his gun and a cat that does not like him.

In *The Big Sleep* (1939), Chandler's best-known novel, General Sternwood sits alone among his hated orchids or lies in bed waiting to die. Carmen Sternwood sits on the steps outside and throws darts at a tree. Vivian Regan lounges in her all-white bedroom drinking scotch. Owen Taylor, the chauffeur, has nothing to do but wipe down two already spotless cars. Agnes Lozelle merely sits behind a desk at Arthur Gwynn Geiger's bookstore and repaints her fingernails. Geiger comes to work at four in the afternoon and goes home to unwind at five-fifteen. Mona Mars has nothing to do but sit in the house behind Art Huck's garage. Lash Canino sits with her. Marlowe does a great deal of sitting in his car or in his office, catching up on his foot-dangling.

The city Chandler described as a "neon slum" is a relentlessly expanding gridiron of boulevards designed for motor traffic among which tiny humans struggle to survive. Chandler saw that the automobile was not only decentralizing American cities but also destabilizing American morals. Automobiles are little houses on wheels; anything can go on inside—and does. Their power, speed, and mobility have a psychological effect on the people who drive them: They make people feel omnipotent. Much of the modern crime epidemic is made possible by automobiles, including armed robberies, drive-by shootings, child abductions, and serial murders.

The anonymity and outright invisibility that automobiles confer bring out passions that people of earlier generations had to suppress. Ironically, it seems that as Western civilization is becoming technologically more advanced, its population is becoming psychologically more primitive. This was the theme of Jean-Luc Godard's famous film *Weekend* (1967), but Godard was only nine years old when Chandler published *The Big Sleep*.

The dominance of the automobile is responsible for the strange, convoluted plots that Chandler's envious detractors deplore and his admirers cherish. Chandler bashers say that they cannot understand his plots—as if they could understand the modern world perfectly and have a problem only with understanding Raymond Chandler.

It is noteworthy that in the opening chapter of *The Big Sleep*, Chandler introduces two automobiles as if they were characters: Carmen's Packard convertible and Vivian's Buick sedan. There is something very sensual about the way Owen Taylor is rubbing down the cars of General Sternwood's sexy daughters. It was necessary for Chandler to introduce automobiles as characters, for they are often more conspicuous than people. For example, Marlowe is aware of being tailed by the gray Plymouth sedan long before he meets its driver Harry Jones.

The Big Sleep could not exist as a story without cars. Marlowe drives to General Sternwood's mansion in West Hollywood, then follows Geiger's cream-colored coupe up Laurel Canyon Boulevard to the sinister bungalow at 7244 Laverne Terrace. Carmen arrives in her Packard and dashes inside to sip wine laced with ether and have her picture taken in the nude. Carmen could never have gotten to Geiger's house without a car; that whole neighborhood could never have existed without cars, because there is no public transportation in the steep Hollywood Hills. Marlowe says, "It seemed like a nice neighborhood to have bad habits in."

Hiney blithely ignores the question of why Chandler's plots were so notoriously complicated. Indeed, Hiney makes so many mistakes or unwarranted assumptions in his summary of *The Big Sleep* that he seems to have it confused with any number of American potboilers and Hollywood B mystery films. For example, he writes, "The gambling debts are settled and the pornographic negatives destroyed by Marlowe." In the story, however, Carmen's promissory notes are never paid off, Vivian's debts to Eddie Mars are not paid off either, and there is only one pornographic negative. According to Hiney, Carmen is "hooked on opium," which is not the case. He says, "Marlowe rummages through criminal LA, buying information and being pistol-whipped as he goes"; yet Marlowe is never pistol-whipped. Hiney states that Carmen kills Sean Regan "on one of her opiate binges"; actually, Carmen suffers from a psychiatric problem accompanied by nymphomania and epileptic seizures.

Hiney's description of *Farewell, My Lovely* (1940) is equally muddled. He calls Jules Amthor a psychiatrist, whereas Amthor is an "international con man" posing as a psychic consultant. Hiney asserts that Lindsay Marriott is killed in Purissima Canyon by his cronies in the blackmail racket, but Marlowe explicitly tells Anne Riordan that Marriott is killed by Helen Grayle (née Velma Valento). Hiney states that Moose Malloy hires Marlowe to find Velma, which suggests that he has confused the novel with the film versions. The English biographer manages to leave out any mention of Anne Riordan, Laird Brunette, and the gambling ship *Montecito*. He summarizes Chandler's novels in such a blithe, simplistic fashion that one might wonder whether he is interested in Chandler as a writer or only as a personality.

Hiney is more comfortable and certainly more accurate when discussing Chandler's youth in England and his alcoholic-befogged visits to England late in his unhappy life. Of the nine chapters, one is titled "From Chicago to Bloomsbury" and another "London License." Americans who think of Chandler as an American writing in the American vernacular about typical Americans in the quintessential American city will be intrigued by the "english" Chandler's bright young English biographer puts on his subject. Still, it is difficult to make Chandler out to be an English writer. American readers are willing to share him with their cousins but will refuse to give him up altogether. Chandler's heart may have remained in England, but his body is buried in his despised, beloved Southern California. In his own words:

What did it matter where you lay once you were dead? In a dirty sump or in a marble tower on top of a high hill? You were dead, you were sleeping the big sleep, you were not bothered by things like that.

Bill Delaney

Sources for Further Study

Atlanta Journal Constitution. July 6, 1997, p. L8.
Booklist. XCIII, April 15, 1997, p. 1404.
Chicago Tribune. June 29, 1997, XIV, p. 2.
Library Journal. CXXII, April, 1997, p. 92.
Maclean's. CX, July 1, 1997, p. 111.
National Review. XLIX, September 29, 1997, p. 58.
The New York Times Book Review. CII, June 22, 1997, p. 12.
Newsweek. CXXX, July 14, 1997, p. 68.
Publishers Weekly. CCXLIV, March 31, 1997, p. 52.
The Spectator. CCLXXVIII, May 17, 1997, p. 39.
The Times Literary Supplement. June 13, 1997, p. 34.
The Washington Post Book World. XXVII, May 18, 1997, p. 3.

REALITY AND DREAMS

Author: Muriel Spark (1918-   )
Publisher: Houghton Mifflin (Boston). 160 pp. $22.00
Type of work: Novel
Time: The 1990's
Locale: England

A film director, seriously injured in a fall, attempts to direct his motion pictures as works of art and live his life as a film

> *Principal characters:*
> TOM RICHARDS, a sixty-three-year-old film director
> CLAIRE, his unfaithful but supportive wife
> MARIGOLD, their unattractive, spiteful daughter
> CORA, Tom's beautiful daughter by his first wife
> ROSE WOODSTOCK, a star actress in Tom's films and his mistress during shootings
> JEANNE, a frustrated film actress
> DAVE, Tom's taxi driver and confidant

Muriel Spark's twentieth novel opens as Tom Richards regains consciousness in a hospital where he is recovering from a nearly fatal fall from a crane he was using while directing a film provisionally entitled *The Hamburger Girl*. The central idea of the film is that a rich man is so struck by a young woman frying hamburgers at a campsite in France that he anonymously bestows a fortune on her and then watches how she copes with her wealth. The plot is pure fantasy, but as the novel progresses readers are shown again and again how fantasy and reality blur and become indistinct, guided, as Tom observes, by "our trade . . . our perceptions and our dreams."

Films have long been the focus of explorations of the thin line between fantasy, dreams, and reality, but Spark's approach to the theme is novel and many-faceted. In the first half of the novel, the main vehicle for the idea is Tom Richards himself, who wonders aloud whether "we were all characters in one of God's dreams" and whose job carries the occupational hazard of confusing film with reality. He has little problem distinguishing real events from imaginary events, but his perception of people seems almost entirely determined by his role as director. While he is filming, for example, he inevitably falls in love and has an affair with his leading lady. When the film is over the affair ends, as if Tom were in love with the role rather than the woman—or, perhaps more accurately, in love with the idea of a star actress. By contrast, the central character in the film, Jeanne (played by an actress also named Jeanne), has no appeal for him because neither the character nor the actress playing her is a star. Similarly, Tom muses frequently on true friendship and inevitably finds that his real friends (or so he believes) are the famous people he has known. Friendship is name-dropping; friends have star quality. In reality, his closest friend in the book is Dave, the taxi driver who drives him aimlessly about London and genuinely listens.

In the second half of the novel, the focus shifts from filmmaking to the mysterious disappearance of Marigold, the unlovely and infuriating product of Tom and Claire's so-called marriage.

Marigold resents her parents' marriage because both partners are flagrantly unfaithful. They in turn resent her because she seems no part of either of them: She is homely in appearance, negative toward everything, has no interest in film, and apparently no affection for either parent. So remote is she from her family that she is not missed for several weeks, and when she is, no one has the slightest idea of where she has gone or whether her disappearance is voluntary.

Paradoxically, however, Marigold is the force that keeps Tom and Claire together: "She kept telling her parents that they had nothing in common, and therefore should divorce, not realising that she . . . was mainly the cause of Claire and Tom's inseparability." Apparently, her voluntary disappearance is motivated at least in part by her desire to drive them apart—in other words, to force them to realize the unreality of their marriage. Ironically, she succeeds only in bringing them closer together.

Marigold is also the hinge between the two parts of this fictional diptych. The main story, centering on Tom, his slow recovery, and his return to the film that occasioned his injuries, is not closely related to the other story—that of Marigold's disappearance and eventual discovery. Marigold provides the link, for her real-life disappearance mirrors an idea Tom has of actually finding the "hamburger girl" and anonymously giving her a large fortune. Eventually he abandons this scheme, only to find that he must expend the same kind of effort in tracking down Marigold who, it turns out, is willfully avoiding everyone so that she may experience poverty and anonymity as part of a book she is writing on unemployment. She also links the two parts in another way, for it is during Marigold's disappearance that Tom slowly begins to appreciate Marigold's potential as a film actress. Physically, she is the antithesis of a beautiful film star, but the more Tom puzzles over the problem of finding someone to play the part of a prophetic Celt in his next film, the more Marigold seems right for the part. Eventually, when Marigold is discovered masquerading as a man and living in a dingy trailer park, Tom does give her the part, which she plays very successfully.

A third link provided by Marigold also involves a secondary theme, the idea of "redundancy," the British term for being fired or laid off from a job. Nearly everyone in the book is redundant in some sense: Tom becomes redundant through his injury; Marigold's husband decides to divorce her, making her a redundant wife; Cora, Tom's beautiful daughter, loses her job in television, as does her husband, Johnny Carr; Jeanne, the frustrated actress in the hamburger girl film, feels neglected by Tom and superfluous in her role; Ralph, Marigold's brother-in-law, loses his job in electronics; Kevin Woodstock, husband of Tom's leading lady, is fired; the husband of one of Tom's nurses loses his job as an auto mechanic; and even Dave's brother is replaced by a cheaper immigrant at the pizza shop. Small wonder that Marigold's book on redundancy and its effects becomes a best-seller.

Juxtaposing these two seemingly unrelated ideas—redundancy and dream/reality—risks allowing this short novel to collapse into parts, but Marigold is a strong enough character to hold the ideas together and even link them without straining. Part of her objection to Tom and Claire is their excess wealth. Claire is an heiress to an American fortune, while Tom enjoys the luxury of a successful film career. Even Marigold has more than enough money. Her undercover research on redundancy, however, has nothing dream-like about it: This is the harsh reality faced by millions of unemployed workers in Britain. Tom's halfhearted attempts to make art out of cinematic commerce, and Claire's generosity toward various charities are of little use in the face of so much suffering. In this sense, Marigold experiences reality while Tom and Claire dream. The tragic expression of the relation between the two ideas is Jeanne's suicide leap from the same crane that occasioned Tom's fall.

Marigold, then, emerges as the most complex and interesting character in the novel. It is unfortunate that Spark did not place her squarely at the book's center and develop her in more detail. Other characters have moments of brilliance: Tom, as he slowly realizes Marigold's acting potential; Claire, as she adroitly handles the tiresome actress Jeanne; Dave, as he listens to and comments shrewdly on Tom's various predicaments and puzzles. None, however, rises to the consistent level of interest created by the unlovely and unlovable Marigold.

The book as a whole moves swiftly from scene to scene, carried along by Spark's sprightly style and gift for dialogue. It is a cinematic book, quickly cutting from character to character and scene to scene. Witty, shrewdly observant, unpretentious, it carries its thematic ideas seriously but not pretentiously. Spark has lost none of her capacity for revealing characters and, through them, the follies and failures of modern times.

Dean Baldwin

Sources for Further Study

Commonweal. CXXIV, May 9, 1997, p. 23.
London Review of Books. XVIII, November 14, 1996, p. 23.
The New York Review of Books. XLIV, July 17, 1997, p. 31.
The New York Times Book Review. CII, May 11, 1997, p. 7.
The Observer. September 15, 1996, p. 17.
Publishers Weekly. CCXLIV, January 27, 1997, p. 76.
The Spectator. CCLXXVII, September 14, 1996, p. 34.
The Times Literary Supplement. September 20, 1996, p. 22.
The Virginia Quarterly Review. LXXIII, Autumn, 1997, p. 130.
Women's Review of Books. XIV, July, 1997, p. 38.

RESURRECTION
The Struggle for a New Russia

Author: David J. Remnick (1958-   )
Publisher: Random House (New York). 398 pp. $25.95
Type of work: History
Time: The 1990's
Locale: Russia

Remnick examines Russian political, economic, and cultural life in the moral vacuum left by the fall of Soviet Communism

Principal personages:
BORIS YELTSIN, first president of the Russian Republic after the fall of Soviet Communism
YEGOR GAIDAR, a key economic adviser to Yeltsin
RUSLAN KHASBULATOV and
ALEKSANDR RUTSKOI, leaders of the old guard in the Russian Parliament
VLADIMIR GUSINSKY, a wealthy media entrepreneur
ALEKSANDR SOLZHENITSYN, the Russian Nobel laureate, who has continued his Vermont exile from his homeland
VLADIMIR ZHIRINOVSKY, a nationalist politician

On December 25, 1991, Mikhail Gorbachev resigned as president of the Soviet Union. When the new year dawned, by agreement of the political entities that composed it, the Soviet Union was dissolved. The creation of Vladimir Ilich Lenin and Joseph Stalin, born in blood in 1917, dubbed "the evil empire" by President Ronald Reagan, had endured some seventy-three years of revolution, civil war, famine, terror, and wars hot and cold. The hopes that arose in the post-Stalin era under Nikita Khrushchev had been dashed by the progressive putrefaction of the Soviet regime that followed under Leonid Brezhnev and his successors. Now the totalitarian creature of Soviet Communism was dead.

What would become of Russia? Could it even be called a "nation," or was it not rather an unstable set of nations making up the vast expanse stretching eastward from European Russia west of the Urals, across the Asian steppes of Siberia to the Pacific? Whatever it was, it had no background in democracy; its populace was docile, accustomed to instructions from above dictating the course of socialist life.

Many observers believed that democracy was—and is—an impossible proposition in this still backward half-Asian, half-European hybrid. No large, civically active middle class—an essential foundation of a free social order—had developed under Communism. Instead, a significant, mostly male, portion of the populace was steeped in alcohol and incivility. By 1993, life expectancy for Russian men had fallen from its 1987 peak of sixty-five to only fifty-nine years—a statistic characteristic of Third World conditions.

Resurrection: The Struggle for a New Russia is David Remnick's second book on Russia, exploring the complex dilemmas of the post-Soviet era. The first, *Lenin's Tomb* (1993), chronicled the decline and fall of the Russian Empire known as the Soviet

Union, based on the author's stint as Moscow correspondent for *The Washington Post*. While not the comprehensive, Russian-novel-sized tome of Remnick's first book, *Resurrection* (whose title plays on Leo Tolstoy's novel and, perhaps unintentionally, on attempts to revive Russia's Christian heritage) constitutes a substantial contribution by a considerable literary and journalistic talent. Remnick, who has become a staff writer for *The New Yorker*, is bilingual and well connected in the key urban centers of Moscow and St. Petersburg. He is an altogether able and fastidious guide to Russia "after the fall." In the end, he insists on an optimistic appraisal of Russia's future, though whether his assessment has sufficient grounds is difficult to judge.

As told by Remnick, the story that unfolds after 1992 is both fascinating and appalling. Economic adviser Yegor Gaidar's "shock therapy" cut state subsidies, which had lowered the prices of everything from bread to subway rides, and began the process of privatizing state property. Society groaned as mass unemployment and ruinous inflation convulsed the economy.

Parliament, protesting this suffering, locked horns with the presidency of Boris Yeltsin. The president won a referendum of support for his policies on April 23, 1993, but a constitutional crisis simmered, then moved to climatic resolution when, in September, Parliament refused to heed a presidential decree dissolving it. As the world looked on via CNN, on October 3-4, units of the Russian army attacked the "White House," as Parliament was known, crushing resistance led by Ruslan Khasbulatov and Aleksandr Rutskoi, parliamentarians longing for the return of the *ancien règime*. That such an event could occur constitutes a stark reminder of the legacy of autocracy that casts a cloud over Russia's attempts to establish democracy.

Apart from the highlights and lowlights of national politics, Remnick surveys the scene of the capital, microcosm of all that is bright, hopeful, and horrible in Russian life after communism. Here readers find signs of the new Russia as varied as a $300 million reconstruction of the historic Cathedral of Christ the Savior, destroyed by Stalin; and the posh Moscow Commercial Club, where tasteless nouveau-riche entrepreneurs await the arrival of media titan Vladimir Gusinsky. It is suggestive and symptomatic that Gusinsky maintains a security force of twelve hundred men to guard his empire.

Remnick devotes an entire chapter to a different kind of titan, Aleksandr Solzhenitsyn, who prepared a triumphal return to Russia after years of exile. Solzhenitsyn's hopes of informing and reforming the conscience of his country, however, proved stillborn. His east-to-west tour of Russia aroused little interest; the young found the great man an often-pompous irrelevance.

Remnick's exploration of the place of Russian literature in the post-Communist era shows the secondary, essentially private place that literature and literary figures occupy in the new Russia. Writers are no longer the prophets, saints, spiritual leaders, and political opposition—"alternative governments"— they once were under czar and commissar alike. They are no longer able to nourish the nation's moral roots; times have changed.

Evident in this account is an underlying theme of the absence of a moral compass that plagues Russia after the fall of communism. The Russia Remnick surveys lacks an identity—it does not know what it is or by what coherent set of beliefs it will live. "One of the most troubling deficiencies in modern Russia," he writes, "is the absence of moral authority. The country lacks the ethical compass provided by Andrei Sakharov, who died in December 1989."

Every society requires rules by which to be governed; it requires basic social norms. Nearly everywhere those norms are premised on religious, legal-moral, or political ideas and beliefs inherited from the past, often centuries or millennia in the making. Material security and well-being, especially in the context of a technologically oriented, postindustrial economy, cannot develop unless everyday social rules are observed—for example, a minimum of taxes collected; basic physical safety; wages and bills paid; the young cared for. Without rules and the moral order to secure them, there is chaos. This is a condition sociologists call "anomie," the absence of what ancient Greece called *nomos*—sacred law or custom.

The Russia described by Remnick is in a state of anomic disarray, lacking a sense of identity. What history and shared ideas identify this people, setting them apart from all others? The old Soviet ideology was one answer to the identity question, but it constituted a denial of the historical past of the various peoples that made up the Soviet empire. With the Soviet Union's demise, Russian politics presents a motley panorama of old Communists, new fascists, Slavophile haters of the West, extreme national chauvinists such as the virulent presidential candidate Vladimir Zhirinovsky, and modern liberal democrats uneasily cohabiting the same political space. In urban civil society, a new generation of youthful, moneyed entrepreneurs with private security guards live next to enormous cohorts of hopeless older workers, struggling professional and other nominally middle-class groups, corrupt, underpaid civil servants, and swarms of ruthless mafia.

Remnick also examines with care the personalist institution of the Yeltsin presidency, especially the problematic character of the president himself. Readers are reminded that Yeltsin spent his career as a Party apparatchik, hardly the environment for a democrat in training. The president's disgraceful policies in the reconquest of Chechnya are a case in point.

The jury is out on the realistic possibility of an eventual successful transition to democracy in Russia. The brief history of Russian politics after 1991 presented by Remnick, capped by the executive's assault on the legislature with tanks and automatic weapons, shows how far the nation is from democratic government. In part this uncertainty stems from Russia's chronic ambivalence toward all things Western, since democracy, though having nearly global appeal, is undeniably a set of Western inventions.

For centuries Russia has maintained a schizoid view of its relationship with the West. On one hand, it has seen itself as inferior—"backward" in manners, culture, and economic development—in comparison with Europe (and later America), and therefore in need of catching up. On the other hand, Russians exhibit a deep distrust of the West, together with nationalist feelings of superiority. Remnick cites Anglo-Russian scholar Isaiah Berlin on this well-known phenomenon. Russia has tended to see itself as intellectually inadequate but emotionally superior. The "Russian soul" is deeper and richer than its impoverished Western counterpart, "cramped, cold, mean, calculating, fenced in, without capacity for large views or generous emotions."

Beyond this ambivalent attitude are perhaps deeper questions of culture and politics. Some scholars, notably Harvard political scientist Samuel P. Huntington, believe that a fault line dividing Western civilization from its Eastern neighbors is drawn by the influence of Western Christianity. Russia, in this view, is beyond the pale, its version of Christianity being Eastern Orthodoxy, product of Constantinople. It was little touched by the Western Renaissance, Reformation, and Enlightenment. All these seminal movements, it is argued, are essential stages on the high road to liberal democracy. Instead, Russia was left relatively uninfluenced by ideas such as the separation of church and state or religious (ideological) toleration, or the Enlightenment love of rationality. Given that it has not followed this Western path to democracy, is Russia condemned to some version of autocracy?

The restraints every society requires on the behavior of its members combine the internal controls of the individual with external controls—a system of rewards and punishments. When self-discipline is weak, either external force such as the state compels restraint or some degree of disorder results. Political "myth" and ideology and religious and philosophical beliefs and ideas are essential supports to prudent behavior. In the case of the Soviet Union, for some time Communist ideology was such a force for self-discipline. Its influence declined during the Brezhnev era, however, as the spiritual and practical hollowness of Communism became increasingly apparent. Under Communism, no competition was allowed to challenge the ideological monopoly of Marxism-Leninism, and consequently once it died, there was no ready replacement. Under a system of state persecution of religion, the influence of Russian Orthodoxy was limited.

After 1991, the need for a foundation for a moral order, for sources of inner restraints, was magnified. Yet no such unifying foundation has emerged or is anywhere in sight. Moscow in particular has become a "wide open" city, where in 1994 alone fifty "bankers" were murdered, and where ubiquitous organized crime is sometimes difficult to distinguish from organized government.

"What is the state without justice," St. Augustine asked, "but a great robber band?" Before 1991, members of the top Soviet bureaucratic class, the "nomenclatura," appeared increasingly like so many organized swindlers. Afterward, however, they were well placed to aggrandize themselves without restraint during what Remnick calls "the biggest property distribution in the history of the world." Organized crime appeared everywhere, more or less openly. Remnick skillfully charts the progress of this social-moral disease:

> So many of the "democrats" became corrupt because they just could not resist temptation. Under Soviet rule, there were fewer temptations; moreover, the regulator was external and strong, even brutal. When the rules of the game changed, it turned out that the moral regulators within the individual had atrophied; when the external regulator was gone, all hell broke loose.

The "struggle for a new Russia," as Remnick subtitles his book, is the search for a way out of this moral morass. Russia is, no doubt, in the process of resurrection, after being crushed by the state and its "opium of the intellectuals," Soviet Marxism. But what is it that is coming to life? A nuclear-armed version of Frankenstein's monster, a new authoritarianism and nationalist state—armed, let it not be forgotten, with nuclear weapons? Or is the world witnessing the first shoots of a Russian spring—a Slavic version of liberal democracy? No one knows, and they will not know for a long time to come.

Charles F. Bahmueller

Sources for Further Study

Business Week. March 17, 1997, p. 14.
The Economist. CCCXLII, March 8, 1997, p. 100.
Foreign Affairs. LXXVI, May, 1997, p. 138.
Los Angeles Times Book Review. March 9, 1997, p. 9.
National Review. XLIX, June 2, 1997, p. 51.
The New Leader. LXXX, March 10, 1997, p. 18.
The New York Review of Books. XLIV, April 24, 1997, p. 13.
The New York Times Book Review. CII, March 16, 1997, p. 7.
Time. CXLIX, March 31, 1997, p. 82.
The Wall Street Journal. March 13, 1997, p. A12.

ROBERT PENN WARREN
A Biography

Author: Joseph Blotner (1923-   )
Publisher: Random House (New York). Illustrated. 585 pp. $35.00
Type of work: Literary biography
Time: 1905-1989
Locale: Kentucky, Tennessee, Connecticut, and Vermont; Italy, France, and England

The first comprehensive biography of the three-time Pulitzer Prize-winning novelist and poet, Joseph Blotner's study details both the triumphs and the tragedies of Robert Penn Warren's personal and professional lives

> *Principal personages:*
> ROBERT PENN WARREN, a poet, critic, novelist, and teacher whose work spanned six decades
> EMMA CININA BRESCIA WARREN, his first wife
> ELEANOR CLARK WARREN, his second wife, also a writer
> ROSANNA PHELPS WARREN SCULLY, the daughter of Eleanor Clark and Robert Penn Warren
> GABRIEL PENN WARREN, Clark's and Warren's son
> ALLEN TATE, a famous poet and critic, and Warren's good friend for sixty years
> CLEANTH BROOKS, a noted literary critic who collaborated with Warren on many of his most important critical texts
> ALBERT RUSSELL ERSKINE, JR., Warren's student at Southwestern College, and later his editor and friend
> KATHERINE ANNE PORTER, the American novelist and short-story writer who was Warren's friend for decades

Robert Penn Warren's was a remarkable life, no matter how one looks at it. He produced more than three dozen books in a career that spanned six decades, from the 1920's to the 1980's. As a fiction writer he published eleven works, including *All the King's Men* (1946), which not only earned for him his first Pulitzer Prize but also has long stood as one of the finest political novels produced in the United States. He also published sixteen collections of poetry, two of which won Pulitzer Prizes among numerous other awards, thus making Warren the only American writer to win the Pulitzer in two different categories. Finally, as a teacher and critic, he helped to shape the terms for the discussions of literature and literary study in America after World War II in a series of important textbooks and critical works.

Warren's personal life was not always a happy one. Born in Guthrie, Kentucky, Warren would always consider the South his home, even though he would rarely live there after childhood. Blinded in one eye in adolescence, he attempted suicide in college when he thought he was losing the sight in the other. Later, his twenty-year marriage to the unstable but demanding Emma Cinina Brescia caused him periods of deep anguish. In spite of these and other problems in the first half of his life, he built a literary career of remarkable distinction and productivity. During his freshman year at Vanderbilt, he was fortunate to have the poet John Crowe Ransom as his English professor, and Warren's career as a writer and teacher was almost foretold in that encounter.

Warren soon joined a group of other bright and talented southern writers, such as Allen Tate and Donald Davidson, and was publishing poetry in their journal, *The Fugitive*, by the early 1920's. Some of these same writers, collectively known as the Southern Agrarians, would produce *I'll Take My Stand*, an important declaration of southern intellectual independence, a few years later. As Blotner explains,

> The basic idea that united the group's core members was clear: the agrarian values of the Old South were the best hope not only for the South in resisting the effects of northern industrialism but also for the rest of America as well.

After graduate work at Berkeley, Yale, and New College, Oxford, as a Rhodes scholar, Warren settled into his life as a teacher, critic, and writer. He taught, among other colleges, at Louisiana State University, the University of Minnesota, and Yale. At Louisiana State, he and his colleague Cleanth Brooks edited *The Southern Review*, one of the most important literary journals to come out of the 1930's, a journal that *Time* magazine in 1940 would call "superior to any other in the English language." He and Brooks then began on a collaboration of some years to correct what they believed were the deficiencies in the field of literary study, and in the next decade produced three of the most important literature textbooks in America: *Understanding Poetry* (1938), *Understanding Fiction* (1943), and *Modern Rhetoric* (1949). These texts became part of the theoretical underpinning for the New Criticism, which would come to dominate the teaching and analysis of literature for the next thirty years. The New Criticism essentially broke away from earlier historical and impressionistic literary criticism, demanding close textual analysis before any interpretation or judgment. What Brooks and Warren first did in *Understanding Poetry*, Blotner shows, was to create

> a text that would translate sophisticated poetic theory into practical application. It would teach a student how to differentiate poetry from prose not only by rhyme and metrics but also by the function of the narrative and descriptive elements, and to go beyond the poet's explicit statement of crucial ideas to apprehend tone and attitude, to follow the function of imagery, and—for the brightest—to savor the operation of ambiguity and irony.

Meanwhile, in addition to his critical texts, Warren had begun writing and publishing not only poetry such as *Thirty-Six Poems* (1936) and *Selected Poems: 1923-1943* (1944) but also novels such as *Night Rider* (1939) and *World Enough and Time* (1949).

The second half of Warren's life would be equally productive but much happier. After his divorce from Cinina in 1951, he married Eleanor Clark, a writer (her *Oysters of Lacmariaquer* would be a national best-seller in 1964) with whom he had a son and a daughter who brightened his life immensely. Warren and his family lived mostly in Connecticut and Vermont, but they spent long periods of travel and writing in France and Italy.

Warren's creative life was not without its disappointments. For some years after his

Selected Poems of 1944, Warren produced no poetry. When he returned with *Brother to Dragons* (1953) and *Promises* (1957), however, it was with renewed poetic gifts and greater power. While he wrote several brilliant short stories ("Blackberry Winter" is probably the best of them), longer fiction was clearly his forte, and he published only one collection of stories in his long career. His later novels—such as *The Cave* (1959) and *Flood* (1964)—never equalled the early popular and critical success of *All the King's Men* in 1946, but he continued to turn them out and at the same time turned increasingly (in the 1950's and 1960's) to nonfiction about his beloved South and its racial troubles, as in *Segregation: The Inner Conflict in the South* (1956) and *Who Speaks for the Negro?* (1965). He ended his career writing poetry, and particularly poetic epics, such as *Audubon: A Vision* (1969) and *Chief Joseph of the Nez Perce* (1983).

Blotner's biography is detailed and comprehensive and maintains the necessary balance between the personal and the literary. He provides a valuable five-page chronology at the very beginning of the book and fifty pages of notes and genealogy at the end. This framework is extremely helpful in describing such a long and productive literary career as Warren's. The volume is divided into seven books of fifty-four chapters and is further broken in the middle by a collection of more than three dozen photographs that provide faces for the many important characters who figured in Warren's life. Warren appears to have known every important literary figure of the twentieth century in his long career, from Robert Frost and T. S. Eliot to Eudora Welty and F. Scott Fitzgerald.

The only problem with Blotner's focus is that he tries to maintain a balance among Warren's various arts, and the fiction naturally gets the greater share. Blotner spends pages in summaries of Warren's complex historical novels, even though these works have clearly declined in significance over the last half of the twentieth century. In manner, Warren was "a craftsman, an intellectual novelist who tended to see a book in terms of problem solving rather than a process of following ardently where the daemon led." In focus, Warren's novels usually reveal his desire "to understand the nature of reality, to achieve a sense of personal identity, and to understand and if possible atone for the transgressions arising out of one's personal portion of original sin." In its themes, Warren's fiction may remind readers of that of Nathaniel Hawthorne or Joseph Conrad in its preoccupation with corruption and guilt. Yet Warren's novels also tend to be filled with sex, violence, and melodrama. William Faulkner, Warren's southern compatriot, had the same elements, but his characters reflected a deeper, almost mythic historical sense that Warren lacked. Nevertheless, other southern writers, such as William Styron (*Lie Down in Darkness*, 1951), were inspired by Warren's work.

If Warren is to be remembered, as he is sure to be, it will be as a poet and as a critic. His poetic career almost spans the twentieth century, from the modernist concerns of Hart Crane and T. S. Eliot—he was just beginning his poetic career in 1922 when *The Waste Land* was published—to the more confessional poetry of Allen Ginsberg and the Beats. Warren's own poetry underwent a similar shift, and his later work is better for the change. Warren was always a master craftsman, but his later poetry, while it retained his intellectual and moral concerns, also became more personal and colloquial. It was this later poetry which would win for Warren two Pulitzers, in 1958 and 1979. "The earlier style—often convoluted, sometimes densely metaphysical—was giving way to a more nearly fluid clarity." Throughout his career, Warren's poetry was marked, as Blotner further notes, by his "impeccable versatile craftsmanship, his profusion of incident, image, and character, and his attempt, at the highest level and with intense personal involvement, to wrest meaning from life through his art." As American author Katherine Anne Porter wrote him, "I love your poetry, I have every one you ever published, you have always been to me first of all a poet, best of all your work." The influences of, and comparisons to, the English poets Thomas Hardy and William Butler Yeats are striking and inevitable.

Likewise, Warren's textbooks revolutionized the study of literature in the United States, and his criticism helped to make literary study more of an art and a science. Unfortunately, he outlived his own revolution, and his last years at Yale were unhappy in part because his methods had been supplanted by newer European theoretical systems (such as structuralism and deconstruction). When *American Literature: The Makers and the Making* appeared in 1973, edited by Warren, Brooks, and R. W. B. Lewis, the New Critical moment had passed, and the two-volume anthology never saw a second edition.

Warren's own practical criticism, however, will outlast his critical theory. In critiques that ranged widely over English and American literature—Warren wrote studies of Samuel Taylor Coleridge, John Greenleaf Whittier, Herman Melville, Theodore Dreiser, and Katherine Anne Porter, among others—Warren broke through the limitations of the New Criticism and modeled for readers an intelligent writer reading other writers, and in so doing left a number of important lessons for students of literature. Not a system, he wrote, but "intelligence, tact, discipline, honesty, sensitivity—those are the things we have to depend on, after all, to give us what we prize in criticism, the insight." Warren left a legacy, less of fiction than of poetry and criticism.

That legacy will live on. One of the last people to interview Warren before his death in 1989 at the age of eighty-three was Ken Burns, the documentary filmmaker who was just starting his study of the Civil War. Warren told Burns to look up the southern novelist and historian Shelby Foote. Burns did, and Foote became, as Blotner notes, the principal commentator for the award-winning series. Warren's judgments and suggestions will no doubt continue to influence American culture for a long time to come.

David Peck

Sources for Further Study

America. CLXXVI, March 22, 1997, p. 33.
Booklist. XCIII, November, 1996, p. 474.

Kirkus Reviews. LXV, January 15, 1997, p. 112.
The New Leader. LXXX, April 21, 1997, p. 19.
The New Republic. CCXVII, October 20, 1997, p. 43.
The New York Times Book Review. CII, March 9, 1997, p. 11.
Publishers Weekly. CCXLIII, November 11, 1996, p. 61.
The Times Literary Supplement. February 28, 1997, p. 5.
The Virginia Quarterly Review. LXXIII, Autumn, 1997, p. 729.
The Wall Street Journal. February 27, 1997, p. A15.
The Washington Post Book World. XXVII, February 23, 1997, p. 5.

SAINTS AND SINNERS
A History of the Popes

Author: Eamon Duffy
Publisher: Yale University Press (New Haven, Connecticut). Illustrated. 326 pp. $30.00
Type of work: History and religion
Time: A.D. 33-1997
Locale: Primarily Rome and elsewhere in Europe

A richly illustrated, vividly written overview of the history of the papacy—from the Apostle Peter to John Paul II—by an eminent Catholic Church historian

Good books normally arise from good ideas, skillfully realized in print. Eamon Duffy's *Saints and Sinners* is an example of a *very* good book in the service of a very questionable idea. A renowned Cambridge University scholar, Duffy was invited by S4C, the Wales television company, to produce a volume to accompany its six-part series on the papacy. As a rule, scholars should refuse such invitations, especially if their field is religion, because one is required to "dumb down" the material, making it appealing to the broadest possible audience. From the start, commercial motivations may dominate. The papacy is ultimately a theological artifact, not justified by its venerability or practical value but by what one makes of Matthew 16:16 ("And I tell you, you are Peter, and on this rock I will build my church"), other scriptural passages, the evolution of authority in the early centuries of the church, the Reformation, and the rival claims of the Eastern Orthodox. For those who cherish the pope and acknowledge his authority, "empirical" and "historical" data always will be secondary. Foremost is the "imagination" of the pope's identity—the willingness to see him as Peter's successor, the vicar of Christ on Earth, and to offer obedience to the church he represents.

Duffy appears to ignore all of this when he explains that this book "is not a work of theology" and that he has "not thought it my business to justify or defend" the evolution of the institution. Readers are thus prepared for a "neutral" history appealing to everyone—and therefore to no one, except perhaps those who want yet another diverting entertainment drawn from the past. Recall, however, the subject: *the popes.* Can tolerant liberal secularism have become so powerful—and the papacy so irrelevant—that it can afford to offer portraits of its worst historic enemy? Has the institution the West once died fighting for (or against) now become so benign as to be settled comfortably alongside *Masterpiece Theater?*

Fortunately, Duffy delivers much more than his statement of intent implies. Acknowledging his own devotion to Catholicism, he confesses that "the story of the popes is a crucial dimension of the story of the providential care of God for humankind in history, the necessary and (on the whole) proper development of powers and responsibilities implicit in the nature of the Church itself." Furthermore, Duffy reports that in writing the book he has become more deeply aware that the papacy, even in its worst moments, has "again and again helped ensure that the local churches of Christendom retained something of a universal Christian vision, that they did not entirely collapse back into the narrowness of religious nationalism, or become entirely subordinated to the will of powerful secular rulers." Finally, Duffy wonderfully reneges on his promise to keep theology at a minimum; rather, he lucidly supplies such theology as is necessary to comprehend issues such as Donatism, Arianism, the Conciliarist position, justification by faith, Modernism, and the other defining arguments by which the Catholic tradition was formed.

Not only is *Saints and Sinners* sustained by strong conviction; clear and lively writing also make the volume extremely appealing. Additionally, the work—printed in Italy—contains superb photographs, maps, reproductions of art, and satirical cartoons. Nearly oversized, it will inevitably take up room on many Catholic coffee tables, but those who ignore its text pay a huge price.

"Upon This Rock," Chapter 1, takes readers from the deaths of Peter and Paul in Rome through the gradual recognition of the apostolic claims of the bishops in Rome, the changes wrought by Constantine's conversion, and the aggressive assertion of Rome's primacy by Leo the Great, pope from 440 to 461. For Leo, who opposed the Eastern view that Rome was but the senior member of "the Pentarchy" (the five patriarchates after the Council of Chalcedon in 451), "the coming of Peter to the centre of empire had been a providential act, designed so that from Rome the Gospel might spread to all the world."

Chapter 2, "Between Two Empires," covers a period that non-Christians call "the dark ages" (461-1000) but that saw foundational developments in the history of the church. Duffy ably narrates the Western dispute with the Byzantine Empire's pronounced tendency to elevate the emperor to the status of Kosmocrator, lord of the world and church; the era of Gregory the Great (590-604), "arguably the greatest Pope ever," which included the mission to England that resulted in the demise of Ireland as an independent center of Christian authority; the melding of Greek and Latin-Roman elements in Rome, creating a "vibrant and solemn religious culture which fascinated and dazzled the newly Christianized peoples of Europe"; the growth of the papal territories; and the emergence under Charlemagne of the Holy Roman Empire, whose head had to receive its crown from the pope in order to possess authority.

"Set Above Nations, 1000-1447" details the rise of "papal monarchy" and the elevation of the institution to full spiritual and temporal primacy in the West. For Protestant readers accustomed to the idea that it required Martin Luther to set in motion the purification of Christianity, Duffy's characterization of the eleventh century as the beginning of the era of papal reform will come as a surprise. Duffy's tangy prose captures well the need for reform after the degradations of the previous century. In theory, the popes were world-orderers; in practice, they "were strictly and often humiliatingly subordinated to the power of the local Roman aristocracy, or to the German ruling house." The venerable idea that no one could judge the pope was belied by the fact that popes often were regularly appointed by an emperor or nobility. As for moral character, the picture often was unbelievably bleak. Benedict IX (1032-1048) "was both violent and debauched, and even the Roman populace, hardened as they were to unedifying papal behavior, could not stomach him. . . . With the help of his family's private army, he was briefly restored in 1045 amid bloody hand-to-hand fighting in the streets of Rome." Thus it was that Emperor Henry III initiated a reform movement that would shortly result in the most famous moment in the history of the papal institution: the humiliation of Henry IV by Gregory VII at Canossa in 1077, when the former begged absolution, standing barefoot in the snows of the Apennines. The pontificate of Innocent III (1198-1216) marked the high point of papal power and influence, when "the finger of the papacy lay on every living pulse" and the claim that popes could release the faithful from their duty of obedience to secular authorities was most decisively asserted. Duffy skillfully shows how the Cluniac reform and other efforts at renewing monastic life lay behind this remarkable development.

Appropriately, "Protest and Division, 1447-1774" is the book's longest chapter. Duffy's intention is to balance the received picture of the Renaissance papacy by detailing the practical challenges to be faced after the Great Schism (a period in which multiple claimants to the office "ruled" simultaneously), the Conciliar movement, and the exciting appearance of Humanism. Duffy does not omit the lurid details of Roman corruption—far from it. Readers are reminded that Alexander VI (Roderigo de Borgia) "flaunted a young and nubile mistress in the Vatican, was widely believed to have made a habit of poisoning his cardinals so as to get his hands on their property, and . . . ruthlessly aggrandized his illegitimate sons and daughters at the Church's expense." Julius II (1503-1513), Michelangelo's great benefactor, donned silver armor and led his own troops against towns that challenged his sovereignty. Also wanting his readers to understand the immense achievements of the Renaissance popes, Duffy focuses more attention on men such as Nicholas V (1447-1455), a great Humanist, the rebuilder of Rome, founder of the Vatican library, and a diplomat who did much to restore peace and unity to the church.

What of Luther, Galileo, Giordano Bruno, and other symbols dear to those who have contempt for the papacy? Here Duffy's determination to keep the book a broad survey will disappoint many. That the church needs constant reform is a persistent theme; Duffy therefore agrees with Luther's attack on indulgences and the penitential system, faulting the popes of the early Reformation period for their failure to grasp the urgency of the situation. Thus, the Council of Trent (1545-1563), which squarely addressed the abuses denounced by Luther, "came a generation too late, a generation during which the split in the Church had widened and hardened." With this he passes on to other matters, noting that the historian can detect "a dialectic of reform— creativity versus conservation." "Conservation" is surely too weak a term for the Inquisition that interrogated Galileo and killed Bruno, but that is the heading under which Duffy places this demonic papal institution. The infamous Torquemada is never mentioned. At the same time, he emphasizes that Copernican science had enjoyed the support and patronage of the papacy, which encouraged the new astronomy and was not inclined to reject the heliocentric theory. Galileo's mistake was that of not allowing the church to introduce the new teaching slowly and in its own time; he forced the "conservative" side to show its face. Concludes Duffy, "The contrast between the earlier toleration and indeed lionizing of Galileo and the injustice of his condemnation was an eloquent sign of the rigidity of Baroque Catholicism."

Chapter 5, "The Pope and the People" (1774-1903), follows Duffy's account of Clement XIV's formal abolition of the Jesuit order in 1773. Caving to pressures exerted by Spain, France, Portugal and Austria—which resented the way the Society thwarted colonial aspirations and "hindered the consolidation of the absolute rule of the monarch within his own domains"—Clement thus banished the primary instrumentality of the Counter-Reformation church. (It would be restored in 1814.) For Duffy, this was the papacy's "most shameful hour," the sign of its powerlessness in the new order established by the absolute monarchies of Europe. The French Revolution would, of course, take the cause of the state to unimaginable lengths in the Civil Constitution of the Clergy, making priests agents of the regime and requiring of them an oath of obedience. This was only a passing phase; in 1794, the cult of Humanity and the Supreme Being was introduced, and the Christian calendar abandoned. Napoleon had master plans that did not include respecting the papal territories. Pius VI negotiated the humiliating Peace of Tollentino, allowing French occupation of Italy. Duffy notes that although this "weak, vain and worldly" man was not a good pope, it is hard to see what goodness in this historical moment would have looked like, for "the monarchies of Europe had hijacked the Church, and pressed religion into the service of the absolute state."

The nineteenth century would witness unimaginable transformations in the relation of the church to governments, cultures, and peoples. The long reign of Pius IX (1846-1878) found the papacy in full-scale reaction against liberalism and the modern state, as the Italian Risorgimento ensured the end of the pope's temporal estate and the elimination of all remnants of political medievalism. At the same time, the Romantic movement had rediscovered the bewitching loveliness of that era; within Catholicism, a fresh sense of the pope's transcendent authority emerged (Ultramontanism). As well, a newly ardent devotion to Mary, the maturation of the cult of the Sacred Heart of Jesus, the rediscovery of Gregorian chant, the phenomenon of Lourdes, and liturgical revival all signified spiritual renewal in the midst of apparent political defeat. Pio Nono's famous "Syllabus of Errors" condemning the idea that "the Roman Pontiff can and should reconcile himself with progress, liberalism, and recent civilization" culminated in the First Vatican Council (1869) and the promulgation of the decree on papal infallibility. Duffy's account is quite detailed here as he attempts to show the sort of severe limitations that hedge this doctrine and the way the process meant defeat for the extreme papal faction. "It is some measure of these restrictions that, since 1870, only one papal statement has qualified as 'infallible,' the definition of the Assumption in 1950," he points out.

The modern shape of the papacy was worked out by Leo XIII (1878-1903). The Vatican came to terms with its loss of territory, its historic resistance to democracy and the liberal state, and its need to become a spokesman for the worker in the face of rampant industrialization. Leo's successors, the eight popes of the twentieth century, are the subject of Duffy's final chapter, "The Oracles of God." Here he treats the controversial matter of the papacy's relations with Nazism, fascism, and communism; the work of Vatican II; and the remarkable pontificate of Pope John Paul II. The latter is the 261st successor to St. Peter and inherits an institution possessing, in Duffy's words, "a spiritual status and prestige greater than at any time since the High Middle Ages." To many, John Paul II seems a backward-looking authoritarian; to others, he is a strong beacon of order and certainty in a confused age. What will the near future bring? Duffy's answer is equivocal: "Only time, and the next Conclave, will reveal which of these directions in their long walk through history the heirs of St. Peter will take."

Leslie E. Gerber

Sources for Further Study

Atlanta Journal Constitution. December 20, 1997, p. C2.
Booklist. XCIV, November 15, 1997, p. 525.
Commonweal. CXXIV, November 7, 1997, p. 24.
The Economist. CCCXLIV, September 6, 1997, p. S16.
Library Journal. CXXII, November 1, 1997, p. 78.
The New York Times Book Review. CII, December 7, 1997, p. 48.
Publishers Weekly. CCXLIV, October 27, 1997, p. 70.
The Washington Post Book World. XXVII, December 14, 1997, p. 13.

SAMUEL BECKETT
The Last Modernist

Author: Anthony Cronin (1926-   )
Publisher: HarperCollins (New York). Illustrated. 645 pp. $30.00
Type of work: Literary biography
Time: 1906-1989
Locale: Ireland, France, Germany, and England

A meticulous portrait of one of the twentieth century's most original writers, one who made a remarkable contribution to the Theater of the Absurd

> *Principal personages:*
> SAMUEL BECKETT, the Irish-born playwright and novelist
> WILLIAM BECKETT, his easygoing, relaxed father, a quantity surveyor
> MARY ROE BECKETT, his moody, difficult mother
> PEGGY SINCLAIR, his first cousin, with whom he had a romantic liaison
> SUZANNE DESCHEVAUX-DUMESNIL, his wife, a piano teacher
> JAMES JOYCE, the Irish poet and novelist, with whom Beckett developed a long-lasting friendship
> R. B. "RUDDY" RUDMOSE-BROWN, a professor of Romance languages at Trinity College, Dublin, and one of the most important influences on the young Beckett's intellectual development

Of late, Samuel Beckett, the 1969 Nobel laureate in literature, has been the object of significant biographical interest. A key literary figure of the twentieth century, this practitioner of the Theater of the Absurd is revealed through insights into his emotional and mental life and through both clever and meaningful allusions to his work. *Samuel Beckett: The Last Modernist* sketches a portrait of a deeply dedicated writer, an "ordinary" Parisian Irishman, a man who was humane, profoundly learned, and unusually sensitive to his surroundings, circle of friends, and professional position.

Samuel Beckett was born May 13, 1906, in the family home in Foxrock, a prosperous suburb on the outskirts of Dublin. He later claimed, however, that his birth date was April 13, Good Friday. He also claimed to have had memories that preceded this date, memories of his fetal existence that include being at the dinner table in his mother's womb shortly before his birth, and overhearing the banal dinner conversation of the guests. Such prenatal memories engendered feelings of entrapment and suffocation in Beckett, as he would later divulge to a psychiatrist.

Beckett was the second son born to William Beckett and Mary Roe, members of an exclusive social class of Dublin society. The Becketts supposed themselves to be descended from Huguenot refugees who had come to Ireland from France after the revocation of the Edict of Nantes in 1685. William Beckett had shown little interest in an academic career; instead, given that his father was a very successful building contractor, responsible for such buildings as the National Library and National Museum in Dublin, he chose a career in quantity surveying, which, at the time, was equivalent to civil engineering and architecture. William Beckett was a shrewd businessman, socially minded, good-natured, and fond of masculine pursuits such as athletics and drinking. Samuel Beckett's mother, who was nicknamed May, was the daughter of the most successful Catholic businessman in Dublin. Somewhat high-strung, May Beckett found the world a rather wicked place but believed that it could be redeemed by religious puritanism. In essence, Beckett's parents were oddly matched: his father adaptable and moderate, his mother extremist and confrontational.

Unlike his brother Frank, his elder by four years, the young Samuel was a thin, sickly baby who cried constantly. As he grew, he became an extremely active child, suffering beatings from his mother, who found his antics inappropriate. A child psychologist might in fact view these acts as suggesting a certain level of disturbance. For example, one of Samuel's diversions was to climb to the top of a tall fir tree in the garden and, stretching out his arms and legs as if for flight, let himself fall, trusting the lower branches to break the impact. The fear of high places, along with recurring nightmares, would haunt Beckett all of his life.

In 1920, at the age of fourteen, Beckett was sent to Portora, an austere Irish Protestant boarding school, where pupils were taught to aspire to "manly" virtues such as truth-telling, trustworthiness, and fair play. Here Beckett was a normal, athletically inclined, clean-cut boy who could be singled out by authorities as a student to be emulated.

When he entered Trinity College in Dublin in 1923, he enrolled in the arts faculty to study modern languages. At this time, Beckett was an intellectually, emotionally, and sexually undeveloped seventeen-year-old who continued to live under his parents' roof. He showed little interest in anything Trinity had to offer other than sports facilities; his passions were golf, cricket, and motorbikes. In addition to theatergoing, Beckett discovered the cinema, notably the masters of comedy and pathos such as Charlie Chaplin, Harold Lloyd, and Buster Keaton. He would later become enamored with the Marx brothers and Laurel and Hardy, once silent movies were no more.

Toward the end of his second year at Trinity, Beckett began to take his studies seriously. One teacher, R. B. "Ruddy" Rudmose-Brown, professor of Romance languages, had a profound and lasting effect on Beckett's intellectual development. Under Rudmose-Brown's tutelage, Beckett read all sixteen of Jean Racine's plays, the influence of which can be seen in his own works as they observe, or closely, the three unities as Racine had derived them from Aristotle. In the autumn of 1927, after a summer trip to Florence on a traveling scholarship, Beckett took his degree, coming first in his class in modern languages and receiving a gold medal as well as fifty pounds.

Thanks to the influence of Rudmose-Brown, Beckett secured a job as a French teacher in Campbell College, Belfast, which was the main alternative to Portora for boys of the Northern Irish Protestant middle class. This experience was an unmitigated disaster. Unable to arrive on time for classes, often absent, departing from the set curriculum, and writing acerbic comments on his students' exercises, Beckett did not perform at an acceptable level. When confronted by the headmaster, who underlined that these pupils were the cream of Ulster, Beckett retorted that yes, they were rich and thick. Since he had been appointed for only one academic year, he was spared the trauma of a dismissal.

Beckett spent that summer in Europe, having wished to visit his aunt Cissie and her family in Kassel, Germany. The main attraction was his seventeen-year-old cousin, Peggy Sinclair, whom he had met several months before when her family visited Dublin. Peggy was at times loquacious and amusing; at other times she was snappish and acted like a spoiled child.

At the end of October, 1928, Beckett moved to Paris to take up a lectureship in English at the prestigious École Normale Supérieure, an appointment arranged through Trinity College. By this time, the French capital was well established as the home of avant-garde modernism. The Exposition des Arts Décoratifs in 1925, with its cubist and modernist outlook, and the innovative creations of Charles-Édouard Jean-neret (Le Corbusier) set the tone for aesthetic renewal. The 1920's in Paris were largely a Surrealist decade, attracting notable expatriates from the English-speaking world such as Ernest Hemingway, F. Scott Fitzgerald, Gertrude Stein, and James Joyce. Beckett was to become a close personal friend of Joyce. Both were Irish, shortsighted, agnostic, apolitical polyglots who were principally interested in Romance languages, and both set a high associative value on the language in which the traditional religions of their forebears had been expressed. Beckett soon became a welcome guest at the Joyce apartment.

During this time, Beckett became involved in the Paris literary scene, receiving a commission to write a piece on Marcel Proust's monumental *À la recherche du temps perdu* (1913-1927; *Remembrance of Things Past*, 1922-1931). He won a poetry contest on the subject of time with his *Whoroscope* (1930), a ninety-eight-line poem based on René Descartes' life. Paris proved a supremely liberating experience for Beckett, now a published author, an intimate friend of various important writers, and a man who had acquired his own literary identity.

After returning to Dublin in 1930 to take up a three-year teaching position at Trinity, Beckett resigned his position in 1932. He was simply too ill at ease speaking in public to be a teacher. Throughout his life, Beckett had suffered from recurring painful ailments, undoubtedly psychosomatic in origin. Certain situations caused him acute stomach upsets, fevers, colds, heart palpitations, dizziness, boils, cysts, facial rashes, or other disturbances. In 1933, William Beckett died from heart failure, and his son, devastated, would mourn his father's loss forever. Therapy that Beckett received in London seemed to assuage his physical ailments as he attempted to take on a more positive outlook about life. When he returned to Dublin in 1935, some of the physical ailments, such as night sweats, returned immediately. At home, Beckett found his mother nervous and depressed, but he comforted himself with the philosophical reflection that her state was no worse than it had often been in the past.

Toward the end of 1937, Beckett returned to Paris, which became his home until his death. He renewed his friendship with Joyce and initiated one with the artist Alberto Giacometti, expelled from the elite circle of Surrealists. Giacometti and Beckett had much in common. They shared late-night walks and a deeply ambiva-lent attitude toward women; they both feared entanglement and found it an obstacle to physical fulfillment. Both frequented prostitutes in the Latin Quarter. Their friendship was gradual in its development and intensely private.

When Adolf Hitler's troops entered Prague in 1939, Beckett realized that war was inevitable. He had become involved with Suzanne Deschevaux-Dumesnil, a piano teacher who was six years his senior. She had a deep understanding and love of music as well as well-developed tastes in literature, and when Beckett embarked on the experimental writing for which he was to become renowned, she was among his first admirers and supporters. She offered keen, perceptive comments on rehearsals of his plays and would become his wife in 1961. Beckett and Deschevaux-Dumesnil fled German-occupied Paris to the southern region of Roussillon, where he played an active role in the Resistance by delivering coded messages when special coordination of activities was required. For his commitment to the movement, Beckett was later awarded the Croix de Guerre.

The writing of *En attendant Godot* (1952; *Waiting for Godot*, 1954) was a liberating experience that Beckett later said saved his sanity. The play is by far the most famous and the most popular of Beckett's works. It evokes his peculiarly gloomy view of human existence, communicated through a profoundly original use of language. Beckett quickly became a well-known French author, yet one whose originality was still largely unknown in the English-speaking world. *Fin de partie* (1957; *Endgame*, 1958) followed *Waiting for Godot* and consolidated the reputation Beckett enjoyed as the writer who knew how to depict alienation in all of its despair and humanity. With his success came requests to mount his plays and to translate them. Beckett was a perfectionist where productions of his works were concerned, distrusting actors and insisting that his written stage directions be meticulously followed.

The awarding to Beckett of the Nobel Prize in Literature in 1969 left him somewhat indifferent: He did not attend the ceremony and believed that Joyce should have received such a distinction. Nevertheless, the award affected his career most dramatically, for thereafter his plays were performed on stage and in film around the world in a variety of languages. Beckett's career was at its zenith.

The 1970's were less hectic for him as he coped with failing sight and lung maladies. In his last years, he continued to write and to supervise productions of his works. His health deteriorated markedly; circulatory and breathing difficulties plagued him until his death in Paris in December 22, 1989, five months after the death of his wife, with whose mortal remains he was interred in the Montparnasse Cemetery.

As paradoxical as it might seem, like all great art, despite its bleakness, incongruities, and pathos, Beckett's work was a celebration of life. *Samuel Beckett* is also a celebration, a celebration of a man whose works have offered provocative, poignant, and engaging glimpses of the human condition, from alienation and isolation to tenderness and hope. Anthony Cronin's style is fluid, human, compelling, and richly documented. The sharpness of detail is at times remarkable—and the portrayal of a man of such enigmatic character and profoundly original inspiration requires nothing less.

Kenneth W. Meadwell

Sources for Further Study

Contemporary Review. CCLXX, April, 1997, p. 218.
Library Journal. CXXII, June 1, 1997, p. 98.
London Review of Books. XVIII, November 14, 1996, p. 8.
The New York Review of Books. XLIII, November 14, 1996, p. 24.
The New York Times Book Review. CII, August 3, 1997, p. 11.
The Southern Review. XXXIII, Summer, 1997, p. 536.
The Spectator. CCLXXVII, September 21, 1996, p. 45.
The Times Literary Supplement. September 27, 1996, p. 3.
The Wall Street Journal. July 11, 1997, p. A12.
The Washington Post Book World. XXVII, July 13, 1997, p. 9.

SAMUEL JOHNSON AND THE LIFE OF READING

Author: Robert DeMaria, Jr. (1948-   )
Publisher: Johns Hopkins University Press (Baltimore, Maryland). Illustrated. 270 pp. $39.95
Type of work: Literary criticism
Time: 1709-1997
Locale: Great Britain

Through an examination of what and how Samuel Johnson read, DeMaria explores the nature of reading from the eighteenth century to the end of the twentieth

Principal personage:
SAMUEL JOHNSON, the famous essayist

In *Printing Technology, Letters, and Samuel Johnson* (1987), Alvin Kernan argued that "Samuel Johnson . . . lived out, in an intense and dramatic manner, the social mutation of writers from an earlier role as gentleman-amateurs to a new authorial self based on the realities of print and its conditions of mechanical reproduction." Kernan thus uses Johnson as a synecdoche for eighteenth century authorship. The social mutations of authors resulted from changes in readership, which expanded in the 1700's. Robert DeMaria, Jr., who has written a biography of Johnson and a study of Johnson's *Dictionary* (1755), uses him to explore the nature of reading in the eighteenth century and beyond, since the approaches to the text that emerged in that period persist.

DeMaria's taxonomy embraces four ways of confronting a text. The first of these is "study," or reading to prepare oneself for life—and in Johnson's case for the afterlife as well, since the Bible was one of the books he studied diligently. So important was the Bible for Johnson that DeMaria devotes a section of his chapter on "study" to this work. Johnson owned a variety of Bibles in various sizes. He carried with him a small copy. When John Jebb, bishop of Limerick, visited Lichfield, Johnson's birthplace, in 1826, the Reverend Canon Hugh Bailye showed the bishop Johnson's pocket Bible, which bore "marks of close and constant study, being folded down, according to his custom, at numerous passages." Johnson preferred to dog-ear his books rather than to annotate them, and the surviving volumes from his library bear few marginal comments. In *Idler* 74 (September 15, 1759), Johnson warned against annotations because these require readers to "load their minds with superfluous attention, repress the vehemence of curiosity by useless deliberation, and by frequent interruption break the current of narration or the chain of reason, and at last [they] close the volume, and forget the passages and the marks together." When studying, Johnson did not wish to be interrupted.

Sir John Hawkins, one of Johnson's oldest friends and earliest biographers, quoted Johnson as saying "that no man read long together with a folio on his table:—Books, said he, that you may carry to the fire, and hold readily in your hand, are the most useful after all." This sentiment may explain why Johnson had a 1743 edition of a three-volume octavo Bible bound in eight volumes and a 1769 edition of a two-volume quarto Bible bound in seven volumes. A later owner of the 1769 work wrote in it that Johnson had rebound the books for "more convenient reading." Even when engaged in serious reading, Johnson sought comfort.

A second kind of study that DeMaria discusses involves the classics. A copy of Adam Littleton's Latin dictionary (1678) at the Lichfield birthplace bears Johnson's inscription, "Sam: Johnson Sept. 7th 1726," his seventeenth birthday. Johnson was reading diligently in Latin authors at this period, less assiduously in the Greeks, whom he read intensively at Oxford University. His period of heavy reading probably ended when he left college in 1729; at least Johnson cultivated the image of a dilatory student thereafter. His memory, however, was prodigious. Hester Thrale, a close friend and biographer of Johnson, reported that when the king of Denmark visited England in 1768, the playwright George Colman took one of the Danish noblemen to visit Johnson. Thinking to impress him by discussing Greek literature, the visitor soon discovered that Johnson preserved a "compendious . . . knowledge of authors, books, and every branch of learning in that language." Johnson later claimed that apart from Thrale's copy of Xenophon, he had "not looked in a Greek book these ten years."

His early reading must have been extensive as well as intensive. When Johnson came to Oxford in 1728, Dr. William Adams, master of Pembroke College, said that the young man "was the best qualified for the University that he [Adams] had ever known come there." Even before matriculating, on his first visit to Oxford to meet his prospective tutor, Johnson astonished the man by quoting from the fifth century grammarian Macrobius.

Macrobius represents another category of books that Johnson studied: compendia of learning. One of Johnson's favorite works was Robert Burton's *Anatomy of Melancholy* (1621), a virtual encyclopedia of curious lore. Johnson claimed that this "was the only book that ever took him out of bed two hours sooner than he wanted to rise." He owned at least two copies, the sixth edition (1652) and the eighth (1676).

The fourth category of books that Johnson studied was the neo-Latin poets and scholars of the sixteenth and seventeenth centuries. Johnson compiled a list of about a hundred books that he took with him to Oxford. This catalog begins with the poems of Joseph Scaliger and ends with those of Julius Caesar Scaliger—two of the most important humanists of the Renaissance. Also represented in this early collection were Erasmus, Daniel Heinsius, Theodore Beza, Marco Girolamo Vida, Claudian, Claudius Quillet, George Buchanan, John Barclay, and William Baxter.

Throughout his life Johnson sought to make himself a part of this erudite community. His first proposed work was an edition of the Latin poems of Angelo Poliziano. Johnson borrowed a copy of Poliziano from Pembroke College in 1734 and never returned it. Less than a month before his death, Johnson compiled a list of projects he was considering. These included a new edition of Claudian, a history of the Renaissance in literature, and a compilation such as Erasmus' *Adagia* (1500). Reading and collecting such books provided a way for Johnson to place himself in the humanist community he longed to join.

His lot forbade him a life of scholarship, and to earn his living as a writer he was compelled to abandon study for other kinds of reading. "Perusal," DeMaria's second category, is still serious reading, but it is undertaken to secure immediate information. Some of Johnson's perusing satisfied personal needs. He was afflicted with melancholy, and he consulted George Cheyne's *English Malady* (1733), which offered advice on diet and on means to combat depression. Cardinal Giovanni Bona's *Manuductio ad coelum* (1671; *A Guide to Eternity*, 1672) served as a spiritual equivalent to Cheyne's physical remedies. Other works Johnson perused for his work, such as when he sought apt quotations to illustrate meaning and usage for his *Dictionary* or to provide information for his edition of Shakespeare (1765) and his *Lives of the Poets* (1779-1781). His perusal often involved reference works. In compiling his *Dictionary*, for example, he used an interleaved copy of Nathaniel Bailey's *Dictionarium Britannicum*, first published in 1730.

DeMaria's third category is "mere reading," which involves less serious matter than study or perusal: "newspapers, narratives, advertisements, and such ephemera as tickets and playbills." Much of Johnson's writing was the stuff of mere reading, from his early employment by Thomas Warren in Birmingham in the early 1730's to his work for Edward Cave on the *Gentleman's Magazine* to his own *Rambler* (1750-1752) and *Idler* (1758-1760). In *Idler* 7 (May 27, 1758), Johnson commented, "One of the principal amusements of the Idler is to read the works of those minute historians the writers of news." Johnson's statement cuts two ways. On the one hand, he is saying that newspaper reading is for the idle, but he also acknowledges in this essay that

> all foreigners remark, that the knowledge of the common people of England is greater than that of any other vulgar. This superiority we undoubtedly owe to the rivulets of intelligence [newspapers] which are continually trickling among us, which every one may catch, and of which every one partakes.

More than a decade later, on March 31, 1772, Johnson again defended journalism: "The mass of every people must be barbarous where there is no printing, and consequently knowledge is not generally diffused. Knowledge is diffused among our people by the news-papers." In "Johnson's *Rambler* and Its Contemporary Context" (*Bulletin of Research in the Humanities* 85 [1982]: 27-64), John Woodruff shows how Johnson drew on newspaper accounts in creating his essays.

The eighteenth century witnessed a proliferation of journalism. Such publications not only provided reading matter but also changed the way people approached other texts, because such ephemera encouraged browsing and less careful reading.

DeMaria's fourth category is "curious reading," which concerns fiction. Johnson contributed a chapter to *The Female Quixote* (1752) by Charlotte Lennox. Here he warned of "Senseless Fictions . . . which at once vitiate the Mind, and pervert the Understanding." He attributed what he called his "unsettled turn of mind" to reading romances, but he did read them. He probably learned to read from Richard Johnson's *The Famous History of the Seven Champions of Christendom* (1687). Another romance of his childhood was *Don Bellianis of Greece*. When he visited Bishop Thomas Percy in the summer of 1764, Johnson read through *Felixmarte of Hircania* (1556). If

Johnson is to be believed, he rarely finished books as he did this one. He told Thrale that the only books, apart from the Bible, that he wished longer were *Don Quixote* (1605, 1615), *Robinson Crusoe* (1719), and *The Pilgrim's Progress* (1678, 1684). On a jaunt in March of 1776, he took with him *Il Palmerino d'Inghilterra* (1553-1554). While he may have chosen the book partly to keep up his Italian, he owned other, more serious volumes in that language that he might have chosen instead.

Johnson argued that such romances were less dangerous than realistic fiction because, as he wrote in *Rambler* 4 (March 31, 1750),

> the reader was in very little danger of making any application to himself; the virtues and crimes were equally beyond his sphere of activity; and he amused himself with heroes and with traitors, deliverers and persecutors, as with beings of another species, . . . who had neither faults nor excellencies in common with himself.

In *Rambler* 97 (February 19, 1751), Johnson excluded Samuel Richardson from his strictures against modern fiction, but Johnson in fact read widely in eighteenth century novels. He claimed to have read Henry Fielding's *Amelia* (1754) in one sitting. He was responsible for the publication of Oliver Goldsmith's *The Vicar of Wakefield* (1766)—DeMaria's dust jacket reproduces part of E. M. Ward's painting of *Dr. Johnson Perusing the Manuscript of "The Vicar of Wakefield"* (1843). As already noted, Johnson was involved in the publication of *The Female Quixote*. His praise of Fanny Burney's *Evelina* (1778) shows that he read that work. Many of Johnson's essays are actually short stories, and his *Rasselas* (1759) is an Oriental tale.

DeMaria's last chapter explores changes in reading brought about by hypertext and the World Wide Web. Unlike pessimists such as Sven Birkerts in *The Gutenberg Elegies: The Fate of Reading in an Electronic Age* (1994), DeMaria does not believe that books will disappear. He does maintain, though, that curious reading and study will become less common as perusal and mere reading expand. One danger that DeMaria sees in computerized texts is the loss of a community of readers, because hypertext allows each person to create individualized narratives and even individualized newspapers. In 1756, Johnson wrote that England had so many authors that "every man must be content to read his book to himself." Hypertext makes every reader a writer and so could produce the solipsistic nightmare that Johnson feared. The vast amount of material available on the World Wide Web, and the nature of that material, may also encourage cursory reading as opposed to more serious engagement with a text.

Because DeMaria has examined a wide range of what Johnson read, his book serves as an intellectual history of the writer and his age. In his *Life of Gray* (1781), Johnson coined the phrase "the common reader." Even if Johnson was an uncommon reader, his central position in the eighteenth century world of letters makes him a good exemplar of the ways in which people approached texts in that period. DeMaria's volume may be studied, perused, and looked into for enjoyment. Altogether, DeMaria has produced a book well worth reading.

Joseph Rosenblum

Sources for Further Study

Choice. XXXV, November, 1997, p. 477.
The Times Literary Supplement. September 5, 1997, p. 36.

THE SASKIAD

Author: Brian Hall (1959-   )
Publisher: Houghton Mifflin (Boston). 380 pp. $23.95
Type of work: Novel
Time: 1984
Locale: Tyler, a suburb of Ithaca, New York

A prose epic that focuses on the maturing of a bright adolescent girl and employs multilayered characters, plot elements, and language that recall Homer's Odyssey

Principal characters:
> SASKIA WHITE, the title character and protagonist, an imaginative adolescent
> LAUREN WHITE, her mother
> THOMAS, her absent father, whose last name remains unspecified
> JANE SINGH (spelled "Sing" by Saskia), her best friend
> BILL (called "Blufferoo" by Saskia), an unproductive writer and Lauren's occasional lover
> JO FLYNN, the mother of "the crew," a group of children Saskia supervises

Brian Hall's *The Saskiad* falls into the broad category known as *Bildungsroman* (novel of education). Like all such works, it has a young protagonist who embarks on an adventure of self-discovery. Authors as diverse as Johann Wolfgang von Goethe, Gustave Flaubert, James Joyce, and J. D. Salinger have written in this genre, so one might think its possibilities for further development limited. Even so, Hall's ability to interweave archaism and contemporary elements makes *The Saskiad* a very different kind of novel.

To begin with what is familiar, twelve-year-old Saskia White, the novel's protagonist, strongly and by her creator's clear intention resembles Telemachus, son of Odysseus, as portrayed in Homer's *Odyssey*. She lives with her mother, Lauren White, in a town near Ithaca, New York (recalling the Ithaca of Odysseus), on a neglected farm that had once been a commune. The general disarray and neglect parallel that of Odysseus' home during his absence.

Saskia has primary responsibility for raising the five children of Jo Flynn, a former communard who has remained on the property. Jo has, in effect, defaulted on her responsibilities as a mother, and except for meals, almost always remains locked in her trailer. Bill, whom Saskia privately identifies as "Blufferoo," has his own trailer, and he stays similarly secluded, presumably writing great works of literature that no one ever sees. Bill occasionally shares Lauren's bed (making him seem like a more successful version of one of Penelope's suitors), but he does this only according to Lauren's own terms and by her own schedule. Lauren's work, which considerably restricts her love life, is organic vegetable gardening. This and her evening job in Ithaca delay the need for her to make any commitment to her lover as efficiently as had Penelope's weaving and unweaving of Laertes' shroud.

Like Telemachus, Saskia has nominal authority in mundane matters during her father's absence; also like Telemachus, she lacks the moral authority that adulthood confers to meaningfully change the conditions under which she and her mother live. She lives amid chaos like many children in contemporary families, yet like Telemachus, her daily existence is an odd mixture of silent resentment and forbearance.

Athena, the goddess of intellect, ultimately becomes the agent of Telemachus' deliverance. It is she, masquerading as Mentor the wise traveler, who initiates Telemachus' search for Odysseus. In Saskia's case, books of varying degrees of acknowledged greatness open an inquiry into her father's imagined past and her evolving conception of her own identity. Homer's *Odyssey* is one of the works Saskia reads, and Saskia's identification of the people and places which surround her acquire an epic flavor, derived partly from Robert Fitzgerald's translation of Homer's poem. Thomas, the father she knows only through hazy memory and an occasional postcard, dwells among the Phaiakians (the mythic island people who rescue the shipwrecked Odysseus and return him at last to Ithaca). Perceptive readers will ultimately discover that Saskia's Phaiakians are in reality Danes.

One of the postcards Thomas sends is a photograph of himself in sailor's clothing. He stands at the ship's railing, a large dog at his side (perhaps like Odysseus' faithful dog Argus), and has an expression of tense control. Because Saskia has read the Horatio Hornblower novels of C. S. Forester, and since she knows that the damaged sailboat she discovered in the garage had belonged to her father, Thomas becomes "The Captain" and she his faithful lieutenant. Her mixed analogy grows more complex once she has read the journals of Marco Polo and has learned of her father's residence on an ashram in India. Thomas becomes the Venetian explorer and acquires a series of adventures in the Mongolian Empire of Kublai Khan. Cornell University, whose towered buildings Saskia can see daily, becomes an impregnable fortress of great wealth similar to Kublai's own, and Saskia vows to take this "castle of Huge Red" by force.

In this rich imaginative mix, readers can see that Saskia not only has a rich imaginative life but also has deep needs and great ambition. Just as she idolizes her absent father, she also idealizes her present but diffident mother. Lauren is, for Saskia, like Apollo's laurel tree: statuesque, with lovely long hair and perhaps like the mythic Daphne herself, who assumed the form of a tree rather than submit to Apollo's advances. Although Saskia takes this analogy no further than Apollo's laurel crown, it perfectly describes a woman who can inspire, like Petrarch's Laura, yet be unresponsive, like Apollo's Daphne.

Since she grows up without television or radio, Saskia's imagination runs deeply. She can recognize the constellations not only because she lives amid the mountains, but also because she identifies the science of astronomy with the Phaiakians, the Danes among whom her father lives. One might expect Saskia to read the popular works of Cornell University astronomer Carl Sagan, but identification with her father leads her to a translated biography of Tycho Brahe, the sixteenth century Danish astronomer whose most famous achievement was discovery of the new star in the constellation

Cassiopeia. The mythic Cassiopeia was the mother of Andromeda, willing to sacrifice her daughter to a sea monster, and this connection adds a dark irony to Saskia's obsession with Brahe.

Brahe's life appears to resemble that of Thomas, at least insofar as what Saskia can learn about her father's past. Brahe's marriage to a peasant strained relations with his family, and Saskia knows of no contact between Thomas and his parents initially. Since she can obtain no clear answers from Lauren, Saskia wonders at the apparent lack of contact between her father's and mother's families and about the origin of the farmland on which she lives. It becomes her own Uraniborg, the name of the observatory Brahe built on the grant of land he received from Frederick II of Denmark. Saskia knows that Frederick's successor, Christian IV, withdrew his support from Brahe because of the astronomer's arrogance. She also knows that some consider Thomas arrogant and that her teachers and schoolmates at Tyler Junior (as she always calls her high school) object to her own behavior as arrogant. For her, this is merely another identification with her absent father.

It is at Tyler Junior that Saskia meets Jane Singh, an attractive girl whose family originated from India but who herself has come from London via Boston. Saskia's attraction to Jane exists on several levels. First, Jane is willowy, naturally graceful, and delicately beautiful—in short, everything Saskia would like to be. Although Jane is only a year older than Saskia, she has had considerably more experience in the world. Jane's complexion is dark, while Saskia's is light. Such contrast extends beyond accidental difference, however, since Jane is sexually experienced, uses marijuana, and has had a history of problems at school. Jane blames her troubles on her parents' severity as well as their fundamental indifference. The two girls quickly form an alliance, and Saskia alters her friend's name to "Sing" because she admires Jane's lyrical grace. With ironic humor, Saskia christens Jane's home "Sing Sing," since Jane considers it her prison.

None of this complex imagining settles the question of Saskia's identity. Her first real chance for self-discovery comes when one of Thomas' postcards invites her on a walking tour of what Hall's readers can identify as northern Denmark. Thomas invites Lauren as well, but she refuses. Appropriately, since she has become Saskia's alter ego, Jane goes in Lauren's place. From this point to its conclusion, *The Saskiad* becomes considerably darker in its implications. Initially, Thomas seems much as Saskia had imagined him. He appears to be an idealistic adventurer in the best sense, an environmental activist who takes the girls to the site of a proposed dam that threatens environmental damage, then single-handedly delays its construction.

Even so, Hall increasingly shows that there is more to the character of Thomas than first appears. A sexual dimension, actually encouraged by Saskia, appears in the relationship of Thomas and Jane, with Jane as Lauren's surrogate and Calypso-like enchantress. The normally inquisitive Saskia does not probe too deeply into either the moral proprieties of this situation or the inconsistencies of the stories Thomas tells about his past.

Thomas returns to the New York farm after a decade of absence; its external order improves, although the sexual tensions become more complicated. Thomas and Lauren reestablish their relationship amid a series of images that recall the Odysseus-Penelope reunion of Homer's *Odyssey*. Thomas has Odysseus' strong ego as well, and one can sense that for Thomas, as for Odysseus, a domestic life will only be temporary.

Homer does not consider the fate of Telemachus, who seems a much more fragile personality than Odysseus. Both Saskia and Telemachus appear to need stability and a sense of place more than do their fathers, disagreeable as the place may be. Hall treats this question with considerable skill in telling the story of Saskia. Almost immediately after Thomas leaves the commune, Saskia leaves too. She trades her identity as Saskia White for that of Jane Dark, a character she bases on her estranged friend Jane Singh. Saskia's experiences in New York City are dark but ultimately short-lived. Upon her return, she appears more reconciled, having learned at least some of the truth concerning her past, but like most people, she is by no means certain of the path her own odyssey will take.

There is even more complex use of motifs and imagery in *The Saskiad* than one can discuss here, primarily because it is so tightly bound up in the novel. There is the recurring motif of drug use in contexts that recall Homer's lotus-eaters, Helen's anodyne, and the Circe *moly* episode. The whole question of identity and identification recalls Odysseus' adventures, particularly with the Cyclops.

As in Homer, wordplay and mythic identification of place are frequent. Word games abound and, as one example, it is not until the final pages of Hall's novel that readers know that 1984, the Orwellian year, is the period of its primary action. They know this only if willing to add a series of roman numerals contained within a message.

Young as she is, Saskia seems to realize from the beginning that although mythic patterns frequently occur in the lives of individuals, the individuals who act life's drama make only short appearances in roles less important than they themselves might think. As Hall has Saskia note, whether of herself, Thomas, Lauren, or Jane, the words that best describe the process of living are "Now you see me, now you . . . "

Robert J. Forman

Sources for Further Study

Booklist. XCIII, December 1, 1996, p. 642.
Boston. LXXXIX, February, 1997, p. 146.
Library Journal. CXXI, November 1, 1996, p. 107.
Los Angeles Times Book Review. January 26, 1997, p. 2.
The New York Times Book Review. CII, January 19, 1997, p. 17.
The New Yorker. LXXIII, March 10, 1997, p. 92.
The Observer. November 24, 1996, p. 18.
Publishers Weekly. CCXLIV, January 13, 1997, p. 49.
The Times Literary Supplement. October 18, 1996, p. 24.
The Washington Post Book World. XXVII, February 9, 1997, p. 8.

THE SELECTED LETTERS OF MARIANNE MOORE

Author: Marianne Moore (1887-1972)
Edited by Bonnie Costello, Celeste Goodridge, and Cristanne Miller
Publisher: Alfred A. Knopf (New York). 612 pp. $35.00
Type of work: Letters
Time: 1905-1969
Locale: Carlisle and Bryn Mawr College, Pennsylvania; and New York City

The letters of modernist poet Marianne Moore reveal the strength of intellect and character that made her such an influential figure

Principal personages:
MARIANNE MOORE, a modernist poet and editor
JOHN WARNER MOORE, her brother, a navy chaplain, referred to as
    Warner or by one of many nicknames
MARY WARNER MOORE, their mother, rarely separated from her
    daughter, referred to as "Mole"
THOMAS STEARNS ELIOT, a poet and early champion of Moore
EZRA POUND, a poet and tireless promoter of new poets, charged with
    treason after World War II for supporting Benito Mussolini
WINIFRED ELLERMAN, known as Bryher, an English writer who edited
    an unauthorized edition of Moore's poetry with H. D.
HILDA DOOLITTLE, known as H. D., a poet and editor, the first to publish
    Moore's poetry in the London journal, *The Egoist*
ALFRED KREYMBORG, a poet and editor who provided Moore with her
    first entry into New York literary society
ELIZABETH BISHOP, the most important of many younger poets whom
    Moore encouraged

In the biographies of fellow poets, Marianne Moore often comes across as a semi-recluse, living with her mother, herself an eccentric and oddly formidable character everyone is afraid to offend. Venerable yet, at the same time, fond of the circus and the Dodgers, Moore wears the aura of the past in these accounts, a revenant of an earlier time when "spinsterhood" could be liberating. This old-fashioned sensibility, however, produced one of the defining voices of modernist verse.

In a letter written late in life, she encapsulates her aesthetic with the words of the German artist George Grosz: "Endless curiosity/ observation and a/ great amount of joy in the thing." Combining joyful curiosity with technical virtuosity, Moore produced highly polished poems that often seem, on first impression, spontaneous and free-form. In one letter, she defines poetry as "entrapped conversation." The result of her fascination with speech rhythms is a free verse based on the strict repetition, line for line, of syllable counts from stanza to stanza. As she explains in a letter to poet Ezra Pound, she never started with the meter, but, as soon as she had a stanza whose rhythm she liked, it set the pattern for the rest of the poem.

Her poetry is often considered difficult despite her passion for clarity and precision. She deals with difficult issues, and the accumulation and compression of detail, with logical connections often left for the reader, make her poems dense. However, a combination of high moral purpose, conceptual depth, close observation, and bracing wit enliven her writing even as she lays bare humanity's frailties.

Marianne Moore was born in Kirkwood, Missouri, just outside St. Louis, in 1887. She lived with her mother Mary and brother Warner in her grandfather's house until his death, after which they moved to Carlisle, Pennsylvania. Moore never met her father, who suffered a nervous breakdown after his business reverses, and she permitted herself little contact with her father's side of the family until her mother's death in 1947.

This suggests the kind of hold Mary had over her children. They were devoted to her, and the three of them comprised a very close-knit family. The family employed its own special language, which included an elaborate system of nicknames drawn from many sources such Kenneth Grahame's *The Wind in the Willows* (1908), where they found the ones that stuck: Warner was Badger, Mary was Mole, and Marianne, often referred to with male pronouns, was Rat.

Except for her four years at Bryn Mawr College, Moore lived with her mother until the older woman's death in 1947. While in college, Moore wrote her mother and brother at least three times a week. In striking contrast to the formal tone of her later correspondence, these early letters are, at times, almost embarrassingly exuberant. Always full of pluck (thinking nothing, for example, of killing and dissecting a stray cat), Moore overflows with passionate accounts of her activities and her crushes on schoolmates. Yet, in the midst of it, she can write,

> Self-possession and a spirit of forgiveness are the things to hold on to, if you want *really*, to be master of your fate. By self-possession, I mean courage and patience. By the other, a real Christ-like desire to aid, tolerate and endure—without any desire to dazzle.

Of course, she wanted to dazzle more than anything. The letters provide a compelling account of her struggle to reconcile the conflicting impulses toward self-assertion and self-mastery. Using a healthy sense of humor to maintain her sanity, she sublimated both drives into a poetry of close observation and sophisticated technique that obscure the personal. With adolescent fervor, she says, in one letter, that writing is merely selfish and puling if it is not great. With this all-or-nothing declaration, she set the bar very high for herself but cleared it with remarkable ease.

After Bryn Mawr, Moore moved back to Carlisle, where she completed a course in a commercial college and taught in the Indian School. It was in Carlisle, between 1909 and 1915, that Moore achieved her distinctive style. After many rejections, she made a very impressive debut. Her first poem appeared in 1915 in the London journal *The Egoist*, and more poems appeared soon after in two important American journals, *Poetry* and *Others*.

In a letter dated May 9, 1915, she writes her brother: "My poems came out this week to the polite oh's and ah's of the neighborhood—Mole is very much disgusted with me for owning up to them." Later that year, Moore's mother advised her not to publish a book of her poetry yet, calling her work, so far, "ephemeral." She reports this as if it were a joke, which is characteristic. Equally characteristic, she heeded her mother's advice, resisting publication until her friends Hilda Doolittle (H. D.) and Winifred Ellerman (Bryher) brought out an edition in England in 1921 without consulting her in advance. In 1918, at the urging of Alfred Kreymborg, editor of *Others*, Moore moved to New York City with her mother, where they lived for the rest of their lives, moving several times between Manhattan and Brooklyn. Her letters make it very clear that Moore was no recluse. Though she rarely ventured far from New York City, she was an enthusiastic consumer of its cultural fare: theater, films, museums, lectures, and sports. In addition, she entered literary society. While she might still gush like a school girl about meeting the Irish poet William Butler Yeats, she was quickly accepted by literary New York as an equal. She impressed everyone as an original, her conversation as striking as her red hair.

At first, she supported herself working in a library while continuing to place poems and reviews with various journals, particularly *The Dial*. One of the most highly respected monthlies in that golden age of little magazines, *The Dial* published her work regularly, marking her as a recognized trendsetter. Then, in 1925, she became the editor, cementing her literary standing.

As an editor, she exchanged letters with many prominent writers, including D. H. Lawrence, Yvor Winters, and Hart Crane. A few of the letters from this period are frosty, even sarcastic, and she made enemies among poets, some of whom thought her old-fashioned and prudish. However, the dominant tone, especially in her lifelong correspondence with such writers as Ezra Pound and T. S. Eliot, is both assured and self-effacing. In contrast to the exuberant college letters, these show that appealing blend of authority and modesty that led William Carlos William to refer to her as "our saint."

She wrote little during her editorial tenure, but the magazine closed in 1929, and the 1930's were productive years. With a growing reputation, she found herself in the position of a role model for younger poets such as Elizabeth Bishop, who became a cherished friend and correspondent. Throughout the 1930's and 1940's, she produced steadily, garnering awards, prizes, and honorary degrees. She responded to them all with gracious humility, downplaying her eminence in her accounts of these honors.

During this period, her mother figures prominently in many of the letters, often as a very precious oddity, cranky but too humorous for offense. There is no question, of course, that Moore considered her mother the most important influence on her writing, and, in the postscript to her 1935 *Selected Poems*, she acknowledges the debt. However, among the photographs included in this book, one taken by Cecil Beaton in 1946 seems to capture something of the burden Moore's relationship with her mother must have placed on her. The poet is in the foreground, and her mother is in the background, sitting down. Mary, farther from the camera, is lit so as to appear to be on same plane as her daughter, but much smaller, like a household god, smiling enigmatically beside Moore, who looks like the weary writer with her muse.

Weary, but indefatigable, and, in 1952, her *Collected Poems* won the National Book Award, the Pulitzer Prize, and the Bolligen Prize. In the aftermath of that, she became a minor celebrity, contributing to more mainstream magazines. Among other assignments, she reported on a trip to the zoo for *Life* and baseball for *Family Circle*. One unfortunate effect of success was a deluge of mail, with as many as fifty letters a day. Though regretting her graciousness to importuning strangers, she gladly encouraged younger poets when she could.

Moore had a stroke in 1963 but continued to lead a full life, even taking in the fights at Madison Square Garden with George Plimpton in 1965 at the age of 77. Her many friends delighted in sending her gifts, especially clothes and flowers, indulging her taste for the stylish. More importantly, she relied on friends to bring her out of herself. "The idea of foregoing visits as one becomes an older and older musketeer and needs them the more, is the apex of folly." It was folly that she avoided until 1969, when a major stroke left her incapacitated until her death three years later.

Critics often point to her poems about armored animals as evidence of her own need for self-protection. The letters make clear that she wore her armor lightly. Whatever she meant in a letter to Elizabeth Bishop about the "heroisms of abstinence," whatever she gave up for her mother's sake, she never grew bitter or brittle. Far from hardening, she became more gracious with time.

In a letter written in 1921, she says, "Duty and self-inflicted hardship as abstract virtues defeat themselves but when rightly applied, are the essence of perfection." Duty and hardship, while suited to a saint, hardly sound likely to produce the kindly and beloved figure that Moore became. This is part of her fascination. She sought a willed return to the spontaneous, to the innocent, which is no more and no less paradoxical or futile than her effort to achieve a technique artless in its perfection.

She chose animals as the subject for many of her poems because they cannot be false to their true nature, while humans can hardly be true to theirs. In her poem "The Frigate Pelican" (1934), she talks about "uniting levity with strength." Moore herself united a strong character with buoyant good humor, but here she means the reader to think of the unity of spirit and body as well.

In animals, the unity is instinctive; one acts with the other. In humans, unity is a moral matter requiring considerable effort because it involves the exertion of spirit against the body. "The spirit cannot submit to the body . . . or its identity is impaired." In a letter attacking the "doctrinaire attitude to degradation and unhope," she laments the vulgarity and crudeness she finds creeping into the poetry of others. She considers this a fake realism, one that ignores the spiritual reality of human dignity.

It is her belief in that dignity that, more than anything, elevates her work. Though the letters rarely mention religion overtly, in one Moore claims an almost priestly role: "We are here to transcend and help others transcend what impairs us." These letters show that Marianne Moore, never blind to human impairments, followed her own advice, making each obstacle she encountered serve poetry as means for aesthetic, even spiritual, ascent.

Philip McDermott

Sources for Further Study

Booklist. XCIV, October 15, 1997, p. 379.
Boston Globe. October 26, 1997, p. N1.
Elle. October, 1997, p. 126.
Los Angeles Times Book Review. CII, October 12, 1997, p. 2.
New York. XXX, November 10, 1997, p. 104.
The New York Times Book Review. CII, November 16, 1997, p. 68.
Paris Review. Issue 135, Summer, 1995, p. 41.
Publishers Weekly. CCXLIV, September 1, 1997, p. 85.
St. Louis Post-Dispatch. November 23, 1997, p. D5.
Yale Review. LXXXV, July, 1997, p. 58.

SELECTED POEMS, 1960-1990

Author: Maxine Kumin (1925-   )
Publisher: W. W. Norton (New York). 294 pp. $27.50
Type of work: Poetry

Prize-winning poet Maxine Kumin offers a vivid, highly readable collection of poems about everyday objects on her New England farm and about the many members of her far-flung family

Although Maxine Kumin is primarily known as a poet, she has published widely in other genres as well, including four novels, eighteen works of juvenile fiction (four coauthored with friend and fellow poet Anne Sexton), one book of short stories, and two books of essays, including the famous volume *To Make a Prairie: Essays on Poets, Poetry, and Country Living* (1980). *Selected Poems, 1960-1990* represents the poet's selection of her own best work from nine volumes, beginning with *Halfway* (1961) and ending with *Nurture* (1989). Although *Connecting the Dots* (1996) is not represented in this collection, Kumin does include a group of four poems from the "Joppa Diary" section of *Up Country* (1972), the book for which she won the Pulitzer Prize in 1973.

Significantly, Joppa is the name of the country road on which her farm (outside Warner, New Hampshire) is located. This farm is the locus of all the natural artifacts she celebrates in her work, including swans, horses, pigs, sheep, dogs, bats, skunks, peas, beans, radishes, tomatoes, trees, and weeds. In an unblinking fashion, Kumin celebrates the precious beauty of each creature without ever losing sight of its inevitable mortality. In her world, beauty depends upon the certain coming of death, and a kind of tragic sense informs the best and most typical of her poems. Beauty and loss always coexist in Kumin's poetic universe.

There is a wholeness and unity to this poetic world, chiefly because she writes about two dominant subjects—nature and the members of her family—and also because she writes with precision and a masterful command of the metaphorical possibilities of the English language. Kumin is a dedicated and careful master of her craft who can somehow divide her time between teaching workshops, writing books, and weeding her garden. A true poet, she is always creating links and connections between one image or perception and another, a process she calls "retrieval." Here, for example, is her telling description of a dog swimming in a pond:

> A dog was swimming and splashing.
> Air eggs nested in his fur.
> The hairless parts of him bobbled like toys
> and the silk of his tail blew past like milkweed.
> The licorice pads of his paws
> sucked in and out,
> making the shapes of kisses.

The moment of that human and canine coexistence is saved forever, preserved in a series of unforgettable similes and metaphors.

In like manner, Kumin, who usually writes in a kind of controlled free verse, can also employ traditional rhyme to achieve powerful effects. The splashing rhythm and echoing sounds of raindrops may have inspired her intricate rhyming in this stanza from "The First Rain of Spring," with its *abaabab* pattern of rhymes and the unusual effect of whole lines echoing one another:

> This is the first rain of spring:
> it is changing to snow in the west.
> The children sleep, closing the ring;
> this is the first rain of spring.
> Darkly, inside the soft nest,
> the children sleep, closing the ring,
> It is changing to snow in the west.

A poem about rain provides a simple introduction to Kumin's major thematic preoccupation, the world of nature, as it is closely observed and studied without sentimentality or false piety. This natural world becomes numinous, almost mystical in its effect on a truly observant writer such as Kumin. In "The Hermit Wakes to Bird Sounds," her use of onomatopoeia links the unique tones and song patterns of New England birds to the common mechanical objects they suggest—typewriters, sewing machines, and pumps:

> The bird who presides at the wellhouse primes the pump.
> Two gurgles, a pause, four squeaks of the handle
> and time after time a promise of water
> can be heard falling back in the pipe's throat.

The animals, like their observer, are fragile members of the biosphere, never knowing if or when they will die. "Sleeping with Animals," for example, is a highly autobiographical poem in which Kumin recounts her nocturnal nurturing of a brood-mare "ten days past due," an event that calls to mind an earlier tragedy. Kumin's universe is not merely defined by birdsongs or beautiful flora but by the juxtaposition of beauty and death. The power of death extends even to the lovely, newborn foals. One foal, she recalls, was "stillborn," another

> One, hours old, dead of a broken spine.
> Five others swam like divers into air,
> dropped on clean straw, were whinnied to, tongued dry,
> and staggered, stagey drunkards, to their feet,
> nipped and nudged by their mothers to the teat.

Kumin evokes this particularized world of nature repeatedly because it is one of the ways she defines herself. The nature poems are not decorative but documentary in nature. She sees herself as intimately involved in the natural environment. In "January 25th," a love poem to her husband, the couple lie together "back to back" in a freezing farmhouse that grew so cold that a "ball of steel wool/ froze to the kitchen window sill." However, the sun rises and covers the pair in "daylight the color of buttermilk," and Kumin addresses her husband in poetry that links them to the hibernating tadpoles and the gradual coming of spring. Thus, the lovers become survivors:

> Lie still; lie close.
> Watch the sun pick
> splinters from the window flowers.
> Now under the ice, under twelve knee-deep layers
> of mud in last summer's pond
> the packed hearts of peers are beating
> barely, barely repeating
> themselves enough to hang on.

Nature, however, is not the only frame of reference in the unfolding story of the poet's life. The other great backdrop is provided by her family history. In fact, *Selected Poems* could be read as a kind of family history, beginning with Kumin's great-grandfather who emigrated from somewhere in Bohemia and who wrote letters to his daughter (Kumin's grandmother) on the official bills of sale from his tailor shop in Newport News, Virginia: "ROSENBERG, THE TAILOR, DEBTOR/ A FULL LINE OF GOODS OF ALL THE LATEST IN/ SUITING AND PANTS."

In "Sperm," she addresses the sexual vigor of her grandfather, who eventually had seventeen grandchildren who would cover his wrinkled face with kisses like "polka dots." This grandfather, she imagines, may have been making love to her grandmother in New York City at the same time that the trolley car

> derailed taking the corner at 15th Street
> in a shower of blue sparks, and Grandmother's
> corset spread out like a filleted fish
> to air meanwhile on the windowsill.

This family saga continues in "The Deaths of the Uncles," perhaps one of Kumin's saddest and most poignant poems on the theme of death and loss. She likens the whole process of writing these poems about family members to "going backward in a home movie." Each one of her uncles is dead, but each is remembered for the virtues and occasional vices of his lifetime. Uncle Mitchell might be taken as an emblem for the group as he eminently suggests the inevitability of change and loss, for Mitchell undergoes a dramatic physical metamorphosis: Once he was "big bellied" and "broad as a rowboat," but then he

> Shrank to a toothpick after his heart attack,
> fasted on cottage cheese, threw out his black cigars
> and taken at naptime died in his dressing gown
> tidy in paisley wool, old pauper thumb in his mouth.

Yet, Mitchell and his brothers were once young and jolly, dressed in knickers, spats, and puttees, entertaining their girlfriends on Kumin's "grandmother's veranda" and "spiking the lemonade." The poet remembers it all, the good and the bad. The reader senses that their deaths preserved and heightened her powers of recollection so that her form of honoring the lost relatives is to create the precise imagery and detailed description employed in this elegy.

In "My Father's Neckties," Kumin uses imagery like a painter applying a few deft touches of color. She suggests her father's personality in a double image in which the lightning bolts of anger merge with the printed design of his neckwear. Kumin sees him in a dream that encapsulates her entire girlhood, "a time of/ ugly ties and acrimony: six or seven/ blue lightning bolts outlined in yellow." He was a man who wore bright colors "recklessly," a man given to hiding out in the "bargain basement of his feelings." By contrast, Kumin's mother, devastatingly sketched in "Life's Work," appears repressed and undeveloped, a stunted personality that ceased to grow after Kumin's grandfather forbade her to go on tour with a violinist, even though she was a "Bach specialist . . . fresh out of the Conservatory." Kumin determines to be her own person and rebels against her parents by choosing to become a swimmer, entering "the water like a knife." The mature poet seizes this image again and places the venue of the freedom-swim in nature, an act of intimacy and bravado: "I hung my bathrobe on two pegs./ I took the lake between my legs." In this place she is utterly welcome; fish twitch beneath her and sing her name.

The most moving of the family poems are those addressed to her daughters and husband. In "Making the Jam Without You," Kumin addresses the poem to a nineteen-year-old daughter who speaks three languages. She has left home to travel in Germany. Kumin reminds her of the bonding that took place in the kitchen, "that harem of good smells," while they ritually prepared blackberry jam under "a white cocoon of steam." Kumin wants to put a dream in her daughter's head because the poet wishes the sweetest and most romantic possibilities for her—an angelic suitor, with whom she might pick giant berries in the mountains and spread the "bright royal fur" of ruby-red jam on fresh bread. In short, the poet donates a fairy-tale fantasy (complete with Prince Charming) to her distant and clearly beloved daughter.

In "Family Reunion," Kumin's daughters return home for a roast pig dinner, with all the trimmings provided from their mother's garden. The good meal ends, and the poet reflects on how their roles and relative positions have changed. Their growth into adulthood is just another form of loss, another adjustment for the poet:

> Wearing our gestures how wise you grow,
> ballooning to overfill our space,
> the almost-parents of your parents now.
> So briefly having you back to measure us
> is harder than having let you go.

Kumin composes many touching elegies for her husband in the pages of *Selected Poems*. Perhaps the most affecting is the poem entitled simply "How It Is." A month after the death of her husband, the poet wears his blue jacket one day, with the following results:

The dog at the center of my life recognizes
you've come to visit, he's ecstatic.
In the left pocket, a hole.
In the right, a parking ticket
delivered up last August on Bay State Road.
In my heart, a scatter like milkweed,
a flinging from the pods of the soul.
My skin presses your old outline.

In a sense, all of the poems in Maxine Kumin's *Selected Poems* are about "outlines" that the poet has touched. The book is a treasure of craft and pure feeling. There is not a dull page—or even a single poem unworthy of rereading. In the midst of a pervasive video culture, Kumin's text reminds the readers of America that life always has more, much more, to offer.

Daniel L. Guillory

Sources for Further Study

Booklist. XCIII, May 15, 1997, p. 1557.
Library Journal. CXXII, June 15, 1997, p. 74.
The New York Times Book Review. CII, August 3, 1997, p. 10.
Ploughshares. XXIII, Spring, 1997, p. 215.
Publishers Weekly. CCXLIV, April 28, 1997, p. 70.

SIMENON
A Biography

Author: Pierre Assouline (1953-   )
First published: Simenon: Biographie, 1992, in France
Translated from the French by Jon Rothschild
Publisher: Alfred A. Knopf (New York). Illustrated. 447 pp. $32.50
Type of work: Literary biography
Time: The twentieth century
Locale: Belgium, France, the United States, and Switzerland

An exhaustive biography of novelist Georges Simenon, creator of Inspector Maigret and author of hundreds of detective and psychological novels

> *Principal personages:*
> GEORGES SIMENON, a prolific Belgian author
> DÉSIRÉ SIMENON, his father
> HENRIETTE SIMENON, his mother
> RÉGINE "TIGY" SIMENON, his first wife
> DENYSE SIMENON, his second wife
> TERESA SBURELIN, his companion during his final years
> MARIE-JO SIMENON, his daughter
> ANDRÉ GIDE, a prominent French writer who championed him

Any account of Georges Simenon's eventful life must deal in superlatives, the most obvious of them literary. "Between 1924 and 1931," estimates Pierre Assouline, the Belgian novelist "published about 190 pulp novels under at least seventeen pseudonyms." This is an extraordinary figure, even when one realizes that most of them were short novels of little consequence. More astonishing still, Simenon went on to write more than two hundred further volumes under his own name, dozens of them featuring the immortal Inspector Jules Maigret of the Paris Judiciary Police.

Who was the man behind this accomplishment? Assouline divides Simenon's life into four parts, each of them set in a particular country and each dominated by a particular woman: Simenon's mother, Henriette, his two wives, Tigy and Denyse, and his final companion, Teresa.

Georges Simenon was born in Liège, Belgium, in 1903. His father, Désiré, was an amiable and easygoing insurance agent whose fondness for timepieces would eventually become an obsession with Georges. His mother, Henriette, was in many ways Désiré's opposite, an ambitious, emotionally repressed woman who made no secret of her preference for Georges's brother. (When the latter eventually died in the French Foreign Legion, Henriette would wonder aloud, "Why did it have to be him instead of you?") One of Simenon's late works, *Lettre à ma mère* (1974; *Letter to My Mother,* 1976) represents an attempt to come to terms with Henriette's bitterness.

At nineteen, already an industrious journalist with one published (albeit minor) novel under his belt, Simenon set out for Paris. A year later, he married a childhood sweetheart, Régine Renchon, nicknamed Tigy. It was during his early years with Tigy that he transformed himself into a virtual writing machine, turning out a seemingly endless series of brief romances and sensational novels under a stable of pseudonyms. Also at this time Simenon met Josephine Baker, an African American entertainer who was the toast of Paris in the 1920's. Simenon was frankly infatuated with Baker and celebrated her sexual appeal in print, although Tigy seems to have been unaware of the relationship that for a while flared between them.

Finally concluding that he had mastered his craft, Simenon began writing under his own name in 1931. His first signed work was *Monsieur Gallet, décédé* (1931; *The Death of Monsieur Gallet*, 1932), a mystery featuring an astute but unassuming French police inspector named Jules Maigret. Second only to Arthur Conan Doyle's Sherlock Holmes in the annals of crime fiction, Maigret would eventually appear in seventy-six novels and collections of short stories, including Simenon's last work of fiction.

At first Simenon sought out a variety of publishers because he wrote so much—certainly more than any one firm could reasonably handle. Even after he moderated his production, however, he changed firms with some regularity, driving bargains that left his publishers reeling. These negotiations made Simenon an increasingly wealthy man, but the attention Assouline devotes to them is sometimes numbing.

Simenon could be relentless in his attempts at self-promotion. He insisted that reprints of one novel be sold with free pairs of handcuffs, resulting in an order for three thousand of the restraints. He launched the Maigret series by renting a nightclub and throwing an "Anthropometric Ball" featuring actors dressed as policemen, prostitutes, and pimps. Another actor appeared as "a butcher in a bloodstained apron." Invitations were printed as booking cards, and fingerprints were taken at the door. The event was attended by more than a thousand guests and was an enormous success.

A vague sensation of ennui led Simenon into a brief period of withdrawal from "ordinary life." There followed a brief period of withdrawal from "ordinary" life. It was during this period—eleven days, later nine, still later seven—that a handful of characters took over Simenon's consciousness, their names drawn from a collection of telephone books. Subsequently Simenon evolved an obsessive method for writing his novels. The writer sharpened his pencils (but kept a typewriter nearby), filled half a dozen pipes, and began his story, completing one chapter a day. The work almost always involved an ordinary, often mediocre, central character driven to his or her limit—and then beyond, into violence and death. The finished manuscript was retyped and presented to Simenon for light editing. Throughout the process the author rigidly maintained the same routine, taking the same walks and wearing the same clothes, that had marked the first day.

Yet Simenon was much more than a writing machine, as critics and fellow writers made clear. One early fan was American novelist and short-story writer Ernest Hemingway, whose severely laconic style paved the way for Simenon's own. Another was novelist André Gide, a mandarin arbiter of French taste whose opinion Simenon valued enormously and whose advice he often sought. As early as 1939, Gide offered the following praise in a literary journal honoring the budding writer: "I consider Simenon a great novelist, perhaps the greatest and most authentic novelist we have in French literature today." Gide routinely annotated his personal copies of Simenon's novels and maintained a file of notes for a projected study, but the work remained unfinished at Gide's death in 1951.

After World War II, Simenon moved with Tigy and their son to the United States. In New York City, he met Denyse Ouimet, whom he hired as his secretary and with whom he immediately began a passionate affair. She soon became a part of the Simenon *ménage*, along with Tigy and a housekeeper with whom Simenon had maintained a long-standing sexual relationship. The arrangement grew increasingly unstable, however, particularly after Denyse bore Simenon a son in late 1949. Within a year, Simenon had divorced Tigy and married Denyse.

In the mid-1950's, Simenon moved his newly reconfigured family to Switzerland, where he built a large, oddly sterile compound. None of the family found peace in the ostensibly orderly realm of Switzerland. Driven by alcoholism, a mania for control (or possibly frustration over Simenon's mania for control), and resentment of her husband's talent, Denyse began to exhibit unmistakable signs of mental instability. At one point she apparently made sexual advances toward their own daughter, Marie-Jo, who would later commit suicide.

Simenon and Denyse separated in the mid-1960's. The writer was to spend his final years with Teresa Sburelin, hired as a housekeeper a few years before. In late 1972, he began yet another novel but found himself unable to advance beyond a few notes. The following year he sent an assistant to the Belgian consulate to change his passport; where once his occupation had read "novelist," he now had "no profession."

The "truth" about this fascinating writer as recounted by Assouline is often different from the "official" version promulgated by Simenon himself, but it is equally arresting. Simenon claimed, for instance, to have had sexual relations with ten thousand women. A marginally more reliable source, Denyse, put the figure at twelve hundred, a sizable figure even when one considers that most of Simenon's partners were prostitutes. In his final work, the lengthy *Mémoires intimes* (1981; *Intimate Memoirs*, 1984), Simenon wrote of the psychological damage that Marie-Jo had suffered at Denyse's hands but seemed unaware that the insatiable sexual appetite he frankly paraded might have had any impact on his daughter's emotional makeup.

Sometimes the "official" version of Simenon's life was helpfully promulgated by others. At the height of his fame as a pulp writer, Simenon agreed to spend twenty-three hours a day for seven days in a glass cage, writing a novel to specifications drawn up by spectators. Years later, a number of commentators remembered the spectacle in detail, but the feat never actually took place. Simenon's publisher broke the contract at the last minute, and in retrospect the frenetic advance publicity the event had generated became the event itself.

The most telling results of Assouline's research involve Simenon's attitude toward Jews and his less than exemplary record during World War II. Although he would later deny it, Simenon was openly anti-Semitic for much of his life, for instance writing a series of articles entitled "The Jewish Peril" for a Liège newspaper when he was eighteen. His attitude did not change with maturity. When handed the task of overseeing the welfare of Belgian refugees fleeing the German invasion of 1940, he had to be forced by his superiors to accept a group of Jews from Antwerp. According to witnesses, however, he carried out his duties with untiring resourcefulness and dedication.

Such duties aside, Simenon acted as if nothing extraordinary were happening. After the war, he claimed to have aided the local French Resistance group by loaning them his Citroën, but the truth is that they helped themselves to the car. He was more than willing to cooperate with Germans and collaborationists anxious to publish his works and film his novels, and he became the object of a series of investigations after the war. His subsequent move to the United States was, it seems, well timed.

Besides this translation, four other biographies of Simenon have appeared in English, the most recent being *Simenon: A Critical Biography* (1987) by Stanley G. Eskin and *The Man Who Wasn't Maigret: A Portrait of Georges Simenon* (1993) by Patrick Marnham. Assouline has profited from unrestricted access to Simenon's private papers and has secured the cooperation of Teresa and his three sons. Still, readers may feel that the obsessive-compulsive aspects of Simenon's life— particularly his endlessly complicated relations with publishers—so dominate Assouline's account that the biographer sometimes loses track of why Simenon should matter to the reader.

Assouline devotes a late chapter, "Style Is Rhythm," to Simenon's working methods, the content of his novels, and his famously spare style. (The reference is to Simenon's revelatory remark "Style is rhythm, the rhythm of the character.") This chapter is as fine a capsule view of Simenon the writer as anyone might hope for but stops just short of evaluating the final worth of his vast creation. Instead, Assouline sums up Simenon's achievement this way: "One hundred ninety-two novels under his own name, about 190 under pseudonyms, hundreds of stories and articles, with 20 or so autobiographical volumes . . . : that was the Simenon continent."

Simenon's best novels include *Le testament Donadieu* (1937; *The Shadow Falls*, 1945), *L'homme qui regardait passer les trains* (1938; *The Man Who Watched the Trains Go By*, 1946), *Pedigree* (1948; *Pedigree*, 1962), *La neige était sale* (1948; *The Stain on the Snow*, 1948), *Le petit saint* (1965; *The Little Saint*, 1965), and *Le chat* (1967; *The Cat*, 1967), and in the judgment of many they are among the best French novels of the mid-twentieth century. They are the reason that this extraordinary, if not always attractive, figure will be read and read about for years to come.

Grove Koger

Sources for Further Study

Booklist. XCIII, June, 1997, p. 1646.
The Economist. CCCXLIV, September 6, 1997, p. 6.
Kirkus Reviews. LXV, April 15, 1997.
Library Journal. CXXII, June 15, 1997.
The Nation. CCLXV, July 28, 1997, p. 25.

National Review. XLIX, September 29, 1997, p. 58.
The New Republic. CCXVII, October 20, 1997, p. 32.
The New York Times Book Review. CII, August 10, 1997, p. 5.
Publishers Weekly. CCXLIV, April 28, 1997, p. 56.
The Spectator. CCLXXIX, September 6, 1997, p. 38.
The Times Literary Supplement. February 5, 1993, p. 9.
World Literature Today. LXVIII, Winter, 1994, p. 83.

SPEAKING FREELY
A Memoir

Author: Nat Hentoff (1925-   )
Publisher: Alfred A. Knopf (New York). 303 pp. $25.00
Type of work: Memoir
Time: 1940's to the present
Locale: Boston and New York City

Journalist Nat Hentoff presents a vivid canvas of personalities, events, and issues ranging from the world of jazz to politics, First Amendment concerns, and his controversial position on abortion

Principal personages:
MARGOT HENTOFF, Hentoff's wife
MALCOLM X, African American radical
LOUIS FARRAKAN, Black Muslim leader
DUKE ELLINGTON, jazz pianist and composer
I. F. STONE, radical journalist
WILLIAM SHAWN, editor of *The New Yorker*
JOHN CARDINAL O'CONNOR, outspoken opponent of abortion

Nat Hentoff has had a remarkable career spanning six decades. He began to work as a journalist at Northeastern University in Boston, where he grew up. There Hentoff established his lifelong devotion to free speech issues, doing battle with the university president who wanted nothing but nice write-ups of sporting events and articles that burnished the school's image. Hentoff protested, affirming his right not only to criticize the school administration but also to publish without censorship. Confronted with an obdurate authority figure, Hentoff resigned.

Hentoff's early career, however, focused primarily on music. He was a devotee of jazz, and he met virtually every important musician working in the Northeast. No musician himself, Hentoff observed performances carefully, consorted with his favorite artists, and gradually built up a resume that made him an authority as a columnist and as an author of liner notes to record albums.

Hentoff learned about more than jazz from geniuses such as Duke Ellington. This master taught Hentoff to appreciate new music and to welcome artists whom Ellington deemed "out of category"—that is, creative musicians who were exploring innovative forms and sounds. This open-mindedness obviously had political implications suited to Hentoff's natural individualism. He admired not only musicians but also political activists such as Malcolm X who challenged the status quo and were unpredictable.

To Hentoff, it did not matter particularly whether he believed in everything someone like Malcolm X stood for. What impressed him about this African American radical in particular was his willingness to speak freely. It amused Hentoff that at his first meeting with Malcolm X he was kept waiting—the only white man in the place—while Malcolm X (unbeknownst to Hentoff) sized up the journalist from a corner. If Hentoff was there to take Malcolm X's measure, Malcolm X wanted Hentoff to know that he was taking Hentoff's.

Such confrontations stimulate Hentoff, who is not one to look for cozy relationships with the people on whom he reports. Even though some of his subjects have become friends, he has continued to argue with them. This includes his wife, Margot, who disapproves of his pro-life position on abortion, and most of his colleagues at *The Village Voice*, for which he has written a column since the 1950's.

Hentoff's journalistic models have been feisty, independent reporters such as I. F. Stone and George Seldes. Stone operated his own newspaper for many years, refusing to hobnob with Washington politicians. Stone drew the ire not only of government officials but also of the press corps, which ostracized him for many years. Stone favored reading tedious but revealing government reports, working up his own analyses rather than relying on off-the-record interviews and deep background briefings, which politicians often use to manipulate the press. Similarly, Seldes was his own man, not only studiously absenting himself from government favors but also harshly criticizing the press for not investigating public figures more vigorously. He was one of the first journalists to report on the media and to examine their own practices.

Although Hentoff might be called a liberal because he has been associated with organizations such as the American Civil Liberties Union (ACLU), he disparages the label. Too often he has found that liberals and other leftists support free speech only when it concerns those who are liberal themselves. When Hentoff developed his pro-life position, he was shunned by colleagues at *The Village Voice*. They did not merely disagree with him; they stopped speaking to him, wanting to punish him for holding what they deemed to be a retrograde opinion. Hentoff is no stranger to harsh criticism, and he does not usually complain of attacks on him. What is more troubling, however, is his colleagues' lack of tolerance for the very expression of opinion.

It was indeed ironic that when Hentoff was invited back to Northeastern University to receive an honorary degree—it took decades for his protest against the university president to be forgiven or forgotten—he learned that many students argued against inviting him because of his pro-life views. His supporters prevailed, though Hentoff went to the event expecting some kind of disruption. It is a mark of his desire to raise First Amendment issues that he was a little disappointed that no one attempted to interrupt his speech. Hentoff likes people to air their grievances, even when they are against him.

Hentoff resigned from the ACLU rather than endorse a policy that resulted in pregnant women not being informed that they had the HIV virus that is a precursor to AIDS. The idea that this information should be kept from them, and that other pro-choice groups supported the ACLU because it opposed the government testing of pregnant women, revolted Hentoff. For him, free speech and the right to know always supersede other items on the ideological agenda or political positions.

If Hentoff is not exactly a liberal, he is hardly a conservative. Although he opposes abortion, he does not support criminal penalties for performing or obtaining abortions. He does not want to punish women or doctors but to make them realize they are taking a human life when they abort a child. He cites several cases in which fetuses with correctable or treatable birth defects have been aborted, and he suggests that respect for human life is eroded when too much attention is focused on the woman's right to choose an abortion.

Hentoff's pro-life position has involved him in friendships with authority figures he could hardly have anticipated liking. John Cardinal O'Connor, for example, reminds Hentoff of his early days in Boston, when as a young Jew he was taunted and beaten by Catholic roughs. Catholic priests still treated Jews as the murderers of Christ, and the Catholic hierarchy did nothing to restrain the outbreaks of violence against Jews. Hentoff finds himself in a strange alliance with O'Connor because of their anti-abortion beliefs. Hentoff presents an O'Connor who is far more open and sensitive than some of his public pronouncements might suggest. When Hentoff harshly criticizes O'Connor for supporting the pope's position that women cannot be priests, O'Connor deals thoughtfully with the reporter's attack. He presents a nuanced—if not entirely candid—argument, conceding that the church might one day change its position. Obviously, O'Connor is not about to contradict the pope, but there is enough elasticity and ambiguity in his reply to Hentoff to show that O'Connor is hardly rigid on the subject. Indeed, on another controversial issue—the acceptance of gays and lesbians—Hentoff reports that O'Connor has met with gay groups and lesbians, impressing at least some of them with his genuine desire to understand their values.

Perhaps O'Connor receives such positive treatment from an initially skeptical Hentoff because O'Connor continues the dialogue. Hentoff notes that O'Connor's predecessor would not even meet with gays or lesbians. The idea that such people can speak freely to a cardinal, and that a weary O'Connor (after a particularly grueling day) does not stop answering Hentoff's hectoring questions, impresses the journalist enormously.

In addition to fascinating chapters on free speech issues and abortion, Hentoff conveys something of what it is like to be a struggling journalist. He often worked for little pay, just to get a chance to write on subjects that interested him. In the case of *The Village Voice*, Hentoff worked for nothing because there were no restrictions on what he could say, and he was given the opportunity to branch out beyond the field of music, where he had first made his reputation.

Hentoff's idea of the ideal editor is William Shawn at *The New Yorker*. Shawn became editor in 1952 after the death of the magazine's legendary founder, Harold Ross. Shawn revered writers and let them publish pieces on topics that interested them. He thought little about what would make the magazine timely; he simply wanted to encourage good writing. He paid his contributors generously and ran very long articles. What *The New Yorker* lacked in timeliness it made up for in the timeless quality of the writing—or to put it another way, because the writing was timeless, it always seemed timely and copies did not go out of date, even if they were read months after publication.

Shawn was always quite formal and correct. Almost everyone called him "Mr. Shawn." He would compliment writers elaborately on their work, even though he sometimes did not publish it, for *The New Yorker* bought many more articles than it could possibly publish. Shawn believed in cultivating talent. This finally got him into trouble with the magazine's new owner, S. I. Newhouse, who fired Shawn. Hentoff believes he never recovered from the blow.

The switch from Shawn and the next editor, Robert Gottlieb, to Tina Brown suggests to Hentoff how degraded journalism has become. Under Brown, Hentoff was summarily retired, just as Shawn had been. To Hentoff, Brown is simply too trendy, preferring shorter articles and pieces that will make instant news. *The New Yorker* is now a magazine too concerned with celebrity, with an organizational structure that thinks writers are interchangeable.

Hentoff does not limit himself to engaging in mere nostalgia; he also shows that Shawn had his faults. He was a paternalistic employer who quashed an attempt to unionize the underpaid staff (not the writers, but the secretaries, fact checkers, and others). Hentoff, who has always believed that employees need their own voice and organization, believes that Shawn destroyed the union effort by suggesting it would spoil the "one big happy family" atmosphere that the magazine fostered.

Hentoff also uses his memoir to settle a few scores. He is especially sore about Black Muslim leader Louis Farrakan, who stated on the network news program *Nightline* that Hentoff was a pro-Zionist reporter who allowed his partiality for Israel to distort his journalism. The program's host, Ted Koppel, let Farrakan's charge go unanswered, and an outraged Hentoff was given brief airtime to rebut the charge, which he did. It still rankles Hentoff, however, that Farrakan has not recanted the accusation and that Hentoff has been regarded, in some quarters, as a propagandist.

Farrakan grew up in Roxbury, Massachusetts, not far from Hentoff's own neighborhood. Given the segregation of those days, the two never met, as Hentoff points out. Ironically, Hentoff remembers hearing in Roxbury a record of Farrakan singing about the sorry fate of black men in a white-dominated world. Hentoff certainly does not deny the sources of Farrakan's grievances, but it is clear he prefers the more just Malcolm X. An honest man, Hentoff does not hide how much Farrakan's charges have hurt, but then Hentoff knows that his own words have wounded others and that free speech is worth the risk of being attacked.

Speaking Freely succeeds as both the record of a journalist's career and as a commentary on the contentious issues of the late twentieth century. Along with Hentoff's earlier memoir, *Boston Boy* (1986), this volume is a provocative and argumentative, but also tolerant, portrayal of an engaging sensibility.

Carl Rollyson

Sources for Further Study

Booklist. XCIII, August, 1997, p. 1869.
George. XI, September 1, 1997, p. 62.
Library Journal. CXXII, September 1, 1997, p. 188.

Los Angeles Times Book Review. September 21, 1997, p. 6.
The New York Times Book Review. CII, October 19, 1997, p. 46.
The Philadelphia Inquirer. October 26, 1997, p. Q3.
Publishers Weekly. CCXLIV, July 28, 1997, p. 61.
The Wall Street Journal. October 6, 1997, p. A20.

THE SPIRIT CATCHES YOU AND YOU FALL DOWN
A Hmong Child, Her American Doctors, and the Collision of Two Cultures

Author: Anne Fadiman
Publisher: Farrar, Straus, and Giroux (New York). 339 pp. $24.00
Type of work: Current affairs
Time: The 1980's
Locale: Merced, California

American medicine and Hmong culture collide over the treatment of a young girl with epilepsy in Merced, California

> *Principal personages:*
> LIA LEE, a young Hmong girl whose severe epileptic seizures confound the American medical establishment
> FOUA LEE, Lia's mother
> NAO KAO LEE, Lia's father
> NEIL ERNST, Lia's doctor at Merced Community Medical Center
> PEGGY PHILIP, Lia's doctor and the wife of Neil Ernst
> DEE KORDA, Lia's foster mother during the period the court removed Lia from her home

The Spirit Catches You and You Fall Down is the riveting narrative of a showdown between modern American medicine and ancient Hmong beliefs, a blow-by-blow account of the battle fought over the body and soul of a very sick young girl. Anne Fadiman's thorough, compassionate, and scrupulously fair presentation of Lia Lee's story provides a balanced and unbiased view of events. Clearly sympathizing with both the girl's family and her doctors, Fadiman examines every facet of a complex situation, while challenging her readers' perspectives on medicine and spirituality.

The Spirit Catches You and You Fall Down alternates chapters on Lia Lee's medical record with accounts of Hmong history, culture, and religion. The author's comprehensive research is evidenced by the inclusion of "Notes on Hmong Orthography, Pronunciation, and Quotations," an extensive bibliography, detailed source notes, and an index. By combining the universality of a family tragedy with a scholarly history of Hmong culture, this book offers a unique and thoroughly satisfying reading experience.

The focal point of this family tragedy is Lia Lee, the fourteenth child of Hmong immigrants Nao Kao and Foua Lee, born in Merced, California, in 1982. The first of the Lees to be born in the United States (and in a hospital), Lia was a healthy baby until she suffered her first seizure at three months of age. Although emergency room doctors at the Merced Community Medical Center initially failed to diagnose Lia's epilepsy (mistakenly treated as a bronchial infection), her family correctly identified her affliction immediately. They understood that Lia was suffering from *qaug dab peg* (the spirit catches you and you fall down), or epilepsy. They believed that her soul, frightened by the sound of their apartment door slamming, fled her body and got lost.

Although concerned for their daughter, they had mixed feelings regarding her condition, because the Hmong (and many other cultures) believe that epilepsy is indicative of special spiritual powers. The Lees "seemed to accept things that . . . were major catastrophes as a part of the normal flow of life. For them, the crisis was the treatment, not the epilepsy." During the following few months, Lia suffered nearly twenty more seizures, was admitted to the hospital seventeen times between the ages of eight months and four-and-a-half years, and made more than one hundred outpatient visits to the emergency room or pediatric clinic. Her medical chart eventually reached five volumes and weighed nearly fourteen pounds, the largest in the history of the hospital. The case frustrated and confounded Lia's doctors, husband and wife Neil Ernst and Peggy Philip, who possessed a "combination of idealism and workaholism that had simultaneously contributed to their successes and set them apart from most of their peers." Although exceptionally conscientious and concerned, Ernst and Philip were hampered in the treatment of Lia not only by their inability to communicate with her parents (hospital translators were seldom available) but also by their ignorance of the Hmong culture. While "failing to work within the traditional Hmong hierarchy . . . [they] not only insulted the entire family but also yielded confused results, since the crucial questions had not been directed toward those who had the power to make decisions."

In an attempt to control her ever-worsening seizures, the doctors placed Lia on a complicated drug regime that would have been difficult for English-speaking parents to follow, let alone the non-English-speaking Lees. The Lees failed to comply with this complicated regimen both because they did not understand it and because they did not want to. As Foua Lee explained:

> The doctors can fix some sicknesses that involve the body and blood, but for us Hmong, some people get sick because of their soul, so they need spiritual things. With Lia it was good to do a little medicine and a little *neeb*, but not too much medicine because the medicine cuts the *neeb*'s effect. If we did a little of each she didn't get sick as much, but the doctors wouldn't let us give just a little medicine because they didn't understand about the soul.

The Lees believed that rather than helping Lia, the drugs were making her worse, and they "didn't hesitate to . . . modify the drug dosage or do things however they saw fit."

In a desperate move, Ernst removed Lia from her devastated parents and placed her with a foster family in an attempt to make sure her medications were administered properly. Lia lived with the Korda family for ten months, during which time Dee Korda scrupulously followed the complicated drug protocol and became devoted to the difficult but lovable Lia. Despite this, Lia deteriorated, improving only when she was put on a new, simpler drug regime. The Lees, shamed that their daughter had been taken from them and shattered by the loss, threatened suicide before Lia was finally returned to the family home.

During her first four months home, Lia improved markedly, suffering only one seizure. The Lees not only complied with her medical protocol but also gave her the best Hmong treatment available, including amulets filled with healing herbs from

Thailand (at a cost of one thousand dollars) and a trip to Minnesota for treatment by a famous *txiv neeb*, or medicine man. Lia's seizures did return, however, and in November of 1986 she suffered massive seizures that could not be controlled. She also suffered septic shock, fell into a coma, and became effectively brain dead. The doctors sent Lia home to die, but she defied their expectations and lived on, although in a vegetative state: quadriplegic, spastic, incontinent, and incapable of purposeful movement. At this point, the Lees became perfect caregivers, keeping the comatose Lia immaculate and well-nourished and lavishing her with attention and love.

Lia's tragedy is placed in context by Fadiman's thoroughly researched chapters on the history of the Hmong. A fiercely independent people, the Hmong, throughout history, have refused to assimilate with any other group. They lived in the mountains of China since 3,000 B.C. without mingling with the Chinese, fighting ferociously to maintain their identity. In the early nineteenth century, when Chinese repression became intolerable, a half million Hmong fled to Vietnam and Laos. In the 1960's, the U.S. Central Intelligence Agency recruited the Laotian Hmong, known as skilled and brutal fighters, to serve in their war against the communists. They suffered massive casualties and devastating destruction of their villages; when the People's Democratic Republic took over the Laotian monarchy in 1975 and attempted to exterminate the Hmong, they were once again forced to flee their homes.

The Lee family succeeded in fleeing Laos in 1979, making their way to a refugee camp in Thailand following a harrowing, twenty-six day journey. After two years in refugee camps, they were able to immigrate to the United States, and, like most Hmong, gravitated to the Central Valley of California. Three of their thirteen children had died from starvation and poor conditions during their flight, and the Lees arrived penniless and illiterate, determined not to be changed by their strange new surroundings.

Clearly, "Lia's case had confirmed the Hmong community's worst prejudices about the medical profession and the medical community's worst prejudices about the Hmong." While the doctors felt that the Lees failure to keep Lia on her initial drug regime contributed to her decline, the Lees felt that the medicine itself contributed to their daughter's condition. A review of Lia's medical records indicated that septic shock rather than epileptic seizures probably caused her vegetative state, septic shock to which her body was susceptible because of the heavy doses of medications she had been receiving. Thus, the Lee's suspicion that the doctors were exacerbating Lia's condition with their treatments was not entirely incorrect, while the doctors' opinion that if Lia's medication had been administered correctly from the start she might not have deteriorated so dramatically may have been accurate as well.

The Spirit Catches You and You Fall Down provides an education in Hmong history and American medicine, a compelling family drama, and a new outlook on the world. When seen from the Hmong perspective, "truths" previously taken for granted come under question and issues of right and wrong are no longer clear-cut when decent, well-meaning people come into direct conflict with one another over them. As the medical establishment increasingly splinters into specialized groups, this book serves as a vivid reminder that the best medicine must always recognize the interconnected-ness of culture, family, body, and soul.

Mary Virginia Davis

Sources for Further Study

Booklist. XCIV, September 15, 1997, p. 184.
Chicago Tribune. November 30, 1997, XIV, p. 3.
Elle. October, 1997, p. 132.
Glamour. XCV, November, 1997, p. 100.
Library Journal. CXXII, September 1, 1997, p. 208.
Los Angeles Times. September 18, 1997, p. E1.
The New Republic. CCXVII, October 13, 1997, p. 31.
The New York Times Book Review. CII, October 19, 1997, p. 28.
Publishers Weekly. CCXLIV, August 11, 1997, p. 393.
San Francisco Chronicle. December 14, 1997, p. 3.

STENDHAL

Author: Jonathan Keates (1946-   )
First published: 1994, in Great Britain
Publisher: Carroll & Graf (New York). 478 pp. $28.00
Type of work: Literary biography
Time: 1783-1842
Locale: Primarily France and Italy

This volume presents the life and works of the bureaucrat, diplomat, journalist, and author Stendhal within the context of the political and social upheavals of his times and against the aesthetic sea change that swept away eighteenth century classicism and brought the birth of nineteenth century Romanticism and realism

Principal personages:
MARIE-HENRI BEYLE, known under the pen name "Stendhal," a major
    French novelist of the early nineteenth century
LOUIS CROZET, a childhood friend and confidant of Stendhal
PIERRE DARU, Stendhal's uncle and benefactor, a French bureaucrat
    under Napoleon
ELENA MARIA METILDE VISCONTINI DEMBOWSKI, one of the great loves
    of Stendhal's life and the inspiration for his work *De l'amour*
HENRI GAGNON, Stendhal's grandfather and a major influence on his
    intellectual development
ADOLPHE DE MARESTE, a friend and correspondent of Stendhal
PROSPER MÉRIMÉE, a French writer and close friend of Stendhal
PAULINE (BEYLE) PÉRIER-LAGRANGE, Stendhal's sister and regular
    correspondent
NAPOLEON BONAPARTE, French emperor whom Stendhal served and
    revered

Marie-Henri Beyle, better known by his pseudonym Stendhal, is a difficult biographical subject. His professional career was varied, the range of his friendships and associations was broad, his intellectual interests were eclectic, and his written work was diverse and uneven. Until the age of thirty-five he was little more than a faceless functionary, a low-ranking cavalry officer and bureaucratic cog in the machinery of Napoleon Bonaparte's empire. Yet through his uncle Pierre Daru, Napoleon's secretary of war, Stendhal was very near the center of power. He took part in Napoleon's campaigns in Italy (1800-1801), Germany (1806), Austria (1809), and Russia (1812) and distinguished himself for bravery and efficiency, which twice earned him an audience with the emperor himself. After the fall of Napoleon in 1814, Stendhal turned to writing. His *Vies de Haydn, de Mozart et de Métastase* (1815; *The Lives of Haydn and Mozart, with Observations on Métastase*, 1817), large portions of which he plagiarized, marked his publishing debut. More significant, if equally erratic, works were *Histoire de la peinture en Italie* and *Rome, Naples et Florence en 1817* (*Rome, Naples and Florence in 1817*, 1818) which followed in 1817 and marked the first appearance of the pen name Stendhal, under which all of his subsequent major writings would appear. "Stendhal," however, was but one of more than two hundred pseudonyms under which Stendhal published, corresponded, and referred to himself in his journals and autobiographical writings. Indeed, his friends coined yet another name, "Jemoi" (I-myself), to characterize the author's principal obsession.

Another obsession for Stendhal was Italy, where he spent close to a third of his peripatetic life. He might well have settled in Milan, a city he grew to love during his first posting there in 1800, had not the suspicions of the city's Austrian occupiers forced his return to France after his most extended stay there from 1814 to 1821. It was in Italy that Stendhal experienced the most intense of his many love affairs, and where he met Elena Maria Metilde Viscontini Dembowski, the unrequited love of his life who inspired one of his best-known works, *De l'amour* (1822; *Maxims of Love*, 1906).

It was also in Italy that the widely read Stendhal began to engage more directly with the intellectual currents of the age. His encounters there with English poet Lord Byron and the circle around Count Ludovico Di Breme introduced him to major figures and ideas of Romanticism, a movement to which, ever since his service in Germany a decade earlier, he had had an ambivalent relationship. As Jonathan Keates observes, "The central paradox of Stendhal's position within the cultural perspective of his age must always be defined by his rigorously selective sympathy with its cult of sensation." A telling indication of Stendhal's aesthetic predilections, which hovered between eighteenth and nineteenth century sensibilities, is the fact that in his musical tastes he preferred Neapolitan composer Domenico Cimarosa to Ludwig van Beethoven and published a gushing biography of Italian composer Gioacchino Rossini in 1823.

During the 1820's Stendhal became a habitué of the Parisian salons (especially that of Étienne-Jean Delécluze) through which he met a number of prominent artists and writers, including Eugène Delacroix, Victor Hugo, Frédéric Jacquemont, and Prosper Mérimée, who became a close friend. Stendhal himself emerged as a witty, outspoken, and slightly eccentric bon vivant whose effervescent cynicism both amused and infuriated his contemporaries. After a visit to England in 1821, Stendhal became a Paris correspondent for various English-language journals (including the *New Monthly Magazine*, the *London Magazine*, and the *Paris Monthly Review*, in which his articles appeared in translation), thus beginning a long and checkered career as a journalist and commentator on literature, art, culture, and society.

Stendhal's first major work of fiction, the novel *Armance*, was published in 1827 (English translation, 1928), but it was his novel *Le Rouge et le Noir* (1830; *The Red and the Black*, 1898) that established the nearly fifty-year-old author as a major personality in French literature. By then, the July Revolution of 1830 had brought the "citizen king" Louis-Philippe to power and a revival of Stendhal's civil service career. At the end of 1830 he was appointed consul-general in Trieste but, owing to the objections of the Austrian government, was soon transferred to Civitavecchia near Rome, where he served as consul-general until his death in 1842. It was during those years that he wrote many of his short stories, autobiographical accounts, and the novel that many consider his greatest work, *La Chartreuse de Parma* (1839; *The Charterhouse of Parma*, 1895).

Keates has written a biography for the general reader that draws heavily upon the full range of French- and English-language Stendhal literature of the past fifty years. His endnotes give adequate accounting of his sources and, in his introduction and suggestions for further reading, he is generous in his acknowledgment of his scholarly debts. The detailed index, however, is spotty and unreliable. Keates is less interested in interpreting his subject than in providing an overview that sets Stendhal's life and works in historical context. It is an ambitious undertaking that involves describing both the varied settings of Stendhal's life and the historical epochs through which he lived, which included the last years of the *ancien régime*, the French Revolution, the rise and fall of Napoleon, the restoration of the Bourbon kings, and the monarchy of Louis-Philippe.

Keates is deft in sketching this framework for Stendhal's life. His descriptions of Grenoble and the mountainous Dauphiné region from which Stendhal came, of the cultural transformations of Paris during the first third of the nineteenth century, of London in the 1820's, and most especially of the Italy and Milan Stendhal so dearly loved, are informative and evocative with a well-balanced combination of historical detail and biographical anecdote. Equally compelling are Keates's excursions into cultural history and his discussions of Stendhal's interests and relationship to larger movements such as Romanticism or the empirical philosophies of the seventeenth and eighteenth centuries. As Keates shrewdly observes,

> Such insistence on the primacy of philosophers over imaginative writers, and on the need to sift the creative impulse through the mesh of theory, says much about Stendhal's whole approach to the business of art. There can seldom have been a novelist who had so little overt interest in the process of fiction, a creative spirit with so little time for the fanciful, or an imaginative writer with such apparent disdain for others working in his own genre.

Stendhal was a man of contradictions, a thinker who lived between and ahead of the times. His famously laconic literary style avoided the grandiloquent gestures of Romanticism, and yet he was in sympathy with the emotional candor of that movement. Stendhal was a precursor of the realists of the later nineteenth century while deploring the crass materialism that was overtaking his age. Keates is a sensitive and sympathetic guide to these various currents of Stendhal's creative activity, and he argues persuasively for the significance of some of the author's lesser-known works, including such unfinished projects as the novel *Lucien Leuwen* (wr. 1834-1835; English translation, 1950) and his *Memoires sur Napoléon* (wr. 1836-1837; memoires on Napoleon). It is a pity that Keates has so restricted his discussions of Stendhal's works because they are among the strongest and best written passages in his biography.

Unfortunately, Keates's book is weakest in fulfilling its avowed purpose of providing a "straightforward birth-to-death narrative" of its subject. Too often Keates's account is confused, repetitious, or awkwardly organized. Important personalities such as Martial Daru, Edouard Mounier, and Adolphe de Mareste are mentioned without adequate introduction, and others, such as Stendhal's influential grandfather, Dr. Henri Gagnon, are unceremoniously dispatched in a subordinate clause. Keates's sentences are often crammed with extraneous details as if he were writing from randomly shuffled note cards; paragraphs frequently hop from subject to subject with little or no attempt at transition. The reader's confusion is exacerbated by Keates's habit of quoting documents, letters, and journal entries without giving dates or adequate identification in the body of the text, and he often sends Stendhal on his travels without first notifying the reader. The result is often an undigested muddle of facts that does little to provide motivation or explanation for Stendhal's admittedly impulsive activities.

The central problem with Keates's narrative is organizational, but careless contradictions and non sequiturs abound. On page 180, readers learn that the Milan of 1816 represented "the most sinister climate of political oppression the modern world had hitherto experienced," and yet on page 236 they learn that in the Milan of 1820 there existed a "relatively peaceful coexistence of the Milanese with their Austrian rulers" whose government used a "comparatively benign approach towards its subjects." Early in the biography, readers are told that young Marie-Henri Beyle found no real friends among his classmates at the École Centrale in Grenoble, and yet at least three (Louis Crozet, Louis de Barral, and Josef Faure) give continuing proofs of their loyalty in the decades to come. Why is it "ironic" that "passion acted as a species of vitamin to creativity"? Where is the contradiction in Stendhal's "unsparing but always alert gaze"?

The situation is aggravated by a number of unfortunate typographical errors, including such confusions of dates as the statement that Stendhal fell in love with his aunt Alexandrine-Thérèse Daru in 1805, whereas the pages that follow make clear that Stendhal's infatuation dated from 1810 and 1811; and the publication date for the first edition of *Racine et Shakespeare* (1823; *Racine and Shakespeare*, 1962) is variously given as 1828 and 1823.

It is perhaps Stendhal's erratic professional career and uncertain creative identity that makes it so difficult to take the measure of the man, and it is only after Stendhal himself settles into middle age that Keates and his readers begin to catch their breath. Stendhal's friend Étienne-Jean Delécluze observed that it was "the conflict of reveries and realities knocking against one another" that made Stendhal "the most incoherent of men," and Victor Hugo observed that Stendhal was "an intelligent man who was also an idiot." Keates, who does not hide his affection for his subject, dutifully notes the contradictions in Stendhal's character and thought, but what he calls Stendhal's "singular and unforgettable personality" remains elusive. Readers learn of his wit but are treated to few of his witticisms; they are given a chronicle of his love life but do not feel the warmth of his passion; they meet his friends but learn too little about the substance of his friendships. In short, this man of so many names and identities remains, even in Keates's sympathetic hands, an enigma. This biography is a tale told from the outside, a succession of keys to so many doors that remain unopened. Its major and not insignificant achievement is to induce readers to return to Stendhal's writings and to discover him for themselves.

Christopher Hailey

Sources for Further Study

Booklist. XCIII, April 15, 1997, p. 1376.
Library Journal. CXXII, April, 1997, p. 92.
New Statesman and Society. VIII, August 4, 1995, p. 37.
The New York Times Book Review. CII, May 4, 1997, p. 13.
Publishers Weekly. CCXLIV, February 10, 1997, p. 72.
The Spectator. CCLXXII, June 25, 1994, p. 25.
The Times Literary Supplement. August 12, 1997, p. 8.
The Wall Street Journal. March 25, 1997, p. A16.
The Washington Post Book World. XXVII, April 13, 1997, p. 9.

STEVEN SPIELBERG
A Biography

Author: Joseph McBride (1947-   )
Publisher: Simon & Schuster (New York). Illustrated. 528 pp. $30.00
Type of work: Biography
Time: 1946-1997
Locale: Primarily Phoenix, Arizona, and Los Angeles, California

McBride presents Steven Spielberg not only as the most successful director in the history of cinema but also the most influential—and least understood—popular artist of the twentieth century

> *Principal personages:*
> STEVEN ALAN SPIELBERG, the noted film director
> ARNOLD MEYER SPIELBERG, his workaholic father, an electrical engineer
> LEAH POSNER SPIELBERG ADLER, his energetic and artistic mother
> AMY IRVING, his first wife
> KATE CAPSHAW, his second wife
> MAX SAMUEL SPIELBERG, the son of Irving and Spielberg
> SASHA SPIELBERG, the daughter of Capshaw and Spielberg
> CHARLES A. "CHUCK" SILVERS, Universal Picture's film librarian and Spielberg's mentor
> SIDNEY J. SHEINBERG, vice president of production for Universal Television
> GEORGE LUCAS, a noted filmmaker, producer, and Spielberg collaborator

It has taken American scholarship a long time to catch up with America's most popular and, arguably, most gifted filmmaker, though *The Steven Spielberg Story*, an uncritical survey written for fans by Tony Crawley, was published as early as 1983 by Zomba Books, London. This was not a book to be taken too seriously, however, and it predates the later, more "serious" films Spielberg would direct, although it does cover the early box-office successes of *Jaws* (1975), *Close Encounters of the Third Kind* (1977), and *E.T.: The Extra-Terrestrial* (1982). Crawley was "encouraged" to write the book by the editor of Marvel Comics' *Starburst* fantasy-film magazine and claims in his acknowledgments that "Steven Spielberg really wrote this book."

In 1986, a joint academic treatment by Donald R. Mott and Cheryl McAllister Saunders entitled *Steven Spielberg* was released by Twayne, but this book was completed too early for a complete treatment of *The Color Purple* (1985), Spielberg's first truly serious adaptation of a major novel. Most academics, however, would shy away from Spielberg. A major exception was Philip M. Taylor's *Steven Spielberg: The Man, His Movies, and Their Meaning* (1992), which expanded its coverage to include everything from *Empire of the Sun* (1987) to *Hook* (1991). Contacted in July of 1997, Taylor explained the genesis of his book. As editor of a series, in 1991 he called twenty-three American scholars in an attempt to find someone willing to write a book on Spielberg, but all declined; Taylor then resolved to write the book himself, because he thought a Spielberg book should be in his series. He was surprised to find that none of the "serious" academics he contacted were interested in linking themselves to Spielberg's star, even though such a book could be lucrative. Taylor then updated his book in 1994 to include coverage of *Schindler's List* (1993). Taylor's book is the main competition to Joseph McBride's *Steven Spielberg: A Biography*.

McBride's biography therefore fills a gap. Though not an academic critic but a reviewer, first for *Variety*, then for *Box Office* magazine, McBride had already written the brilliantly iconoclastic *Frank Capra: The Catastrophe of Success* (1992). As an industry insider, McBride was able to interview people who knew and worked with Spielberg over the years, and the book is derived from more than three hundred interviews. It runs to more than five hundred pages but is still 250 pages shorter than the earlier Capra book. It is more thoroughly researched than John Baxter's competing book *Steven Spielberg: The Unauthorized Biography* (1997), which, according to one reviewer, was blemished by factual errors and even misquoted the most famous line of all the Spielberg movies: "E.T., phone home."

Despite McBride's diligent research, his biography falls short of his earlier treatment of the popular director Capra, which began with a retrospective account of a trip the aging Capra made to Sicily very late in his career. That initial portrait of Capra set the tone for the book by demolishing Capra's lovable popular image with deft satiric strokes and presented him as a mean-spirited and ungenerous person, to the consternation of his many fans. By contrast, the Spielberg book is far less controversial and more pedestrian. The first one hundred pages trace the boy's home life from Cincinnati to New Jersey to Arizona to California, recalling far too many boyhood pranks while demonstrating young Steven's obsession with filmmaking and his rejection in some quarters as a Jewish outsider, particularly at Saratoga High School, near the Santa Clara Valley.

McBride devotes rather too many pages to Spielberg's childhood and adolescence, even if there is arguably some merit to his speculations about the "Peter Pan syndrome" and the characterization of Spielberg as the boy who did not want to grow up from a childhood that was fragmented and rootless, though neither especially happy nor especially miserable. Spielberg's father, Arnold, was an engineer who worked for RCA in New Jersey, then for General Electric in Phoenix.

McBride attempts to set the childhood history against the later films Spielberg would make—none too convincingly, let it be noted, until page 75, when Elliott of *E.T.* is compared to the younger Steven, who was neglected by his workaholic father. Yet how much needs to be said about a scruffy, brainy kid whose childhood fantasies are tied to films? Feeling obliged to list every film and television show that might have influenced the wunderkind prodigy Spielberg was to become, McBride puts the reader to sleep.

Spielberg's parents were divorced in 1965, about the time he graduated from high school. They were both educated and unconventional people, and their son grew up something of a loner and an outsider, though he had many friends in Arizona. After the divorce, the boy lived with his father and enrolled at California State College in Long Beach. His grades were uneven, not good enough to gain entrance at the well-established film school at the University of California, Los Angeles, or the University of Southern California. Spielberg was more interested in hanging out at Universal Studios, where he gained his most useful education as a tyro filmmaker. For him, college was relatively pointless; he was particularly frustrated when he was given a C in a television production course—to the later chagrin of the professor who taught the course.

McBride devotes another hundred pages to the college years and Spielberg's apprenticeship at Universal. Thus one-third of the book passes before one comes to a discussion of Spielberg's first directorial assignment in feature filmmaking at Universal, *The Sugarland Express* (1974). At the same time, however, Spielberg's directorial development is carefully traced through work he directed for television, especially the "Eyes" segment, starring Joan Crawford, for the television series pilot *Night Gallery* (1969); "Par for the Course," done for *The Psychiatrist* (1971); and the made-for-television chase film *Duel* (1971). McBride effectively provides a context for Spielberg's indisputable talent, but Spielberg the person remains oddly remote and untouched—which is to say, unrevealed—by McBride's carefully researched narrative. The young Spielberg seems as work obsessed as his father had been. The core events of his career are carefully rehearsed and described, but beyond that McBride can only speculate about the young man's spiritual development.

Spielberg's detractors would argue that there was no spiritual development, that Spielberg's talent was wasted on projects that were merely entertaining and had no lasting significance other than the records set at the box office. Spielberg himself would later dismiss the likes of the Indiana Jones series as "popcorn movies," but ultimately he took on projects that were clearly more ambitious. *The Color Purple* may be seen as a pivotal project. Spielberg reshaped Alice Walker's novel to suit his own purposes and took much of the edge off the relationship that develops in that story between Celie (Whoopi Goldberg), Walker's heroine, and her friend Shug Avery (Margaret Avery). McBride describes the controversy that arose over the way African American husbands and fathers were presented in the film, but he simply does not seem to grasp Spielberg's real achievement in *The Color Purple*, which is the sentimental manipulation he accomplished by restructuring Celie's reconciliation with his estranged husband and her reunion with her long-lost sister, which is more Spielberg's invention than Walker's.

Spielberg's two most mature pictures, *The Color Purple* and *Empire of the Sun*, are dismissed as secondary and uneven films, mere stepping-stones toward the final achievement of *Schindler's List*, the film that earned Spielberg the acceptance and recognition that he craved from the Academy of Motion Picture Arts and Sciences. If this is the story McBride has to tell, it is truncated and simplified. The British director David Lean, much admired by Spielberg, gave up on plans to adapt J. G. Ballard's autobiographical novel to the screen because, he told Kevin Brownlow, "it hasn't got a dramatic shape." *Empire of the Sun* is interesting precisely because of the dramatic shape Spielberg's film was to achieve, but McBride's evaluation is blinkered by his determination to show how the film was shaped by Spielberg's "own thematic concentration on the painful process of growing up."

In the simplified design of Spielberg's life McBride's book posits, Spielberg had to "grow up" before he could undertake such an adult topic as *Schindler's List*, so all one needs to do is to trace Spielberg surrogates through the child actors of his films to "understand" his development. "The kid in *E.T.* that Henry Thomas played was as much who Steven Spielberg was when he made that movie as the kid in *Empire of the Sun* was when he made *Empire of the Sun*," McBride informs the reader, quoting as psychological authority Bob Gale, a friend and collaborator of Spielberg and Robert Zemeckis on the weak, even infantile *1941* project.

The biography does a competent job of documenting Spielberg's technical skills. McBride spends a great deal of time covering the production histories of *Jaws* and *Close Encounters of the Third Kind*, the latter being regarded as a far more serious picture and treated as a remake of an amateur film Spielberg made in high school, *Firelight*, begun in 1963 and completed in 1964. *E.T.: The Extra-Terrestrial* is also covered in considerable detail because if fits McBride's thesis that Spielberg's most popular film is "a disguised emotional autobiography" of the director. Even if this thesis is believable, it puts a heavy emphasis on a movie that some might dismiss as kid stuff, though extraordinarily successful kid stuff. Yet even at the age of fifty in 1996, after the critical acclaim of *Schindler's List*, Spielberg, with a newfound sense of responsibility, expressed a desire to shift "back and forth from entertainment to socially conscious movies"—a well-established pattern, given the fact that *Jurassic Park* was also released in 1993, the year of *Schindler's List*.

Overall, McBride makes about as strong a case for Spielberg as anyone could. "The disdain of the self-styled intellectual elite for this great popular artist reminded me of the condescension with which such Golden Age directors as Hitchcock, Hawks, and Capra were treated in the prime of their careers," McBride writes in his acknowledgments. To him, as also to Taylor, it seemed "that first-rate writers on film and academic scholars were shunning Spielberg as if he were unworthy of sustained attention."

Since "Spielberg himself declined to be interviewed" for the book, this is not an "authorized" biography. Many of Spielberg's friends and associates likewise refused to cooperate, notably Sidney J. Sheinberg (who as vice president of television production at Universal Studios supported Spielberg unfailingly during the early years), MCA president Lew Wasserman, Kathleen Kennedy, Frank Marshall, John Williams, John Melius, and Richard Dreyfuss, all of whom could have been immensely helpful. Spielberg's mother, Leah Adler, spoke with McBride by telephone but was finally convinced by her son not to cooperate. Arnold Spielberg, on the other hand, did agree to a single interview.

McBride seems more timid in writing this book than he was in writing his book on Capra, and one hopes this is not a consequence of Spielberg's obvious power and influence in Hollywood. The author demonstrates that Spielberg has lied about his age, that the director was born in 1946, not 1947 as frequently reported. The only other controversial issue raised in the book is the tragedy of the helicopter crash during the late-night filming of *Twilight Zone*, which killed actor Vic Morrow and two nonprofessional child performers, but in this instance Spielberg's involvement seems peripheral at best. Spielberg has suggested that he may write his own autobiography someday, but until that day arrives, McBride's biography should be the main source for those interested in the director's career.

James M. Welsh

Sources for Further Study

Booklist. XCIII, April 15, 1997, p. 1374.
Commentary. CIV, August, 1997, p. 68.
Empire. May, 1997, p. 145.
Los Angeles Times Book Review. July 13, 1997, p. 8.
The New York Times Book Review. CII, June 15, 1997, p. 24.
The Observer. April 13, 1997, p. 18.
Publishers Weekly. CCXLIV, April 28, 1997, p. 65.
Sight and Sound. VII, August, 1997, p. 30.
The Times Literary Supplement. July 18, 1997, p. 18.
The Washington Post Book World. XXVII, June 29, 1997, p. 3.

STONEWALL JACKSON
The Man, the Soldier, the Legend

Author: James I. Robertson, Jr. (1930-   )
Publisher: Macmillan (New York). Illustrated. 950 pp. $40.00
Type of work: Biography
Time: 1824-1863
Locale: The United States and Mexico

The private life and military exploits of Thomas "Stonewall" Jackson, the second most popular Confederate general in the War Between the States and the man Robert E. Lee considered his right arm

Principal personages:
THOMAS J. JACKSON, known as "Stonewall" from his regiment's stand at
    the First Battle of Manassas
LAURA JACKSON ARNOLD, his sister, secular in religious views,
    pro-Union in politics
ELLIE JACKSON, his first wife from a pro-Union family
ANNA JACKSON, his second wife, later the "Widow of the Confederacy"
ROBERT E. LEE, the commander of the Army of Northern Virginia
JAMES LONGSTREET, the senior of "Lee's Lieutenants"

There must somewhere be a comment about Stonewall Jackson that James Robertson missed. If so, it is buried in some totally obscure manuscript. If ever a book about Jackson were to be considered definitive, this is it.

Thomas "Stonewall" Jackson had been a preeminent Confederate hero from the moment his Valley campaign (spring, 1862) revived the hopes of Southern patriots who were reeling from a series of Union victories. His death a year later after the Battle of Chancellorsville, where he was shot accidentally by Southern sentries, was considered by contemporaries to be the most severe blow ever dealt the Confederacy; and they later chose to believe that the "Lost Cause" might have been saved had "Stonewall" lived. Such a pivotal figure could not be ignored by historians, who eagerly seized upon his oddities of behavior and quirks of personality to create the "Tom Fool" Jackson legend, the man who rode around with one arm in the air, sucking on lemons, a religious fanatic who combined God and war to become the scourge of Lincoln's generals.

Robertson makes great effort to revise this legend. He succeeds only partially. In truth, Jackson was an oddity. He was taciturn to a fault, repeatedly putting his forces into difficult situations that could have been avoided by telling his subordinates something, anything, about his intentions. Such revelations were not possible, however, because Jackson expected obedience in the same blind manner that he himself gave it (to the harm of his cause, especially at Seven Days). He honored the Sabbath so punctiliously that he would do nothing on the seventh day except fight, and he took no personal credit for any success—every victory was the Lord's. This belief in God having a design for each human being freed him from all concern for personal danger and from any fear that he was driving his men too hard or asking too much of them. His poor health led him to exercise regularly and to adopt a diet of bread, buttermilk, and fresh fruit (hence the lemon legend); his love of stimulants (even coffee) caused him to avoid them as much as possible.

Much about Jackson's personality is explained by his being orphaned in childhood, the rest by his physical weakness. His full height was just short of six feet, but he was so debilitated throughout his youth that he considered reaching 166 pounds a great achievement. He was slow in thought, slower in speech. Everything he learned came through concentrating every power, and he was inarticulate in explaining what he had mastered except to repeat it exactly; hence, he learned to rely solely on repetition and memorization. This was not a trait likely to be compatible with success in society—Jackson's lack of the social graces was almost legendary—but it goes far to explain his methodical approach to combat. Jackson believed in a completely ordered and disciplined life, and he found a justification for this belief in his Presbyterian God, a deity who knew what He was doing and what He expected of true Christians.

Jackson, however, is not to be so easily pigeonholed. Photographs reveal a handsome soldier, private letters indicate a playful and passionate husband, and anecdotes show a caring and compassionate man. As a young man, Jackson taught a slave how to read, although that was against the law (and the slave promptly used his new talent to escape). While he was a faculty member at the Virginia Military Institute (VMI), Jackson established a Sunday school for poor whites and slaves, although that was technically against the law. He quickly learned that when he was not present to lead services and instruction, attendance declined from one hundred to far fewer, and his first act after the victory at the First Battle of Manassas was to write a brief note to the church at Lexington, Virginia, enclosing his check for support of the school (which came as a great disappointment to the congregation that anticipated a blow-by-blow account of the battle). He loved Mexico and for a while contemplated settling there. His dream of marrying some local young woman faded under deeper study of the reality of religious life there and the unstable political situation, but he came to love the Spanish language, which he spoke fluently for the rest of his life. Although he never spoke for or against slavery as an institution, he saw it and state's rights as part of an inscrutable divine plan that only heretics would try to change; his model society was one in which rulers took the responsibility for governing according to Biblical rules, and the model slaveholder who treated his servants fairly and humanely fit Jackson's views much better than the radicals in the North who were challenging every tradition that the state and family represented.

Jackson was a hero of the Mexican War but one who never sought to exploit it for fame or personal advancement; he saw how discipline, training, leadership, and personal example could affect the results of combat. His appointment at VMI was a poor match of talents to subject, and he was never considered a star of the faculty or the community, but he developed skills in making young men accomplish unpleasant tasks. His marriages were arranged as secretly as anything in his military career, and he bore the deaths of infant children and his beloved first wife with the same stoicism he displayed on the battlefield; he was deeply distressed, but he carried on. In short, Jackson's every experience up to 1861 seemed part of a plan to prepare him for the challenge of command in a great war.

Nevertheless, there was great initial reluctance both in the high command and among the troops to expect much of the taciturn mathematics professor, and rumors of his odd habits and religious practices caused many to think that it was a mistake to entrust him with any command. His strict methods ran contrary to the anarchic democracy of the volunteer army, but they quickly proved themselves in the test of combat: Units which had been slackly commanded performed poorly, whereas Jackson's troops earned the sobriquet "the Stonewall Brigade" at the First Battle of Manassas.

Jackson's Valley campaign raised popular expectations so high that his performance at Seven Days came as a severe disappointment. Subsequent generations of historians strained to explain how, in Lee's first campaign, neither man seemed to have done well, yet Jackson and Lee obtained their goal of driving Union general George McClellan from the gates of Richmond. Douglas Southhall Freeman criticized Jackson's actions (or lack of action) in his seminal history *Lee's Lieutenants* (1942-1946), thereby concentrating historians' attention on the mistakes which cost the Confederacy its best chance to destroy the Union army totally. Robertson defends Jackson's reputation stoutly, arguing that exhaustion, lack of sleep, heat and humidity, and illness, along with strange roads, incorrect maps, Lee's vague instructions (or lack of orders or incorrect ones), and Jackson's penchant for carrying out orders exactly (no more and no less) all combined to give the impression of a commander who was repeatedly tardy and unaggressive. In this, as in his efforts to dispel the myths of eccentricity, Robertson is less than fully successful. He does, however, succeed in modifying most extreme mythologizing and eliminating some widely held errors.

There may have been blame to share for the mistakes of Seven Days, but it is much easier to criticize when one knows for certain that McClellan was not going to counterattack, concentrating his superior forces against isolated Confederate forces or even striking straight for Richmond. Hindsight is much more certain than any wisdom Lee or Jackson possessed.

In subsequent combats, Jackson urged more speed and daring than Lee or the other generals were willing to risk. Jackson was probably wrong: His armies lacked the means to pursue a defeated foe with the speed and determination needed to destroy him. On the other hand, if Jackson had been correct, the South might have won its independence. Around such points swirl long-lasting controversies, and since Lee's plans, daring as they were, did not work, might not Jackson's have been successful? Alternatively, given the argument that Lee's aggressiveness wore down the Confederate forces unnecessarily, would Jackson's have simply led to a quicker exhaustion of the South? If so, Jackson would not have complained—he believed that wars should be short, violent, and decisive; but then, since the Lord was on his side, he did not expect defeat.

Among the debunked myths are Jackson's activities at Harpers Ferry at the beginning of the war: He did not change the hours that trains could pass through the town and later confiscate the rolling stock; the engines he dismantled and transported overland came from Martinsburg. At the Second Battle of Manassas, Jackson's goal was to cut the Orange and Alexandria Railroad, not to occupy Manassas Junction itself; when the opportunity presented itself, however, he seized it. In short, Jackson had the gift of innovating creatively while conforming to the general plan. Lee recognized this genius, entrusting him with an independent corps for risky flanking marches at the Second Battle of Manassas and the Battle of Chancellorsville, something he did not do with any other general. When Lee invaded Maryland on the Antietam campaign, he entrusted Jackson with the capture of Harpers Ferry, where a strong garrison was a dangerous threat to the Confederate rear. Jackson's swift attack on Maryland Heights, the key to the defenses, his placement of artillery on heights he had studied at the beginning of the war, and the relentless bombardment all caused the garrison to surrender in time for Jackson to get his forces to Sharpsburg to reinforce Lee's badly outnumbered troops against determined Union assaults.

The secrets to Jackson's success are no secret: train troops relentlessly, drill them for speed and effectiveness, teach them that their strength and endurance is far greater than they could ever have believed, inspire them by personal example, tolerate no excuses, and stress the importance of discipline and secrecy. He emphasized speed and maneuver, encouraging his troops to strike at outnumbered and unprepared enemies, seize the high ground and exploit it, and to follow up victory with swift pursuit. Jackson wanted his troops to recognize that war is terrible and therefore should be short, and since the shortest way to peace is by victory, the waging of war should be conducted with all one's heart, spirit, and mind; remembering that the inscrutable ways of the Lord determine all outcomes will free the spirit from guilt and hesitation, allowing God's warrior to concentrate all his resources on the immediate matter at hand. In the midst of death, Jackson could remain absolutely calm. This attitude had a marvelous effect upon his troops, who worshiped him. Alternatively, a flashing glance from his deeply browed eyes coerced awe and obedience.

Little of this was the result of raw native talent. Whatever Jackson achieved, he did by efforts as determined and relentless as those he had applied to mathematics as a youth, to mastering the intricacies of artillery drill at West Point, and to learning some social graces in order to court his wives. Stonewall Jackson, man and warrior, is best understood as the personification of the motto he lived by: "You may be what ever you resolve to be."

William L. Urban

Sources for Further Study

American History. XXXII, August, 1997, p. 10.
Atlanta Journal Constitution. September 28, 1997, p. M2.

Civil War Times Illustrated. XXXVI, June, 1997, p. 12.
Kirkus Reviews. LXV, January 1, 1997, p. 48.
Library Journal. CXXII, February 15, 1997, p. 142.
The New York Times Book Review. CII, March 16, 1997, p. 23.
Publishers Weekly. CCXLIV, February 3, 1997, p. 86.

STOPS

Author: Joel Sloman
Publisher: Zoland Books (Cambridge, Massachusetts). 92 pp. $19.95
Type of work: Poetry

Stops *is a difficult collection of postmodernist poems in which the images often startle but do not form logical structures*

Joel Sloman's *Stops* is a difficult but often amusing book of poems. Sloman is a postmodernist poet who consciously avoids the usual coherent and rational structures of earlier poetry. In the book's preface, Denise Levertov claims that in his postmodernist method, "Sloman neither jumps nor falls over that brink: the means by which he stretches our expectations of language and continually surprises us are not erosions of grammar and syntax, but swifter adjacencies than we are used to, even after decades of familiarity with the dictum, 'one perception must lead immediately to another perception.'" The connections and relationships of lines or parts of poems, therefore, can seem arbitrary, but Sloman is challenging and goes beyond the reader's usual sense of coherence. He provides a defense and description of his method in the poem (like most, titled by its first line) "While an ugly green house in a pale light." The speaker poses the question: "Is it an affective disorder to be unable to comprehend any/ but logical steps?" His concept of meaning is that it "spreads from each thing like a potion/ in wine."

The reader must be prepared for swift juxtapositions and leaps from one image to another to get any pleasure out of these poems. There is, however, another clue to Sloman's method: He claims that the personifications in the book "become performers in my own dramas put on by my own touring opera company." He personifies clouds, trees, and houses in nearly every poem in the book. Sloman claims that they are "neighborhood players in a spiritual realm that reverberates with persistent moral and other philosophical dilemmas. . . ." This may be making too large a claim for these playful poems, but the use of repeated images that take on human characteristics is central to Sloman's poetics.

The poems are arranged into three groups. "It rains on elms' tall pillars" is a good introduction to Sloman's method. There are the familiar trees that introduce the poem, and there is a reversed perspective: "The baby's garden dwarfs its house. . . ." It is a child's world with its playfulness and freedom. It is "Nursery world" in which all are commanded to "Yield." One of the important themes in the book is freedom from institutions or social restraints; the natural or child's world is consistently juxtaposed to forces that would limit that freedom.

"It's all having an impact on me" presents an oppressive monochrome world that is "proud to be obliterating" the joy of "broadcasted laughter." As they often do in these poems, images of darkness oppose the world of freedom and pleasure; in this poem, it is "Espresso warps" and "Dark nostrils." The conclusion is mocking as the "tug on her arm" is "merely her headphone cord" that provokes "an elegantly superior expression." Presumably, the mechanical image calls forth this "superior expression," but it is not very clear. Sloman's logic of contrasting images of variety to monochromatic ones, mechanical to natural ones, is clear, but the resolution of this and other poems is not.

"Am I closer to thee, dotted world?" describes a computerized world made of "pixel" and "chip." The speaker throws himself "out of bed with a martial arts grunt." He is, presumably, preparing himself for the encounter with the "dotted world" that is curiously addressed in archaic language as "thee." That world of "black shapes" sails from "port to port" in an amusing pun. The resolving line of the poem, however, is uncertain. "They are walking in wind and companionship." Who are "they?" Is it the speaker and this world of "black shapes?" Is he now "closer" to that world? Or does the world of pixels walk in companionship with its own elements? That seems to be the most likely interpretation, but there is no certainty of meaning in these poems.

"Dirty windows dull the known brightness" uses the familiar dark and light imagery. The dark seems about to envelop the world as "the negative inside asserts itself"; however, the "sameness" is "a limited sameness." Sameness takes on negative aspects in the poems and is consistently set against variety and multiplicity. Positive images of smiles and flowers are then evoked. The last stanza brings another figure into the poem: "In our love display/ we are vulnerable. . . ." The beloved is not identified but shares the values of the speaker. Their love is opposed to the monochromatic world of darkness and dirt. Furthermore, they cannot be controlled by "rulers"; "We need wiggle room." The concept of needing freedom and space is clear, and "wiggle room" captures the idiosyncratic and childlike desire found in this and many other poems.

"Zurbaran" is one of the few titled poems, and it describes a still life by seventeenth century Spanish painter Francisco de Zurbarán. The description takes on symbolic overtones. Everything besides the "saint's left forearm is horizontal" and threatening as it "leads indirectly to another place/ shifting the blame." The last line is puzzling: "Streaked glass lets in today's color-hating light." The glass of the window apparently lets in the light that then illuminates the painting. Why this should be "color-hating" is unclear. Perhaps it hates the abundance of Zurbarán's imagined world of color. Here art seems to be superior to nature.

The second group of poems uses Sloman's repeated images and themes. "My mode is evasion, her clothes summer white" deals with a world of birds. One bird is described in detail as he "swoops along a slanted parcel of air inches above a/ pointed wavelet." The description is technical in its "slanted parcel of air," and the "pointed" wavelets is very precise. The last line locates the poem in Sloman's world of art and the imagination: "Diving, it wriggles through a movie soundtrack of closely/ miked breath and bubbles." Nature is turned into the fantasy land of the movies as the gull performs his tricks to a recording microphone. The bird "wriggles," very similar to the demand for "wiggle room" in an earlier poem.

"This is an articulation of my deepest values" seems, on the surface, to be a philosophical poem, but the "values" that are articulated are very personal ones. The images that follow the first line seem to be negative rather than propagating any "values." There is a "despairing lettered sign" and the artificial "gold streaked in streaked vinyl." The second stanza reverses that movement with bird images that are connected to love: "My hand pets your hard cheek, your throat./ Our feathers are erect, a song pipes, cheers, and breaks." The poem ends in a playful list of those values after asserting that "Accepting my values is my sole value." These values are various and contrasting: "It might be the physical universe, it might be my eyes, it might/ be my principles and disposition." Sloman seldom states anything directly, and the conditional mood of this supposed announcement of his deepest values is typical.

"All the while a sea of floes" is an interesting poem that works from the familiar cloud images to something deeper. The poem begins with a "sky of clouds" that are compared to a sea with "peaks point out." This sets the speaker's heart "racing," but only to conform "to routine/ all day." Some trivial conversation follows: "How was/ your/ weekend?" The answer and the final image reverse the trivial passage and the cloud image: "Mine was/ anesthetizing/ thank goodness/ looking/ forward/ to dark." Does the "dark" mean death, which would be a deeper obliteration than being anesthetized? It is inviting to read it this way, although Sloman does not use traditional images or symbols, so his intent remains uncertain.

The poems in the third group are similar to those in the other groups; however, the first poem in this group, "Recitative," is a prose poem. The first part of the poem is a meditation on the "irrecoverable" nature of the "past." Sloman describes the past as "chaotic" and claims that history is "porous." What had been a logical discussion of the past then shifts into a series of loosely related sentences. The lack of connections, presumably, demonstrates his thesis about the past. The tone in this latter section is playful and willful as Sloman announces, "I'd like to return to the forties" and then declares "There was something special about the thirties." The last lines of the poem shift from history to fabrics as Sloman claims "Wearing cotton is a sensuous link to history." The last line explores another aspect of clothing: "Wearing leather and fur resurrects the animal in me."

"Burning" is a rather different poem in its evocation of a personal memory. "My father was in charge of the library./ He marched back and forth on sentry duty." Such an activity sounds like the institutional confinement that Sloman opposes in a number of poems. He does seem to distance himself from that confinement as he asks, "Are landscapes inheritable?" The question is not answered, but the past is once more irrecoverable: "Ages of steam and iron and illumination quickly fled." The poem ends with contrasting images of "violets" that are not limited to one color: "Some were purple, others mostly white with purple centers,/ still others veined with a purple that looked nearly charcoal." The depth of the "charcoal" purple image is very effective.

Sloman's poetry is very similar to that of John Ashberry, and "Resistance is Futile" is, perhaps, the best example of the Ashberry style. The poem begins with some unnamed "they" destroying everything: "They will eat anything, even sun." Later, "They wished even more people had been killed." The countermovement is the arrival of "spring," although this is accomplished "by virtue of a technicality." The speaker is mired in "complete unhappiness," but all the images seem positive. There are leaves that "charge en masse," and the street is filled "with golden pollen"; however, "They ate it all, leaving us nothing."

"I am a *boulevardier* in Paris" is an interesting poem. The speaker announces that "My ambition is to study science. . . ." The science that he will study is seen in an amusing and juxtaposed list: "Atomic structure/ Sex lives/ Bridge construction. . . ." All of his studies will stress the "subtext" rather than the text. The speaker then talks of returning to "sum this up." The last section of the poem speaks of a change in "our method of transportation" and cleaning "The dome and ironwork. . . ." We will, "At this time of day, stare at maps." The resolution apparently is to turn our place into another Paris with "domes and ironwork." The "maps" and the new "method of transportation" will make an imaginative world that will equal Paris.

The last poem in the book is titled "Sonnet," and it does have fourteen lines, although it does not follow the structure of any sonnet that came before. The poem begins with the weather falling "apart," then moves to the speaker feeling "unease in your bony hands." The "clouds" make an appearance, as do insects, but the speaker makes no connection to the natural world, instead talking of his loneliness: "I sip from solitude's diversionary clarity." The last two lines of the poem undo the whole scene, "Sit side by side, elbows on the counter./ Efface this memory with 'a brush of the sponge.'" This is another example of life being turned into a work of art that can then be effaced.

Stops is a puzzling book of poems that is likely to find a limited but devoted audience. There is a sameness in the use of imagery that does link poem to poem; however, the sudden and surprising juxtapositions make every poem new. Sloman does have an eye for the absurd image and a firm control of the poetic line, although the lines lack resonance and are often too playful to be effective.

James Sullivan

Source for Further Study

Publishers Weekly. CCXLIV, September 22, 1997, p. 77.

STRAIGHT MAN

Author: Richard Russo (1949-   )
Publisher: Random House (New York). 391 pp. $25.00
Type of work: Novel
Time: A week during spring semester, sometime in the early 1990's
Locale: West Central Pennsylvania College, in Railton

Hank Devereux, interim chair of English at a third-rate college, resorts to comically drastic but finally successful means to secure a budget while shaking himself, some foes, and some friends out of a twenty-year torpor

Principal characters:
    WILLIAM HENRY (HANK) DEVEREUX, JR., discontented, not quite
        down-and-out chair of the West Central Pennsylvania College English
        department
    WILLIAM HENRY DEVEREUX, SR., Hank's father, a famous critic-teacher
    LILY DEVEREUX, Hank's job-seeking wife
    ANGELO CAPICE, Hank's colorful father-in-law
    JULIE DEVEREUX RUSSELL, Hank and Lily's younger daughter, whose
        rocky marriage troubles Hank
    DICKIE POPE, malignant campus executive officer
    TEDDY BARNES, Hank's paranoid predecessor as chair
    JACOB ROSE, dean of liberal arts
    PAUL ROURKE, Hank's archenemy
    FINNY COOMB, closet homosexual
    BILLY QUIGLEY, department drunk
    RACHEL, loyal department secretary
    GRACIE DUBOIS, department poet whose verse Hank mocks
    TONY CONIGLIA, resident sage and foil for Hank

Richard Russo's *Straight Man* invalidates the widely held notion in academe that nothing happens in a department during an interim chair's watch. Up to a point, fiction mirrors life in Russo's most ambitious novel, his fourth. William Henry (Hank) Devereux, Jr., who teaches creative writing, was appointed as department chair pro tempore only because he was considered safe. For the last twenty years engulfed in stagnant grievances and unfulfilled ambitions, the crabby English faculty at West Central Pennsylvania College assume they can rely on him, as undistinguished as they, not to muddy the academic waters with change. They are wrong. Russo devotes nearly four hundred pages to Hank's mind-over-matter reinvention of himself.

"In English departments the most serious competition is for the role of straight man," Hank tells himself early in the novel. Wearing a fake nose and glasses, he has just mock-accused one of his tormentors, a female poetaster, of sexual harassment. "You weren't turned on yesterday?" he jokes. Yesterday, the poet, Gracie DuBois, had bashed him for an unsubtle slight uttered at a department meeting. For overplaying the role of straight man, Hank had to summon the janitor to extricate the coils of Gracie's notebook from his nostril.

Paul Rourke, the dour "eighteenth century man," is Hank's most persistent enemy. Rourke charges him with trying to make everything into a joke but never being funny.

In this novel's terms, Rourke is more right than he thinks. Hank functions like Hawkeye Pierce in *M*A*S*H*; he detests the fraud and cant he sees everywhere, especially in himself, and pretends to laugh at his self-entrapments to keep from crying.

Straight Man pivots skillfully between the two meanings of its title. Russo never quite allows his protagonist's moral focus to be obliterated by all the verbal shenanigans; it is merely disguised. Crunch time comes after still another fruitless confrontation with the slimy Dickie Pope, campus executive officer. Hank grabs a goose from the campus pond (he had dubbed the goose Finny that very morning, after the department transvestite) and, with TV cameras churning while dignitaries cut the ribbon for a grand, new engineering complex, he threatens to kill it or another like it (he really means ducks) every day until the English department gets its funding. "This is a nonnegotiable demand," Hank shouts above the cheers of the crowd and camera crew. "I want the money on my desk by Monday morning, or this guy will be soaking in orange sauce and full of cornbread stuffing by Monday night."

The comic effect would be spoiled if Hank had to make good his threat. Several ducks, mysteriously dead, turn up, and Hank is blamed by everyone from students and colleagues to Railton's animal rights advocates. The placing of blame and the accusations do not matter: The duck threat defuses the force of the administration's rigid authority. Hank has introduced a human factor whose workings will be slow but sure. The comic ploy allows the reader to infer the effect on Hank of twenty years of departmental sloth and "the increasingly militant ignorance" of students. In this one bold-if-bluffing stroke, he has taken on the administration and the union. He calls a pox on both houses and in the process upholds his most dearly held motto, drawn from the philosophical rule of Occam's razor: "Entities should not be multiplied unnecessarily."

For Hank Devereux, invoking Occam's urge to simplify becomes a check on any tendency to self-indulgence. Its implications are profound, but application is difficult. In dealing with his domestic problems, including the residual effects of his teacher-critic father's early defection from the family, Hank reminds his wife Lily that lies and pretenses always require more lies and pretenses—a clear violation of Occam.

"I'm not an easy man," Hank confesses in a seven-page prologue. "The kind of man I am, according to those who know me best, is exasperating. I was . . . an impossible child." Even more so is his father. William Henry Devereux, Sr., never functions as a character in the book but instead is a galvanic presence—or rather, absence—in his son's life. When Hank was nine years old, having "lobbied" two years for a dog and "earned" one, he fled the house rather than accept the pet his father brought him: not the puppy he wanted but an aged dog that became available when a retired colleague went into a nursing home.

> A purebred, rust-colored Irish setter, meticulously groomed, wonderfully mannered, the kind of dog you could bring into a house owned by the university, the sort of dog that wouldn't really violate the no pets clause, the kind of dog . . . you'd get if you didn't really want a dog or to be bothered with a dog. It was like a painting of a dog, or a dog you'd hire to pose for a portrait, a dog you could be sure wouldn't move.

Fittingly, upon his return, Hank finds that the dog has died. Forty years later, he will name his dog Occam.

Hank's skewed relationship with his father is a dissonant echo from offstage. "I have inherited from my father most of what I had hoped to avoid," Hank reflects in characteristic self-deprecation. His father is a womanizing "academic opportunist" whose successful books follow fashion. They enable him to move among the best schools and couple with eager graduate students at each ivy port. As *Straight Man* opens, the father, whom Hank has not seen in years, is returning to Railton, all the worse for wear.

"When all is said and done, I'm an English professor, like my father [but] he's been a successful one," Hank laments. He landed in Railton because of a critically praised but nonselling first novel, *Off the Road*, the remaindered copies of which, for reasons not explained, still sell in the campus bookstore for the original price. Hank has written nothing for twenty years except satirical columns for the local paper. He effaces any bitterness by remembering Occam's razor, "which strongly suggests that I am a one-book author. Had I been more, I'd be more. Simple."

The more Hank's Hawkeye persona takes over—his verbal high jinks of apparent self-mockery and real disdain for town and gown—the more all authority falls under suspicion. Gossip is the currency of the flawed, which the faculty certainly are; soon, even tenured professors fear the rumor that there is a list, demanded by the higher-ups, of faculty who can be fired to ease the budget crisis. "Not all lousy teachers can become administrators," Hank jokes when his paranoid predecessor demands to know if he is on the blacklist. When the hated Dickie Pope, well-named campus executive officer, praises Hank's duck-killing ploy, Hank is suspicious. Because Pope has never shown a sense of humor, Hank concludes that he thinks it was funny "in the same way that stabbing me through the throat with an ice pick would be funny."

Hank Devereux's is a world in which cynicism is a given and the worst truth that someone can come up with about any person or event is the most consequential truth. Because Hank is the reader's only guide, most of the characters except for him are monochromatic, and the plot is hostage to his lightly veiled self-pity.

Dialogue is what Russo does best. As in his previous novel, *Nobody's Fool* (1993), the tone of the writing conveys the same low-key, wiseacre intelligence as its characters. The most affecting are the walk-ons: Mr. Purdy, the self-made man of means who admiringly pursues Hank's mother because she has "class"; Angelo, Hank's father-in-law, who sent his daughter off to receive the education he lacked and from which he naïvely believed she would achieve affluence but otherwise remain unchanged; and Bodie Pie, of women's studies, whom Hank fantasizes as having a lesbian tryst with his wife.

Somewhat in the manner of nineteenth century Russian novels, Russo concludes with an epilogue, a flash-forward from April to August, tying up neatly—perhaps too neatly—some dangling strands. Hank's father died in July, but not before father and son have come full circle, burying Occam as they had buried the old dog the nine-year-old Hank had not wanted. Paul Rourke, appointed dean, now exchanges politic smiles with his enemy. By disappearing, Rourke's usually stoned second wife has made it easier for Rourke to entertain the chancellor. Jacob Rose is out as dean but in with Hank's lovely secretary, Rachel; they have married and are building a house on property bought from Hank. Brooklyn-born Tony Coniglia, slow in racquetball but fast on wise repartee, has the best chance to get out of the academic boonies; he is awarded a working sabbatical at the University of Pittsburgh.

If, as H. G. Wells wrote, James Joyce was a writer with a cloacal obsession, Russo may be said in *Straight Man* to have one with the human bladder. Hank haunts rest room urinals awaiting passage of a kidney stone, a problem he shares with his father. His urologist hints that his ailment may be more serious. When Hank turns down the deanship and relinquishes his tenure, he sees it as the symbolic equivalent of passing the stone. Given a clean bill of health, Hank will see a collection of his columns into print and resume writing fiction. Although his marital situation is never quite clear— Lily is mysteriously job-hunting in Philadelphia throughout most of the book—the reader is led to believe it has improved when Lily is promoted to a principalship in Railton. Daughter Julie rejoins her husband Russell in Atlanta.

The final pages of the epilogue bring most of the male characters together, as if for a curtain call. They have gathered in Tony Coniglia's small hospital room to cheer him up; he is to be kept overnight after heart fibrillations. They exchange stories all have told before. Looking for "some form of concentrated significance" in the scene, Hank finds himself calling the roll:

> I knew these men. I'd known them for twenty years. When we met we were all married. A few of us still were. A few more were divorced. A few more were re-married and trying again. Some of us had betrayed fine women. Some of us had been ourselves betrayed. But here we were, tonight at least, drawn together by some need, as if we were waiting for a sign. And I was one of their number.

Faced with a moral crisis that required more than his customary accommodations to self-deception, Hank finds at the end of this rich chronicle of self a new phenomenon: inner growth.

Richard Hauer Costa

Sources for Further Study

Atlantic Monthly. August 1997, p. 97.
Booklist. May 15, 1997, p. 1541.
Chicago Tribune. August 3, 1997, XIV, p. 3.
The Christian Science Monitor. October 6, 1997, p. 14.
The Chronicle of Higher Education. XLIII, August 8, 1997, p. B8.
Library Journal. CXXII, June 15, 1997, p. 99.
Los Angeles Times Book Review. September 21, 1997, p. 8.
The New York Times Book Review. CII, July 6, 1997, p. 10.

Publishers Weekly. CCXLIV, May 12, 1997, p. 56.
San Francisco Chronicle. July 6, 1997, p. REV4.
Time. CL, July 14, 1997, p. 84.
USA Today. July 3, 1997, p. D6.

A SUPPOSEDLY FUN THING I'LL NEVER DO AGAIN
Essays and Arguments

Author: David Foster Wallace (1962-   )
Publisher: Little, Brown and Company (Boston). 353 pp. $23.95
Type of work: Essays

Writing in a high-voltage, colloquial style, novelist David Foster Wallace focuses his unique and sardonic wit on the icons of American popular culture in the 1990's

Reading David Foster Wallace is like riding a verbal roller coaster or being catapulted by some zany carnival ride that twists and turns one's perspective, flips the world upside down, and creates a kaleidoscope of blurred colors and rapidly alternating images. His prose is a nonstop language experience, immersing the reader in varieties of slang, four-letter words, technical terminology, academic jargon, and outright linguistic inventions. Only Wallace, for example, would describe the overly solicitous and nervously busy crew of a cruise ship as "amphetaminic," the same Wallace who, just as casually, evokes a colloquial ambiance with words like "stuff" and "hellacious." The poet W. H. Auden once remarked that a poet was anyone who loved language and, in this regard, Wallace must be ranked as a kind of poet of pop culture, even though he is known as a writer of short stories, essays, and novels. His intense, high-pressured use of language becomes a kind of poetry within his work. No matter what the subject—drugs, county fairs, tennis, cruise ships, *film noir*, or television (his obsession)—the reader is invariably awed by Wallace's subtle and witty manipulations of language.

The essays in *A Supposedly Fun Thing I'll Never Do Again* are the expanded "director's cut" versions (according to Wallace) of shorter pieces, many originating as assignments from editors at *Harper's* magazine. Other essays appeared in *Esquire*, *Premiere* (a film journal), and *The Review of Contemporary Fiction*. These journals and periodicals give a hint of Wallace's stature within the literary community and also summarize his broad interests in the field of contemporary culture. The revised versions of the essays and their publication between the covers of one book closely follow the appearance of Wallace's massive tome of a novel, *Infinite Jest* (1996), a long (1,079 pages) exploration of television, commercialism, addiction, tennis, and adolescence; in short, the same preoccupations of *A Supposedly Fun Thing I'll Never Do Again*. The very same themes appeared in Wallace's first novel, *The Broom of the System* (1987) and in his collection of short stories, *Girl with Curious Hair* (1988). Thus, there is a clear thematic wholeness in Wallace's oeuvre as well as a consistency of tone. Wallace is not merely an excruciatingly precise observer of the surface and depth of American life, but he is also a witty and downright humorous interpreter of social situations, a comic genius who has been compared to English satirist Jonathan Swift. In *Infinite Jest*, for example, Wallace spoofs our national tendency to commercialize everything by creating a future society where even the years will have corporate sponsors. Only rarely does Wallace remove his ironic mask.

The seven essays that constitute *A Supposedly Fun Thing I'll Never Do Again* should not be read, however, as scholarly articles, despite their origins in prestigious literary venues. These seven pieces, ranging in length from eight pages ("Greatly Exaggerated") to ninety-seven ("A Supposedly Fun Thing I'll Never Do Again"), and comprising such topics as food, television, state fairs, tennis, old age, tornadoes, and films, are distinctly personal documents offering Wallace's unique "arguments" or complicated conversations with the reader. Wallace is less interested in proving a point or creating some abstract hierarchy of ideas than in simply sharing a vision. He wants readers to try to perceive the world through his eyes, even for a moment. Hence, he includes two essays on tennis because, to him, it remains one of the few beautiful and heroic activities in human life. After all, the essay, as a literary form, derives from the French *essayer*, "to try," and Wallace tries hard, in the manner of a tennis hero, serving one ball after another. He downloads the equivalent of a whole hard drive of vocabulary on the reader and, in vulnerable moments, even confesses some awkward and morbid truths about himself.

The opening essay, "Derivative Sport in Tornado Alley," one of the two pieces on tennis, is a highly nostalgic and brutally honest account of Wallace as a young tennis champion growing up in the tiny village of Philo, Illinois, a lonely and isolated dot on the prairie. Although the essay is eloquently detailed on the lore of tennis courts, rackets, and tournaments, Wallace manages a literary hat trick (the equivalent of a powerful backhand) by combining his insights into tennis, the vagaries of the weather (wind and tornadoes), and the spatial dimensions of the broad, flat prairie. The author uses the precision of physics or mathematics (Wallace majored in mathematics at Amherst, where he graduated *summa cum laude* in 1985) and the aesthetic vision of a landscape painter or photographer to write some unusually compelling and vivid prose:

> When I left my boxed township of Illinois farmland to attend my dad's alma mater in the lurid jutting Berkshires of western Massachusetts, I all of a sudden developed a jones for mathematics. I'm starting to see why this was so. College math evokes and catharts a Midwesterner's sickness for home. I'd grown up inside vectors, lines and lines athwart lines, grids—and, on the scale of horizons, broad curving lines of geographic force, the weird topographical drain-swirl of a whole lot of ice-ironed land that sits and spins atop plates.

This specimen is vintage Wallace—honest, pensive, witty, and linguistically playful with street-talk ("jones") and highly elevated ("catharts") and technical ("vectors") diction. The honesty continues in Wallace's self-deprecating portrait of himself as a lonely, alienated youth, a "math-wienie" who could only beat his opponents by exasperating them with his mathematically regular style of playing, which was boring but effective. Wallace is quite open about his shortcomings in tennis and in other departments of life. He has given interviews about his addictions to drugs, alcohol, and tobacco. The drug rehabilitation sequences in *Infinite Jest* derive from painful personal experience. Wallace takes a cold, clinical measure of himself in the other essay on tennis, concluding that, although he may have once possessed impressive amateur skills, he was never on the plane of world-class players, a fact that clearly rankles.

The unabashed hero-worship for professional athletes stands out clearly in "Tennis Player Michael Joyce's Professional Artistry as a Paradigm of Certain Stuff About Choice, Freedom, Discipline, Joy, Grotesquerie, and Human Completeness," an essay that comes closer to mainstream journalistic style than any other piece in the book. It is the one rare instance where Wallace drops the comic mask and lets a dreamy and unfulfilled self emerge. Even though Wallace reports the minutiae of a day in the life of a typical tennis professional (while throwing in interesting tidbits about the history and rules of the sport), he is really writing about himself and his deepest longings and frustrations.

There is a poignantly sad side to Wallace, who has described himself in interviews as being a "nerd" and who is sometimes socially awkward. There are moments in some of the other essays where Wallace actually hides himself in his room, a kind of reflex action for him, a sort of existential "duck and cover." He wants to watch but not to be watched, and that fundamental sense of alienation empowers him to write most persuasively about the central icon of contemporary American culture—television.

Even though the diction is idiosyncratic, the arguments are sometimes partially developed, and the transitions from point to point or section to section is often awkward and wooden, "E Unibus Pluram: Television and U.S. Fiction" is an intellectual beacon in the murkiness of contemporary life. The essay has more wisdom on such subjects as alienation, loneliness, passivity, and the effects of watching (and accepting) the fraudulence of television than a whole library of books on these subjects. This essay absolutely defines the ethos of the generation that came of age in the 1980's and the subsequent works of art produced by that age group (Wallace's very own demographic niche) that occupies the space between the so-called Baby Boomers and Generation X'ers.

Wallace makes the central point that television, with its prepackaged plots and personalities, has become the preponderant reality for young writers, whose stories all sound like television programs because the writers don't actually know anything else. His biggest worry is that television induces an ironic stance in its audience while simultaneously insulating itself from irony; in short, television, as a medium, has no responsibility except to create audiences and garner attention. Its power is so devastating that Wallace can offer no way out, so the essay simply stops—it doesn't end with any kind of conclusive argument or synthesizing metaphor. In a way, "E Unibus Pluram" stands out as the most honest and intelligent effort in the book, not merely because Wallace is generally free from irony but also because his frustration is plainly evident. He seeks transcendence but cannot find it, and he will not stoop to bluffing or dishonesty in the service of a rhetorically neat ending.

By comparison, "Greatly Exaggerated," the shortest essay in the book and a kind of primer of postmodern criticism, is neatly done and shows all the marks of good craftsmanship and tight thinking. Yet, it is something of a lightweight in the company of the powerhouses that occupy the book, and it tends to read a little like a graduate school seminar paper, albeit a clean and elegant one. Its absence would not have altered the book materially, or, perhaps, its contents could have been included in the "E Unibus Pluram" essay. The subject Wallace tackles in "Greatly Exaggerated" (as in "reports of my death have been greatly exaggerated") is the death of the author, or the attacks, by postmodern critics, on the very existence of authors. Clearly, Wallace does believe in authors; as a practitioner, he has little choice. The notion of the film-author, or *auteur*, provides Wallace with a grounding orientation for his other major essay, "David Lynch Keeps His Head."

By following director David Lynch around the set of *Lost Highway* (1996), Wallace had an excellent opportunity to report on the behind-the-scenes activities of film-makers. The genuine subject, however, is the mind of Lynch, not the Lynch who made the successful science fiction classic *Dune* in 1985 (which had too much big studio control, in Wallace's view) but the Lynch of *Blue Velvet* (1986) and the television series *Twin Peaks*. Lynch is an *auteur* precisely because he has a vision, one that cannot be paraphrased. However, it is clear that the narrative techniques and fundamental assumptions of Lynch are also shared by Wallace. The writer praises the filmmaker for creating a multilayered reality, where evil and good not only coexist but are also indistinguishable, where the possible and the impossible both occur. Hence, Wallace praises the scene in *Lost Highway* where a man calls himself on the telephone and engages in a conversation with himself, all in "real" time. That kind of quirky universe is exactly the sort that Wallace tried to evoke in his fictional works, especially *Infinite Jest*.

The two remaining essays, "Getting Away from Already Being Pretty Much Away from it All" and the title piece, "A Supposedly Fun Thing I'll Never Do Again," are both log-style reports on public events: in the first instance, the Illinois State Fair and, in the second, a week-long cruise in the Caribbean aboard a luxury liner. Wallace's descriptions of food (from corn dogs to a cocktail called the Slippery Nipple), carnival rides, tourists, and social classes are as well written as anything done by Tom Wolfe, the master "new journalist." The general air of unreality on the ship and on the fairgrounds also recalls "gonzo" journalist Hunter Thompson at his best.

On the final page of the book, Wallace returns to dry land after his Caribbean cruise, ready to face the "real world," as will the readers who have accompanied him on his unfailingly lively and comic excursions.

Daniel L. Guillory

Sources for Further Study

The Antioch Review. LV, Spring, 1997, p. 249.
Artforum. XXXV, Summer, 1997, p. 15.
Booklist. XCIII, February 15, 1997, p. 996.
Chicago Tribune. March 9, 1997, XIV, p. 1.

Library Journal. CXXII, January, 1997, p. 100.
Los Angeles Times. February 7, 1997, p. E2.
The New Republic. CCXVI, June 30, 1997, p. 27.
The New York Times Book Review. CII, March 16, 1997, p. 11.
Newsweek. CXXIX, February 17, 1997, p. 63.
Publishers Weekly. CCXLIII, December 30, 1996, p. 47.
The Review of Contemporary Fiction. XVII, Summer, 1997, p. 265.
Time. CXLIX, April 14, 1997, p. 89.
The Washington Post Book World. XXVII, February 2, 1997, p. 13.

TEXACO

Author: Patrick Chamoiseau (1953-   )
First published: 1992, in France
Translated from the French and Creole by Rose-Myriam Réjouis and Val Vinokoruv
Afterword by Rose-Myriam Réjouis
Publisher: Pantheon Books (New York). 401 pp. $27.00
Type of work: Novel
Locale: Martinique

Winner of the 1992 Prix Goncourt, France's most prestigious literary award, Texaco *is the epic story of the development and survival of Martinican Creole culture and identity through the postslavery period to the present as exemplified through the evolution of a shantytown*

Principal characters:
>   MARIE-SOPHIE LABORIEUX, the founder of Texaco, a sprawling shantytown situated outside Fort-de-France on the island of Martinique
>   ESTERNOME LABORIEUX, her father, a former plantation slave
>   IDOMÉNÉE CARMÉLITE LAPIDAILLE, her mother, also a former plantation slave
>   ADRIENNE CARMÉLITE LAPIDAILLE, the twin sister of Idoménée
>   THE URBAN PLANNER, also known as THE CHRIST, whose task is to raze Texaco
>   TI-CIRIQUE, a Haitian who settles in Texaco and introduces Marie-Sophie to language and literature
>   OISEAU DE CHAM, THE WORD SCRATCHER, the writer who interviews Marie-Sophie and records her story

Texaco, a richly woven narrative tracing 150 years of postslavery Caribbean history, recounts the establishment and evolution of Texaco, a shantytown established, in close proximity to Fort-de-Prince, Martinique, by Marie-Sophie Laborieux. In his novel, which won France's most prestigious literary award, the Prix Goncourt, in 1992 and which has been translated into fourteen languages, Patrick Chamoiseau's voice resonates in affirmation of Martinique's Creole history and identity. Chamoiseau— novelist, playwright, and essayist—is profoundly cognizant of the complex process of *métissage* and creolization that has led to the development of a Martinican collective consciousness. Throughout *Texaco,* one is keenly aware that he wishes to chronicle Martinican society, history, and oral traditions through a literary language that is all-encompassing. The importance of memory as communicated through the spoken word reflects the distinctiveness of Creole culture, embedded in orality, and is underlined on every page of this lyrical, poignant, and powerful work. Much like the poet and diplomat Saint-John Perse, born in Guadeloupe, or the African American novelist Toni Morrison, Chamoiseau creates a universe rich in history, epic in its allegoric nobility, and compelling in its exotic fullness.

Texaco offers a poetic continuation to *Au Temps de l'antan* (1988; *Creole Folktales,* 1994), in which Chamoiseau reveals the magical power of the storyteller, once imprisoned by slavery and colonialism and wishing now to inform and amuse, to elucidate the past and the future. *Texaco*'s narrative is interwoven with short sequences—often in relation to the past of a particular character—and interspersed with extracts from the fictive notebooks of Marie-Sophie and the words of the urban planner. This framework is introduced by a short history of Martinique and of Texaco, a historical and mythical rendering of the past that includes allusions to the lives of certain characters as well as landmark dates such as the mass importation of black African slaves in 1680, the abolition of freedom decreed in the French colonies in 1848, the slave rebellion in Martinique in the same year, and the election of the renowned poet Aimé Césaire in 1945 as mayor of Fort-de-France, where in 1948 there were riots that led to an exodus to the site of Texaco. The documentary feel of these initial pages reinforces Chamoiseau's intention to classify and articulate the evolution of Martinican land and society through the ages he has devised to reflect this development: the Age of Longhouses and Ajoupas (3000 B.C. to A.D. 1680), the Age of Straw (1823? to 1920), the Age of Crate Wood (1903 to 1945), the Age of Asbestos (1946 to 1960) and the Age of Concrete (1961 to 1980). Against this backdrop, the words and deeds of Chamoiseau's characters serve to affirm Martinican belonging, identity, and society, which were born from centuries of colonialism and slavery as well as the cultural influences of East Indian, African, and Chinese workers imported to Martinique after former slaves refused to work in the fields.

Texaco is, consequently, an epic narrative of reality and fantasy, recounted by its heroine and founder, Marie-Sophie Laborieux, to Oiseau de Cham (an obvious wordplay on the author's name), the Word Scratcher, as a result of the city council's desire to raze the shantytown. Her story, a jewel of Martinican oral literature, is that of her quarter, whose name reflects the presence of the petroleum company, as it embraces her personal history, that of the island, and an abundance of other both anodyne and compelling details relating to important events and characters, such as the abolition of slavery, the eruption of Mount Pelée, the political ascent of Aimé Césaire, the poet descendant from former slaves, to the mayorship of Fort-de-France, the creation of Martinique as an official department of France, and a visit of Charles de Gaulle.

While endeavoring to reconstitute the death of a storyteller, Solibo Magnifique—a character depicted by Chamoiseau in his *Solibo Magnifique* (1988; Solibo the magnificent)—the Word Scratcher comes to meet his "Source," Marie-Sophie, an old woman whose parents were a mulatto man and a black woman. Captivated by her mixture of Creole and French, by the sentences that whirl about her, he preserves—first in written form and then by recording—her narratives, which follow no specific chronology.

The novel opens in allegorical fashion, with an account of how the urban planner, known as the Christ, is hit by a stone while entering Texaco, now linked by road to what is known as "City" (translated from the Creole *l'Enville*), that is, Fort-de-France. The juxtaposition of shantytown and city bespeaks the evolution of Martinican society, the mixture of French and Creole culture and the disadvantaged position occupied in the social hierarchy by the latter. Judged insalubrious by the city council, Texaco has become an object of the urban planner's scrutiny. To understand Texaco is to follow Marie-Sophie as she traces her own genealogy, the movement of freed slaves, and the population expansion that occurred outside City.

Gradually, the reader comes to form a chronological history of the deeds and events recounted by Marie-Sophie in her interviews with the Word Scratcher. One learns of the birth of Esternome Laborieux, her father, the first slave born on a plantation whose main house was called the Big Hutch. The landowner was known simply as the Béké, and his wife as the Lady. Békés are white Creoles, descendants of old, established colonial planter families. Fluent in Creole, they speak accented French. A house servant in the Big Hutch, Esternome was granted freedom for having saved the life of his master after the latter was attacked by a demented slave and poisoned by a filthy bayonet. Esternome received what is called his savanna freedom, that is to say, freedom granted to him without any act of notary, tax, or mandatory food pension. The Béké set Esternome free to do what he wished.

Idoménée Carmélite Lapidaille, the mother of Texaco's founder-to-be, was born— with a twin sister, Adrienne Carmélite—a slave on a plantation near Fort-de-France. The plantation Béké sold Adrienne seven days after her birth. Years later, the death of Marie-Sophie's mother coincided with the end of the plantation system, rendered archaic and inefficient by an ever-growing sugar factory industry.

Working as a cleaning woman for an old mulatto, Idoménée progressively lost her eyesight, until she became blind. Her mistress deposited her unceremoniously at the Bethlehem Asylum but returned days later to fetch her because her pet parrots, lamenting the absence of the slave woman, had plucked out their eyes and wailed continuously. By this time, however, Idoménée had found her way to City and in the street recognized the scent of her sister, Adrienne. She had previously taken Esternome under her wing, and so the three lived together in the Quarter of the Wretched, which soon became absorbed by the advancing City.

Once Marie-Sophie was born, she and her elderly parents lived in a crate wood hutch, for which rent was paid by the income from Esternome's vegetable gardens and by Idoménée's meager earnings from selling fritters. In order to sell her wares, Idoménée was guided into City by Marie-Sophie, her mother's eyes.

Upon the death of her mother, Marie-Sophie forsook her schooling and took over her mother's work of making and selling fritters. Esternome died after being beaten for an accumulation of overdue rent. He died in his hutch, describing to his daughter the images and events that flickered through his memory. These words gave Marie-Sophie the will and legacy that inspired her to found Texaco.

One day, Marie-Sophie discovered a gentle slope near the petroleum company's lands, overlooking City on the other side of the harbor. In this area, close to a mangrove swamp, she eventually erected her own hutch out of bamboo poles, canvas, and rusted sheets of tin. Surrounded by rounded hills, overlooking the Caribbean and feeling its winds, she founded on this magical spot what was to be known as Texaco.

Marie-Sophie's hutch attracted other hutches, and gradually the shantytown took shape, spreading over the slopes, invading the mangrove swamp on long stilts, and surrounding the petroleum reservoir tanks. Police expulsions and the dismantling of hutches in all states of construction punctuated the gradual process, initiated by Marie-Sophie, that resulted ultimately in the creation of Upper Texaco, sculpted into the cliff, and Lower Texaco, at the mercy of the tides.

This conglomeration of souls, hutches, and desires crystallized in Marie-Sophie's soul and imparted to her the profound meaning of a space collectively nurtured by the Creole identity. She began to write down the echoes of the past and the words of her father, whom she called "my Esternome," in notebooks, which are excerpted in the novel. She discovered the act of writing, the beauty of filled pages, the promise of blank pages, and the urgency felt once the first word is liberated. A newcomer to Texaco, Ti-Cirique, a Haitian, attempted to disentangle her sentences and spoke to her of the importance of language, simple, precise, and powerful, and of the world of literature.

As Texaco continued to spread over the slopes, City and its officers became alarmed. The city planner who visited the shantytown had been sent to assess the possibility of razing it. Ultimately, he came to realize that the community he was visiting was in fact a collectivity formed of likeness and uniqueness, a microcosm of his own society, and for this reason deserved the same material support as City. Shortly after his departure, the rehabilitation of Texaco began, first by the installation of electrical lines—to be the first of modern comforts—with the city council's express intent of acknowledging its existence and, most important, respecting its integrity without making it into a smaller City. Thus Marie-Sophie's struggles to receive formal validation of her community, with its uniqueness and complexities, proved victorious.

Her death shortly thereafter brings to a close this monumental account of the history of Texaco. The novel closes by suggesting the difficulties inherent in all types of social change. The future of Texaco seems assured; however, the results of its rehabilitation remain unclear.

It is impossible to read *Texaco* without noting its rich language. Written in what the translators refer to as Mulatto French, a bookish and dictionary-styled language used by mulattos in order to facilitate socioeconomic betterment, and Creole French—a mixture of Carib, Old French, Spanish, English, East Indian, Arabic, and African words—the text moves in a predominantly French matrix. *Texaco* is a song celebrating history, identity, and desire. It is an eloquent homage to Creole culture and society, and its poetry underlines the power and nobility of human will in action, the beauty of the epic struggle.

Kenneth W. Meadwell

Sources for Further Study

Chicago Tribune. March 23, 1997, XIV, p. 4.
Los Angeles Times Book Review. March 2, 1997, p. 7.

National Review. XLIX, May 5, 1997, p. 54.
The New Republic. CCXVI, April 28, 1997, p. 45.
The New York Review of Books. XLIV, August 14, 1997, p. 45.
The New York Times Book Review. CII, March 30, 1997, p. 13.
The New Yorker. LXXIII, March 24, 1997, p. 82.
The Observer. March 9, 1997, p. 16.
Publishers Weekly. CCXLIII, December 9, 1996, p. 61.
The Times Literary Supplement. March 21, 1997, p. 22.

TIMEQUAKE

Author: Kurt Vonnegut (1922-   )
Publisher: Putnam (New York). 219 pp. $23.95
Type of work: Novel and memoir
Time: 1922-2010
Locale: The United States

Vonnegut mixes his personal memoirs with observations on writing, life, and death into the framework of an abandoned novel about the near future, in which he himself is a leading character

Principal personages:
KURT VONNEGUT, the author and narrator
JANE MARIE COX VONNEGUT, his deceased first wife
JILL KREMENTZ, his second wife, a photographer
BERNIE VONNEGUT, his recently deceased older brother, a physicist
ALICE (ALLIE) VONNEGUT, his deceased sister, whose children he adopted
ALEX VONNEGUT, his uncle

Principal characters:
KILGORE TROUT, an aging, long out-of-print science fiction writer
DUDLEY PRINCE, an African American guard at the American Academy of Arts and Letters, who rescues Trout's manuscripts from the trash
MONICA PEPPER, the academy's executive secretary and the narrator's future wife

Kurt Vonnegut has come unstuck in time.

If this, his last book, proves to be true, be prepared for a nasty jolt at 2:27 P.M. on February 13, 2001. At that moment, the universe will suffer a crisis in self-confidence and stop expanding. The result will be a "timequake," in which Vonnegut and everyone and everything else will go back to February 17, 1991. Then the universe will resume expanding, and everyone will relive the next ten years exactly as they did the first time. However, although everyone will know precisely what is coming, no one will be able to do a thing about it. People will live through the timequake like actors in plays ("artificial timequakes") controlled by a script that denies them free will. Those who die before 2001 may enjoy being restored to life in 1991, but they will die again, exactly as they did the first time, before the timequake ends.

Real trouble does not begin, however, until the timequake returns everyone to February 13, 2001. Unprepared for the abrupt restoration of their free will, people are immobilized. Those who happen to be walking stumble and fall; those operating vehicles and machinery have accidents, and so on. Ten years of being on automatic pilot leaves almost everyone too numb to cope on their own.

Ironically, the first person to gather his wits and respond intelligently is the aging and ostensibly dissolute science fiction writer Kilgore Trout (who appears in many of Vonnegut's previous novels). Blessed with a rich, if unprofitable, imagination, Trout alone recognizes what is happening when the timequake ends, and he takes vigorous action. To help others come to their senses, he tells them: "You were sick, but now you're well again, and there's work to do." His words become the mantra that helps the entire world readjust to having free will. (Unfortunately, Trout is not awarded the Nobel Prize that Vonnegut promised him in *Breakfast of Champions* in 1974.)

Such is the plot loosely tying together what is surely Vonnegut's most eccentric book. Its fictional storyline may be thin, but Vonnegut's explanation of how he came to write it—which is also related in bits and pieces throughout *Timequake*—is of great interest. That story begins with Vonnegut's birth.

Born on Armistice Day in 1922, Vonnegut reached the age of seventy-three in 1995. He then realized that he had achieved a greater age than either of his parents and declared that he had lived too long. Moreover, he announced that this book would be his last. His completion of the book, therefore, signaled his literary death. The exact moment evidently occurred around late April, 1997, when he wrote *Timequake*'s last pages—an epilogue eulogizing his brother Bernie. The timing was ironic, as Mark Twain, one of Vonnegut's literary idols, died on almost the same date in 1910 when he, like Vonnegut, was five months into his seventy-fifth year. So it goes.

Categorizing any Vonnegut book as fiction, nonfiction, or something else is a tricky business. Lines separating fact and fiction in his novels often grow fuzzy, then disappear—especially when Vonnegut slips himself in as a character. Vonnegut's sudden appearances in *Slaughterhouse-Five* (1969), for example, remind readers that he, like his fictional protagonist Billy Pilgrim, was a German prisoner in Dresden during World War II. That novel's description of the Allied firebombing of Dresden, therefore, seems more real than imagined. In contrast, Vonnegut's appearance in the entirely imaginary Hooverville of *Breakfast of Champions* is something different—a more contrived device, evidently designed to startle readers and remind them of his authorial presence.

Timequake takes metafiction to a new level, opening with this disclaimer: "All persons, living and dead, are purely coincidental." What follows is not so much a novel as a rambling meditation about a novel, in which Vonnegut slips back and forth into the very fiction he describes. One moment he comments on a problem he had while writing the book; the next moment he describes his conversation with Kilgore Trout as if Trout were a real person. Even more startling is his casual mention of the fact that, in 2010, he will be married to Monica Pepper (a fictional character), although his present wife, Jill Krementz, is still very much alive.

Bizarre transitions such as these will delight Vonnegut's regular readers, while leaving those unfamiliar with his work merely bewildered and unable to pick up on the book's underlying humor and often devastating wit. The book's jacket blurb may not exaggerate in calling *Timequake* a "literary form such as the world has never seen before," for it would be difficult to name the book's structural peer. How much of its odd structure is deliberate, however, is unclear. The parallels already noted between Vonnegut's and Mark Twain's latter years may be suggestive. *Timequake* repeatedly reveals Vonnegut's fascination with Mark Twain. Is Vonnegut, to some extent, deliberately mimicking him?

Vonnegut's description of how he came to write *Timequake* recalls Mark Twain's account of how he wrote *Pudd'nhead Wilson* (1894). After a long struggle with a manuscript containing two incompatible storylines, Mark Twain claimed to have "pulled one of the stories out by the roots, and left the other one," in what he called "a kind of literary caesarean operation." Vonnegut applies a similar metaphor to his creation of *Timequake*, which his prologue compares to the huge marlin caught by Ernest Hemingway's title character in *The Old Man and the Sea* (1952). Its old fisherman lashes his gigantic catch to the side of his boat and spends days getting back to shore, only to discover that sharks have eaten away the marlin's flesh. What the man should have done, Vonnegut points out, was hack off chunks of marlin meat, leaving the rest for the sharks.

Vonnegut faced a similar problem in 1996, when he found himself

> the creator of a novel which did not work, which had no point, which had never wanted to be written in the first place. *Merde!* I had spent nearly a decade on that ungrateful fish, if you will. It wasn't even fit for shark chum.

What he then did was akin to Mark Twain's "literary caesarean operation." He decided to "fillet" his fish and throw the rest away. The result was *Timequake*—a collection of fishy chunks with neither skeleton nor any other discernible structure other than the ten-year loop of the "timequake." The curious book that survived Vonnegut's operation contains scattered bits and pieces of passages originally written for the original book, which he calls *Timequake One*. A long section on Abraham Lincoln's assassination, for example, is reduced to a terse anecdote in *Timequake*.

Timequake's apparently random insertions of passages from *Timequake One* recall Vonnegut's familiar technique of sprinkling synopses of Kilgore Trout stories throughout his earlier novels. *Timequake* itself includes summaries of more Trout stories. Trout's habit of disdainfully trashing the manuscripts of these stories after finishing them proves to be a key element in the book's purely fictional storyline.

Several interrelated themes run through *Timequake:* the devaluation of literacy, the declining meaning of human skills, and the inevitably of death. Vonnegut repeatedly bemoans the two "deaths" his literary career has suffered. The first came after he began writing professionally, supporting his family by feeding short stories to the insatiable appetite for fiction of magazines of the early 1950's. When television came along, it drew people away from magazine fiction, forcing Vonnegut to turn to novels. His old impulse to create short stories survived, however, and was expressed in the synopses of Kilgore Trout books that appear throughout his novels.

Vonnegut's second, and final, literary death has been caused by the spread of computers and electronic entertainments, which he charges are killing both literacy and creative skills in general. This time, there is no other literary form to which he can turn.

Vonnegut's report of his literary death may, however, prove to be exaggerated. *Timequake* reveals that he will live until at least 2010 (exactly one hundred years after Mark Twain's death). Will he really go through the coming years without writing another book? On the other hand, perhaps he is not kidding when he claims to have lived too long. *Timequake* is obsessed with mortality. Almost all of its sixty-four chapters allude to at least one or another form of death: accidental deaths, deaths from illness, individual deaths, mass deaths, and, particularly, suicides. Vonnegut repeatedly mentions the deaths of his mother, first wife, and sister and devotes his epilogue to the death of his brother. *Timequake* also frequently mentions specific wars and incidents of mass destruction.

What, if anything, all this has to do with the book's imaginary timequake might be illuminated by examining the dates that encompass this timequake. It begins on February 13, 2001, in the first year of the next millennium—a significant date in itself. Moreover, the choice of February 13 may also be important: February 13, 1945, is the date on which Vonnegut and Billy Pilgrim cowered in the deep cellar of a Dresden slaughterhouse with other prisoners of war as Allied bombers rained flaming death on tens of thousands of German civilians on the surface. Vonnegut's real-life experience in helping to clean up the heaps of incinerated bodies was a transforming moment in his life. His 1969 publication of *Slaughterhouse-Five* about the bombing has been called his catharsis for that experience, but *Timequake* suggests otherwise—that the destruction of Dresden still haunts him.

The date at the other end of the timequake, February 17, 1991, is also suggestive. On that historical date, the United States and its allies were busy pounding Iraq because Saddam Hussein's army had occupied Kuwait and threatened world access to low-priced petroleum. In that war, as in World War II, the allies were not above incinerating civilians—though this time they did it on live television with high-tech missiles rather than crude firebombs. Around February 17, the Cable News Network (CNN) broadcast graphic images of the flaming destruction inflicted by an American missile on a civilian air-raid shelter.

Curiously, despite *Timequake*'s frequent references to specific wars and their devastation, it fails to mention the Gulf War by name. Its only acknowledgement of that conflict appears in chapter 7—a vague allusion to "blasting the bejesus out of some Third World country because of petroleum." So it goes.

That caveat aside, it appears that Vonnegut's imaginary timequake begins and ends on dates symbolizing the pointless incineration of innocent civilian enemies in the midst of horrifying wars. Could it be that modern conflicts, particularly the Gulf War of early 1991, rekindled Vonnegut's painful memories of World War II and Dresden and moved him to start writing a book he could not finish satisfactorily?

Despite its evident obsession with death, *Timequake* is also about finding joy in life. A "plausible mission of artists," Vonnegut writes, "is to make people appreciate being alive at least a little bit." Pleasure, however transitory, is certainly a primary reason most of Vonnegut's readers will read this book. The book is not likely to provide many with the satisfaction that his earlier books, with their flesh and skeletons still intact, offer, but its humor should, nevertheless, offer readers much to raise their spirits, if not to make them laugh aloud. As Vonnegut's Uncle Alex would say, if that isn't nice, what is?

R. Kent Rasmussen

Sources for Further Study

Booklist. XCIII, August, 1997, p. 1849.
Charleston. XI, November, 1997, p. 55.
The Nation. CCLXV, October 20, 1997, p. 33.
The New York Times Book Review. CII, September 28, 1997, p. 14.
The New Yorker. LXXIII, October 6, 1997, p. 43.
Newsweek. CXXX, September 29, 1997, p. 78.
The North American Review. CCLXXXII, September, 1997, p. 41.
Publishers Weekly. CCXLIV, August 4, 1997, p. 63.
Time. CL, September 29, 1997, p. 95.
The Times Literary Supplement. September 26, 1997, p. 22.

TO BE AN AMERICAN
Cultural Pluralism and the Rhetoric of Assimilation

Author: Bill Ong Hing
Publisher: New York University Press (New York). 243 pp. $29.95
Type of work: Current affairs

A challenge to "anti-immigrant" sentiment, drawing on extensive studies of the economic impact of immigration as well as the author's experience as an immigration lawyer

Bill Ong Hing is the author of an excellent history of U.S. immigration policy, *Making and Remaking Asian America Through Immigration Policy, 1850-1990* (1993). Asian Americans have traditionally been relegated to the periphery in overviews of immigration history, but, in that book, Hing showed that they belong at the center of the story. Hing, a professor of law at the University of California at Berkeley and executive director of the Immigrant Legal Resource Center in the late 1990's, has devoted much of his career to immigration law and has represented many immigrants in deportation hearings. In addition, he has served as counsel to the international law firm Baker and McKenzie.

Scholar, activist, and legal expert, Hing thus brings an unusual range and depth of experience to his new book, *To Be an American: Cultural Pluralism and the Rhetoric of Assimilation.* The title is slightly misleading, since a good chunk of the book— roughly six of its eleven chapters—is given to challenging and contextualizing what Hing regards as virulent attacks on recent immigrants, largely Asians and Latinos. The subject is extremely important, and if Hing's treatment of it is unsatisfactory, his failure is instructive, illuminating certain habits of thought that are pervasive in the immigration debate.

The matter of perception versus reality is a good starting point to gain a sense of Hing's project and its limitations. Many Americans have the notion that immigrants are taking jobs from native-born workers and lowering the wages of those who remain employed. In some cases, this perception has been fueled by studies purporting to show that immigrants are a drain on the economy (meanwhile, other studies come to the opposite conclusion). In other cases, it is based chiefly or exclusively on firsthand experience or anecdotal evidence.

As anyone who has plowed through some of the dueling reports on immigration and the economy knows only too well, the issues are devilishly complex. There are so many variables that neither "side" can claim decisive victory in this debate. Hing has mastered an impressive body of research, and his own conclusion is that immigrants clearly benefit the economy in the long run, though he concedes some pockets of dislocation for native-born workers and some extra, short-term expenses for states (such as California) where immigrants are disproportionately concentrated. Here he seeks to be a voice of reason, arguing that the widespread perception of immigrants as a financial burden is not supported by the facts.

It must be said that Hing does not deal adequately with some of the economic concerns provoked by the massive influx of immigrants and refugees in the wake of the 1965 reforms in U.S. immigration policy. For example, one significant issue is the skyrocketing number of recently arrived elderly immigrants who are dependent on government aid. Most of these elderly immigrants were admitted under provisions of family reunification, and their sponsors in the United States had to swear that they had the financial resources to support the aging family members who were joining them. Once arrived, however, many of these immigrants went on welfare, and there was no enforcement of the sponsors' obligation. The welfare reform legislation of 1996 sought to address this problem by eliminating key benefits to legal immigrants who are noncitizens, but—after protests from a variety of groups—many of those benefits were reinstated.

However, far more fundamental than the treatment of various disputed questions in recent immigration history is the way Hing frames his entire argument. "Is there any doubt," he asks rhetorically, "that we are experiencing one of the most potent periods of anti-immigrant fervor in the United States?" There is, indeed, some doubt. In fact, one wonders how a scholar as knowledgeable as Hing could put forward such a thesis—and advance it as a truth so obvious as to be beyond doubt. The immigration total for the 1990's has been near a record high. Despite the 1995 recommendations of the congressionally appointed U.S. Committee on Immigration Reform calling for a substantial reduction in legal immigration, the 1996 legislation focused on illegal immigration and procedural issues. How can Hing's perception be so radically removed from reality?

Hing cites as evidence the passage of Proposition 187 in California, an initiative that would exclude children of illegal immigrants from public schools and bar them and their families from public medical care. However, one must wonder if this initiative will ever be put into practice, or if it will, as most observers believe, be struck down on constitutional grounds. Further, Hing writes, "Congressional proposals that would reduce legal immigration by a third . . . receive strong bipartisan support." The unwary reader may gather from this that the passage of such proposals is imminent or even that they have been enacted as legislation. How strong is "strong"? Not strong enough to pass such legislation in Congress—in 1996, it wasn't even close. In short, even as he sets out a formidable array of data to counter the alleged misperceptions of critics who focus on the economic impact of immigration, Hing himself is guilty of misperception—and misrepresentation—on a global scale.

Hing's mention of the proposals to reduce legal immigration by one-third raises another question about his project. One might suppose that, in a heavily documented book of nearly 250 pages on the subject of immigration, the author would, at some point, be obligated to explain what he deemed to be a desirable level of immigration and why. That is, he would be obligated to engage the hard questions that Barbara Jordan and her Committee on Immigration Reform wrestled with: How many immigrants should be admitted to the United States each year, and how should we decide whom to admit?

Hing simply does not answer these basic questions. One can infer that he believes that a very high level of immigration is desirable, but he does not explain why. Why are proposals to "reduce legal immigration by a third" ipso facto evidence for "anti-immigrant fervor"? Why does Hing characterize the people who make such proposals as simplistic and fearful, lumping together racists such as David Duke with principled critics of U.S. immigration policy? Is there a magic number—one million immigrants a year, for example—that is good, while 750,000 would be bad and 500,000 terrible? Again, why? How does one decide?

By his failure to address such questions straightforwardly, Hing leaves the reader with the impression that, like all too many immigrant advocates, he is ultimately just another spokesperson for a special interest group. Clearly, that is not his intention. Hing wants to communicate a larger vision of the common good, rooted in what he calls "cultural pluralism." In his first chapter, he describes growing up in Superior, Arizona, a copper-mining town of about five thousand people where his family ran a small grocery store. The population was mostly Mexican American, but there were also American Indians—Navajo and Apache—African Americans, Caucasians of varied European descent, and representatives of other national and ethnic groups. Without sugarcoating the scene, Hing gives a vivid and appealing picture of cultural pluralism at work.

The trouble comes when one tries to connect this picture—or Hing's portrait of his client Rodolfo Martinez Padilla, a hardworking Mexican immigrant who is the subject of chapter 2—with the policy issues raised by immigration. While there are no doubt bigoted readers who are so ethnocentric that they would find the racial mixing Hing celebrates distasteful, and while there are surely readers whose prejudices would not allow them to acknowledge the existence of the many immigrants like Rodolfo, these pictures cannot begin to bear the weight that Hing places on them.

It would be perfectly possible, for instance, for a reader to share Hing's sense of the preciousness of America's unique diversity while believing, at the same time, that legal immigration should be significantly reduced and illegal immigration more efficiently policed. Certainly, one could eat dinner at a Vietnamese restaurant, go home and listen to some Cuban music, and then, without contradiction, write a letter to one's congressional representative about the brazen failure of immigrants' sponsors to meet their obligations and the abysmal failure of the Immigration and Naturalization Service to enforce these obligations.

The first thing that Hing must do to advance a real conversation on immigration is to acknowledge that one need not be simply *for* or *against* immigrants and immigration—that there are many gradations and that many issues arising from immigration must be treated on their own merits rather than as a litmus test of one's standing as a good cultural pluralist. Second, Hing must considerably refine his notion of "assimilation." He refers, at various points, to "race-assimilationists," advocates of "Anglo-conformity," and others whose views he considers wrong and destructive. However, he fails to make clear, in any comprehensive way, what issues are at stake in the matter of assimilation.

On the one hand, Hing argues that immigrants assimilate naturally to the larger culture; the point here is that the fears of a balkanized America are unfounded. On the other hand, he argues that assimilation as an ideal (the melting pot of lore) is undesirable. He does not seem to notice the contradiction. In fact, his first point has more to recommend it than his second. Assimilation is happening all the time, willy-nilly, less by the directives of any group (such as assimilationists) than by an extraordinarily complex and relentless convergence of social and technological change. At many evangelical Christian colleges in the United States, students were forbidden to see movies even into the 1960's. By the 1990's, students at those same colleges were writing essays on the films of Oliver Stone. That is assimilation with a vengeance.

Hing concludes with a call for Americans to "think in terms of inclusion rather than exclusion." The sentiment is nice, but it does not answer any hard questions. Is an American Jew who marries a non-Jew embodying the principle of inclusion and cultural pluralism or contributing to what some have called "the second Holocaust," eroding the distinctive identity of the Jewish people? If cultural pluralism is to be more than a cover for interest groups and more than an expression of vague pieties, Hing and others must wrestle more explicitly and more persuasively with such questions.

John Wilson

Sources for Further Study

Booklist. XCIII, February 15, 1997, p. 980.
Choice. XXXV, November, 1997, p. 571.
The New York Times Book Review. CII, April 27, 1997, p. 34.

TOWARD THE END OF TIME

Author: John Updike (1932-   )
Publisher: Alfred A. Knopf (New York). 334 pp. $25.00
Type of work: Novel
Time: 2020
Locale: Suburban Massachusetts, north of Boston

> *In this, his forty-eighth book and his eighteenth novel, Updike returns to familiar territory—affluent, WASP suburbia—but renders it with a postmillennial twist that provides some perspective for this prolific writer's customary subjects: sex and the meaning of life*

Principal characters:
BEN TURNBULL, a sixty-six-year-old retired investment adviser
GLORIA, Ben's somewhat younger and vastly more energetic wife
DEIRDRE, a former prostitute, Ben's drug-addicted young mistress

John Updike began his career as one of America's most skilled and most revered novelists forty years ago with the publication of *The Poorhouse Fair* (1959), a parable about social disintegration revolving around an old man and set twenty years in the future. Now, on the verge of the turn of the millennium, Updike has written another novel with a similar premise. *Toward the End of Time* is set in the year 2020, after the federal government has disintegrated in the wake of the Sino-American nuclear war. The old man this time is Ben Turnbull, a sixty-six-year-old retired investment adviser who lives in considerable comfort on eleven choice waterfront acres located in the WASP suburbs north of Boston. Much has changed in this world of the future: There is no cross-country transportation, food shortages are the rule of the day, and the worthless greenback has been replaced by sienna-colored regional scrip called "welders," honoring a Republican governor who oversaw Massachusetts toward the end of the twentieth century.

Ben experiences only modest discomfort as the result of America's postmillennial, postwar breakdown. He is rich in his retirement (not only did he succeed in his professional life, but he also married money when he took his second trip to the altar), and his wealth enables him to buy some kind of "protection" from a couple of low-life extortionists who promise to guard him and his property from the threat posed by lawless, mixed-race youths streaming out of urban ghettos. Ben also is able to go on enjoying some of the pastimes traditionally pursued by affluent retirees toward the end of the previous century, such as golf, and his vigorous second wife, Gloria, keeps up a steady round of visits to the hair stylist, the pedicurist, the aerobics salon, and the ladies' luncheon club. In many respects, the lives of these two proceed with the undiminished regularity of the seasons.

Ben, however, has begun to suspect that time is not as reliable as it once seemed, and he decides to make a play for immortality by keeping a journal. His journal—which ostensibly is the narrative of *Toward the End of Time*—opens with the first snowfall of the year and traces the events of his life over the next year. Perhaps it is more accurate to speak of the events of the narrator's "lives," however, because part of what Updike seems to be attempting to address in this novel is the permeability of time and space.

Toward the End of Time opens with two epigrams, one of which is taken from a 1986 essay by mathematician and science writer Martin Gardner: "We cannot tell that we are constantly splitting into duplicate selves because our consciousness rides most smoothly along only one path in the endlessly forking chains." One of Gardner's areas of expertise is quantum mechanics, and Ben—as well as his creator—seems to have done considerable reading in this area of late. Ben, who declares himself uncomfortable with fiction and whose favored reading material includes *Scientific American*, occasionally interrupts his narrative of day-to-day existence to enter the mind-set of another individual—an ancient Egyptian tomb robber, a murdered medieval monk— who existed, or exists, on an altogether different path. He seems to be able to do this because he lives in a world no longer governed by the accepted rules, one that includes not only Mexico as a land of economic promise but also two moons (one of them human-made) overhead and a new life form below: life-threatening, insect-sized, inorganic "metallobioforms" that sprang up out of the postwar nuclear detritus.

Ben had always been most alive below the waist. In the new world that exists toward the end of time, his sex life, too, seems to be slipping into an alternative universe. Much of the story line of the novel revolves around a deer that Gloria wants to destroy because it is eating her beloved garden. Urged by his wife to shoot the animal, Ben instead comes to believe that he has perhaps shot Gloria. In any event, his wife has disappeared, and her place in the household and in Ben's bed is taken over by Deirdre, a young prostitute whose tawny skin and blunt nose are reminiscent of the doe Ben was supposed to have destroyed. Like the deer, Deirdre steals Gloria's property—the family silver instead of dormant tulip bulbs—and like the deer she seems to come from a netherworld Ben cannot hope to understand. Although he muses over evidence that Neanderthal man and the more advanced Cro-Magnon man who was the true forebear of *Homo sapiens* apparently coexisted for a time and may even have interacted, Ben cannot seem to comprehend that he has slipped onto another path along the forking chains.

One day Deirdre simply slips away, as Gloria returns from a trip to Singapore. Just as suddenly, and simply—and seemingly inevitably—Ben loses touch with that part of himself that had always formed the core of his identity. Having spent most of his life obsessed with sex, he is now robbed by time of what had been most dear to him. Just at the moment he begins to intuit this change that carries with it the beginning of the end of his life, Ben has an out-of-body experience. He encounters Aaron Chafetz, his young new doctor, in the locker room, and "Another universe, thinner than a razor blade" slices into the room as Ben recalls the last time they met. That time he was naked, and Dr. Chafetz was examining his prostate gland. This time, however, it is the doctor who is naked, and one of Ben's alter egos, seizing the advantage of being fully clothed, stages an ugly scene in which he is a Nazi tormenting a helpless prisoner (Chafetz) at a concentration camp.

Out-of-body experiences often accompany traumatic events and are also said to precede death. Ben's recent prostate examination had been a painful one, and recollecting it gives rise to the subconscious awareness that it was a sign of the beginning of the end. Indeed, a few days later Ben discovers that he has prostate cancer. He is treated for the disease, and he suffers all the indignities that accompany prostate surgery, chief among them incontinence and impotence. Time has taken its toll on Ben, and although there are indications that he may regain his old life, it is clear that the world has moved on without him. His last sexual partner had been a fourteen-year-old girl who was part of a gang of teenagers who camped out on Ben's eleven acres and who represented the next generation of enforcers. After Gloria manages to get rid of them—perhaps with the collusion of FedEx, which seems to be taking on the role of government—as well as the marauding doe, Ben is deprived of an outlet for his desire.

Toward the End of Time is an old man's book, a winter's tale. (Updike even names the first wife Ben lost "Perdita," after the lost wife in William Shakespeare's *A Winter's Tale*.) Like his protagonist, Updike is in his sixty-sixth year and clearly meditating on the end of things. Critics have noted that Ben Turnbull is an avatar of Updike's longest-lived fictional alter ego, Rabbit Angstrom, whom the author killed in 1990 in *Rabbit at Rest*, the fourth in a celebrated series of novels. The death appears to have been premature, as Ben greatly reminds readers of the libidinous Rabbit. It is altogether fitting that Harry Angstrom should reappear as another person in a postmillennial world where alternative universes intersect and time is a permeable dimension. Precisely because *Toward the End of Time* is set in postmillennial America, however, Ben is a vastly more introspective individual than Rabbit.

This change in Updike's protagonist is unfortunate, because the narrative breaks devoted to quantum mechanics, string theory, and the origins of consciousness—as well as Updike's attempts to dramatize these theories by having Ben relive past lives—weigh down *Toward the End of Time*. Although the familiar Updike terrain of adulterous WASP suburbia once again comes alive, the more experimental sections of the book prove to be rough going. It may be a noble aim to have one's hero meditate on the afterlife rather than on his groin, but it comes as a relief when Ben complains about his prostate problems. Readers recognize that Ben, like Rabbit Angstrom, is an exploitative cad, but his flaws are ones most people share to some degree, and perhaps it is only human nature to prefer to read—and write—about sex rather than the meaning of existence per se. In any event, most readers approach a work of fiction with the expectation that it will contain more grubbing about in the muck than reaching for the stars through higher mathematics.

Exploring mathematical proofs of God's existence is one of Updike's recent obsessions, one he also indulged in *Roger's Version* (1986). Like his latest novel, *Roger's Version* was a less than fully achieved work. Updike has stumbled before, in works such as *S.* (1988) and *Brazil* (1994)—in fact, almost every time he has strayed from the contemporary suburban turf he has made his own. Like most writers, Updike writes best when he writes about what he knows best, and what he knows best is not just the diurnal round of middle-class existence in late twentieth century America but also what it connotes. He may be unsurpassed in his portrayal of, say, wife-swapping in the 1960's (as in *Couples* [1968]), but sex is clearly not his entire subject.

A still life might picture a dead rabbit and half a grapefruit, but the object of the painting is not simply to portray these items as skillfully and realistically as possible. Instead, through their placement and juxtaposition, painters use them to convey symbolic meanings, ranging from statements of faith, to memento mori, to social commentary. Updike, who studied fine art and drawing at Oxford University in the 1950's, has become one of the finest practitioners of the English language by translating the still life into words and making such statements.

Toward the End of Time opens with the snows of early November and closes, one year later, with this observation of another natural phenomenon: "The weather is so warm a multitude of small pale moths have mistakenly hatched. In the early dark they flip and flutter a foot or two above the asphalt, as if trapped in a narrow wedge of space-time beneath the obliterating imminence of winter." No other novelist writing today manages to do so much with the marvels the natural world presents for human examination and edification. *Toward the End of Time* may be a failed novel, but between its opening sentence and that incredible ending, it offers some wonderful writing. Updike still manages to perform some breathtaking feats.

Lisa Paddock

Sources for Further Study

Atlanta Journal Constitution. October 5, 1997, p. L10.
Booklist. XCIII, August, 1997, p. 1849.
The Boston Globe. October 19, 1997, p. 1.
The Economist. CCCXLV, November 15, 1997, p. 14.
The Los Angeles Times. October 5, 1997, p. BR2.
The Nation. CCLXV, November 3, 1997, p. 62.
The New Republic. CCXVII, November 17, 1997, p. 38.
The New York Review of Books. XLIV, December 4, 1997, p. 32.
The New York Times Book Review. CII, October 12, 1997, p. 9.
The New Yorker. LXXIII, December 8, 1997, p. 116.
Newsweek. CXXX, October 13, 1997, p. 78.
Publishers Weekly. CCXLIV, August 4, 1997, p. 62.
The Wall Street Journal. October 8, 1997, p. A20.
The Washington Post. November 2, 1997, p. WBK 5.

TRAPPED IN THE NET
The Unanticipated Consequences of Computerization

Author: Gene I. Rochlin (1938-   )
Publisher: Princeton University Press (New Jersey). 293 pp. $29.95
Type of work: Current affairs

A sober analysis of the subtle and long-term implications of computerization in a variety of organizational contexts, especially in the U.S. military

The trap in *Trapped in the Net* refers to the blind drive of modern society to computerize every aspect of human activity in the interest of efficiency and productivity. Gene Rochlin, a professor of energy and resources at the University of California, Berkeley, casts this "computer trap" in a wider net by examining the impact of networked computer technology on the organizations in which individual computer users function.

In a sweeping history of computerization, Rochlin underscores the apparent organizational ambivalence of the machine itself. While early mainframe computers operated under a centralized and vertically organized administration, the more horizontal orientation of later small digital computers offered individual users greater freedom and control. Such democratization, Rochlin notes, was temporary. New technologies such as the Internet increase the computer's involvement in task management, emphasize standardization and conformity, and significantly reduce the autonomy of individual users.

Rochlin credits the computer with revolutionary social and organizational changes comparable to those caused by the printing press and the telephone. These changes are analyzed in terms of the scientific management theory proposed early in the twentieth century by Frederick W. Taylor, who applied the principles of production engineering to business management. Rochlin sees computerization as part of the same Taylorist pattern of organizational control, rational modeling, and analysis pursued by American industry since Henry Ford invented the production line. Skilled labor and craftspeople yield to standardized labor, and the technical staff that keeps the automated machinery in operation becomes more important than the workers who use the equipment.

The manifold benefits of computerization disguise the ways computers alter not only individual human activities but also the very structure of human organizations. Rochlin is particularly worried that preprogrammed machines do not readily allow human operators to acquire the expertise necessary to deal with unexpected events and problems. While computers can perform highly complex computations upon large amounts of data, they are only tools that require monitoring and control by knowledgeable humans. Yet many aspects of the computer, such as its high response speed, make human intervention difficult when things go wrong and inhibit the ability of human controllers to develop and maintain full cognitive awareness of the enterprise.

The core of *Trapped in the Net* is a series of case studies examining the consequences and long-term problems of computerization in specific occupational contexts. Three particular incidents illustrate the ramifications of electronic trading of stocks and commodities. In the stock market crash of October, 1987, the sheer volume of sell orders by computerized trading programs turned what should have just been a bad day into an automated and electronic panic. On July 19, 1995, the volume of transactions led to a complete halt in trading activity at the National Association of Securities Dealers Automated Quotations market (NASDAQ). The collapse of the British banking firm Barings P.L.C. in 1995 resulted from the unscrupulous computerized dealing of one employee. For Rochlin these incidents illustrate a breakdown in traditional, hierarchal control over financial activities and a dangerous diffusion of powers horizontally across an electronic network. Because trading activities in the virtual marketplace take place not in banks or on market floors but over an interactive network, the influence of both brokerage firms and their regulatory agencies is weakening. Rochlin worries that such an electronically transformed market is unstable and vulnerable to fluctuations due to single transactions, fraud, and theft. He fears the possible domino effect of automated electronic trading and anticipates the need for new financial regulatory structures to monitor the activities of all electronic users.

The crux of the organizational problem created by computerized automated processes is a significant decline in human expertise and in the role of human actors and decision makers. For example, accountability is dispersed in an organization such as Eurotransplant, an electronic facilitator of organ transplants that relies upon other institutions such as hospitals and shipping services to complete its tasks via a centralized computer and an international database. When such an intricate network errs, who is responsible? So, too, naval duty officers value the training and experience needed to interpret, evaluate, and control data generated from a variety of electronic sources. They speak of "having the bubble," of retaining a coherent sense of all the interconnected elements in a ship's system, including combat status, observation, and weaponry. The possibility of operational error increases significantly if personnel fail to maintain an on-going and comprehensive status assessment.

In several case studies, including United Airlines flight 811 from Hawaii to New Zealand in 1989, Rochlin notes how the flying experience and knowledge of a commercial airline pilot, not the support of electronic equipment, saved lives. A similar conclusion is reached by examining airline crashes caused by verifiable human error, such as that of a British Midland 737 in 1989. For Rochlin this disaster was caused by a "representational failure," by misinterpretation of the information provided by the navigation systems. Pilots should be active flyers as well as "flight-system managers" who operate computerized controls in a glass cockpit. Airplane operators need more situational awareness, not more automated and computerized controls. They require the expertise and training to know when to use and when to override automated controls.

So, too, air traffic controllers have fought to retain their handwritten flight progress strips in the face of increasing automation and electronic-generated data. Controllers argue that such human input is essential to maintaining a sense of traffic, to "having the bubble." Rochlin agrees and suggests that the management of such complicated technical systems requires the awareness of complex and subtle cognitive maps on the part of human operators. To the extent that computerization diminishes such awareness, public safety is placed at risk. The goal of any computerized operation should be to assist, not to replace, human judgment. Rochlin argues that using automation to avoid human error in routine situations may actually be counterproductive and even dangerous. Humans learn through trial and error, and elimination of this educational process leaves humans vulnerable and inexperienced in moments of crisis. Despite the popular view that automated systems are designed to eliminate inefficiency, Rochlin argues both for technical and human redundancy to avoid equipment failures or judgment errors, and for the slack time needed for experienced human operators to make critical decisions.

Rochlin's most compelling examples of the dangerous long-term effects of computerization come from the military. Surveying the growth of modern warfare and logistics, beginning with the reforms of Frederick the Great in the seventeenth century, he follows the debate between advocates of new military technologies and traditionalists who emphasize the importance of well-drilled soldiers and expert marksmen in warfare and fear that technological changes would transform the very nature of the military. Rochlin suggests that these fears are justified.

Most U.S. wars have been wars of attrition in which victory was achieved by wearing down the enemy via sheer mass of human and industrial resources. Only with the successful employment of atomic weaponry in World War II did the U.S. military begin to advocate significant use of technology, which became a career path for ambitious officers. The Vietnam conflict persuaded both the American military and people that a new generation of high-technology weapons was needed. While computer technology made possible more complex and sophisticated human-operated systems such as the B-1 bomber, Rochlin also notes a trend in the post-Vietnam era away from manned systems in favor of self-controlled and pre-programmed systems such as the Tomahawk cruise missile. In the age of the all-volunteer army the American soldier has become a remote operator instead of a personal fighting machine, and the focus of American miliary power has shifted from the fighting soldier to the technocrat, from an emphasis on seniority and leadership to technological know-how. To Rochlin the American military organization is becoming more like the modernistic corporation, with its reliance on automated electronics packages, detailed micromanagement, sophisticated forms of rapid communication, and highly coordinated vertical chains of command. In fact, the small, professionalized military's need for high-technology systems of C^3I (command, control, communications, and intelligence) run by well-trained personnel has resulted in a marked decrease in the percentage of combat soldiers who man weapons in favor of the technological and support crews who design and control them. The balance between the fighting tooth of the armed forces and their logistical tail has become distorted in the last two decades.

Three instances of malfunctioning technology illustrate the changes imposed by computerization upon the decision-making process in a combat environment. In each case, advanced electronic warfare systems contributed to disastrous cognitive errors. In the downing of a Libyan airliner by the Israeli Air Force in 1973, Rochlin notes that both the Libyans and the Israelis acted correctly based upon a reasonable interpretation of the information that technology made available to them. The Libyans thought they were in Egypt while the Israelis were convinced that they were dealing with a hostile flight. Similarly, in the attack of an Iraqi Mirage jet on the USS *Stark* in 1987, both the failure of the U.S. ship to take evasive action or use its defensive weapons effectively, and the Iraqi decision to attack were, for Rochlin, the result of "complementary errors of interpretation." The Iraqis assumed the hostility of the American ship, while the crew of the *Stark* hesitated to assume similar motives for the Iraqis. While navy investigators assumed that the downing of Iran Air flight 655 by the missile cruiser USS *Vincennes* in 1988 was the result of either individual or group error, Rochlin argues that possible mistakes in information gathering and interpretation were ignored and that the decision-making system on the ship did not process evidence correctly. In other words, despite the *Vincennes*'s very sophisticated information system, its operating organization failed under the stress of crisis. Rochlin questions the wisdom of using highly automated equipment in an environment that is inevitably human-oriented and action-centered, and in unpredictable combat situations.

Similar conclusions are drawn from an examination of American operations in the Gulf War against Iraq, which Rochlin considers more of a war game than a real combat situation, since the Iraqis lacked the ability to use effective electronic countermeasures against American weaponry and communication systems. While the American military appeared satisfied with the performance of its technology in the Gulf War, Rochlin warns that performance assessment of individual weapons or systems must be accompanied by an overall evaluation of the integrated system of technological tools and human organization. So, too, consideration of the vulnerabilities inherent in the complex organizations needed to support advanced technological systems must be factored into the analysis of their cost and performance. In this context, Rochlin notes that in the Gulf War, civilian employees had to take over many of the support roles traditionally performed by military personnel, and that the war's C^3I problems included ever-increasing demand for intelligence data, a parallel increase in the volume of communications, and the exposure of the communications system to electronic and physical interference.

From this analysis Rochlin concludes that technology has transformed warfare. The front lines and mass attacks of traditional attrition warfare are being replaced by the nonlinear operations of "maneuver warfare," in which small military units move quickly and independently. More ominously, Rochlin warns that on future battlefields, integrated command-and-control systems may remove all discretion from individual soldiers and units. While concerns about the long-term organizational consequences have slowed down implementation of computerization in other fields, such as air traffic control, Rochlin fears that the American military, falling into a Taylorist trap, believes that real war problems conform to predetermined models and are solvable by advanced planning and increased technology. The consequences of this electronic net may someday prove fatal.

Thomas J. Sienkewicz

Sources for Further Study

Booklist. XCIII, May 15, 1997, p. 1547.
Choice. XXXV, December, 1997, p. 669.
New Scientist. CLIV, July 5, 1997, p. 46.
The New York Times Book Review. CII, September 7, 1997, p. 23.
Publishers Weekly. CCXLIV, March 24, 1997, p. 65.
The Virginia Quarterly Review. LXXIII, Autumn, 1997, p. 134.

TUMBLE HOME

Author: Amy Hempel (1951-   )
Publisher: Scribner (New York). 155 pp. $21.00
Type of work: Short stories

Seven new short-short fictions and a novella from a master miniaturist who gets the most out of the minimalist's adage, "Less is more"

Amy Hempel is the author of two previous collections of short fiction, *Reasons to Live* (1985) and *At the Gates of the Animal Kingdom* (1990), tightly controlled, highly compressed stories that happen swiftly, and unfold unexpectedly: quick, flash-flood-like fictions driven by situational and verbal acrobatics. Hempel is brave enough to embrace uncertainty in her struggle to write stories of unpredictable and lasting power. Such masterful, tiny palm-of-the-hand dramas as "In a Tub," "In the Cemetery Where Al Jolson Is Buried," and "The Harvest" are already considered new classics—daring stories propelled by unpredictable blasts of language. Hempel's debut collection immediately attracted national attention, for its voice, vision, and sensibility were unmistakably quirky and inimitably new. Her second book delivered unconditionally, uncompromisingly, on the promise of the first. Now, in *Tumble Home*, her third assembling of fiction, Hempel has hit the mark once again.

Ironically, Hempel's characters are far less secure as persons than she has become as a writer. They are transient, always looking for a new place to call home. As the title *Tumble Home* suggests, they exist in a constant state of "tumbling," for even when they do arrive at any given place, and even though they might want to stay, something always keeps them from feeling rooted, from feeling a sense of comfort or at-homeness in their own home.

Such is the situation in "The Annex," the story of a woman whose house is directly across the street from a cemetery. As she explains, "From every window in the front of our house, when you look out, that gravestone is what you see." The gravestone is that of a five-month-old baby—the narrator exclaims, "five *unborn* months!" She is haunted, each day, not only by the revisited vision of that headstone but by the presence of a visitor—the mother of this five-month-old—who becomes, for the woman of the house, a menacing, threatening trespasser. "I can almost believe," she confesses, "that somewhere is the person who could look across the street and see a vision of perfect peace." For her, the recurring sight of the child's grave marker and a grieving mother is too much to bear. She will never be at rest, at peace, even in her own home. Like many of the other characters found in this collection, she has found not a reason to live, but reason to flee.

It is not always perfectly clear which way Hempel's fleeing characters ought to go. This is certainly the case with Jack, the on-the-run, on-the-road protagonist of "Sportsman," who, when faced with the hardcore loneliness of an empty house after his wife Alex leaves him, heads east to upstate New York, to stay for a little while with a pair of old friends. Upon his arrival—after driving virtually nonstop across the country, stopping only to sleep at the side of the road (to avoid staying at cheap motels that struggle and end up failing to replicate the comforts and appearances of home)— Jack hopes to relocate his old self here in the company of Vicki and her husband, referred to only as "the doctor." The two of them proceed, in an effort to help Jack, to fix him up with a date/visit with their psychic friend Trina, who predicts "a turbulent year ahead with the love of his life." Jack, a man who believes that "there was nothing wrong with faking your way to where you belonged," finds solace in the simple fact that "the psychic had not said that Alex was the love of his life. He had *assumed* that was who she was talking about." This simple, anticipated possibility—the piece of fiction projected by a total stranger—of somebody else stirring up friction in his love life is enough to keep Jack hoping, enough to give him a renewed, although falsely optimistic, vision of who and what he might be pulled toward next.

In "Weekend," a very short piece of fiction (although it is not the briefest story in this collection—the shortest is a single-paragraph/single-sentence sliver of a tale called "Housewife"), Hempel captures the organized chaos of a country-day picnic among city people getting away from city life. It is a portrait of grown men and women going back home to the nonchalant pace of childhood, back to that falling-into-love phase of honeymoon romance, of life before kids, of casual attire and weekend whiskers, of women whispering, beneath the heated breath of a good-night kiss, "Stay, stay," instead of "Go."

Hempel is a chronicler of a generation of characters always on the go, always coming from someplace else, never native to the place they are calling home. They are, in short, guests, new arrivals, like the narrator of "The New Lodger" and of the title entry—the novella "Tumble Home." The woman who narrates "The New Lodger" returns to a beachside bar for what is now her third and possibly final time, at a place where, years before, she nearly drowned. She seems to be coming back to take care of unfinished business. Despite the picturesque quality of the place, "people have lost their lives on the way to this beach, or on the way home from it." In this place of personal danger, a part of her was born the day she almost drowned, while another part died. Here, she says,

> I'll stay for as long as it takes. I will not get in touch with anyone on my list. Not the friends of friends who live nearby, whose gardens I must see, whose children I must meet. Nor will I visit the famed nature preserve, home of a vanishing tern. Why get acquainted with what will be left, or leaving?

So she sits, in a corner booth at the Soggy Dollar bar, with an array of postcards fanned out on the table—like palm-sized stories—"trying not to say the same thing on every one."

This, the desire to mix it up, not to say the same thing, not to rewrite the same story formulaically, over and over again, could be attributed to Amy Hempel herself, as a writer of fictions that are never predictable, never conventional, a writer who is always daring to put the pen in a place it has never been put before, to move away from what has previously arrived. This is the true trademark of an artist—always looking ahead to what comes next, looking for a new place to go. Hempel in this way is not unlike her characters.

At the same time, though, one cannot mistake an Amy Hempel story, for every sentence that she writes bears her signature—verbal wizardry, wit, the recursive grace of the composition, the way her stories seem to spool outward, word by word, sentence by sentence, governed not by plot or story but always by language, for it is language, the language of perception, that always plows the way.

This is especially true of the title entry from this collection, an epistolary novella—Hempel's strongest and longest piece of fiction. "Tumble Home" unfolds slowly, precisely, through a series of anecdotal reports or responses sent into the world (specifically to a man whom the narrator has met only once) by a woman who is a "guest" staying at a "home" for the mentally, spiritually, and emotionally estranged. The composer of this long letter—a letter that brings this book to its lyrical, grace-filled close—approaches, sometimes even achieves (at least on the page) moments of brief, never-before-seen clarity, grace, and perhaps even transcendence. Early in "Tumble Home," at the beginning of this letter, the writer puts forth this question: "How can I possibly put an end to this when it feels so good to pull sounds out of my body and show them to you." The appropriate answer is "Don't." That is, "Don't put an end to it—because we want more."

Hempel's short-short fiction—some have mislabeled her a minimalist, a term that suggests a reductiveness of language and a starkness of vision that simply do not characterize her—sometimes leaves one wanting more. The reader wants more, hungers for more, not because there is not enough but because of how much is packed in so few words, so few strokes of the pen. The vitality and energy of Hempel's sentences give such sweet pleasure that they stimulate greed—a desire for more, more, more.

"Tumble Home," with its feel of a short novel, will satiate even the heftiest of reader appetites. Reading "Tumble Home" is like finding the lost notebook of an unknown poet whose voice is pure melody, pure longing—a music maker who sings sentences of sheer and astonishing beauty, sentences that weave back and forth between past and present, memory and revelation, looking in some way to reconcile "the pull of the old home, pulling apart the new." This fissure in this narrative's fabric, the turbulence between the old and the new, the interior versus the exterior, gives rise to the tension in this terse little novel. Little by little the letter-writer uncovers, unveils, the reasons and burdens that have brought her to this point, to this place. "Everyone here is better than they were there, 'there' being anywhere else."

The relation between here and there is best summed up by a Hempel character in another story, who points out insightfully that "you can't make an entrance until you've established your exit." This is to say that one needs a place to be from, a place to leave from, in order to find that other place, or places, where one belongs, to which one must go. One must continue going to whatever or wherever comes next.

What will come next from Hempel herself? It seems possible, as a natural evolution from the success of the novella, that her follow-up effort could be that long-awaited, much-longed-for first novel—the work that will say for itself, will announce to even the loudest of naysayers, that Hempel not only has arrived but is here to stay. For even in a time that has been christened a golden age or renaissance of the American short story, there still exists a certain pressure on writers of short stories to write a novel—fueled by the false notion that writers have not fully arrived or have not fully apprenticed themselves until they become novelists. There is a prejudice that short stories are simply not enough, that they are an inferior, a minor form: popular songs compared to symphonies. This notion is a hot-air balloon that can quickly be popped by the mere drop-of-the hat mention of one name: Anton Chekhov, the great Russian short-story writer. It is important to remember other writers who happen, who perhaps even choose, to look past the temptations of the novel in favor of the short story: Raymond Carver, Alice Munro, André Dubus, Stuart Dybek, Tobias Wolff, Rick Bass. To this list should be added the name of Amy Hempel, a writer who has not merely stopped for a visit but has come to stay, to take up permanent residence in the house of the contemporary short story.

Peter Markus

Sources for Further Study

Booklist. XCIII, May 1, 1997, p. 1478.
Elle. XII, May, 1997, p. 92.
Kirkus Reviews. LXV, March 15, 1997, p. 402.
Los Angeles Times Book Review. July 27, 1997, p. 7.
Mirabella. May, 1997, p. 77.
The New York Times Book Review. CII, July 27, 1997, p. 9.
Newsweek. CXXIX, April 28, 1997, p. 78.
Publishers Weekly. CCXLIV, March 10, 1997, p. 47.
The Washington Post Book World. XXVII, April 13, 1997, p. 6.

THE UNDERPAINTER

Author: Jane Urquhart (1949-   )
Publisher: Viking (New York). 340 pp. $22.95
Type of work: Novel
Time: The 1890's to the 1970's
Locale: Upstate New York; Ontario, Canada; France; and New York City

An elderly painter, reflecting on the past, sees the damage his calculated detachment has done to his arts, his friends, and his own self-esteem

> *Principal characters:*
> AUSTIN FRASER, a painter
> SARA PENGELLY, his model and mistress for fifteen years
> GEORGE KEARNS, Austin's friend, proprietor of a china shop
> VIVIAN LACEY (VI DESJARDINS), a beautiful, heartless young woman
> AUGUSTA MOFFAT, a nurse, George's friend and lover
> MAGGIE PIERCE, a nurse, Augusta's friend

In her three earlier novels, as well as in her poetry and her short fiction, Jane Urquhart has considered such matters as reality and illusion, the everyday world and the realm of the imagination, and the temptation to escape from life, which, she suggests, is probably experienced, to some degree, by every human being capable of reflective thought. In *The Whirlpool* (1986), characters are mesmerized by Niagara Falls and the flight into death that it offers them; in *Changing Heaven* (1990), art is presented as a man's refuge from the demands of love; and, in *Away* (1993), women fall under the spell of the supernatural, the wilderness, and their own power to rewrite reality. All of these novels focus on women. *The Underpainter* deals with the same issues, but, in it, the women are presented obliquely because the narration is entrusted to a man.

The selection of Austin Fraser as a narrator is somewhat surprising, since the central fact of his life is his refusal to become attached to anyone or anything, which, he is persuaded, is the way to produce great art. In the end, however, Fraser's art suffers because, as his fellow artist Rockwell Kent comments, he has no feeling for his subjects. Similarly, Fraser fails as a human being, not only because he never allows himself to love, but also because, since he never develops the capacity to empathize with others, he does great harm to those who care for him. When, at the age of eighty-three, Fraser realizes his mistake, he is alone in a sterile house with no company except his memories, some images, and his artifacts.

The Underpainter begins with a prologue which, though admittedly tantalizing, is a bit confusing. The scene is a deserted Canadian mining village in the dead of winter. An unnamed woman, who lives there alone, opens the telegram she has just received and sets out on foot for Port Arthur, some twenty-two miles away. Then, the narrator intervenes. He is merely imagining these events, he says, and adds that they took place forty years before. Finally, he introduces himself. He is Austin Fraser, he says, and he was the person who called the woman to Port Arthur.

In the main part of the book, Fraser is not so laconic; he routinely introduces characters by name and explains who they are, at least externally. However, readers of *The Underpainter* are not permitted to be passive observers. In the first place, they must develop their own working timetables. Fraser's narrative is governed by memory rather than by chronology, jumping back and forth in time and moving just as suddenly from one location to another. The author does provide some help: She has her narrator drop in exact dates fairly frequently, and she also has him mention his age and the ages of the other characters often enough that, with a little effort, one can keep track of the action. There is, however, still more to be done by Urquhart's readers. Even though, as the book proceeds, Fraser is working toward a degree of revelation, a narrator as insensitive as he will inevitably be blind to subtleties. He may not understand the implications of the actions of others or of their comments to him. It is, therefore, left to the reader to put the pieces together, to imagine the emotions that the self-centered Fraser cannot understand, and to feel the pain that Fraser refuses to experience or even to acknowledge.

The metaphor indicated by Urquhart's title, then, comes to have a complex significance. On the obvious level, underpainting is a term drawn from art: It refers to what is first placed upon a canvas. After embarking on what he called his "new" style, Fraser began as an "underpainter" with a realistic scene or figure. Then, he began overpainting, adding layer after layer to cover up his initial effort. Fraser's greatest fear was that his underpainting would be revealed; in fact, he has sometimes held paintings for years in order to make absolutely sure that no chemical action would occur that would cause the shapes he deliberately obscured to rise to the surface. Since the critics titled one series of Fraser's paintings *Erasures*, it is obvious that they understood his intention. Early in *The Underpainter*, Fraser also makes it clear that the pattern of his life is exactly like that of his painting. He has always set about to blank out reality.

However, when one applies the underpainting-overpainting concept to the novel itself, it is clear that Urquhart is forcing her narrator and her readers to reverse the process. Step-by-step, they must remove layer after layer of overpainting until reality appears before them. That intention explains the air of mystery in the prologue, and that process determines the structure of the book because, even if Fraser's memories appear to be random and uncontrolled, his creator knows exactly what she is doing.

Each of the three sections of the novel, for example, has a clear purpose and a specific subject. The first, which takes up almost one-third of the book, is entitled "The Lake Effect." It begins with Fraser's recollections of the woman mentioned in the prologue, Sara Pengelly, who has died and left him all she owns: her isolated house on the north shore of Lake Superior. There, for fifteen summers, Fraser had lived with her, using her freely, both as his model and as his mistress. Then, suddenly deciding on a change of painting style, he packed up and left for New York City. Eventually, however, Fraser returned to Rochester, New York, the town where he was born. In retrospect, Fraser realizes that his mother and his father represented the two attitudes toward life between which he would later have to choose. His mother had a great imagination and gothic tastes: She liked to take her son on long walks along the

Genesee River gorge and into the Mount Hope cemetery. She died, however, when Fraser was nine, and he was left with his father, who, at that time, shrank from any displays of emotion. Driven into himself, Fraser had already begun to become the person who would find so appealing the doctrine of detachment propounded by his mentor, Robert Henri. Now, Fraser is struck by the similarity between his own passionate mother and Rockwell Kent, whose view of life he rejected in favor of that of Henri.

The narrative now jumps to the momentous summer of 1913, when Fraser's father, who had become wealthy, acquired a lakeside home in Davenport on the north shore of Lake Ontario. There, Fraser found a friend, George Kearns, who, like him, was interested in art but, unable to afford art school, spent his time painting designs on articles to be sold at the China Hall. George had two passions: Vivian Lacey, who liked to flaunt her power over young men like him, and a small collection of valuable china. At the end of the summer, George left for France but not before demonstrating his affection for Fraser. If anything should happen to him, he said, his beloved collection was to go to his friend Fraser.

The section concludes with more memories of Sara and with an interesting comment. Fraser's reason for avoiding Sara all those years, he now knows, was not that he did not want to see her but that he could not bear for Sara to find out who he really was.

Fraser's reasons for feeling such profound guilt are made clear in the second and longest section of the book, "Night in the China Hall." Fraser now introduces a new character, Augusta Moffat, and repeats her life story as she told it to him during the night they spent together in the China Hall. Augusta was reared on a farm near Davenport, became a nurse, and served in France. There, she first met George, who had been wounded. She also met Maggie Pierce, another nurse, and they became friends. After the hospital was shelled and Maggie died, Augusta was sent home to be hospitalized until she recovered from shell shock. After her release, she became George's companion, and, over the years, little by little, together they rebuilt their lives.

Since Fraser is trying to make sense out of his own life, not that of Augusta, it is logical that, from time to time, he would abandon her story in order to think about his own. He remembers how he broke off his friendship with Kent because his friend had told him an unpleasant truth: that Fraser's painting was flawed because it was so cold. He also keeps thinking about his relationship with Sara. Fraser's new understanding of himself becomes evident when he comments that, where he used to feel that he would never forgive either Kent or Sara, now he wonders whether they ever forgave him.

What Fraser most needs, however, is some sense of forgiveness for what he did to George and Augusta. He had not set out to harm them, but, nevertheless, his carelessness in driving the glamorous Vi Desjardins, or Vivian Lacy, to Davenport to see George, twenty-four years after their last disastrous encounter, as certainly results in tragedy as if Fraser had acted out of malevolence.

In the final section of the novel, "Ontario Lake Scenery," Fraser returns to his past with Sara and to the planned reunion at Port Arthur. As he hinted at the beginning of the novel, he did not see her. Now, the reason is evident: He did not want her to see him for what he was. The only amends he could make for what he did to her was to spare her his presence; the only amends he could imagine for what he did to George and Augusta was to painstakingly piece back together the china George broke when he discovered what had happened to the woman he loved.

By the end of *The Underpainter*, all of the secrets have been told, all of the references explained. However, this is not a simple story, in part because it deals with the complexities of human nature, in part because it admits the degree to which human beings and the landscape are intertwined. The symbolism is complicated. Darkness, the north, and water are all important in the book, but their significance is constantly shifting. In the prologue, Sara sees the ice as a road to the man she loves; on the other hand, Fraser's mother, who thinks of the north as profoundly spiritual and sees the wild Genesee River as a symbol of life, imagines, in her final delirium, that she is skating north on the Lake Ontario ice, drawn inexorably toward death.

However, it is the very complexity of structure and symbolism that makes *The Underpainter* so haunting. Life, Urquhart suggests, is much like the lakes that are so important in her landscape. One must either accept it all, calm and storm, life and death, or avoid risk by remaining forever on the shore. At the end of the novel, Fraser, seeing how foolish he has been, changes his attitude and reverses the direction of his art. His final painting, he says, will be a self-portrait, and it will include everyone and everything in his experience, even the uncaring Vivian, even the bitterest cold of winter. Fraser will entitle it "The Underpainter," for that is what, at last, he has chosen to be.

Rosemary M. Canfield Reisman

Sources for Further Study

Booklist. XCIV, September 15, 1997, p. 212.
Library Journal. CXXII, September 1, 1997, p. 221.
Maclean's. CX, September 15, 1997, p. 85.
The New York Times Book Review. CII, November 23, 1997, p. 28.
Publishers Weekly. CCXLIV, November 24, 1997, p. 48.
The Times Literary Supplement. November 28, 1997, p. 22.

THE UNDERTAKING
Life Studies from the Dismal Trade

Author: Thomas Lynch (1948-   )
Publisher: W. W. Norton (New York). Illustrated. 202 pp. $23.00
Type of work: Essays
Time: 1948-1996
Locale: Milford, Michigan; Ireland; and London, England

Funeral director and poet Thomas Lynch reflects on his primary profession and ponders what funerals reveal about the attitudes of the living

Principal personages:
THOMAS LYNCH, the author, who decided to follow the professional footsteps of his father and become a funeral director
ROSEMARY and EDWARD LYNCH, the parents of the author, both deceased
NORA LYNCH, Thomas's Irish cousin who bequeaths to him her cottage in Ireland
HENRY NUGENT, a poet who finds new love after his nasty divorce
STEPHANIE, a young girl killed by a cemetery marker in a freak accident
MARY JACKSON BANCROFT and WILBUR JOHNSON, two senior citizens of Milford who instigate a fund drive to restore the bridge to the town's old cemetery
RUSS READER, a four-hundred-pound eccentric who insists on being cremated after his death
MATTHEW SWEENEY, a poet and hypochondriac
DR. JACK KEVORKIAN, the real-life pathologist whose mission to assist suicides earns him the mortal hatred of Thomas Lynch

To write a book about the business and philosophical thoughts of a funeral director that is neither morbid nor sensationalist in nature is a rather challenging endeavor. To think seriously about death and what a culture does with its dead bodies is bound to raise some readers' discomfort, especially when it is carried out with deliberation and humanistic decorum. People who expect harrowing stories of grave robbers, desecrations, or lurid, near-pornographic accounts of the details of autopsies, embalmings, and the effects of physical decay on the human body will be disappointed by Thomas Lynch's serious collection of essays concerning his somber trade.

However, a reader who is willing to engage in a silent philosophical discourse on the nature of humanity's concern with the mortal remains of its species will find *The Undertaking* very rewarding reading indeed. Throughout the nicely illustrated, black-jacketed book, two major points emerge upon which its author, a published poet and practicing mortician, insists.

The first is Lynch's expressive belief that funerals do not matter to the dead, who are beyond earthly concerns. The author reiterates at the somewhat overwritten beginning of his text that "the dead don't care" what is or is not done to them. Instead, Lynch argues with conviction, a funeral is a chance for the living to come to terms with the universal fact of death.

Second, like William Gladstone, the nineteenth century English prime minister, whom he quotes upon this occasion, Lynch believes that the manner in which a culture disposes of its dead says everything about it. What value and meaning people ascribe to life, Lynch argues, can best be deduced if one observes how they care about burial, cremation, or other modes of disposal for their dead. Once death is perceived as a mere "nuisance," as Lynch fears is happening in America at the end of the twentieth century, life itself has become devalued and dehumanized.

Funerals, therefore, exist to comfort the living and to give meaning to life. That is the double message of *The Undertaking*. To convince the reader of this message, Lynch takes his readers on a guided tour of his life, the lives of his family and his friends, and the deaths that bring him his customers. Thus, there are many memorable characters peopling Lynch's interrelated essays, and the reader quickly encounters a fascinating variety of the still living, the once living, and the long dead. For reasons of confidentiality, many characters have been slightly altered or are composites of many real people, yet Lynch's narrative makes every one of his fictional creations as real as the members of his family who reappear so often in his musings.

Corresponding to the deeply personal nature of his essays, Lynch offers some rich insights into his own character, which he sees as inextricably linked to his family history. Thus, *The Undertaking* contains many loving lines commemorating the author's deceased parents, Rosemary and Edward Lynch. Here, the son admires the Catholic faith of his mother, which saw her raise nine children and which sustained her as she was dying from cancer in her early sixties. Juxtaposed to Rosemary's faith that God would protect the family from all serious harm, Thomas evokes his father's constant fear that something untoward may befall his children: Daily dealings with death as a funeral director have alerted his father to the fact that no life is safe from a fatal accident.

The father's worries nearly find ghastly confirmation when Thomas drunkenly falls from a third-floor fire escape landing at college but, miraculously, suffers no serious damage. In 1969 and at the age of twenty-one, after his brush with death, Lynch searches for his roots in Ireland and meets his cousins Tommy and Nora Lynch, who live bachelor lives in an ancient cottage on the country's west coast. Without indoor plumbing or running water, the cottage appears, to the young American visitor, as a link to a more natural past.

With a wink at the reader, Lynch offers the hypothesis that as bathrooms become part of the house, the acts of birthing and dying are moved away from home, resulting in their being seen as vague embarrassments. Frequently, Lynch begins with a point in his personal life or an event encountered while working in his profession and moves beyond to a poignant criticism of contemporary American culture. What angers Lynch are all forms of dishonesty, beginning with crafty euphemisms designed to cover up facts of life and ending with diatribes against the usefulness of his trade by American critics of the funeral industry.

A culture that does not respect its dead, Lynch argues, is in mortal danger of losing its respect for the living. Those who perceive as wasted the land set aside to honor and commemorate the dead, *The Undertaking* insists, are close to losing their sense of the value and meaning of life. As Lynch cynically ponders the possibility of a "Golfatorium" (a golf court atop a cemetery that allows people to pursue leisure activities while visiting the dead), the reader can sense a serious outrage at contemporary efforts to minimalize the space set aside to reflect on earthly life's ultimate destination.

Lynch is quick and generous to let the reader in on his own blemished but generally successful life. When his first marriage ends in divorce, he tells of how the stresses of being a single parent to four young children nearly drive him to alcoholism. This is a danger that Lynch escapes when he decides not to drink anymore whenever he is in America; he lives up to his decision.

Once Lynch, like his poet friend Henry Nugent, finds new love, he finds balance and new strength to maintain his position as comforter for the bereaved. Consequently, *The Undertaking* is at its very best when Lynch's writing resembles his deeply humanistic, caring, and comforting professional stance, writing with compassion about those who suffer and those who are in danger of losing a sense of the value of life by discarding their duties toward the dead too quickly, too shabbily, or too neglectfully.

On the other hand, when Lynch tries his hand at a more lighthearted approach, his puns and jokes often appear a bit flat, tired, or overwrought; they do not always ring true to the persona of the author. Yet, there are times when Lynch is genuinely funny and witty in his reflections on "the dismal trade." His observation on the similarity of pastoral-sounding names such as "Grand Lawn" for golf courses, new housing developments, and cemeteries, for example, is right on the mark.

Thus, among the many incidents connected to his business life, Lynch offers sometimes amusing, sometimes harrowing, and sometimes inexplicable anecdotes. Among the more lighthearted characters is Russ Reader, a practical joker weighing in at four hundred pounds. Alive, Russ loudly tells Lynch that he wants to be cremated; his ashes should be scattered from a hot air balloon over the town. When he dies, however, Russ's widow and surviving nine children give him a traditional Irish wake and bury him on a fine plot in the town's cemetery after a full church service.

Lynch's rendition of the lives and deaths of his townspeople are not always as uplifting. One harrowing tale is that of the twelve-year-old Stephanie, who is killed when some youngsters throw a cemetery marker from a freeway bridge at the van in which she is driving with her parents. Again, Lynch ponders questions of destiny, divine cosmic oversight, or pure chance: Minutes before the fatal accident, Stephanie had changed places with her young brother, who would have been killed in her stead had he not switched seats.

While death comes unexpectedly to many, *The Undertaking* also provides a glimpse at those who look ahead with planning and foresight to their final moments. Understandably, Lynch chides most attempts at "pre-planning" a funeral as misguided folly—a funeral is, after all, for the living mourners who should be allowed to design it according to their needs. Therefore, he pokes fun at his Irish friend Matthew

Sweeney, who, through his imagined illnesses, seems to live out his funeral while still walking the streets of London.

Lynch also admires his neighbors in town who, upon the initiative of strong-willed octogenarian actress Mary Jackson Bancroft and her ally Wilbur Johnson, convince the county to pay for the replacement of the old bridge leading to Oak Grove Cemetery. In keeping with his stance that the living owe respect to the dead for the sake of the living themselves, such an act of good citizenship meets with his undivided approval.

Throughout *The Undertaking*, Lynch has crafted a voice refreshingly free of cant or sanctimony. At times, his interest in the living appears crystal clear, such as when he defines love as "that unencumbered approval by another . . . for your presence in their lives" or finds a day "so beautiful you regret you will die."

When it comes to the contentious issues of abortion and physician-assisted suicide, Lynch's outrage moves his tone to almost fever pitch. In his essay on his fictional "Uncle Eddie," Lynch powerfully expresses his overtly hostile distaste for Dr. Jack Kevorkian as he inveighs against this pathologist's methods in a nearly polemical voice. For the sake of rhetoric, Lynch's hold on human history also becomes shaky. "The birth of new life" has not always been met with universal joy and wonder; the ancient Greeks disposed of unwanted babies by exposing them in the wilderness, and infanticide has a long, sad history.

There are a few moments when a reader may wonder why an author who is also a poet did not check his spelling more carefully. It is odd that an undertaker does not appear to know that a person is "hanged" and never "hung" in common English language.

Minor problems of tone and form aside, *The Undertaking* presents a moving, witty, and deeply thoughtful reflection on an occupation which is, as Thomas Lynch rightfully asserts, as old as the dawn of human consciousness, when the Neanderthals first began to bury their dead. Lynch's main theses, that funerals are indicative of the living people's attitudes toward life and that they are designed for their solace and comfort, rings very true. His warnings against turning death into an embarrassment in dire need of camouflage, cover-up, and forgetfulness appear to be of equal soundness. Lynch's final advice to readers invited to funerals to "see it till the very end," to accept the reality of death and treat it with honor and dignity, sounds very valuable and true to the heart of the human condition.

R. C. Lutz

Sources for Further Study

Bloomsbury Review. XVII, May, 1997, p. 19.
BMJ: British Medical Journal. September 20, 1997, p. 755.
Boston Globe. July 27, 1997, p. N14.
The Nation. CCLXIV, June 9, 1997, p. 28.

The New York Times Book Review. CII, August 17, 1997, p. 12.
Publishers Weekly. CCXLIV, May 5, 1997, p. 184.
The Spectator. CCLXXVIII, May 3, 1997, p. 37.
The Times Literary Supplement. May 2, 1997, p. 26.
USA Today. January 6, 1998, p. D8.
The Village Voice. July 1, 1997, p. 61.
The Wall Street Journal. September 15, 1997, p. A20.

UNDERWORLD

Author: Don DeLillo (1936-)
Publisher: Scribner (New York). 827 pp. $27.50
Type of work: Novel
Time: 1951-1997
Locale: United States and Kazakhstan

The Cold War and its aftermath are the subjects of Don DeLillo's latest, and longest, look into postwar dread

> *Principal characters:*
> NICK SHAY, waste management analyst
> MATT SHAY, his brother
> JAMES COSTANZA, their missing father
> ALBERT BRONZINI, science teacher
> KLARA SAX, formerly his wife, later a famous artist
> ESMERELDA, homeless twelve-year-old who is raped and murdered in the Bronx
> SISTER EDGAR, teacher
> LENNY BRUCE, irreverent, blackly humorous stand-up comic
> VIKTOR MALTSEV, trying to merchandise nuclear explosions in Kazakhstan

Big novels can generate big interest: Vikram Seth's 1,349-page *A Suitable Boy* (1993); Thomas Pynchon's *Mason and Dixon* (1997), a mere 773 pages but twenty years in the making; and now Don DeLillo's *Underworld*, 827 pages in just five years from conception to auction. The million dollars Scribner paid for the right to publish *Underworld* is admittedly small potatoes compared to the seventeen million dollars Stephen King demands but is still surprising given DeLillo's reputation as a serious writer of brilliant but hardly mainstream fiction. Even a million dollars, however, has its price in the quid pro quo world of modern publishing: The usually self-effacing DeLillo has had to do his part to publicize his book. DeLillo bashers, whose numbers are legion among the politically and aesthetically conservative, may find some irony here, some not so subtle connection among auction price, publicity hype, and the blinding speed with which *Underworld* was nominated for the National Book Award (it lost) and (like *Mason and Dixon*) became, very briefly, a best-seller. Has the novelist appreciated by many and dismissed by some for his sardonic critiques of American consumer culture perhaps sold out? Or is it that *Underworld* demonstrates all too well the consumer culture's ability to absorb and turn a profit on anything, its own critics included? Thankfully, even a dark late-capitalist cloud may have its silver post-Marxist lining, generating interest in, as well as royalties for, one of the very few American novelists who has something interesting to say about modern American life.

Underworld is DeLillo's biggest book, but is it also his best? No, but only because all of his last four novels have been, for all their differences, equally good, and both collectively and individually better than just about anything else published during the same period (1985 to 1997) by any other American writer. Louise Erdrich comes close, but only Philip Roth, in the wildly inventive work he has published from *The Counterlife* (1987) through *American Pastoral* (1997), has produced anything as consistently interesting, intelligent, and inventive as *White Noise* (1985), *Libra* (1988), *Mao II* (1991), and *Underworld*. Although not DeLillo's best novel, *Underworld* is surely his most ambitious, an 827-page "damage check" on the effects of the Cold War. The novel began to take shape shortly after DeLillo saw a news item on the fortieth anniversary of Bobby Thompson's game-winning home run in the final game of the playoff series between the (then) New York Giants and Brooklyn Dodgers. As DeLillo learned at the local library, "the shot heard round the world," as the *New York Daily News* called it, occurred on the same day that the Soviets conducted their second atomic bomb test; indeed, the two stories appeared side by side on the front page of *The New York Times*. Playing on that coincidence and surreal journalistic juxtaposition, the novel's fifty-page prologue starts the narrative ball rolling: the home run ball that is part holy grail and part fool's gold but mainly a MacGuffin, a plot device. Like the bomb, it offers opportunities for paranoid plots to hatch and develop, worming their way through *Underworld* while at the same time offering temporary relief from Cold War fears and uncertainty.

"Is this when history turned into fiction?" one character asks. Making much the same point in 1960, Philip Roth wondered whether American novelists could any longer compete with an American reality that had become more fantastic than anything the writer could imagine. Novels as different as *Portnoy's Complaint* (1969), *Operation Shylock* (1993), and Robert Coover's *The Public Burning* (1977) provide one kind of answer, *Underworld* quite another. There is nothing outrageous or grotesque about *Underworld*, other than its size and scope. Indeed, DeLillo seems to be up to nothing more, and nothing less, than what Giants sportscaster Russ Hodges recalls having done early in his career in working up radio re-creations of big league games: "Somebody hands you a piece of paper filled with letters and numbers and you have to make a ball game out of it." Letters and numbers on a sheet of paper become players on the field and the crowd in the stands, right down to the kid with the cowlick—or, in DeLillo's case, a black kid named Cotter Martin who skips school, jumps the gate, and ends up with the home run ball. Part of the understated brilliance of this richly detailed and intricately plotted novel derives from the way DeLillo pans back and forth between history and fiction, players and crowd, and the public and personal, not just in the prologue (at the game) but throughout the novel. His postmodern version of the 1950's television show *The Big Picture* continually shreds and frays into a series of fitful glimpses before recomposing itself into a panoramic long shot. Not surprisingly, films (and paintings) figure prominently, including the premiere of a long-lost film by the great Russian director Sergei Eisenstein (or rather by DeLillo, playing fast and loose with history), of course titled *Underworld*.

"We can't see the world clearly," one character contends, "until we see how nature is organized." The same may be said of *Underworld*. From its beginning at the Polo Grounds on that serendipitous day that two shots are heard round the world (and a reproduction of Brueghel's painting *The Triumph of Death* torn from *Life* magazine floats down into the hands of FBI Director J. Edgar Hoover to become one more object of his obsessive desire), the novel explodes ahead to 1992, to a vast work in progress under way at a remote Air Force base, where famous artist Klara Sax and her crew are painting 230 mothballed B-52's. From there, the novel painstakingly works its way back, counting down the decades to the day after "the shot heard round the world," to October 4, 1951 (and another shot, this one louder but more personal), before exploding ahead once again, more briefly this time, to 1997. The basic idea behind the novel's structure may not be new (think of Martin Amis's *Time's Arrow*, 1991), but it is certainly effective. What disconcerts is not just the sense of déjà vu; it is DeLillo's putting the cart of effect before the horse of causality. For all its disorienting maneuvers, vast cast of characters, and varied settings, *Underworld* achieves a Poe-like unity of effect, and well it might, for *Underworld* is in many ways "The Fall of the House of Usher" updated and writ large, its horror not of Germany but of the soul, the Cold War and post-Cold War soul.

Language is key. "He speaks in your voice, American, and there's a shine in his eye that's halfway hopeful." The shine is not only in the eye; it is in the rhythm too, the better to measure the distance between the aw-shucks, can-do optimism and the undertone of Cold War dread that follows. Although written in familiar DeLillo-ese, the novel spans the full range of narrative voices (first, second, third) and postwar American idioms. There are the author's signature lines ("She ran her hand through his fire retardant hair") and surreal couplings (the wildlife refuge that doubles as a firing range, the Abo Elementary School and Fallout Shelter), the parodies and echoes, the Whitmanic lists delivered in Buster Keaton deadpan, the authentic-sounding Lenny Bruce routines, and the wondrously visceral and transparently idiomatic language of the novel's longest section, full of sounds and smells, local Bronx humor, and 1950's street slang.

The novel's unity of effect also derives from the vast network of parallels and repetitions that create the illusion of a connectedness at once paranoid and purposeful. This theme, obsessively pursued in *Libra*, develops just as insidiously in *Underworld*: Random events intertwine to form arbitrary but seemingly coherent narratives. Chance occurrences—the home run and the test blast, for example—first intersect, then breed and proliferate. Here are the raw materials of absurd hope and paranoid fear so brilliantly overdetermined as to very nearly credit what the *Underworld* undermines as it explores and exposes modern forms of connectedness, from radio and television to the Internet and World Wide Web.

"Do you believe in me?" asks the man who will sell the home run ball he has stolen from his son to the man who will buy it on faith alone (including the faith that his son will cherish it, which he won't). Belief is everywhere in the novel but takes a decidedly contemporary form of half-believing in everything while having conviction in nothing. Where the desire to believe manifests itself in bizarre forms, the hunger for transcendence becomes just another growth area for the consumer culture that develops alongside, perhaps in response to, Cold War dread. DeLillo's attitude toward his characters' lives of quiet desperation, their misplaced faith in conspiracy theories and consumer culture, is, like Nathanael West's a half century earlier, at once satiric and sympathetic. As the graffiti artist turned community activist Ismael Munoz explains to two Roman Catholic nuns, "Some people have a personal god, okay. I'm looking to get a personal computer. What's the difference, right?"

Spurious transcendence is not all that the consumer culture produces. There is also the waste that forms "the secret history, the underhistory" of these decidedly un-Chaplinesque modern times. What to do with all the proliferating forms of waste, from garbage, feces, and inner cities to outdated aircraft and spent plutonium? Flush it, pile it, bury it, burn it, nuke it, turn it into art. In Phoenix, the city that rises downwind from the ashes of so many atomic tests, lives the novel's protagonist, Nick Shay (née Nicholas Costanza). Formerly of the Bronx, Nick is now a major player in the international waste management business. He believes in waste and its future, finding temporary relief from post-Cold War dread in "great thick proposals in thick binders," in everyday rituals such as running and recycling, in reading voraciously (or is it obsessively?), and in endlessly rearranging his bookshelves, on one of which sits the home run ball that Manning sold for $34.50 and Nick bought years later for $34,500, the ball that Nick, a Dodger fan, claims is about losing, not winning, about the pitcher Branca, not the batter Thompson. Nick's journey from the Bronx to Phoenix reflects the sea change in American life in the latter half of the twentieth century, as Nick Carraway's leaving the Midwest and his family's hardware business for the Northeast and a career in stocks and bonds did in *The Great Gatsby*. DeLillo's Nick does not leave his father, however; his father, a numbers runner, leaves him, murdered by the mob, according to the version Nick prefers to believe. Nick's younger brother—"A police sketch made from seven different people—that was Matt"—has his own version: Their father simply walked out.

Underworld's pages overflow with characters walking in and out. They may not be the fully rounded characters of earlier fiction, but neither are they the lifeless "Xerox copies" faulted by some reviewers. They are clearly postmodern subjects—cultural constructs—but they are also parents, spouses, children, neighborhood acquaintances, business associates, teachers, celebrities, fans, and artists. All play their parts, and all deal with waste in one way or another, although few as consciously as Nick, or artist Klara Sax with her "methods of transforming and absorbing junk," or stand-up comic Lenny Bruce shrieking "We're all gonna die" onstage during the Cuban Missile Crisis. The characters are central to *Underworld*, but their individual and private lives are played out against the looming background of their times. "This is what the twentieth century feels like," Lenny Bruce tells his audience after rubbing and licking a condom onstage. The reader may well say the same thing after reading *Underworld*. Here are the contradictions, the low-level, everyday dread that the end of the Cold War has done little if anything to assuage, the feelings of "strangulated rapture" beyond "logical explanation"; here too is a world that goes well beyond history's "record of events" into DeLillo's brand of fiction, which "comes out of another level of experience . . . out of dreams, daydreams, fantasies, delirium." *Underworld* is the late twentieth century's delirious underhistory. It is Brueghel's *Triumph of Death* in postmodern drag, a fantastically wrought scarlet letter throwing its "lurid gleam along the dark passage-way of the interior" of American life, hauntingly true to that life in ways unimaginable to less ambitious and more conventionally realistic contemporary American writers.

Robert A. Morace

Sources for Further Study

Atlantic. October, 1997, pp. 113-116.
The Economist. CCCXLIV, November 8, 1997, p. 94.
Gentleman's Quarterly. September, 1997, pp. 193-196.
Harper's. November, 1997, pp. 72-75.
The Nation. CCLXV, November 3, 1997, p. 18.
The New Republic. CCXVII, November 10, 1997, p. 38.
The New York Review of Books. XLIV, September 6, 1997, p. 4.
The New York Times Book Review. CII, October 5, 1997, p. 12.
The New Yorker. LXXIII, September 15, 1997, p. 42.
Newsweek. CXXX, September 22, 1997, p. 84.
People. October 13, 1997, p. 33.
Publishers Weekly. CCXLIV, August 11, 1997, p. 261.
The Review of Contemporary Fiction. XVII, Fall, 1997, p. 217.
San Francisco Chronicle. September 21, 1997, pp. Book Review 1, 6.
Time. CL, September 29, 1997, p. 89.
Vanity Fair. September, 1997, pp. 202, 204.

THE UNTOUCHABLE

Author: John Banville (1945-   )
Publisher: Alfred A. Knopf (New York). 368 pp. $25.00
Type of work: Novel
Time: The late 1970's, with flashbacks ranging over an entire lifetime
Locale: London, Russia, France, and Ireland

One of the last of Britain's spies from the 1930's is exposed, and he composes a memoir presumably to explain himself but which reveals ironically his life and cloudy motivation for treason

Principal characters:
> VICTOR MASKELL, the narrator, an art scholar and former spy
> SERENA VANDELEUR, a writer interviewing Maskell for a biography
> BOYSTON "BOY" BANNISTER, an ardent fellow spy and schoolmate of
> 　　Maskell who eventually seeks refuge in Russia
> ALASTAIR SYKES, another spy and schoolmate of Maskell
> QUERELL, a novelist and associate of Maskell whom he believes has
> 　　informed on him
> VIVIENNE BREEVORT, Maskell's estranged wife
> NICHOLAS BREEVORT, Vivienne's brother and eventual member of
> 　　Parliament

The Untouchable is a complex, intriguing novel that extends and further develops concerns John Banville has explored in previous works (*The Book of Evidence*, 1989; *Ghosts*, 1993; and *Athena*, 1995). This is the first novel to follow the Freddy Morrow trilogy, and here Banville turns his attention to a fictional reworking of Sir Anthony Blunt's exposure as a spy in 1979. Victor Maskell is another of Banville's reflective, self-regarding narrators who uses the narrative to explain and rationalize his actions.

The novel opens immediately after Maskell has been identified by the "PM" (Prime Minister Margaret Thatcher) in the House of Commons. Although he avoids reporters, he does grant a series of interviews to Serena Vandeleur, a writer preparing a book on Morrow's exploits who seeks an explanation as to why Blunt spied for the Russians, an answer that he consistently evades.

A vain, self-involved man, Maskell writes not so much to confess as to compete with others who would define and describe his life. Son of a Northern Ireland bishop, he attended Cambridge in the 1930's where he flirted with Marxist ideology and eventually joined some fellow students in becoming a spy, a word he particularly despises because he refuses to see himself as adventuresome or daring.

He recalls his college days, his journey to Russia, spying during World War II, his development as a scholar of Nicolas Poussin's art, his marriage into the influential Breevort family, and his immersion in the gay lifestyle of his era. For all of his successes and influence, Maskell is an oddly unambitious figure who describes himself as "in remission all my life." He often finds himself in life-altering situations as a result of impetuous or dubious decisions. He joins the cell of future spies despite the fact that he does not believe in the Soviet Union nor in the perfectibility of the workers' condition, proposes to Vivienne Breevort, knowing he does not love her and certainly does not want a family, and maintains a lifelong acquaintance with the novelist Querell while always disliking him. His chief attribute is his capacity for dissembling: "I am a great actor, that is the secret of my success."

During the war he works for the British Secret Service in the code-breaking center at Bletchley Park, all the while feeding vital information to the Russians. After the war, because of his accomplishments as an art scholar and connections with the royal family, he is placed in charge of cataloging the royal art holdings, knighted, and awarded a sinecure as Keeper of the Royal Pictures. He assiduously avoids his family in Ireland and his wife and children in England while he devotes himself to art, his gay relationships, and a life of privileged irresponsibility. Life is a game or entertainment, and when he is exposed and stripped of these privileges, Maskell continues to play a game with Vandeleur and the reader, teasing with halfhearted excuses and motives for his actions.

As in previous novels, art and artistic appreciation are central to an understanding of Banville's latest work. In *The Book of Evidence*, for instance, the protagonist kills a housemaid while stealing a painting, and in *Athena* the same protagonist is inducted into a world of crime when he is commissioned to catalog some paintings by Flemish artists. Similarly, Maskell is another self-proclaimed authority on art and a devotee of aesthetic bliss. Also like Freddy Morrow, Maskell loses his connection with life as he immerses himself fully in his artistic passions.

Early in the narrative he tells Vandeleur that "Art was all that ever mattered to me," warning her and the reader that any sense of devotion or duty is subservient to his dedication to aesthetic perfection, the one realm where order is achievable. In fact, his greatest sense of loyalty is to Poussin's *The Death of Seneca*, which he purchased in his youth. No matter where he goes or the vicissitudes of his life, Maskell stands in awe of that work, describing and evaluating its every nuance. When he learns that the Spanish Brigades have been defeated by Franco, he does not pause in his study of another Poussin painting and even comments that the "two events, the real and the depicted, were equally far off from me in antiquity."

He continually sees himself and others in artistic terms—he, a latter-day Seneca as interpreted by Poussin, and others as caricatures, worthy of scorn, derision, or lofty tolerance. One explanation for his treason issues from his putative belief that most art criticism is fascist because it is comparative, whereas Marxist art will "emphasise the progressive elements in art." Maskell often uses the word "amusing" to describe signal events, not because of their humorous nature but in the sense of "a test of the authenticity of a thing, a verification of its worth," and it is this quality of authenticity and worth that inheres in art itself, what Maskell calls the "only thing in my life that was untainted."

A central irony of the novel, however, is that art may actually be the source of Maskell's undoing. As he reviews the tatters of his life, he hearkens back to the day he found his beloved Poussin and suddenly wonders if perhaps that purchase was actually designed to put him in the debt of those who would manipulate him for the rest of his life. Art, then, is not only his greatest consolation but also his greatest weakness, and, in a final irony, the painting around which he has constructed an entire sense of purpose and self may actually be a forgery he was incapable of discerning.

The issue of identity, as in earlier novels, is also paramount and is tied closely to the theme of art. Maskell approaches his self-exploration as an art restorer would an ancient masterpiece: "I shall strip away layer after layer of grime—the toffee-coloured varnish and caked soot left by a lifetime of dissembling—until I come to the very thing itself and know it for what it is. My soul. My self." His concern—always—is with himself, admitting, for instance, that anything he did was first and foremost for himself rather than for any cause or nation. Everything pales in comparison to his thorough self-regard and vanity.

Maskell is many things to many people, and his life is a parade of different roles and selves that he dons and doffs—husband, brother, son, father, art scholar, patriot, traitor—a cavalcade in which he eventually loses himself. Initially, Maskell describes himself as an actor, someone presumably in control of these myriad selves. He can be anything and revels in the idea of a life of continuous alternatives. As he comments, "You are never required to *be yourself.* . . . It is the power to be and not be, to detach oneself from oneself, to be oneself and at the same time another."

Behind these remarks lies the assumption that there is some central Victor Maskell who simply eludes detection and emerges when he chooses to do so. Yet, in becoming a double or quadruple (or other multiple) agent, one whose allegiances are lost in a maze of poses, Maskell's ultimate sense of self eludes readers and finally him. An important metaphor for his condition is offered when he visits the institution that will house his brother, and he wanders into the dayroom containing scores of disheveled patients. "The room looked like nothing so much as the inside of my own head: bone white, lit by a mad radiance, and thronged with lost and aimlessly wandering figures who might be the myriad rejected versions of my self, of my soul."

With all that he has rejected and discarded, Maskell comes to the profoundly uncomfortable realization that there is no true self. He has become, in effect, something akin to a painting of himself—a version, a representation, an interpretation of Victor Maskell—while the model of Maskell has been lost years ago. When he discovers how treasonously he has been treated and that the cornerstone of his life, the Poussin painting of Seneca, has crumbled, he further discovers that his children may not be his and that he has been cuckolded by an associate for whom he has felt lofty disdain.

Banville's manipulation of the subjective narrator is nothing short of brilliant. Like a narrator from a Robert Browning monologue, Maskell is a self-betrayed figure. He is proud and arrogant in his intellectual and cultural superiority; no one is his equal, including the king of England, with whom he has an interview when requested to perform a royal favor. The reader must see evidence of his exceptionality while at the same time sensing the Achilles' heel which will be his destruction. More than Browning, though, it is Vladimir Nabokov who provides a model for Maskell. Like Humbert Humbert in *Lolita* (1955), Maskell is a witty, pernicious voice who inveigles, persuades, and disgusts his audience. Like Humbert, Maskell delights in the witty aside and the trenchant turn of phrase. Both Humbert and Maskell are trapped figures, men whose abundant cleverness abandons them at crucial moments and who close their narratives as defeated outcasts.

A subtle but persistent element in Banville's fiction is concern for Irish life and culture. His novels *Birchwood* (1973) and *The Newton Letter* (1982) explore the "Big House" theme; however, later novels have not referred so overtly to Irish experience. Nevertheless, Banville skillfully grafts Irish attributes onto a most British scoundrel. Maskell is Anglo-Irish, and as in so much of Irish literature, such a person is one of divided loyalties and identities. Characters are continuously commenting on his ethnicity, and he often pauses in the hurly-burly of his narrative to reflect upon his Irishness.

In a particularly revealing aside he mentions that his nineteenth century ancestors converted to the Church of Ireland to escape the famine, and thus the attributes of disloyalty and self-protection are given a sense of familial precedent. He often daydreams of returning to the countryside of Carrickdrum in his youth, and when he fears exposure, he imagines himself hiding in the hills of Ireland like a Fenian rebel on the lam from the oppressor. Although he is thoroughly acculturated to the life of the British aristocracy, he admires the Irish Republican Army, which has recently exploded a bomb in London. "All that rage, that race-hatred. We should have been like that. We would have had no mercy, no qualms. We would have brought down a whole world."

When Serena Vandeleur interviews Maskell, she asks over and over for his motivation. He prevaricates and slithers away, until she fires the most provocative possibility: "What did you think you would achieve by betraying your country and your country's interests? Or was it because you never thought of this as your country? Was it because you were Irish and hated us?" The possibility is indeed intriguing but finally facile; Banville, of course, wants to explore Irish themes but at the same time keep Maskell as elusive as possible.

The Untouchable is further proof that Banville is a major writer. His prose is supple, fluid, and exactingly precise. Few writers in the 1990's can capture the slight changes in emotional register that he so deftly manages. Aside from the intricacies of a byzantine plot and the ability to limn characters so exactingly, Banville reminds us that fiction is the art of words, and a writer of such ravishing prose is a true writer indeed.

David W. Madden

Sources for Further Study

Booklist. XCIII, April 15, 1997, p. 1389.
Commonweal. CXXIV, June 20, 1997, p. 25.
Library Journal. CXXII, April 15, 1997, p. 116.

Los Angeles Times Book Review. April 20, 1997, p. 2.
National Business Review. May 23, 1997, p. 36.
The New York Review of Books. XLIV, May 29, 1997, p. 17.
The New York Times Book Review. CII, June 8, 1997, p. 10.
Publishers Weekly. CCXLIV, April 14, 1997, p. 52.
The Times Literary Supplement. May 9, 1997, p. 20.
The Wall Street Journal. May 9, 1997, p. A16.
World Literature Today. Autumn, 1996, p. 958.

UTOPIA PARKWAY
The Life and Work of Joseph Cornell

Author: Deborah Solomon (1957-   )
Publisher: Farrar Straus Giroux (New York). 426 pp. $30.00
Type of work: Biography
Time: 1903-1972
Locale: New York City

A stirring, elegantly written biography of a major artist who anticipated by decades the mixing of classical and popular arts, producing boxes and collages that retain an aura of mystery and exquisite form

> *Principal personages:*
> JOSEPH CORNELL, an American artist known for his works of assemblage
> ROBERT CORNELL, his brother, afflicted with cerebral palsy
> HELEN CORNELL, his mother
> JOSEPH CORNELL, his father
> MARCEL DUCHAMP, his friend and precursor in the art of assemblage

Reviewers of Deborah Solomon's authoritative work remark that Joseph Cornell ought to be a dull subject for a biography. Except for four years at a preparatory school in Massachusetts, he never traveled outside the state of New York. He was a recluse who worked in Manhattan but lived very quietly in Queens. What major artist lives in an outer borough of the city? The glamour has always been in Manhattan, and if a New York artist did live anywhere else, it should be Brooklyn. Queens is philistine and middle-class to the New York art crowd.

Worse yet, Cornell died a virgin. He had no stormy love affairs and lived most of his life with his mother and brother. He accepted dull, unambitious jobs in the textile industry. He engaged in none of the self-dramatization and invention that mark the lives of many modern artists. He had none of the flamboyance of the Surrealists (who influenced his art) or the menace that made the abstract expressionists dangerous and sexy. Cornell's life, in short, lacked action. He did not even commit suicide. Rather, he died quietly at home.

At best, perhaps a biographical essay, a miniature of Cornell's life akin to his small-scale boxes, would seem in order—not a four-hundred-page-plus biographical narrative. Yet Solomon has been able to fashion a fascinating, probing account that never flags as she delicately describes Cornell's life and art. She shows how he found a way to be an artist when most people would have assumed that he had no affinity for art at all. He developed a vision and a craft that his fellow artists, and later the public, found enchanting, and he created a career for himself without compromising any of his principles. Cornell's is, in retrospect, a triumphant life, even though he himself despaired and questioned his right to call himself an artist.

Cornell became an artist in his late twenties, having shown till then little aptitude for art or for making a success in the world. He was drawn to art by an inquisitive nature and a desire to collect and treasure objects that others might consider junk. Art became his only medium of full expression after years of self-denial and withdrawal from the world.

Cornell grew up in Nyack, New York, the oldest son of Joseph and Helen Cornell. His father, a textile salesman, seems to have had an aesthetic sense that he conveyed to his son—though the son hardly knew it, since he was dominated by his demanding mother, Helen, who was thrown into bitter confusion when her husband died young and left her to fend for herself. As the oldest boy, Joseph not only took his father's place but became a principal caretaker of his younger brother Robert, afflicted with cerebral palsy. Helen Cornell never considered working; she lived on a small inheritance and then in part on her son Joseph's salary.

Joseph did poorly at preparatory school, earning mostly C's and D's. He was not granted a diploma. Shortly after returning home, he got a job through family connections with a wool manufacturer. It was during these early years that he began to haunt the bookshops on Manhattan's Fourth Avenue, visit galleries, and occasionally go to the theater. These were exciting forays for an otherwise shy and timid man. He never rebelled, never sought girlfriends, and never lived by himself. He felt it his duty not merely to take care of his brother but to amuse him and make sure that Robert lived as cheerfully as possible. Both of the Cornell sisters eventually moved away from home and established families of their own; they felt guilty about the fact that Joseph was left to shoulder nearly the whole burden of his mother and brother, yet they were determined to have lives of their own.

In these unpromising circumstances, Joseph Cornell turned to collage and box making. He seems to have been inspired by Max Ernst, Pablo Picasso, and Marcel Duchamp. Both Picasso and Duchamp were famous for their appropriations of other artists' work. Picasso plagiarized openly from virtually all the great artists. Duchamp went further, producing an art not so much for the eye as for the mind, a conceptual art whose subject was art from an unconventional perspective. Thus Duchamp put a mustache on the *Mona Lisa*, transforming Leonardo da Vinci's famous painting into an androgynous, modern questioning of human identity. Duchamp also excelled in producing what he called "ready mades," or "found art," selecting objects not thought of as art and presenting them in an artistic context. Literally anything, including a men's urinal, could then become art in Duchamp's view.

An avid collector of photographs, films, theater programs, and an incredible array of items from five-and-dime stores, Cornell realized that he could put together his sense of the world in the art of the box. He learned carpentry skills and worked in his basement and garage, and late at night in his kitchen. Here he showed his independence—not only standing up to his mother's complaining about the mess his art made in the house but also ignoring the art world of New York, where most artists believed that they had to promote themselves.

Cornell had no training in art. He could not draw or paint; he never attempted sculpture. Late in life he tried to remedy his lack of formal training by sitting in on classes at Queens College. Yet even in his sixties, as a world-renowned artist, Cornell felt just as estranged from traditional art education and the art world as he had in his twenties. No amount of recognition from friends such as Duchamp and Willem De Kooning could assuage his feelings of unworthiness.

Yet Cornell took pride in his work and refused to exploit his genius. He did not market himself, although he did want the public to see his work—especially children, who were his favored audience. Early on, the boxes were advertised as toys by one gallery owner—not an inapt description, except that unlike toys, the boxes were not merely amusements or playthings but were as intricate and sophisticated as great paintings and sculptures. Cornell's boxes explore how the artist puts together the world. Solomon points out that his Lauren Bacall box, for example, is modeled on the penny arcade games Cornell loved as a child. A wooden ball careens through the box, passing the Manhattan skyline and flicking past Bacall's face with a momentum that is reminiscent of the fleeting images of film. The box is at once a tribute to Bacall and a comment on how film captures people's childlike imaginations. Bacall, by the way, loved the box.

It is a tribute to Solomon's tact and confidence that she does not belabor the symbolism of Cornell's work. It is not the symbolism so much as the exquisite sense of form that makes Cornell's boxes art, subtle constructions of the imagination that repay study. Indeed, it upset Cornell when art critics conducted deep analyses of his work. As Solomon suggests, Cornell was a fan of art—films, opera, the theater, literature, and painting—and his work is meant to demonstrate his enthusiasms and the mystique he found in creativity and the imagination.

It becomes obvious—so that Solomon does not have to say it in so many words—that the box, the miniature, was a perfect expression of Cornell's limited life. His work was the antithesis of the expansive abstract expressionist canvas. Yet like his more robust contemporaries, Cornell was breaking new ground in art. He saw beauty, for example, in the shapes of pharmacy bottles; he took the utilitarian and showed that a part of its usefulness consisted in its wonderful design. Art did not have to be on a wall or in a museum.

As Solomon concludes, no other artist remained as faithful to the art of assemblage as Cornell or has explored its variety as skillfully. For all of his independence, however, Cornell suffered from doubts about the worth of his work. He wished that he could draw, just as he wished that he could have sexual relationships with women. Perhaps most astounding and cheering is his efforts in his sixties to reach out to women and to young people, to share his feelings. It was too late for him to commit himself to others, and he lived a lonely, depressed existence after his mother and brother died, but he did not abandon his efforts to break out of his self-imposed shell.

What stopped Cornell from emerging completely? He suspected that his isolation and sexual repression made him a better artist—that he poured his feelings into his work. In small doses, he could admit his yearnings to others. Neighborhood doctors, for example, would listen to Cornell in his kitchen saying that he wanted to make love to women. Although many women found the emaciated, unkempt artist unattractive, he did find a few who reciprocated his romantic yearnings and even allowed him some physical intimacy.

Cornell disliked it when he was called a hermit or recluse. He believed that he had his own ways of being involved with the world. He kept a diary, for example, which Solomon rightly suggests was an effort not only to understand himself but to reveal himself to others. Whatever his doubts about his work, he knew that he had an artistic legacy, and he wanted his work to remain intact as a collection. He was, however, refreshingly immune to the artistic virus of jealously. He seemed not to care at all where his place was in the pecking order of reputations. If he was competitive, it was with himself.

Solomon brings Cornell brilliantly to life. This biographer does not seem to be capable of writing a dull sentence. Occasionally she interjects a very personal reading of a Cornell box, which adds to the flavor of her book, for it shows how intimate and suggestive Cornell's art is. Her biography also charts the uneven but progressive recognition of Cornell's importance in the art world and beyond. There are many amusing scenes with important people who make a pilgrimage to Cornell's house on the aptly named Utopia Highway. There is a very funny scene, for example, with the actor Tony Curtis (an avid painter as well) showing his boxes for Cornell's approval. Typically, Cornell would look at Curtis, look at Curtis's box, and then look at Curtis, never saying a word about the actor's homage to the artist.

Cornell liked attention and hated it. There were days when he announced that he was receiving visitors. There were days when he would not answer the door. He was quaint—Victorian in many ways—and yet very modern in his wide-ranging tastes and openness. He enjoyed receiving a visit from Yoko Ono. Yet it was just as much of a thrill for a neighborhood child to appear, giving Cornell a chance to show off his collages and boxes. For Cornell, there was no conflict between entertainment and art, between enjoying film stills and portraiture. As much as any artist of the modern era, he reveals a unifying sensibility through which potentially the whole world can be contained in the box of his art.

Carl Rollyson

Sources for Further Study

Art News. May, 1997, p. 109.
Booklist. XCIII, February 15, 1997, p. 991.
Boston Globe. March 26, 1997, p. D4.
Chicago Tribune. March 23, 1997, XIV, p. 1.
Elle. XII, March, 1997, p. 150.
The New Republic. CCXVI, June 30, 1997, p. 38.
The New York Review of Books. XLIV, August 14, 1997, p. 28.
The New York Times Book Review. CCII, March 23, 1997, p. 11.
Publishers Weekly. CCXLIV, January 13, 1997, p. 60.
The Wall Street Journal. March 19, 1997, p. A16.
The Washington Post Book World. XXVII, May 4, 1997, p. 9.

VIRGINIA WOOLF

Author: Hermione Lee (1948-   )
First published: 1996, in Great Britain
Publisher: Alfred A. Knopf (New York). Illustrated. 893 pp. $39.95
Type of work: Literary biography
Time: 1882-1941
Locale: London and other locations in England

In this substantial biography, Hermione Lee explores the life and work of one of the outstanding writers of the twentieth century, Virginia Woolf

Principal personages:
    ADELINE VIRGINIA WOOLF (née STEPHEN), the British novelist and
      essayist, feminist, and most famous member of the Bloomsbury group
    LEONARD WOOLF, her husband, an essayist, editor, and publisher
    VANESSA BELL (née STEPHEN), her sister, a painter
    LESLIE STEPHEN, her father, creator of the *Dictionary of National
      Biography*

Virginia Woolf has long been celebrated by feminists. After all, she is the writer who passionately argues for women's rights in her essay "A Room of One's Own" (1929). She has also become one of the prime writers in the literary canon—the works that are studied and discussed at the university level. Such groundbreaking novels as *Mrs. Dalloway* (1925) and *To the Lighthouse* (1927) brought fresh, innovative approaches to fictional narratives and earned Woolf a reputation as a modernist. Fortunately, Hermione Lee's book is a welcome addition to the numerous studies of this well-known but little understood woman.

One of the most interesting aspects of *Virginia Woolf* is that it is a biography about a writer who had a lifelong obsession with the challenges posed by the very nature of biography. That very keen interest stems, in part, from the fact that her father was the famous Sir Leslie Stephen, a workaholic writer who devoted much of his life to the *Dictionary of National Biography*. Woolf rejected the traditional notion of biography as a life reduced to just so many words on a page, calling it "poppycock." However, many of her major works are concerned with this problem, from the straightforward biography *Roger Fry* (1940), to the autobiographical *To the Lighthouse*, to the fictional mock-biography *Orlando* (1928). That Lee devotes her first chapter ("Biography") to this very issue augurs well for her own essay in the genre and is no mean feat of courage. A lesser writer would probably have ducked the problem and given instead a simple presentation of the known facts, but all to the detriment of the finished product. With admirable candor, Lee sets out the would-be biographer's dilemma in facing Woolf's life. The recurring questions include the possibility of sexual abuse in her childhood, the nature of her mental illness, her husband's character, and her social attitudes. Various critics have already made up their minds regarding these issues, making the biographer's task as treacherous as threading one's way though the proverbial minefield. This is not to say that objectivity should be the biographer's goal, for writers cannot screen out their own prejudices and political leanings. Thus, Lee's admission of this is as honest as it is brave: "There is no such thing as an objective biography, particularly not in this case."

Another problem that Lee confronts is the fact that this life is one of the mind. Woolf's many battles were intellectual and emotional, and they unfolded in a life that appeared to be outwardly uneventful. Though the future novelist never traveled beyond the confines of Europe, her family life provides a rich source of material for the biographer. Like many women of the Victorian period, Adeline Virginia Stephen endured the ignominy of watching her brothers attend the best schools while she was forced to stay at home. Lee's account of Woolf's childhood is fascinating in its depiction of someone who was always something of an outsider. It is true that the lack of a formal education excluded certain career opportunities from her, but it also allowed her to develop her own independent voice. She was a true autodidact, and what she lacked in formal education she made up for through sheer intellectual voracity. Woolf was one of the great readers of her time, no doubt inspired, in part, by her father's example. Sir Leslie Stephen was a formidable personality by any standard. Best known for his work as the editor of the *Dictionary of National Biography*, he numbered writer Thomas Hardy among his friends.

One great service rendered by Lee's book is the effective manner with which she attempts to sort out the complex web of family relationships in Woolf's life. It was a large clan. When the widowed Sir Leslie married Julia Duckworth (also widowed), he already had a daughter and she had two sons and a daughter. Together, their union produced two boys and two girls. Lee makes it clear that these complicated relationships played a vital role in Woolf's status as an outsider, particularly in reference to the Duckworth boys. As already stated, Lee eschews any notion of objectivity. This does not mean, though, that her purpose is to bend Woolf's life to her own set of prejudices. Rather, Lee's goal is to present the most balanced account possible when dealing with the more contentious issues in the writer's life. When conflicts arise among various accounts on a given issue, or when there are gaps in her knowledge, she provides what information is known and leaves the rest to the reader. It is a method that is most effective in dealing with Woolf's relationship with the children from her mother Julia's first marriage, the Duckworths. The controversy centers on Woolf's half brothers George and Gerald Duckworth, who were, respectively, fourteen and twelve years older than she. According to Woolf's own account, Gerald sexually abused her by fondling her genitals when she was a small child. She believed that her feelings of shame and guilt over her body were caused, in part, by this incident. Woolf only mentioned it twice in her writings, late in life and after Gerald's death. The other instances of probable abuse were perpetrated by George, who reportedly kissed and fondled her after taking her to her first social engagements when she was in her late teens. Again, feelings of shame crop up here. It would be easy to seize upon these incidents, as many critics have, and simply condemn her half brothers' behavior as yet another example of the Victorian patriarchy and its suppression of women. Yet Lee's procedure of reporting the known facts with little commentary works well here.

Woolf's family relations were much more complicated than mere resentment toward her Duckworth brothers. Although she did loathe George, it was Gerald who offered to publish some of her early fiction. Lee is also to be lauded for her discussion of the consequences of this probable sexual abuse. Woolf, after all, was a writer, and Lee takes care to trace the effects of these incidents upon the fiction that her subject was so adept at creating. Although Woolf never directly incorporated these incidents into her novels, Lee sees a connection between the fears of some of her characters and the writer's own painful memories.

The main reason that so many critics focus upon these incidents is to gain some insight into Woolf's lifelong battle with mental illness. Beginning at the age of thirteen, Woolf suffered five major breakdowns and may have made just as many suicide attempts. Indeed, her final, successful suicide attempt (drowning herself in the river Ouse) occurred when she feared the consequences of yet another such breakdown. As with the topic of sexual abuse, Lee adopts a welcome voice of reason as she contends with the issue of mental illness. Lee notes Woolf's valiant struggle with these episodes at a time when medicine could only offer ineffective and often harmful treatments. After carefully weighing the fragmentary evidence (Woolf's medical records have not survived), Lee characterizes Woolf's breakdowns as examples of bipolar disorder. In spite of this considerable handicap, Woolf displayed an astonishing capacity for work. Her reading interests ranged from the ancient Greeks to her contemporaries, and her wide knowledge of English history is reflected in such novels as *Orlando*. Woolf's writings include voluminous diaries and countless letters, in addition to the published work of novels, short stories, essays, and book reviews. This accounts for the fact that any biography of this woman will amount to little more than a work in progress. It is true that each generation will have to make its own assessment of Woolf, but one must also contend with the fact that additional letters continue to crop up with some degree of frequency.

Lee's book superbly integrates the published work with the life of its creator, and it should be noted that the emphasis is more upon the latter than the former. In other words, Lee's book is more concerned with providing a narrative account of the writer's life than issuing critical appraisals of her works. The biographer demonstrates that Woolf did far more than slave away in a lonely garret. She and husband Leonard were intimately connected with the arts, and this is evidenced by their establishment of the Hogarth Press in 1917. And Lee is quite fair in her appraisal of Woolf's capacity as a critic in this regard. She was a champion of T. S. Eliot and an early publisher of his poem *The Waste Land* (1922), a landmark in twentieth century literature; she failed, however, to recognize James Joyce's talent, even refusing to publish his revolutionary novel *Ulysses* (1922). Lee's biography also clarifies one of the most significant influences upon Woolf's conception of literature: painting. Ironically, this most gifted of English writers owed much of her aesthetic judgment to that most visual exponent of the arts. Again, Woolf's connection with the Stephen clan comes into play through her sister Vanessa Bell. The latter was an accomplished painter, and she also designed the covers and created the illustrations for Woolf's books. Lee is correct to point out the significance of painting in the novels, particularly in *To the Lighthouse*. She misses the importance of this visual art, however, in Woolf's use of language. Even the most casual reader of *Orlando* cannot fail to notice the function of color in Woolf's figures of speech. Lee is to be praised, though, for her examination of Roger Fry's role in this area. He organized an exhibition of French sculptures and paintings in 1910 under the title "Manet and the Post-Impressionists," something that proved to be a watershed in Woolf's conception of art. For both the budding writer and the art world, it marked a distinct break between the Edwardian and Georgian periods. In practice, it meant a new freedom for Woolf in her writing, with a greater stress upon color and texture over formal realism.

Yet Fry was only the most visible aspect of what has come to be known as the Bloomsbury group, the artistic milieu that formed such an important part of much of Woolf's career. Lee is to be commended for clarifying the role of this important entity, which is often invoked but rarely defined. This group, which met at various times from 1910 into the 1920's, included individuals whose interests ranged from publishing to interior decoration. For Woolf, it meant participation in an exclusive intellectual-artistic clique that included novelist E. M. Forster (but not T. S. Eliot). This is an important part of Lee's biography because it reveals something that cannot be gleaned from Woolf's writings. It is an unfortunate fact that Woolf was rather snobbish, a proud participant in an elite of like-minded individuals. Yet Lee's biography also makes clear the dangers of assigning Woolf to specific categories. Although she was one of the most famous members of Bloomsbury, she would be the last person to identify herself as such. Always the outsider, she also distinguished herself from feminists and lesbians, with whom she was closely associated. Lee's excellent biography reveals much about this elusive personality, but one is left wishing for more.

Cliff Prewencki

Sources for Further Study

Booklist. XCIII, May 1, 1997, p. 1474.
The Economist. CCCXLI, December 7, 1996, p. 12.
London Review of Books. XIX, January 23, 1997, p. 3.
Los Angeles Times Book Review. August 3, 1997, p. 4.
The New Leader. LXXX, June 30, 1997, p. 15.
The New Republic. CCXVII, September 29, 1997, p. 33.
The New York Times Book Review. CII, June 8, 1997, p. 13.
The Observer. September 15, 1996, p. 16.
Publishers Weekly. CCXLIV, March 24, 1997, p. 65.
The Spectator. CCLXXVII, November 23, 1996, p. 44.
The Times Literary Supplement. September 20, 1996, p. 28.

W. B. YEATS: A LIFE
Volume I: The Apprentice Mage, 1865-1914

Author: R. F. Foster (1949-   )
Publisher: Oxford University Press (New York). Illustrated. 640 pp. $35.00
Type of work: Literary biography
Time: 1865-1914
Locale: Ireland and England

In this volume of a projected two-part authorized biography, historian R. F. Foster considers the first fifty years in the life of William Butler Yeats, the major poet in English of the twentieth century

Principal personages:
WILLIAM BUTLER YEATS, the Irish poet, playwright, and nationalist
JACK BUTLER YEATS, his father
MAUD GONNE, an Irish actress and political activist, Yeats's great love
LADY AUGUSTA GREGORY, a literary and theatrical collaborator with Yeats
ANNIE HORNIMAN, a financial backer of the Irish theater movement and sometime amanuensis of Yeats
JOHN QUINN, an Irish American supporter of Yeats

William Butler Yeats is the major poet of the twentieth century in English. He also, arguably, is modern Ireland's most significant figure, looming large not only for his contributions to the country's literature (as critic, playwright, and fiction writer as well as poet) but also for his work in establishing an Irish theater, reviving Irish mythology, and promoting nationalism and other political causes. By the age of twenty-one, in 1886, he was publishing prolifically, and because of his literary, theatrical, and political activities, he remained an influential public presence in Ireland for more than five decades, until his death in 1939.

Yeats has been the subject of many biographical and critical studies, including *W. B. Yeats, 1865-1939* (1943), written by Joseph Hone; Richard Ellmann's *The Man and the Masks* (1948); and A. Norman Jeffares's *W. B. Yeats: A New Biography* (1989). Yeats himself wrote a number of autobiographical accounts and memoirs, beginning with *Reveries* in 1916, which he included (somewhat revised) in *Autobiographies* a decade later. R. F. Foster's study, the first volume of which ends in Yeats's fiftieth year, stands apart from its predecessors for three reasons: Foster is a historian, not a literary scholar, and thus brings a different perspective to his subject; Hone, Yeats's first biographer, was a journalist who was close personally and professionally to Yeats (whose widow sanctioned the book, and to whom the copyright reverted after Hone's death) and lacked scholarly background and detachment; and finally, most earlier biographers use Yeats's own thematic arrangement (in *Autobiographies*) as their pattern, eschewing chronology and tracing such elements as romanticism, occultism, and nationalism through his life. Foster the historian has written a day-by-day, chronological life, concerned more with what Yeats did than with what he wrote, stressing the man's influence on those around him rather than the relationship between Yeats and his writings. In sum, Foster primarily focuses on Yeats as a force in twentieth century Irish history, the intellectual as public activist, and in this first of his two projected volumes, presents a portrait of the artist as a young man.

William Butler Yeats was born on June 13, 1865, in a Dublin suburb. His father, John Butler Yeats, was a barrister who preferred the artist's life, so WB, as everyone called him, and his three siblings (two others died very young) passed some of their childhood in near poverty. They spent long periods, however, with their mother and her family in Sligo, western Ireland, where the Pollexfens had servants and a governess to care for the children. This was only one aspect of a bifurcated life, for John Butler Yeats, his wife Susan, and their children also lived for a time in London.

Years later, William spent long periods in that city, joining its literary circles and becoming acquainted with fellow writers, initially through the Rhymers Club but also by other social means. Through the years, then, he developed links of varying kinds with Padraic Colum, Edward Dowden, Ernest Dowson, Lord Dunsany, Edmund Gosse, James Joyce, John Masefield, George Moore, A. E. (George Russell), George Bernard Shaw, and Arthur Symons. Although he occasionally sought solitude to write (often retreating in summers to the Coole Park home of Lady Augusta Gregory, his sometime collaborator and patron), Yeats's creative impulses seemed to thrive on social and intellectual interaction.

Although many of these activities involved him in conflict and controversy, they also filled gaps left by his sporadic formal education. An indifferent student in high school, he was bored by art school, years later describing the experience as "destructive of enthusiasm." His father was a better teacher, of geography and chemistry as well as literature, reading aloud to his son Honoré de Balzac, Charles Dickens, Sir Walter Scott, and Thomas Babington Macaulay. Later, in his twenties, the younger Yeats read extensively at the British Museum and Dublin's National Library and also borrowed friends' books. His eclectic reading led him to an interest in English poets, particularly William Blake, Percy Bysshe Shelley, and Edmund Spenser; in Ireland's literature, folklore, mythology, and the Irish language; and also in sixteenth century occult and mystic writings.

Descended from a long line of Protestants through both parents, Yeats never embraced orthodox Christianity but was attracted to the quasi-mysticism of Blake and Shelley and to theosophy, Neoplatonism, and spiritualism. Foster shows how these interests not only met Yeats's spiritual needs but also shaped his actions (he partici-pated in séances, for example), influenced his work (leading him to write poems and plays about Ireland's heroic past and Irish myths), and nurtured his involvement in the Irish nationalist movement.

Although he did not marry until 1917, women also played an important part in his intellectual development, beginning with a cousin, Laura Armstrong, whom he met briefly in 1882 and then corresponded with for a time. More significant presences, in addition to Lady Gregory, were Olivia Shakespear, Annie Horniman, and Maud Gonne. Shakespear, two years older than Yeats, was a novelist whom he met in 1894;

the two became lovers the next year, soon after she married. Although they drifted apart, they resumed their relationship years later, when she introduced him to Ezra Pound, her son-in-law, who became Yeats's secretary for a time.

Annie Horniman was an heiress whom Yeats met in 1890, when they joined an occult group, the Hermetic Order of the Golden Dawn, whose members followed the theosophical teachings of Madame Helena Blavatsky and other spiritualists. Horniman became infatuated with Yeats, plied him with gifts, and courted a marriage proposal from him. Although he resisted the romantic advances, he tolerated her, and during bouts of his recurring eye problems, she was his amanuensis. She also became an important financial backer of the Irish theater movement, but her day-to-day involvement led to conflicts with others, and she eventually detached herself from the Abbey. In 1907, however, she provided the funds for the publication of Yeats's *Collected Works*, and he borrowed money from her the next year.

Maud Gonne, an actress and nationalist eighteen months younger than Yeats, stands apart from the other women with whom Yeats had close relationships, for he was deeply in love with her for many years, although she persistently denied him marriage. They met for the first time in January, 1889, and—he recalled later—"the troubling of my life began." A believer in reincarnation and the occult and a devotee of Madame Blavatsky, she participated with Yeats in Golden Dawn. One of the most openly political persons in his circle at the end of the century, she demonstrated against Queen Victoria's Diamond Jubilee in 1897 and campaigned against the British in the Boer War. During an affair in France with a journalist-politician, Gonne had two children, one of whom died. When she revealed this secret life to Yeats late in 1898, she also confessed to having loved him for years but rejected the possibility of marriage; they resolved upon an asexual commitment to each other, spurred by the belief that they had been brother and sister in an earlier incarnation.

Despite her emotional and spiritual attachment to Yeats and her declared aversion to sex and marriage, Gonne did marry John MacBride of the Irish Republican Brotherhood and a leader of the anti-British South African agitation. The match was a failure, the pair legally separated in a few years, and the British executed MacBride in 1916 for his role in the Easter Uprising. Gonne continued to serve Yeats as creative inspiration and symbol throughout his career, and he transformed her in his poetry into the ideal of Irish womanhood. The 1902 poem "Adam's Curse," more than any other of his works, reflects both the passion and the hopelessness of his love for her. The shifting fortunes of their relationship notwithstanding, they worked closely together in the Irish theater movement.

As early as 1897, Yeats had enlisted the support of Lady Gregory and others for the Celtic Theatre (soon renamed the Irish Literary Theatre) in Dublin, to present prose and verse plays about modern and legendary Ireland. After resolving difficulties over a performing license, they publicized their efforts, gained prominent endorsers, raised money, and secured a facility, the venture debuting at Dublin's Antient Concert Rooms with Yeats's verse drama *The Countess Cathleen* and Edward Martyn's *The Heather Field*. The latter, a more traditional play, was the popular and critical success of this premier double bill. A second season's plays were presented in Dublin's Gaiety Theatre, which suggested a step forward; however, by 1901 the experiment had run its course, perhaps doomed by the elitism of its promoters.

A year later, under the aegis of Frank and William Fay's Irish National Dramatic Society, Maud Gonne appeared at Dublin's St. Teresa's Hall in Yeats's *Cathleen ni Houlihan*, and the prospect of a new theater group emerged. Yeats's assessment of the Fays' efforts was generous: "in very truth, a National company, a chief expression of Irish imagination." He became its president, Gonne a vice president, and with the help of Horniman and others, the INDS found a permanent home. The Abbey Theatre opened December 27, 1904, and under a ruling triumvirate of Yeats, Lady Gregory, and John Millington Synge, the Abbey went on the road, to England and Scotland. Despite personal intrigues and cultural wars, Yeats's dream had been realized and a major element in the Irish renaissance achieved.

Further problems, tragedies, and triumphs lay ahead for Yeats. For example, when the opening of Synge's *The Playboy of the Western World* at the Abbey in January, 1907, caused riots because of its unconventional portrayal of Irish women, Yeats called the police, provoking a confrontation with his associates. Two years later, Synge's death at the age of thirty-eight significantly affected Yeats, for he believed that the young playwright had represented artistic freedom against Catholic middle-class parochialism. According to Foster, the death "would haunt WBY for the rest of his life, inspiring a continual elegy in prose and verse." It came soon after a milestone event for Yeats, the publication in 1908 of his *Collected Works* in eight volumes. A daring, even audacious, project for a writer in his early forties—implying, as Lytton Strachey put it, "a claim to a recognised and permanent place in the literature of a nation"—the enterprise enjoyed a respectful critical reception.

The establishment of an Irish theater, the publication of the *Works*, and Synge's death, all occurring within a few years, marked the end of Yeats's apprenticeship and the start of his life as Ireland's preeminent man of letters. Official recognition of this position came when the king granted him a Civil List pension—a guaranteed annual income of 150 pounds. Although it was ironic that an incipient Irish nationalist would receive royal largess, Yeats had become increasingly estranged from Irish life; while continuing to be involved with the Abbey, he was spending more time in London. He also made a second and then a third trip to the United States. His first lecture tour, in 1903, under the aegis of the Irish American lawyer John Quinn, had been a huge success, establishing him as a writer of great promise; when he returned in 1910 and 1913, he was greeted as an eminent literary figure.

As he neared his fiftieth birthday, Yeats increasingly used the lecture platform and his poetry for political purposes, as in "September 1913," which Foster says "stands with the great polemics of literature." Indeed, Yeats was moving in tandem with his countrymen, who were on the threshold of an epic confrontation with the British. The title of his 1913 collection is apt: *Poems Written in Discouragement*. Foster concludes his book with Yeats writing *Reveries*, an autobiographical account of his first half-century. His achievements thus far had been remarkable, but ahead lay greater poetry and acclaim, more forays into spiritualism, and eventually marriage and children.

Foster skillfully reveals the emergence of greatness as he presents his detailed, almost day by day, account of Yeats's apprenticeship. He is an admiring biographer but has not written a hagiography. Nor is his book a study of Yeats's works; he deals more with the process of composition than with interpretation. The plethora of biographical detail and careful delineation of the social, intellectual, political, and spiritual milieu provide the basis for others to engage in exegesis. With this first volume of *W. B. Yeats: A Life*, Foster has provided Yeats scholarship with an invaluable resource.

Gerald H. Strauss

Sources for Further Study

America. CLXXVII, August 30, 1997, p. 27.
Choice. XXXV, October, 1997, p. 296.
Los Angeles Times. May 9, 1997, p. E3.
The Nation. CCLXIV, May 12, 1997, p. 51.
The New York Times Book Review. CII, April 6, 1997, p. 10.
Publishers Weekly. CCXLIV, March 3, 1997, p. 55.
The Sewanee Review. CV, Spring, 1997, p. 251.
The Times Literary Supplement. April 11, 1997, p. 21.
The Wall Street Journal. April 23, 1997, p. A16.
The Washington Post Book World. XXVII, April 20, 1997, p. 6.

WAIST HIGH IN THE WORLD
A Life Among the Nondisabled

Author: Nancy Mairs (1943-   )
Publisher: Beacon Press (Boston, Massachusetts). 212 pp. $20.00
Type of work: Autobiography

Having lived with multiple sclerosis (MS) for twenty years, Mairs presents her physical and emotional experiences as a person trapped in her wheelchair amid persons and in a society insensitive to her lifestyle

Principal personage:
NANCY MAIRS, a wheelchair-bound writer with multiple sclerosis (MS)

Diagnosed in 1972 when she was a twenty-nine-year-old wife, mother, and writer, Nancy Mairs faced a mysterious, incurable, degenerative neurological disease. Over the years, she became more and more physically limited, until in 1992 she became wheelchair-bound.

In her earlier nonfiction books—*Plaintext: Deciphering a Woman's Life* (1986), *Remembering the Bone House: An Erotics of Place and Space* (1989), *Carnal Acts* (1990), *Ordinary Time: Cycles of Marriage, Faith, and Renewal* (1993), and *Voice Lessons: On Becoming a (Woman) Writer* (1994), all of which are partially autobiographical—Mairs includes some reflections on her crippling illness. *Waist High in the World: A Life Among the Nondisabled* is her first attempt to capture for the reader the entirety of her private and public life with multiple sclerosis (MS).

Mairs introduces the reader to her wheelchair-bound world not in a way that will make the nondisabled reader feel good but rather in a way that will awaken this reader to the reality of Mairs's world. Her tone does not reflect self-pity or nostalgia; rather, it is marked by realism—tough realism, tempered by humor. As readers of Mairs's earlier books know, she is absolutely honest, always.

Mairs's purposes are several. First, she wants to reach out to others suspecting or knowing that they have MS or a similar severe disability, to assure them that "a life commonly held to be insufferable can be full and funny." Second, she wants to bring the experience of being a disabled person to nondisabled readers, to make these readers see Mairs as she is. She wants the disabled also to see themselves as she sees them: in ways that are mostly negative, not from deliberate ill will but from a sort of blindness to the reality of the human being who is disabled. Finally, as more and more disabled persons are living longer lives, Mairs argues that the world can be adjusted in ways that will enable them to live, if not totally full lives, at least lives as full as possible. For this to happen, though, there must be changes in human attitudes and societal space.

What Mairs refuses to do is replicate those media stories that give their audience a romantic picture of life with MS. This book will not make the nondisabled reader feel good, nor will it convince the world that the disabled are able to overcome all of their problems, or at least get along with a cheerful attitude. At the same time, Mairs never asks for, indeed mocks at, attitudes of either pity or admiration for the disabled. For these reasons, she predicts that her book will not make the best-seller list, and she is right. Yet because of its unflinching realism, this book is a significant contribution to the literature about human beings with disabilities.

Mairs's purposes are served by her structure, which is topical rather than chronological. She writes first about her private life and second about her life in the public sphere.

The first half of Mairs's text, "Home Truths," is just that: a description of coping with basic life functions in the home, day by day, with an ill and deformed physical body. She has no privacy, though she loves solitude, because she cannot dress, eat, bathe, or go to the bathroom without someone's assistance. She cannot cook or do laundry or clean. She is dependent. What is this like?

Mairs points out her good fortune in having her husband, George, as a loving caretaker who gives her the comfort of a relationship so close that he knows her needs almost instinctively. Also, Mairs tell the reader, their physical intimacy continues—without intercourse, but very satisfying. Nevertheless, Mairs fears for the time when George can no longer help, because either his melanoma cancer returns or he simply ages. She fears living her last days without someone to give her the care she must receive daily, without George's willingness to help her live a full life. She fears being exiled to a nursing home. At the same time, Mairs feels guilt for the strain she puts on her family members because her need for care keeps increasing; she feels guilt for her inability to offer them ordinary kindnesses, such as visiting or helping out when a need arises.

As she writes about her full range of emotions, not only guilt and fear but also anger, frustration, embarrassment, envy, and anxiety, Mairs does not allow herself any self-pity. Rather, she has learned to practice her brand of courage: adapting herself to each progressive lessening of independence, but doing so as a person in control of, rather than controlled by, MS. She has done what she could for herself as long as possible but has also let go when necessity demanded, in every case—from her earliest losses, such as becoming unable to take long walks, to her latest, becoming wheelchair-bound.

In this first section Mairs also writes of the impact of MS on her spirituality. Mairs, a convert to Catholicism, embraces a Catholic Worker-style faith, one committed to acts of mercy, to helping others. As she became more and more deprived of the ability to serve others and increasingly dependent on those who would serve her, she took charge of herself and found other avenues for serving. One such avenue, says Mairs, is listening, at which she feels she has become better. Her primary way of serving others, she has decided, is her writing. This gift, she explains, "has always been an act of oblation and nurturance, my means of taking the reader into my arms, holding a cup to her lips, stroking her forehead, whispering jokes into her ears." Thus, the reader finds in Mairs's account of her personal life and her inner life a fierce spirit that has propelled her forward even as her body has deteriorated—but not without periods of anger and frustration at the great, unalterable difficulties.

Mairs moves out of her home and becomes more political in the second part of *Waist High in the World*. In this "Wider World" she experiences being other, or invisible, rejected by uninviting persons and spaces. To challenge the first reaction, a sort of kindly or embarrassed or pitying attitude toward her, Mairs gives multiple examples of such an attitude and its resultant behaviors, in sharply phrased anecdotes from her own experience and observation. Her wry tone protects the reader from feeling attacked, but her honesty calls the reader to a similar honesty, an admission of some of the behaviors she describes.

As in the first section, Mairs continues to point out that the disabled are not "other"; they are human beings, just like the nondisabled. She and her disabled counterparts laugh and cry, strive for a full life, fall in love. This book forcefully challenges the nondisabled to examine their attitudes and behaviors when they meet the disabled in a social context. Mairs admits that in recent years there has been positive change in society's attitudes toward the disabled; she does feel greater acceptance. More change is needed, however, and she wants this change sooner rather than later.

In terms of social space, Mairs credits the Americans with Disabilities Act of 1990 (ADA) for some success in addressing the needs of the disabled. Still, such accommodation is not a universal requirement. Mairs would have accessibility for the disabled be required in all new construction of both private and public buildings. A home bought by a young couple should be accessible not only to the disabled who want to visit them but also to the couple themselves when they age and lose some of their mobility. The failure to make every home accessible reveals a blindness to the reality of modern society. Few would see this; few would disagree.

Universal accessibility for and acceptability of the disabled is, Mairs argues, good for both the disabled and society. Businesspersons who do not see the possibility for employment in a person who is disabled lose qualified workers while denying the disabled a full life. Also, businesses that are not accessible to the disabled lose profits while denying the disabled a full life. Mairs's viewpoint is both practical and ethical.

Tourism is the fastest-growing industry in America in the 1990's, so one wonders at the travel difficulties Mairs has faced when out in public either to sell her books or to enjoy an adventure. Mairs is very assertive, able to fight for her rights and to adapt herself in trying situations. Yet why should any person who wants to leave her home or her immediate surroundings have to overcome so many barriers to mobility? Airports and airlines, in particular, thus far exempt from ADA regulations, often treat Mairs more like freight than like a person.

Yet not always, she adds. At the same time that she laments the problems she has faced, Mairs points out places where her traveling needs have been met. For example, her home city of Tucson has done well by the disabled. She notes, however, some recent downgrading even there, as public monies have become tighter. In general, the current nondisabled-citizen attitude toward government assistance and funding for those in need of society's aid worries Mairs. As far as she is concerned, human beings have an obligation to help other human beings as needed. It is that simple.

While accessible-space issues might not be new to some readers, the significance of the ethical issues of abortion and euthanasia for the disabled might be. The aborting of a fetus when amniocentesis shows a birth defect and the granting of freedom to choose one's time of death concern Mairs, although she is pro-choice in both cases. Her concern focuses on a dangerous attitude that might lurk behind society's discussions of abortion and euthanasia: that using abortion and euthanasia for the extermination of the disabled and the elderly, considered by some burdens on society, is feasible. Mairs, who has been in a state of suicidal depression more than once, believes that even a hint that persons with physical limitations are expendable could nudge some into self-destruction.

This is probably one of the most important insights that Mairs shares with her nondisabled readers. What Mairs asks again and again is that the disabled hear that life as they live it is valid, that they, just as they are, are a welcomed and valued part of society. This is her plea.

In a final chapter, Mairs waxes both personal and metaphysical. She and her family moved from New England to Tucson, Arizona, from the compact East to the sprawling West, just before her disease was diagnosed and her writing career took off. In the land of space and individualism, she has neither mobility nor independence. So she asks, is she a Western writer or not? Yes, she answers, the West suits her both symbolically and metaphysically, for in her deepest being she feels "a vastness within which my yearning spirit must grapple with my recalcitrant flesh perpetually." This captures the writer well.

For a person with serious disabilities to live a full life, the reader learns from Nancy Mairs's frank picture of her body and her spirit, requires effort from both the disabled and the nondisabled. Mairs makes a persuasive and witty case for her ideal world: a world in which all doors and all hearts are open to her.

Francine Dempsey

Sources for Further Study

Booklist. XCIII, January 1, 1997, p. 790.
Inside MS. XV, Summer, 1997, p. 25.
Kirkus Reviews. LXIV, January, 1997, p. 158.
Library Journal. CXXI, December, 1996, p. 132.
Los Angeles Times. March 30, 1997, p. E1.
Mainstream. XXI, December, 1996, p. 14.
The Nation. CCLXIV, April 14, 1997, p. 32.
The New York Times Book Review. CII, March 2, 1997, p. 19.
Publishers Weekly. CCXLIII, November 4, 1996, p. 56.
The Washington Post Book World. XXVII, February 2, 1997, p. 4.
Women's Review of Books. XIV, March, 1997, p. 8.

WALKER PERCY
A Life

Author: Patrick H. Samway (1939-   )
Publisher: Farrar Straus Giroux (New York). 506 pp. $35.00
Type of work: Literary biography
Time: 1916-1990
Locale: Mississippi, Louisiana, Alabama, and New York

A meticulously researched but constrained retelling of Walker Percy's life

> *Principal personages:*
> WALKER PERCY, a southern novelist, amateur semiotician, and
>   nonpracticing doctor
> MARY "BUNT" PERCY, his wife
> SHELBY FOOTE, his lifetime friend, a Civil War novelist
> WILL PERCY, his uncle and guardian

Since Walker Percy's death from cancer in 1990, the critical industry surrounding his work has gained momentum. Patrick Samway's biography of Percy comes second after *Pilgrim in the Ruins: A Life of Walker Percy* (1992) by Jay Tolson, which received favorable reviews and the Southern Book Award for Nonfiction in 1993. Since Samway has been working on his biography since 1987, one can only speculate on how this competing biography affected his work in progress. While Tolson dramatizes Percy's struggle to transform himself from a practicing doctor into a successful writer, Samway in contrast seems reluctant to dramatize his subject at all, preferring to let the reader draw his or her own conclusions about Percy's behavior. In his drive to write a "biography without holding prior theory or thesis," Samway may be more honest about his findings than Tolson, but his work lacks coherency and continuity as a result. One wishes he had arrived at a thesis after researching to help bind his study together. Too often, this book reads like a collection of inadequately synthesized notes, and for this reason Samway shows up some of the dangers of being overly respectful and selfless when telling the story of another person's life.

The literary editor of *America*, a weekly Catholic journal, Samway brings to this project his Jesuit training, which seems to have merited Percy's approval. When Samway offered to write the biography, Percy replied, "There is no one I'd rather entrust such a project to." Perhaps Percy felt that Samway could explore Percy's conversion to the Catholic Church and his faith's subsequent effect on his fiction with greater exactitude than other biographers. Samway was also able to speak to the Percys frequently during the last three years of Walker Percy's life, and by doing so gradually amassed a large group of friends, fellow writers, and relatives to help him assemble enough information for the biography.

Despite this large pool of data, Samway resists the biographical tendency to interpret Percy's fiction in the light of his life's experiences, even though he does use Percy's writings to help describe key places and scenes in his life. In turn, Samway's use of Percy's descriptions shows up the lack of description in his own prose. For example, while Samway often describes houses well, he tends to leave out physical detail in his descriptions of people, letting the reader learn about them largely through their actions. Thus, most of the supporting cast of Percy's life seems underdeveloped and at times unclearly related to Percy. Too often, Percy himself seems to slip right through the net of his life story, a feat no doubt made possible by his theories concerning the unknowability of the self and his private, reticent, easygoing personality.

Samway's thorough biographical method does help us picture Percy's early years. We learn that Percy came from two prominent, if high-strung, Alabama families. Percy was born during World War I, in 1916, to Mattie Sue and Leroy Percy, his father an up-and-coming lawyer in the Birmingham area. Within a year of his birth, Percy's grandfather on his father's side shot himself, perhaps due to manic depression. Later, when Percy was just thirteen, his father shot himself in turn with a shotgun, again seemingly because of depression, leaving his widowed mother with little to do but move back in with family in Athens, Georgia, and finally onto Greenville, Mississippi, where she too mysteriously died when she drove her car off a small bridge into a creek. Although the evidence was unclear, Percy believed that she also had committed suicide. Percy and his two brothers were then adopted by their uncle Will Percy, a poet and writer of the memoir *Lanterns on the Levee* (1941), and from then on Percy worked hard to settle in with the Greenville community, socializing easily and getting good grades at the local high school. Although not visibly affected by the many suicides in his family, Percy would later characterize his writing as, in part, an argument with his absent parents.

If it were not for his parents' tragic deaths and his early penchant for writing poetry for the high school paper, one could hardly distinguish Percy as in any way more remarkable than his classmates. He met Shelby Foote in high school and they developed a friendship that would eventually flower into a mutually supportive literary relationship, but otherwise he did not show much notable interest in writing. At the University of North Carolina at Chapel Hill, where he studied literature, science, and math, Percy was known for his filmgoing and for reading Robert E. Lee's biography on the front porch of his fraternity house.

Percy might never have written at all if he had not encountered tubercular patients at Bellevue Hospital when studying at Columbia's College of Physicians and Surgeons. Percy contracted the illness himself and suddenly found himself bedridden for months in a New York State sanatorium. By pulling him away from his career as a doctor, his bout with tuberculosis suddenly freed up Percy to meditate on his career. While ill, Percy read the works of Søren Kierkegaard, Albert Camus, Jean-Paul Sartre, Fyodor Dostoevski, Nikolai Gogol, Leo Tolstoy, and others, and suddenly he began to explore what his scientific training could not answer: what it is like to be a specific human being who is going to die. To answer this question, Percy turned to fiction.

Samway also ably discusses Percy's conversion to Catholicism. For much of his life, raised as a Presbyterian, Percy paid little attention to religion. After largely recovering from tuberculosis, however, Percy began writing essays and fiction in earnest, married Mary "Bunt" Bernice, and converted to Catholicism, all in rapid succession. Though reticent about his faith, Percy would defend it from all attacks, seeing it as a gift of grace in the midst of a particularly murderous century. While his friend Shelby Foote wrote to Percy about the lack of any good Catholic art for centuries, Percy's editor and mentor Caroline Gordon found something new in his Catholic perspective that would prove a boon for his fiction. By providing insights from Gordon, Samway illustrates how the "Protestant *mystique*" of most writers of the period had turned into the worst kind of worn-out convention. In contrast, Catholicism gave writers such as Percy and Flannery O'Connor a moral tradition to build upon. Catholic writers, in a sense, already know who made the cosmos; the question becomes how to find one's place within it. While Percy's belief led to a slight didacticism in his later works, it also helped him frame the questions for his mature fiction.

During this key moment in his life, the period in between being a doctor and becoming a writer, something major happened, a kind of coalescing of Percy's powers that came from his brush with mortality, a time to step aside to take stock that suddenly transformed all of his memories into material for fiction. In the process, Percy hit upon a new way to graft the existential concerns of Gabriel-Honoré Marcel, Kierkegaard, Camus, and Sartre onto the landscape of the South. This method freed up New Orleans, a place normally found to be too overladen with its colorful Creole heritage to be easily written about, to be a setting for Percy's first published novel, *The Moviegoer* (1961). It is precisely because the lead character, Binx Bolling, could be anywhere with his existential concerns that New Orleans functions so well in the novel. Through his philosophical musings, Percy found a way to neatly incorporate the values and the landscape of the old chivalric South into contemporary fiction.

While Jay Tolson found an intense restless mind underneath Percy's relaxed southern gentleman facade, thus forming the tension that led to his writing, Samway does not tell us why Percy wrote as much as he did. Even before writing *The Moviegoer*, Percy produced a surprising amount of published essays about semiotics, naming, symbol-making, and alienation from his relative isolation in the suburbs around New Orleans. Repeatedly, Percy tried to use his understanding of science to answer questions about human identity. His forays into language theory helped him to understand his adopted daughter Ann's deafness. The pictures of alienation in his essays—a man on a train unknowingly traveling through New Jersey—prepare the way for scenes in his fiction. Percy demonstrated how an understanding of place helps ground alienated human identity, and in this way he justified his turning to fiction to help answer existential questions. Between writing apprentice novels, debating aesthetics with Shelby Foote, and writing these essays, Percy prepared the philosophical groundwork for the novels of his maturity.

Samway supplies all this information in a dry prose that sometimes seems fragmentary, as if he sometimes had trouble knowing what to incorporate in his research and what to leave out. For instance, Samway will sometimes include discussions of peripheral figures such as Paul Green, a playwright who lived in Greenville during Percy's high school days, without clearly connecting him to Percy. Samway may have wanted to depict the cultural ambiance of the time, but his refusal to speculate about connections can leave the reader wondering why he brought up Green to begin with. At another point, Samway includes an exhaustive list of medical professors at Columbia that could only concern those who know them in the profession. Elsewhere, Samway fails to smoothly blend in World War II events with Percy's day-to-day affairs, even though Percy was doubtless affected by them. In these cases Samway fails to combine his information into a coherent whole, again the possible result of the lack of a guiding thesis.

When *The Moviegoer* received the National Book Award, Percy, always a shy man in public, had to suddenly confront the vagaries of fame. He awkwardly promoted his book on the *Today* show, dealt with mixed reviews and phone calls from strangers, and from then on suffered bouts of depression between writing books. Later in his writing career, secure in his fame and increasing scholarly attention, Percy's story became an increasingly repetitive series of award ceremonies, speeches, and retreats back to Covington to write. Some of the later novels, such as *Lancelot* (1977), did not get very good critical or public receptions, and Samway is careful to emphasize the positive as much as he can, even though Percy confessed that he learned the most from bad reviews. Ironically, Percy mentions that a William Faulkner biography had left out all of the good parts because his surviving relatives cleaned up Faulkner's story for posterity. Writing for the same publisher as Percy's—Farrar, Straus and Giroux—and working with Percy's relatives, Samway seems to have done some of the same whitewashing for Percy. For instance, there is a hint of an affair between Percy and one of his friends, the much younger Lyn Hill, and Percy writes at one point about how much younger women are drawn to him, but Samway again keeps his respectful distance from making any conclusions in this area.

Ultimately, Samway's respectful distance from Percy and his unwillingness to draw conclusions from his findings limits his otherwise thorough study of the author. When Percy describes himself as a "bad Catholic, a lazy writer, and a sinful man," one wishes Samway would produce more evidence of what he meant. Again and again, the samples from Percy's writings reveal a more vividly colorful personality than the man Samway describes.

Roy C. Flannagan

Sources for Further Study

America. CLXXVI, May 24, 1997, p. 28.
Atlanta Journal Constitution. July 20, 1997, p. L9.
Booklist. XCIII, March, 1997, p. 1221.
Chicago Tribune. May 25, 1997, XIV, p. 5.
Commonweal. CXXIV, July 18, 1997, p. 22.
Library Journal. CXXII, March 1, 1997, p. 76.

The New Leader. LXXX, June 30, 1997, p. 17.
The New Republic. CCXVII, September 8, 1997, p. 41.
The New York Times Book Review. CII, June 8, 1997, p. 17.
Publishers Weekly. CCXLIV, March 24, 1997, p. 64.

WALKING IN THE SHADE
Volume Two of My Autobiography, 1949-1962

Author: Doris Lessing (1919-   )
Publisher: HarperCollins (New York). 404 pp. $27.50
Type of work: Autobiography
Time: 1949-1962
Locale: London

*The second volume of Doris Lessing's autobiography, chronicling the 1950's in postwar London, her first fiction success (*The Grass Is Singing*), her political life in and out of the Communist Party, and her writing process*

Principal personages:
    DORIS LESSING, novelist
    PETER, her son
    "JACK," her lover, a psychiatrist refugee from Czechoslovakia
    CLANCY SIGAL, American Trotskyist writer, also her lover
    MRS. SUSSMAN, her therapist

Doris Lessing, born in 1919 in Persia (present-day Iran), grew up in Southern Rhodesia (present-day Zimbabwe) with immigrant white-settler parents, spent the war years in Salisbury protesting in leftist groups the conditions of black people, and there wrote her first novel. The first volume of her autobiography, *Under My Skin* (1994), chronicles her life until she left Africa for London. This second volume covers the years 1949-1962, from her arrival in London with no resources but the unpublished manuscript of *The Grass Is Singing* (eventually published in 1950) to the publication of *The Golden Notebook* (1962). Both volumes are wonderful evocations of place and time, and in each, one very much hears Doris Lessing's wise tone, unique in all of literature. It is this mentoring tone that is so distinctive in her novels, the sense that the narrator is sitting in the room with the reader, just talking. That tone remains in the autobiographies: There is always a double vision of the narrator's present voice juxtaposed against her views in the past.

The title of this volume, *Walking in the Shade*, refers to the epigraph from "On the Sunny Side of the Street," a popular song from the 1930's. In a larger sense, it evokes Lessing's coming to terms with communism: first, her joining the party, then later her leaving the party as the details of Joseph Stalin's purges became known in the 1950's. The "shade" signifies her outsider political position, both in and out of the party, for she was always aware of the contradictions inherent in being a communist. In a very real sense, this is a book about the politics of the 1950's more than it is a book about the making of a writer.

Lessing went to London at the very beginning of the Cold War, and she went with a leftist political consciousness, nurtured by her experiences in southern Africa. Almost overnight, communism became suspect, because when World War II ended, the Soviet Union was no longer one of the Allies. The Western communist community became cut off. Still, the McCarthy era was never as frightening in England as in the

United States (there was no equivalent there of the House Committee on Un-American Activities), and the British Isles harbored many American and Canadian leftist comrades-in-exile.

Lessing structures the book around the different houses she occupied in London over the course of a dozen years. Each address was in a different part of London, from a garret in the western immigrant area of Denbigh Road, to Church Street in Kensington, to Warwick Road in southwest London, back to central London near the BBC, and finally to Somers Town and an old house she bought and remodeled in Charrington Street. In each part, Lessing not only describes her living situation and sundry housemates but also includes a section of "The Zeitgeist, or How We Thought Then," recounting in telling detail people's attitudes in those times. In her wise tone, Lessing recalls the "feel" of the era—from the bombed-out buildings and bad food and worse coffee of postwar England to the Cold War shift in attitude and something so seemingly simple as the coming of television and the subsequent death of working-class culture.

With a new Labour government, people all over the world looked to England after the war as a place of hope for the future. Lessing, along with thousands of others from around the old British Empire, emigrated to London. Along with many others, she came with a dream of an egalitarian society, founded on communist ideals. She participated in communist groups throughout the decade, even as she was becoming disillusioned with the Communist Party. Her pertinent descriptions of leftists refusing to accept the information then being leaked to the West about the numbers of people tortured and killed by Stalin are devastating. The most startling of her assertions are that Stalin, not Adolf Hitler, should be considered the arch villain of the twentieth century; that there have been lies for decades about the numbers killed during the 1930's and 1940's in the Soviet Union; that the numbers of casualties during World War II were always inflated by adding the numbers of their own citizens killed on Stalin's orders; and that the reason for the cover-up was the military alliance with the Soviet Union against Germany. Lessing cites a figure of eight million Russians lost, not the twenty million often given by the Soviet Union itself.

As with most movements, people still believed in the ideals, even as they turned a blind eye or excused the excesses of Stalin. Lessing understands her own complicity in this. In England, as elsewhere in the West, people needed to continue to believe in the possibility of an egalitarian society, so the protests against the arms race and particularly against nuclear weapons were led by leftist groups. The Campaign for Nuclear Disarmament, the Committee of a Hundred, and the Easter Aldermaston Marches culminating in mass demonstrations in Trafalgar Square were all a part of Lessing's political life in the 1950's. She reveals how corrupt these groups were, right down to the puppet leader who told an aging Bertrand Russell exactly what to write and say. The antiwar movement in England in the late 1950's, she notes, was the genesis of the anti-Vietnam War movement of the 1960's in the United States.

As a successful leftist writer (*The Grass Is Singing* was reviewed favorably and reprinted several times), Lessing was a member of one of the very first delegations of foreign writers allowed into the Soviet Union in the 1950's. This was the beginning of an era of many delegations, all arranged by various Soviet committees: peace delegations, socialist delegations, and groups of miners, musicians, artists, and teachers. All were tightly controlled in their itineraries, contacts, and discussions. At a visit to a collective farm on Lessing's trip, a peasant dared to step forward and say that all was not positive, that foreigners were told lies, that the Russian people had terrible lives, and that communism was horrific. Pulled back by his comrades, he spent the rest of the visit silently staring at the Western visitors. Everyone knew that such behavior would land the man in the Gulag. Several in the delegation nevertheless rationalized the incident as the ravings of an envious man.

In 1956, at the Twentieth Party Congress in Moscow, Nikita Khrushchev revealed to the world (some of) the crimes of Stalin, but many of the faithful Western comrades refused to believe, saying that Khrushchev had been bought off by the Central Intelligence Agency or the capitalist press. Lessing was one of those who wondered why Khrushchev had not told the whole truth, ten times worse than the details he gave. She says it was hard to let go of her belief in the ideals of the communist system, but Khrushchev's confession changed her: "Now I knew that everything I had been clinging on to was nonsense." It also was in 1956 that she went back to southern Africa, courtesy of the Soviet cultural attaché in England. A Prohibited Immigrant in South Africa and Southern Rhodesia, she was nevertheless permitted entry. Always in touch with the black expatriate African community in London and acquainted with all the political leaders, such as Kenneth Kaunda of Northern Rhodesia (now Zambia) and Babu Mohammed of Zanzibar, Lessing interviewed people in four countries. Her book *Going Home* (1957) describes that trip.

Many of her friends and comrades were devastated and literally went mad as a result of their disillusionment on learning about the real horrors of communism. Lessing writes movingly of the experience of breakdown, that descent into madness, in several of her novels, among them *The Golden Notebook*, *The Four-Gated City* (1969), and *The Summer Before the Dark* (1973). She says that she was able to deal with the possibility of madness in herself by writing about it in her characters: "I write myself out of those potentials for disaster." Her generation's predilection for "disorder and extremity" came from World War I; she tells of her parents' psychological destruction by that war. Lessing's father lost a leg and spent a year in the hospital, taken care of by Nurse McVeagh, later his wife. Lessing's mother had lost her first sweetheart by drowning after his ship was torpedoed by a German sub. After their marriage, they went first to Persia and then to Southern Rhodesia to start a new life, but the war was a permanent part of their lives and thus of daughter Doris's.

The Golden Notebook was an attempt to give form to the "extreme compartmentalization" and then breakdown that the belief in communism had fostered in a whole generation of people, people whose childhoods were permanently scarred by World War I. "Old, young; black, white; men, women; capitalism, socialism; these great dichotomies undo us, force us into unreal categorisation, make us look for what separates us rather than what we have in common." The book was mostly misread, Lessing says, reviewers latching onto the woman versus man "sex war" theme. It came to be called the "Bible of the Women's Movement" in the late 1960's and 1970's because of its honesty in detailing women's situation—with children, with men, and with their own sexuality (it was one of the first novels to discuss menstruation). Lessing is bitter about readers and reviewers who demand that all writing must be autobiographical, wanting to identify this or that character with the author, refusing myth, legend, and fable—products of the imagination—and assuming that they can find "the truth" in factual detail.

When she had finished *The Golden Notebook*, Lessing says she had written herself out of the "package"—the package of her Western education blinders. She was ready to learn a new way. She began by studying various forms of Buddhism, then Hinduism, but soon she realized that the Western "individualist" style would not work—she must have a teacher, a mentor, in order to find her way and to submit to a spiritual discipline. The teacher she found was Idries Shah, a Sufi (Islamic mystic); from that time on, "this was my real life," she writes. Her later works all reflect her work with parable, mysticism, and nonlinear ways of thinking, especially *The Memoirs of a Survivor* (1974), *Briefing for a Descent into Hell* (1971), and her speculative fiction series, *Canopus in Argos: Archives* (five-novel series collective published in 1992).

Walking in the Shade also is about Lessing's writing process—how she wrote and how she managed as a single parent with a young child. Her usual habit was to write on a portable typewriter for most of the day while Peter was at school. She would pace about the room, smoke, and take quick catnaps to clear her mind between long sessions of composing. Lessing cannot suppress her creative storytelling urges, and the book is stuffed with dramatic sketches, often introduced with "A scene:." She is also a master at different styles and uses pastiche as brilliantly as she did in *The Golden Notebook* itself. She rewrites the beginning section of *The Golden Notebook* as if it were a society column to tweak the critics who complained that her male characters were all unpleasant. Lessing also chronicles her relations with the publishing industry, then and now, and her connections with agents and with theater and television producers.

The book's greatest weakness is its sometimes extreme allusiveness, with no explanations provided for readers not familiar with the intellectual scene in 1950's London. Although the anecdotes about her encounters with Nelson Algren, Kenneth Tynan, John Osborne, J. P. Donleavy, Shelagh Delaney, Brendan Behan, and even the more famous Bertrand Russell or Henry Kissinger are interesting or amusing, often the name-dropping is simply boring.

The book's greatest strength is its honesty in explaining and reliving the mind-set and attitudes of the Cold War decade from the perspective of a former communist. As she says, "To have been a communist but not now to be one was normal and described most of the people one met." Her work in this autobiography is an extraordinary attempt to get past the lie of memory to the honesty of how and why she thought and acted as she did at the time. Lessing's double vision and voice are always heard, guiding the reader with the wise tone of the teacher and mentor that she remains.

Margaret McFadden

Sources for Further Study

Booklist. XCIII, August, 1997, p. 1844.
Library Journal. CXXII, September 15, 1997, p. 75.
The Nation. CCLXV, October 13, 1997, p. 31.
National Business Review. October 31, 1997, p. 42.
The New York Times Book Review. CII, September 14, 1997, p. 16.
The New Yorker. LXXIII, November 17, 1997, p. 108.
Publishers Weekly. CCXLIV, August 11, 1997, p. 392.
Times Literary Supplement. Dec. 5, 1997, p. 6.
The Wall Street Journal. October 15, 1997, p. A21.
Women's Review of Books. XV, November, 1997, p. 5.
World and I. December, 1997, p. 256.

WEST WIND
Poems and Prose Poems

Author: Mary Oliver (1935-   )
Publisher: Houghton Mifflin (Boston). 63 pp. $21.00
Type of work: Poetry

Mary Oliver knows that the world is filled with people who feel that their lives are missing some important dimension, and she writes for those who have not yet willed themselves to be explorers of what nature has to offer

Mary Oliver is one of a small handful of poets who has had both critical and popular success. She has won both a Pulitzer Prize and a National Book Award. Her readers include many people for whom poetry is a small part of their reading life. That is, she has managed to win an audience among the general reading public that usually, when it turns to poetry at all, turns to practitioners of warm, fuzzy, amateurish drivel. By widening the audience for serious, accomplished poetry, Oliver has done a great service to poetry itself. *West Wind*, her ninth full-length collection, is presented to that larger audience as well as to the audience already committed to poetic excellence.

In design, *West Wind* looks like a small coffee table book. The shape of the book is odd, almost square, its extra-wide pages giving more than the usual breathing space to Oliver's poems. There is an extra half-title page following the contents, its verso blank, and then the first section divider, with its verso blank as well. Sections end on recto pages, leaving blank versos ahead of the next divider. All in all, a luxurious display of white space frames the poetry, although two short-lined poems are set in double columns, thus confined to one page rather than spread over two. The book design, with is unusual juxtapositions of typography and open space, hints at the spiritual, ascendant quality of Oliver's writing. It is as if the print is the heavy world and the marks one makes upon it, and the generous frame of white is the silent ecstatic state one can enter through and beyond it.

Not conventionally (or institutionally) religious, these poems nevertheless are poems of faith and miracle. Oliver is attentive to miracle in the natural world; or, closer to it, the miracle of the natural world. Her gift of words is to serve by celebrating and sharing her rapture of beholding and belonging. Oliver's stance, then, is much like English poet Percy Shelley's in his "Ode to the West Wind," and her title pays homage to this far more ostentatious poet-priest of nature.

Her collection has three parts in a structure of diminuendo. The first part, containing twenty-six poems, comprises the bulk of the book. The second section, titled "West Wind," is a thirteen-part numbered sequence. The final section is a single poem, "Have You Ever Tried to Enter the Long Black Branches," which recapitulates Oliver's major themes. The shape of the book, then, enacts a movement toward silence.

The first part is introduced by a quotation from A. Gilchrist's *Life and Works of William Blake* (1863). In the company of "persons of a scientific turn," Blake heard them declaiming upon the great distances between planets and how long it takes for light to reach the earth. Blake responded, "'Tis false! I was walking down a lane the other day, and at the end of it I touched the sky with my stick." Similarly, Oliver can stand rooted in this world and feel herself transported to the heavens. Her imagination, like that of the great Romantic poets, closes the distances between the everyday and the extraordinary, the temporal and the eternal. These remarks should not suggest that Oliver's work is old-fashioned. She is a skillful practitioner of contemporary free verse. One of her characteristic devices is the grammatical parallelism first honed into a vigorous poetic technique by Walt Whitman. Stretches of such poems as "Spring," "Stars," "Morning Walk," and "Dog" use this device to advantage, the power of enumeration and accumulation driving the emotional register to crescendo after crescendo. In "Morning Walk," Oliver describes the fate of whelks:

> they come one by one
> to the shore
>
> to the shallows
> to the mussel-dappled rocks
>
> to the rise to dryness
> to the edge of the town

Streams of propositional phrases and longer structures roll and carry Oliver's images in a processional fugue.

A less frequently used device, but one that also sends out a wave-like pulse, is the stanza in which successive lines begin further and further from the left-hand margin. This is the technique of "The Rapture"—one of those poems that most compactly announces Oliver's own credo—and "Shelley," which gives specific reference to the key images in Shelley's credo poem "Ode to the West Wind." "At the Shore" uses a similar technique in uneven groupings rather than the four-line stanzas favored in the aforementioned two poems as well as "Little Summer Poem Touching the Subject of Faith" which includes the following passages:

> And, therefore, let the immeasurable come.
> Let the unknowable touch the buckle of my spine.
> Let the wind turn in the trees,
> and the mystery hidden in dirt
>
> swing through the air.
> How could I look at anything in this world
> and tremble, and grip my hands over my heart?
> What should I fear?

As one might expect, many of Oliver's poems take their focal points and titles from a single natural kind. "Seven White Butterflies," "Black Oaks," "Pilot Snake," "Maples," "The Osprey," and "Fox" are among those works in which Oliver often goes beyond appreciative and moving description to enter a world of imagined sensibility. For Oliver, a plant or animal is uniquely itself but also a map of the larger creation. Each, too, is a challenge to human knowing and human language. Particularly in "Fox," Oliver addresses the issue of interplay between the thing out there, the experience that flows through her, and the role and limits of language. Her poem is at once about the fox, the poet's response, and the process of the poem. The poet, watching carefully, chooses "among the vast assortment of words/ that it should run again and again across the page" until the reader will "shiver with praise" as Oliver has done.

Oliver, then, combines several hallmark concerns of English Romantic poetry in her strikingly contemporary work. Like her literary ancestors, she pays attention to nature itself somewhat less than she pays attention to how it moves her. Her response, as in the lines from "Little Summer Poem" quoted previously, borders on an ecstatic mysticism. Like them also, she is concerned with the poet's mission as an intermediary between nature's expressiveness and humankind. However, as did Shelley and John Keats, Oliver finds this mission is complicated by the ultimate failure of language to handle the task. In "Stars" she claims, "Here in my head, language/ keeps making its tiny noises," suggesting her distance from the rest of the created world. Then she asks:

> How can I hope to be friends
> with the hard white stars
>
> whose flaring and hissing are not speech
> but a pure radiance?

Nevertheless, the impulse to make language do as well as it can to conjure within readers the voices and expressive force of the natural world drives Oliver on.

"Three Songs," found in the first part of the book, is a sequence of prose poems. The title is somewhat ironic, these pieces being at first sight the least lyrical in the collection. Except for the lack of functional lineation, however, there is nothing to distinguish these compositions from Oliver's other work. "Three Songs" anticipates the scattering of prose poems found within part 2, "West Wind." Oliver's attitude toward the prose poems seems a bit uneasy. On the one hand, she needs to call attention to their difference by giving the collection the subtitle "Poems and Prose Poems." In "Three Songs," she asks if prose can sing. Yet in "West Wind" she allows an unself-conscious mixing of these types, downplaying the distinction.

The untitled sections of "West Wind" do not form a markedly cohesive unit. The conceptual and formal ranges are not significantly different from those in part 1, and if the individual units in the sequence had titles, they could be interchanged with the poems found in that initial section. One difference, however, perhaps enough to justify the sequence notion, is the frequent reference to an ambiguous "you," as if the poems were written with a specific listener in mind. The references to "you" give a dramatic heightening to these poems, suggesting the ongoing inner story of a relationship. Many segments of "West Wind" are among the strongest poems in the collection: Numbers 3, 6, 11, and 13 seem to cry out for titles and independence.

The final section of *West Wind*, "Have You Ever Tried to Enter the Long Black

Branches," is a masterpiece of its kind and deserves the special emphasis it receives both as a poem standing alone and as the poem that concludes this fine collection. For power of expression and mastery of technique, it is rivaled only by "Am I Not Among the Early Risers" of part 1. Both are certain to take their places as anthology pieces. In the closing poem, Oliver addresses her readers, challenging them to enter into other lives as well as into the very being of leaf, water, and wing. She knows that the world is filled with people who feel that their lives are missing some important dimension, and she is sure that they have not willed themselves to be explorers of what nature has to offer. She frets that we are "breathing just a little, and calling it a life" while there is so much more that life will offer if we risk to accept it. Just as "Am I Not Among the Early Risers" presents Oliver's own fulfilling lifetime of habits, so the culminating poem insists that this fulfillment is sharable, that it could—and perhaps should—be duplicated by others. Her accomplishment in this fine collection is to persuade readers that they can share her intense joy.

Philip K. Jason

Sources for Further Study

Booklist. XCIII, June 1, 1997, p. 1648.
Boston. LXXXIX, May, 1997, p. 119.
Library Journal. CXXII, July, 1997, p. 87.
Publishers Weekly. CCXLIV, June 30, 1997, p. 73.

WHAT THE LIVING DO

Author: Marie Howe (1950-   )
Publisher: W. W. Norton (New York). 91 pp. $21.00
Type of work: Poetry

These poems form an elegy for Howe's brother John, who died at age twenty-eight; in coming to terms with his death, Howe reflects on their early family life and on her adult relationships with family, friends, and lovers

The traditions of the elegy include not only a statement of the mourner's grief at the death of the subject but also, usually, a documentation of that grief with an account of the past relationship between the subject and speaker. Moreover, elegies of the past usually concluded by offering some sort of consolation from which the survivors might take heart. Although the late twentieth century challenged many of poetry's traditional forms, the essential elements of the elegy remain perceptible in Marie Howe's volume *What the Living Do*, a collection of poems that memorializes her brother John, who died at age twenty-eight, and that also marks the deaths of other people important to the poet. The mode of these poems, however, has much in common with the work of contemporary poets such as Sharon Olds; Howe's voice is personal and colloquial, and her descriptions of her relationships with the people to whom this book is dedicated are often detailed and frank. However, her purposes are those that have always been associated with the elegy—to find meaning in the suffering and deaths of loved ones and to find a means by which the survivors can somehow redeem their losses.

Poems in the first section of the volume record events from the speaker's childhood; her brother figures in these poems, but he is not their main focus. A central theme of this section concerns the sexuality of children. "Sixth Grade," for example, relates how a gang of neighborhood twelve-year-olds harasses the speaker and a friend one summer. As the bullying increases, so does its sexual suggestion. Only the speaker's direct appeal to a friend of her brother defuses the violence that seems imminent. In "Practicing," the poet records the long sessions of "practice" kissing she shares with other seventh-grade girls as they prepare for the real kisses they will soon share with boys.

This section also portrays conflicts between the speaker's father and the family's children. The book's first poem, "The Boy," relates how the speaker's older brother runs away from home to prevent his father from cutting his hair. He runs to a nearby vacant-lot hangout, and, after a few days, the speaker is sent to coax him home with the promise that there will be no reprisals. When the brother returns, the father shaves his head; the brother refuses to speak for the next month. This poem makes a sort of epigraph for this section of the book. It concludes:

> What happened in our house taught my brothers how to leave, how to walk
> down a sidewalk without looking back.
>
> I was the girl. What happened taught me to follow him, whoever he was,
> calling and calling his name.

The most painful revelation of this section concerns the speaker's sexual abuse by her father. "The Mother" portrays a passive woman who cannot defend her daughter against the abuse she knows is going on. Only the older brother offers to help her. He sits like "an exiled prince grown hard in his confinement" in his attic bedroom, designing dream buildings for a drafting class and listening while their father enters the speaker's bedroom across the hall. When the father leaves, he goes to his sister and sits with his arm around her: "I don't know if he knows he's building a world where I can one day/ love a man."

The next section begins to detail John's decline and death, beginning with "For Three Days." The title refers to the three days in which the speaker has tried to think of another word for "gratitude," the gratitude she feels at her brother's escape from a death that seemed almost certain as the family gathered around him in the intensive care unit. At the same time, Howe notes, guiltily, that she had already begun to imagine him dead and to plan what she would write about him. The poem ends with a reference to Jesus' raising of the dead Lazarus. When Lazarus's sister saw him alive, Howe says, she was "crushed . . . with gratitude and shame." (Howe uses a similar biblical reference to Lazarus's sisters Mary and Martha toward the end of this collection in "Memorial," a poem about the death of a friend.)

Howe's editing of *In the Company of My Solitude: American Writing from the AIDS Pandemic* (1995, edited with Michael Klein) suggests that her brother John was dying of AIDS; the character Joe, who appears in this section, may have been John's lover. The focus of this section, however, is on the slow-motion process of death rather than on its clinical details or the politics of its cause, and the details will seem familiar to anyone who has watched the gradual decline of a loved one. The process is painfully slow and painfully inevitable. Meanwhile, life goes on outside the sickroom in all its heedless beauty. "Rochester, New York, July 1989" depicts a summer evening in which children ride bicycles and the air is full of the scents of grass and lilac. Someone is sitting with John, while, from an apartment below, the piano teacher keeps her promise to play softly for him. The music of Frédéric-François Chopin drifts up to the sitter's ears so softly that it may go unnoticed until it stops, "the way you know a scent from a flowering tree once you've passed it." The theme of dying's quiet is restated in "Without Music"; Howe labels the silence: "Somebody sleeping. Someone watching somebody sleep."

John's death is recorded in the poem "Faulkner." On the day of his death, Joe is reading William Faulkner's novel *As I Lay Dying* (1930) for an English course. He tries to tell the speaker about the plot (a complex one in which the mother's death is related from many points of view), and, in the evening, while waiting for the inevitable arrival of relatives bearing food, the speaker tries to read the novel but stops, unable to concentrate. Instead, through the next few days, she recalls a line from another Faulkner novel, *The Sound and the Fury* (1929), in which the idiot brother Benjy recalls his sister's smell.

The section ends not with the death itself or the poem "The Grave" (relating the speaker's visit to John's grave a year after his death) but with "One of the Last Days," in which she recalls telling John that she loves him as much as he loves Joe; his ironic response is that she might need to begin looking for someone else.

The poems of the next section deal with life after John's death and suggest how one traumatic event can become bound up with others that happen at roughly the same time as the first. Two characters who appear in the section are the poet Jane Kenyon (who died in 1995) and the speaker's lover James. In "Wanting a Child," she thinks about her physical love for James and about Jane Kenyon, lying in the hospital, already bald from chemotherapy. The speaker finds something about the simplicity of Kenyon's situation to be almost enviable. Although it is a snowy night, a vase of daffodils sits on the fireplace mantle in the speaker's house, somehow evoking the poem's opening statement that "trees endure/ what we/ don't want—the long dead months before the appalling blossoms."

Instead of blossoming into childbirth, however, the speaker quarrels with James, and, for a time, they are estranged. The quarrel is recorded in "Watching Television," where the speaker describes a nature special in which a spider carries around the egg sac containing her hundreds of babies. The speaker says that the real subject of the quarrel was never stated, but the spider image suggests that it concerned having a child. The images of emptiness at the end of the poem imply both barrenness and the drained relationship: "Anything I've ever tried to keep by force I've lost." In the empty months following the speaker's estrangement from James, Jane Kenyon dies. "Prayer" unites the themes of love and death in a time when "the man I love has forgotten my smell." Howe goes on:

> And Jane is dead,
>
>   and I want to go where she went,
>
> where my brother went,
>
> and whoever it is that whispered to me
>
> when I was a child in my father's bed is come back now . . .

The "whisperer" murmurs the frightening news that her life will always be as full of anxiety and estrangement as it is now. Only with effort does she recall another, more hopeful, story that lingers in the back of her mind. That hope is validated in the next poem, "Two or Three Times," where she recalls the fragile radiance her father seemed to emit during those two or three times when he tried to quit drinking, the same cracked light she sees from James as he returns, bringing her a deli tray, coffee, and a Danish. Their reunion is described in several poems at the end of this section, reminding the reader that it was her brother John who enabled the speaker to love a man.

The collection's last two poems confirm the consolation in this elegy. Having established the past life she shared with her brother and having documented the pain of his death, the speaker now recalls "What the Living Do." In the harsh realities of daily life in a bitter winter, the annoyances of clogged drains and spilled coffee, and, behind those annoyances, the deep pain of loss, she still finds moments when she cherishes her own living and sees that cherishing as a kind of memorial to John. The collection's last poem pictures a dog, Buddy, who leaps up in excitement when he hears the word "walk," thinking it refers to him. The dog cannot understand the difference between the sign and the thing itself: "how we can talk about something when/ it's not/ even there . . . the way I talk about John." The consolation people find in death lies in their memories of those they have loved.

The poems of this collection are, for the most part, very accessible in language and syntax. Most of them use a long line, colloquial diction ("that silly Buddy" the speaker calls the dog), and the settings of everyday life (households, winter landscapes, a street corner near the video store). A minor exception may lie in the numerous proper names: These poems seem so autobiographical that the reader soon attaches some of the personages of the poems to the persons named on the dedication page and identifies the poems' speaker as identical to the writer Marie Howe, a violation of the practice that separates a poem's persona from its composer. Such an identification, however, is probably not dangerous in a volume as personal as this.

This volume's simplicity should not be taken to imply prosiness, however. The clarity of Howe's imagery (the daffodils on the mantle, a vase of purple tulips, the sound of snowplows or of Chopin) and the rhythms of her language, whether in long lines or, as in "The Kiss," in short lines, all remind the reader that the elegy, traditionally, is poetry and that the significance of its memorial is established, in part, by the way its language suggests that this death is worthy of our attention.

One reads not so much to learn about others' losses as to understand and even, perhaps, to redeem one's own. That is why Howe has chosen to tell readers what the living do.

Ann D. Garbett

Sources for Further Study

Commercial Appeal. November 16, 1997, p. G3.
Library Journal. CXXII, October 15, 1997, p. 65.
Ploughshares. XXIII, Winter, 1997, p. 221.
Publishers Weekly. CCXLIV, October 27, 1997, p. 71.

WHEN THE SONS OF HEAVEN MEET THE DAUGHTERS OF THE EARTH

Author: Fernanda Eberstadt (1960-   )
Publisher: Alfred A. Knopf (New York). 404 pp. $25.00
Type of work: Novel
Time: The late 1980's
Locale: New York City

Isaac Hooker, a homeless vagrant, Harvard drop-out, short-order cook, and frame-shop employee, paints a biblical narrative and becomes the toast of the art world—but at what cost?

Principal characters:
    ISAAC HOOKER, an artist, age twenty-five, from Gilboa, New Hampshire
    DOROTHEA (DOLLY) DIEHL GEBLER, the head of the Aurora Foundation
      for the Arts
    ALFRED GEBLER, the director of the Aurora Foundation for the Arts, a
      gourmand who married money—and spends it
    CASEY HANRAHAN, Isaac's college friend, now with the Aurora
      Foundation
    WILLA PERKINS, the creator of *Ajax*, an avant-garde opera, and an artist
      with the Aurora Foundation

In this brilliant novel, Isaac Hooker (a character loosely based on artist Jean Michel Basquiat and about whom Fernanda Eberstadt has written in two previous novels, *Low Tide*, 1985, and *Isaac and His Devils*, 1991) is a small town New Hampshire wunderkind who, when awarded a scholarship to Harvard, drops out and goes to New York City, "which everyone came to, on the supposition that here he would be better equipped to execute his life's work, whatever it might be." A mugging, a broken arm, a bout of homelessness, and a total of two years of down-and-outness lead, by a series of deftly narrated chances and happenstances, to an art class in a Henry Street residence for homeless men, where Isaac works in the kitchen. He watches then joins the class and finds salvation "hungry as a thief for orange and scarlet and green and purple crayons, for dry, whispery charcoals, thick sheets of empty paper." However, "every subject in the world" seems to be a "brightly colored cluster bomb" and every memory has "a fizzing fuse on it waiting to blow up in your face." After some days of staring at the paper, he begins to draw what is in his memory: his room in Gilboa and the home that he left there. Creating pictures is now all he wants to do, and his drawings of empty rooms reek of loneliness and guilt. Then he begins to draw people— specifically, a tribe of dead people, including his father in his coffin. "Something big had changed," and Eberstadt permits readers to view this birth of an artist, to witness his struggles first with memory, then with materials and technique and the fires of creation. The discovery of the demands of unrelenting recognition and their consequences will come next. First, however, Isaac has to survive. Eberstadt must plot his way out of Henry Street.

Depending on a lucky coincidence to resolve a plot is considered amateurish, but allowing it to begin one is brilliant (Oedipus at the crossroads, for example). Therefore, Isaac must discover that he is not alone. Acting on a hint from a friend, Isaac goes unannounced to the Aurora Foundation for the Arts to seek work, perhaps as an installer or a framer, but his encounter with Alfred Gebler, director of the Foundation, ends disastrously: Isaac has been directed into Alfred's office and has seated himself in the Director's chair, making himself quite at home, his homeless smell and dress contrasting sharply with the white purity of the Foundation. Alfred, outraged at this unseemly intrusion by this "ogre," throws Isaac out of his office. Wandering, Isaac stops by Washington Square Park for rounds of speed chess, where he encounters, by chance, a friend from college, Casey Hanrahan, who has a job with Aurora and to whom Aurora has given "a hundred thousand dollars and five thousand feet of exhibition space to fill." Casey promises to win Isaac a second audience with Alfred at a later date, but Isaac insists on going back the same evening to retrieve his oil sticks, which he left behind in Alfred's office. Encountering a lonely Alfred, a man who made "frantic efforts never to be alone," Isaac not only retrieves his oil sticks but also receives dinner, a night on the town, and an invitation to the opening of Willa Perkins's opera and the party at the Geblers's afterward. Thus, he enters the cosseted world of foundations and the New York art "scene" of the 1980's, his chance encounter with a long-lost friend abruptly and arbitrarily reversing his fortune. Thus begins Isaac's association with the people who provide place and comfort and a measure of peace for those artists "lucky" enough to be chosen beneficiaries of Aurora's wealth.

Readers are wary, however. Early and sudden material success often destroys the artistic talent, whatever the medium. Still, artistic genius is heaven-sent, the inspired, mad artist a "son of heaven." In this novel, Isaac emerges as one of these sons of heaven who, indeed, meets and grapples and couples with the daughters of the earth. The result, as figured in Eberstadt's rich and succulent novel, is wonderfully worth reading.

Eberstadt structures the novel like a symphony, exploring fully and richly its principal themes of the connections, often ironic, of art and wealth, and the rise and fall of the artist in the rich world of capitalism. A number of subsidiary motifs balance, shade, and darken the whole. Its reasonably straight-forward narrative—interpreted with necessary (and marvelously skillful) flashbacks to fill in background about characters, the Aurora Foundation, and the art world of New York City—chronicles the passion of Isaac, characterizing not only individuals but also the city of New York and, indeed, postmodern America. These themes include: immigration, high society, the sundering of the iron curtain, the city, the country, class, poverty and homelessness, wealth and conspicuous consumption, marriage, infidelity, and, above all else, art. Eberstadt renders each in action, dialogue, and exquisitely rich detail; her mastery of keen observation and the English language is apparent in every sentence.

The New York art scene, in particular, is the setting for much of the action—the cozy if angst-ridden environment of pretentious yet hopeful artists ranging from "installers" and "performance" charlatans, safe from discovery that they are, indeed, quite naked, to artists whose capacity for suffering, whether in Eastern Europe or New York City itself, informs their painting, music, or dance and whose talent for rendering that experience in various media yields art that engrosses, overwhelms, and trans-forms. Artists of both sorts have been swept up in the benevolent clutches of the Aurora Foundation, the beneficiaries (and perhaps victims) of the largesse of Dorothea ("Dolly") Gebler and her husband Alfred. Dolly (and her wealth) comes from a Chicago family whose social circle includes people so rich that they "don't know where the kitchen is." Dolly, trying, at one point, to resolve her own ambiguity about her inherited wealth, notes that her father had

> made his fortune from scratch . . . . had nothing to feel guilty about . . . was a smart man who knew the world and worked like a galley slave till the day he died. . . . But for the next generation, everybody hates you on principle, and quite right, too. I remember our nursemaid pinching us when nobody was looking. Why not? She was the eldest of six children, she'd gone to work at fourteen, she couldn't bear the sight of these petted princesses in velvet coats and patent-leather shoes with their superior snobbish little attitudes, throwing tantrums if their ponies weren't ready on time. That's part of what I mind about money—it makes one very silly and ignorant, being so cut off from reality.

However, instead of being "careless" people, such as Daisy and Tom Buchanan in F. Scott Fitzgerald's *The Great Gatsby* (1925), the Geblers, motivated by Dolly's passionate belief that art can (and should) change the world, create the Aurora Foundation to pour millions "into exhibiting all that was most advanced in a setting pure as an ice palace." It is quite different from her father's foundation: Charles Diehl, having made his fortune in pharmaceuticals, had set up his foundation in Chicago and gave money to museums, universities, and orchestras. Dolly, unsuccessful in her attempts to control her father's foundation upon his death, took her portion of the income from the company and established Aurora in New York City with her husband Alfred, whose devotion to the pleasures of the sensual contrasts starkly with Dolly's devotion to promoting the idea that art can change the world. She backs up her belief by spending freely: "Mrs. Gebler didn't believe in nickel-and-diming; she thought art could change the world, and that anything that aimed for less wasn't interesting. She was unperturbed by the incongruity of her situation: a capitalist queen, a woman of conservative instincts and worldview, using her riches to subvert capitalism." Her work was not, however, without criticism. Under attack for promoting "the transcen-dency of individual talent," for validating an oppressive power structure, Aurora becomes the means for Eberstadt to wittily treat the theme of political correctness with a refreshing irony.

Another major theme is that of the city versus the country: the vitality and excitement of the city, its wealth and energy, its danger and destructiveness, contrasting strongly with the creative and restorative power of the country. Nothing, however, is as simple as it seems. The frozen landscapes of Isaac's New Hampshire home, with its stark interiors and gaunt, emotionally straited inhabitants, provide him with inspiration and an emotional foundation, and the quiet, Long Island country home of the Geblers gives him the place and the peace to create. The city, however, tests and tries each artistic move, mugs and makes its creator and, finally, with its excess of wealth and distraction, cripples or destroys the creative capacity.

Eberstadt's keen intelligence, her powers of observation, her knowledge, and her control of language (particularly diction and cadence) make for prose that is always rich, always right, always a treat to read and savor. She excels in encapsulating, in a deft sentence or two, the world of art, the intensity of its creation and the occasional banality of its reception, idolization, and commercialization. This description of Willa Perkins's career at the opening of her opera provides a good example:

> [Willa]... having spent the seventies performing in basement gyms and the eighties scooping up European commissions for ten-hour spectacles in Stuttgart and Cologne, had at last come home famous, an American phenomenon magnetic enough to attract this small pride of bejewelled lionesses in taffeta and skinny legs, accompanied by husbands wearing double-breasted suits and velvet slippers, men who were wondering why they had allowed their wives to drag them below Fiftieth Street and how soon they could get to bed, for word had already got out that the piece was very long.

Here, she skillfully suggests the tensions between the work of an artist and the world of foundation largesse. Even more successful is her economical rendering of Isaac's initial resistance to Dolly's offer of the country home at Goose Neck as a place to work, succumbing finally to the gift of time and place, trusting "that his new calling was sufficient antagonist to the old demons. Besides, now he had a body of work to get done, a patroness who believed in him, a Manhattan dealer who might be willing to exhibit his paintings." As he works on his drawings for each element of his painting *When the Sons of Heaven Meet the Daughters of the Earth*, he must teach himself how to accomplish the particular effects his vision has proffered him—rendering fog by rubbing wood ash directly on the paper, considering how "to place his splayed girl more convincingly upon" the lush "slipperiness of decaying tree trunks, the curling sheen of ivy underfoot, the clayey declivity of the bank," deciding how "to angle the ram so that you could see his body sidelong but also his yellow eyes and horns, could tell he was not approaching but was backing away, the act discharged. There was an antinomianism he enjoyed in having this rank, ambiguous son of God come down to rut with the earthly daughter, taking the shape not of a lamb, but of a ram." The completed painting, a canvas of six feet by eight feet, marks Isaac as a throwback, in some senses, to an earlier, more narrative art than New York is accustomed to seeing. With the backing of the Geblers, Isaac takes the town by storm. And then what? After the teas, the cakes, the ices? After the receptions and studio visits? What project? What vision? The education of the artist has yet another course to complete, and, along the way, he and his principal supporter must learn even more about love and distance.

Theodore C. Humphrey

Sources for Further Study

Art in America. LXXXV, July, 1997, p. 29.
Artforum. XXXV, June 1, 1997, p. 25.
Booklist. XCIII, March, 1997, p. 1109.

Harper's Bazaar. March, 1997, p. 278.
Library Journal. CXXII, March 1, 1997, p. 101.
Los Angeles Times. June 23, 1997, p. E3.
Maclean's. CX, June 23, 1997, p. 52.
The New York Times Book Review. CII, March 30, 1997, p. 8.
Publishers Weekly. CCXLIV, January 20, 1997, p. 391.
The Times Literary Supplement. August 22, 1997, p. 23.
Vanity Fair. CLXXXIX, March, 1997, p. 132.
Vogue. CLXXXVII, March, 1997, p. 318.
The Wall Street Journal. March 10, 1997, p. A16.

WHITTAKER CHAMBERS
A Biography

Author: Sam Tanenhaus
Publisher: Random House (New York). 638 pp. $35.00
Type of work: Biography
Time: 1901-1961
Locale: New York; New Jersey; Washington, D.C.; and Maryland

A comprehensive, sympathetic biography of the Communist spy and valiant anti-Communist whose testimony against former government official Alger Hiss became a cause célèbre that helped to define the Cold War era

> *Principal personages:*
> WHITTAKER CHAMBERS, an American Communist turned anti-Communist activist
> JAY VIVIAN CHAMBERS, his father
> LAHA CHAMBERS, his mother
> RICHARD CHAMBERS, his brother
> ESTHER CHAMBERS, his wife
> ALGER HISS, a government official and president of the Carnegie Endowment for World Peace whom Chambers accused of espionage for the Soviet Union
> PRISCILLA HISS, Alger's wife
> HENRY LUCE, the owner of Time, Inc., Chambers's employer
> RICHARD NIXON, the congressman most responsible for advancing the Hiss-Chambers investigation
> BERT ANDREWS, a newspaperman who worked with Nixon to expose Hiss
> LLOYD PAUL STRYKER, Hiss's flamboyant defense attorney in his first trial
> THOMAS MURPHY, the prosecutor of Hiss's two perjury trials

In many respects the Hiss-Chambers investigation and trial can be viewed as shaping the Cold War era. Although Alger Hiss continues to have some partisans today, most historians agree that Whittaker Chambers's testimony has been vindicated and that he did expose Hiss and others as members of an extensive Soviet espionage ring. In addition to a narrative that amply reveals Hiss's culpability, Sam Tanenhaus gives *Whittaker Chambers: A Biography* an appendix that sets out the overwhelming evidence against Hiss and explains his futile efforts to refute it.

Tanenhaus approaches his story in measured, objective tones. He does not minimize Chambers's weaknesses or spare his subject criticism, but the biographer does maintain a sympathetic tone and respect for a figure still vilified by remnants of the Left and consecrated as a saint by the Right. Chambers was more complicated than these labels suggest, and Tanenhaus deserves considerable praise for his finely tuned accounts of Chambers's changing moods and political positions.

Who was Whittaker Chambers? Tanenhaus takes a conventional approach, beginning with a childhood troubled by his father's confused sexuality and his brother

Richard's suicide. Jay Vivian Chambers was bisexual, a condition that made him miserable and hard on his family. He left home for long periods, lived with other men, and endured the contempt of family members who regarded him as unmanly and perverted. His son did not realize that his father was bisexual until years later, when he found himself attracted to both men and women and the center of more than one ménage à trois. Named for his father, he abandoned Jay Vivian for his mother's family name, Whittaker, and staked out an identity as a Communist and writer during his years at Columbia University.

Chambers had a formidable intellect and imagination. His professors at Columbia considered him the best of his generation, and fellow students—such as the art critic Meyer Shapiro and the literary critic Lionel Trilling—swore by his integrity as well as his genius. Chambers produced some of the best proletarian fiction and became an editor of *The New Masses*. His rebellious streak ended a promising education at Columbia, which was followed by episodes of bumming around the country and working as a manual laborer. He lived the life of a proletarian that most leftists only dreamed of.

Chambers had been a conservative before he was a Communist, but it is clear that he engaged in a lifelong quest for a spiritual and political solution to his agonized need for meaning, and that his return to a religious and traditional position later in life constituted not so much a betrayal of radicalism as an extension of his earliest yearnings for salvation. Marriage, family, and a farm represented his attempts to settle down, yet he could not forswear a life of action and political involvement—first as a member of the Communist underground, then as a writer for *Time*, and finally as a government witness against former Communists and spies.

Chambers had an independent spirit that balked at Communist Party discipline, a spirit he could control only as long as he thought the Communist Party represented human renewal and an antidote to the corruption of capitalism. Seeing the Party from the inside, however, convinced him that Communism was more corrupt than the system it sought to subvert. He broke with the party in the late 1930's, fearing for his life but eventually establishing a respected, if controversial, position at *Time* as an extraordinary book reviewer and scourge of liberals and Communists.

Chambers first approached the government in 1939 with information about Communists in the Roosevelt administration. Although he named Hiss and others as officials who were passing sensitive secret government information to the Soviets, Chambers was largely ignored as the country mobilized for World War II. The Federal Bureau of Investigation (FBI), for example, was more concerned with Nazi infiltrators than with Communists, especially after the United States and the Soviet Union became allies.

After the war, the political climate began to change. The Republican Party gained seats in Congress, and much of President Franklin Roosevelt's New Deal program became suspect. The House Committee on Un-American Activities (HUAC) investigated Communist influence in Hollywood, the labor unions, and government. Yet such congressional investigations were often done sloppily and for obvious political gain.

HUAC abused its witnesses and destroyed the careers of people who were labeled Communists or fellow travelers (those aiding the Communist cause).

Tanenhaus follows Richard Nixon's biographers and other historians who credit Nixon with reviving and legitimizing the anti-Communist crusade. Nixon and HUAC investigator Robert Stripling were alone in believing Chambers's charges that Hiss had been and perhaps still was a Communist. Hiss had had a brilliant career in government, culminating in his work at Yalta alongside Roosevelt. As president of the Carnegie Endowment for World Peace, Hiss was one of the most important postwar opinion makers. It was dreadful to think that he had advised the ailing Roosevelt at Yalta, where to many anti-Communists it seemed Roosevelt had capitulated to Soviet designs in Eastern Europe and elsewhere.

Tanenhaus is adept at showing how the odds were against Chambers and Nixon. Hiss had impeccable references. He dressed well, moved elegantly, and was unflappable in his assertion of innocence. Chambers was fat, disheveled-looking in his rumpled suits, and an admitted Communist who had lied and deceived others for nearly a decade and had perjured himself in testimony before government committees. Nearly all the important columnists wrote sympathetic profiles of Hiss. Only the daily newspapers, Tanenhaus reports, tried to report evenhandedly on the case.

Hiss could not be charged with espionage, because the statute of limitations had run out. Based on Chambers's testimony and Hiss's denials, however, Hiss was tried for perjury. On the one hand, the government had a strong case. Chambers testified in detail about Hiss's habits and intimate life. Chambers possessed government documents in Hiss's handwriting. Chambers's wife Esther corroborated his story and testified to her friendship with Hiss's wife, Priscilla. The government was able to show that Priscilla had typed documents on her typewriter that matched those in Chambers's possession. On the other hand, Hiss alleged that Chambers could have stolen the documents from Hiss's office because of lax government security. Hiss intimated that Chambers was a delusional writer who had concocted a fanciful story, and Priscilla Hiss corroborated her husband's staunch denials of any involvement with Communists or espionage. Most of all, Hiss stood on his impeccable public record.

The first perjury trial ended in a hung jury—precisely the outcome that Hiss's attorney, Lloyd Paul Stryker, had sought. Stryker did not believe that he had the evidence to exonerate his client, but he had thought that by dwelling on Chambers's unsavory background he could create enough doubt in the jury to ensure that it could not reach a unanimous verdict. After all, the government could not show how Chambers had acquired Hiss's documents, and Hiss did not deny knowing Chambers (under the pseudonym George Crosley). It was just possible, in other words, that the parts of the Hiss and Chambers versions that overlapped accounted for the fact that both men admitted knowing each other and yet fashioned such different interpretations of what their friendship had meant.

Even so, the first trial ended with eight of twelve jurors ready to convict Hiss. Tanenhaus treats Hiss as an arrogant liar who thought that he could bluff his way out of a jam. The wise course would have been to continue Stryker's tactics in a second trial. Instead, Hiss hired a lawyer who went all out for his exoneration. Thus Hiss's lawyer had to resort to theories about how a typewriter could be constructed to mimic Priscilla Hiss's machine. Such a machine was produced, but it took more than a year to manufacture, and it still had flaws that allowed experts to tell the difference between it and Priscilla's typewriter. Even more important, according to Tanenhaus, was the change in political climate. Before the Hiss trial, less than half of the American public believed that there had been a Communist conspiracy inside the U.S. government. After the first Hiss trial, a majority of the American people were prepared to believe not only in Hiss's guilt but also in a widespread Communist espionage ring.

Although Chambers and Nixon triumphed, they were vilified for years in the liberal press. Tanenhaus shows that Nixon certainly played the Hiss case to his political advantage and that Chambers became a political partisan close to Nixon and other Republicans. Yet the idea that Chambers made up his evidence, or that exposure of Hiss and other spies was simply a political attack on the New Deal, is untenable. Nixon was a first-rate investigator, and much of his work was corroborated by Bert Andrews, a *Herald Tribune* journalist initially skeptical of Chambers's charges. The evidence against Hiss has only strengthened in recent years.

Although Chambers became a patron saint of the Right in the last ten years of his life, he developed a more nuanced politics than most of the ideologues who supported him. He was initially sympathetic to Joseph McCarthy, but Chambers realized that McCarthy's thuggish tactics seriously damaged the anti-Communist cause. Yet he did not publicly repudiate McCarthy or the excesses of anti-Communism. In private, he expressed his reservations to conservatives such as William F. Buckley, Jr., whose *National Review* grew in part out of Chambers's apocalyptic view of a world in struggle against a Communist conspiracy.

Except during the trials, Esther Chambers receives little attention in this book. How she interacted with her husband, and why she believed strongly in him, is never explained. Besides sifting the evidence at the end of the biography, Tanenhaus might have teased out the implications of the Hiss-Chambers case. It did considerable damage to the American Left that is still not well understood because of the focus on the evils of McCarthyism. Certainly the witch-hunting associated with the reckless McCarthy constitutes a deplorable episode in American history. Yet so is the blindness of many liberals who insisted on Hiss's innocence even in the face of mounting, irrefutable evidence. As reporter Rebecca West put it, the Hiss-Chambers case was like the Dreyfus trial in reverse. Whereas Alfred Dreyfus was pronounced guilty before he was tried, largely because he was Jewish, Hiss was pronounced innocent before the evidence against him was carefully assessed because he was a New Deal liberal. The Hiss-Chambers case can seem a relic of the past in the post-Cold War world, yet it demeaned political dialogue in ways that still deform America's civic life.

Lisa Paddock

Sources for Further Study

America. CLXXVII, July 19, 1997, p. 25.

Chicago Tribune. March 16, 1997, p. 3.

Commentary. CIII, February, 1997, p. 61.

The Economist. CCCXLIII, June 21, 1997, p. 6.

Houston Chronicle. March 2, 1997, p. 27.

Los Angeles Times. March 2, 1997, p. 4.

The Nation. CCLXIV, February 17, 1997, p. 27.

The New Republic. CCXVI, April 14, 1997, p. 38.

The New York Times Book Review. CII, March 9, 1997, p. 5.

The New Yorker. March 17, 1997, pp. 112-17.

Publishers Weekly. CCXLIII, December 16, 1996, p. 48.

Time. CXLIX, March 10, 1997, p. 88.

The Times Literary Supplement. June 6, 1997, p. 9.

USA Today. March 27, 1997, p. D6.

The Wall Street Journal. February 20, 1997, p. A18.

The Washington Post Book Review. March 9, 1997, p. 1.

THE WHOLE SHEBANG
A State-of-the-Universe(s) Report

Author: Timothy Ferris (1944-   )
Publisher: Simon & Schuster (New York). Illustrated. 464 pp. $25.00
Type of work: Science

Beginning with the big bang theory, Ferris provides an accessible, nontechnical overview of the history, current theories, and future direction of modern cosmological research

Henry David Thoreau noted in his masterpiece, *Walden*, "The universe is wider than our views of it." His observation sprung more from intuition than scientific knowledge of the whole scale structure of the cosmos. It was not until the twentieth century that Thoreau's 1847 pronouncement on the state of the universe would be substantiated by scientific evidence. Extraordinary discoveries, especially in the fields of astronomy and physics, have forever changed our perceptions of the universe and of our place in it.

The advent of dynamic new theories, as well as cutting-edge technology, gave birth to the infant science of cosmology and propelled it into adulthood. Exotic ideas such as the big bang, black holes, quantum leap, and the space-time continuum were eagerly explored by the scientific community. Such concepts even became part of pop culture as science fiction writers appropriated them as literary devices. Timothy Ferris, respected science writer and professor emeritus of journalism at the University of California at Berkeley, addresses these and other abstract concepts in *The Whole Shebang: A State-of-the-Universe(s) Report*. Shunning mathematical equations and convoluted interpretations, Ferris offers an engrossing, comprehensive, and comprehensible report on how science views not only the beginning of creation but the current—and future—state of the universe as well. His lucid treatment of difficult concepts such as quantum uncertainty, relativity, inflationary models of the universe, and "string" theory aids the general reader in understanding the puzzling structure of the universe as it is understood by astronomers and physicists.

Beginning with a historical overview, Ferris traces how the human perception of the universe has changed over time. He covers familiar ground as he hits the highlights: Ptolemy's epicycles, Copernicus's sun-centered universe, Kepler's laws of planetary motion, Galileo's concept of inertia, Newton's law of gravity, Einstein's theory of relativity, the much-debated Hubble constant, and finally the big bang theory, which shapes our modern concept of "the beginning." Ferris's discussion of this material may be familiar to some readers. But to those who have little background in physics or astronomy, understanding these theories is vital to comprehending other, more difficult concepts presented later in the book.

One of the most engaging chapters in the book comes early on when Ferris launches into a discussion about the controversy surrounding the theory of black holes. These strange objects defy our earth-bound perceptions of space and time as they gobble up stars unlucky enough to cross their paths. Their masses are so dense and their gravitational fields so strong that nothing nearby can escape their feeding frenzies. As space curves around itself, past, present, and future become indistinct from one another within the black hole, cut off from the rest of the universe. Current research indicates that black holes, once thought to be rare, are quite common. Found at the centers of galaxies, they are responsible for the annihilation of millions of suns. From the basics of thermodynamics to the weird world of wormholes, Ferris's coherent discussion of black holes, while based on solid science, still manages to convey the wonder cosmologists feel as they strive to understand the properties of these peculiar objects.

Ferris's account concerning the unraveling of the mystery surrounding black holes is engrossing enough, but he also gives the reader a glimpse of the personal side of science when he recounts the David and Goliath-like battle between graduate student Jacob Bekenstein and famed cosmologist Stephen Hawking. Bekenstein pondered the problem of black hole entropy. He believed that, contrary to prevailing opinion, black holes possessed entropy and that entropy, if boosted by outside forces, could increase the disorder inside the black hole. Even though it was believed that no information could escape a black hole, Bekenstein's theory suggested that the contents of a black hole could leak out into space. Hawking, one of the foremost theorists of black hole dynamics, took issue with Bekenstein's hypothesis. A tug-of-war ensued between Hawking, Bekenstein, and their followers that revealed much about not only the nature of black holes but the inner workings of the scientific community as well.

This is only one example of the many fascinating vignettes that pepper Ferris's account. Ferris effectively uses these inside stories to shed light on the politics, power, and quest for truth that drives, and sometimes divides, the scientific community. Yet controversy often brings an opportunity for growth and new understanding, even for established scientists. Concerning the outcome of the Bekenstein-Hawking debate, Ferris writes: "But then—to his 'horror,' as he recalled the moment—Hawking found that his calculations offered no escape from the conclusion that a *non*-rotating black hole will also emit particles. Bekenstein was right."

Hawking's realization dramatically underscores Thoreau's assertion that the nature of the universe often transcends our best attempts to understand it. Nevertheless, considerable progress has been made. Einstein's theory of relativity, as well as atomic theory, have laid the foundation for much of what we know about the stuff from which the universe is fashioned. Ferris dubs matter "frozen energy," an image that is easier to grasp than Einstein's mathematical equation "$E=mc^2$." Frozen energy resulted from the swift cooldown of the incredibly hot elements forged during the first three minutes of the big bang. Ferris's compelling narrative of those first few minutes in the life of the universe captures all the violent beauty of the beginning of time.

The story continues to unfold as Ferris addresses the problem of dark matter, using David Weinberg's playful "Dark Matter Rap" as a frame for his discussion. He moves on to the large-scale structure of the universe and to cosmic evolution. But then he shifts his focus from the vast reaches of the cosmos to the unimaginably tiny world of quarks, bosons, and other exotic subatomic particles. Although the concepts of quantum theory are sometimes difficult to grasp, the persistent reader will find this material at once fascinating and mind-bending. Ferris quotes the late Danish physicist Niels Bohr concerning the paradoxical nature of quantum theory: "If someone says that he can think about quantum physics without becoming dizzy, that shows only that he has not understood anything whatever about it."

A discussion of symmetry, supersymmetry, and broken symmetry follows. This lays the foundation for understanding more complicated principles involving superstring theory and inflationary models of the universe. Ferris is careful to explain symmetry clearly, and, for the most part, he succeeds. Nonetheless, there are times when he strives too hard and other times when he does not try hard enough. For example, when he addresses the problem of mapping the electron and its antimatter counterpart, the positron, he writes that "the electron has the same mass and spin as the positron, but opposite electrical charge. (Electrons have negative charge, positrons positive.)" The parenthetical statement is almost too simplistic, particularly when one considers that this fact is more or less generally known. Then several pages later, during a discussion of John Schwartz and Michael Green's quest to resolve anomalies connected with string theory, this sentence appears: "Ten years of work had led them to a single hypothesis; technically stated, it was that the anomalies disappeared when one calculated one-loop amplitudes with either of two internal gauge symmetry groups." Ferris does say that the hypothesis is "technically stated," but he fails to give a nontechnical explanation for the benefit of the general reader. Even though there are only a few a instances where some principles are overexplained and some underexplained, the ones that do occur prove frustrating to the reader trying to make sense of difficult concepts.

As Ferris continues to explore the wonderland of quantum physics, things get more and more curious. Recent theories suggest that subatomic particles are actually tiny strings of space from which the fabric of the universe is woven. Ferris's enthusiasm for string theory is obvious as he waxes eloquent about its mathematical beauty. He ponders the paradox of how nothing can be made out of nothing and exclaims, "Everything *is* nothing, in a sense, for all is made of space, which in this context means pure geometry." The terrain gets steeper to negotiate when he addresses the reasons why we are aware of only four dimensions of the original ten that existed at the birth of the universe. He acknowledges that "ten dimensional mathematics . . . is dizzying," but the vivid, concrete images he employs to illustrate abstract concepts bring lofty mathematical principles down to earth.

Ferris's erudite discussion of string theory sets the stage for an exploration of one of the most astounding—and hard to prove—theories presented in the book. Chaotic inflation, as conceived by physicist Andrei Linde, proposes that our universe "ballooned out of the spacetime of a preexisting universe." The startling implication is that our universe is one of many in an eternally evolving multiverse. Ferris's gift for imagery again makes difficult ideas plain as he speculates that the structure of the multiverse resembles a collection of bubbles springing from space-time foam, each bubble constituting an individual universe governed by its own laws and inaccessible to other universes. This inaccessibility is one of the reasons why chaotic inflation cannot be substantiated. Yet Ferris is so taken with the multiverse notion that he subtitles his book "The State-of-the-Universe(s) Report." The theory also inspires him to poetry and prophecy: "The history of the cosmos is darker than the depths of the sea, and its myriad futures richer and less predictable than all the unpainted paintings and uncomposed songs yet to emerge from the minds of all the humans to be born from now till the sun goes red and dies."

Finally, in the last chapter of the book, Ferris tackles an issue he has tried to avoid all along: What has God got to do with all of this? Ferris acknowledges that current research in quantum mechanics resonates with what the mystics have known for thousands of years: The universe is everywhere deeply interconnected. Earlier he gives spirituality its due when he claims that "some of the most important scientific and philosophical thinking in history has been impelled by mystical motives." Yet he still questions whether science can tell us anything about the nature and existence of God. If readers expect a yes or no answer to this intriguing question, they will be sadly disappointed. While taking neither the believer's nor the atheist's side, Ferris walks down the middle road and concludes, "Cosmology presents us neither the face of God, nor the handwriting of God, nor such thoughts as may occupy the mind of God. This does not mean that God does not exist, or that he did not create the universe, or universes. It means that cosmology offers no resolution to such questions." Some scientists would no doubt castigate Ferris for bringing religion into what they believe should remain a purely scientific discussion. Yet in view of the fact that no intellectual discipline remains isolated from social, psychological, political, or spiritual influences, Ferris's "Contrarian Theological Afterward" is an appropriate ending to a fascinating and provocative book.

Pegge Bochynski

Sources for Further Study

Air and Space Smithsonian. XII, June, 1997, p. 86.
Astronomy. XXV, July, 1997, p. 108.
Discover. XVIII, August, 1997, p. 86.
Library Journal. CXXII, February 15, 1997, p. 159.
Los Angeles Times Book Review. May 18, 1997, p. 4.
Natural History. CVI, March, 1997, p. 12.
New Scientist. CLIV, April 19, 1997, p. 46.
The New York Review of Books. XLIV, June 12, 1997, p. 16.
The New York Times Book Review. CII, May 11, 1997, p. 9.
Publishers Weekly. CCXLIV, February 24, 1997, p. 70.
The Wall Street Journal. June 17, 1997, p. A16.

WILLIAM FAULKNER
The Making of a Modernist

Author: Daniel J. Singal (1944-   )
Publisher: The University of North Carolina Press (Chapel Hill). Illustrated. 357 pp. $29.95
Type of work: Literary criticism and literary biography

Daniel Singal uncovers the largely unresolved conflicts between Victorian and Modernist values in the life and career of William Faulkner, as well as detailing how these conflicts enhanced Faulkner's novels

As Daniel J. Singal notes early in this important study of William Faulkner, more critical work has been done on the Mississippi writer than on any author working in English, save William Shakespeare. There would appear to be little room for still another critical study in this crowded library, but Faulkner is clearly the greatest novelist to emerge in the United States in the twentieth century, perhaps ever, and the breadth and depth of his fiction leave plenty of room for more work, especially such a valuable critical study as this one.

The key question that Singal answers is this: How did Faulkner—born in 1897, with no formal education and from the small town of Oxford, Mississippi, in what is arguably the most culturally backward area in the country—produce *The Sound and the Fury* (1929) and *Absalom, Absalom!* (1936), two of the most intellectually complex and significant works of twentieth century American literature? The answer gets to the heart of this study. Singal's focus is on the nature and extent of Faulkner's thought, and he describes in great detail the ideas—from early Freudian psychology to a progressive reading of Southern history—that were to grow in Faulkner's fertile mind. The mystery of Faulkner's breadth and intelligence, Singal shows, lies in the structure of that thought, for Faulkner was torn throughout his career between two major historical cultures,

> the Victorian one into which he had been born in late-nineteenth-century Mississippi, and the Modernist one he discovered and absorbed through his extensive readings. . . . It is this very conflict of cultures within him, never entirely resolved even late in his life, that provides the crucial key to making sense of Faulkner.

The Victorian culture that Faulkner inherited in rural Mississippi still carried the cavalier tradition, an image of the South "as an aristocratic society organized in quasi-feudal fashion and blessed with remarkable stability and cohesion." Such a culture, carrying as it did a number of distorted notions (about women and black people, for example) was to be a terrible burden on many of its twentieth century heirs.

Early in his writing career, however—first in New Orleans with Sherwood Anderson, then in Paris viewing the multiple experiments in the arts, and finally back in Oxford with his Harvard-educated friend and mentor Phil Stone—Faulkner was learning the most important lessons of Modernism. As in the fiction of James Joyce, whom Faulkner admired immensely, Modernist thought represented "an attempt to restore a sense of order to human experience under the often chaotic conditions of contemporary existence" and "to combat the allegedly dishonest conception of existence that the Victorians had introduced." Modernism reflected the notion of a universe where nothing was ever predictable and where moral values would be in a constant state of flux, and insisted "on confronting the ugly, the sordid, and the terrible, for that is where the most important lessons are to be found." In stark contrast to Victorianism, Modernism rejected the idea of some innocent past and demanded instead that writers confront "reality" fully, no matter how painful that process might turn out to be.

> All his life Faulkner would struggle to reconcile these two divergent approaches to selfhood—the Victorian urge toward unity and stability he had inherited as a child of the southern rural gentry, and the Modernist drive for multiplicity and change that he absorbed very early in his career as a self-identifying member of the international artistic avant-garde.

Put simply, as Singal so convincingly does, there would be two William Faulkners throughout his career, two central selves: the old-fashioned country gentleman and the contemporary writer. The first would live most of his adult life in shabby splendor in "Rowan Oak," the southern mansion he bought and refurbished, but the second would shock his conservative neighbors in book after book. Part of the power of Faulkner's fiction came from this bipolarity, the tension between these two writing selves as they struggled for control of the man and of the writer.

Two immediate examples jump to mind from the many in Singal's pages. Faulkner's most memorable characters are in a constant search for self, struggling between the demands of competing ways of life. Quentin Compson in *The Sound and the Fury*, for example, is unable to reconcile his nineteenth century Southern heritage to the modern world, and he ends up drowning himself in Cambridge. Thomas Sutpen, the central character in *Absalom, Absalom!*, on the other hand, reinvents himself in the swamp outside Jefferson where he builds his mansion, and throws away one skin to don another. These and so many other major Faulkner characters are in a constant quest for *identity*, a true self; like their creator, they never satisfactorily achieve it. Faulkner's lifelong search to reconcile the warring cultures within himself would find expression in his own strongest fictional characters.

On another level, Faulkner's female characters also can be more easily understood using Singal's analysis. In Faulkner's treatment of women, "If his Modernist self deeply admired . . . liberated women, the Victorian part of him required that the narratives in which they appeared duly punish them for their sins, either through death or through some form of mutilation." Characters such as Candace Compson, the voiceless center of *The Sound and the Fury*, and Charlotte Rittenmeyer, the heroine of *The Wild Palms* (1939), represent in different ways how this tension was released within their creator.

Singal's study moves easily between biography and literary analysis, between the life and the work, and the balance is a necessary one because so much of Faulkner's power comes out of his identification with the South he had grown up in and was still struggling to come to grips with until the end of his life. Singal shows the role that Faulkner's Confederate great-grandfather and namesake, Colonel William Falkner

[sic], played in his life. He outlines the troubled lifelong relationship with Estelle Oldham and understands the release that Hollywood work in the 1930's offered to the writer living within such a marriage and working in such a small town as Oxford. He draws on all the available evidence, medical and psychological, to conclude that the clear drop-off in Faulkner's creativity after 1940 may have come as a result of a drunken fall that resulted in hypoxic encephalopathy (lowered blood circulation to the brain). He also describes the happy coda that Faulkner's last few years as a writer-in-residence at the University of Virginia provided to the novelist. Singal's "Notes" of thirty-five pages and bibliography of fifteen indicate that he has consulted all available sources for this study.

Most important, Signal's use of Faulkner's life helps to illuminate the literature. Faulkner's success did not come easily. After several faltering starts as a writer (*Soldiers' Pay* in 1926 and *Mosquitoes* in 1927), Faulkner suddenly found his true voice in 1929 in *Sartoris* and *The Sound and the Fury*. What he discovered was Yoknapatawpha County, the rural home country that he transformed into his own fictional universe.

> Indeed, turning to a familiar setting allowed Faulkner to give his Modernist perspective a firm rooting and thus a degree of depth it had not previously enjoyed—much as Joyce had found when writing of Dublin. One might even say that it proved the final and essential step in establishing his eventual cultural balance, enabling him at last to create a true Modernist or authorial self to counter the still vigorous Victorian sensibility with which he had been endowed.

What Faulkner discovered in writing his first Yoknapatawpha County novels was "a series of techniques that at last allowed him to render in literary terms the conflicts taking place inside him." Writing about his own region (in and around the fictional county seat of Jefferson) gave Faulkner for the first time "the tools he needed for his basic quest of comprehending the inner dynamics of southern culture and diagnosing its ills." Writing these novels, Singal understands, Faulkner

> had discovered the artistic value, from a Modernist standpoint, of his own roots, both personal and regional. He had learned how provincial materials could be put to cosmopolitan uses. Most of all, through the employment of tropes borrowed from Freudian theory he had acquired the means of dealing directly with the cultural pathology he perceived within himself and the South—with its obsessive attachment to a mythic past, its repression of vital human instincts, its illusive and destructive pursuit of purity, and its incestuous closed-mindedness.

The best fiction of Faulkner's career would center on Yoknapatawpha County, and Singal charts it in chapters devoted to the major works Faulkner produced. His analysis of *The Sound and the Fury* moves between depictions of the Compson family and the forces that are squeezing them, but also between the Victorian cultural mores that spell their downfall and the Modernist literary techniques that Faulkner uses to tell their stories. He misreads Quentin as the book's central character (the silent, absent Caddy, the object of her three brothers' various obsessions, is really the center of the novel), but he does a brilliant job with the rest of the novel, particularly the end, where he shows the importance of the commemorative statue of the Confederate soldier in the town square, which finally quiets the bellowing Benjy.

Singal also has brilliant analyses of the Modernist techniques in *As I Lay Dying* (1930); he even uncovers significant ideas in the potboiler *Sanctuary* (1931), including the role of Temple Drake and the significant contrast between the male characters Popeye and Horace Benbow. His analysis of *Light in August* (1932) reveals those competing forces heightened (especially in the character of Joe Christmas) in tensions between light and dark, past and present, male and female, and black and white.

Signal rightly sees *Absalom, Absalom!* (1936) as Faulkner's crowning achievement, and his analysis penetrates it on many levels: the almost cubist mode of the story's telling, its exposure of the historical and cultural forces that have been the South's undoing in the twentieth century, the role of Sutpen's house and its "design," and the heroic parts that Charles Bon and Judith Sutpen play in that tragedy. Most important, Singal sees that

> Faulkner in writing *Absalom, Absalom!* was attempting to locate what he sensed was an essential and tragic truth about the old planter class that the region's reigning mythology had tended to omit or repress—a flaw that had proved of enormous consequence in shaping the South right up to his own day, giving rise to the havoc so vividly depicted in *The Sound and the Fury.* Sutpen thus stands as the founder not so much of the actual, historical South but of the southern psyche.

Singal's brilliant analyses work because his theoretical approach only heightens his reading of the individual novels. Instead of standing in the way, his understanding of the cultural forces that competed within Faulkner help to unlock the novels. Using what can best be called a New Historicist understanding of Faulkner's fiction, Singal never allows his theory to overwhelm his sensitive responses to the complex psychological and aesthetic creations that are Faulkner's novels.

David Peck

Sources for Further Study

Atlanta Journal Constitution. September 21, 1997, p. L12.
Library Journal. CXXII, October 15, 1997, p. 62.
New Criterion. XVI, September, 1997, p. 61.
The Washington Post Book World. XXVII, September 28, 1997, p. 13.
Washington Times. September 21, 1997, p. B8.

THE WISDOM OF THE BODY

Author: Sherwin B. Nuland
Publisher: Alfred A. Knopf (New York). 395 pp. $26.95
Type of work: Biology and ethics

A fascinating account of how the body works, combining an engrossing drama of human disease and recovery with a quest for the spirit, which Nuland believes motivates the wisdom of the body

Sherwin B. Nuland is a clinical professor of surgery at Yale University, where he also teaches medical history and bioethics. He is also the author of the acclaimed *How We Die* (1994). Nuland is writing for a general audience, although he does not skirt complex explanations of human biology. (Consulting the glossary at the back of the book provides help with his scientific explanations.) Wisely, he begins his book with a riveting incident in an operating room before launching into more difficult passages about how the body works and about his philosophy of life. Nuland writes well, although he has a tendency to indulge in purple prose. He needs the discipline of describing the operating room and biological processes, it seems, because when he lets go of this material, his prose can be sophomoric—especially when he engages in silly puns. As he admits, surgeons are a rather arrogant and self-regarding group. He usually manages to keep his own ego in check, though, as he submits himself to considering the wonder and mystery of the body, acknowledging that for all of his skill and learning, there are many diseases that simply defy explanation or treatment.

Nuland suggests that in most cases bodies take care of themselves. There are innumerable self-correcting mechanisms in the body. It is constantly fighting off and killing cancer cells, renewing itself, and compensating when some part of its system is hurt. Nuland suggests that this "wisdom of the body" is not merely a material phenomenon. It has developed over centuries into automatic functions of which people remain unaware. Moreover, cells, tissues, organs—indeed all parts of the body—have become not merely machines but living organisms that are driven not by themselves but by some spirit that is greater than the sum total of the body's parts. Nuland does not claim to know what this spirit is. But he does insist that the body cannot be explained entirely in terms of its biology. There is another organizing principle at work, which can be explored if it cannot be entirely explained.

Nuland is no mystic. He has little tolerance for simplistic beliefs in mind over matter. For every patient with a will to live who has triumphed over a seemingly fatal illness, there have been just as many—even more—with the same fighting spirit who have succumbed to dreadful diseases. Neither a materialist nor a spiritualist, Nuland sets himself the difficult problem of fathoming the interaction between self and soul, so to speak. Nuland bases his quest for a realm beyond the material on the observation that much of the body has developed to a point well beyond what is needed for mere survival.

Even if Nuland's search for the transcendent principle is discounted, his absorbing accounts of surgery suggest a bond between doctor and patient that cannot be understood in pure material terms. A case in point is Marge Hansen, a vigorous woman in her forties who thought that she was suffering from no more than muscle strain. When her problem persists, and when she is suddenly rushed to an emergency room because her midsection is swelling with blood so rapidly that she looks like a pregnant woman, Nuland is called in to deal with a situation that has the attending obstetrician perplexed to the point of panic. Hansen is not pregnant, and the origin of her rapid blood loss eludes detection. With only a few minutes to save her, Nuland plunges into her body, holding up her spleen, examining its vessels, searching for the site of the bleeding. He finds the source of the blood flow in an aneurysm of the splenetic artery—a weakened area that had ballooned into a blood bubble that had burst and caused her internal hemorrhage. Hansen's case was so rare that even a veteran surgeon like Nuland had never seen it before.

What impresses Nuland about this operation is the bond he felt between himself and Hansen. He did not know her name at the time of the operation, and he points out that the draping of a patient's body during surgery is not merely for antiseptic reasons but to shield the surgeon from too personal an involvement with the patient. Yet there is something about the energy he derives from the operation, from his later account to his wife about how he had saved the woman's life, that provokes him to contemplate what he means by the wisdom of the body. He suggests that human life has organized itself around not merely its own survival but around a will to triumph over such exigencies.

Nuland does not think it merely accidental that a surgeon's skill and a patient's body collaborate—in Hansen's case—in survival and a desire to celebrate life. As he describes his cases, a kind of choreography emerges between patient and doctor. Sharon Fisher, for example, fights her increasing awareness that the lump in her breast is not merely the kind of benign tumor that often appears in pregnant woman's breasts. On the examining table, she is already apprehensive—as is Nuland, though he masks his concern with measured but encouraging words. Nuland provides a detailed account of the examination—interspersing his accounts with Fisher's words about what she was feeling at the time. The tumor is large—two to three inches in diameter—and it is thick and hard, with irregular folds. An inflammation is a telltale sign of a site filled with cancer cells. A biopsy later reveals that cancer has spread to two of the lymph nodes. The prognosis is not good. Fewer than half of women with breast cancer in Fisher's state survive five years after surgery.

Nuland's treatment of Fisher is tactful. He does not tell her everything, only what he believes she needs to know to make sound decisions. His decision may seem arrogant. Who is he to decide how much she needs to know? Yet he makes a persuasive case that it is important to maintain a patient's equilibrium. What he knows about other cases similar to Fisher's may not be applicable to her. Each body is unique, he points out, and to tell her that her statistical chances of survival are slim may not be relevant to the way her body will respond to treatment.

Fisher does survive well beyond the five-year mark—a feat that she attributes to a positive attitude and to her supportive husband. Nuland does not want to contradict his patient, but he knows that patients in similar circumstances have not survived. He tries to understand why.

The remaining chapters of *The Wisdom of the Body* explore the central nervous system, searching for an explanation of how the body adjusts to the foreign elements that attack it. Like the psychological equilibrium Nuland tries to maintain with his patients, the body seems to have its own mechanisms of adjustment to upsets and attacks—a phenomenon to which he alludes in a chapter title, "Sympathy and the Nervous System." Like the nervous system, each part of the body—the cells, for example—have their own ways of maintaining a steady state.

Yet Nuland wants to avoid biological determinism. Human beings are not merely the sum of the systems that keep them alive, he insists. Nor are they merely the victims of genetic defects. In a particularly moving case, he describes the life of Kirk Selden, born with Down syndrome. Kirk's mother admits that her first reaction to Kirk's birth was depression. It took her two weeks to get over the idea that her baby was not perfect. Doctors advised her to avoid a deep attachment to the child. She could take Kirk home and prepare for the day (when he was five or six) that he would be institutionalized, or she could institutionalize him immediately, or she could face the heartache of trying to raise him to adulthood. She chose the third course when it became apparent that her husband loved Kirk and wanted him home.

In Kirk's case, at least, much of the genetic defect was overcome by a loving home with parents who included their son in all of their activities. So powerful was their love and support of Kirk that even the Seldens' younger adopted son began to look out for Kirk, teaching him things like riding a bicycle. Although Down syndrome tends to soften bodies, Kirk became a power lifter and won medals at the Special Olympics for athletes with disabilities. Rather than becoming a burden to his family, he became a source of special pride. His subnormal IQ meant that it was difficult for him to participate in team sports, but power lifting, an individual sport, is just one example of how Kirk and his family found activities in which he could excel. The consequences and implications of Kirk's story are wide-ranging, Nuland points out. Not only Kirk's family but also his neighborhood accepted him as a normal person, and children treated him as an equal.

Nuland realizes that he is recounting extraordinary stories and that the lives of most children with Down syndrome are not so positive. But that is his point. Biologically, there is no difference between Kirk and other children with Down syndrome. It is the environmental factors that account for his success, factors motivated by what Nuland calls, in another chapter title, "The Act of Love." What is sometimes called free will is this human ability to act upon the givens of biology, to organize them in new ways.

In one of his last chapters, Nuland quotes Sir Charles Sherrington's classic essay "The Wisdom of the Body," which calls the workings of this planet a "tour de force" that ought to provoke in its inhabitants a sense of wonder. Only out of this sense of wonder, of possibility, is free will—the ability to organize life into new patterns—possible. Nuland argues that the body already knows this—that its ability to organize itself is a response to the wonder of the universe. Human minds must follow what human bodies are prepared to tell them, Nuland concludes. We do not grasp all we need to know about the wisdom of the body, but only through continual exploration of biology and environment can we hope to understand why life itself leaves poets such as William Wordsworth "breathless with adoration"—to quote the last words of Nuland's inspiring book.

Carl Rollyson

Sources for Further Study

Booklist. XCIII, March 15, 1997, p. 1202.
Library Journal. CXXII, April 15, 1997, p. 108.
Los Angeles Times Book Review. May 25, 1997, p. 9.
New Scientist. CLV, August 2, 1997, p. 44.
The New York Times Book Review. CII, May 25, 1997, p. 15.
Publishers Weekly. CCXLIV, March 24, 1997, p. 64.
Science News. CLI, June 21, 1997, p. 378.
Time. CXLIX, March 12, 1997, p. 91.
U.S. News and World Report. CXXII, June 30, 1997, p. 65.
The Wall Street Journal. May 7, 1997, p. A16.

THE WITCH OF EXMOOR

Author: Margaret Drabble (1938-   )
Publisher: Harcourt Brace & Company (New York). 281 pp. $23.00
Type of work: Novel
Time: Mid-1990's
Locale: Southern England

Another of Margaret Drabble's biting explorations of middle-class English life, centered on one family's perplexity about how to deal with their eccentric, self-willed mother

> *Principal characters:*
> DANIEL PALMER, a barrister
> PATSY PALMER, his wife
> SIMON PALMER, their son
> EMILY PALMER, their daughter
> GRACE D'ANGER, Daniel's sister, a neurologist
> DAVID D'ANGER, Grace's husband, an academic and politician
> BENJAMIN D'ANGER, Grace and David's son
> ROSEMARY HERZ, Grace and Daniel's sister
> NATHAN HERZ, Rosemary's husband, an advertising executive
> FRIEDA HAXBY PALMER, eminent sociologist and scholar, mother of the
>   Palmers
> WILL PAINE, lodger at the Palmers' house

Three well-off, middle-class, middle-aged English couples gather in the Hampshire countryside for a pleasant weekend of conversation, tennis, good food, and relaxation. There is only one problem, which dominates the weekend, even though no one really wants to talk about it: What should the Palmer family do about their formidable, eccentric mother—a noted author and thinker—who has abandoned her old life and without explanation has gone to live in a run-down former hotel by the sea in Exmoor, in the West Country? Why has she done this? Is she mad? What is she plotting? How is she going to allocate her money in her will? These are the questions to be considered by Frieda Haxby Palmer's three offspring—Daniel, Grace, and Rosemary—who have never been very fond of their mother, nor she of them.

Such is the opening scene in Margaret Drabble's fifteenth novel. As the story unfolds, it becomes clear that the Palmers, in spite of their relative affluence, are not a family to be much envied. In fact, the ominous first two sentences of the novel, "Begin on a midsummer evening. Let them have everything that is pleasant," suggest as much, at the same time drawing attention to the godlike powers of the narrator. Drabble enjoys doing this. Throughout the novel, as in many of her previous novels, she adopts the role of intrusive narrator, thus providing herself with a chance to explore, usually with a caustic and disparaging eye, the state of mid-1990's, post-Thatcher Britain, in which the ruthlessness of the free market has triumphed and few people bother to talk anymore about social justice. This is a left-leaning view of the "state of the nation" that will be familiar to anyone who has read previous Drabble novels. Indeed, *The Witch of Exmoor* is in some ways an update, ten years later, of *The*

Radiant Way (1987), which examined, unfavorably, the Thatcherite Britain of the 1980's.

The Palmers are professionally employed, complacent about their comfortable position in the scheme of things, and unwilling to change. Daniel is a lawyer, Grace is a neurologist, and Rosemary is in arts administration. Of the spouses, two are outsiders: Nathan Herz, Rosemary's husband, is Jewish, an advertising executive from a lower-middle-class background; and David D'Anger, Grace's husband, is an aristo-cratic, expatriate Guyanese, a charming, ambitious academic, journalist, and parlia-mentary candidate. It is through David that one of the novel's main themes is brought out. At the Hampshire weekend, David initiates a game he calls the Veil of Ignorance, in which participants have to decide whether, if they were to discover the principles on which a just society were to be founded, they would be willing to accept these if they did not already know what place they would occupy in the society. Would they press the button to make it happen? Their response is for the most part summed up by Daniel, who says, "I gave up any hope of any kind of social justice years and years ago. What I have, I hold. That's my motto." Drabble, as narrator, pours considerable scorn on this notion:

> The middle classes of England. Is there any hope whatsoever, or any fear, that anything will change? Would any of them wish for change? Given a choice of anything more serious than decaffeinated coffee or herbal tea, would they dare to choose?

The narrator's view of the current state of Britain is equally plain and censorious. After informing the reader that David is haunted by his vision of a fair society, she breaks in, "Is this possible, you ask, in the late twentieth century? . . . Surely we know better now? . . . Lecturers and professors still discuss the concept of the fair, the just and the good. But they have no connection with a world of ring-roads and beef-burgers, with a world of disease and survival." This point is forced home later when it transpires that Nathan has taken on a project to "update" the image of the National Health Service. The assumption is that, political realities being what they are, there is no chance of providing adequate health care for everyone, so advertising wizards must use their tricks to ensure that people simply expect and are happy with less.

Such social commentary aside, the tale that unfolds around the mad "Witch of Exmoor" and her eerie castle is admirably gothic. Frieda is in fact not mad at all, although her family might be forgiven for thinking her so. After all, she has been behaving strangely: She has taken up smoking, discovered a sudden passion for Wagnerian opera, and abandoned her car in the middle of a London traffic jam and tried to give it away. On top of that, she has produced an unreadable, overresearched historical novel that departs completely from her previous works of social history and has effectively destroyed her reputation. When Patsy hears Frieda on the radio spouting mystical nonsense about her connections with Sweden's seventeenth century Queen Christina—the subject of the book—the family is convinced that she is, to put it colloquially, off her rocker.

The Palmers are concerned about what their mad mother is likely to do with their inheritance (which they do not really need), although they are rather cagey about what they say to each other about it. Their anxiety increases when Frieda mysteriously disappears. Several weeks later, her body washes up on the coast (it appears that she fell from a cliff). In her will, they discover, she left everything to her favorite grandson, the precocious, too-good-to-be-true Benjamin, who reacts to his good fortune by becoming sick, then becomes progressively sicker as time goes by. His illness is of the mind, not the body, but his parents, David and Grace, seem strangely incapable of doing anything to improve the situation.

In the meantime, Rosemary has discovered that she is in ill health and may have to rely on the unreliable National Health Service, Nathan is worried about losing his job, and Daniel and Patsy's son, Simon, who is an Oxford student, steadily sinks into drug abuse, although at the time no one seems to notice. Things are not going well for the complacent Palmers, and one almost expects the narrator to break in and gloat, for she clearly does not care much for these, her characters.

There is one character in the novel who is presented in a sympathetic light, and that is Will Paine, a half-black working-class young man from Wolverhampton in the English Midlands. The fact that he is not purebred English, seems, in this novel, to be an advantage. Will has been in prison for selling marijuana, but he is a decent, honest, and sensible lad. Patsy Palmer took pity on him and offered him a room in the attic, from which he emerges now and then, early in the novel, to help with odd jobs. Patsy's compassion eventually wears out, and she evicts him. The exigencies of the plot eventually take Will to Frieda's castle, where he manages to persuade an initially hostile Frieda to allow him to stay and do some maintenance work. Frieda soon gets fed up with him and bribes him to leave. Flush with money, Will flies to the Caribbean, the homeland he has never seen, where he has to lie low for a while because the English police suspect, wrongly, that he had a hand in Frieda's disappearance.

The irony of the novel is that Will, a man born with no natural advantages, ill-educated and unsure of himself, is the character who eventually has the most success. He moves on from Trinidad to Sydney, Australia, where he is apprenticed to a landscape gardener and his life flourishes in every way.

What Drabble intends to convey by this is subject to different interpretations. Will's success might be seen as negating the frequent insistence on the lack of social justice. After all, Will succeeds even though all the odds are against him. He does not spend his time complaining about his position; indeed, the opposite is true. Even when he is in difficulties, he regards himself as lucky. His eventual success might seem to imply—whether or not this is what Drabble intended—that what counts most is individual character, not a person's given place in society or the nature of that society. On the other hand, it is perhaps to the point that Will finds himself only because he is willing to take the risk of traveling abroad, away from the stifling rigidity of English society.

The note of hope sounded by Will Paine—if that is what it is—also can be found in the closing episodes of the novel. The emphasis shifts to the younger generation—to Benjamin, and to eighteen-year-old Emily, daughter of Daniel and Patsy. Benjamin eventually is set on the road to recovery through the attentions of Lily McNab, a child psychiatrist. It turns out that, like many gifted children, Benjamin has suffered under the weight of parental expectations. To use Drabble's metaphor about the elder Palmers, Benjamin is thick in the mud of the life that has been mapped out for him before he has had a chance to find out who he really is. Early in the novel, he is presented as the perfect child: studious and scholarly, imaginative and hardworking, and popular with his peers. When he plays with his friends, he tells them he has special powers, and they believe him. His parents encourage him to regard himself as special. Lily McNab, on the other hand, tries to show him that he is not as special or as predestined as he had thought. He does not always have to be the best, but can choose to be ordinary. Benjamin pretends to go along with this, but secretly he still believes he has a special destiny. Drabble implies that it will not be easy for him to seek out this destiny, but at least he is ready to make his own choices, a development conveyed by the delicious image of young Benjamin biting into a particularly sweet candy—the sort that his parents would never let him eat—and slowly savoring it.

As for Emily, she is dispatched to Frieda's house to sort out the dead woman's papers. She sets out, full of youthful energy and confidence, on a glorious winter day. Implications of renewal are strong, and the narrator's description of her as "wise young virgin" does not seem to be ironic. While Emily is at Frieda's house, she has a shock when a deer, chased by hounds, crashes into the house and takes refuge under a table. The mounted hunters gather, but Emily, rising to the occasion like an avenging angel, says she is giving the deer sanctuary and orders the hunters to leave the property. And they do: "The undifferentiated mass of black-jacketed, white-stocked, fawn-breeched, red-nosed, hair-netted, khaki-jacketed, black-booted folk begins to mumble, thin, retreat. Emily tosses her golden mane and scrambles back over her window-sill." Thus are the English middle classes at play put to rout, and youth and unsullied innocence, at least for a moment, has its triumph.

Bryan Aubrey

Sources for Further Study

Artforum. Winter, 1997, p. 32.
Booklist. XCIII, May 15, 1997, p. 1539.
Library Journal. CXXII, June 15, 1997, p. 96.
The Nation. CCLXV, October 13, 1997, p. 33.
The New York Times Book Review. CII, October 19, 1997, p. 15.
The New Yorker. LXXIII, November 3, 1997, p. 107.
The Observer. October 20, 1996, p. 17.
Publishers Weekly. CCXLIV, June 16, 1997, p. 44.
The Times Literary Supplement. October 11, 1997, p. 26.
The Wall Street Journal. September 24, 1997, p. A20.

WITH CHATWIN
Portrait of a Writer

Author: Susannah Clapp
Publisher: Alfred A. Knopf (New York). 240 pp. $23.00
Type of work: Literary biography
Time: 1940-1989
Locale: Mostly New York and various locations in England

With Chatwin *is an absorbing, elegantly and economically written account of the abbreviated career of one of the twentieth century's most chimerical and captivating travel writers*

> *Principal personages:*
> BRUCE CHATWIN, a preternaturally beautiful, preternaturally gifted British writer who traveled the world in search of oddities that he wove into uncategorizable narratives
> ELIZABETH CHATWIN, his independent, American-born wife
> SUSANNAH CLAPP, Chatwin's first editor and longtime friend

With Chatwin is a title meant to allude to that of Bruce Chatwin's breakthrough book, *In Patagonia* (1977), and also, as biographer Susannah Clapp states, "to the helping hand that friends of the Victorian explorers used to claim they had provided." As his biographer chronicles, Chatwin did travel to places that others longed to go. Many of these others in fact went with him, but none of them came away with the original insights Chatwin managed to marshal into some of the most unique travel-oriented prose written this century. Even before his early death in 1989 of AIDS, Chatwin was the stuff of legend, a figure who gave off much heat and light in which others longed to bask. He did have a gift for friendship, and like the Victorian explorers, he did not get where he got on his own.

Chatwin clearly was one of a kind, blessed with great beauty and even greater charisma. Born in the dark days of World War II in Sheffield, England, he was the son of a solicitor and a housewife. He had a seemingly unremarkable British upbringing that, typically, he would later embroider. Failing to win a scholarship to Oxford, in 1958 Chatwin joined the Sotheby auction house in London as a porter. He had always had an eye for the rare and beautiful, but as was ever the case, he landed in this situation through connections and impeccable timing. Sotheby's experienced a period of explosive growth during the late 1950's and 1960's, and Chatwin rose rapidly through the ranks. By the time he left the auction house in 1966, he had been made a director of the firm and headed two departments, Antiquities and an entirely new one devoted to art of the Impressionists.

While working at Sotheby's, Chatwin began his travels and began to make important connections in the world of the monied elite. In 1961, for example, he was sent to the French Riviera to inveigle writer Somerset Maugham out of his collection of Impressionist paintings. As Clapp reports, for a time the "blond boy" did not mind being used by his superiors at Sotheby's as bait as well as an art expert. He went to New York, Switzerland, and Paris, then to more exotic locales: Afghanistan, Persia, and Egypt.

He became famous for the prodigious feats of his discerning eye. Then, mysteriously, he became afflicted with an eye disease.

In his 1987 book *The Songlines*, Chatwin gave the following account of his reasons for leaving Sotheby's:

> One morning, I woke up blind.
>
> During the course of the day, the sight returned to the left eye, but the right one stayed sluggish and clouded. The eye specialist who examined me said there was nothing wrong organically, and diagnosed the nature of the trouble.
>
> "You've been looking too closely at pictures," he said. "Why don't you swap them for some long horizons?"

This version of events is characteristic of Chatwin's manipulation of facts: They were in his renditions usually embellished and rendered poetic, but grounded in a fundamental truth. He was indeed troubled with eye problems—usually brought on by stress—all his life. By 1966, he had grown weary of the sharp practice and toadying associated with art dealership. He was burdened by an overabundance of ornament. After returning from a leave of absence spent in the arid Sudan, he told his wife, Elizabeth—whom he had met at Sotheby's and married in the summer of 1965—that he wanted to study archaeology at the University of Edinburgh.

Although initially she approved of her husband's desire to study in Edinburgh, Elizabeth found the city less than agreeable. After a short while, her husband felt the same way about the university and about archaeology. "I started liking people who had no garbage to leave. I wanted to find the other side of the coin," he said. He wanted to study nomads. He wanted to *become* a nomad—and he did.

About this time, Chatwin also became a writer. Before he left on the journey that would produce *In Patagonia*, he spent three years in the early 1970's working off and on for the London *Sunday Times* magazine. Before he took the job, he had no regular source of income and was bogged down in a book on nomads that seemed to be going nowhere. At the *Times*, he received lavish travel budgets and was given a free rein—for a time. Then the editor who was his champion was replaced with another who thought Chatwin's writing "all purple prose and self-indulgence." Harold Evans, then editor of the *Times* proper, handed down a budget-cutting directive that made specific mention of Chatwin. It was time to move on.

Later in life, when he described his departure from the newspaper, Chatwin declared that he had simply telegrammed the office: "Gone to Patagonia." No one was ever able to produce this telegram, but all agree that the extravagance of such a gesture would be typical of Chatwin. He did not entirely sever his connection with the *Sunday Times*, where he had learned a kind of journalistic discipline that vastly improved his writing, but his departure for South America did mark for him the beginning of his career as a writer.

Clapp, who edited *In Patagonia*, declares that Chatwin's first book changed the standard for travel writing forever. An admixture of fact and fiction, it contains a high degree of autobiographical material while remaining true to Chatwin's commitment to objectivity. Like its author, the book is fraught with paradox, but somehow its contradictions add up to a pleasing whole. *In Patagonia* was widely praised on its publication in 1977 and won two important literary awards.

Chatwin's next book, *The Viceroy of Ouidah* (1980), a portrait of a slave trader in Dahomey, was more fiction than travel writing, but when Chatwin's third book, *On the Black Hill* (1982) appeared, it won the Whitbread Award as the best first novel of the year. Clearly the literary establishment did not know what to make of Chatwin. *On the Black Hill* concerns brothers who are farmers in the Welsh border country, and it is the only one of Chatwin's six books to be set in England. The protagonists of *On the Black Hill* are identical twins and, according to novelist Edmund White, Chatwin had intended also to make them lovers. He did not do so, but Clapp speculates that the dualities in the book speak to Chatwin's own dilemmas, including his bisexuality. Although he remained married to one woman for most of his adult life, Chatwin also had many lovers of both sexes. Around the time he was writing *On the Black Hill*, he was contemplating moving into a Welsh cottage with dress designer Jaspar Conran, one of two men whom at the end of his life Chatwin said he had loved.

Chatwin also had some extremely close friendships with men that seem not to have been tinged with sexuality. In the early 1980's, novelist Salman Rushdie traveled through Australia with him while Chatwin collected material for his next book. That book, *The Songlines*, a discursive meditation on Aboriginal culture, featured a primary character named Arkady whose role it was to debate with another character named Bruce. Arkady, Chatwin later said, was based on Rushdie. Rushdie declared both characters to have been Chatwin in disguise. The identity of the two writers received an ironic twist after Chatwin's death, when Rushdie, who had just had a price put on his head for publishing the iconoclastic novel *The Satanic Verses* (1988), became the center of media interest at Chatwin's memorial service.

Chatwin was already ill when he began work on *The Songlines*; by the time it was finished, he seemed to be on the verge of death. Chatwin proved to be no more forthcoming about having AIDS than he had been about his sexuality. He told friends that he was being treated for a rare fungus that he had picked up in China—perhaps from eating a black egg in Lijiang or as a result of visiting the Hong Kong bird market. As always, Chatwin evinced a weakness for ornament, preferring to embellish the truth. The fact that this particular ailment is exotic and actually exists made it even more irresistible. Of course, like many AIDS sufferers, Chatwin wanted to deny that he was infected with a virus that carried both a stigma and a death sentence. Like many others, he was in denial. In 1988, he wrote a letter to the *London Review of Books* in response to a recent article on AIDS, arguing that the disease had not been proven to be fatal.

For a time, Chatwin's health did improve—enough, in fact, for him to produce yet another book, *Utz* (1988), a novella about a Czech collector of porcelain. By the time he had completed the manuscript, however, Chatwin's health had declined precipitously. Too weak to edit the book himself, he turned most of the decision making over to Clapp. *Utz* was finally published in September, 1988. By the following January, Chatwin was dead.

Chatwin's funeral, like his life, was the stuff of legend. Toward the end, he had developed an interest in the Greek Orthodox Church, and a memorial service was held for him at the Greek Cathedral of St. Sophia in London. Friends who attended the funeral were fascinated by the exotic nature of the service, conducted by black-robed priests with flowing beards whose only intelligible word was "Bruce." It was a ceremony worthy to be called Chatwinesque, a word that had entered the lexicon while the author was still alive.

Eloquent, exotic, aesthetic, and—above all—changeable, Chatwin devoted as much energy during his forty-eight years to creating his own myth as he did to manipulating words on the page. Much debunking naturally followed his death. Clapp has done a superior job of injecting some balance into the debate about Chatwin and his achievements. Not a true—or at least traditional—biography, *With Chatwin* nevertheless provides a strong sense of the man. Clapp was herself a feature of the gorgeous web he wove about himself, but she does not intrude on the story, instead letting readers come to their own conclusions about who Chatwin was and what he accomplished. Although it presents a roughly chronological account of Chatwin's life and works, *With Chatwin* is short on fact and long on anecdote. This approach seems thoroughly appropriate for a book about such a contradictory character. Chatwin was always on his way to some new place, and all most people knew of him came from a fleeting glimpse. When she was putting together an entry on Chatwin for the *Dictionary of National Biography*, Clapp asked Elizabeth for details of her husband's domestic habits. Elizabeth responded with merriment: "Well, you could say he was hardly ever at home."

Chatwin remains an enigmatic figure after *With Chatwin*. There is much more to be written about the man and his myth, but it is to Clapp's credit that she leaves readers wanting to know more about his brief and brilliant life.

Lisa Paddock

Sources for Further Study

Artforum. Winter, 1997, p. 7.
Booklist. XCIII, July, 1997, p. 1770.
Geographical Magazine. LXIX, April, 1997, p. 62.
The Guardian. January 21, 1997, p. 2.
Los Angeles Times Book Review. August 31, 1997, p. 9.
The New York Review of Books. XLIV, December 4, 1997, p. 6.
The New York Times Book Review. CII, September 28, 1997, p. 23.
Publishers Weekly. CCXLIV, June 23, 1997, p. 77.
San Francisco Chronicle. August 10, 1997, p. REV3.
The Times Literary Supplement. February 14, 1997, p. 13.
The Washington Post Book World. July 27, 1997, p. 1.

WITHIN THE CONTEXT OF NO CONTEXT

Author: George W. S. Trow (1943-   )
First published: 1981
Publisher: Atlantic Monthly Press (New York). 119 pp. $20.00; paperback, $11.00
Type of work: Essay and cultural criticism

A critique of television drives an often trenchant and impassioned exposé of what the author perceives as the fundamental unreality at the heart of contemporary American culture

Within the Context of No Context may be simply described as the reissue of a book first published in 1981. The description would, however, be misleading in its simplicity. Before there was the book, there was the essay in *The New Yorker*; the book actually consisted of two essays from *The New Yorker*, one of which has been dropped from the current edition. It is the title essay of the book, by critical consensus the stronger of the two, that is now reprinted, along with a new introduction that can be called an essay in itself. The topic, simply put, is television; again, however, the simple way of putting it may not be the most accurate. To reissue sixteen years after a first appearance in book form what was originally a magazine piece, ostensibly on a topic that many would consider ephemeral at best, is a step sufficiently exceptional as to suggest that some rather strong claims are implicitly being made for George W. S. Trow's essay. To what extent does the essay justify such claims?

A longtime contributor to *The New Yorker*, Trow is also an accomplished playwright, writer of short stories, and novelist. Before the original publication of *Within the Context of No Context*, Trow had had two plays produced off-Broadway; short stories originally published in *The New Yorker* were gathered in book form as *Bullies* in 1980. A short novel, *The City in the Mist*, was published in 1984, three years after *Within the Context of No Context*. Trow's work has been favorably reviewed, although some critics seem troubled by what they regard as an elitist air. The critical question may be whether his work as a whole exposes elitism or exemplifies it. The same issue can arise very specifically in relation to *Within the Context of No Context*. Readers may eventually forget some of Trow's subtler points, but no one who reads this book is ever likely to forget that Trow, as he repeatedly reminds readers, attended Exeter School and Harvard University.

Yet it would be too easy to dismiss Trow's frequent references to his relatively privileged background as mere one-upmanship. Trow is offering in this book a global critique of what he sees as the failings of an American culture that has television at its center, but he never pretends to pure objectivity. He is, on the contrary, careful to define his perspective. He is, first of all, a member of a particular generation, the one that grew up in the years following World War II. The malaise of this generation, their sense of abandonment, is his deep subject. He never claims that the culture he sees will be seen in the same terms by someone whose generational frame of reference is radically different from his own. He is also the product of a particular family history and bears the burden of expectation that comes from that background. In a defining image, Trow recalls his father's fedora and the expectation that, as his father's son, he would on arriving at manhood don a fedora of his own. Yet he has never been able to wear a fedora except ironically. Finally, he is self-consciously the product of privilege. In short, what Trow offers is cultural criticism, intended as generally valid, yet honestly uttered from a particular perspective.

These observations, however, do not entirely resolve the issue of elitism. When someone of Trow's background and accomplishments turns his attention to television, or to popular culture in general, suspicions immediately arise. Are readers in for yet another denunciation of popular culture for being popular? When he makes the sweeping claim that no good has come of television, Trow opens himself to the charge of aristocratic prejudice. If readers, especially readers who do not share Trow's background, are to be dissuaded from that charge, Trow's critique must transcend attitude. What does Trow offer in the way of ideas?

The idea of no context (in the book, sometimes rendered as "no-context") seems an appropriate place to start. According to Trow, "The work of television is to establish false contexts and to chronicle the unraveling of existing contexts; finally, to establish the context of no-context and to chronicle it." The state of no-context to which Trow refers seems to be the consequence of a loss of a sense of history. History, as summarized by Trow, is the record of growth, conflict, and destruction, and all of these are interfered with by television. The benefits of history reveal themselves in a deepened sense of context, a sharpened awareness of the relations of background and foreground. That, at any rate, is the old history. The New History (Trow's capitalization) is the history of demographics, the history of no-history. This New History is little more than a record of preferences, in which nothing is judged, everything is merely counted. It scarcely matters whose preferences are recorded; those of a child weigh as much as those of an adult.

Trow finds a telling instance of no-context in a moment from *Family Feud*, a highly rated show at the time of the essay's original composition. *Family Feud* was a quiz show; yet this quiz show did not test the contestants' knowledge of any body of information. Rather, in a moment representative of the show, and if Trow is right, of a major tendency in American culture of the late 1970's and early 1980's, the host "asked contestants to guess what a poll of a hundred people had guessed would be the height of the average American woman. Guess what they've guessed. Guess what they've guessed the *average* is." As Trow comments, there is no reality, not a fact in sight.

New England, says Trow, is history. A complex of personalities, events, conditions adds up, over time, to New England. Yet within the context of no context, New England is merely a complex of characteristics, put on display in a television commercial in which a properly costumed "New England" woman stands on a carefully chosen, or skillfully constructed, "New England" porch and pours some sort of artificial dessert topping (the product advertised) over her New England cherry cobbler. Gertrude Stein is supposed to have said of Oakland, California, that there isn't any there there. Within the context of no context, it seems, there is no there anywhere.

The degeneration of the historical sense is reflected also in the degeneration of gossip. People as well educated as Trow might be expected to despise gossip, or at least to regard it as a paltry thing compared to history. In fact, Trow does explicitly place gossip beneath history, but, he insists, the current age is beneath gossip. Gossip, he points out, depends on violation. The best gossip of the century arose out of the relationship of England's Edward VIII and Wallis Simpson, later the duke and duchess of Windsor, and what made it delicious was the clarity of the violation involved. What made it interesting, moreover, was a clash of contexts, a rejection of inhibiting contexts, which included the context of British history itself.

In place of gossip, what one has within the context of no context is merely synthetic talk. When one turns to *People* magazine, one may be looking for gossip, but one will look in vain. The people in *People* are not properly subjects of gossip, because their actions violate nothing, occur in no inhibiting contexts. Nor is the discourse of *People* a violation in itself, since its revelations are not made within any context of propriety, reticence, or discretion.

The place of celebrity within the context of no context is another of the key ideas of the book. When people still lived in history, they lived within a multiplicity of contexts, in the realm of the middle distance. Now, as the middle distance has fallen away, there remain only two grids, the grid of two hundred million and the grid of intimacy. There is national life, or the shimmer of it, and there is intimate life, with nothing between. The power of celebrities, the source of their fascination for others, is that for them there is no distance between the two grids. Thus they, and only they, are complete.

The replacement of history by demographics is the replacement of the record of growth, conflict, and destruction by the record of the expression of preferences. Choice, as one might expect, assumes a peculiar role within the context of no context. In its noble form, now largely abandoned, the aim of choice is to choose successfully; in its debased form, dominant in the late 1990's, the aim is to be endlessly choosing. Trow does not apply his observations to the pro-choice movement, but is it a symptom of where Americans are that one of the most recognized movements of the period Trow is writing about brackets the question of whether abortion is the right choice in favor of the declaration that choice itself must be defended?

Clearly, *Within the Context of No Context* is a book provocative enough to impel the reader in intellectual directions that might surprise and disturb the author. The provocation can be located in the book's manner, in which one discerns the influence of Friedrich Nietzsche and Roland Barthes, as well as in its matter. Sustained, coherent argument is not for Trow. The book is divided into brief segments, some as short as a single sentence, none longer than a few pages. The style is often aphoristic. There is no amassing of evidence. Even factual examples are rare. The categories into which Trow divides his material can seem arbitrary or mystifying. This is the rhetoric of a writer who will not stoop to persuade. Either the reader gets the point or not. Can this fairly be restated in elitist terms: either the reader is one of us or not?

All of this is often brilliant, always provocative, yet not ultimately satisfying.

Surprisingly, perhaps, the book's gravest weakness may lie in the author's failure to deal adequately with context. In the introductory essay, "Collapsing Dominant," Trow tells of an encounter in Alaska with a man who is frighteningly certain that all films are made from one political motive: to strip Americans of their freedom. Trow responds by pointing out that the purpose of films is to make as much money as possible, and this, rather than some political agenda, determines most of what is seen on the screen. It is ironic, then, that at times in the book Trow himself sounds like a highly and expensively educated urban version of his man from Alaska, in need of someone to coach him in ordinary cynicism. Television, such a mentor might point out, is primarily an advertising medium; it can be understood only when placed in the context of consumer capitalism. Yet it is precisely in this sort of contextualizing that the book most obviously falls short.

It falls short, if less obviously, in other respects as well. How much, finally, does Trow know about the lives of people who read *People*, or indeed of people who watch *Family Feud*? How deeply does he care about these people? Although one senses a passion in the author, it seems a passion aroused by offenses to his refined sensibility, a passion that has little to do with compassion.

In his introductory essay, Trow offers his own evaluation, from the perspective of seventeen years later, of the original *Within the Context of No Context*. He now finds in the essay the expression of an informed confusion. He also finds that the period for which the formulation of the essay was valid is coming to an end. This raises again the question introduced at the beginning of these remarks. If, in the judgment of the author, the essay expresses an informed confusion about a period that is coming to an end, why does it appear in a new edition in 1997? Perhaps *Within the Context of No Context* is the sort of book best appreciated when it is happily discovered on a library shelf or in the aisles of a used book store. It certainly deserves to be read. Whether it had to be reissued is another question.

W. P. Kenney

Sources for Further Study

Library Journal. CXXII, April 1, 1997, p. 134.
Los Angeles Times Book Review. May 18, 1997, p. 10.
New York. XXX, May 12, 1997, p. 59.
The New York Times Book Review. CII, April 6, 1997, p. 6.
Vanity Fair. March, 1997, p. 182.

WOBEGON BOY

Author: Garrison Keillor (1942-   )
Publisher: Viking (New York). 305 pp. $24.95
Type of work: Novel
Time: The 1990's
Locale: Upstate New York and Lake Wobegon, Minnesota

Radio personality and author Garrison Keillor weaves a witty tale of love and midlife crisis for his protagonist John Tollefson, a transplanted native of Keillor's fictional town of Lake Wobegon

Principal characters:
> JOHN TOLLEFSON, a forty-something radio station manager living in upstate New York, originally from Lake Wobegon, Minnesota
> ALIDA FREEMAN, a history professor at Columbia University and John's significant other
> HOWARD FREEMAN, a lawyer and friend of John
> BYRON AND MARY TOLLEFSON, John's parents

Wobegon Boy is the ninth book by celebrated author and radio personality Garrison Keillor. To fans of his weekly two-hour public radio program, *A Prairie Home Companion*, he provides more of the same: humorous anecdotes about small-town midwesterners, probably based on real people he knew growing up in the small town of Anoka, Minnesota, in the 1940's and 1950's. In *Wobegon Boy*, he takes these anecdotes and weaves them into a novel-length saga about a forty-something native of the fictional town of Lake Wobegon, who takes a job as a radio station manager at a small college in upstate New York.

John Tollefson, Keillor's protagonist, begins his narrative in Minneapolis, reminiscing about his childhood in Lake Wobegon. He was born to Lutheran parents, his father a "Dark" Lutheran, his mother a "Happy" Lutheran. According to John, the Dark Lutherans "believed in the utter depravity of man and separation from worldly things and strict adherence to the literal truth of Scripture," while the Happy Lutherans "believed in splashing some water on babies and confirming the little kids and then not worrying about it, just come every Sunday and bring a hot dish." John believes himself to be a Happy Lutheran. He sums up his mother's teachings thus: "Cheer up, Make yourself useful, Mind your manners, and, above all, Don't feel sorry for yourself."

He graduated in history from the University of Minnesota and went east at the age of thirty to avoid marrying his college sweetheart. There, he got a job as a radio station manager at St. James College in Red Cliff, New York. According to John, St. James is popularly known as a charitable institution that services "financially gifted parents of academically challenged students." Here, he functions peaceably for some ten years, settling in at St. James, establishing his preference for classical music on the radio, buying a home, and making friends with a local lawyer, Howard Freeman.

It is in Red Cliff, at his fortieth birthday bash, that he meets the love of his life,

Alida, who happens to be Howard's sister. Alida is a history professor at Columbia University, working on a book about an obscure Norwegian immigrant named Bolle Balestrand. John and Alida, who lives in New York City, establish a fairly comfortable relationship. They live apart during the week, each pursuing his or her own career, and spend their weekends together, alternately in the city at Alida's apartment or in Red Cliff at John's. They enjoy fine cuisine, which John prepares, and good wine. John, however, is growing tired of the single life and is beginning to think about marriage. Alida, on the other hand, who experienced the painful divorce of her parents, is in no hurry to tie the knot. She likes things just the way they are.

Despite his fairly upbeat long-distance romance with Alida, John's life begins to fall apart. He and Howard sink their life savings into starting a farm restaurant, Gibbs Farm, which will serve fresh produce grown on the premises. The venture is fraught with problems, however, from the moment they hire a New Age contractor named Steve. Steve, it turns out, is an old friend of Howard. They met when they toured the country together in a circus (Howard was a mime). Steve has grandiose visions of turning Gibbs Farm into his magnum opus and spares no expense in its creation, much to the financial woe of John and Howard, who are threatened with bankruptcy.

Worse yet, John's love of classical music is challenged at St. James when a new dean tries to force talk radio into the programming. At the same time, allegations of sexual harassment are made against John, who told a joke about a douche bag at a party and offended a female guest. John is called upon to answer for his actions but refuses to apologize.

A climax of sorts is reached when John's taciturn father Byron dies, and John returns to Lake Wobegon to attend the funeral. There, he reunites with the rest of his family, which is quite a mixed bag. His mother, Mary, was the one who found his father dead, slumped on the basement stairs with a bag of frozen peas clutched in his hand. In characteristic stoic Lutheran fashion, Mary removed the bag of peas from Byron's hand and placed them in the refrigerator before calling 911—and later serves them for dinner when her grown children arrive home for the funeral. John's ailing older brother drives up from Minneapolis. His older sister flies in from Tucson with her "partner" April. His younger brother, a born-again Pentecostalist, flies in from Dallas, and his younger sister, who still lives in town with her minister husband, comes over. Their gathering, of course, engenders even more reminiscences. Alida pleasantly surprises John by arriving unexpectedly for the funeral.

In the end, John, ever the romantic, decides to throw in the towel as station manager at St. James as well as restaurateur at Gibbs Farm and moves to New York City to marry Alida and live happily ever after, or the closest approximation for a Lutheran.

John's is a rather pedestrian life enlivened by the strings and strings of anecdotes that Keillor weaves into this charming tale. His fans will find themselves on familiar ground when John recalls such Wobegon landmarks as the church of Our Lady of Perpetual Responsibility, the Chatterbox Cafe, the Sidetrack Tap, Skoglund's Five and Dime, and Ralph's Pretty Good Grocery, all of which have figured prominently in Keillor's weekly radio monologues.

Not all of the anecdotes are necessarily new. Keillor once again dusts off such old chestnuts as the story of John's aunt, Mildred Tollefson, the embezzling bank employee who fled to South America: "People always said that Mildred was as normal as the day is long, but days get short in the winter." Another familiar tale is that of the talking toilet seat, installed by a Wobegonian man in order to drive his unemployed sister-in-law out of the house; of course, the trick fails in humorous fashion. There is also a nod to the Living Flag, an annual event in Lake Wobegon, "whereby four or five hundred people wearing red, white, or blue caps stood in tight formation, making the Stars and Stripes with the tops of their heads." These stories will be familiar to Keillor's many longtime listeners and fans, but, as with John's uncle Art, "He has told this story hundreds of times, often to the same individuals on consecutive days, but frequent usage has not taken the shine off it for him."

Keillor is a marvelous storyteller, and it is during these humorous anecdotes, both new and old, that he truly hits his stride in *Wobegon Boy*. He has a unique ability to see humor in what most people would consider to be very mundane places and situations. Keillor deftly describes Minnesota as a place where romance has been supplanted by the weather: "either winter is just over with or winter is on the way again. Or else it's winter." Keillor is a master of acute understatement. He describes the people of Lake Wobegon as the kind who "looked at the outside world with suspicion, as a place where you send your money and nothing comes back." He says of Wobegonians that they talk "so slow you can hear the grass grow between the sentences." At one point, he even compares, to great effect, the dull, obvious chitchat of his relatives with a Samuel Beckett play. Yet, despite these satirical digs, a love of home and sense of pride in his background shine through. Throughout Keillor's story of John Tollefson is the overwhelming conviction that, wherever John goes and whatever he does, he is and always will be a Wobegonian in his heart.

No one is immune to Keillor's skewering, least of all himself, as reflected in his depiction of his protagonist, with whom he has much in common. At one point, John's sister Judy cautions Alida about John: "Don't believe what this man tells you about Lake Wobegon. He hasn't been around here for years. He's living in the past." Later, John stakes out a New York bookstore, surreptitiously repositioning Alida's new book to better vantage and spying on the customers perusing the shelves. One can see Keillor himself in John's place:

> As I turned to leave, I noticed a woman looking at Alida's book. A woman with wild black hair, in a white suit and black T-shirt, who read a couple pages, glanced at Alida's picture on the back flap, and put it under her arm. A reader! Someone who was actually going to sit and soak up those sentences so laboriously composed, eat that permanent banquet arranged at lavish expense.
> A reader! I was overjoyed. I wanted to shake her hand. I wanted to invite her to the wedding.

Keillor's facetiousness is right on the money. Success as a fiction writer is not easy, and Keillor obviously has firsthand knowledge of the difficulties faced in the modern-day publishing industry.

Nevertheless, as evidenced by his long-running weekly radio program and nine books, Keillor has found success with his "little town that time forgot." He appears to have an infinite number of stories to tell and a ready audience to tell them to. Unlike his protagonist's taciturn father Byron, who was not interested in making new friends because it would take too long to tell them all his stories, Keillor continually reaches out to listeners and readers, new and old, by finding the extraordinary in the ordinary.

C. K. Breckenridge

Sources for Further Study

Booklist. XCIV, October 1, 1997, p. 276.
Entertainment Weekly. October 31, 1997, p. 101.
Library Journal. CXXII, December, 1997, p. 153.
National Review. XLIX, December 8, 1997, p. 50.
The New York Times Book Review. CII, October 26, 1997, p. 14.
People Weekly. XLVII, December 8, 1997, p. 43.
Publishers Weekly. CCXLIV, September 29, 1997, p. 66.
USA Today. November 26, 1997, p. D13.
The Washington Post Book World. XXVII, November 30, 1997, p. 1.

THE WOMEN

Author: Hilton Als (1961-   )
Publisher: Farrar Straus Giroux (New York). 145 pp. $21.00
Type of work: Memoir
Time: 1932-1991
Locale: New York City

In his idiosyncratic work, Hilton Als seeks to explain his homosexuality with his self-identification with women and reflects on the lives of black literary artists Dorothy Dean and Owen Dodson

Principal personages:
HILTON ALS, the author, who tells of his childhood experiences and
     juvenile discovery of his homosexuality
MARIE ALS, his beloved mother, who died of diabetes
CYPRIAN WILLIAMS, his remote father
DOROTHY DEAN, a Harvard-educated black intellectual who looked for
     love among gays and whites
OWEN DODSON, a black poet and dramatist who was young Als's mentor
     and lover
AN ANONYMOUS JANITOR, a black pederast who had sexual relations
     with a ten-year-old Als
LOUISE LITTLE, the mother of Malcolm X, preferred over her son by the
     author

Overall, Hilton Als's startling book remains difficult to categorize. Even though parts of it deal with the life of its author, *The Women* functions both as multiple memoir and a platform for social and intellectual criticism by the outspoken and opinionated Als. Written in a deliberately unconventional style, the book's three chapters focus on Als's mother and his relationship with her, the doomed life of the black intellectual Dorothy Dean, and the author's interaction with one of his first literary mentors and lovers, the critic and author Owen Dodson.

Thus, a reader who does not mind Als's almost mannerist style and his deliberate refusal to write a conventional autobiography will find *The Women* a stimulating intellectual feast. The book is very wide-ranging and reflects on subjects as varied as Als's boyhood, possible reasons for homosexual behavior, and the author's critical evaluation of the African American writers of the Harlem Renaissance of the early and mid-twentieth century.

Als's commemorative description of his mother Marie Als's hard but determined life introduces a person whose strength of will seems unsurmountable. Born on the Caribbean island of Barbados, she emigrated to New York City to be near the father of her next four children. Among them was the young Als, who never established a close relationship with his biological father Cyprian Williams. Instead, he grew up admiring the iconoclastic will of his mother and sought to emulate the lifestyle of his unnamed sister, eleven years his senior.

For Als, this identification with his mother and favorite sister, his desire to live in their worlds, was what made him become an "auntie man." This is the term men on Barbados use derogatorily to describe what they consider an effeminate homosexual. Als takes up the term with pride and unflinchingly reports his encounter with a black janitor, who sexually abused the ten-year-old boy. Yet Als does not view that encounter in these terms; *The Women* calls it a seduction of the man by the boy. Here, a reader may differ with Als, but the author's startling statements and ideas force a critical reflection and confrontation.

Similar to Norman Mailer's apparently paradoxical self-description as a "White Negro" in his *Advertisements for Myself* (1959), Als calls himself a "Negress." Als uses this term repeatedly to indicate his self-avowed identification with his mother and his sisters, to whom he applies the word as well. By using this term, usage of which is discouraged in contemporary standard English because of its negative, derogatory associations, Als deliberately tries to shock the reader and establish a certain sense of radical self-esteem. This follows the custom of some homosexuals who have claimed the originally pejorative term "queer" for themselves and is indicative of how close *The Women* runs along the cutting edge of cultural upheavals in the late twentieth century. Moreover, "Negress" clearly denotes a female sexual identity, which is obviously different from his own biological makeup. By applying the term to himself, Als persistently reminds his readers that he believes that his gender identity has crossed the physical lines of biology. For Als, a "Negress" is a culturally and personally determined position of the self, and in his book, either sex can use this startling description. For the reader, this idea certainly offers plenty of food for thought.

As so often in *The Women*, the contemplation of his family life, with its special dynamics, serves Als as a starting point for his literary and cultural criticism. Taking his sister's resistance to her status as "Negress," and her and his mother's command that Als act more masculine, Als compares their difficulty with themselves and his homosexuality to the family of Malcolm X. Taking on Malcolm X, Als declares that Malcolm hated his mother because she lived like what Als calls a "Negress." For Als, Louise Little was an admirable person who was misunderstood by her famous son, and *The Women* praises her qualities. To present the reader with his vision of Little's world, Als tries to imagine what she would have written in her own autobiography, taking his cues from quotes of her son's famous text. This is certainly of interest to the reader, as are many of Als's critical asides. Yet the question remains to what extent Als projects himself and his own ideas and viewpoints onto this other, deceased, person who has not left such a written account of her life.

As with Louise Little, his mother, and his favorite sister, Als is similarly fond of his father's outspoken but alcoholic sister, whom he venerates as another like person. Als views her drinking as a reaction to the many disappointments in her life, ranging from a stillborn son to a bad marriage. Again, *The Women* presents the reader with a point of view which invites intellectual discussion.

The second part of *The Women* is only remotely linked to the first and third part, which focus more directly on Als's life. The book's middle part tells instead of the tragic life of black intellectual Dorothy Dean, who was much beloved by New York

City's homosexuals who gave her a splendid memorial service in the spring of 1987 after her death from lung cancer at age fifty-four.

The Women's generous portrait of Dean may have some roots in the affinity which its author feels toward this outcast, misplaced, and unique person who defied all conventional attempts at categorization. This is, of course, a position similar to the one Als is staking out for himself in his book. Born in 1932, and one of the few middle-class African American women attending the elite colleges of Radcliffe and Harvard, Dean saw herself as the perennial outsider, according to Als. Isolated from the experience of the majority of black people in America during these years, Als quotes from Dean's copious writings to illustrate his point that she felt her uniqueness very intensely.

Because they were similarly outcast, Als writes, Dean soon began to associate with "closeted" white homosexuals during her college years. Intellectually and spiritually attracted to these men, among them Dean was able to overcome the barriers of race but foundered in the face of different sexual orientations. Her ardent love affairs with gay men inevitably faltered and left Dean with a growing problem with alcohol and substance abuse.

Moreover, while white gay men could hide behind an artificial facade of hetero-sexuality, Als argues, Dean, even though she felt differently, could never hide her race and overcome the latent and overt racism which lingered in the world beyond her colleges and socially elevated world. For Als, this inability to hide a physical and biological body links up to his own biological maleness, which is with him in spite of his desire to be like a black woman.

When Dean got pregnant by a French musician while studying abroad, she gave up the boy for immediate adoption and sank into deep depression. Returning to America during the 1960's, the gay scene of New York City bestowed glamour and cultural approbation on the unique, witty, but unfortunately rather self-destructive Dean.

With the waning of the counterculture and the advent of the 1970's, however, Als indicates that Dean had lost her grip on the fiercely competitive "in" world of the avant-garde of New York City. The newly liberated gays thrived less on the wit and intellectual fun that Dean provided and more on the leather and chains of new sadomasochistic establishments. For Dean, another affair with a homosexual cocaine dealer failed. Disappointed and in ill health, Dean moved to Colorado in 1980. For Als, however, her life was exemplary, and he clearly admires her struggle to survive in a world where her race and sexual orientation made her an outsider among outsiders.

The final part of *The Women* returns to Als's life and his encounters with his first mentor and elderly lover, the black poet, dramatist, and literary critic Owen Dodson. Their relationship began when a female tutor sent the thirteen-year-old Als to her friend Dodson for some free books. Immediately the two hit it off with one another, and when Als turned fifteen in 1976, they become lovers.

As Als describes it, his mother and sister feared that Dodson was turning Als into a homosexual. For the author, this is ironic, since he states that he already felt as such before meeting the older mentor. Like Dodson, who disliked women because he felt he was competing with them for male lovers, Als felt that jealousy and envy motivated his family since he was shifting his attention away from them and to the old man. When Als broke off his affair with Dodson at age nineteen, he did so in obedience to his mother's and sister's wishes. Yet he describes his act as one of betrayal. Dodson's death three years later occurred before the two had a chance to meet again.

While the last chapter of *The Women* is as courageously open in its descriptions of its subjects' sexual actions as the preceding chapters, Als makes clear that his attraction to Dodson was not purely sexual. What attracted him, in the words of his memoir, which doubles as a small biography of Dodson, was Dodson's sense that literary criticism was an act of public performance, a view shared by Als. Another characteristic Als found attractive about Dodson was his knowledge of, but personal disrespect for, the authors of the Harlem Renaissance. This group of black writers, who worked from the 1920's to the 1940's, was privately ridiculed by Dodson. Als felt sympathy for Dodson's personal view that the writers of the Harlem Renaissance, including Zora Neale Hurston, Langston Hughes, and Countee Cullen, were too repressed and middle class in their aspirations. Rather than radically embracing a black culture different from that of the whites, Als and Dodson felt, the "New Negro" writers of the Harlem Renaissance became sanctimonious in their desire to obtain for blacks a culture modeled after white lifestyles and ideals.

Dodson's alcoholism was greeted with a mixture of fascination and bewilderment by the young Als. Their first sexual encounter took place after Dodson had to leave a dinner party in his apartment and retreat to his bedroom because of alcohol-induced vomiting. Als describes his own reactions as free of revulsion or discomfort as he followed the older man to his bed. Again, the reader is confronted with a radical vision of an exceptional lifestyle.

Throughout, *The Women* is an intensely personal and unique book. It is also radically open in its presentation of its subject matter. Whether Als chronicles Dean's ultimately doomed quest to find love, tells of his mother's unconventional relationship with his father, or illustrates his own actions and thoughts as a black homosexual, *The Women* never covers up unfortunate occurrences. Honest and opinionated, Hilton Als presents a style and viewpoint which is genuinely his own. *The Women* is certainly a remarkable book.

R. C. Lutz

Sources for Further Study

Artforum. XXXV, November, 1996, p. S14.
Houston Chronicle. February 16, 1997, p. Z23.
Library Journal. CXXI, September 1, 1996, p. 198.
Los Angeles Times. November 13, 1996, p. E8.
The New York Times Book Review. CII, January 5, 1997, p. 7.
The New Yorker. LXXII, December 16, 1996, p. 108.
Publishers Weekly. CCXLIII, September 23, 1996, p. 65.
San Francisco Chronicle. January 12, 1997, p. REV3.

WOMEN AND THE COMMON LIFE
Love, Marriage, and Feminism

Author: Christopher Lasch (1932-1994)
Edited by Elisabeth Lasch-Quinn
Publisher: W. W. Norton (New York). 196 pp. $23.00
Type of work: Essays, history, and women's issues

These essays represent Lasch's revision of the common contemporary understanding of the history of marriage, women, and the evolution of feminism in Western society from the seventeenth century until today

The daughter of the late American historian Christopher Lasch is editor of this volume of his spirited essays on women, romantic love and marriage, and feminism. All but one of the essays had been published elsewhere. Lasch's ruminations on what he considered important questions in these realms occupied his thinking and influenced his work for many years. Questions about the place of women in society, the connections between love and marriage, and the roots of feminist thought have yielded conclusions not always congruent with reality, according to Lasch. The most recently written essay in the collection, "Bourgeois Domesticity," was near completion at the time of the author's death from cancer in 1994. In the two years that preceded his passing, Lasch himself chose which of his essays were to be included here. The selection is a good representation of his thought and its development, rather than a reflection of the mind of the editor.

Lasch's aim is to demonstrate the connections between contemporary feminism and an emerging preference for intimacy as a basis for marriage. He critiques some facile and incomplete conclusions about society past that he believes infect modern thought. He believes that today's extensive reliance on processes and institutions that are the legacy of the Enlightenment and its worship of reason has produced a new paternalism, heir to the patriarchy of past generations. Rather than increasing and assuring freedom for the family and for women, twentieth century professionalization has rendered modern life nearly devoid of intimacy and imagination and has bound it to a new form of oppression. The hegemony of reason has produced a magnifying glass that brings so much light and heat that it burns away the very life it scrutinizes.

The book is divided into two sections. Part 1, "Manners and Morals," presents a historical cameo of life as it was lived and recorded prior to the modern era. The section includes four essays, somewhat uneven in what they offer the reader but clear in what they are trying to accomplish: laying the groundwork for Lasch's conclusions. Lasch contends that much of what has been written about past institutions and practices is inaccurate, or at best incomplete. Some literature from the past, especially drama, may have exaggerated certain aspects of male-female relationships. The accuracy of the picture is further compromised when viewed by contemporary historians, feminists, and others through a murky lens, clouded by preoccupations with the abstract question of gender. Lasch sees this as the wrong question.

Part 2 offers his vigorous and sometimes caustic commentary on modern society and its chroniclers. It includes, for example, some rather direct shots at Carol Gilligan, one of feminism's contemporary heroes. This seems to be the more successful section of the book. Its representative essays are more even than those in part 1, and it takes on the concrete issues of modern feminist and male scholarship with a decisive cutting edge. Lasch's assertion that society has moved "from patriarchy to neopaternalism" informs its content.

In the first essay, "Comedy of Love and Querelles des Femmes," the author enters the persistent debate about the nature and place of women in society. Lasch questions the common wisdom that medieval courtly life reflected misogyny. His read on the period suggests that rather than a "diatribe against womanhood," the quarrels over women that are represented in the literature of the time were really intended as lighthearted play, in which both sexes are the target of satire. The author shifts the question from abstract thinking about women to the actual status of women as lovers and as wives. He defines the issue not as a detached dispute about whether women are equal to men in general but as an exploration of the relative equality of women in different social constructs. This theme, the need to locate questions about women in historical context rather that to distill them into a dualistic mind-body dichotomy, is consistent throughout the essays.

Selections in the first section of the book are not evenly rendered. Some are so generously punctuated with quotations and ideas from other sources that the casual reader may be reluctant to continue. The second essay, a review of a book by Jean Hagstrum, abandons the reader to mine Lasch's themes and thinking in the ore of another's work. Yet Lasch is not reticent in presenting his reaction to Hagstrum's position. This review becomes another opportunity to reassert Lasch's belief that the contemporary imagination and emotional horizon have reached a state of poverty.

His piece exploring England's move to suppress clandestine marriages in the mid-eighteenth century illustrates that such marriages actually realized the ideal of romantic love as part of marriage more than the expedient arranged marriages that were the custom. The new law was imposed to regularize the contractual process of marriage, navigating the various intersecting religious streams and the interests of families and prospective spouses. The law's result, however, was to bring marriage more fully under the control of the prevailing bourgeois morality, with its standards of thrift and delay of immediate gratification. This piece of legislation represented the relentless movement toward the "therapeutic state" that Lasch details in the book's final essay.

The hindsight of history soon verified that the middle-class bulwark of marriage, purporting to offer a refuge and terminus for the "fashionable" but economically dependent woman, was not a panacea for the ills that intruded on both private and public life. Women were encouraged to become "useful rather than ornamental" (Hannah More) and seek a marriage of egalitarian friendship rather than transient passion, which rendered women "either slaves or tyrants" (Mary Wollstonecraft). This change for women, which Lasch sees as originating within the domestic circle itself, is the prodrome and catalyst to women's activism in the greater community. He contends that feminism was in fact fanned by the flame of the domestic hearth rather than a reaction to it. It was in the kitchen that the caldrons of feminist thinking began to boil.

Having set the stage for his own position on modern life in part 1, Lasch exposes his ideas more fully in part 2. The state of women and of the common life in the 1990's today may not be better than it was in previous eras. Five essays unpack Lasch's read on the rise of the suburbs, modern scholarship that separates the worlds and wisdom of men and women, and the final triumph of the institutions erected on the altar of reason to regulate the lives of women and the home.

Postwar patterns divided the arenas of men and women in a way unprecedented in history. The suburban migration produced for the first time a physical distance between "women's work" and that of men. This physical separation, a radical extension of the nineteenth century privatization of the domestic sphere with the onslaught of the Industrial Revolution, resulted in a situation that no nineteenth century reformist could have predicted. For Lasch, it produced the "suburbanization of the American soul." Rather than nourishing the anorexic feminine spirit with productive work significant to the greater society, activity that might overcome the isolated "make-work" context of housewifery, suburban living eventually pushed women to buy the common commodity of the marketplace: that work is valuable only if it is paid. Yet ingesting a large bite of the corporate pie has produced little more than an oversized stomachache and a recurring appetite. It has not cured the hunger for meaning. The feminist movement, seeking baptism and redemption in the spill of corporate capitalism, has been instead engulfed by its values and seems doomed to be drowned in its demands. Lasch sees no "progress" here. His corrective is to transform the structures of contemporary capitalism. This clarion call places him among the most political of feminists.

Perhaps the best essay in the collection is the whimsically titled "Gilligan's Island." Assuming that the reference was to the defunct television show, readers may well be caught off guard to find an incisive critique of the other Gilligan, Carol. Lasch does an exemplary job of analyzing her research, probing its holes and exposing its flaws. He notes, for example, the ambivalence Gilligan exhibits in her treatment of women's difference from men.

Especially interesting is Lasch's commentary on the research done at Laurel School, a kindergarten through senior high all-girls' institution in a suburban community. Contrary to some feminist wisdom, such as that in practice at Laurel, Lasch believes that what girls need, instead of increased doses of care and self-esteem, is an exposure to a wider worldview, one that includes impersonal rather than individualistic ideals, experiences of the marketplace as well as those of tight-knit relationships among women. He even indulges the suggestion that girls could profit from exposure to literature taken from the now-suspect dead white men's corpus. Even those without firsthand knowledge of Laurel School will find Lasch on target with his analysis of the retreat of late twentieth century women into the comfort of an all-female cocoon.

The chrysalis must, inevitably, yield the butterfly. Shelter from the wider reality cannot prepare even the most vulnerable and delicate to cope effectively with the exigencies of their context.

Men's studies do not escape Lasch's equal-opportunity critique. In documenting the multiplication of male-oriented books that parallel the introspective examinations of gender in women, he laments that "the market for self-pity . . . is inexhaustible." The preoccupation with gender in both burgeoning literary collections, according to Lasch, "tends to coarsen our sensibilities rather than to refine them. It replaces historical explanation with formulas, rips ideas out of context and often strengthens the very stereotypes it seeks to discredit."

The transference of dominance over women from former to contemporary masters is underlined in the final essays of the book. "The therapeutic state" is Lasch's term for modern society, which he believes has changed the venue of authority over women from a patriarchal overlord to a therapeutic one. The liberal state advanced a number of official and professional persons: doctors, social workers, juvenile authorities—all sorts of "official" personnel that keep "a watchful eye on the pathology of the nuclear family," lest it err in its historic task. Lasch is clear in his prescription. "What the family needs," he asserts, "is a policy on officials, designed to keep them in their place."

Elisabeth Lasch-Quinn can be proud of this tribute to her father, which, although begun at his deathbed, emerges in the light of day to catch the sun of good sense for the contemporary reader. As a woman, she need not be disquieted by his critique of feminism. His treatment seems balanced, fair, and more successful than many. For a further look at Christopher Lasch's views on the family, the reader may investigate *Haven in a Heartless World: The Family Besieged*, written in 1977.

Dolores L. Christie

Sources for Further Study

Boston Globe. March 23, 1997, p. N17.
First Things. February, 1997, p. 40.
Library Journal. CXXII, January 1, 1997, p. 127.
Los Angeles Times Book Review. January 12, 1997, p. 10.
New Statesman. CXXVI, March 21, 1997, p. 53.
The New York Times Book Review. CII, January 19, 1997, p. 8.
The Observer. March 16, 1997, p. 17.
Public Interest. Fall, 1997, p. 116.
The Times Literary Supplement. July 11, 1997, p. 13.
The Washington Post Book World. XXVII, March 9, 1997, p. 8.
The Wilson Quarterly. XXI, Winter, 1997, p. 96.

WOMEN WITH MEN

Author: Richard Ford (1944-   )
Publisher: Alfred A. Knopf (New York). 255 pp. $23.00
Type of work: Short stories
Time: 1975 and undefined
Locale: Montana and Paris

Three stories by 1995 Pulitzer Prize winner Richard Ford about a young boy coming of age in Montana and grown men seeking identity in Paris

Principal characters:
> MARTIN AUSTIN, married businessman
> JOSÉPHINE BELLIARD, a French woman Martin meets
> CHARLEY MATTHEWS, writer and college professor
> HELEN CARMICHAEL, his traveling companion, a former student
> LAWRENCE, a seventeen-year-old living in Montana
> DORIS, his aunt

Until he won the Pulitzer Prize in 1995 for *Independence Day*, Richard Ford was best known for his generally well-received novel *The Sportswriter* (1986), to which his Pulitzer Prize winner is a sequel of sorts. The central character of the two novels, Frank Bascomb, has been compared with Arthur Miller's Willy Loman and John Updike's Harry Angstrom as a middle-class American comic-tragic hero. The novels themselves have been called masterful works of great fiction that will ensure Ford's place as a great American writer.

Admirers of the short story will best remember Ford as the author of *Rock Springs* (1987), a collection that has guaranteed Ford a place in textbook anthologies, especially with the title story as well as with "Communist" and "Great Falls," stories that focus on adolescent boys trying to find someone on whom to model their lives and on displaced men unable to establish any sense of identity or stability.

In this new collection of three long stories, or short novels, Ford is still concerned with the painful initiation of adolescent males and the dilemma of lost and drifting middle-aged men, but these "new" fictions have neither the comprehensive voice and vision of Ford's highly praised novels nor the tight, metaphoric technique of his best stories. In the two pieces that focus on American men in Paris—"The Womanizer" and "Occidentals"—the central characters are unsympathetic and not particularly wise; they have no humor, they drift passively through relationships, and they affect others only negatively. "Jealous" is the best of the lot, but only because Ford seems much more comfortable focusing on a young man in Montana, a country he obviously knows well, than on middle-aged men adrift in Paris, a city that he seems to know only as a prototypical European site of American dreams and disillusionment.

"The Womanizer" first appeared in *Granta* in the summer of 1992, while "Jealous" was published in *The New Yorker* in November, 1992. "Occidentals" apparently is previously unpublished. The collection is so lackluster that one is tempted to suggest, perhaps uncharitably, that Ford's publisher wished to capitalize quickly on his Pulitzer

Prize visibility and urged him to "put together" this collection out of whatever he had lying around. Perhaps not, but the book does not promise to add significantly to Ford's reputation or career. Even the title seems to be something an editor devised to stitch together some disparate and desultory pieces.

The title of "The Womanizer" suggests what thematic focus Ford is trying to explore in the first story. The answer to the unspoken question, "What is a womanizer?," according to Ford's take on the topic, is that he is a disengaged, passive romantic. Although such a passive character as Martin Austin may very well have been a typical character of the minimalist-realist trend in the late 1980's and early 1990's, he seems dated here. The plot is simple enough: Martin, a forty-four-year-old businessman, married with no children, meets Joséphine Belliard, a French woman in her thirties, who is in the midst of divorcing her husband. Although Martin is not unhappy with his wife, he wants to do "something extraordinary," saying to the bemused and more sophisticated Joséphine, "I'd like to make you happy somehow."

Although Martin's wooing of Joséphine seems romantically motivated, it is, in practice, indecisive and indifferent. Joséphine is not passionately interested in Martin, asking him directly at one point what he wants from her, and Martin does not seem passionate about her, telling her at one point, "This is real life. We could be lovers." When he talks to his wife on the phone, he perversely tells her he is going out to dinner with a woman. Although he does not hint to his wife of a sexual involvement with Joséphine, he lets her know that he is not really interested in their relationship either. After being back home in America only one day, his indifference to his wife drives her away, and he impulsively flies back to Paris. Even this drastic act of leaving his job and his wife, however, has no real energy about it. When he arrives back in Paris and calls Joséphine, she is as indifferent to him as she was before.

The story reaches its contrived climax when Martin takes care of Joséphine's young son Leo while she goes to see her lawyer. While in the park, Martin is so distracted by his recent actions, his own weak and indecisive romanticism, and Joséphine's indifference that he allows Leo to be kidnapped and sexually assaulted. When the boy is found, the mother informed, and the police report made, Joséphine confronts Martin with the ultimate angry retort to his "womanizing" idealization: "It is not a game. You know? Maybe to you it is a game." Finally, as if the reader is not astute enough to grasp Ford's thematic interest in the story, Joséphine spits out, "You don't know who you are. . . . Who are you? . . . Who do you think you are? You're nothing." The story ends with Austin still in Paris, admiring his wife for the fact that she "had felt a greater sense of responsibility than he had; a greater apprehension of life's importance, its weight and permanence."

Although Charley Matthews, the central character in "Occidentals," is a college professor in Paris to meet with his editor and the translator of his first novel, he seems very much like Martin Austin—passive, indifferent, and disengaged. One can hardly imagine he would be capable of writing a novel. His traveling companion is Helen Carmichael, one of his former students, with whom he has had an affair for two years. Charley vaguely knows she had "cancer of the something" the year before. He is not in love with Helen, but is with her because she seems to make no more demands on him than he does on her.

Charley's one source of disappointment and woe, the narrator relates, is his defeated marriage, about which he has written his novel, *The Predicament*. The title comes from Charley's knowledge that he and his wife's hating each other was easier than trying to love somebody else and that it would have been better for them to set aside their differences and call it a marriage. How to do this was precisely the predicament he could not resolve.

Paris is a series of disappointments for Charley. His editor changes his plans and cannot meet him, the weather is bad, and Helen is not feeling well. Nothing much of significance happens in the story until its climax. Charley and Helen meet two other Americans, Beatrice and Rex, but they add little to an understanding of Charley's identity, which seems, after all, to be the central concern of the story. In a far-fetched anecdote that is supposed to be symptomatic of his aimless romanticism, Charley happens to remember that a woman he once had an affair with in America now lives in Paris, and he just happens to have her phone number in his wallet. He calls her, but like Martin Austin in "The Womanizer," he does not really know what he wants from her. When she is only mildly interested that he has called and tells him that her husband is now with her, Charley does not tell her he is in Paris.

The story comes to a climax when Charley returns to his hotel to discover that Helen has taken an overdose of pills because she knows she is dying of cancer. In her suicide note, she makes a Ford-forced literary connection between her cancer cells and Charley's novel: Both seem to represent all of life. Helen's death has no more effect on Charley than her life has had. He merely thinks he will have to take a chance with his faulty French and find someplace to eat his dinner alone. The novel ends with a sort of coda when Charley meets his translator and seems to come to some under-standing about his life. The last paragraph has him thinking that he had "learned something. He had commenced a new era in his life." There is nothing in Charley's character or Ford's prose to help the reader understand what Charley has learned or what this new era will be; consequently, there is nothing to make the reader really care.

"Jealous" is more successful than the two middle-aged-men-in-Paris stories, not only because it is set in Montana, where Ford lived for a time—and thus seems an area with which he is more engaged—but also because it is told from the point of view of the seventeen-year-old boy at its center, rather than from the talky limited omniscient point of view that seems to go on endlessly with explanations and ruminations in "The Womanizer" and "Occidentals."

The story takes place on the day before Thanksgiving in 1975. Lawrence has been living with his father in a rural area, but on this day he is going to go to Seattle, Washington, to visit his mother. His mother's sister, Aunt Doris, a sexy free spirit, is going to accompany him on the train. The plot focuses on their misadventures in the town of Shelby while waiting for the train. Doris meets a man in a bar whom the sheriff and deputies come looking for on suspicion of murdering his wife. The man is killed in a shootout in the bar. After Doris and Lawrence are questioned, they board the train for Seattle. Although Ford does not make it clear what effect the killing of the man in the bar has on the boy, the story ends with him sitting in the train feeling calm for the first time in his life.

The voice of the boy is similar to the voices of the young men in *Rock Springs*. The problem is, what worked in 1987 when Ford's collection was published, and perhaps even what worked in 1992, when this story was published in *The New Yorker*, does not necessarily work now. As in the two Paris stories, there is little engagement and no real sense of involvement; instead, there is a kind of trendy minimalist passivity and simplistic blue-collar realism parading as honesty and down-to-earth truth.

Only one scene in the story, when Lawrence and his aunt are sitting in her car after the killing, has a sense of danger and mysterious involvement. Doris asks the boy to hold her because she is so cold. "'You need to warm me up,' she whispered. 'Are you brave enough to do that? Or are you a coward on the subject?'" As he feels her breathing under her coat, she says, as if she were sorry about something, "Oh, my. You've got everything don't you? You've just got everything." This sexually suggestive encounter with his aunt seems to have little to do with the boy's coming of age. In short, readers cannot be sure what advance on his life this one day before Thanksgiving has made.

In an interview in 1987, at the high point of Ford's success with *The Sportswriter* and *Rock Springs*, he told an interviewer that he started to write novels because he got sick of writing bad stories, sending them off, and getting them back in a short amount of time. Now that he has won the Pulitzer Prize, Ford does not have to worry too much about sending off stories and getting them back, but perhaps he should start worrying again about writing bad stories.

Charles E. May

Sources for Further Study

Booklist. XCIII, May 15, 1997, p. 1540.
Los Angeles Times Book Review. July 13, 1997, p. 2.
The New York Times Book Review. CII, July 13, 1997, p. 5.
The New Yorker. LXXIII, December 15, 1997, p. 155.
North and South. December, 1997, p. 114.
Publishers Weekly. CCXLIV, May 12, 1997, p. 57.
San Francisco Chronicle. June 15, 1997, p. REV3.
The Times Literary Supplement. August 29, 1997, p. 23.
The Wall Street Journal. June 27, 1997, p. A13.
The Washington Post. July 8, 1997, p. E2.

¡YO!

Author: Julia Alvarez (1950-   )
Publisher: Algonquin Books of Chapel Hill (Chapel Hill, North Carolina). 309 pp. $18.95
Type of work: Novel
Time: The 1960's to the 1990's
Locale: New York City, New England, and the Dominican Republic

Julia Alvarez presents Dominican American author Yolanda García through the eyes of sixteen diverse characters whose lives have intersected with hers in various ways

Principal characters:
YOLANDA MARIA GARCÍA, a Dominican transplanted to the United
    States, where she has a career as a writer
CARLOS GARCÍA, her father, a physician
LAURA GARCÍA, her mother
CARLA GARCÍA, her oldest sister
SANDI GARCÍA, her middle sister
FIFI GARCÍA, her youngest sister
LUCINDA MARIA VICTORIA DE LA TORRE, her cousin
PRIMITIVA (PRIMI), the Garcías' maid
SARITA, Primi's daughter, who becomes a physician
DOUGLAS MANLEY, Yolanda's third husband
JORDAN GARFIELD, Yolanda's college English professor
MARIE BEAUDRY, Yolanda's landlady, an abused wife

What readers learn about Yolanda García, the protagonist of this novel, they glean through sixteen discrete sections, all of which directly concern Yolanda. Many of these sections are interconnected. People who have known Yolanda reveal facets of her personality as they relate their encounters with her. From their revelations emerges a well-developed and complex portrayal of a multifaceted creative artist.

The arrangement of the separate portions, each about twenty pages long, is vital to the cohesiveness of the book. Although any of the sections might be read meaningfully as separate entities, it is their placement that justifies identifying the book as a novel rather than a collection of character sketches or short stories.

Yolanda is permitted to tell her own story only in the dialogue she has with the characters of each section, identified by such designations as "The Sisters," "The Mother," "The Caretakers," "The Maid's Daughter," and "The Third Husband." The result is a carefully structured novel from which the protagonist emerges as one of the best developed protagonists in recent literature. Alvarez's structure, perfect for the telling of her highly autobiographical tale, allows for the presentation of a central character more complex and diverse than she would have seemed had any other method of presentation been used.

The clue to the novel's autobiographical nature lurks in the title itself. *Yo* is both a shortened form of Yolanda and the Spanish word for "I." Readers, however, must be cautioned to remember that *¡Yo!* is a work of fiction and cannot be read as an autobiography presumed to be accurate in all of its details.

Each of the sketches in this novel, along with presenting one or more characters as they interact with Yo, deals with some global theme. A political current relating to the despotic dictatorship of strongman Rafael Trujillo in the Dominican Republic underlies many of the individual sketches, in which Alvarez also deals with such broad and compelling matters as political oppression, spousal abuse, homosexuality, acquired immunodeficiency syndrome (AIDS), poverty and exploitation in the Third World, the problems faced by immigrants trying to reestablish themselves in alien cultures, and the effects of the creative temperament on those whose lives intersect with the life of an artist.

Alvarez has already dealt chillingly with the Trujillo regime in her novel *In the Time of the Butterflies* (1995). She returns to this theme, although somewhat less stridently, in ¡*Yo!*. She also presented the García family in some detail in *How the García Girls Lost Their Accents* (1991).

The first section of ¡*Yo!*, called "Prologue," consists of one sketch, "The Sisters." It, like each sketch in the book, is identified with a descriptor, in this case "fiction." Other sections have such descriptors as "nonfiction," "poetry," "revelation," "confrontation," "characterization," and "tone," suggesting that Alvarez, a professor who was teaching writing at Middlebury College in Vermont when she wrote this book, perhaps composed along with her students, producing a sketch for each week of a sixteen-week semester, each sketch reflecting some major aspect of composition and contributing to an overall piece of creative writing, in this case a compelling novel.

The prologue is central to the novel as a whole. Yolanda García's sisters are uneasy about the liberties their sister takes in her writing with bits of private information she possesses about members of the family. They are concerned, as is Yolanda's mother in the first sketch in part 1, with what they regard as a violation of their privacy by a sister and daughter who, as the novel continues, is shown to be a natural storyteller but whose stories have sometimes created threatening situations.

The very last sketch, "The Father," touches on this subject as Carlos García, a member of the Dominican underground during the early years of his marriage, recalls how Yolanda, as a small child in Trujillo's Dominican Republic, placed the family in grave danger. Watching a movie with the family's neighbor General Molino, she boasted that her father—living in a dictatorial society where the possession of firearms by civilians was strictly banned—had a bigger gun that the one carried by the cowboy in the film.

This sketch is particularly telling because it contains the veiled suggestion that Molino took some sexual liberties with the small child. Bouncing Yolanda on his knee and tickling her from time to time, the general says, watching the television screen, "Ay, look at that big gun, Yoyo!" to which she replies, "My papi has a bigger gun!" The sexual implications here are inescapable.

These sexual implications relate to various aspects of Yolanda's sexual development and possibly suggest why she has married three times. The book's sexual undercurrent is handled discreetly and well, with the most direct and obvious sexual revelations being made in the sections entitled "The Stalker," whose descriptor is "tone," "The

Suitor," whose descriptor is "resolution," and "The Night Watchman," whose descriptor is "setting."

Each section carries its own specific theme that relates to a prevailing social or political crosscurrent. "The Landlady," whose descriptor is "confrontation," makes a strong feminist statement about spousal abuse. Marie Beaudry, who becomes Yolanda's landlady, suffers frequent beatings from a brutish husband who drinks too much. Like many abused wives, she denies that she is being abused, while blaming herself for motivating her husband's beatings. Yolanda finally confronts Clair Beaudry, the abusive husband, then forces Marie to confront him and to turn her life around.

This section reveals Yolanda striving for tenure at the college in which she teaches. She needs a quiet place in which to work, but having signed a lease on the apartment the Beaudrys own, located above their own home, she finds that she cannot work there because their noise as they fight intrudes on her space, upsetting her greatly.

Also, when the first rains come, she realizes that Clair Beaudry has, quite without conscience, rented her an apartment that floods in wet weather. The first flood destroys much of the material she has been working on in preparation for writing the book that she hopes will assure her being granted tenure.

Clair's reluctance to release Yolanda from her lease precipitates the confrontation that results, at Yolanda's instigation, in Marie's liberating herself from her abusive marriage. Clair Beaudry has reached the conclusion that Yolanda is a lesbian, although she is not, and accuses his wife of being drawn into Yolanda's web.

Yolanda does have a close lesbian friend, Tammy Rosen, but the two are no more than friends. Yolanda also has been close to a male homosexual, Jordan Garfield, her college English professor, with whom she has maintained contact through the years. Garfield, married for more than thirty years, finally leaves his wife, Helena. He soon enters into a homosexual relationship with a much younger colleague, Matthews, who eventually takes a teaching job in San Diego, putting the two a continent apart.

Their relationship, nevertheless, continues on a long-distance basis, with Garfield counting the time until he can retire, which will enable him to live with Matthews. Before this dream can be realized, however, Matthews reveals that he is dying of AIDS. Garfield, ever the caregiver, takes him in and tends him throughout what remains of his life.

Alvarez is particularly sensitive in presenting the details of relationships that skirt the fringe of what society regards as normal and usual. She also retains a great consistency in developing her characters. Garfield, for example, is ever the caring person, fully aware of his commitment and responsibility to others.

A major concern in this novel is the Dominican Republic. Carlos García has immigrated with his wife and four daughters to the United States, giving up his profession, medicine, to do so. Only after years of doing menial work is he finally able to be certified to practice medicine in his adopted country.

The family brings Primitiva, who worked for Laura García's family in the Dominican Republic, to the United States to be their maid. She eventually is able, with their help, to bring her daughter, Sarita, to live with her. The entire Primitiva/Sarita episode is intriguing in that it deals with a problem common in societies where large numbers of people are oppressed and live in grinding poverty. Primitiva, apparently, was impregnated by the husband of the family for whom she worked in the Dominican Republic, the well-to-do de la Torre family, from which Laura García comes. Primitiva's illegitimate daughter is, in all probability, the cousin of the García girls, although her social position is quite different from that of their cousin Lucinda, who also appears in the novel.

Sarita is bright and is not bound by the social constraints that keep Lucinda from obtaining a college education, so, ironically, Sarita becomes a physician while Lucinda, brought back to the Dominican Republic before she has finished her formal education, is never able to have a career. The message is clear: Immigration to the United States places enormous hurdles before Third World people, but as both Carlos and Sarita demonstrate, the United States is also a land of great opportunity in which immigrants of any social class can ultimately succeed and become contributing members of society.

Alvarez's technical experiments in this novel are noteworthy. Whereas most of the sketches focus on a central character who has in one way or another been a part of Yolanda García's life, two of the sketches, "The Sisters" and "The Caretakers," present two central characters who have had some crucial contact with the protagonist. Alvarez's most daring section, however, is "The Wedding Guests," in which the author experiments with the presentation of her narrative through the eyes of several characters, presented in brief segments, to whom she has introduced her readers earlier in the novel. This section, for all of its technical complexity, succeeds admirably and helps achieve a unity that adds an overall coherence to the larger work.

In *¡Yo!*, Alvarez consistently addresses the question of what it is to be a sensitive creative artist in the modern context and to be dissociated from one's native society. In this regard, *¡Yo!* is similar in its nostalgic tone to Cristina García's *Dreaming in Cuban* (1992) and *The Agüero Sisters* (1997).

The sensitivity that Yolanda García demonstrates, while in all likelihood part of her birthright, also has to do with her day-to-day encounters, many of them sexually based, although the author does not write in prurient detail about such encounters. In many of the sketches she touches on the subject of sexuality. Sexuality is emphasized in such sketches as "The Stalker," "The Suitor," "The Watchman," and "The Caretakers," but nearly all the book's pieces suggest through some subtle innuendo a sexual undercurrent skillfully but arcanely planted.

R. Baird Shuman

Sources for Further Study

The Atlantic. CCLXXIX, February, 1997, p. 110.
Booklist. XCIII, September 15, 1996, p. 180.

Chicago Tribune. January 26 1997, XIV, p. 2.
Hispanic. X, March, 1997, p. 68.
Library Journal. CXXI, October 1, 1996, p. 124.
Los Angeles Times. March 23, 1997, p. E1.
Ms. VII, March, 1997, p. 82.
The New York Times Book Review. CII, February 9, 1997, p. 19.
Publishers Weekly. CCXLIII, December 16, 1996, p. 38.
The Virginia Quarterly Review. LXXIII, Summer, 1997, p. 95.
The Washington Post Book World. XXVII, January 19, 1997, p. 9.

MAGILL'S
LITERARY ANNUAL
1998

BIOGRAPHICAL WORKS BY SUBJECT
1977-1998

ABEL, LIONEL
   Intellectual Follies (Abel) (85) 451

ABERNATHY, RALPH DAVID
   And the Walls Came Tumbling Down
   (Abernathy) (90) 39

ACHESON, DEAN
   Dean Acheson (McLellan) (77) 197

ADAMS, ABIGAIL
   Descent from Glory (Nagel) (H-84) 121

ADAMS, CHARLES FRANCIS
   Descent from Glory (Nagel) (H-84) 121

ADAMS, HENRY
   Descent from Glory (Nagel) (H-84) 121
   Five of Hearts, The (O'Toole) (91) 295
   Letters of Henry Adams, 1858-1892, The
   (Adams) (84) 441
   Letters of Henry Adams, 1892-1918, The
   (Adams) (90) 516

ADAMS, JOHN
   Descent from Glory (Nagel) (H-84) 121
   Faces of Revolution (Bailyn) (91) 279
   John Adams (Ferling) (93) 413

ADAMS, JOHN G.
   Without Precedent (Adams) (H-84) 497

ADAMS, JOHN QUINCY
   Descent from Glory (Nagel) (H-84) 121
   John Quincy Adams (Nagel) (98) 472

ADAMS, MIRIAM "CLOVER"
   Five of Hearts, The (O'Toole) (91) 295

ADLER, MORTIMER J.
   Philosopher at Large (Adler) (78) 654

AGEE, JAMES
   James Agee (Bergreen) (85) 473

AGEE, JOEL
   Twelve Years (Agee) (82) 854

AIKEN, CONRAD
   Conrad Aiken (Butscher) (89) 207
   Selected Letters of Conrad Aiken (Aiken)
   (79) 652

AKHMATOVA, ANNA
   Akhmatova Journals, 1938-41, The
   (Chukovskaya) (95) 19
   Anna Akhmatova (Reeder) (95) 38
   Nightingale Fever (Hingley) (82) 555

ALABI, PANTO
   Alabi's World (Price) (91) 10

ALEXANDER
   Search for Alexander, The (Lane Fox) (81) 712

ALLEN, FRED
   Province of Reason (Warner) (H-85) 368

ALLEN, PAULA GUNN
   I Tell You Now (Swann and Krupat, eds.) (88) 413

ALLENDE, SALVADOR
   Overthrow of Allende and the Politics of Chile,
   1964-1976, The (Sigmund) (78) 630

ALS, HILTON
   Women, The (Als) (98) 874

ALSOP, JOSEPH "JOE"
   Taking on the World (Merry) (97) 802

ALSOP, STEWART
   Taking on the World (Merry) (97) 802

ANDERSON, SHERWOOD
   Sherwood Anderson (Anderson) (85) 820
   Sherwood Anderson (Townsend) (88) 817

ANGELOU, MAYA
   All God's Children Need Traveling Shoes
   (Angelou) (87) 25
   Singin' and Swingin' and Gettin' Merry like
   Christmas (Angelou) (77) 738

ANGERMEYER, JOHANNA
   My Father's Island (Angermeyer) (91) 614

ANTHONY, SUSAN B.
   Elizabeth Cady Stanton, Susan B. Anthony,
   Correspondence, Writings, Speeches (Stanton
   and Anthony) (82) 214

ANTIN, MARY
   Province of Reason (Warner) (H-85) 368

ARBUS, DIANE NEMEROV
   Diane Arbus (Bosworth) (96) 174

ARENDT, HANNAH
   Between Friends (Arendt and McCarthy) (96) 73
   Hannah Arendt (Hill, ed.) (80) 395
   Hannah Arendt (Young-Bruehl) (83) 322

ARLETTY
   Six Exceptional Women (Lord) (95) 724

ARNOLD, MATTHEW
   Life of Matthew Arnold, A (Murray) (98) 500
   Matthew Arnold (Honan) (82) 518

ARTAUD, ANTONIN
   Antonin Artaud (Artaud) (77) 52
   Antonin Artaud (Esslin) (78) 68

ASHE, ARTHUR
   Days of Grace (Ashe and Rampersad) (94) 213

ATTLEE, CLEMENT
   Attlee (Harris) (H-84) 33

AUDEN, W. H.
   Auden (Davenport-Hines) (97) 79
   W. H. Auden (Carpenter) (82) 923
   W. H. Auden (Osborne) (80) 860

AUSTEN, JANE
   Jane Austen (Honan) (89) 409
   Jane Austen (Nokes) (98) 468
   Jane Austen (Tanner) (87) 435
   Life of Jane Austen, The (Halperin) (85) 564

AUSTER, PAUL
   Hand to Mouth (Auster) (98) 374

BAGWELL, ORLANDO
   I've Known Rivers (Lawrence-Lightfoot) (95) 384

BAKER, RUSSELL
   Good Times, The (Baker) (90) 309
   Growing Up (Baker) (83) 317

BAKHTIN, MIKHAIL
   Mikhail Bakhtin (Clark and Holquist) (86) 608
   Mikhail Bakhtin (Morson and Emerson) (92) 500

BALCH, EMILY GREENE
   Province of Reason (Warner) (H-85) 368

BALDWIN, JAMES
   James Baldwin (Leeming) (95) 388
   Talking at the Gates (Campbell) (92) 795

BALLARD, MARTHA
   Midwife's Tale, A (Ulrich) (91) 596

BIOGRAPHICAL WORKS BY SUBJECT

DONOVAN, WILLIAM J.
Donovan (Dunlop) (H-83) 99
DOOLITTLE, HILDA. *See* H. D.
DORR, HARBOTTLE, Jr.
Faces of Revolution (Bailyn) (91) 279
DORRIS, MICHAEL
Broken Cord, The (Dorris) (90) 76
DOS PASSOS, JOHN
Dos Passos (Carr) (85) 194
John Dos Passos (Ludington) (81) 464
Life Sentences (Epstein) (98) 504
DOSTOEVSKY, FYODOR
Dostoevsky (Dostoevsky) (77) 230
Dostoevsky, 1821-1849 (Frank) (77) 236
Dostoevsky, 1850-1859 (Frank) (84) 244
Dostoevsky, 1860-1865 (Frank) (87) 212
Dostoevsky, 1865-1871 (Frank) (96) 202
Selected Letters of Fyodor Dostoevsky
(Dostoevsky) (88) 806
DOTY, MARK
Heaven's Coast (Doty) (97) 368
DOUGLAS, KIRK
Ragman's Son, The (Douglas) (89) 692
DOUGLASS, FREDERICK
Frederick Douglass (McFeely) (92) 232
DRAKE, SIR FRANCIS
Sir Francis Drake (Sugden) (92) 757
DREISER, THEODORE
Theodore Dreiser, 1871-1907 (Lingeman)
(87) 847
Theodore Dreiser, 1908-1945 (Lingeman)
(91) 798
DRYDEN, JOHN
John Dryden and His World (Winn) (88) 438
DU BOIS, W. E. B.
W. E. B. Du Bois (Lewis) (94) 847
DUKAKIS, MICHAEL
What It Takes (Cramer) (93) 874
DULLES, ALLEN
Dulles (Mosley) (79) 170
DULLES, ELEANOR
Dulles (Mosley) (79) 170
DULLES, JOHN FOSTER
Dulles (Mosley) (79) 170
John Foster Dulles (Pruessen) (H-83) 229
DU MAURIER, DAPHNE
Daphne du Maurier (Forster) (94) 204
DUNBAR-NELSON, ALICE
Give Us This Day (Dunbar-Nelson) (86) 349
DUNNE, JOHN GREGORY
Harp (Dunne) (90) 364
DU PONTS, THE
Blood Relations (Mosley) (81) 93
du Pont Family, The (Gates) (80) 240
DURANT, ARIEL
Dual Autobiography, A (Durant and Durant)
(78) 280
DURANT, WILL
Dual Autobiography, A (Durant and Durant)
(78) 280
DURHAM, JIMMIE
I Tell You Now (Swann and Krupat, eds.) (88) 413

EARLS, FELTON
I've Known Rivers (Lawrence-Lightfoot) (95) 384
EATON, EDITH MAUDE. *See* SUI SIN FAR

EBAN, ABBA
Abba Eban (Eban) (78) 1
Decisions in Crisis (Brecher and Geist) (81) 228
EDEN, ANTHONY
Another World, 1897-1917 (Eden) (78) 59
EDISON, THOMAS ALVA
Edison (Clark) (78) 284
Streak of Luck, A (Conot) (80) 790
EDWARD VII
Edward VII (St. Aubyn) (80) 264
Uncle of Europe (Brook-Shepherd) (77) 861
EDWARD VIII
King Edward VIII (Ziegler) (92) 403
EHRLICH, GRETEL
Solace of Open Space, The (Ehrlich) (86) 840
EHRLICHMAN, JOHN
Witness to Power (Ehrlichman) (H-83) 473
EINSTEIN, ALBERT
Albert Einstein (Einstein) (80) 19
EISENHOWER, DWIGHT DAVID
Diary of James C. Hagerty, The (Hagerty)
(H-84) 125
Eisenhower, Vol. I (Ambrose) (H-84) 141
Eisenhower, Vol. II (Ambrose) (H-85) 120
Eisenhower and the Cold War (Divine) (82) 195
Eisenhower Diaries, The (Eisenhower) (82) 199
Eisenhower the President (Ewald) (82) 205
Eisenhower's Lieutenants (Weigley) (82) 210
Hidden-Hand Presidency, The (Greenstein)
(H-83) 190
ELEANOR OF AQUITAINE
Eleanor of Aquitaine (Seward) (80) 277
ELIADE, MIRCEA
Ordeal by Labyrinth (Eliade) (83) 572
ELIOT, ANDREW
Faces of Revolution (Bailyn) (91) 279
Parallel Lives (Rose) (84) 662
ELIOT, GEORGE
George Eliot (Ashton) (98) 335
Woman of Contradictions, A (Taylor) (91) 909
ELIOT, T. S.
Eliot's New Life (Gordon) (89) 262
Letters of T. S. Eliot, The (Eliot) (89) 488
Lives of the Modern Poets (Pritchard) (81) 520
Pound/Williams (Pound and Williams) (97) 675
T. S. Eliot (Ackroyd) (85) 932
T. S. Eliot (Bush) (85) 937
ELIZABETH I
Elizabeth Regina (Plowden) (81) 272
Elizabethan Deliverance, The (Bryant) (H-83) 114
First Elizabeth, The (Erickson) (H-84) 164
ELLIS, HAVELOCK
Havelock Ellis (Grosskurth) (81) 412
ELLISON, RALPH
Collected Essays of Ralph Ellison, The (Ellison)
(96) 128
EMERSON, RALPH WALDO
Emerson (Barish) (91) 249
Emerson (Richardson) (96) 222
Emerson Among the Eccentrics (Baker) (97) 239
Emerson in His Journals (Emerson) (83) 224
Ralph Waldo Emerson (McAleer) (85) 717
Waldo Emerson (Allen) (82) 902
ENGELS, FRIEDRICH
Selected Letters (Marx and Engels) (83) 722
EPSTEIN, JOSEPH
With My Trousers Rolled (Epstein) (96) 818

BIOGRAPHICAL WORKS BY SUBJECT

MACDONALD, ROSS
    Ross Macdonald (Bruccoli) (85) 766

MacLEISH, ARCHIBALD
    Archibald MacLeish (Donaldson) (93) 28
    Letters of Archibald MacLeish (MacLeish)
       (84) 436

McLUHAN, MARSHALL
    Letters of Marshall McLuhan (McLuhan) (89) 484
    Marshall McLuhan (Gordon) (98) 542
    Marshall McLuhan (Marchand) (90) 562

MACMILLAN, HAROLD
    Harold Macmillan (Fisher) (H-83) 185
    Harold Macmillan, 1894-1956 (Horne) (90) 352
    Harold Macmillan, 1957-1986 (Horne) (90) 358
    Past Masters, The (Macmillan) (77) 610
    War Diaries (Macmillan) (H-85) 474

MacNEICE, LOUIS
    Louis MacNeice (Stallworthy) (96) 444

McPHERSON, JAMES ALAN
    World Unsuspected, A (Harris, ed.) (88) 984

MADISON, JAMES
    Mr. Madison's War (Stagg) (H-84) 303
    Witnesses at the Creation (Morris) (86) 959

MAHLER, ALMA SCHINDLER
    Gustav Mahler, 1892-1904 (La Grange) (96) 321

MAHLER, GUSTAV
    Gustav Mahler, 1892-1904 (La Grange) (96) 321

MAILER, NORMAN
    Lives of Norman Mailer, The (Rollyson) (92) 445
    Mailer (Mills) (83) 428

MAIRS, NANCY
    Ordinary Time (Mairs) (94) 594
    Voice Lessons (Mairs) (95) 835
    Waist High in the World (Mairs) (98) 814

MALAN, RIAN
    My Traitor's Heart (Malan) (91) 624

MALCOLM X
    Malcolm (Perry) (92) 474

MALENKOV, GEORGY MAKSIMILIANOVICH
    All Stalin's Men (Medvedev) (H-85) 12

MALLARMÉ, STÉPHANE
    Throw of the Dice, A (Millan) (95) 782

MALRAUX, ANDRÉ
    Lazarus (Malraux) (78) 515

MANDELSTAM, OSIP
    Nightingale Fever (Hingley) (82) 555

MANET, ÉDOUARD
    Art and Act (Gay) (77) 67

MANN, HEINRICH
    Brothers Mann, The (Hamilton) (80) 119

MANN, THOMAS
    Brothers Mann, The (Hamilton) (80) 119

MANSFIELD, KATHERINE
    Collected Letters of Katherine Mansfield,
      1903-1917, The (Mansfield) (85) 106
    Collected Letters of Katherine Mansfield,
      1918-1919, The (Mansfield) (88) 165
    Katherine Mansfield (Tomalin) (89) 427

MAO, MADAME. See JIANG QING

MAO ZEDONG
    Mao (Terrill) (81) 549
    People's Emperor (Wilson) (81) 645
    Uncertain Partners (Goncharov, Lewis, and Xue)
      (95) 809

MARIE DE L'INCARNATION
    Women on the Margins (Davis) (96) 826

MARKHAM, BERYL
    Straight on till Morning (Lovell) (88) 865

MARLBOROUGH, DUKE OF. See CHURCHILL,
JOHN

MARLOWE, CHRISTOPHER
    Reckoning, The (Nicholl) (95) 639

MARQUAND, JOHN PHILLIP
    Marquand (Bell) (80) 517

MÁRQUEZ, GABRIEL GARCÍA. See GARCÍA
MÁRQUEZ, GABRIEL

MARSHALL, GEORGE C.
    General of the Army (Cray) (91) 333
    George C. Marshall, 1945-1959 (Pogue) (88) 346
    Marshall (Mosley) (H-83) 283

MARSHALL, LAURENCE K.
    Province of Reason (Warner) (H-85) 368

MARSHALL, THURGOOD
    Dream Makers, Dream Breakers (Rowan)
      (94) 252

MARX, KARL
    Karl Marx (Padover) (79) 349
    Selected Letters (Marx and Engels) (83) 722

MARY TUDOR
    Bloody Mary (Erickson) (79) 64

MASON, BOBBIE ANN
    World Unsuspected, A (Harris, ed.) (88) 984

MASTERS, HILARY
    Last Stands (Masters) (83) 386

MATHER, COTTON
    Life and Times of Cotton Mather, The
      (Silverman) (H-85) 256

MATISSE, HENRI
    Matisse (Schneider) (H-85) 303

MATTHIESSEN, PETER
    Indian Country (Matthiessen) (H-85) 241
    Snow Leopard, The (Matthiessen) (79) 685

MAUGHAM, W. SOMERSET
    Maugham (Morgan) (81) 559

MAYER, LOUIS B.
    Empire of Their Own, An (Gabler) (89) 278

MAYHEW, JONATHAN
    Faces of Revolution (Bailyn) (91) 279

MEAD, MARGARET
    With a Daughter's Eye (Bateson) (H-85) 507

MEDAWAR, PETER
    Memoir of a Thinking Radish (Medawar) (87) 541

MEHTA, VED
    Ledge Between the Streams, The (Mehta)
      (85) 539
    Sound-Shadows of the New World (Mehta)
      (87) 802
    Stolen Light, The (Mehta) (90) 758
    Up at Oxford (Mehta) (94) 823

MEITNER, LISE
    Lise Meitner (Sime) (97) 526

MEIR, GOLDA
    Decisions in Crisis (Brecher and Geist) (81) 228

MEITNER, LISE
    Lise Meitner (Sime) (97) 526

MELLONS, THE
    Mellons, The (Koskoff) (79) 434

MELVILLE, HERMAN
    Herman Melville (Parker) (97) 373
    Melville (Robertson-Lorant) (97) 568

MENCKEN, H. L.
    Diary of H. L. Mencken, The (Mencken) (91) 211

Time of Stalin, The (Antonov-Ovseyenko)
(82) 845
Uncertain Partners (Goncharov, Lewis, and Xue)
(95) 809
STANTON, ELIZABETH CADY
Elizabeth Cady Stanton, Susan B. Anthony,
Correspondence, Writings, Speeches (Stanton
and Anthony) (82) 214
In Her Own Right (Griffith) (H-85) 230
STAPLES, BRENT
Parallel Time (Staples) (95) 594
STEGNER, WALLACE
Wallace Stegner (Benson) (97) 871
STEIGER, ROD
Leaving a Doll's House (Bloom) (97) 494
STEIN, GERTRUDE
Six Exceptional Women (Lord) (95) 724
STEINBECK, JOHN
John Steinbeck (Parini) (96) 398
Steinbeck and Covici (Fensch) (80) 780
True Adventures of John Steinbeck, Writer, The
(Benson) (85) 927
STENDHAL
Lion for Love, A (Alter) (80) 497
Stendhal (Keates) (98) 726
STEPHEN, THOBY
Bloomsbury (Edel) (80) 88
STERN, RICHARD
Sistermony, A (Stern) (96) 716
STEVENS, MAY
Working It Out (Ruddick and Daniels, eds.)
(78) 937
STEVENS, WALLACE
Lives of the Modern Poets (Pritchard) (81) 520
Parts of a World (Brazeau) (84) 668
Wallace Stevens (Doggett and Buttel, eds.)
(81) 879
Wallace Stevens (Longenbach) (92) 859
Wallace Stevens, 1879-1923 (Richardson) (87) 927
Wallace Stevens, 1923-1955 (Richardson) (89) 882
STEVENSON, ADLAI
Adlai Stevenson and the World (Martin) (78) 6
STEVENSON, ROBERT LOUIS
Footsteps (Holmes) (86) 297
Robert Louis Stevenson (Calder) (81) 694
Robert Louis Stevenson (McLynn) (96) 655
STEVENSON, WILLIAM S.
Man Called Intrepid, A (Stevenson) (77) 475
STIEGLITZ, ALFRED
Georgia O'Keeffe (Robinson) (90) 289
Stieglitz (Lowe) (H-84) 426
STIMPSON, CATHARINE R.
Working It Out (Ruddick and Daniels, eds.)
(78) 937
STONE, CHARLES A.
Province of Reason (Warner) (H-85) 368
STOWE, HARRIET BEECHER
Harriet Beecher Stowe (Hedrick) (95) 296
STRACHEY, LYTTON
Bloomsbury (Edel) (80) 88
Great Friends (Garnett) (81) 386
Love in Bloomsbury (Partridge) (82) 504
STREICHER, JULIUS
Julius Streicher (Bytwerk) (H-83) 234
STRINDBERG, AUGUST
August Strindberg (Lagercrantz) (85) 32

STUART, JESSE HILTON
Jesse (Richardson) (85) 494
STYRON, WILLIAM
Darkness Visible (Styron) (91) 184
SUI SIN FAR
Sui Sin Far/Edith Maude Eaton (White-Parks)
(96) 732
SULLIVAN, LOUIS
Louis Sullivan (Twombly) (87) 499
SUN YAT-SEN
Sun Yat-sen (Schiffrin) (81) 777
SUSLOV, MIKHAIL ANDREYEVICH
All Stalin's Men (Medvedev) (H-85) 12
SWIFT, JONATHAN
Swift, the Man, His Works, and the Age
(Ehrenpreis) (84) 849
SZILARD, LEO
Portraits (Shils) (98) 639

TALESE, GAY
Unto the Sons (Talese) (93) 842
TALLMOUNTAIN, MARY
I Tell You Now (Swann and Krupat, eds.) (88) 413
TATE, ALLEN
Poets in Their Youth (Simpson) (83) 608
TAYLOR, FREDERICK WINSLOW
One Best Way, The (Kanigel) (98) 607
TEASDALE, SARA
Sara Teasdale (Drake) (80) 741
TENNYSON, ALFRED, LORD
Poetry of Tennyson, The (Culler) (78) 665
TENSKWATAWA
Shawnee Prophet, The (Edmunds) (H-84) 409
TERTZ, ABRAM
Voice from the Chorus, A (Tertz) (77) 892
THANT, U
View from the UN (Thant) (79) 809
THATCHER, MARGARET
Downing Street Years, The (Thatcher) (94) 248
Iron Lady, The (Young) (90) 429
Path to Power, The (Thatcher) (96) 573
THEROUX, PAUL
Old Patagonian Express, The (Theroux) (80) 619
Riding the Iron Rooster (Theroux) (89) 726
THOMAS, DYLAN
Collected Letters of Dylan Thomas, The
(Thomas) (87) 132
THOMAS, EDWARD
Great Friends (Garnett) (81) 386
THOMAS, NORMAN
Norman Thomas (Swanberg) (77) 570
THOREAU, HENRY DAVID
Henry Thoreau (Richardson) (87) 387
Thoreau's Seasons (Lebeaux) (85) 895
THORNTON, NAOMI
Working It Out (Ruddick and Daniels, eds.)
(78) 937
THURBER, JAMES
James Thurber (Kinney) (96) 389
TOKLAS, ALICE B.
Six Exceptional Women (Lord) (95) 724
TOLKIEN, J. R. R.
Letters of J. R. R. Tolkien, The (Tolkien) (82) 448
Tolkien (Carpenter) (78) 851

BIOGRAPHICAL WORKS BY SUBJECT

TOLSTOY, LEV
 Tolstoi in the Sixties (Eikenbaum) (83) 816
 Tolstoi in the Seventies (Eikenbaum) (83) 821
 Tolstoy (Wilson) (89) 845
 Tolstoy and Gandhi, Men of Peace (Green)
  (H-84) 447
 Tolstoy's Letters, Vol. I and Vol. II (Tolstoy)
  (79) 754

TOOMER, JEAN
 Jean Toomer, Artist (McKay) (85) 489
 Wayward and the Seeking, The (Toomer) (81) 904

TORRIJOS, OMAR
 Getting to Know the General (Greene) (H-85) 168

TOTH, SUSAN ALLEN
 Blooming (Toth) (82) 55
 Ivy Days (Toth) (85) 466

TREVOR, WILLIAM
 Excursions in the Real World (Trevor) (95) 214

TRILLIN, ABE
 Messages from My Father (Trillin) (97) 573

TRILLIN, CALVIN
 Messages from My Father (Trillin) (97) 573
 Remembering Denny (Trillin) (94) 692

TRISTAN, FLORA
 Flora Tristan's London Journal, 1840 (Tristan)
  (82) 288

TROGDON, WILLIAM. See HEAT-MOON,
 WILLIAM LEAST

TROLLOPE, ANTHONY
 Anthony Trollope (Glendinning) (94) 29
 Trollope (Hall) (92) 825

TROTSKY, LEON
 Leon Trotsky (Howe) (79) 368

TRUMAN, BESS
 Dear Bess (Truman) (H-84) 117

TRUMAN, HARRY S.
 Conflict and Crisis (Donovan) (78) 210
 Counsel to the President (Clifford, with
  Holbrooke) (92) 123
 Dear Bess (Truman) (H-84) 117
 Harry S. Truman and the Modern American
  Presidency (Ferrell) (H-84) 185
 Truman (McCullough) (93) 810
 Truman's Crises (Gosnell) (81) 836
 Tumultuous Years (Donovan) (H-83) 435

TRUTH, SOJOURNER
 Sojourner Truth (Painter) (97) 772

TSVETAYEVA, MARINA
 Letters (Pasternak, Tsvetayeva, and Rilke)
  (86) 514
 Marina Tsvetaeva (Feiler) (95) 464
 Marina Tsvetaeva (Karlinsky) (87) 520

TURGENEV, IVAN
 Gentle Barbarian, The (Pritchett) (78) 340
 Turgenev (Schapiro) (80) 832
 Turgenev Letters (Turgenev) (84) 879

TWAIN, MARK
 Making of Mark Twain, The (Lauber) (86) 561
 Mark Twain A to Z (Rasmussen) (96) 452
 Mark Twain's Letters (Twain) (89) 535

TYNAN, KENNETH
 Life of Kenneth Tynan, The (Tynan) (88) 482

UNAMUNO, MIGUEL DE
 Private World, The (Unamuno) (85) 701

UPDIKE, JOHN
 Self-Consciousness (Updike) (90) 725

VALIAN, VIRGINIA
 Working It Out (Ruddick and Daniels, eds.)
  (78) 937

VAN BUREN, MARTIN
 Martin Van Buren (Niven) (H-84) 298

VANCE, CYRUS
 Hard Choices (Vance) (H-84) 180

VAN GOGH, VINCENT
 Van Gogh (Sweetman) (91) 843

VANN, JOHN PAUL
 Bright, Shining Lie, A (Sheehan) (89) 125

VANZETTI, BARTOLOMEO
 Justice Crucified (Feuerlicht) (78) 487

VARGAS LLOSA, MARIO
 Fish in the Water, A (Vargas Llosa) (95) 239

VASSILTCHIKOV, MARIE
 Berlin Diaries, 1940-1945 (Vassiltchikov) (88) 95

VELÁZQUEZ, DIEGO RODRÍGUEZ DE SILVA Y
 Velázquez (Brown) (87) 907

VERGHESE, ABRAHAM
 My Own Country (Verghese) (95) 515

VIDAL, GORE
 Palimpsest (Vidal) (96) 561
 Screening History (Vidal) (93) 707

VIZENOR, GERALD
 I Tell You Now (Swann and Krupat, eds.) (88) 413

VOLTAIRE
 Voltaire (Mason) (82) 885
 Voltaire (Orieux) (80) 850

VONNEGUT, KURT
 Palm Sunday (Vonnegut) (82) 609
 Timequake (Vonnegut) (98) 760

VOROSHILOV, KLIMENT YEFREMOVICH
 All Stalin's Men (Medvedev) (H-85) 12

WALEY, ARTHUR
 Great Friends (Garnett) (81) 386

WALKER, ALICE
 Working It Out (Ruddick and Daniels, eds.)
  (78) 937

WARNER, HARRY
 Empire of Their Own, An (Gabler) (89) 278

WARNER, JACK
 Empire of Their Own, An (Gabler) (89) 278

WARNER, SYLVIA TOWNSEND
 Letters (Warner) (84) 432
 Scenes of Childhood and Other Stories (Warner)
  (83) 679

WARREN, EARL
 Earl Warren (Pollack) (80) 255
 Earl Warren (White) (H-83) 109
 Memoirs of Earl Warren, The (Warren) (78) 567
 Super Chief (Schwartz) (H-84) 435

WARREN, ROBERT PENN
 Robert Penn Warren (Blotner) (98) 678

WASHINGTON, GEORGE
 Cincinnatus (Wills) (H-85) 78
 David Humphreys' "Life of General Washington"
  (Humphreys and Washington) (92) 147

WAT, ALEKSANDER
 Aleksander Wat (Venclova) (97) 18
 My Century (Wat) (89) 571

WATKINS, PAUL
 Stand Before Your God (Watkins) (95) 752

WATSON, RICHARD
 Philosopher's Demise, The (Watson) (96) 581

WAUGH, EVELYN
    Diaries of Evelyn Waugh, The (Waugh) (78) 258
    Evelyn Waugh (Hastings) (96) 237
    Evelyn Waugh, 1903-1939 (Stannard) (88) 293
    Evelyn Waugh, 1939-1966 (Stannard) (93) 275
    Letters of Evelyn Waugh, The (Waugh) (81) 489
WAYNE, JOHN
    John Wayne's America (Wills) (98) 477
WEBB, BEATRICE
    Letters of Sidney and Beatrice Webb, The (Webb
    and Webb) (79) 378
WEBB, SIDNEY
    Letters of Sidney and Beatrice Webb, The (Webb
    and Webb) (79) 378
WEBER, MAX
    Max Weber (Diggins) (97) 559
WEBSTER, DANIEL
    Daniel Webster (Bartlett) (79) 143
    Daniel Webster (Remini) (98) 221
    Great Triumvirate, The (Peterson) (88) 363
    One and Inseparable (Baxter) (H-85) 339
    Province of Reason (Warner) (H-85) 368
WEEKS, EDWARD
    Writers and Friends (Weeks) (83) 928
WEIL, SIMONE
    Simone Weil (Fiori) (90) 738
    Simone Weil (Nevin) (93) 736
    Utopian Pessimist (McLellan) (91) 838
WEISSTEIN, NAOMI
    Working It Out (Ruddick and Daniels, eds.)
    (78) 937
WEIZMANN, CHAIM
    Chaim Weizmann (Reinharz) (86) 111
WELCH, DENTON
    Journals of Denton Welch, The (Welch) (85) 504
WELCHMAN, GORDON
    Hut Six Story, The (Welchman) (H-83) 201
WELLES, ORSON
    Orson Welles (Leaming) (86) 709
WELLS, H. G.
    Great Friends (Garnett) (81) 386
    Group Portrait (Delbanco) (83) 312
    H. G. Wells (West) (85) 380
    Invisible Man, The (Coren) (94) 410
    Rebecca West (Rollyson) (97) 684
WELTY, EUDORA
    Conversations with Eudora Welty (Prenshaw)
    (85) 137
    Eudora Welty's Achievement of Order (Kreyling)
    (81) 288
    One Writer's Beginnings (Welty) (85) 663
WERFEL, FRANZ
    Franz Werfel (Jungk) (91) 313
WEST, DOROTHY
    Richer, the Poorer, The (West) (96) 641
WEST, JESSAMYN
    Woman Said Yes, The (West) (77) 928
WEST, REBECCA
    Rebecca West (Glendinning) (88) 732
    Rebecca West (Rollyson) (97) 684
    Young Rebecca, The (West) (83) 932
WHARTON, EDITH
    Feast of Words, A (Wolff) (78) 314
    Letters of Edith Wharton, The (Wharton) (89) 475
    No Gifts from Chance (Benstock) (95) 544
WHITE, E. B.
    E. B. White (Elledge) (85) 209
    Letters of E. B. White (White) (77) 413

WHITE, KATHARINE S.
    Onward and Upward (Davis) (88) 630
WHITE, PATRICK
    Flaws in the Glass (White) (83) 257
    Patrick White (Marr) (93) 619
    Patrick White (White) (97) 656
WHITE, STANFORD
    Evelyn Nesbit and Stanford White (Mooney)
    (77) 260
WHITE, T. H.
    Great Friends (Garnett) (81) 386
WHITE, THEODORE H.
    In Search of History (White) (79) 314
WHITEHEAD, ALFRED NORTH
    Alfred North Whitehead, 1861-1910 (Lowe)
    (86) 5
    Alfred North Whitehead, 1910-1947 (Lowe)
    (91) 20
WHITMAN, WALT
    Walt Whitman (Kaplan) (81) 883
    Walt Whitman (Zweig) (85) 984
    Walt Whitman's America (Reynolds) (96) 806
WHITNEY, DOROTHY PAYNE
    Whitney Father, Whitney Heiress (Swanberg)
    (81) 921
WHITNEY, WILLIAM COLLINS
    Whitney Father, Whitney Heiress (Swanberg)
    (81) 921
WIDEMAN, JOHN EDGAR
    Brothers and Keepers (Wideman) (85) 57
    Fatheralong (Wideman) (95) 227
WIDEMAN, ROBBY
    Brothers and Keepers (Wideman) (85) 57
WIESEL, ELIE
    All Rivers Run to the Sea (Wiesel) (96) 18
WILBERFORCE, WILLIAM
    Wilberforce (Pollock) (79) 862
WILDE, OSCAR
    Oscar Wilde (Ellmann) (89) 630
WILDE-MENOZZI, WALLIS
    Mother Tongue (Wilde-Menozzi) (98) 567
WILDER, THORNTON
    Enthusiast, The (Harrison) (84) 272
    Journals of Thornton Wilder, 1939-1961, The
    (Wilder) (86) 491
    Thornton Wilder (Simon) (80) 815
WILHELM II
    Last Kaiser, The (Tyler-Whittle) (78) 509
WILLIAM, DUKE OF CLARENCE
    Mrs. Jordan's Profession (Tomalin) (96) 465
WILLIAMS, CHARLES
    Charles Williams (Hadfield) (84) 153
WILLIAMS, GEORGE WASHINGTON
    George Washington Williams (Franklin) (86) 332
WILLIAMS, TENNESSEE
    Five O'Clock Angel (Williams) (91) 291
    Memoirs (Williams) (77) 494
    Tom (Leverich) (96) 756
WILLIAMS, WILLIAM CARLOS
    Lives of the Modern Poets (Pritchard) (81) 520
    Pound/Williams (Pound and Williams) (97) 675
    William Carlos Williams (Mariani) (82) 946
WILLS, CHERYL
    I've Known Rivers (Lawrence-Lightfoot) (95) 384
WILSON, ANGUS
    Angus Wilson (Drabble) (97) 48

CATEGORY INDEX

1977-1998

ANTHROPOLOGY. *See* SOCIOLOGY,
ARCHAEOLOGY, and ANTHROPOLOGY

ARCHAEOLOGY. *See* SOCIOLOGY,
ARCHAEOLOGY, and ANTHROPOLOGY

AUTOBIOGRAPHY, MEMOIRS, DIARIES, and
LETTERS
Abba Eban (Eban) (78) 1
Accidental Autobiography, An (Harrison) (97) 1
Adieux (Beauvoir) (85) 1
Aké (Soyinka) (83) 10
Akhmatova Journals, 1938-41, The (Chukovskaya)
(95) 19
Albert Einstein (Einstein) (80) 19
All God's Children Need Traveling Shoes (Angelou)
(87) 25
All Rivers Run to the Sea (Wiesel) (96) 18
Always Straight Ahead (Neuman) (94) 11
America Inside Out (Schoenbrun) (H-85) 22
American Childhood, An (Dillard) (88) 25
American Life, An (Reagan) (91) 24
American Requiem, An (Carroll) (97) 38
And the Walls Came Tumbling Down (Abernathy)
(90) 39
Angela's Ashes (McCourt) (97) 43
Anne Sexton (Sexton) (78) 54
Another World, 1897-1917 (Eden) (78) 59
Answer to History (Mohammad Reza Pahlavi) (81) 47
Antonin Artaud (Artaud) (77) 52
Anything Your Little Heart Desires (Bosworth) (98) 68
Arna Bontemps-Langston Hughes Letters, 1925-1927
(Bontemps and Hughes) (81) 57
Around the Day in Eighty Worlds (Cortázar) (87) 45
Arrivals and Departures (Rovere) (77) 62
As I Saw It (Rusk) (91) 56
Asking for Trouble (Woods) (82) 28
Assault on Mount Helicon (Barnard) (85) 27
Atlantic High (Buckley) (83) 29
Autobiography of a Face (Grealy) (95) 56
Autobiography of Values (Lindbergh) (79) 43

Becoming a Doctor (Konner) (88) 77
Becoming a Man (Monette) (93) 62
Berlin Diaries, 1940-1945 (Vassiltchikov) (88) 95
Bernard Shaw, 1856-1898 (Holroyd) (89) 89
Bernard Shaw, Collected Letters, 1926-1950 (Shaw)
(89) 84
Better Class of Person, A (Osborne) (82) 45
Between Friends (Arendt and McCarthy) (96) 73
Beyond the Dragon's Mouth (Naipaul) (86) 56
Blessings in Disguise (Guinness) (87) 71
Blind Ambition (Dean) (77) 96
Bloods (Terry) (H-85) 48
Blooming (Toth) (82) 55
Blue-Eyed Child of Fortune (Duncan, ed.) (93) 91
Born on the Fourth of July (Kovic) (77) 115
Borrowed Time (Monette) (89) 112
Boston Boy (Hentoff) (87) 84
Boswell (Boswell) (78) 140
Boyhood (Coetzee) (98) 134
Breaking Ranks (Podhoretz) (80) 101
Breaking with Moscow (Shevchenko) (86) 81
Broken Cord, The (Dorris) (90) 76
Bronx Primitive (Simon) (83) 80
Brothers and Keepers (Wideman) (85) 57
Burning the Days (Salter) (98) 138
Byron's Letters and Journals, 1822-1823 (Byron)
(81) 108
Cassandra (Wolf) (85) 74
Chance Meetings (Saroyan) (79) 92
Charles Darwin's Letters (Darwin) (97) 148
Chief, The (Morrow) (86) 121
Childhood (Sarraute) (85) 89
China Men (Kingston) (81) 137
Chinabound (Fairbank) (H-83) 61
Christopher and His Kind (Isherwood) (77) 158
Clear Pictures (Price) (90) 104
Clinging to the Wreckage (Mortimer) (83) 127
Cloak of Light, A (Morris) (86) 140
Cloister Walk, The (Norris) (97) 160
Collected Letters, 1911-1925 (Shaw) (86) 145
Collected Letters of Dylan Thomas, The (Thomas)
(87) 132

CATEGORY INDEX

BIOGRAPHY. See also LITERARY BIOGRAPHY

Canaris (Höhne) (80) 125
Captain Kidd and the War Against the Pirates (Ritchie) (87) 99
Captain Sir Richard Francis Burton (Rice) (91) 123
Catcher Was a Spy, The (Dawidoff) (95) 104
Catherine, Empress of All the Russias (Cronin) (79) 80
Catherine the Great (Haslip) (78) 155
Catherine the Great (Troyat) (81) 117
Caught in the Web of Words (Murray) (78) 160
Cavour (Mack Smith) (86) 105
Chaim Weizmann (Reinharz) (86) 111
Chairman, The (Bird) (93) 138
Chaplin (Robinson) (86) 116
Charles Darwin (Bowlby) (92) 83
Charles Darwin (Brent) (82) 87
Charles Darwin (Browne) (96) 90
Charles Fourier (Beecher) (88) 138
Charles Stewart Parnell (Lyons) (78) 169
Charles the Second (Hutton) (91) 132
Charmed Lives (Korda) (80) 141
Churchill (Morgan) (H-83) 65
Citizen Cohn (von Hoffman) (89) 164
Clarence Darrow (Weinberg and Weinberg) (81) 152
Claude Monet (Tucker) (96) 120
Colonel, The (Smith) (98) 202
Conspiracy So Immense, A (Oshinsky) (H-84) 100
Conversations with Nietzsche (Gilman, ed.) (88) 199
Cornwallis (Wickwire and Wickwire) (81) 203
Cromwell (Howell) (78) 219
Custer and the Little Big Horn (Hofling) (82) 161
Daniel Defoe (Backscheider) (90) 143
Daniel Webster (Bartlett) (79) 143
Daniel Webster (Remini) (98) 221
Darrow (Tierney) (80) 188
Darwin (Desmond and Moore) (93) 196
David Bomberg (Cork) (88) 238
David Humphreys' "Life of General Washington" (Humphreys and Washington) (92) 147
Dean Acheson (McLellan) (77) 197
De Gaulle, 1890-1944 (Lacouture) (91) 192
De Gaulle, 1945-1970 (Lacouture) (93) 219
Descartes (Gaukroger) (96) 170
Diane Arbus (Bosworth) (96) 174
Disraeli (Bradford) (H-84) 135
Disraeli (Weintraub) (94) 239
Dönitz, the Last Führer (Padfield) (H-85) 115
Donovan (Dunlop) (H-83) 99
Dorothy Day (Coles) (88) 252
Dream Makers, Dream Breakers (Rowan) (94) 252
Dulles (Mosley) (79) 170
Du Pont Family, The (Gates) (80) 240
Earl Warren (Pollack) (80) 255
Earl Warren (White) (H-83) 109
Edison (Clark) (78) 284
Edmund Burke (Ayling) (90) 198
Edward Hopper (Levin) (96) 214
Edward Sapir (Darnell) (91) 245
Edward VII (St. Aubyn) (80) 264
Eisenhower, Vol. I (Ambrose) (H-84) 141
Eisenhower, Vol. II (Ambrose) (H-85) 120
Eisenhower the President (Ewald) (82) 205
Eleanor of Aquitaine (Seward) (80) 277
Eleanor Roosevelt, 1884-1933 (Cook) (93) 253
Elizabeth Regina (Plowden) (81) 272
Eminent Elizabethans (Rowse) (H-84) 147
Emma Goldman (Wexler) (H-85) 125
Empire of Their Own, An (Gabler) (89) 278
Eva Perón (Fraser and Navarro) (82) 249
Evangelist of Race (Field) (82) 256
Evelyn Nesbit and Stanford White (Mooney) (77) 260
Faces of Revolution (Bailyn) (91) 279
Family (Frazier) (95) 222
FDR, 1933-1937 (Davis) (87) 276

FDR, 1937-1940 (Davis) (94) 278
FDR (Miller) (H-84) 158
FDR (Morgan) (86) 269
Felix Frankfurter and His Times (Parrish) (H-83) 140
Fidel (Szulc) (87) 282
Fidel Castro (Quirk) (94) 287
Figures in a Western Landscape (Stevenson) (95) 231
Fire and Water (de Jonge) (81) 335
First Churchill, The (Thomson) (81) 344
First-Class Temperament, A (Ward) (90) 258
First Elizabeth, The (Erickson) (H-84) 164
First in His Class (Maraniss) (96) 263
Fitzgeralds and the Kennedys, The (Goodwin) (88) 323
Five of Hearts, The (O'Toole) (91) 295
Force of Nature (Hager) (96) 286
Ford (Lacey) (87) 297
Franco (Preston) (95) 257
Frank Capra (McBride) (93) 298
Frank Lloyd Wright (Secrest) (93) 303
Franklin of Philadelphia (Wright) (87) 303
Frederick Douglass (McFeely) (92) 232
Freud (Clark) (81) 357
Freud (Gay) (89) 311
Fulbright (Woods) (96) 294
Gandhi (Brown) (91) 321
Gates (Manes and Andrews) (94) 335
Gaudier-Brzeska (Silber) (98) 331
General of the Army (Cray) (91) 333
Generations (Clifton) (77) 318
Genius (Gleick) (93) 308
Genius in Disguise (Kunkel) (96) 303
George Bancroft (Handlin) (H-85) 162
George C. Marshall (Pogue) (88) 346
George Washington Carver (McMurry) (82) 310
George Washington Williams (Franklin) (86) 332
Georgia O'Keeffe (Robinson) (90) 289
Giacometti (Lord) (86) 343
Gladstone (Jenkins) (98) 344
God's Chinese Son (Spence) (97) 339
God's Fool (Green) (86) 354
Gold and Iron (Stern) (78) 354
Goldwyn (Berg) (90) 303
Grant (McFeely) (82) 338
Great Harry (Erickson) (81) 391
Great Melody, The (O'Brien) (93) 316
Great Triumvirate, The (Peterson) (88) 363
Guggenheims (Davis) (79) 260
Gustav Mahler, 1892-1904 (La Grange) (96) 321
Harold Macmillan (Fisher) (H-83) 185
Harold Macmillan, 1894-1956 (Horne) (90) 352
Harold Macmillan, 1957-1986 (Horne) (90) 358
Harriet Beecher Stowe (Hedrick) (95) 296
Harry Hopkins (Adams) (78) 375
Harry S. Truman and the Modern American Presidency (Ferrell) (H-84) 185
Havelock Ellis (Grosskurth) (81) 412
Helene Deutsch (Roazen) (86) 402
Henry Cabot Lodge and the Search for an American Foreign Policy (Widenor) (81) 416
Herbert Hoover (Burner) (80) 400
Himself! (Kennedy) (79) 273
His Holiness (Bernstein and Politi) (97) 388
Hitler (Stone) (81) 434
Hitler and Stalin (Bullock) (93) 349
Hitler of History, The (Lukacs) (98) 396
Hornes, The (Buckley) (87) 410
House of Morgan, The (Chernow) (91) 432
Hugo Black and the Judicial Revolution (Dunne) (78) 418
Hugo L. Black (Ball) (97) 415
Huxley (Desmond) (98) 411
Imaginative Landscape of Christopher Columbus, The (Flint) (93) 365

CATEGORY INDEX

CATEGORY INDEX

Money (Hacker) (98) 562
One World, Ready or Not (Greider) (98) 612
Pop Internationalism (Krugman) (97) 666
When Work Disappears (Wilson) (97) 880

EDUCATION
Among Schoolchildren (Kidder) (90) 34
Call of Stories, The (Coles) (90) 81
Content of Our Character, The (Steele) (91) 170
Cultural Literacy (Hirsch) (88) 223
Higher Superstition (Gross and Levitt) (95) 301
Howard Mumford Jones and the Dynamics of Liberal
   Humanism (Brier) (95) 329
Innumeracy (Paulos) (90) 420
John Dewey and American Democracy (Westbrook)
   (92) 388
Literature Lost (Ellis) (98) 512
Number Sense, The (Dehaene) (98) 603
Recalcitrance, Faulkner, and the Professors (Wright)
   (91) 701
Savage Inequalities (Kozol) (92) 712
Seeing Voices (Sacks) (90) 720
Small Victories (Freedman) (91) 750
Soul of the American University, The (Marsden)
   (95) 744
There Are No Children Here (Kotlowitz) (92) 813
Vocation of a Teacher, The (Booth) (90) 854

ENVIRONMENT. See NATURE, NATURAL
   HISTORY, and the ENVIRONMENT

ESSAYS
a long the riverrun (Ellmann) (90) 1
Actual Minds, Possible Worlds (Bruner) (87) 11
After Henry (Didion) (93) 1
Against the Current (Berlin) (81) 9
Agon (Bloom) (83) 1
AIDS and Its Metaphors (Sontag) (90) 19
Americans at War (Ambrose) (98) 64
—And I Worked at the Writer's Trade (Cowley) (79) 24
Anthropologist on Mars, An (Sacks) (96) 47
Arguifying (Empson) (89) 46
Around the Day in Eighty Worlds (Cortázar) (87) 45
Art & Ardor (Ozick) (84) 44
Art in the Light of Conscience (Tsvetaeva) (93) 36
Art of Telling, The (Kermode) (84) 49
Art of the Novel, The (Kundera) (89) 54
Art of the Personal Essay, The (Lopate, ed.) (95) 47
Artificial Wilderness, An (Birkerts) (88) 68
Aspects of the Present (Mead and Metraux) (81) 62
At Home (Vidal) (89) 59
Avoidance of Literature, The (Sisson) (80) 40
Bachelorhood (Lopate) (82) 40
Bad Mouth (Adams) (78) 81
Balancing Acts (Hoagland) (93) 45
Barthes Reader, A (Barthes) (83) 44
Bartleby in Manhattan (Hardwick) (84) 82
Beyond Geography (Turner) (81) 82
Beyond the Dragon's Mouth (Naipaul) (86) 56
Black Athena Revisited (Lefkowitz and Rogers, eds.)
   (97) 114
Black Holes and Baby Universes and Other Essays
   (Hawking) (94) 94
Borges, a Reader (Borges) (82) 63
Bottom Translation, The (Kott) (88) 116
Boy Scout Handbook and Other Observations, The
   (Fussell) (83) 70
Breathing Under Water and Other East European
   Essays (Barańczak) (91) 105
Bully for Brontosaurus (Gould) (92) 69
Burning Forest, The (Leys) (86) 86
But Do Blondes Prefer Gentlemen? (Burgess) (87) 94

Camera Age, The (Arlen) (82) 73
Camera Lucida (Barthes) (82) 78
Catbird's Song, The (Wilbur) (98) 156
Celebrations and Attacks (Howe) (80) 136
Choice of Days, A (Mencken) (81) 142
City of Bits (Mitchell) (96) 112
Collected Essays of Ralph Ellison, The (Ellison)
   (96) 128
Collected Essays of Robert Creeley, The (Creeley)
   (90) 108
Collected Prose (Lowell) (88) 173
Collected Works (Metcalf) (98) 199
Complete Collected Essays (Pritchett) (93) 179
Complete Prefaces, 1889-1913, The (Shaw) (95) 145
Complete Prose of Marianne Moore, The (Moore)
   (87) 165
Congregation (Rosenberg, ed.) (88) 189
Correspondent Breeze, The (Abrams) (85) 142
Cosmic Code, The (Pagels) (83) 156
Crooked Timber of Humanity, The (Berlin) (92) 133
Cutting Edges (Krauthammer) (86) 208
Cycles of American History, The (Schlesinger)
   (87) 183
Daguerreotypes and Other Essays (Dinesen) (80) 180
Dark Brain of Piranesi and Other Essays, The
   (Yourcenar) (85) 152
Days of Obligation (Rodriguez) (93) 204
Dead Elvis (Marcus) (92) 157
Devil Problem, The (Remnick) (97) 210
Desire in Language (Kristeva) (81) 231
Destructive Generation (Collier and Horowitz)
   (90) 168
Doing What Comes Naturally (Fish) (90) 190
Don't Tell the Grown-ups (Lurie) (91) 231
Down the River (Abbey) (83) 205
Earthly Delights, Unearthly Adornments (Morris)
   (79) 175
Economists, The (Silk) (77) 251
Edward Hoagland Reader, The (Hoagland) (80) 260
Eiffel Tower and Other Mythologies, The (Barthes)
   (80) 269
Empire of Signs, The (Barthes) (83) 230
Encounters with Chinese Writers (Dillard) (85) 223
End Papers (Breytenbach) (87) 242
Essays (Knox) (90) 219
Essays, Articles and Reviews of Evelyn Waugh, The
   (Waugh) (85) 238
Essays in Appreciation (Ricks) (97) 256
Essays in Feminism (Gornick) (80) 302
Essays of E. B. White (White) (78) 295
Essays of Virginia Woolf, 1904-1912, The (Woolf)
   (88) 288
Essays of Virginia Woolf, 1912-1918, The (Woolf)
   (89) 283
Essays of Virginia Woolf, 1919-1924, The (Woolf)
   (90) 222
Ethics (Foucault) (98) 289
Eudora Welty (Prenshaw, ed.) (81) 283
Europe, Europe (Enzensberger) (90) 227
Every Force Evolves a Form (Davenport) (88) 298
Examined Life, The (Nozick) (90) 231
Experience of Place, The (Hiss) (91) 275
Eye of the Story, The (Welty) (80) 200
Faith in a Seed (Thoreau) (94) 274
Fame and Folly (Ozick) (97) 269
Familiar Territory (Epstein) (80) 310
Fate of the Earth, The (Schell) (83) 244
Fatheralong (Wideman) (95) 227
Figures of Thought (Nemerov) (79) 209
Flower and the Leaf, The (Cowley) (86) 288
Forever Young (Cott) (79) 231
Friday Book, The (Barth) (85) 307
Giving Good Weight (McPhee) (80) 358

929

931

CATEGORY INDEX

CATEGORY INDEX

CATEGORY INDEX

CATEGORY INDEX

CATEGORY INDEX

CATEGORY INDEX

CATEGORY INDEX

TITLE INDEX

1977-1998

969

TITLE INDEX

TITLE INDEX

TITLE INDEX

TITLE INDEX

Poems, The (Yeats) (85) 692
Poems New and Selected, 1962-1992 (Van Brunt) (94) 641
Poems of Paul Celan (Celan) (90) 673
Poems of Stanley Kunitz, 1928-1978, The (Kunitz) (80) 665
Poet and Dancer (Jhabvala) (94) 645
Poet as Journalist, The (Whittemore) (77) 623
Poetical Works of Federico García Lorca (García Lorca) (93) 637
Poetics of Aristotle, The (Halliwell) (88) 706
Poetry and Repression (Bloom) (77) 627
Poetry into Drama (Herington) (86) 742
Poetry of Tennyson, The (Culler) (78) 665
Poets in Their Youth (Simpson) (83) 608
Poets, Poetics, and Politics (Humphries) (93) 642
Poet's Work (Gibbons, ed.) (80) 668
Poet's Work, The (Nathan and Quinn) (92) 623
Point, The (D'Ambrosio) (96) 589
Polish Complex, The (Konwicki) (83) 611
Polish Officer, The (Furst) (96) 593
Political Liberalism (Rawls) (94) 649
Political Life of Children, The (Coles) (87) 665
Political Repression in Nineteenth Century Europe (Goldstein) (H-84) 342
Politician, The (Dugger) (H-83) 348
Politics and Ideology in the Age of the Civil War (Foner) (81) 661
Politics in Black and White (Sonenshein) (94) 654
Politics of Energy, The (Commoner) (80) 671
Politics of Recovery, The (Romasco) (H-84) 347
Politics of Rich and Poor, The (Phillips) (91) 674
Polonaise (Read) (77) 632
Pop Internationalism (Krugman) (97) 666
Pope's Rhinoceros, The (Norfolk) (97) 671
Porcupine, The (Barnes) (93) 646
Portable Jack Kerouac, The (Kerouac) (96) 597
Portage to San Cristóbal of A. H., The (Steiner) (83) 616
Portraits (Shils) (98) 639
Portraits of the Artist in Exile (Potts, ed.) (80) 675
Possessing the Secret of Joy (Walker) (93) 651
Possession (Byatt) (91) 679
Postscript to *The Name of the Rose* (Eco) (85) 697
Pound/Ford, the Story of a Literary Friendship (Pound and Ford) (83) 621
Pound/Lewis (Pound and Lewis) (86) 747
Pound/Williams (Pound and Williams) (97) 675
Poverty and Compassion (Himmelfarb) (92) 627
Power and Principle (Brzezinski) (H-84) 351
Power Game, The (Smith) (89) 658
Power on the Left (Lader) (80) 680
Power to Lead, The (Burns) (H-85) 363
Powers That Be, The (Halberstam) (80) 684
Practicing History (Tuchman) (82) 647
PrairyErth (Heat-Moon) (92) 632
Prayer for Owen Meany, A (Irving) (90) 677
Praying for Sheetrock (Greene) (92) 636
Preacher King, The (Lischer) (96) 601
Prehistoric Avebury (Burl) (80) 688

Preparing for the Twenty-first Century (Kennedy) (94) 658
Presence of Ford Madox Ford, The (Stang, ed.) (82) 652
Presidency of Lyndon B. Johnson, The (Bornet) (H-84) 355
President Kennedy (Reeves) (94) 662
Price of Power, The (Hersh) (H-84) 361
Price Was High, The (Fitzgerald) (80) 693
Prick of Noon, The (De Vries) (86) 752
Pride of Family (Ione) (92) 641
Primacy or World Order (Hoffmann) (79) 551
Primary Colors (Klein) (97) 679
Primary Colors, The (Theroux) (95) 613
Prince of Our Disorder, A (Mack) (77) 637
Principle of Hope, The (Bloch) (87) 670
Printing Technology, Letters, and Samuel Johnson (Kernan) (88) 710
Prisoner's Dilemma (Powers) (89) 663
Prisoners of Hope (Hughes) (84) 705
Private Demons (Oppenheimer) (89) 668
Private World, The (Unamuno) (85) 701
Prize, The (Yergin) (92) 645
Prize Stories 1978 (Abrahams, ed.) (79) 556
"Probable Cause" *and* "Beyond Reasonable Doubt" (Shapiro) (93) 75
Problems and Other Stories (Updike) (80) 697
Problems of Dostoevsky's Poetics (Bakhtin) (85) 706
Prodigal Child, A (Storey) (84) 711
Profane Art, The (Oates) (84) 716
Professing Poetry (Wain) (79) 561
Profession of the Playwright, The (Stephens) (93) 655
Professor of Desire, The (Roth) (78) 669
Progress and Privilege (Tucker) (H-83) 352
Progress of Love, The (Munro) (87) 677
Progressive Presidents, The (Blum) (81) 665
Promethean Fire (Lumsden and Wilson) (H-84) 366
Promise of Light, The (Watkins) (94) 667
Promise of Pragmatism, The (Diggins) (95) 617
Promise of Rest, The (Price) (96) 606
Promised Land, The (Lemann) (92) 650
Prophets of Past Time (Dawson) (89) 674
Protecting Soldiers and Mothers (Skocpol) (94) 671
Proust Screenplay, The (Pinter) (78) 673
Providence (Brookner) (85) 712
Province of Reason (Warner) (H-85) 368
Provinces (Miłosz) (92) 656
Psychopathic God, The (Waite) (78) 677
Puffball (Weldon) (81) 670
Pugilist at Rest, The (Jones) (94) 676
Puritan Way of Death, The (Stannard) (78) 682
Purple America (Moody) (98) 643
Purple Decades, The (Wolfe) (83) 626
Pursued by Furies (Bowker) (96) 610
Pursuit of Power, The (McNeill) (H-83) 357
Pushcart Prize, III, The (Henderson, ed.) (79) 565
Puttermesser Papers, The (Ozick) (98) 648

Quality of Mercy, The (Shawcross) (H-85) 373
Quantity Theory of Insanity, The (Self) (96) 615

993

TITLE INDEX

TITLE INDEX

AUTHOR INDEX

1977-1998

AUTHOR INDEX

AUTHOR INDEX

BOWKER, GORDON
    Pursued by Furies (96) 610
BOWLBY, JOHN
    Charles Darwin (92) 83
BOWLES, JANE
    Out in the World (86) 723
BOWLES, PAUL
    In Touch (95) 372
    Collected Stories, 1939-1976 (80) 151
BOYD, BRIAN
    Vladimir Nabokov, The American Years (92) 854
    Vladimir Nabokov, The Russian Years (91) 856
BOYD, WILLIAM
    Ice-Cream War, An (84) 363
BOYERS, ROBERT
    Atrocity and Amnesia (86) 43
BOYLAN, CLARE
    Holy Pictures (84) 347
BOYLE, KAY
    Fifty Stories (81) 325
    Words That Must Somehow Be Said (86) 966
BOYLE, NICHOLAS
    Goethe (92) 247
BOYLE, T. CORAGHESSAN
    East Is East (91) 240
    Greasy Lake and Other Stories (86) 372
    If the River Was Whiskey (90) 406
    Road to Wellville, The (94) 709
    Tortilla Curtain, The (96) 764
    Without a Hero (95) 880
    World's End (88) 988
BRADBURY, MALCOLM
    Rates of Exchange (84) 721
BRADBURY, RAY
    Death Is a Lonely Business (86) 222
    Stories of Ray Bradbury, The (81) 769
BRADFORD, SARAH
    Disraeli (H-84) 135
BRADLEE, BEN
    Good Life, A (96) 316
BRADLEY, DAVID
    Chaneysville Incident, The (82) 82
BRADLEY, MARION ZIMMER
    Mists of Avalon, The (84) 561
BRADLEY, OMAR N., and CLAY BLAIR
    General's Life, A (H-84) 171
BRADSHER, HENRY S.
    Afghanistan and the Soviet Union (H-84) 1
BRADY, FRANK
    James Boswell (85) 479
BRADY, KRISTIN
    Short Stories of Thomas Hardy, The (83) 747
BRALY, MALCOLM
    False Starts (77) 269
BRANCH, TAYLOR
    Parting the Waters (89) 649
BRANDYS, KAZIMIERZ
    Warsaw Diary, A (84) 926
BRATHWAITE, EDWARD KAMAU
    MiddlePassages (95) 486
    X/Self (88) 999
BRAUDEL, FERNAND
    Perspective of the World, Vol. III, The (H-85) 353
BRAUNBEHRENS, VOLKMAR
    Mozart in Vienna, 1781-1791 (91) 606

BRAUTIGAN, RICHARD
    Sombrero Fallout (78) 785
BRAVERMAN, KATE
    Palm Latitudes (89) 639
BRAZEAU, PETER
    Parts of a World (84) 668
BRECHER, MICHAEL, and BENJAMIN GEIST
    Decisions in Crisis (81) 228
BRECHT, BERTOLT
    Bertolt Brecht Short Stories, 1921-1946 (84) 86
BREDIN, JEAN-DENIS
    Affair, The (87) 15
BREITMAN, RICHARD
    German Socialism and Weimar Democracy
      (82) 315
BRENT, PETER
    Charles Darwin (82) 87
BRESLIN, JAMES E. B.
    Mark Rothko (94) 504
BREWER, JOHN
    Pleasures of the Imagination, The (98) 634
BREYTENBACH, BREYTEN
    End Papers (87) 242
    True Confessions of an Albino Terrorist, The
      (86) 913
BRIDGMAN, RICHARD
    Traveling in Mark Twain (88) 907
BRIER, PETER
    Howard Mumford Jones and the Dynamics of
      Liberal Humanism (95) 329
BRIGHTMAN, CAROL
    Writing Dangerously (93) 887
BRIMELOW, PETER
    Alien Nation (96) 9
BRINK, ANDRÉ
    Chain of Voices, A (83) 101
    Writing in a State of Siege (84) 983
BRINKLEY, ALAN
    Voices of Protest (H-83) 449
BRINKLEY, DAVID
    Washington Goes to War (89) 887
BROCH, HERMANN
    Hugo von Hofmannsthal and His Time (85) 410
BRODER, DAVID S.
    Changing of the Guard (81) 127
BRODKEY, HAROLD
    Runaway Soul, The (92) 698
    Stories in an Almost Classical Mode (89) 822
    This Wild Darkness (97) 816
BRODSKY, JOSEPH
    Less Than One (87) 471
    On Grief and Reason (97) 644
    So Forth (97) 766
    To Urania (89) 840
BROMBERT, VICTOR
    Victor Hugo and the Visionary Novel (85) 969
BROMWICH, DAVID
    Hazlitt (85) 363
BRONK, WILLIAM
    Life Supports (82) 466
    Vectors and Smoothable Curves (84) 905
BROOK-SHEPHERD, GORDON
    Archduke of Sarajevo (H-85) 33
    Uncle of Europe (77) 861
BROOKHISER, RICHARD
    Founding Father (97) 306

AUTHOR INDEX

BURNS, KEN, et al.
Civil War, The (91) 137
BURNS, RIC, et al.
Civil War, The (91) 137
BURROWS, DAVID
Sound, Speech, and Music (91) 759
BURSTON, DANIEL
Wing of Madness, The (97) 885
BURUMA, IAN
Wages of Guilt, The (95) 840
BUSCH, FREDERICK
Closing Arguments (92) 94
Girls (98) 340
Long Way from Home (94) 479
BUSH, CLIVE
Dream of Reason, The (79) 165
BUSH, RONALD
T. S. Eliot (85) 937
BUTLER, JON
Awash in a Sea of Faith (91) 65
BUTLER, ROBERT OLEN
On Distant Ground (86) 685
Tabloid Dreams (97) 792
BUTSCHER, EDWARD, editor
Conrad Aiken (89) 207
Sylvia Plath (78) 809
BUTTEL, ROBERT, and FRANK DOGGETT, editors
Wallace Stevens (81) 879
BUTTERFIELD, HERBERT
Origins of History, The (82) 604
BUZZATI, DINO
Siren, The (85) 825
BYATT, A. S.
Angels and Insects (94) 25
Babel Tower (97) 87
Matisse Stories, The (96) 457
Possession (91) 679
BYRON, GEORGE GORDON, LORD
Byron's Letters and Journals, 1822-1823 (81) 108
Lord Byron, Selected Letters and Journals
(83) 418
BYRON, WILLIAM
Cervantes (79) 84
BYTWERK, RANDALL L.
Julius Streicher (H-83) 234

CAHILL, THOMAS
How the Irish Saved Civilization (96) 343
CAINE, BARBARA
Victorian Feminists (93) 851
CALASSO, ROBERTO
Marriage of Cadmus and Harmony, The (94) 508
Ruin of Kasch, The (95) 669
CALDER, ANGUS
Revolutionary Empire (82) 675
CALDER, JENNI
Robert Louis Stevenson (81) 694
CALISHER, HORTENSE
Mysteries of Motion (84) 593
On Keeping Women (78) 613
CALISHER, HORTENSE
In the Palace of the Movie King (95) 359
CALLAHAN, DANIEL
What Kind of Life (91) 886
CALVET, LOUIS-JEAN
Roland Barthes (96) 664

CALVINO, ITALO
Difficult Loves (85) 184
If on a winter's night a traveler (82) 380
Italian Folktales (81) 450
Marcovaldo (84) 509
Mr. Palomar (86) 620
Road to San Giovanni, The (94) 705
Six Memos for the Next Millennium (89) 799
Under the Jaguar Sun (89) 872
CAMILLE, MICHAEL
Master of Death (97) 555
CAMPBELL, BEBE MOORE
Your Blues Ain't Like Mine (93) 896
CAMPBELL, JAMES
Talking at the Gates (92) 795
CAMPBELL, JEREMY
Grammatical Man (83) 301
Winston Churchill's Afternoon Nap (88) 964
CAMPBELL, JOSEPH
Inner Reaches of Outer Space, The (87) 429
CAMPBELL, MARY B.
World, The Flesh, and Angels, The (90) 921
CAMUS, ALBERT
First Man, The (96) 268
CANETTI, ELIAS
Torch in My Ear, The (83) 827
CANIN, ETHAN
Emperor of the Air (89) 268
Palace Thief, The (95) 586
CANNON, LOU
Reagan (H-83) 362
CANTOR, JAY
Krazy Kat (89) 445
CANTOR, MILTON
Divided Left, The (79) 157
CANTOR, NORMAN F.
Inventing the Middle Ages (93) 394
Sacred Chain, The (95) 678
CANTY, KEVIN
Stranger in This World, A (95) 769
CAPPS, WALTER H.
Unfinished War, The (H-83) 440
CARDOZO, NANCY
Lucky Eyes and a High Heart (79) 409
CAREY, PETER
Oscar and Lucinda (89) 626
Tax Inspector, The (93) 775
CARLYLE, THOMAS, and JOHN RUSKIN
Correspondence of Thomas Carlyle and John
Ruskin, The (83) 153
CARO, ROBERT A.
Years of Lyndon Johnson, Means of Ascent, The
(91) 919
Years of Lyndon Johnson, The Path to Power,
The (H-83) 478
CAROTENUTO, ALDO
Secret Symmetry, A (83) 709
CARPENTER, HUMPHREY
Benjamin Britten (94) 75
Serious Character, A (89) 779
Tolkien (78) 851
W. H. Auden (82) 923
CARR, VIRGINIA SPENCER
Dos Passos (85) 194
CARROLL, JAMES
American Requiem, An (97) 38
Mortal Friends (79) 462

1015

AUTHOR INDEX

DALE, ALZINA STONE
  Outline of Sanity (83) 582
DALLEK, ROBERT
  American Style of Foreign Policy, The
    (H-84) 11
  Franklin D. Roosevelt and American Foreign
    Policy, 1932-1945 (80) 328
  Lone Star Rising (92) 450
D'ALPUGET, BLANCHE
  Turtle Beach (84) 886
D'AMBROSIO, CHARLES
  Point, The (96) 589
DANGERFIELD, GEORGE
  Damnable Question, The (77) 188
DANIELS, KATE
  White Wave, The (85) 1023
DANIELS, PAMELA, and SARA RUDDICK, editors
  Working It Out (78) 937
DANTE ALIGHIERI
  Inferno of Dante, The (96) 376
DANTICAT, EDWIDGE
  Krik? Krak! (96) 406
DARNELL, REGNA
  Edward Sapir (91) 245
DARNTON, ROBERT
  Great Cat Massacre and Other Episodes in French
    Cultural History, The (H-85) 183
DARR, ANN
  Cleared for Landing (79) 113
DARWIN, CHARLES ROBERT
  Charles Darwin's Letters (97) 148
DAVENPORT, GUY
  Da Vinci's Bicycle (80) 195
  Eclogues (82) 185
  Every Force Evolves a Form (88) 298
  Hunter Gracchus, The (97) 419
  Table of Green Fields, A (94) 783
DAVENPORT, JOHN, and DYLAN THOMAS
  Death of the King's Canary, The (78) 238
DAVENPORT-HINES, RICHARD
  Auden (97) 79
DAVIDSON, EUGENE
  Making of Adolf Hitler, The (78) 552
DAVIDSON, JAMES WEST, and MARK HAMILTON
    LYTLE
  After the Fact (H-83) 10
DAVIE, DONALD
  Collected Poems, 1970-1983 (84) 183
  Czesław Miłosz and the Insufficiency of Lyric
    (87) 189
  These the Companions (83) 787
  Under Briggflatts (91) 833
DAVIE, MICHAEL, and ANNE CHISHOLM
  Lord Beaverbrook (94) 488
DAVIES, JOHN
  History of Wales, A (95) 309
DAVIES, NORMAN
  Europe (97) 260
DAVIES, ROBERTSON
  Cunning Man, The (96) 144
  Lyre of Orpheus, The (90) 548
  Murther and Walking Spirits (92) 535
  Rebel Angels, The (83) 641
  What's Bred in the Bone (86) 939
  World of Wonders (77) 952
DAVIS, DAVID BRION
  Slavery and Human Progress (H-85) 411

DAVIS, JOHN H.
  Guggenheims (79) 260
DAVIS, KENNETH C.
  Two-Bit Culture (85) 952
DAVIS, KENNETH S.
  FDR, 1933-1937 (87) 276
  FDR, 1937-1940 (94) 278
DAVIS, LINDA H.
  Onward and Upward (88) 630
DAVIS, NATALIE ZEMON
  Women on the Margins (96) 826
DAVIS, PETER
  Hometown (83) 344
DAWIDOFF, NICHOLAS
  Catcher Was a Spy, The (95) 104
  In the Country of Country (98) 419
DAWKINS, LOUISA
  Natives and Strangers (86) 644
DAWSON, CARL
  Prophets of Past Time (89) 674
DAWSON, JOHN W., JR.
  Logical Dilemmas (98) 517
DAY LEWIS, C.
  Complete Poems of C. Day Lewis, The (93) 184
DAYAN, MOSHE
  Moshe Dayan (77) 513
DEAN, JOHN W., III
  Blind Ambition (77) 96
DEARBORN, MARY
  Happiest Man Alive, The (92) 266
DE BEAUVOIR, SIMONE. See BEAUVOIR,
    SIMONE DE
DEBRECZENY, PAUL
  Other Pushkin, The (84) 657
DE GALBA, MARTÍ JOAN, and JOANOT
    MARTORELL
  Tirant lo Blanc (85) 907
DEGLER, CARL N.
  In Search of Human Nature (92) 338
DE GRAND, ALEXANDER
  Italian Fascism (H-83) 224
DEHAENE, STANISLAS
  Number Sense, The (98) 603
DEIGHTON, LEN
  Blitzkrieg (81) 88
DE JONGE, ALEX
  Fire and Water (81) 335
  Life and Times of Grigorii Rasputin, The
    (H-83) 264
DEKKER, GEORGE
  American Historical Romance, The (88) 31
DELANY, PAUL
  D. H. Lawrence's Nightmare (80) 223
DELANY, SAMUEL R.
  Stars in My Pockets like Grains of Sand
    (85) 860
DELBANCO, NICHOLAS
  About My Table (84) 1
  Group Portrait (83) 312
DeLILLO, DON
  Libra (89) 496
  Mao II (92) 479
  Names, The (83) 515
  Players (78) 661
  Ratner's Star (77) 647
  Running Dog (79) 617

1019

AUTHOR INDEX

JOHANNSEN, ROBERT W.
  To the Halls of the Montezumas (86) 887
JOHANSON, DONALD C., and MAITLAND A.
  EDEY
  Lucy (82) 514
JOHNS, RICHARD, and DAVID HOLDEN
  House of Saud, The (H-83) 195
JOHNSON, CHARLES
  Being and Race (89) 80
  Middle Passage (91) 591
  Sorcerer's Apprentice, The (87) 795
JOHNSON, DAVID ALAN
  Founding the Far West (93) 293
JOHNSON, DENIS
  Already Dead (98) 23
  Fiskadoro (86) 279
  Jesus' Son (94) 427
  Resuscitation of a Hanged Man (92) 679
JOHNSON, DIANE
  Dashiell Hammett (84) 212
  Le Divorce (98) 490
  Persian Nights (88) 683
  Terrorists and Novelists (83) 783
JOHNSON, GEORGE
  In the Palaces of Memory (92) 342
JOHNSON, JAMES WELDON
  Selected Writings of James Weldon Johnson, Vol.
    I and Vol. II, The (96) 694
JOHNSON, PAUL
  Birth of the Modern, The (92) 52
  History of the Jews, A (88) 392
  Modern Times (H-84) 306
JOHNSON, RONALD
  Ark (97) 62
JOHNSON, SAMUEL
  Letters of Samuel Johnson, The (93) 444
JOHNSTONE, ROBERT M., JR.
  Jefferson and the Presidency (79) 331
JOLLEY, ELIZABETH
  Foxybaby (86) 306
  Well, The (87) 958
JONES, ARCHER
  Civil War Command and Strategy (93) 153
JONES, ARCHER, RICHARD E. BERINGER,
  HERMAN HATTAWAY, and WILLIAM N.
  STILL, JR.
  Why the South Lost the Civil War (87) 980
JONES, DAVID RICHARD
  Great Directors at Work (87) 362
JONES, DOUGLAS C.
  Arrest Sitting Bull (78) 72
JONES, EDWARD P.
  Lost in the City (93) 491
JONES, J. SYDNEY
  Hitler in Vienna, 1907-1913 (H-84) 207
JONES, JAMES
  Whistle (79) 843
JONES, LOUIS B.
  California's Over (98) 147
  Ordinary Money (91) 647
  Particles and Luck (94) 611
JONES, MADISON
  Last Things (91) 503
JONES, PRESTON
  Texas Trilogy, A (77) 812

JONES, R. V.
  Wizard War, The (79) 888
JONES, STANLEY
  Hazlitt (91) 381
JONES, THOM
  Cold Snap (96) 124
  Pugilist at Rest, The (94) 676
JONG, ERICA
  Fanny (81) 309
  How to Save Your Own Life (78) 413
JORDAN, HAMILTON
  Crisis (H-83) 93
JORDAN, JUNE
  Technical Difficulties (93) 779
  Things That I Do in the Dark (78) 826
JOWITT, KEN
  New World Disorder (93) 559
JUDD, ALAN
  Ford Madox Ford (92) 218
JUDIS, JOHN B.
  William F. Buckley, Jr. (89) 908
JUDSON, HORACE FREELAND
  Eighth Day of Creation, The (80) 273
JÜNGER, ERNST
  Aladdin's Problem (93) 6
JUNGK, PETER STEPHAN
  Franz Werfel (91) 313
JUST, WARD
  American Ambassador, The (88) 20
  Echo House (98) 277
  Jack Gance (90) 445

KADARE, ISMAIL
  General of the Dead Army, The (92) 242
KADOHATA, CYNTHIA
  Floating World, The (90) 273
  In the Heart of the Valley of Love (93) 374
KAEL, PAULINE
  Reeling (77) 662
KAFKA, FRANZ
  Letters to Friends, Family, and Editors (78) 526
  Letters to Ottla and the Family (83) 401
KAGAN, DONALD
  On the Origins of War and the Preservation of
    Peace (96) 528
KAHLO, FRIDA
  Diary of Frida Kahlo, The (96) 182
KAHN, DAVID
  Hitler's Spies (79) 281
KAHN, HERMAN, WILLIAM BROWN, and LEON
  MARTEL
  Next 200 Years, The (77) 559
KALB, MADELEINE G.
  Congo Cables, The (H-83) 80
KAMIN, LEON J., R. C. LEWONTIN, and STEVEN
  ROSE
  Not in Our Genes (H-85) 329
KAMINER, WENDY
  Women Volunteering (H-85) 516
KAMMEN, MICHAEL
  Machine That Would Go of Itself, A (87) 503
  Mystic Chords of Memory (92) 545
KANIGEL, ROBERT
  One Best Way, The (98) 607
KAPLAN, BARRY JAY, and NICHOLAS MEYER
  Black Orchid (78) 100

AUTHOR INDEX

AUTHOR INDEX

PURDY, JAMES
  In a Shallow Grave (77) 380
PUTNAM, HILARY
  Renewing Philosophy (94) 696
PYM, BARBARA
  Academic Question, An (87) 1
  Crampton Hodnet (86) 194
  No Fond Return of Love (83) 536
  Some Tame Gazelle (84) 809
  Unsuitable Attachment, An (83) 855
  Very Private Eye, A (85) 964
PYMAN, AVRIL
  History of Russian Symbolism, A (95) 305
PYNCHON, THOMAS
  Mason and Dixon (98) 546
  Slow Learner (85) 830
  Vineland (90) 844
PYRON, DARDEN ASBURY
  Southern Daughter (92) 775

QUANDT, WILLIAM B.
  Decade of Decisions (78) 243
QUERRY, RON
  Death of Bernadette Lefthand, The (94) 217
QUINN, ARTHUR, and LEONARD NATHAN
  Poet's Work, The (92) 623
QUINN, SUSAN
  Mind of Her Own, A (88) 558
QUIRK, ROBERT E.
  Fidel Castro (94) 287

RABAN, JONATHAN
  Bad Land (97) 91
  Foreign Land (86) 302
  Hunting Mister Heartbreak (92) 314
  Old Glory (82) 580
RABINOWITCH, ALEXANDER
  Bolsheviks Come to Power, The (77) 109
RABINOWITZ, DOROTHY
  New Lives (77) 549
RADOSH, RONALD, and HARVEY KLEHR
  Amerasia Spy Case, The (97) 28
RADOSH, RONALD, and JOYCE MILTON
  Rosenberg File, The (H-84) 388
RAMPERSAD, ARNOLD
  Jackie Robinson (98) 458
  Life of Langston Hughes, 1902-1941, The
    (87) 489
  Life of Langston Hughes, 1941-1967, The
    (89) 501
RAMPERSAD, ARNOLD, and ARTHUR ASHE
  Days of Grace (94) 213
RANDALL, WILLARD STERNE
  Thomas Jefferson (94) 797
RANDERS-PEHRSON, JUSTINE DAVIS
  Barbarians and Romans (H-84) 39
RANSOM, JOHN CROWE
  Selected Essays of John Crowe Ransom (85) 797
RANSOM, ROGER L., and RICHARD SUTCH
  One Kind of Freedom (78) 622
RAPPAPORT, LEON, and GEORGE M. KREN
  Holocaust and the Crisis of Human Behavior, The
    (81) 439
RASMUSSEN, R. KENT
  Mark Twain A to Z (96) 452

RATUSHINSKAYA, IRINA
  Grey Is the Color of Hope (89) 330
RAUCH, JONATHAN
  Kindly Inquisitors (94) 436
RAVIV, DAN, and YOSSI MELMAN
  Every Spy a Prince (91) 271
RAWLS, JOHN
  Political Liberalism (94) 649
READ, PIERS PAUL
  Married Man, A (80) 522
  Polonaise (77) 632
REAGAN, RONALD
  American Life, An (91) 24
RECTOR, LIAM
  Sorrow of Architecture, The (85) 855
REED, RALPH
  Active Faith (97) 9
REED, ISHMAEL
  Reckless Eyeballing (87) 690
  Shrovetide in Old New Orleans (79) 681
  Terrible Twos, The (83) 778
REEDER, ROBERTA
  Anna Akhmatova (95) 38
REEVES, HUBERT
  Atoms of Silence (H-85) 39
REEVES, RICHARD
  American Journey (H-83) 46
  President Kennedy (94) 662
REEVES, THOMAS C.
  Life and Times of Joe McCarthy, The
    (H-83) 270
  Question of Character, A (92) 660
REICH, CARY
  Life of Nelson A. Rockefeller, 1908-1958, The
    (97) 506
REICH, ROBERT B.
  Work of Nations, The (92) 919
REID, PANTHEA
  Art and Affection (97) 66
REILLY, ROBIN
  William Pitt the Younger (80) 873
REINHARZ, JEHUDA
  Chaim Weizmann (86) 111
REISCHAUER, EDWIN O.
  Japanese, The (78) 459
REMINI, ROBERT V.
  Andrew Jackson and the Course of American
    Democracy, 1833-1845 (H-85) 28
  Andrew Jackson and the Course of American
    Empire, 1767-1821 (78) 50
  Andrew Jackson and the Course of American
    Freedom, 1822-1832 (82) 11
  Daniel Webster (98) 221
REMNICK, DAVID
  Devil Problem, The (97) 210
  Lenin's Tomb (94) 458
  Resurrection (98) 673
RENFREW, COLIN
  Archaeology and Language (89) 41
REUTHER, VICTOR G.
  Brothers Reuther, The (77) 124
REYNOLDS, DAVID S.
  Walt Whitman's America (96) 806
REYNOLDS, MICHAEL
  Hemingway, The American Homecoming
    (93) 325

1053

ROOKE, LEON
Shakespeare's Dog (84) 784
ROOT-BERNSTEIN, ROBERT SCOTT
Discovering (90) 186
ROREM, NED
Knowing When to Stop (95) 427
ROSE, PHYLLIS
Parallel Lives (84) 662
ROSE, STEVEN
Lifelines (98) 508
ROSE, STEVEN, R. C. LEWONTIN, and LEON J. KAMIN
Not in Our Genes (H-85) 329
ROSEN, JONATHAN
Eve's Apple (98) 299
ROSENBERG, DAVID, editor
Congregation (88) 189
ROSENBERG, TINA
Haunted Land, The (96) 330
ROSENBERG, WILLIAM G., and MARILYN B. YOUNG
Transforming Russia and China (H-83) 426
ROSENFIELD, ISRAEL
Invention of Memory, The (89) 400
ROSENGARTEN, THEODORE, editor
Tombee (87) 875
ROSENTHAL, M. L., and SALLY M. GALL
Modern Poetic Sequence, The (84) 570
Sailing into the Unknown (79) 632
ROSSABI, MORRIS
Khubilai Khan (89) 432
ROSSNER, JUDITH
Attachments (78) 77
ROTH, HENRY
Diving Rock on the Hudson, A (96) 190
From Bondage (97) 319
Mercy of a Rude Stream (95) 482
ROTH, JACK J.
Cult of Violence, The (81) 215
ROTH, PHILIP
American Pastoral (98) 45
Anatomy Lesson, The (84) 26
Counterlife, The (88) 204
Deception (91) 188
Facts, The (89) 288
Ghost Writer, The (80) 354
Operation Shylock (94) 581
Patrimony (92) 615
Professor of Desire, The (78) 669
Sabbath's Theater (96) 672
Zuckerman Unbound (82) 981
ROTHENBERG, GUNTHER E.
Art of Warfare in the Age of Napoleon, The (79) 38
ROTHMAN, ELLEN K.
Hands and Hearts (H-85) 195
ROUDINESCO, ELIZABETH
Jacques Lacan (98) 463
ROVERE, RICHARD H.
Arrivals and Departures (77) 62
Final Reports (H-85) 141
ROWAN, CARL T.
Dream Makers, Dream Breakers (94) 252
ROWSE, A. L.
Eminent Elizabethans (H-84) 147
ROY, ARUNDHATI
God of Small Things, The (98) 357

RUBIN, LOUIS D., JR., editor
History of Southern Literature, The (86) 426
RUDDICK, SARA, and PAMELA DANIELS, editors
Working It Out (78) 937
RUDMAN, MARK
Millennium Hotel, The (97) 586
RUÍZ, RAMÓN EDUARDO
Great Rebellion, The (81) 396
RUKEYSER, MURIEL
Collected Poems, The (80) 148
RUNYON, RANDOLPH PAUL
Reading Raymond Carver (93) 669
RUSH, NORMAN
Mating (92) 490
RUSHDIE, SALMAN
Haroun and the Sea of Stories (91) 376
Imaginary Homelands (92) 324
Moor's Last Sigh, The (96) 478
Satanic Verses, The (90) 711
Shame (84) 788
RUSK, DEAN
As I Saw It (91) 56
RUSKIN, JOHN, and THOMAS CARLYLE
Correspondence of Thomas Carlyle and John Ruskin, The (83) 153
RUSS, JOANNA
How to Suppress Women's Writing (84) 353
RUSSELL, JEFFREY BURTON
History of Heaven, A (98) 387
Lucifer (H-85) 272
Mephistopheles (87) 553
RUSSO, JOHN PAUL
I. A. Richards (90) 401
Straight Man (98) 745
RYAN, ALAN
John Dewey and the High Tide of American Liberalism (96) 393
RYAN, PAUL B., and THOMAS A. BAILEY
Hitler vs. Roosevelt (80) 404
RYBCZYNSKI, WITOLD
Home (87) 402
Most Beautiful House in the World, The (90) 582
RYMER, RUSS
Genie (94) 345

SÁBATO, ERNESTO
On Heroes and Tombs (82) 585
SACHAR, HOWARD M.
Diaspora (86) 226
History of the Jews in America, A (93) 340
SACKS, OLIVER
Anthropologist on Mars, An (96) 47
Island of the Colorblind and Cycad Island, The (98) 454
Man Who Mistook His Wife for a Hat, The (87) 516
Seeing Voices (90) 720
SAFRANSKI, RÜDIGER
Schopenhauer and the Wild Years of Philosophy (91) 711
SAGAN, CARL
Broca's Brain (80) 116
SAGAN, FRANÇOISE
Silken Eyes (78) 776
Unmade Bed, The (79) 791

AUTHOR INDEX

AUTHOR INDEX

VICKERS, BRIAN
    Appropriating Shakespeare (94) 33
VIDAL, GORE
    At Home (89) 59
    Creation (82) 151
    1876 (77) 256
    Empire (88) 275
    Hollywood (91) 423
    Lincoln (85) 570
    Palimpsest (96) 561
    Screening History (93) 707
    Second American Revolution, The (83) 700
    United States (94) 819
VIERECK, PETER
    Archer in the Marrow (88) 46
VINCENT, GÉRARD, and ANTOINE PROST,
    editors
    History of Private Life, Riddles of Identity in
        Modern Times, A (92) 294
VIVANTE, ARTURO
    Run to the Waterfall (80) 736
VLASTOS, GREGORY
    Socrates (92) 766
VOGELGESANG, SANDY
    American Dream Global Nightmare (81) 31
VOLLMANN, WILLIAM T.
    Atlas, The (97) 76
    Fathers and Crows (93) 288
    Rifles, The (95) 647
VON ABELE, RUDOLPH
    Cage for Loulou, A (79) 70
VON BAEYER, HANS C.
    Rainbows, Snowflakes, and Quarks (H-85) 379
VON HOFFMAN, NICHOLAS
    Citizen Cohn (89) 164
VONNEGUT, KURT
    Bluebeard (88) 107
    Deadeye Dick (83) 174
    Galápagos (86) 326
    Hocus Pocus (91) 413
    Jailbird (80) 436
    Palm Sunday (82) 609
    Slapstick (77) 749
    Timequake (98) 760

WADE, BRENT
    Company Man (93) 176
WAGNER-MARTIN, LINDA
    Sylvia Plath (88) 874
WAGNER, BRUCE
    I'm Losing You (97) 423
WAGONER, DAVID
    Collected Poems, 1956-1976 (78) 197
    First Light (84) 299
    Who Shall Be the Sun? (79) 852
WAIN, JOHN
    Pardoner's Tale, The (80) 640
    Professing Poetry (79) 561
WAITE, ROBERT G. L.
    Psychopathic God, The (78) 677
WAKOSKI, DIANE
    Emerald City of Las Vegas, The (96) 218
    Jason the Sailor (94) 422
    Man Who Shook Hands, The (79) 414
WALCOTT, DEREK
    Arkansas Testament, The (88) 52
    Fortunate Traveller, The (82) 293
    Midsummer (85) 609

    Omeros (91) 643
    Star-Apple Kingdom, The (80) 777
WALDRON, ARTHUR
    Great Wall of China, The (91) 368
WALKER, ALICE
    Color Purple, The (83) 139
    In Search of Our Mothers' Gardens (84) 368
    Meridian (77) 501
    Possessing the Secret of Joy (93) 651
    You Can't Keep a Good Woman Down (82) 976
WALKER, MARGARET
    Richard Wright, Daemonic Genius (89) 722
WALL, STEPHEN
    Trollope (90) 827
WALLACE, ANTHONY F. C.
    St. Clair (88) 790
WALLACE, DAVID FOSTER
    Girl with Curious Hair (90) 299
    Infinite Jest (97) 446
    Supposedly Fun Thing I'll Never Do Again, A
        (98) 750
WALSER, MARTIN
    No Man's Land (90) 619
WALSER, ROBERT
    Selected Stories (83) 734
WALSH, JOHN EVANGELIST
    Into My Own (89) 390
WAMBAUGH, JOSEPH
    Glitter Dome, The (82) 325
WANGERIN, WALTER, JR.
    Book of Sorrows, The (86) 77
WARD, GEOFFREY C.
    First-Class Temperament, A (90) 258
WARD, GEOFFREY C., et al.
    Civil War, The (91) 137
WARNER, MARINA
    From the Beast to the Blonde (96) 290
WARNER, ROGER, with HAING NGOR
    Haing Ngor (89) 335
WARNER, SAM BASS, JR.
    Province of Reason (H-85) 368
WARNER, SYLVIA TOWNSEND
    Letters (84) 432
    One Thing Leading to Another (85) 658
    Scenes of Childhood and Other Stories (83) 679
WARREN, EARL
    Memoirs of Earl Warren, The (78) 567
WARREN, ROBERT PENN
    Being Here (81) 76
    Now and Then (79) 501
    Rumor Verified (82) 704
    Selected Poems, 1923-1975 (78) 753
WARREN, ROSANNA
    Each Leaf Shines Separate (85) 204
WASHINGTON, GEORGE, and DAVID
    HUMPHREYS
    David Humphreys' "Life of General Washington"
        (92) 147
WASSERSTEIN, BERNARD
    Secret Lives of Trebitsch Lincoln, The (89) 762
WAT, ALEKSANDER
    Lucifer Unemployed (91) 545
    My Century (89) 571
WATKINS, PAUL
    Promise of Light, The (94) 667
    Stand Before Your God (95) 752